Compendium of Early
Mohawk Valley Families

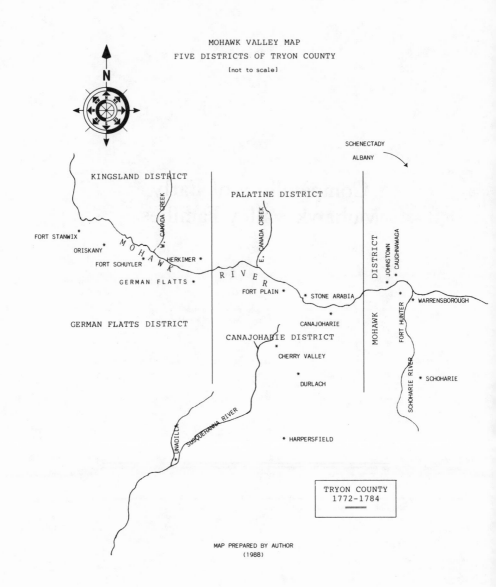

MOHAWK VALLEY MAP
FIVE DISTRICTS OF TRYON COUNTY
[not to scale]

N

SCHENECTADY
ALBANY

KINGSLAND DISTRICT

PALATINE DISTRICT

W. CANADA CREEK

E. CANADA CREEK

FORT STANWIX *

ORISKANY *

FORT SCHUYLER

HERKIMER *

GERMAN FLATTS *

MOHAWK

RIVER

FORT PLAIN *

* STONE ARABIA

MOHAWK   DISTRICT

JOHNSTOWN *

* CAUGHNAWAGA

FORT HUNTER *

* WARRENSBOROUGH

GERMAN FLATTS DISTRICT

*
CANAJOHARIE

CANAJOHARIE DISTRICT

*
CHERRY VALLEY

*
DURLACH

SCHOHARIE RIVER

* SCHOHARIE

SUSQUEHANNA RIVER

* UNADILLA

* HARPERSFIELD

TRYON COUNTY
1772-1784

MAP PREPARED BY AUTHOR
(1988)

COMPENDIUM
of Early
MOHAWK VALLEY
FAMILIES

Maryly B. Penrose, C.G., A.S.I.

Volume 2

 Genealogical Publishing Co., Inc.

Published by Genealogical Publishing Co., Inc.
1001 N. Calvert Street, Baltimore, Maryland 21202
Library of Congress Catalogue Card Number 90-81619
International Standard Book Number, Volume 2: 0-8063-1281-5
Set number: 0-8063-1279-3
Made in the United States of America

TABLE OF CONTENTS

VOLUME 1

VOLUME 2

NASH

Birth/Baptism

Nasch, James & Anna [?]: Anna Catharina, b. 3/7/1784; bapt. 3/7/1784 (DRGF:81). Sponsors: John Osteroth & Anna Catharina.

Death Record

Nash, [?], (infant of Joh. Nash, Jr.), d. 9/5/1823, Germanflats; buried in the church cemetery in the same place (RDH:288)

Tryon County Militia

Nash, James   [Appendix A]

1790 Census

Nash, James   [Appendix B]
Nash, Johnston

NATES

Birth/Baptism

Nates, Christopher (of Gaiesberg) & Susanna [?]: Martinus, bapt. 4/25/1790 (SJC:26). Sponsors: Andreas Smith & Magdalena Smith.

NAZIERT

Birth/Baptism

Naziert, Daniel & Lena [?]: Margretha, bapt. 6/17/1777 (DRGF:24). Sponsors: Carl Kurn & Margreth.

NEALEY (also see NEELY)

Marriage

Nealey, Mathew m. Elizabeth McKenney, both of Remsonsbush, 11/21/1791 (JDR:#100)

NEALSON (also see NIELSON)

Marriage

Nealson, Allen m. Jane McGlasion, both of Schenectady, 1/26/1786 (JDR:3)

1790 Census

Neilson, Allen   [Appendix B]

NEAR

1790 Census

Near, George   [Appendix B]
Near, Jacob

NEEF

Birth/Baptism

Neef/Neeve/Nef, Jacob & Catharina (Angst): Jacob, bapt. 5/12/1765 (DRC:14); Henrich, b. 9/10/1769, bapt. 9/20/1769 (RDSA:97); Abraham, b. 2/15/1772 (LTSA:42); Elizabeth, bapt. 10/26/1777 (DRC:45). Sponsors: Jacob Neef & Barbara Neef (re:1); Philipp Schafer & his wife, Elisabetha (re:2); Jacob Bosshard & his wife (re:3); Hendrick Bushart & Elizabeth

Bushart (re:4).

Neef, John J. & Martha (Beckwith): Elisabeth, b. 9/25/1790; bapt. 2/5/1791 (DRC:94). Sponsors: Jacob Neef & his wife.

NEELEN

Marriage

Neelen, Michael m. Bethay Coren, 7/13/1794 (DRGF:211)

NEELY (also see NEALEY)

1790 Census

Neely, John   [Appendix B]

NEHER

Birth/Baptism

Neher, Jacob & Maria [?]: Maria, b. 2/3/1795 (LTSA:88). Sponsors: Andreas Dillebach, Magdalena Loescher.

Neher, Johannes & Elisabet [?]: Casparus, b. 9/27/1792 (LTSA:75). Sponsors: Conrad Neher, Elisabeth Koch.

NELLES see NELLIS

NELLIS

Marriage

Nelles, Georg m. Cath. Dussler, 11/14/1771 (LTSA:282)

Nelles, Georg m. Maria Catharin Stahlee (dau. of Ad: Stahlee), 1/17/1786 (DRGF:203)

Nelles, Jacob m. Christina Fuchs, 1/12/1768 (RDSA:184)

Nelles, Johannes m. Anna W. Fox, 5/14/1782 (DRGF:196)

Nelles, Johannes m. Maria Dussler, 9/4/1781 (DRGF:195)

Nelles, Peter Henr: m. Elisabeth Sneider (dau. of Ludw. Sneider), 9/20/1785 (DRGF:202)

Nelles, Peter Wilh: m. Catharina Tyghart (dau. of Sev: Tyghart), 11/17/1784 (DRGF:200)

Nelles, Theobald (widower, Canajoharie) m. Elisabetha Bell (widow of Johannes Bell, Little Falls), 12/13/1761 (RDSA:170)

Nelles, Wilhelm m. Catharin Stroobeck, 11/9/1781 (DRGF:195)

Nelles, Wilhelm m. Dorothea Tyghart (widow), 9/1/1783 (DRGF:198)

Nelles, Wilhelm m. Maria Waggoner, 4/27/1786 (DRGF:203)

Birth/Baptism

Nellis, Adam & Dorothea [?]: Catharina, b. 6/2/1770 (LTSA:32). Sponsors: Joannes Glok, Jr. & his wife.

Nellis, Andreas & Maria Barbara [?]:
Catharina, b. 9/16/1753 (LTSA:8); Dorothea,
b. 8/3/1764, bapt. 8/12/1764 (RDSA:49).
Sponsors: Catharina Fuchs [Fox], Henrich
Wallrath (re:1); Wilhelm Fox & his wife,
Margretha (re:2).

Nellis, Andreas, Jr. & Elisabeth [?]: Johann
Joseph, b. 5/7/1778, bapt. 5/10/1778
(LTSA:52); Peter, b. 11/27/1780, bapt.
12/3/1780 (DRGF:40); Elisabetha, b. 5/8/1783,
bapt. 5/19/1783 (DRGF:72). Sponsors: Joh.
Joseph Wagner, Dorothea Nellis (re:1); Peter
Warmoeth & Anna (re:2); Georg Waggoner &
Elisabetha (re:3).

Nellis, Andrew (Canajoh. Castle) & Elisabeth
[?]: Heinrich, bapt. 5/22/1791 (SJC:43).
Sponsors: Peter Deygert & Sara Deygert.

Nellis, Christian & Christina [?]: Catharina, b.
11/14/1764, bapt. 11/18/1764 (RDSA:52);
Elisabeth, b. 6/21/1767, bapt. 6/30/1767
(RDSA:76); Johannes, b. 12/5/1769
(LTSA:29); Jacob, b. 11/26/1771 (LTSA:40).
Sponsors: Catharina Frej [Frey] & Jacob Klock
(re:1); Elisabetha & Theobald Nolles (re:2);
Joannes Kaiser, Anna Clok (re:3); Jacob Klok
& his wife (re:4).

Nellis, Dewald & Anna [?]: Jo[h]annes, b.
12/10/1755 (LTSA:23); Elisabeth, b. 9/11/1757
(LTSA:22); Anna, b. 10/18/1759 (LTSA:23);
Margaretha, b. 9/1/1761 (LTSA:23); Dorothea,
b. 2/5/1763 (LTSA:23). Sponsors: Henrich
Dillenbach & his wife, Barbara (Schultz) (re:1);
Werner Casselman, Anna Nellis (re:2); Henrich
Dillenbach & his wife, Barbara (Schultz) (re:3-
5).

Nellis, George & Elisabeth [?]: Johannes, b.
11/22/1778; bapt. 12/28/1778 (LTSA:55).
Sponsors: Johann Tussler, Elisabeth Knieskern.

Nellis, Henrich & Anna [?]: Maria Elisabetha,
b. 8/20/1769 (LTSA:29). Sponsors: Cunrad
Hahn & his wife.

Nellis, Henrich (of Palatine) & Catharina [?]:
Catharina, bapt. 12/27/1789 (SJC:21);
Margretha, bapt. 10/16/1791 (SJC:49).
Sponsors: John Nellis & Maria Hellmer (re:1);
Johannes Nelles & Margretha Klock (re:2).

Nellis, Henrich & Elisabeth [?]: Henrich, b.
4/30/1784; bapt. 5/16/1784 (DRGF:83).
Sponsors: Marcus Dussler & Elisabeth Helmer.

Nellis, Henrich & Margaretha [?]: Johann
Willhelm, b. 8/17/1769 (LTSA:29); Johann
Werner, b. 9/25/1771 (LTSA:39). Sponsors:
William Nelles & his wife (re:1); Hennrich
Dillenbach, Elisabetha Jaker (re:2).

Nellis, Joh. Georg & Maria Elisabeth [?]: Anna
Maria, b. 1/15/1762, bapt. 2/11/1762
(RDSA:31); Johann Georg, b. 8/27/1765, bapt.
9/10/1765 (RDSA:57); Wina, b. 1/14/1770,
bapt. 1/28/1770 (RDSA:99). Sponsors: Anna
Maria Majer & Johannes Christman (re:1);
Johann Georg Dachstaeder & his wife (re:2);
Sabina & Joh[?] Friedrich Helmer (re:3).

Nellis, Johannes & Anna [?]: Wilhelm, b.
2/?/1783, bapt. 2/16/1783 (DRGF:67); Anna,
b. 6/12/1797 (LTSA:99). Sponsors: Wilhelm
Fox & Anna Eva (re:1); Jacob Schnell & Maria
(re:2).

Nellis, Johannes & Magdalena [?]: Jo[h]annes,
b. 7/7/1770 (LTSA:32); Anna, b. 8/10/1772
(LTSA:44). Sponsors: Joannes Christoph
Schulz, Jr., Elisabetha Wagner (re:1); Peter
Wagner, Anna Lambmann (re:2).

Nellis, John (Canajoharie) & Lea [?]: Maria,
bapt. 9/22/1793 (SJC:81). Sponsors: Georg

Haus & Maria Haus.

Nellis, John (Palatine) & Delia [?]: Margretha, bapt. 1/5/1793 (SJC:70). Sponsors: Friderich Bam & Elisabeth Bam.

Nellis, John J. (Palatine) & Catharina (Weber): Peter, bapt. 4/12/1792 (SJC:57). Sponsors: Peter C. Fox & Nancy Nelles.

Nellis, Ludwig & Eva [?]: Peter, b. 10/27/1790 (LTSA:66). Sponsors: Peter Fuchs, Elisabet Nelles.

Nellis, Peter & Catharina [?]: Johannes, bapt. 5/13/1792 [Palatine] (SJC:59); Maria, b. 11/8/1795 (LTSA:92). Sponsors: John Nelles & Delia Deygert (re:1); Severinus Deichert & Gertraut (re:2).

Nellis, Philip & Elisabeth [?]: Eva, b. 7/17/1781, bapt. 7/22/1781 (DRGF:46); Pieter, b. 9/21/1783, bapt. 11/11/1783 (DRGF:77); Jacob, b. 6/24/1795 (LTSA:90: Eva, b. 7/19/1797 (LTSA:99). Sponsors: Delia Joh: Nelles & Georg Saltzmann (re:1); Pieter Fox & Catharina Fox (re:2); Jacob Schnell & Maria (re:3); Jerg Ekert, Anna Waggoner (re:4).

Nellis, Philip & Maria [?]: Elisabet, b. 10/18/1797 (LTSA:100). Sponsors: Lips [Philip] Nellis & Elisabet.

Nellis, Philipp & Elisabetha [?]: Hennrich, b. 2/21/1771 (LTSA:35); Anna, b. [?]; bapt. 9/13/1778 (LTSA:54). Sponsors: Dewald Maerkel & his wife (re:1); Johannes Hess, Anna Hess (re:2).

Nellis, Robert & Anna [?]: Christina, b. 1/10/1755 (LTSA:10); Barbara Elisabetha, b. 2/24/1756, bapt. 3/7/1756 (RDSA:16); Wilhelmus, b. 9/11/1761, bapt. 9/20/1761

(RDSA:28); Maria, b. 8/3/1763, bapt. 8/7/1763 (RDSA:41); Margretha, b. 8/12/1765, bapt. 9/1/1765 (RDSA:57); Lea, b. 1/4/1770, bapt. 1/21/1770 (RDSA:99). Sponsors: Christian [?], Lea Hagedorn (re:1); Maria (dau. of Henrich Merckel) & Hermanus (surviving unmarried son of Sam Hagedorn) (re:2); Wilhelm (son of Georg Koppernoll) & Anna (dau. of Christian Nelles) (re:3); Margretha Finck & Johannes Laux (re:4); Johannes Spaltzberger & Anna Merckel (re:5); Henrich Merckel & Margretha (re:6).

Nellis, Theobald & Elisabetha [?]: Theobaldus, b. 7/13/1766; bapt. 7/20/1766 (RDSA:66). Sponsors: Christian Nelles & Christina.

Nellis, Wilhelm & Catharina [?]: Christian, b. 10/27/1782; bapt. 11/3/1782 (DRGF:64). Sponsors: Albert Lentler & Sussanna Hess .

Nellis, Wilhelm & Maria [?]: Catarina, b. 12/11/1792 (LTSA:76); Jacob, b. 9/28/1796 (LTSA:97). Sponsors: Wilhelm Wagner, Catarina Deichert (re:1); Isaac Walrat & Margaret (re:2).

Nellis, Wilhelm & Maria Dorothea (Salzmann/Saltsman): Margaretha, b. 2/21/1753 (LTSA:7); Maria Elisabeth, b. 2/24/1755 (LTSA:11); Henrich, b. 10/14/1756 (LTSA:20). Sponsors: Henrich Nellis, Margaretha Merckl (re:1); Henrich Salzmann & wife, Maria Elisabetha (re:2); Henrich Wallrath, Ludwig Nellis, Elisabetha Kaiser (re:3).

Death Record

Nellis, [?], (child of George P. Nellis), d. 3/8/1813, age 5 years, 1 month (DFP:96)

Nellis, [?], (child of Lips [Philip] Nellis), d.

578

11/14/1806, age 8 yrs., 7 mos., 8 days (DFP:91)

Nellis, [?], (child of Peter Nelles), d. 2/17/1812, age 5 months, 5 days (DFP:94)

Nellis, George, (legitimate son of George Nelles), b. 3/4/1788; d. 10/3/1789; buried 10/4/1789 (DFP:80)

Nellis, Margaret, (wife of Sylvenus Nellis), d. 12/12/1853, age 68 years; buried Fort Plain Cemetery, Minden (FPC 56:43g)

Nellis, Maria Elisabeth, (widow of George Nellis), d. 4/21/1806, Germanflats, age 79 years, 8 months; buried in the new cemetery in Herkimer (RDH:256)

Nellis, Peter W., d. 3/?/1813, age 53 years, 7 months, 10 days; buried 3/9/1813 (DFP:96)

Nellis, Sylvenus, d. 12/9/1850, 62 yrs., buried Fort Plain Cemetery, Minden (FPC 56:43g)

Probate Abstract

Nellis, Adam A., (of Oppenheim), will dated 9/3/1827; probated 10/25/1828. Legatees: wife, Anna; sons, Jonas and Adam; daus., Polly (wife of David Fikel), Nancy (wife of Henry Zielley), Eve. Executor: son, Jonas. Witnesses: Henry Markell, Christopher Fox, Joseph J. I. Clock, Joseph Klock. (WMC 57:272)

Nellis, Christian, (of Palatine), will dated 11/28/1807; probated 10/11/1808. Legatees: sons, John C. and Jacob C.; daus., Margaret (wife of Henry I. Bellinger) & Elizabeth (wife of John J. Klock, Jr.). Executors: two sons & Jacob J. Klock. Witnesses: Christian Klock, Peter March, Cornelius C. Beekman. (WMC 56:159)

Nellis, Johannis, (of Palatine), will dated 10/9/1806; probated 5/17/1813. Legatees: wife [not named]; sons, John, Peter, Jost and William; daus., Delia (wife of Peter P. Ehle), Nancy (wife of Peter C. Fox) and Magdalene (wife of Jacob Keller). Executors: son, Jost; George Waggenor. Witnesses: Peter Marckel, Jacob Snell, Jr., Henry Snell. (WMC 56:387)

Nellis, Ludwig, (of Palatine), will dated 8/8/1809; probated 1/17/1810. Legatees: wife, Elizabeth; sons, John, Ludwig (decd. and his son, Peter); daus., Mary (wife of John Anthony Peck), Margareth (wife of Christopher W. Fox), Catharine (wife of George Shultis), and Elizabeth (wife of Adam Kilts). Executors: George Saltsman, Jacob Snell and John Frey. Witnesses: Peter and Elizabeth Markell, Jacob Snell. (WMC 56:160)

Nellis, Peter, (of Oppenheim), will dated 2/24/1813; probated 5/3/1822. Legatees: wife, Roxina/Rosina[?]; sons, Joseph, William, Daniel and Warner; daus., Mary, Nancy and Betsey; brother, John W. Executors: Peter C. and Frederick Fox. Witnesses: Frederick Fox, Benjamin Brown, W. L. Cochran. (WMC 57:173)

Nellis, Peter H., (of Oppenheim), will dated 5/28/1814; codicil dated 8/2/1814; probated 5/9/1815. Legatees: wife, Sally; sons, Warner, Benjamin, Robert Henry, Levi and Abraham (5 sons); daus., Margrate, Anna, Merean and Elizabeth. Executors: John C. Nellis, Jacob H. Failing, David Anderson, Jr. Witnesses: Jacob Flander, Ludwig Haring, Cornelius C. Beekman (to the will); John and Peter Hase; & Cornelius C. Beekman (to the codicil). (WMC 56:394)

Nellis, Peter I. [J.?], (of Oppenheim), will dated 9/10/1815; probated 5/6/1816. Legatees:

wife, Caty; sons, Daniel and Ira; only dau., Lenah; father and mother-in-law, Daniel and Catharine Fox. Executors: John Nellis, Jacob A. Keller, David Fox. Witnesses: Frederick Fox, William Nellis, John Claus. (WMC 56:397)

Nellis, William, (of Palatine), will dated 1/17/1821; probated 2/28/1826. Legatees: wife, Mary; sons, Peter, Jacob and Garrit; daus., Anna and Catherine (wife of Michael Shultis); granddau., Anna Putman. Executors: son, Peter; William Waggoner, Peter P. Waggoner. Witnesses: John C. Lipe, William and George Waggoner. (WMC 57:185)

Tryon County Militia

Nellis, Andreas	[Appendix A]
Nellis, Christian	
Nellis, George	
Nellis, Henry	
Nellis, Henry N.	
Nellis, Jacob	
Nellis, John	
Nellis, Joseph	
Nellis, Ludwig	
Nellis, Peter	
Nellis, Philip	
Nellis, William	

Pension Abstract

Nellis, George, b. 10/18/1751; m. Elisabeth Dusler, 10/19/1771; d. ca. 1820, Minden, Montgomery Co., N.Y. Children: Johannes, b. 11/23/1778; Christina, b. 2/2/1792 (m. George Shout); Robert, b. 10/21/1793; Hannah (m. Henry Murphy); Catharine (m. Leonard Shall); Lana (m. Jacob J. Cramer). George served as a private in Col. Jacob Klock's 2nd. Regt., Tryon Co. Militia. (RWPA: #W21834)

Nellis, George H., b. 6/27/1767, Canajoharie, Albany Co., N.Y.; resident of Canajoharie, Montgomery Co. on 2/9/1844. George H. enlisted in April 1778 "by the leave and direction of his father who had provided for him a gun & other equipment" and "also furnished with a fife upon which he was taught to play"; he was in Capt. Adam Lipe's Co., Col. Samuel Clyde's 1st. Regt., Tryon Co. Militia and was ordered to drive a team for drawing timber for construction of Fort Clyde; he enlisted again in 1779 into the same regiment and drove the team and dug trenches for setting pickets to enclose the said fort; he was on garrison duty at Fort Clyde from 1780 to 1782 and "when the force at the garrison was weak that he should play upon his fife to deceive the indians"; George stated that his total service time amounted to two and one half years. (RWPA: #R7581)

Nellis, John D., b. 12/10/1755, son of David Nellis, Canajoharie, N.Y.; m. [not named: widow of Solomon Keller who was killed in the battle of Oriskany], 2/15/1780; resident of Whitestown, Oneida Co., N.Y. on 12/11/1839. John D. enlisted in 1775 and served in Capt. John Hess' Co., Col. Jacob Klock's 2nd. Regt., Tryon Co. Militia; John D. was employed by Col. Jacob Klock (who lived about a mile from John D. Nellis' home) as an express rider in 1780 for a period of one year; he witnessed in the same year "the burning of his father's David Nellis house and barn set on fire by the Indians and Tories"; John D. fought in the battles of Oriskany and Johnstown. (RWPA: #R7582)

Nellis, John L., b. 12/3/1762 or 1763, Palatine, N.Y.; resident of his birthplace in Montgomery Co. on 9/20/1832. John L. entered the military early in 1778 and served at various times until the fall of 1782; he was a private, corporal and drummer under Capts. Christopher W. Fox, Henry Miller and John Sholl in the regiments of Cols. Jacob Klock, Waggoner, Harper, Brown and Willett; John L. was a participant in the battles of Stone Arabia, Lampman, Turlock and Johnstown; he was discharged after serving one year, eight months and nineteen days. (RWPA: #S23820)

Nellis, Joseph, b. 1758/9; resident of Oppenheim, Montgomery Co., N.Y. in 1832. Joseph served in the military from 1775 until his discharge sometime in 1781; he was a private in Col. Jacob Klock's 2nd. Regt., Tryon Co. Militia; Joseph was engaged in the battles of Oriskany, Brown, Failing and Klock. (RWPA: #S14017)

Nellis, William, m. Mary Waggoner, 4/28/1786, Palatine, N.Y. by Rev. Abraham Rosencrantz; d. 6/23/1821, Palatine, Montgomery Co. (Mary Nellis, b. 1762/3; resident of Palatine, N.Y. on 1/29/1841.) Children: Jacob W. Nellis. William was a private in Capt. John Hess' Co., Col. Jacob Klock's 2nd. Regt., Tryon Co. Militia from 1779 through 1782; he also served in Col. Samuel Clyde's 2st. Regt., Tryon Co. Militia. (RWPA: #R7583)

1790 Census

Nelles, George   [Appendix B]
Nellis, Adam
Nellis, Andrew
Nellis, Christian
Nellis, David
Nellis, George
Nellis, Henry
Nellis, Henry W.
Nellis, John (2)
Nellis, John D.
Nellis, John H.

Nellis, Ludwick
Nellis, Peter W.
Nellis, Philip
Nellis, Robert
Nellis, William
Nellis, Yost

NELSON

Death Record

Nelson, [?], (infant child of George Nelson), d. 4/?/1823, age [not stated]; buried Cherry Valley Presbyterian Church cemetery (PCV:79)

Pension Abstract

Nelson, Moses, b. 1/?/1765, Cherry Valley, N.Y.; m. Dolly [?], 11/16/1787, Stillwater, Saratoga Co., N.Y.; d. 8/11/1845 or 8/12/1845, Plainfield, Otsego Co., N.Y. (Dolly Nelson, b. 1766/7; resident of Rome, N.Y. in 1846.) Children: Eunice, b. 9/23/1789 (m. James Hays). Moses enlisted from Cherry Valley on 3/20/1780 and served as a private for eleven months in Capt. John Denny's Co. of the N.Y. Line; he was taken prisoner by the Indians at Cherry Valley and held for two years in captivity. Moses was a resident of Westmoreland, Oneida Co., N.Y. on 11/11/1832 when he applied for pension. (RWPA: #R7586)

NENTZELL

Death Record

Nentzell, Conrad, b. Germany; d. 3/16/1792; buried 3/17/1792 (DFP:82)

NESLEY see NESTEL

NESTEL

Marriage

Nestel, Georg m. Elisabeth Majer (widow), 9/25/1781 (DRGF:195)

Nestel, George m. Elisabeth Misselis (dau. of Gerret Misselis), 4/8/1760 (RDSA:168; LTSA:278)

Nestel, Gottlieb m. Barbara Elis. Dillenbach, 10/29/1771 (LTSA:282)

Nestel, Martin m. Catharina Cuntermann, 9/13/1792 (RDSA:197)

Nestel, Martin, Jr. m. Elisabeth Dillenbach (dau. of Henrich Dillenbach), 4/10/1764 (RDSA:173)

Nestel, Peter (of Cherry Valley) m. Catherine Farqason (of Cherry Valley), 1/11/1826 (PCBC:51)

Birth/Baptism

Nestel, Andres & Gertraut [?]: Heinrich, b. 5/19/1793 (LTSA:78). Sponsors: Heinrich Walrat, Delia Deichert.

Nestel, Georg & Elisabeth [?]: Maria Catharina, b. 6/11/1761, bapt. 6/14/1761 (RDSA:27); Georg, b. 10/17/1762, bapt. 10/24/1762 (RDSA:35); Johann, b. 6/21/1767 (RDSA:76); Joann Michael, b. 1/27/1769, d. 7/23/1769 (LTSA:25); Gottlieb, b. 6/29/1770 (LTSA:32); Adam, b. 5/11/1772 (LTSA:43). Sponsors: Maria [?] & Casper Nessel (re:1);

Bath Koch & his wife (re:2); Johann Chryst Dillenbach & Anna Maria (re:3); J. Mich. & Gottlieb Nestel, Magd. Dillenbach (re:4); Gottlieb Nestel, Barbara Dillenbach (re:5); Adam Vorri, Catharina Margaretha Beker (re:6).

Nestel, Georg & Elisabeth [?]: Johannes, b. 7/7/1782; bapt. 7/9/1782 (DRGF:59). Sponsors: Fritz Raspach & Catharina.

Nestel, Gottlieb & Barbara Elisabetha [?]: Maria, b. 5/26/1772 (LTSA:43); Magaretha, b. 11/6/1773 (LTSA:45); Johannes, b. 3/9/1778, bapt. 3/22/1778 (LTSA:52); Elisabeth, b. [?]; bapt. 3/27/1780 (LTSA:60); Carolina, b. [?]; bapt. 3/27/1780 (LTSA:60); Martin, b. 4/8/1782, bapt. 4/14/1782 (DRGF:57); Barbara Elis., b. 56/7/1791 (LTSA:68). Sponsors: Andraeas Dillenbach & his wife (re:1); Joh. Lescher & his wife (re:2); Johannes Koch & Magdalena (re:3); Carl Salome Friderici, Heinrich Tillenbach, Elisabeth Teigert (re: 4 & 5); Martin Nostel & Elisabeth (re:6); Martin Nestel, Elisabeth Koch (re:7).

Nestel, Heinrich & Elisabet [?]: Elisabet, b. 10/29/1792 (LTSA:70); Joh. Baltas, b. 2/24/1796 (LTSA:93). Sponsors: Martinus Dillebach, Elisabet Koch (re:1); Balthas Dillebach & Elisabet (re:2).

Nestel, Joh. Martin & Anna Maria [?]: Johann Peter, b. 7/17/1753 (LTSA:7); Elisabetha, b. 9/20/1755 (LTSA:15); Dorothea Magdalena, b. 8/23/1764, bapt. 9/2/1764 (RDSA:49). Sponsors: Maria Emig, Hannes Kaiser (re:1); Peter Deigert, Elisabetha Kaiser (re:2); Dorothea & Johannes Teughard; Magdalena Dillenbach & Casper [?] (re:3).

Nestel, Martin & Elisabetha [?]: Henrich, b.

COMPENDIUM

11/27/1764, bapt. 11/27/1764 (RDSA:52); Martinus, b. 11/3/1766, bapt. 11/16/1766 (RDSA:69); Catharina, b. 7/27/1770 (LTSA:33); Johannes, b. 2/19/1772 (LTSA:41); Elisabeth, b. 3/31/1780, bapt. 4/9/1780 (LTSA:60). Sponsors: Henrich Dillenbach & Margretha Sutz (re:1); Martinus Dillenbach Jun. & Mar Lena Dillenbach (re:2); Andraeas Dillenbach & his wife (re:3); Johannes Lescher & his wife (re:4); Gerrhardt Loescher & Catharina (re:5).

Death Record

Nestel, [?], (Mr.), d. 1808, age 77 years, 9 months, 3 days (DFP:91)

Nestel, Conrad, (son of Peter Nistle), b. 1/26/1810; d. 4/4/1810, age 1 month, 6 days; buried 4/5/1810 (DFP:93)

Nestell, John, b. 1795; d. 1863; buried Ames Rural Cemetery, Canajoharie (ARC:8)

Nestell, Sarah Voorhees, (wife of John Nestell), b. 1799; d. 1888; buried Ames Rural Cemetery, Canajoharie (ARC:8)

Probate Abstract

Nestel, Gottlieb, (of Palatine), will dated 1/4/1812; probated 6/27/1812. Legatees: wife; sons, John, Henry, Martinis and Peter; daus., Mary (wife of John Cnouts), Margaret (wife of John Righter), Ustena, Barbel and Elizabeth (wife of Peter Righter). Executors: son, John; David Zielly, Jacob Sarfos. Witnesses: Henry Nestel, Jacob Sarfos, David Zielly. (WMC 56:385)

Nestel, John, (of Palatine), will dated 11/17/1813; probated 1/11/1815. Legatees: mother; brothers, Henry, Martinus (& his son,

John M.), Peter (& his children and Barber); sisters, Ustena, Barber, Mary, Margaret, Elizabeth (& her dau., Barber); sister's son, John Knouts. Executors: Martines M. Nestel, David Zielley. Witnesses: John Dillenbach, Abraham Sternberg, Peter Wilhelm Domeier. (WMC 56:393)

Nestle, John M., (of Cherry Valley), will dated 10/26/1827; probated 9/7/1828. Legatees: sister, Maria Lewis (& her Benjamin); sisters, Caty, Eliza and Nancy Barbary; brothers, Sylvester, George, Martin and Daniel. Executors: Sylvanus Tygert, John Warner, John Devendorf. Witnesses: Delos White, John McFee, James McFee. (WMC 57:271-272)

Tryon County Militia

Nestel, Andrew   [Appendix A]
Nestel, George
Nestel, Gotlieb
Nestel, Henry
Nestel, Martin

Pension Abstract

Nestel, Gotlieb, resident of Palatine, N.Y. when he enlisted in Col. Jacob Klock's 2nd. Regt., Tryon Co. Militia as a private; he was wounded in the eye by the oversetting of a baggage wagon on a march in the year 1777. Gotlieb was disabled and a record of him can be found in the American State Papers, Class 9, p. 94. [There is no application by Gotlieb Nestel for a pension, although he is listed in the file.]

Nestle, Martin, b. ca. 1760; m. Catharine [?], 10/?/1778 by Rev. Pick; resident of Oppenheim, Montgomery Co., N.Y. on 2/16/1821; d. 7/27/1827. (Catharine Nestle, b. 1753/4; resident of Brutus, Cayuga Co., N.Y.

on 4/11/1837.) Martin enlisted from Stone Arabia in August 1776 and was a matross [gunner's assistant] in the N.Y. Regt. of Artillery under the command of Col. John Lamb; he served in Capt. Fleming's Co. and fought in the battles of Oriskany and Johnstown. (RWPA: #W16354)

1790 Census

Nesley, William   [Appendix B]
Nestle, Andrew
Nestle, Godlip
Nestle, Martin

NESTLE see **NESTEL**

NEUBERG

Birth/Baptism

Neuberg, Wilhelm & Catharina [?]: Margaretha, b. 9/30/1770 (LTSA:33). Sponsors: Sebastian Holzhoeffer, Margaretha Devin.

NEUHOFF (also see NYHOOF)

Marriage

Neuhoff, Johannes m. Lena Fungie (widow), 7/21/1785 (DRGF:202)

Birth/Baptism

Neuhof, Johann & Magdalena [?]: Benjamin, b. 7/5/1791 (LTSA:68). Sponsors: Peter

Steller, Dorothea Wik.

NEWCOMB

1790 Census

Newcomb, Eleazer   [Appendix B]

NEWELL

1790 Census

Newell, Elisha   [Appendix B]

NEWKIRK

Marriage

Newkirk, Charles (Major) m. Gertruyd Schuyler (widow of Major Schuyler), [no date: follows 11/19/1793] (DRGF:210)

Birth/Baptism

Newkirk, Cornelis & Cornelje [?]: Abraham, b. 10/9/1762; bapt. 10/31/1762 (RDSA:36). Sponsors: Wilhelm Quackenbusch & Rahel Newkerck.

Newkirk, Gerrit A. & Nancy (Cosaadt): Elsje, b. 11/6/1776, bapt. 1/5/1777 (DRC:40); David, b. 4/1/1778, bapt. 5/18/1778 (DRC:48); Stephen, b. 3/10/1785, bapt. 7/13/1785 (DRC:74). Sponsors: David Prime & Elsje Prime (re:1); [none named] (re:2); [none named] (re:3).

Newkirk, Gerrit C. & Nelylche (Quackenbush): Johannis, b. 7/25/1772, bapt. 7/25/1772 (DRC:22); Maria, b. 12/18/1775, bapt. 2/3/1776 (DRC:36). Sponsors: Johannis Newkerk & Rachel Newkerk (re:1); Abram Quack & Maria Quack (re:2).

Newkirk, Gerrit C. & Rachel (Gardenier): Samuel, b. 4/6/1791; bapt. 5/8/1791 (DRC:97). Sponsors: Samuel Gardenier & Mareitje Gardenier.

Newkirk, Johannes & Neeltje (Colier): Rachel, b. 2/28/1791; bapt. 4/10/1791 (DRC:96). Sponsors: Johanis Newkerk & Rachel Newkerk.

Newkirk, Johannes & Rachel (Knute): Arie Gerretse, b. 6/12/1773, bapt. 7/3/1773 (DRC:25); Annatje, b. 7/29/1776, bapt. 8/10/1776 (DRC:39). Sponsors: Gerrit Newkerk & Elshe Pruin (re:1); Jacob Putman & Annatje Putman (re:2).

Newkirk, William J. & Deborah (Hanson): Rachel, b. 4/19/1791; bapt. 5/15/1791 (DRC:98). Sponsors: Peter Hanson & wife.

Probate Abstract

Newkirk, Abraham, (of Glen), will dated 3/13/1830; probated 7/26/1830. Legatees: wife [not named]; sons, Garret A., Abraham (decd. and his Cornelius Garrison and Abraham); daus., Eleanor (wife of John Little John), Maria (wife of Harmanus Mabee). Executors: wife; son, Garret A. Witnesses: Albert Coggeshall, Howland Fish, Cornelius H. Putman. (WMC 57:277)

Newkirk, Garret Cornelius, (of the town of Florida), will dated 7/6/1808; codicil dated 9/29/1820; probated 1/7/1822. Legatees: sons, Gerrit, Abraham, William, Cornelius (& his Cornelius, Mary, Margaret); dau., Mary. Bequest: "twenty shillings in right of primogeniture" to his eldest son, Gerrit. Executors: sons, Gerrit and William. Witnesses: John Becker, John Newkirk, William Lauder (to the will); (codicil mentions grandson, Corenlius Newkirk, decd.); Albert, John and Francis Newkirk (witnesses to codicil). (WMC 57:173)

Newkirk, Gerrit I., (of the town of Florida), will dated 9/16/1815; probated 1/31/1820. Legatees: wife, Mary (her father of Schenectady); daus., Rachel, Hester, Tinetta (all married); Nancy, Nelly and Mary (single); sons, Albert, John and Francis. Executors: three sons. Witnesses: John Becker, William Newkirk, Barrent Martin. (WMC 57:169)

Newkirk, John, (of Montgomery Co.), will dated 1/15/1793; probated 1/5/1807. Legatees: wife, Rachel; dau., Nancy; sons, William, John and Garret (large family bible). Executors: Garret I. Putman; wife; son, Garret. Witnesses: James Hazard, Daniel McMichel, William Snook. (WMC 56:155)

Newkurk, Charles, (of Palatine), will dated 8/27/1822; probated 2/26/1823. Legatees: wife, Gertrude; brothers, Andrew and Conradt; nephew, Henry (of Conradt); sisters, Margaret, Anna, Blondana Southwick, Mary (wife of Junis Van Waggoner & her dau., Polly Morris); nephews, Charles, Jr. (& his son, Charles C.; & Charles, Jr.' wife, Elsie & their dau., Anna Maria); Charles N. Sweet. Bequest: Land in Lysander, Onondaga Co.; Manlius, Onondaga Co.; Cincinnatus, Cortland Co. Executor: nephew, Charles Nukerck, Jr. Witnesses: Peter C. Fox, Daniel C. Fox, Gabriel L. Cooper. (WMC 57:175)

Tryon County Militia

COMPENDIUM

Newkirk, Abraham   [Appendix A]
Newkirk, Benjamin
Newkirk, Garret
Newkirk, Gerrit C.
Newkirk, Gerrit
Newkirk, Jacob
Newkirk, John

Pension Abstract

Newkirk, Garret, b. 1760, son of Garret C. Newkirk, Florida, N.Y.; m. Rachel Gardinier, 6/2/1787, Caughnawaga, N.Y.; d. 11/12/1839, Florida, Montgomery Co., N.Y. Garret enlisted in 1779 and served as a private in Capt. William Snook's Co., Col. Frederick Fisher's 3rd. Regt., Tryon Co. Militia; his total service time amounted to one year, five months and nine days at the time of his discharge. (RWPA: #W24339)

Newkirk, Jacob, m. Caty [?], 8/24/1782 or 8/25/1782, Florida, N.Y.; d. 12/19/1793. (Caty Newkirk, b. 7/24/1760/1; resident of Glen, Montgomery Co., N.Y. on 6/2/1838.) Jacob enlisted from Florida in 1777 and was a private in Capt. Samuel Pettingell's Co., Col. Frederick Fisher's 3rd. Regt., Tryon Co. Militia; he was a participant in the battle of Oriskany; Jacob served for six months in 1779 as guide and interpreter under Col. Peter Gansevoort and Gen. James Clinton in an expedition [Sullivan's] to the Indian country; he was taken prisoner by the enemy in 1780 while serving in Col. Harper's Regt. and carried to Canada where he was held until his exchange eighteen months later. (RWPA: #W19912)

Newkirk, William J., b. 1765; m. [wife not named]; resident of Florida, Montgomery Co., N.Y. from childhood through 9/19/1832; d.

2/22/1849, Montgomery Co., N.Y. Children: Douw, Nicholas, Margaret, Helen, Maria Ann (m. [?] Quackenbush); Deborah (m. [?] Stack); Rachel (m. [?] Johnson). [These children were all living at the time of their father's death in 1849.] William J. volunteered in 1779 and was under the command of Capt. Jacob Gardinier at the blockhouse called Fort Fisher situated at Sacondaga; he "volunteered and actually went to take one Harry [Henry] Hare a British Spy whose family resided at Florida while he [Henry Hare] had been engaged in travelling back and forth to & from Canada as a Spy: That Captain William Snook commanded the Company in taking Hare. That they surrounded the house at the Night and made him a prisoner & he was hung as a Spy at Canajoharie"; William J. was taken prisoner in 1780 and conveyed to Niagara where he remained for three years; he resided with Col. Butler "who had been formerly acquainted with this deponents family" and remained with him "between One & two years taking care of his Horses". (RWPA: #R7623)

1790 Census

Newkerk, Garrit C.   [Appendix B]
Newkerk, Garrit Corns.
Newkerk, Garrit I.
Newkerk, Jacob
Newkerk, John
Newkerk, William
Newkirk, Garrit

NEWMAN

Birth/Baptism

Newman, Joseph & Elisabeth [?]: Johannes, b. 7/7/1784, bapt. 8/1/1784 (DRGF:85); Stephan, bapt. 9/16/1792 [Palatine Dist.] (SJC:64).

Sponsors: Johannes Bajer & Elisabeth Baader (re:1); Stephan Caming[?] & Debora Caming[?] (re:2).

Tryon County Militia

Newman, Joseph   [Appendix A]

Pension Abstract

Newman, Joseph, m. Elizabeth Boyer, 1776; d. 3/20/1843. Children: Nancy, John, Joseph, Robert, Stephen, Elizabeth, Mary, David, b. 1799/1800 (resident of Verona, Oneida Co., N.Y. on 4/21/1853). [Nancy, John and Mary were all deceased by 8/3/1853.] Joseph enlisted on 5/1/1777 in the Continental Line of Massachusetts under Capt. Alvord in the town of Colerain and also served under Col. Elmore in Gen. Wooster's Brigade; he then enlisted in Col. Jacob Klock's 2nd. Regt., Tryon Co. Militia and on 3/2/1780 was taken prisoner by the enemy and transported to Canada where he escaped, but was recaptured and remained in captivity until 5/21/1783. (RWPA: #R7626)

1790 Census

Newman, Abner   [Appendix B]
Newman, John

NEWNAN

1790 Census

Newnan, Kirby   [Appendix B]

NEWTON

Death Record

Newton, Joseph W., d. 9/13/1838, age 33 years; buried sect. 4, Colonial Cemetery, Johnstown (JC:185)

Probate Abstract

Newton, Joseph, (of Fundiesbush [Fondasbush], will dated 4/13/1812; probated 4/21/1812. Legatees: wife [not named]; sons, William and George; daus., Nelley, Mary and Bettey. Executors: William Newton, Robert Mitchell, Archibald McIntyre. Witnesses: Robet Mitchell, Peter McKinlay, Edmund G. Rawson. (WMC 56:384)

NICHLEY

1790 Census

Nichley, Michael   [Appendix B]

NICHOLAI

Birth/Baptism

Nicholai, Michael & Maria Barber [?]: Johannis, b. 11/31/1778, bapt. 12/28/1778 (DRC:51); John Michel, b. 11/11/1780, bapt. 11/20/1780 (DRC:57). Sponsors: Johannis Alt & Geertruy Alt (re:1); Johannis Hartel & Regina Hartel (re:2).

Nicoli, Michael & Mary [?], Stillwater: Henry, bapt. 10/22/1783 (JDR:15).

COMPENDIUM

NICHOLS

Marriage

Nicols, Stephan m. Elisabeth Cornute, 12/5/1792 (DFP:47)

Birth/Baptism

Nicolls, William (of Schneidersbusch) & Catharina (Reay): John, b. 5/12/1788; bapt. 1/10/1789 (SJC:8). Sponsors: Simon Nicolls & Anna Nicolls.

Death Record

Nichols, [?], (widow), d. 5/14/1837, age [not stated], of infirmities of age; buried Cherry Valley Presbyterian Church cemetery (PCV:87)

Nichols, Zachariah, d. 12/28/1835, age 67 years, of Dropsy; buried Cherry Valley Presbyterian Church cemetery (PCV:86)

Probate Abstract

Nichols, Samuel, (of Salisbury), will dated 5/13/1808; probated 7/1/1808. Legatees: daus., Bethia Witt, Mary Harris, Lydia Streeter and Lucy Lee; grandsons, William, Benejah, Willard and Samuel Randall; granddaughter, Opah Randall; grandchildren, Warren, Seth and Anson Nichols. Executor: grandson, Samuel Randall. Witnesses: Elijah Ford, Rebekah Ford, Henry Shaw. (WMC 56:158)

1790 Census

Nichols, Hesekiah   [Appendix B]
Nichols, John
Nichols, Simeon
Nichols, Thomas
Nichols, William

NICHOLSON

1790 Census

Nicholson, Peter   [Appendix B]

NICKSON

Birth/Baptism

Nickson, Tho & Ann [?]: Margaret, bapt. 7/14/1740 (FH:11A). Sponsors: Tho Burrows, Sophia Peters, Arriyaentie Vedder.

NICOLAUS

Birth/Baptism

Nicolaus, Jacob & Elisabet [?]: Barbara, b. 2/5/1795 (LTSA:88). Sponsors: parents.

NIELSON (also see NEALSON)

1790 Census

Nielson, Ball   [Appendix B]
Nielson, Thomas
Nielson, William

NIEMAN

Marriage

Nieman, Christian Earnest m. Maria Christina Kurn, 2/14/1760 (RDSA:166; LTSA:278)

588

Birth/Baptism

Niemand, Christian Ernst & Maria Christina [?]: Catharina, b. 10/24/1760; bapt. 11/2/1760 (RDSA:23); Gottlieb, b. 4/28/1763, bapt. 5/8/1763 (RDSA:39). Sponsors: Catharina (dau. of Georg Koppernoll) & Georg Kurn (re:1); Gottlieb Nostel & Magdalena Kurn (re:2).

NIER

Marriage

Nier, Conrad m. Anna Fox, 1/18/1795 (RDSA:200)

Birth/Baptism

Nier, Caspar & Margretha [?]: Margretha, b. 7/28/1769; bapt. 8/3/1769 (DRGF:19). Sponsors: Margretha Kasselmann & Johannes Hauss.

Nier, George (Gaisberg) & Elisabeth [?]: Catharina, bapt. 7/24/1791 (SJC:44). Sponsors: Georg Preiss & Catharina Preiss.

Nier, Jacob (Canajoharie) & Catharina [?]: Johannes, bapt. 2/3/1793 (SJC:71). Sponsors: Johannes Ougspurger & Susanna Ougspurger.

NIERSCH

Birth/Baptism

Niersch, Caspar & Anna [?]: Eva, b. 7/16/1776; bapt. 7/28/1776 (DRGF:19). Sponsors: Eva van Sleick & Johannes Bierhaus.

NIGHT

1790 Census

Night, John   [Appendix B]

NIKERSON

Birth/Baptism

Nikerson, Elind (of Palatine) & Margretha [?]: Nathannel, b. 10/19/1784, bapt. 10/18/1789 (SJC:18); John, b. 4/22/1787, bapt. 10/18/1789 (SJC:19); Elias, b. 4/8/1789, bapt. 10/18/1789 (SJC:19). Sponsors: John Ries & Catharina Ries (re:1); Conrad Klock & Margretha Baxter (re:2); Warner Farbus & Mary Haus (re:3).

Nikerson, Kasyas[?] (Canajoharie) & Betel [?]: Georg Matheus, bapt. 1/29/1792 (SJC:53). Sponsors: [none named].

NOFF

1790 Census

Noff, Richard   [Appendix B]

NORTH

1790 Census

North, Gabriel   [Appendix B]
North, Robert

NORTHHOOP

1790 Census

Northhoop, Nathaniel   [Appendix B]

NORTMAN

Marriage

Nortman, George m. Sarah Hunt, Warrensbush, 9/15/1787 (JDR:#70)

Birth/Baptism

Nortman, Marcus Henr. & Mary [?], Marlattsbush: Christian, bapt. 1/12/1785 (JDR:10).

NORTON

1790 Census

Norton, Christopher   [Appendix B]
Norton, Zebulan

NOTEN

1790 Census

Noten, Gideon A.   [Appendix B]

NOYES

1790 Census

Noyes, Amos   [Appendix B]

Noyes, Nehemiah
Noyes, Samuel

NURSE

1790 Census

Nurse, Jonathan   [Appendix B]
Nurse, Joshua

NUTTING

1790 Census

Nutting, Simeon   [Appendix B]

NYHOOF (also see **NEUHOFF**)

Birth/Baptism

Nyhoof, Johannes & Magdalena [?]: Johannes, b. 6/1/1782; bapt. [?] (LTSA:60). Sponsors: Severinus Wick and wife.

———

OAKH (also see **OCH**)

OAKLY

1790 Census

COMPENDIUM

Oakly, John   [Appendix B]

OAKS

1790 Census

Oaks, Samuel   [Appendix B]

OATHOUT

Probate Abstract

Oathout, Johas, (of Minden), will dated 6/11/1803; probated 7/14/1821. Legatees: wife, Maria; dau., Lidia; unborn child. Executors: Abraham and Volkert D. Oathout. Witnesses: Elias Garlock, Peter G. Fox, Henry V. Oathout. (WMC 57:171-72)

OBELL

1790 Census

Obell, Luke   [Appendix B]

OBERAKER

Birth/Baptism

Oberaker, George/Jerg & Jannetche/Jannike [?]: Anna, b. 12/19/1788 (LTSA:61); Sara, bapt. 12/9/1792 [Canajoharie] (SJC:67). Sponsors: Jacob Keller & Maria (re:1); Kneles Krankheit & Anna Krankheit (re:2).

Oberaker, George (of Gaiesberg) & Johanna [?]: Daniel, bapt. 4/25/1790 (SJC:26). Sponsors: Daniel Fort & Anna Nier.

OBERHEISER

Birth/Baptism

Oberheiser, Bernhard & Catarina [?]: Elisabet, b. 5/19/1793 (LTSA:79). Sponsors: Jacob Klock, Elisabet Nelles.

OBITS

1790 Census

Obits, Michael   [Appendix B]

OBYRN

Birth/Baptism

Obyrn, Thomas (Yukersbush) & Magdalena [?] (Palatine): Maria, bapt. 8/4/1792 (SJC:62); Johannes, bapt. 2/8/1794 (SJC:90). Sponsors: Joel Haid & Betel Haid (re:1); Samuel Asch & Catharina Yoran (re:2).

OCH

Birth/Baptism

Och, Johannes Georg & Sussanna [?]: Ernestina Catharina, b. 3/14/1766, bapt. 6/18/1766 (RDSA:65); Petries, b. 3/15/1767, bapt.

4/29/1767 (RDSA:75); Maria Barbara, b. 8/1/1776, bapt. 8/3/1776 (DRGF:19); Johann Henrich, b. 5/27/1779, bapt. 5/31/1779 (DRGF:35). Sponsors: Ernestina & Johannes Bellinger (re:1); Pieter Weber & Anna Weber (re:2); Johann Georg Sneck & Maria Barbara (re:3); Henrich Schaffer & Catharina Margretha (re:4).

Tryon County Militia

Och, George   [Appendix A]

1790 Census

Oakh, George   [Appendix B]

OCHS

Marriage

Ox, Johann Nicolaus m. Maria Fox, 1/6/1767 (RDSA:180)

Birth/Baptism

Ochs, Johann Nicolas & Maria [?]: Johann Nicolaus, b. 5/14/1769, bapt. 7/11/1769 (RDSA:95); Pieter, b. 10/9/1778, bapt. 11/8/1778 (DRGF:32). Sponsors: Johann Friedrich Bellinger & his wife H[?] (re:1); Johannes Fox & Anna (re:2).

OCHSNER

Marriage

Oxner, Johannes m. Gertraut Orndorff (dau. of Con: Orndorff), 6/30/1793 (DRGF:210)

Birth/Baptism

Ochsner, Nicolaus & Maria [?]: Johannes, b. 8/16/1767; bapt. 10/24/1767 (RDSA:79). Sponsors: Johannes Bellinger & his wife, Maria.

Death Record

Oxner, Gertraud, (wife of Johannes Oeschsener, from Columbia), d. 6/24/1818, age 45 years; buried in the cemetery near the church in the same place (RDH:276)

ODELL

Birth/Baptism

Odell, Levi (of Oswego) & Elisabeth [?]: Margaretha, bapt. 3/15/1789 (SJC:12). Sponsors: Georg Young & Margaretha Wallrath.

1790 Census

Odell, Luke   [Appendix B]

OFDAK

Birth/Baptism

Ofdak, Abram & Hannah (Deline): Abraham, b. 6/12/1794; bapt. 7/20/1794 (JDR:10).

OFENHAUSER

Birth/Baptism

Ofenhauser, Sebastian (of Palatine) & Catharina [?]: Anna Catharina, bapt. 2/22/1789 (SJC:10). Sponsors: Johannes Hess & Anna Hess.

OGDEN

Birth/Baptism

Ogden, Jonathan & Caty (Synes): Lean, b. 9/20/1790; bapt. 1/8/1791 (DRC:93). Sponsors: [none named].

Tryon County Militia

Ogden, Daniel, Sr.   [Appendix A]
Ogden, David

Pension Abstract

Ogden, David, b. 6/?/1764; m. Susannah Goodrich, 11/15/1788, Otego, Otsego Co., N.Y.; d. 10/30/1840, Franklin, Delaware Co., N.Y. (Susannah Ogden, b. ca. 1771; resident of Franklin, N.Y. on 10/10/1843.) Children: Abner (eldest child); David, b. 6/5/1792 (third child); Eleanor, b. 1802/03; Sally, b. 1809/10. [David Ogden, Jr. (b. 6/5/1792); m. Sarah McCall, 1/5/1815. Sarah (McCall) Ogden, b. 1/7/1794, dau. of Deacon Ira and Mary McCall. Children: Miriam, b. 10/15/1815; Ira, b. 9/3/1817, d. 8/18/1825; Linus, b. 12/20/1819; Suran, b. 2/16/1822; Chaney [son], b. 6/1/1824; Mary, b. 4/7/1826.] David enlisted in Caughnawaga in April 1778 and served nine months as a private in Capt. Vroman's Co., Col. Fisher's 3rd. Regt.; enlisted in April 1780 as a private in Capt. Walker's Co., Col. Weissenfel's Regt.; he was in skirmishes at Johnstown & Caughnawaga;

David was stationed at Fort Stanwix and on 3/2/1781, while cutting wood for the garrison, he was captured by a body of Indians and Tories under Brant, carried to Niagara and held there until the fall of 1782 when he was conveyed to Oswego; on 6/20/1783 David made his escape and crossed the Oswego River in a canoe, swam across Three River Point and proceeded up Oneida Lake to the Mohawk River and reached German Flatts on 6/25/1783, having been a prisoner for two years, three months and nineteen days. (RWPA: #W24364)

1790 Census

Ogden, Daniel   [Appendix B]
Ogden, Daniel, Jr.
Ogden, David
Ogden, John
Ogden, Richard

OHENS

Birth/Baptism

Ohens, Daniel & Rosina [?]: Nicolaus, b. 8/6/1791 (LTSA:84); Elisabet, b. 3/1/1794 (LTSA:84). Sponsors: [none named].

OHR

Marriage

Ohr, Jacob (son of Anthon Ohr, decd.) m. Anna Jordan (dau. of Georg Jordan), 2/1/1791 (DFP:43)

COMPENDIUM

OHRENDORFF

Marriage

Ohrndorff, Conrad m. Catharina Schumacher, 6/12/1770 (RDSA:189)

Ohrndorff, Friedr. (widower) m. Maria Petri (widow of Marc. Petri), 11/28/1786 (DRGF:204)

Ohrndorff, Henrich Fridr: m. Anna Sternberger (dau. of Jac: Sternberger), 7/1/1788 (DRGF:205)

Birth/Baptism

Ohrendorff, Conrad & Catharina [?]: Anna Eva, b. 3/10/1778, bapt. 3/20/1778 (DRGF:29); Margretha, b. 2/18/1781, bapt. 2/25/1781 (DRGF:42); Henrich, b. 1/17/1783, bapt. 1/28/1783 (DRGF:67); Elisabetha, b. 7/25/1785, bapt. 8/17/1785 (DRGF:100). Sponsors: Anna Eva Ohrndorff & Rudolph Schumacher, jur. (re:1); Margretha Cox & Nicolaus Rosencrantz (re:2); Stophel Yates, Mjr. & Maria (re:3); Georg Ittig & Elisabetha Bellinger, widow (re:4).

Ohrendorff, Friederich & Anna Eva [?]: Elisabetha, b. 11/28/1759, bapt. 12/9/1759 (RDSA:18); Anna Eva, b. 6/30/1763, bapt. 7/17/1763 (RDSA:41); Johann Henrich, b. 8/12/1765, bapt. 9/10/1765 (RDSA:57). Sponsors: Elisabeth, wife of Nicolaus Fheling (re:1); Anna Eva, wife of Christian Gettmann (re:2); Johann Henrich Majer & Anna Maria (re:3).

Ohrendorff, Friedrich & Barbara [?]: Johann Friedrich, b. 8/19/1778, bapt. 8/23/1778 (DRGF:31); Lena, b. 8/6/1780, bapt. 9/28/1780 (DRGF:40); Henrich, b. 2/23/1784,

bapt. 3/7/1784 (DRGF:81); Maria, b. 8/1/1785, bapt. 8/3/1785 (DRGF:99). Sponsors: Joh: Friedrich Ittig & Anna Maria Peiffer (re:1); Conrath Volmer & Lena (re:2); Henrich Orndorff & Catharina Volmer (re:3); [?] Ittig & Maria (re:4).

Ohrendorff, Georg & Elisabeth [?]: Elisabeth, b. 10/1/1776, bapt. 10/6/1776 (DRGF:21); Anna Eva, b. 5/2/1778, bapt. 5/3/1778 (DRGF:30); Georg, b. 1/1/1782, bapt. 1/1/1782 (DRGF:53); Wilhelm, b. 9/15/1783, bapt. 12/28/1783 (DRGF:78). Sponsors: Barbara Folmer & Joh: Friedr: Ittig (re:1); Jacob Petri & Maria (re:2); Johannes Hesse & Margretha (re:3); Joh. Wilhelm Volmer & Elisabeth Wohleben (re:4).

Ohrendorff, Peter & Catharina [?]: Friedrich, b. 9/4/1777, bapt. 9/14/1777 (DRGF:26); Maria Catharina, b. 4/14/1780, bapt. 4/18/1780 (DRGF:38); Anna Eva, b. 2/9/1783, bapt. 3/4/1783 (DRGF:68); Margretha, b. 8/6/1785, bapt. 8/17/1785 (DRGF:100). Sponsors: Fritz Ohrndorff & Elisabeth Peiffer (re:1); Joh: Michael Ittig & Catharina (re:2); Andrees Pfeiffer & Dorothea Schumacher (re:3); Henrich Ohrndorff & Margreth Pfeiffer (re:4).

Death Record

Ohrendorf, Catharina, (wife of Conrad Ohrendorf, Innkeeper in Columbia), d. 2/24/1814, age 65 years, 2 months, 15 days; buried in the field near the church cemetery in the same place (RDH:269)

Ohrendorf, Frederick, b. 1720, Canajoharie; d. 8/8/1802, Germanflats, age about 82 years; buried Germanflats Church cemetery. (Being publicly strengthened with the Sacrament of the Holy Supper in the presence of the Congregation, eight days later, after an illness

594

of five months, in the weakness of old age, he piously expired.) (RDH:248)

Ohrendorf, Johannes Conrad, (son of Henry & Bolly (Tuneclef) Ohrendorf, from Columbia), d. 3/15/1814, age 4 months, 19 days; buried near his uncle belonging to the church (RDH:270)

Ohrendorff, Barbara, (wife of Frederick Ohrendorf; born: Fulmer), d. 2/22/1821, age 63 years; buried near the stone church (RDH:280)

Ohrendorff, Conrad, (Innkeeper), d. 3/4/1819, Columbia, age 71 years, less 10 days; buried on his own land near the church in the same place (RDH:277)

Ohrendorff, Dorothea, (wife of William Ohrendorf; born: Werner), d. 9/13/1821, age 36 years; buried near the stone church [Germanflats] (RDH:281)

Ohrendorff, Maria, (widow of [?] Ohrendorf; born: Crantz), d. 6/22/1818, Germanflats, age 74 years; buried in the cemetery near the stone church (RDH:276)

Tryon County Militia

Ohrendorph, Fred., Jr.   [Appendix A]
Ohrendorph, Frederick, Sr.
Ohrendorph, George
Ohrendorph, Peter

1790 Census

Ohrendorff, Conradt   [Appendix B]
Ohrendorff, Frederick, Sr.
Ohrendorff, Peter
Orendorph, Frederick, Jr.

OHRSMANN

Birth/Baptism

Ohrsmann, John & Margaretha (Muller): Maria, b. 2/3/1788; bapt. 2/26/1788 (RDSA:116). Sponsors: Valentin Frolich & Maria (born: Hadenbeck).

OIN

Birth/Baptism

Oin, Abraham & Sara [?]: Thomas, b. 5/17/1794 (LTSA:84). Sponsors: Johannes Lawx & Eva.

OLDEN

1790 Census

Olden, Prince   [Appendix B]

OLDMAN

1790 Census

Oldman, [?]arant   [Appendix B]
Oldman, Frederick

OLEA

1790 Census

Olea, Gilbert   [Appendix B]

OLEN

OLLER

OLENDORFPH (also see ULENDORFF)

OLIN

Birth/Baptism

Olin, William & Ariaantje (Wimpel): Isaac, bapt. 9/13/1761 (DRC:5); Reyer, bapt. 1764 (DRC:12). Sponsors: Isaac Coljer & Annaatje Coljer (re:1); William Snogh & Susanna Mebie (re:2).

OLINE

OLIVER

OLMSTED

Probate Abstract

Olmsted, Lewis, (of Northampton), will dated 1/8/1812; probated 5/3/1813. Legatees: wife, Sarah; son, Jay; dau., Betsey. Executors: wife, Joseph Spier, Isaac Brown. Witnesses: Justus and Betty Olmsted, Calvin Rice, Joseph Spier. (WMC 56:387)

Pension Abstract

Olmstead, Ashbel, b. 6/?/1763, Simsbury, Hartford Co., Conn., son of Daniel Olmstead; wife [not named]; resident of Triangle, Broome Co., N.Y. on 8/6/1832. Children: Luman (resident of Triangle, N.Y. in 1852). Ashbel enlisted from his home in Simsbury, Conn. in July 1780 and served on various tours of duty to 12/24/1781; he was a private under Capt. Adonijah Burr, Col. Mead's Regt.; Capt. Giles Pettibone, Col. Chauncy Pettibone's Regt.; Capt. John Churchill, Col. John Mead's Regt.; and Capt. Billing, Col. Herman Swift's Regt. [In 1790, Ashbel Olmstead was a resident of Whites, Montgomery Co., N.Y.] (RWPA: #S23346)

Olmstead, Daniel, b. 1749, Simsbury, Hartford Co., Conn; m. Rosannah Tuller, 11/22/1782, at Simsbury; d. 8/11/1836. (Rosannah Olmstead, b. 1762/3; resident of Whitestown, Oneida Co., N.Y. on 9/13/1838; d. 6/14/1853.) Children: Chanle, b. 6/4/1785;

Elihu, b. 3/11/1787; Mettee, b. 11/19/1789; Daniel, b. 4/15/1791; Liman, b. 8/6/1793; Elijah, b. 7/19/1795; Orrin, b. 7/13/1798; Oliver, b. 3/4/1800; Luke, b. 5/10/1802. Daniel enlisted from Simsbury, Conn. in 1776 and served on various tours of duty through 1780; he was a private under Capt. Ebenezer Fitch Bissell's Co., Col. Jedediah Huntington's Regt.; Capt. Abel Pettibone's Co., Col. Enos' Regt.; in 1779 Daniel was a corporal for six months; in 1779 and 1780 he was made a sergeant in Capt. Gatlin's Co., Col. Arnold's Regt.; Daniel participated in the battles of Long Island and White Plains. (RWPA: #W19936)

Olmstead, Gamaliel, b. 1759, Conn.; m. Elizabeth Baker, 4/21/1798, Utica, Oneida Co., N.Y.; d. 7/3/1832. Children: Ester, b. 9/8/1801; Charles, b. 8/28/1805; Mary, b. 12/27/1808; Henry, b. 5/8/1811; Laury, b. 2/6/1817. Gamaliel enlisted as a private in the Town of New Hartford, Litchfield Co., Conn. on 2/1/1778 and served as a private in a company commanded by Capt. Joseph Walker in the Conn. Line; he was in the battles of Rhode Island and Springfield, N.J.; he was discharged from military service on 2/1/1781. [Gamaliel Olmstead was a resident of Whites, Montgomery Co., N.Y. in 1790. He applied for his pension from Whites (later called Whitestown, Oneida Co., N.Y. where he was living on 4/18/1818.] (RWPA: #W5435)

1790 Census

Olmsted, Ashbel   [Appendix B]
Olmsted, Barton
Olmsted, Gamaliel

OMSTEAD

1790 Census

Omstead, Henry   [Appendix B]

ONEAL

1790 Census

Oneal, John   [Appendix B]

ONES

1790 Census

Ones, Essenetus   [Appendix B]

ONY

Birth/Baptism

Ony/Ogny, John (Field Dist.) & Mary [?]: Junys[?], bapt. 1/7/1791, age 8 years (SJC:36); John, bapt. 1/7/1791, age 5 years (SJC:36); Robert, bapt. 1/7/1791, age 3 years (SJC:36); Margretha, bapt. 4/28/1791 (SJC:41). Sponsors: Heinrich Mayer & Anna Eva Mayer (re:1); John Mayer & Mary Mayer (re:2); Andreas Mayer & Catharina Mayer (re:3); Georg Hellmer & Margretha Hellmer (re:4).

OOLEY

1790 Census

Ooley, Henry   [Appendix B]

COMPENDIUM

OOLMAN (also see ULMAN)

Marriage

Oolman, Barent m. Echje Crommel, 11/14/1773 (DRC:158)

Oolman, John m. Maria Hoff, 8/25/1779 (DRC:162)

Birth/Baptism

Oolman, Barent & Eche (Crommell): Maria, b. 6/1/1775, bapt. 7/9/1775 (DRC:34); Maria, b. 11/11/1782, bapt. 1/4/1783 (DRC:64); Fredrik, b. 5/29/1787, bapt. 7/15/1787 (DRC:85). Sponsors: Harmanis Crommell & Catrina Crommell (re:1); David Luis & Maria Luis (re:2); Fredrik Ulman & Naatje Ulman (re:3).

Oolman, John & Catrina (Hoff): Frederick, b. 4/10/1781, bapt. 9/4/1781 (DRC:68); Catrina, b. 3/22/1783, bapt. 5/11/1783 (DRC:66). Sponsors: Frederick Oolman & Maria Hoff (re:1); Herms. Crommell & Catrina Crommell (re:2).

OOSTRANDER

Birth/Baptism

Oostrander, Henderick & Elizabeth (Schuivets): Willem, b. 10/1/1778; bapt. 1/3/1779 (DRC:51). Sponsors: Joseph Prentip & Annatje Prentip.

OPIZ

Birth/Baptism

Opiz, Michael & Anna [?]: Margaret, b. 8/15/1794 (LTSA:87). Sponsors: Cornelius Wem, Margaret Boshart.

ORENIENS

Birth/Baptism

Oreniens, Johatan & Regina [?]: Catarina, b. 2/5/1790 (LTSA:71). Sponsors: John Smit & Beiol.

ORLOB

Birth/Baptism

Orlob, Wilm & Maria [?]: Anna Maria, b. 4/6/1757 (LTSA:21). Sponsors: Johannes Kesler & his wife, Anna Maria.

ORTON

1790 Census

Orton, David   [Appendix B]

OSBURN

1790 Census

Osburn, Samuel   [Appendix B]

OSMAN

COMPENDIUM

Death Record

Osman, Isajas, (Language Professor, from Livonia), d. 3/4/1812, age 64 years; buried in the new cemetery at Herkimer (RDH:265)

1790 Census

Osman, Henry   [Appendix B]

OSTERHOUT

Birth/Baptism

Osterhout, Cornelius & Sarah (Hallenbek): Elisabetha, b. 9/11/1781, bapt. 9/19/1781 (DRGF:48); Baata, b. 3/28/1786, bapt. 4/21/1786 (DRC:78). Sponsors: Elisabeth Brunner & Friedrich Mohr (re:1); Abram Kidds & Baata Hallenbek (re:2).

Osterhout, Friedrich & Elisabeth [?]: Pieter, b. 1/28/1782; bapt. 2/1/1782 (DRGF:54). Sponsors: Pieter Fox & Anna Bellinger.

Probate Abstract

Ousterout, Frederick, (of Oppenheim), will dated 10/6/1815; probated 6/4/1816. Legatees: wife, Elizabeth; sons, Frederick, George, Abraham, Peter and Henry; daus., Eva Frame and Elizabeth Smith; grandchildren, Elizabeth and Joshaway Ousterot. Executors: Peter and George Ousterout. Witnesses: Daniel Hyde, George Klock, Patrick Kennedy. (WMC 56:397)

Tryon County Militia

Osterhout, John   [Appendix A]

1790 Census

Osterhout, Cornelius   [Appendix B]
Osterhout, Frederick
Ousterhout, John

OSTERMAN

Marriage

Osterman, Christian m. Elizabeth Nukirk, 7/8/1777 (DRC:161)

Birth/Baptism

Osterman, Christian & Elizabeth (Newkirk): Peter, b. 5/4/1778, bapt. 5/10/1778 (DRC:47); Christina, b. 2/1/1782, bapt. 2/3/1782 (DRC:60); William, bapt. 12/26/1784 at age 9 weeks (DRC:69); Elisabeth, b. 4/15/1787, bapt. 4/16/1787 (DRC:84). Sponsors: [none named] (re:1); Joseph Pattingle & Christina Oosterhout (re:2); John Werdt & Annatje Niewkerk (re:3); Gerrit C. Niewkerk, Jr. & Elisabeth Metselaer (re:4).

Pension Abstract

Osterman, Christian, b. 1756; m. Elisabeth Nukirk, 7/8/1777, Dutch Ref. Church, Caughnawaga, Tryon Co., N.Y.; d. 3/5/1839. (Elisabeth Osterman, b. 1756/7; resident of Guilderland, Albany Co., N.Y. on 7/18/1839.) Children: [not named in application; but a son-in-law, Elias Gray, is mentioned in the file]. Christian enlisted in March 1778 from Tryon Co. and was a private in Capt. Robert McKean's Co., Col. Wynkoop's Regt. of the N.Y. Line; Christian fought in the battle of Johnstown; he was allowed a pension on 11/2/1818 while a resident of Duanesburgh,

599

COMPENDIUM

Schenectady Co., N.Y. (RWPA: #W21876)

1790 Census

Ostroman, Christian   [Appendix B]

OSTEROTH

Birth/Baptism

Osteroth, Frederick (of Yukersbusch) & Elizabeth (Klock): Johannes, b. 1/3/1785, bapt. 1/9/1785 (DRGF:92); Eva, bapt. 1/3/1790 (SJC:21); Elisabeth, bapt. 10/24/1792 (SJC:66). Sponsors: Johannes Glock & Anna Margreth (re:1); Conrad Hellegas & Eva Hellegas (re:2); Henrich Mayer & Anna Mayer (re:3).

Osteroth, John & Catharina [?]: Anna Eva, b. 12/28/1777, bapt. 3/4/1778 (DRGF:29); Johann Nicolas, b. 11/7/1780, bapt. 1/?/1781 (DRGF:41); Catharina, b. 11/19/1784, bapt. 3/25/1785 (DRGF:94). Sponsors: Johannes Steph: Franck & Anna Eva (re:1); Johannes Bellinger & Maria (re:2); Friedrich Hess & Bally (re:3).

Tryon County Militia

Osteroth, Frederick   [Appendix A]

OSTRAM

Marriage

Ostram, John m. Nancy Lane, both of Marlatsbush, Montgomery Co., 2/7/1787 (JDR:3)

Birth/Baptism

Ostrom, John & Nancy (Lane), Marlatsbush: Henricus, bapt. 4/18/1790 (JDR:15); Elizabeth, bapt. 3/11/1792 [Note: surname incorrectly noted as OSTERMAN.] (JDR:13).

1790 Census

Ostrom, Thomas   [Appendix B]
Ostrum, John
Ostrum, Joshua

OSTRAND

Birth/Baptism

Ostrand, John & Sarah (Concklin), Newtown: Sarah, bapt. 7/3/1785 (JDR:23).

OSTROM see OSTRAM

OSTRUM see OSTRAM

OTTMAN

Probate Abstract

Ottman, Christopher, (of Canajoharie), will dated 1/21/1820; probated 9/5/1820. Legatees: sons, Henry and Philip; daus., Eva and Elizabeth. Bequest: Seats in Currys Town Church to sons, Henry and Philip. Executors: son, Henry; Henry Antis, John S. Clement. Witnesses: John Malich, John Alpaugh, Henry

600

COMPENDIUM

I. Antis. (WMC 57:170)

<u>1790 Census</u>

Otman, Christian   [Appendix B]
Otman, William

OUDERKERK

<u>Birth/Baptism</u>

Ouderkerk, Abraham m. Mary [?]: Abraham, bapt. 8/27/1738 (FH:4); Hannah, bapt. 9/21/1740 (FH:11A). Sponsors: Joseph Clement, Wm. Prentop Junr, Anna Clement (re:1); Will. Prentop Jur, Engeltie Hanse, Elizabeth Prentop (re:2).

OUGSPURGER

<u>Birth/Baptism</u>

Ougspurger, Johannes (Canajoharie) & Susanna [?]: Elisabeth, bapt. 2/3/1793 (SJC:71). Sponsors: Georg Nier & his wife.

OULTSAVER (also see ULSHEVER)

<u>1790 Census</u>

Oultsaver, Bastian   [Appendix B]

OVERACKER

<u>1790 Census</u>

Overacker, George   [Appendix B]

OVERBACK

<u>1790 Census</u>

Overback, Benjamin   [Appendix B]

OWENS

<u>1790 Census</u>

Owens, Isaac   [Appendix B]

OWER

<u>1790 Census</u>

Ower, John   [Appendix B]

OX see OCHS

OXNER see OCHSNER

601

COMPENDIUM

PABST

Birth/Baptism

Pabst, Adam & Maria [?]: Margreth, b. 8/8/1767; bapt. 9/24/1767 (RDSA:77). Sponsors: Maria Margretha & Peter Ziegler.

PADDOCK

1790 Census

Paddock, Jobe   [Appendix B]
Paddock, Peter

PADGET

Probate Abstract

Padget, James, (of Glen), will dated 7/14/1825; probated 10/25/1830. Legatees: sons, James, Robert and John; granddau., Sally Clayton; daus., Barbary, Sarah, Jane, Rebecca and Mary. Executors: son, James; John Wilcox. Witnesses: Edd. Dykeman, Robert Robison, Cornelius H. Putman. (WMC 57:278)

PAGE

1790 Census

Page, Abraham   [Appendix B]
Page, Isaac
Page, John
Page, Jonathan

PAINE

1790 Census

Paine, Ezra   [Appendix B]
Paine, Joshua
Paine, Philip

PALMATEER

Tryon County Militia

Palmateer, John   [Appendix A]
Palmateer, Thomas
Palmateer, William

PALMER

Marriage

Palmer, Amaziah m. Rebecca Hubble, Balltown, Albany Co., 4/9/1782 (JDR:1)

Palmer, J., Esq. (of Stillwater) m. Mercy Keyes (of Canajoharie), 4/1/1826 (PCBC:51)

Death Record

Palmer, Gershon, d. 5/1/1830, age 69 years, of Consumption; buried Cherry Valley Presbyterian Church cemetery (PCV:84)

Palmer, Hannah, d. 9/26/1831, age 67 years, of Cholera Morbus; buried Cherry Valley Presbyterian Church cemetery (PCV:85)

1790 Census

Palmer, Benjamin   [Appendix B]
Palmer, Ichabod B.

602

COMPENDIUM

Palmer, Nathan

PALNATON

1790 Census

Palnaton, John   [Appendix B]

PALSLI

Birth/Baptism

Palsli, Andrew (of Palatine) & Lea (Pikard): Maria, bapt. 2/15/1789 (SJC:9); Anna, bapt. 12/12/1790 (SJC:35); Margretha, bapt. 5/20/1792 (SJC:59); Niclaus, bapt. 10/22/1793 (SJC:84). Sponsors: Jacob Palsli & Maria Pikard (re:1); Jacob Fehling & Anna Fehling (re:2); Heinrich Pikard & Anna Eva Ris (re:3); Niclaus Pikard & Barbara Pikard (re:4).

Palsli, Johannes & Catharina [?]: Jacob, bapt. 11/3/1788 (SJC:5). Sponsors: Jacob Hubel & Maria Hubel.

PAPA

Death Record

Papa, [?], (wife of Ernst Papa), b. 3/3/1759; d. 10/8/1808, age 49 years, 7 months, 5 days (DFP:92)

PARCEL

1790 Census

Parcel, Jacob   [Appendix B]
Parcel, Paul

PARIS

Birth/Baptism

Paris, Daniel & Catharine [?]: Isaac, b. 4/19/1799, bapt. 7/21/1799 (JPC:15); William Saunders, bapt. 4/5/1801 (JPC:19).

Paris, Daniel & Maria [?]: Delia, b. 7/11/1785; bapt. 7/17/1785 (DRGF:99). Sponsors: Jacob Perris & Maria.

Paris, Isaac & Catharina [?]: Isaacus, b. 12/25/1761, bapt. 1/1/1762 (RDSA:29); Margretha, b. 1/7/1766, bapt. 1/12/1766 (RDSA:61); Franciscus Ludovicus, b. 12/17/1767, bapt. 12/25/1767 (RDSA:81). Sponsors: Ludwig Feyl & Sophia Lepper (re:1); Margretha & Conrad Lepper (re:2); Peter Sutz & his wife, Elisabeth (re:3).

Death Record

Paris, Ann Mary, (dau. of Daniel & Catharine Paris), d. 7/25/1821, age 10 years, 5 months; buried sect. 5, Colonial Cemetery, Johnstown (JC:185)

Paris, Catharine, d. 8/4/1806, age 68 years; buried sect. 5, Colonial Cemetery, Johnstown (JC:185)

Paris, Franz Ludwig, d. 7/16/1796, age 28 years & 6 months, less one day; buried 7/18/1796 (DFP:89)

603

Paris, Joh. Adam, (son of Ludovici Paris), d. 10/9/1804, Herkimer, age 22 years, 4 months, 11 days; buried in the cemetery near the church at Herkimer (RDH:253)

Paris, Margaret, (dau. of Daniel & Catharine Paris), d. 9/30/1821, age 17 years, 25 days; buried sect. 5, Colonial Cemetery, Johnstown (JC:185)

Paris, Pierre Jane [sic.] , (son of Daniel & Catharine Paris), d. 10/26/1812, age 10 years, 2 months, 20 days; buried sect. 5, Colonial Cemetery, Johnstown (JC:185)

Paris, William, (son of Daniel & Catharine Paris), d. 2/5/1812, age 7 months, 15 days; buried sect. 5, Colonial Cemetery, Johnstown (JC:185)

Probate Abstract

Paris, Isaac, (of [not stated]), will dated 3/26/1790; probated 6/21/1790. Legatees: his mother [not named]; brothers, Daniel (not yet of age), and Francis (land at Torloch). Executors: Rev. John Daniel Gros, Corn[elius] Glen and Barent Blecker (both merchants of Albany), Paul Hochstrasser. Witnesses: Richard Young, Arnold Willkens, Robert McFarlan. (WMC 56:146)

1790 Census

Paris, Anthony   [Appendix B]
Paris, Catherine

PARKEL

1790 Census

Parkel, Nathaniel   [Appendix B]

PARKER

Marriage

Parker, William m. Nanse Freeman, both of Settles Barrack, 11/2/1789 (JDR:#83)

Birth/Baptism

Parker, Edward & Anne (Milligan), Warrensborough: Elizabeth, bapt. 1/9/1786 (JDR:13).

Death Record

Parker, Emma, (dau. of William & Elizabeth Parker), d. 9/1/1841, age 2 years, 6 months; buried sect. 10, Colonial Cemetery, Johnstown (JC:185)

Parker, William, (son of William & Elizabeth Parker), d. 8/22/1835, age 1 year, 4 months; buried sect. 10, Colonial Cemetery, Johnstown (JC:185)

1790 Census

Parker, Andress   [Appendix B]
Parker, Asa
Parker, Daniel (2)
Parker, Edward
Parker, Elijah
Parker, Elijah, Jr.
Parker, Henry
Parker, Jason
Parker, Jonathan (2)

PARKHOUSE

1790 Census

Parkhouse, Frederick   [Appendix B]

PARKIE

Death Record

Parkie, [?], (widow of Jacob Parkie, from Schyler-Town), d. 11/24/1813, age 95 years; buried in the public cemetery in the same place (RDH:268)

Parkie, Polly, (wife of Peter Parkie, Jr.), d. 12/25/1818, Shyler, age 24 years; buried in the same place (RDH:277)

PARKMAN

1790 Census

Parkman, Alexander   [Appendix B]

PARKS

1790 Census

Parks, David   [Appendix B]
Parks, Ezra
Parks, John
Parks, Joseph
Parks, Robert
Parks, Squire

PARKSON

1790 Census

Parkson, Reuben   [Appendix B]
Parkson, Silvanus

PARMELLA

1790 Census

Parmella, Amos   [Appendix B]

PARRY

1790 Census

Parry, Archer   [Appendix B]

PARSEE

Death Record

Parsee, Henry, (son of T. B. & Mary Parsee), d. 4/15/1839, age 18 months, 7 days; buried sect. 6, Colonial Cemetery, Johnstown (JC:185)

Parsee, John, (son of T. B. & Mary Parsee), d. ?/15/1830, age 9 months, 17 days; buried sect. 6, Colonial Cemetery, Johnstown (JC:185)

PARSHALL

1790 Census

COMPENDIUM

Parshall, Israel   [Appendix B]

PARSONS

Probate Abstract

Parsons, Joseph, (of the Town of Amsterdam), will dated 3/9/1813; probated 6/7/1820. Legatees: wife, Hannah. Executors: Paris Otis (of Galway), Thomas Hewit (of Broadalbin), Harvey Bartlett (of Amsterdam). Witnesses: John Brower, John W. Cady, Thomas Beekman. (WMC 57:170)

1790 Census

Parsons, Chatwell   [Appendix B]
Parsons, Eli
Parsons, Moses

PATCHIN

1790 Census

Patchin, Freegift   [Appendix B]
Patchin, John, Jr.

PATER

1790 Census

Pater, Francis   [Appendix B]

PATERSON

Birth/Baptism

Paterson, John & [?], Warrensborough: Henry, bapt. 7/16/1780 (JDR:15); William, bapt. 7/21/1782 (JDR:24).

Patterson, James & Maria [?]: Nelly, b. 3/23/1768; bapt. 7/4/1768 (RDSA:87). Sponsors: John Darnthe & Catharina van Sleuk.

1790 Census

Paterson, James   [Appendix B]
Patterson, Edward
Patterson, James

PATRICK

1790 Census

Patrick, Robert   [Appendix B]

PATRIDGE

1790 Census

Patridge, Thomas   [Appendix B]

PATTESON

Tryon County Militia

Patteson, Adam   [Appendix A]

COMPENDIUM

PAUL

Marriage

Paul, Joseph m. Juliana Stein, 3/11/1765 (RDSA:175)

PAULDING (also see PAWLING)

1790 Census

Paulding, Henry   [Appendix B]

PAUTER

1790 Census

Pauter, John   [Appendix B]
Pauter, Lodowick

PAWLING (also see PAULDING)

Death Record

Pawling, Elizabeth, (wife of Capt. Henry Y. Pawling), d. 10/16/1826, age 69 years; buried sect. 3, Colonial Cemetery, Johnstown (JC:185)

Pawling, Henry Y., (Captain, a soldier of the Revolution), d. 8/16/1825, age 69 years; buried sect. 3, Colonial Cemetery, Johnstown (JC:185)

Probate Abstract

Pawling, Elizabeth, (widow of Henry, of Johnstown), will dated 10/7/1826; probated 3/14/1827. Legatees: Henry Pawling Lounsberry, Christopher D. Lounsberry; Henry Pawling Davis (of James); Henry Pawling Burk (of John); Rachel (of Christopher D. Lounsberry); Rachel Winne; niece, Catherine (wife of Daniel B. Davis); nephew, Daniel B. Davis; niece, Elizabeth Buxton. Executor: Daniel B. Davis. Witnesses: William I. Dodge, Patience Dodge, Eliza Hoffman. (WMC 57:267)

Pawling, Henry, (of Johnstown), will dated 6/19/1795; probated 5/24/1827. Legatees: wife, Elizabeth; brother, John. Executors: Wife; James Lansing, John Davis. Witnesses: Jonathan Clayton, William Dunlap, James Lansing. (WMC 57:268)

PEACOCK

Probate Abstract

Peacock, Hugh, (of the town of Florida), will dated 9/15/1799; probated 10/9/1799. Legatees: wife, Jane; brothers, David and Robert (of Great Britain). Executors: John Crull, Thomas Keachy. Witnesses: Jeremiah McCartney, Robert McCrady, Hugh Sample. (WMC 56:150)

PEAK

1790 Census

Peak, James   [Appendix B]

PEAS

COMPENDIUM

1790 Census

Peas, Samuel   [Appendix B]

PEASE

Probate Abstract

Pease, William S., (of Broadalbin), will dated 2/10/1826; probated 5/2/1826. Legatees: wife, Jane; Daniel Pease's second son, Lewis. Bequest: Mortgage signed by Nathaniel Ruggles, dated 4/24/1824, Bridgeport, Conn.; Note dated 5/1/1810, Huntington, Conn., by Levi & Albert Edwards; Notes dated 6/8/1825, Canaan, Col. Co., N.Y., by Daniel Pease and Phineas Cook; Notes dated 5/20/1825, Nassau, N.Y. by John B. Pease; Notes dated 6/18/1822, Nassau, N.Y. by Truman Norton; Note dated 5/?/1826, Broadalbin, by Trustees M.E. Church, Fondasbush, Broadalbin; Note dated 1/28/1823, Lenox, by Joseph Norton. Executor: Lewis Pease. Witnesses: Doddridge Smith, Alerin Fuller, Judah Sowle. (WMC 57:264)

1790 Census

Pease see House   [Appendix B]

PECK

Birth/Baptism

Peck, Cobus & Catrina (Meebe): Harmanus, b. 11/9/1786; bapt. 1/29/1787 (DRC:82 & 86). Sponsors: Harmanus Meebe & Susanna W[?].

Peck, John & [?] (Van Nost?): John, b.

7/16/1791; bapt. 7/28/1791 (DRC:99). Sponsors: Francis [?] & [?].

1790 Census

Peck, Harmanus   [Appendix B]
Peck, Jedediah
Peck, Joseph
Peck, Luman

PEEK

Birth/Baptism

Peek, George & Florah (Blake), Schenectady: Annah, bapt. 4/26/1802 (JDR:10).

Probate Abstract

Peek, Jacobus, (of the town of Florida), will dated 6/11/1823; probated 6/14/1827. Legatees: wife, Nancy; sons, Cornelius, John, Joseph (of Princetown), and Henry; daus., Catlina (wife of Tunis Van Olinda), Caty (wife of Samuel Bant) and Elizabeth. Executors: sons, Cornelius, Joseph and John. Witnesses: Garret Stephens, Harmonus Peek, Th. X. Harman, Jr. (WMC 57:268-269)

1790 Census

Peek, Moses   [Appendix B]

PEEKLE

1790 Census

Peekle, John   [Appendix B]
Peekle, John, Jr.

608

COMPENDIUM

PELLENDOM

1790 Census

Pellendom, James   [Appendix B]

PELLETT

1790 Census

Pellett, Silas   [Appendix B]

PERCY

Tryon County Militia

Percy, Ephraim   [Appendix A]

PERKINS

Probate Abstract

Perkins, William, (of Duanesburgh, Albany Co.), will dated 5/30/1794; probated 8/17/1795. Legatees: wife, Elizabeth; son, William; dau., Elizabeth. Executors: wife and friend, Charles Wright (of Sandersfield, Mass.). Witnesses: Adoniram[?] Kimball, Benjamin Jacobs, Benjamin Egelston, Isaac Delamater. (WMC 56:148)

1790 Census

Perkens, Silas   [Appendix B]
Perkins, Nathaniel

PERRY

Birth/Baptism

Perry, Elizabeth & [?]: Benjamin, bapt. 3/9/1739/40 (FH:10). Sponsors: Joseph Clement, James Elwood, Anna Clement.

Death Record

Perry, Zilpha, (wife of Gidion Perry), d. 8/2/1849, age 32 years; buried sect. 12, Colonial Cemetery, Johnstown (JC:186)

1790 Census

Perry, George H.   [Appendix B]
Perry, Jonas
Perry, Jonathan
Perry, Nathan
Perry, Thomas

PERSON

Deed Abstract

Persen, Christopher [by Samuel Clyde, Sheriff of Montgomery Co.] (by a Writ of Fieri Facias against Christopher Persen for debts owed to James Richey in the sum of L30.6.7.) to Matthew Cannon and James Dickson. Instrument dated 5/22/1786; recorded 6/22/1786. Description: All of the lands belonging to Christopher Persen situated in Old England District, in a patent containing 9,000 acres granted to Richard Wells, and known as Lot #27 (100 acres). Samuel Clyde on 10/11/1785 exposed to sale at public vendue and did sell the land (Lot #27) to Matthew Cannon and James Dickson. Consideration: L34.10.0., which was paid to James Richey for

COMPENDIUM

his debt and damages. Witnesses: Tunis Van Wagenen, James Cannon. (MVL:8)

1790 Census

Person, Pool   [Appendix B]

PERSONS

Probate Abstract

Persons, James, (of [not stated]), will dated 1/22/1810; probated 2/15/1810. Legatees: wife, Hannah; sons, James, Oliver, Gurdon and John; daus., Mercy, Hannah and Lynda (wife of Daniel Bowen). Executors: sons, John and Gurdon. Witnesses: Isaac and John Thrall, Eli'h Cheadel. (WMC 56:161)

PESAUSIE

Tryon County Militia

Pesausie, John   [Appendix A]

PESOS

Death Record

Pesos, [?], d. ?/?/1831, age 63 years; buried Presbyterian Church cemetery, Cherry Valley (PCV:84)

PETERS

Tryon County Militia

Peters, Joseph   [Appendix A]
Peters, Joseph, Jr.

1790 Census

Peters, Benjamin   [Appendix B]
Peters, Samuel

PETERSON

1790 Census

Peterson, Zachariah   [Appendix B]

PETISS

1790 Census

Petiss, John   [Appendix B]

PETRY

Marriage

Petry, Daniel m. Maria Huber, 7/25/1784 (DRGF:200)

Petry, Daniel Jac: m. Anna [Paul] Seghner, 4/9/1791 (DRGF:207)

Petry, Fritz m. Eva Ohrndorff (dau. of Conr: Ohrndorff), 8/31/1794 (DRGF:211)

Petry, Heinrich m. Maria Loux, 4/26/1789 (RDSA:194)

COMPENDIUM

Petry, Johann Dieterich (son of Johann Jost Petri, Little Falls) m. Catharina Klock (dau. of Johannes Klock, Canajoharie), 3/31/1761 (RDSA:169)

Petry, Johann Jost (M.) m. Catharina Kessler, 5/5/1766 (RDSA:179)

Petry, Johann Jost (son of Johannes Petri) m. Anna Barbara Windekker, 10/24/1769 (RDSA:188)

Petry, Johannes Diet: m. Anna Eva Bellinger (dau. of Ad. Bellinger), 7/17/1787 (DRGF:205)

Petry, Johannes J: Diet: m. Gertraud G: Demuth, 12/26/1786 (DRGF:204)

Petry, Johannes Joh: m. [?] A. Bellinger, ?/25/1795 [date: between Oct./Dec.] (DRGF:213)

Petry, Marcus m. Elisabeth Walker (formerly wife of Ephraim Walker & dau. of Henry Killy), 2/3/1796 (DFP:54)

Petry, Wilhelmus, Dr. (Burnetsfield) m. Margretha Salome Wolff, 12/22/1766 (RDSA:180)

Birth/Baptism

Petry, Heinrich & Maria [?]: Heinrich, b. 4/22/1790 (LTSA:65). Sponsors: Peter Laux, Elisabeth Koch.

Petry, Henrich (Royal Grant) & Magdalena [?]: Magdalena, bapt. 10/23/1791 (SJC:49). Sponsors: Adam Garlach & Dorothea Zimmermann.

Petry, Jacob & Maria [?]: Georg, b. 5/20/1777,

bapt. 6/1/1777 (DRGF:23); Jacob, b. 12/31/1779, bapt. 2/1/1780 (DRGF:38); Catharina, b. 2/15/1784, bapt. 3/7/1784 (DRGF:81); Delia, b. 2/15/1784, bapt. 3/7/1784 (DRGF:81). Sponsors: Georg Ohrndorff & Elisabeth (re:1); Jacob Smaal & Maria (re:2); Johann Michael Ittig & Catharina (re:3); Jno. Wieth & Delia (re:4).

Petry, Joh: Dieterich & Elisabeth [?]: Lena, b. 7/14/1776; bapt. 7/15/1776 (DRGF:19). Sponsors: Werner Tyghart & Helena.

Petry, Joh: Dietrich & [?]: Catharina, b. 2/18/1777; bapt. 3/7/1777 (DRGF:22). Sponsors: Jacob Kessler & [?].

Petry, Joh. Jost D: & Maria Elisabeth [?]: Daniel, b. 11/5/1777, bapt. 11/9/1777 (DRGF:27); Lorentz, b. 9/2/1781, bapt. 12/26/1781 (DRGF:52); Elisabeth, b. 2/23/1784, bapt. 3/13/1784 (DRGF:82). Sponsors: Daniel Petri & Elisabeth Kesslar (re:1); Henrich Zimmermann & Anna Zimmermann (re:2); David Majer & Catharina Zimmermann (re:3).

Petry, Johann Dieterich & Catharina [?]: Catharina, b. 12/21/1761, bapt. 1/16/1762 (RDSA:30); Johann Jost, b. 2/14/1763, bapt. 2/26/1763 (RDSA:38); Johannes, b. 2/17/1765, bapt. 5/27/1765 (RDSA:55). Sponsors: Catharina (dau. of Jacob Foltz) & Johannes (son of Hannes Klock) (re:1); Johann Jost (son of Marcus Petri) & [?] (re:2); Johannes Klock & Catharina Foltz (re:3).

Petry, Johann Jost & Maria Eva [?]: Delia, b. 5/12/1760, bapt. 5/25/1760 (RDSA:20); Catharina, b. 11/4/1763, bapt. 11/7/1763 (RDSA:42). Sponsors: Anna (dau. of Henrich Merckel) & Wilhelm (son of Georg Coppernoll) (re:1); Catharina Herder & Georg Friderich

COMPENDIUM

Helmer (re:2).

Petry, Johann Jost (son of Marcus) & Catharina [?]: Anna Maria, b. 8/31/1766, bapt. 9/15/1766 (RDSA:68); Anna Eva, b. 2/29/1768, bapt. 4/18/1768 (RDSA:85); Margretha, b. 3/5/1770, bapt. 3/22/1770 (RDSA:101); Johanes, b. 3/6/1776, bapt. 3/24/1776 (DRGF:16); Johann Jost, b. 6/19/1777, bapt. 7/6/1777 (DRGF:24). Sponsors: Anna Maria & Johannes Heering (re:1); Jacob Petri & Anna Eva Petri (re:2); Elisabeth Kessler & Dieterich Petry (re:3); Jacob Grantz & Elisabeth Joh: Kessler (re:4); Jacob Kesslar & Delia (re:5).

Petry, Johann Marcus & Anna Maria [?]: Cordelia, b. 5/10/1764, bapt. 6/9/1764 (RDSA:47); Elisabeth, b. 3/29/1766, bapt. 5/5/1766 (RDSA:64). Sponsors: Catharina Foltz & Johann Jost Petri (re:1); Elisabeth Petri & Jacob Kessler (re:2).

Petry, Johannes & Barbara [?]: Anna Elisabeth, b. 7/13/1776, bapt. 7/21/1776 (DRGF:19); Christian, b. 5/14/1782, bapt. 5/26/1782 (DRGF:58). Sponsors: Georg Zimmermann & Anna Elisabeth (re:1); Henrich Joh: Glock & Maria (re:2).

Petry, Johannes (of Schneidersbusch) & Dorothea [?]: Johann Jost, b. 2/15/1789; bapt. 3/20/1789 (SJC:12). Sponsors: Johann Jost Petri & Eva Petri.

Petry, Johannes & [thought to be Margretha as named in baptismal record (LTSA:12)]: Margretha, b. 7/8/1761; bapt. 7/28/1761 (RDSA:27). Sponsor: Margretha, wife of Christian Ittig.

Petry, Johannes M. & Dorothea [?]: Eva, b. 10/30/1776, bapt. 11/3/1776 (DRGF:21); Johannes, b. 11/10/1777, bapt. 12/8/1777

(DRGF:27); Johann Marcus, b. 7/26/1779, bapt. 7/30/1779 (DRGF:36); Delia, b. 3/3/1781, bapt. 3/21/1781 (DRGF:43); Adam, b. 11/24/1782, bapt. 12/1/1782 (DRGF:64); Jacob, b. 11/20/1784, bapt. 12/25/1784 (DRGF:91). Sponsors: Johannes Eisenmann & Elisabeth (re:1); Johannes Kesslar & Catharina (re:2); Jacob Kesslar & his wife, Elisabeth (re:3); Jacob Kesslar & Delia (re:4); Joh: Adam Bellinger & Maria Elisabeth (re:5); Jacob Petri & Maria (re:6).

Petry, Marcus D. & Margretha [?]: Daniel, b. 1/14/1779, bapt. 1/17/1779 (DRGF:33); Pieter, b. 10/9/1781, bapt. 12/31/1781 (DRGF:52); Elisabeth, b. 1/25/1784, bapt. 2/28/1784, d. 2/28/1784 (DRGF:81). Sponsors: Daniel Petri & Gertraut Bellinger (re:1); Pieter Bellinger & Delia (re:2); Johannes Bellinger & Catharina Petri (re:3).

Petry, Marcus J: & Maria [?]: Catharina, b. 7/14/1768; bapt. 9/1/1768 (RDSA:89). Sponsors: Johannes Petri, jun. & Catharina Crantz.

Petry, Marcus, Jr. & Elisabeth [?]: Henrich, b. 4/15/1764, bapt. 5/10/1764 (RDSA:47); Catharina, b. 12/1/1765, bapt. 12/3/1765 (RDSA:59); Johannes, b. 3/12/1768, bapt. 3/17/1768 (RDSA:84); Johannes, b. 5/1/1770, bapt. 5/25/1770 (RDSA:102). Sponsors: Nicolas Schmidt & his wife, Anna Maria (re:1); Catharina & Henrich Hergheimer (re:2); Johannes Champel & Eva Meyer (re:3); Johannes Smidt & Margretha Kasselmann (re:4).

Petry, Wilhelm/William, Dr. & Margretha Salome [?]: Catharina, b. 9/15/1767, bapt. 10/23/1767 (RDSA:79); Anna, b. 3/19/1770, bapt. 3/22/1770 (RDSA:101); Wilhelm, b. 10/12/1781, bapt. 12/31/1781 (DRGF:52);

Maria, b. 12/9/1784, bapt. 12/19/1784 (DRGF:91); Margretha, b. 3/15/1791, bapt. 4/30/1791 [parents of German Flats] (SJC:41). Sponsors: Catharina & Friedrich Bellinger (re:1); Anna Weber & Jost Smidt (re:2); Adam Smidt & Sara (re:3); Georg Fried: Petri & his wife (re:4); Heinrich Harter & Catharina Harter (re:5).

Death Record

Petry, Barbara, (widow of Johannes Petry), d. 2/25/1807, Herkimer, age 55 years, 11 months, 7 days; buried in the cemetery in the town of Little Falls, near the church in the same place (RDH:258)

Petry, Catharina, (dau. of Conrad Petry), d. 9/20/1814, Columbia, age 2 years; buried in the cemetery near the church in the same place (RDH:270)

Petry, Catharina, (left behind dau. of Wm. Petry, M.D., from Herkimer), d. 2/5/1814, age 46 years, 4 months, 20 days; buried in the cemetery of the new church in Herkimer (RDH:269)

Petry, Daniel, (farmer), d. 12/26/1821, Herkimer, age 68 years; buried in the cemetery near the church in town (RDH:282)

Petry, Elisabetha, (widow of Daniel Petry; born: Foltz), d. 3/3/1807, Herkimer, age 85 years, 3 months, 3 days; buried in the new cemetery in Herkimer (RDH:258)

Petry, Joseph D., (honest resident), d. 8/14/1822, Herkimer, age 59 years, 6 months; buried in the cemetery near the new church in a corner [manhemie] near the Herkimer limits (RDH:284)

Petry, Margaretha Salome, (wife of William Petry; born: Wolf), d. 1/18/1820, Herkimer, age 70 years, 10 months, 9 days; buried in the cemetery near the church in the same town (RDH:279)

Petry, Maria, (wife of Jacob Petry), d. 5/27/1808, Herkimer, age [?] (died in childbirth); buried with one infant who subsequently died, in the cemetery near the Herkimer church (RDH:260)

Petry, Maria, (wife of Heinrich Petri & maiden name: Laux), b. 6/4/1768; m. 4/26/1789; d. 5/8/1790; buried 5/10/1790 (RDSA:232)

Petry, Maria, (wife of Jacob Petry, from Columbia), d. 6/8/1813, age 63 years; buried in the cemetery of the new church in the same place [Herkimer?] (RDH:268)

Petry, William, b. 12/7/1733, in Nierstein near Mainz, situated on the Rhine, in the Electoral Palatinate; d. 8/20/1806, Herkimer, age 72 years, 8 months, 13 days; buried in the cemetery near the church in Herkimer. (A very accomplished surgeon, in this place called Doctor of Medicine. An austere man, yet heartily devoted to religion, particularly the Reformed religion, and in politics a genuine Republican, an Elder of the church at Herkimer for many years; died very suddenly of dysentery, and was buried in the cemetery near the church in Herkimer in the presence of a large gathering.) (RDH:256)

Tryon County Militia

Petry, Daniel	[Appendix A]
Petry, Deterich	
Petry, Jacob	
Petry, Johannes	
Petry, Johannes Jost	

COMPENDIUM

Petry, John Marx
Petry, Joseph
Petry, Marx

Pension Abstract

Petrie, Richard Marcus, son of Marck Petrie &
nephew of Richard Petrie; m. Catharine
Bellinger, 6/?/1770 or 6/?/1771, at the home
of Catharine's father, Col. Peter Bellinger, in
Little Falls, N.Y.; d. 8/6/1777. (Catharine
Petrie, b. 1751/2; m. 2nd. (following death of
Richard Marcus Petrie), John Bellinger [d.
2/?/1820]; resident of Danube, Herkimer Co.
on 6/6/1838; [brother: Peter P. Bellinger, b.
4/24/1760; also resided in Danube, N.Y. in
1838].) Children of Richard M. & Catharine
Petrie: [two children]; one named: Catharine
(resident of Lysander, Onondaga Co., N.Y. in
1853). Children of John & Catharine Bellinger:
David (resident of Danube, N.Y. in 1854).
Richard Marcus served as an ensign from the
beginning of the Revolution in Capt. Bell and
Capt. Jacob Small's Cos., Col. Peter
Bellinger's Regt. of the Tryon Co. Militia; he
assisted in the construction of Forts Stanwix
and Dayton; he went on expeditions to
Johnstown, Unadilla and Ticonderoga; Richard
M. was promoted to the rank of lieutenant; he
was killed in the battle of Oriskany on 8/6/1777
and after the battle Richard M.'s body was
found and buried by a party of friends and
neighbors. (RWPA: #R729)

1790 Census

Petree, Catherine   [Appendix B]
Petrie, Barbara
Petrie, Daniel
Petrie, Honyost
Petrie, Honyost, Jr.
Petrie, Jacob
Petrie, John

Petrie, John D.
Petrie, John M.
Petrie, Marks
Petrie, Richard
Petrie, William

PETTEBONE

1790 Census

Pettebone, Amasa   [Appendix B]

PETTEGROVE

1790 Census

Pettegrove, Thomas   [Appendix B]

PETTEYS

Probate Abstract

Petteys, Peleg, (of Charleston), will dated
4/24/1830; probated 7/26/1830. Legatees: wife,
Martha; sons, Richard, Hiram, Robert L.,
James, Valentine and George; dau., Ann; owns
mortgage in town of Camden given by Isaac
Wheeler. Executors: wife; son, James.
Witnesses: Robert Lawton, John Ross, Noadiah
Potter. (WMC 57:277)

PETTINGELL

Marriage

Pettengal, Benjamin m. Abelone Shoots, Warrensborough, 4/6/1786 (JDR:3)

Pettengall, Philip m. Ruth Cox, both of Warrensborough, 3/1/1792 (JDR:#110)

Pittegal, Joseph m. Anna Bennet, 11/9/1785 (DRC:164)

Birth/Baptism

Pettengall/Pettengell, Benjamin & Abelone (Shoots): Abigail, bapt. aged 5 wks., 1/18/1789 [parents of Florida, Montgomery Co.] (JDR:9); Nanse, bapt. 2/24/1793 [parents of Warrensbush] (JDR:21); Elizabeth, b. 5/5/1797, bapt. 6/4/1797 (JDR:14); John, bapt. 8/18/1799, age 18 days (JDR:18). [parents of Florida, Montgomery Co. for final two baptisms]

Pettengell, Joseph (son of Samuel) & Margaret (Evan), Florida: Joseph, bapt. 1/2/1799 (JDR:18); Margaret, bapt. 1/8/1803 (JDR:21).

Pettengell, Joseph (son of John Pettengall) & Nanse (Bennet), Warrensborough: Abigail, bapt. 2/22/1790 (JDR:9); Elizabeth, bapt. 2/15/1792 (JDR:13); Evah, bapt. 5/?/1796 (JDR:13).

Pettengell, Martin & [?] (Colley): Elizabeth, bapt. 2/8/1795 (JDR:13).

Pettengell, Peter & Mary (Snook): Elizabeth, bapt. 5/12/1793 [of Warrensborough] (JDR:13); Cornelius, bapt. 6/20/1797, age 5 wks. & 4 days [parents of Florida] (JDR:11).

Pettengell, Samuel & Marjory (Cooley), Warrensbush: Peter, bapt. 4/9/1787 (JDR:21); Peter, bapt. 3/18/1788 (JDR:22); Nancy, bapt. 3/30/1794 (JDR:21).

Pettingell, Jacob & Christina (Snoock): Gertrury, b. 11/7/1790, bapt. 1/6/1791 (DRC:92). Sponsors: Martin Pattingal & Christina Pattingal.

Pettingell, Samuel & Elizabeth (Klyne): Maragriet, b. 5/?/1775, bapt. 5/27/1775 (DRC:33); Hendrik, b. 1/14/1777, bapt. 6/20/1777 (DRC:43). Sponsors: John Magraw & Maragriet Megraw (re:1); Hendrik Snock & Catrina Snock (re:2).

Tryon County Militia

Pettingell, Henry   [Appendix A]
Pettingell, Jacob
Pettingell, John
Pettingell, Joseph
Pettingell, Samuel
Pettingell, William

Pension Abstract

Pettingell, Joseph, b. 1763; (father: [not named] died in the battle of Oriskany with the captain of his company, Samuel Pettingell); m. Anna [?], 6/?/1785; resident of Cicero, N.Y. on 10/14/1834 when his application for pension was rejected for lack of proof of service; d. 1/1/6/1842. (Anna Pettingell, d. 3/10/1837.) Joseph stated in his application that he enlisted at Florida, N.Y. in the spring of 1779 and served for three years as a private in Capt. William Snook's Co., Col. Volkert Veeder's Regt.; Joseph fought in the battle of Johnstown. (RWPA: #R8152)

Pettingell, William, b. 5/2/1758, son of Samuel Pettingell, Florida, N.Y.; resident of Milford, Otsego Co., N.Y. on 10/16/1832. William enlisted in May 1776 and served in his father's [Capt. Samuel Pettingelll] Co., Col. Frederick Fisher's 3rd. Regt., Tryon Co. Militia; he was

COMPENDIUM

stationed at Fort Herkimer and marched with his company to Johnstown where Sir John Johnson surrendered his arms in the same year; in 1777 William was in the battle of Oriskany where "his father Capt. Pettingel was killed at that time"; he continued service in the militia under Capts. William Snook and Peter Yates through 1779. (RWPA: #S18163)

1790 Census

Pettingell, Wiliam   [Appendix B]
Pettingill, Benjamin (2)
Pettingill, Joseph (2)
Pettingill, Martin
Pettingill, Samuel

PETTIT

Probate Abstract

Pettit, Jabez, (of Palatine), will dated 2/8/1813; probated 2/12/1813. Legatees: wife, Susannah; sons, Thomas, Moses and Abraham. Executors: Witman Hering, Chancey Hutcheson, Daniel Bedford. Witnesses: John Cochran, Peter Sharp, John Wood, Daniel Bedford. (WMC 56:386)

PFEIFFER (also see PIPER)

Death Record

Pfeiffer, Johannes, (skilled carpenter from German Flats), d. 4/12/1811, age 35 years, 9 months (died of consumption); buried in the [Clepsattle cemetery in Germanflats] (RDH:263)

Probate Abstract

Pifer, Andrew, (of Minden), will dated 5/2/1816; probated 2/14/1818. Legatees: wife, Maria. Executors: wife; Augustus I. Diffendorff. Witnesses: Henry Diefendorf, Nicholas Garloch, Abram Arndt. (WMC 57:166)

1790 Census

Pfyfer, Andrew   [Appendix B]

PFLANZ

Birth/Baptism

Pflanz, Johannes/Hannes & Margaretha [?]: Anna Eva, b. 4/10/1754 (LTSA:9); Johanes, b. 4/1/1756 (LTSA:18). Sponsors: Peter Adami, Anna Eva Contrimann (re:1); Conrad Contriman, Catharina Rosner (re:2).

PHANORMUN

1790 Census

Phanormun, Daniel   [Appendix B]

PHELAN

Death Record

Phelan, Rowena, (Miss.), d. 7/4/1848, age 15 years, of Spinal affection [infection] terminating in dropsy on the brain; buried Cherry Valley Presbyterian Church cemetery (PCV:88)

616

COMPENDIUM

PHELPS

Marriage

Phelps, Henry J. (of Canajoharie) m. Elen Hodge (of Canajoharie), 11/24/1832 (PCBC:52)

Probate Abstract

Phelps, Joab, (of Johnstown), will dated 12/15/1830; probated 4/25/1831. Legatees: Joab Phelps, Jr.; Sylvester Phelps; Sally Phelps; Rosell Phelps. Executors: Joab and Sylvester Phelps. Witnesses: Eli Phelps, Abigail Phelps, Clusta Phelps (all of Mayfield). (WMC 57:280)

1790 Census

Phelps, Abijah   [Appendix B]
Phelps, Jacob
Phelps, James
Phelps, Jedediah
Phelps, John
Phelps, Joseph
Phelps, Rufus
Phelps, Silas

PHILIPS

Marriage

Philips, Hermanes m. Annatje Crommel, 5/22/1767 (RDSA:182)

Philips, Johannes m. Catharina Majer (dau. of Henry Majer), 11/21/1784 (DRGF:200)

Philips, John m. Eva Levis, 11/7/1792 (DFP:46)

Philips, Simon m. Margaretha Lewis, 12/30/1793 (DFP:50)

Philips, William (widower) m. Balli Lodrigs, 6/8/1769 (RDSA:186)

Birth/Baptism

Philips, Abram & Sarah (Evertse): Abram, b. 4/24/1782, bapt. 5/3/1782 (DRC:62); Johannis, b. 2/?/1787, bapt. 3/18/1787 (DRC:83). Sponsors: Philip Philipse & Maria Evertse (re:1); Arend D. Putman & Catrina Van Brakelen (re:2).

Philips, Adam (of Palatine) & Elisabeth [?]: Niclaus, bapt. 1/20/1791 (SJC:38). Sponsors: Adam Nelles & Anna Dumm.

Philips, Christian & Elizabeth (Koel): Nicholas, b. 2/28/1791; bapt. 4/17/1791 (DRC:96). Sponsors: Nicolas Daxteder & his wife.

Philips, George & [?]: Thomas, bapt. 1/16/1742/3 (FH:19). Sponsors: Edward Mills, John Mills.

Philips, Glas & Elisabetha [?]: Elisabeth, b. 3/22/1755 (LTSA:12). Sponsors: Henrich Dagstetter, Elisabetha Philips.

Philips, Harmanus & Annatje (Crommell): Elizabeth, b. 8/26/1773, bapt. 9/20/1773 (DRC:26); Cobus, b. 12/11/1776, bapt. 1/5/1777 (DRC:40); Maria, b. 12/28/1779, bapt. 1/24/1780 (DRC:55); Margritje, b. 5/2/1785, bapt. 6/6/1785 (DRC:73). Sponsors: David Lewis & Meritje Lewis (re:1); Harmanis Crommell & Catrina Crommell (re:2); Abram Flipse & Eva Miller (re:3); Benjamin England & Maria Kuiller (re:4).

Philips, Jacob & Anna (Hover): Jacob, b.

617

10/28/1781, bapt. 1/2?/1782 (DRC:60); Elizabeth, b. 6/22/1783, bapt. 7/20/1783 (DRC:66); Jury, b. 4/23/1785, bapt. 8/21/1785 (DRC:75); Hendrick, b. 3/4/1791, bapt. 4/17/1791 (DRC:96). Sponsors: Adam Everse & Dorothea Doxteder (re:1); Benjamin England & Eliz. Doxteder (re:2); Jury Docksteder & Barber Docksteder (re:3); George Acre & Lena Acre (re:4).

Philips, Jacob/Cobus & Lena (Quack/Quakkenbosh): Elizabeth, b. 11/28/1780, bapt. 12/31/1780 (DRC:58); Abram, b. 8/27/1782, bapt. 9/22/1782 (DRC:64); Doretha, b. 7/9/1786, bapt. 7/24/1786 (DRC:81). Sponsors: John Lenardson & Anna Philipse (re:1); Abram Philipse & Sara Philipse (re:2); Martin Gardenir & Dorethea Gardenir (re:3).

Philips, Johannes & Jannetje (Delyne): Elizabeth, b. 10/29/1779, bapt. 11/12/1779 (DRC:54); Johannis, b. 10/13/1781, bapt. 11/11/1781 (DRC:59); Lewis, b. 3/4/1786, bapt. 3/18/1786 (DRC:78). Sponsors: Abram Philpse & Elizabeth Philipse (re:1); Philip Philipse & Angenietje Delyne (re:2); Barent Ter Williger & Jannetje Ter Williger (re:3).

Philips, John & [?], Warrensborough: Jane, bapt. 2/13/1779 (JDR:15).

Philips, John & Alida (Printup): Jannetjie, b. 4/21/1772 (DRC:22); Willem, bapt. 12/28/1777 (DRC:46); Joseph, b. 10/25/1780, bapt. 12/7/1780 (DRC:57). Sponsors: Arent Bradt Esqr. & Effie Bradt (re:1); Joost Staal & Polly Staal (re:2); John Hale & Susanna Hale (re:3).

Philips, John V. & Hannah (Russel): Dorithy, b. 5/?/1790; bapt. 8/1/1790 (DRC:88). Sponsors: Volkert Philipse & Dorithy Phlipse.

Philips, Lewis & Marrigriet (Hatkok): Elizabeth, b. 8/13/1772, bapt. 8/23/1772 (DRC:22); Johannis, b. 1/14/1775, bapt. 2/13/1775 (DRC:32). Sponsors: Hanse Hotkok & Mariche Philipsey (re:1); Timothy Leendersen & Catje Leendersen (re:2).

Philips, Ludwig & Maria Margaretha [?]: Philipp, b. 4/18/1770 (LTSA:31). Sponsors: Philipp Philipps & his wife.

Philips, Philip & Annatje (Ritch): Maria, b. 5/14/1786; bapt. 6/5/1786 (DRC:80). Sponsors: Harnanus Crommell & Catrina Crommell.

Philips, Philip & Elizabeth (Wanner): Annaatje, bapt. 10/16/1763 (DRC:10). Sponsors: Henderck Daksteder & Catarina Daksteder.

Philips, Philip & Margaret [?]: Mary, bapt. 4/13/1735 (FH:1); Catharine, bapt. 1/25/1738/9 (FH:5); Margaret, bapt. 6/21/1741 (FH:14); Dorothy, bapt. 1/13/1744/5 (FH:26). Sponsors: Peter Conyn, Sarah Conyn, Eliza Phillpse (re:1); Philipp Phillipse Jur, and his wife; Mary Sixbury (re:2); Abraham Quakenbos, Mary Quakenbos (re:3); Marte Van Olinde & his wife; Helena Van Olinde (re:4).

Philips, Philip, Jr. & Polly (Brader): Philip, bapt. 2/?/1785 at age 4 weeks (DRC:71). Sponsors: John Brader & Elizabeth Brader.

Philips, Volkert & Dorothea (Smith): Meritje, b. 3/14/1785, bapt. 5/1/1785 (DRC:72); Catrina, b. 2/7/1787, bapt. 3/4/1787 (DRC:83, 87). Sponsors: John Wemph & Meritje Hanson (re:1); Isaac Davis & Catrina Davis (re:2).

Philips, Volkert & Mary (McDonald): John, bapt. 1758 (DRC:1); [?], b. 11/26/1772, bapt. 12/28/1772 (DRC:23); Barent, b. 12/26/1774, bapt. 1/13/1775 (DRC:32); Folkert, b. 11/26/1776, bapt. 12/25/1776 (DRC:40); Michel, b. 11/10/1779, bapt. 11/19/1779 (DRC:54); Maragrita, b. 1/8/1782, bapt. 2/16/1782 (DRC:61). Sponsors: John Smith & Anna Barber Smith (re:1); James CoolCraft & Fransynche CoolCraft (re:2); Petrus Conyne & Maragrita Wemph (re:3); Derick Groat & Yanney Groat (re:4); John B. Wemple & Maria Wemple (re:5); John & Alida Van Eps (re:6).

Philips, Wilhelm & Jannitje [?]: Hanna, b. 9/20/1767; bapt. 9/24/1767 (RDSA:77). Sponsors: Lena & Pieter Serves.

Philips, Wilhelm & Maria [?]: Benjamen, b. 3/31/1772 (LTSA:42). Sponsors: Ebenezer Philips, Nanci Adams.

Philips, William & Hannah (Huisman/Huise): Catrina, b. 4/4/1782, bapt. 5/5/1782 (DRC:62); James, b. 2/25/1784, bapt. 5/11/1784 (DRC:69); Albert, b. 10/20/1785, bapt. 5/22/1786 (DRC:78). Sponsors: Philip Fredric & Catrina Fredric (re:1); John McGraw & Maragrita McGraw (re:2); [none named] (re:3). [Note: See next baptismal record.]

Philips, William & Hannah (Houseman), Florida: Cornelius, bapt. 1/29/1797 (JDR:11); Evah, bapt. 12/13/1799, age 5 wks. (JDR:14); Sarah, bapt. 3/22/1802 (JDR:24).

Philips, William & Mary [?]: John, bapt. 10/12/1740 (FH:12); Mary, bapt. 4/24/1743 (FH:20); Cornelius, bapt. 2/9/1745/6 (FH:29). Sponsors: John Boen, Will Sixbury, Susannah Boen (re:1); John Barclay, Gerrittie Barclay, Eliz Wemp (re:2); Cornelius Boen, Isaac Wemp, Anna Sixberry (re:3).

Philips, William & Sussanna (Wimp): Debora, bapt. 12/11/1762 (DRC:8). Sponsors: Dowe

Funda & Debora Wimp.

Probate Abstract

Phillips, Lewis, (of the town of Florida), will dated 9/28/1816; probated 3/22/1820. Legatees: sons, Philip, John, David and Lewis; daus., Elizabeth Siver, Mary Gano[?], Peggy Dean and Hannah. Executors: sons, Lewis and David; William Van Olinda. Witnesses: Samuel O. Riggs, David Crane, Nicholas I. De Graff. (WMC 57:170)

Phillips, William, (of Broadalbin), will dated 4/14/1828; probated 10/18/1828. Legatees: wife, Elizabeth; sons, Samuel, Holder, Gorton and Benjamin; daus., Betsy, Sally Chase and Katharine Chase; grandsons, William Phillips, John Phillips, Elijah and Jabez Phillips; granddau., Lellis Phillips. Executors: Samuel Phillips, Holder Phillips. Witnesses: John and Alex Stewart, Enoch Honeywell. (WMC 57:272)

Phillips, William, (of the town of Florida), will dated 1/30/1821; codicil dated 11/29/1823; probated 6/17/1824. Legatees: wife [not named]; daus., Caty, Hannah, Margaret, Sally and Maria; sons, James, Hamilton, Henry, William and Cornelius. Executors: sons, Cornelius and William. Witnesses: Aaron Haring, Ethan Akin, Lodowick Putman (to the will); May' Turnbool, Michael McCabe, Deodatus Wright (to the codicil). (WMC 57:179)

Tryon County Militia

Philips, Abraham   [Appendix A]
Philips, Harmanus
Philips, Henry
Philips, Jacob
Philips, James

Philips, John
Philips, Lewis
Philips, Phillip
Philips, Volkert
Philips, William

Pension Abstract

Phillips, Abraham, b. 3/?/1751/2, Caughnawaga [now Johnstown], N.Y.; resident of Ephratah, Montgomery Co., N.Y. on 9/20/1832. Abraham enlisted in September 1775 from Johnstown and served at various times as a private and batteauman until 1783; he was in the regts. of Cols. Fisher, Cox, Veeder, Willett and Klock; Abraham fought in the battle of Oriskany. (RWPA: #S9986)

Philips, Jacob, b. 3/20/1750, Caughnawaga, N.Y.; resident of Root, Montgomery Co., N.Y. on 9/19/1832; d. 2/19/1835. Jacob enlisted on 3/1/1776 and served a nine month tour of duty in Capt. Jacob Shaver's Co.; he enlisted again on 3/1/1777 and served for nine months in Capt. John Clute's Co., Col. Christopher Yates' Regt.; Jacob was at the taking of Burgoyne in 1777 and fought in the battle of Johnstown; he continued serving nine month tours of duty each year through 1782. (RWPA: #S11238)

Phillips, John, b. 1758, Johnstown, N.Y.; (brother: Abraham Philips [RWPA: #S99861]); resident of Pamelia, Jefferson Co., N.Y. on 9/11/1832. John enlisted for nine months in 1777 and served in Capt. John Clute's Co. in the batteau service on the Hudson River transporting army stores from Albany up to Fort Edwards; he volunteered again in March 1778 and served for nine months in Col. Christopher Yates' Regt. as a batteauman; John "saw Burgoyne when he laid down his arms" and he was a participant in the battle of

Johnstown. (RWPA: #R8200)

Phillips, John m. Hannah Russell, [date not given] in the home of Barent Vrooman's father in Montgomery Co., N.Y.; d. 12/?/1814, Schoharie, N.Y. (Hannah Philiips, b. 1766/7; lived in the home of Barent Vrooman prior to her marriage; resident of Michias, Cataraugus Co., N.Y.) Children: [four youngest not named]; Doroty, b. 5/?/17??; Betsy, b. 2/3/1792; Volkert, b. 6/12/1794; Peggy, b. 5/20/1796; Daniel, b. 4/?/1799; Caty, b. 8/20/1802; John P., b. 1/16/1804; Jonah, b. 1/18/1806; William, b. 8/20/1808. Hannah Phillips stated in her deposition of 9/22/1847 that "her husband [John] was a resident of Montgomery Co. during the Rev. War and lived near Johnstown. She has often heard her husband tell that he served in the Rev. War". (RWPA: #R8192)

Phillips, John, m. Yaniche Deline, July/August 1779, Johnstown, N.Y.; d. 4/15/1835, Pamelia, Jefferson Co., N.Y. (Yanniche/Jinney Phillips, b. 1753/4; d. 5/20/1835, Pamelia, N.Y.) Children: Elizabeth, b. 1780/1 (widow of Christian Casselman in 1839); John, b. 1782/3; Lewis, b. 1788/9; Nancy, b. 1790/1 (m. Garet Francisco); Benjamin, b. 1795/6. [All children living in 1829; John and Nancy deceased by 1844.] John served as a private from Johnstown early in the war and was in Capt. John Davis' Co., Col. Frederick Fisher's 3rd. Regt., Tryon Co. Militia; he fought in the battle of Oriskany; John enlisted for one year in 1778 under Capt. Simon De Graf in the batteau service on the Hudson and Mohawk Rivers; he also served from the spring of 1781 through the fall of 1782, for a total of eighteen months, in Col. Marinus Willett's Regt. (RWPA: #S23844)

COMPENDIUM

1790 Census

Philips, Abraham (2)   [Appendix B]
Philips, Adam
Philips, Amaziah
Philips, Christian
Philips, Hermanus (2)
Philips, Jacob
Philips, James
Philips, John (6)
Philips, John, Jr.
Philips, Philip (2)
Philips, Philip, Jr.
Philips, Philip, Sr.
Phillips, [?]
Phillips, Elijah
Phillips, John
Phillips, Lewis
Phillips, Richard
Phillips, Thomas

PHILIPSEY

Probate Abstract

Philipsey, John, (farmer, of Montgomery County), will dated 8/13/1811; probated 4/26/1815. Legatees: wife; sons, Peater, Abraham, Harmanes, Sime, John and Philipe. Executors: friends, John Philipsey, Jr. and John T. Lenardson. Witnesses: John T. Lenardson, Andrew Tine, Isaac H. Vosburgh. (WMC 56:394)

PHILIPSON

Marriage

Philipson, Lewis m. Margretha Hadkok, 12/13/1768 (RDSA:186)

Philipson, Philip m. Balli Brodder, 10/3/1769 (RDSA:187)

Philipson, Volckert m. Marytje MacDannel, 9/29/1764 (RDSA:173)

Birth/Baptism

Philipson, Abraham & Catharina [?]: Marytje, b. 12/21/1762, apt. 1/30/1763 (RDSA:37); Agnittje, b. 1/24/1765, bapt. 2/17/1765 (RDSA:54). Sponsors: Margritha Phlipsen & Henrich Hoff (re:1); Marytje & Sam van Etten (re:2).

PHILLS

Death Record

Phills, Abraham, (son of Philipp & Ann Phills), d. 10/1/1837, age 5 years, 3 months, 16 days; buried sect. 11, Colonial Cemetery, Johnstown (JC:186)

Phills, Matilda Ann, (dau. of Abraham Morrel; wife of Phillip Phills), d. 3/29/1836, age 22 years; buried sect. 11, Colonial Cemetery, Johnstown (JC:186)

PHILPOT

Probate Abstract

Philpot, Spencer, (of Johnstown), will dated 9/16/1807; probated 10/22/1807. Legatees: sisters, Mary, Eliza, and Margaret. Executor: John McCarthy. Witnesses: Clement Sadlier, M.B. Hildreth, P.H. Bostwick. (WMC 56:156)

PHITIS

1790 Census

Phitis, Philip   [Appendix B]

PHLYSSE

Birth/Baptism

Phlysse, Philip & [?]: Neeltie, bapt. 3/3/1744/5 (FH:27). Sponsors: David Quackenbos, Ann Quackenbos, Rachel Van Alen.

PHOENIS (also see **PHOENIX**)

Birth/Baptism

Phoenis, Michael & Barbara [?]: Anna Elisabeth, b. 11/12/1779; bapt. 11/21/1779 (LTSA:58). Sponsors: Christoph. Empie, Anna Schill.

PHOENIX (also see **PHOENIS**)

Tryon County Militia

Phoenix, Michael   [Appendix A]

PICCARD

Birth/Baptism

Piccard, John & Kinyet (Bratt): Catrina, b. 2/25/1787; bapt. 6/11/1787 (DRC:85).

Sponsors: Hendrik Bratt & Catrina Bratt.

PICK

Marriage

Pick, Dietrich Christoph Carl August Andreas (the Rev. Minister, Preacher of the Reformed Congregations at Canajoharie and Stone Arabia) m. Elisabeth Leib (3rd. dau. of Capt. Adam Leib, at Canajoharie), 3/10/1789, married by Rev. Mr. Dyslie in Palatine District (DFP:39)

PICKEN

Marriage

Picken, Samuel m. Sophia Syber, 10/2/1792 (DFP:46)

PICKERT

Birth/Baptism

Pickert, Conrad & Anna Margaretha [?]: Catharina, b. 4/24/1754 (LTSA:9). Sponsors: Henrich Wallrath, Rahel Pickert.

Pickert, Conrad (Schneidersbusch) & Catharina [?]: Maria, bapt. 12/25/1791 (SJC:51). Sponsors: Johann Dieterich Petri & Maria Pikard.

Pickert, George (Gaiseberg) & Maria [?]: Magdalena, bapt. 5/16/1790 (SJC:27). Sponsors: John Counterman & Maria Pikard.

COMPENDIUM

Pickert, Joh. & Maria [?]: Anna Margaretha, b. 1/25/1775; bapt. 2/19/1775 (LTSA:48). Sponsors: Nicol. Pickert, Margaretha Stanzel.

Pickert, Johannes & Anna Rosina (Contrimann/Countryman): Niclas, b. 11/6/1752 (LTSA:6); Anna, b. 5/11/1754 (LTSA:9); Maria Margaret, b. 3/11/1756 (LTSA:16). Sponsors: [none named] (re:1); Conrad Contrimann, Rahel Pickert (re:2); Johannes Pflanz & his wife, Maria Margaretha (re:3).

Pickert, Johannes (of Palatine) & Anna Margretha [?] (Caneserago): Peter, bapt. 2/6/1791 (SJC:39); Adam, bapt. 2/18/1793 (SJC:73). Sponsors: Peter [?] & Margretha, his wife (re:1); Adam Gerlach & his wife (re:2).

Pickert, Joseph (Palatine Town) & Magdalena (Fort): Andreas, bapt. 11/16/1788 (SJC:6); Benjamin, bapt. 7/17/1791 (SJC:44); Rudolf, bapt. 11/17/1793 (SJC:85). Sponsors: Christian Pletas & Catharina Fort (re:1); Benjamin Ellwood & Elisabeth Ellwood (re:2); Rudolf Koch & Anna Koch (re:3).

Pikert, Hartman & Dorotea [?]: Anna Eva, b. 1/25/1795 (LTSA:87). Sponsors: Jacob Pikert, Anna Eva Stamm.

Probate Abstract

Pickert, Bartholomew, (of Manheim), will dated 3/13/1813; probated 7/19/1813. Legatees: wife, Catherine; daus., Polly, Anny and Rebecca; sons, Jonas, Bartholomew, Abel and Zachariah. Executors: wife; Anthony Kaufman. Witnesses: John and Peter Pickert, Henry Boyer. (WMC 56:388)

Pickert, Bartholomew, (of Manheim), will dated 3/9/1804; probated 2/11/1809. Legatees:

wife, Maria Catherine; sons, Frederick and John; daus., Dina (wife of William Kissner), Eche (wife of Elijah Goodell) and Maria (wife of Gerret Van Slyke). Executors: William Feeter, Anthony Kaufman. Witnesses: Johannes Keller, Frederick Windecker, Jr., Hendrick Keller, Jr. (WMC 56:159)

Pickert, George N., (of Minden), will dated 1/20/1829; probated 3/21/1831. Legatees: wife, Catharine; sons, Abraham and Martin; daus., Lany and Delean; grandson, John Brookman. Executors: wife; son, Abraham; brother-in-law, Jacob Bettinger. Witnesses: Isaac Elwood, John A. Conterman, Margaret Conterman. (WMC 57:281)

Tryon County Militia

Pickert, Adolph	[Appendix A]
Pickert, Conrad	
Pickert, George	
Pickert, Jacob	
Pickert, John	
Pickert, Nicholas	

1790 Census

Pickard, Isaac	[Appendix B]
Pickard, Nicholas	
Pickart, Bartholimew	
Pickart, John	
Pickart, Joseph	
Pickerd, Adolph	
Pickerd, Conradt	
Pickerd, George	
Pickerd, John	
Pickerd, Nicholas I.	

PICKLE

COMPENDIUM

Birth/Baptism

Pickle, Johannes & Madelena (Salman): Anna Mari, b. 11/1/1780; bapt. 11/12/1780 (DRC:57). Sponsors: Hannis Pickle & Anna Mari Pikkle.

Probate Abstract

Pickle, Johannis, (of Stone Arabia), will dated 10/22/1803; probated 10/31/1803. Legatees: wife, Anna Maria; Lutheran Church of Stone Arabia ($250.00 for bell); son, Johannes (now residing in Germany, at a place called Oberbesinger in der Grasshoft Sicht 12 Stund von Frankfort am Mayn); Margaret, Elizabeth (12 Stund von Frankfort am Mayn). Executors: Rev. Philip Groz, Johannis Cook, Henry Shier. Witnesses: Peter Steller, John B. Cook, Sefrnes Wek. (WMC 56:152-153)

1790 Census

Pier, David	[Appendix B]
Pier, Ernest	
Pier, John	
Pier, Solomon	
Pier, Thomas	

PIERCE

Tryon County Militia

Pierce, Ephraim	[Appendix A]

1790 Census

Pierce, Abner	[Appendix B]
Pierce, Ephraim	

PIER

Marriage

Pier, Philip m. Anna Magdalena Helmer, 12/15/1741 (LTSA:1)

Piere, Ernest m. Sophia Maria Hayny, 12/7/1784 (DRGF:200)

Birth/Baptism

Pier, Georg Philipp & Anna Magdalena (Helmer): Johannes Ernestus, b. 11/3/1743 (LTSA:1); Anna Sophia, b. 3/23/1751 (LTSA:1); bapt. 3/23/1751 (RDSA:10). Sponsors: Joh. Leonhard Helmer, Barbara Elisabetha Dagstater (re:1); Philip Helmer, Anna Margaretha Nellis (re:2).

PIERSON

Death Record

Pierson, Abram V., (son of Eli & Amanda Pierson), d. 8/27/1851, age 6 years; buried sect. 1, Colonial Cemetery, Johnstown (JC:186)

PIKE

1790 Census

Pike, Jarvis	[Appendix B]

PILGRIM

COMPENDIUM

Birth/Baptism

Pilgrim, Dieterich (Palatine) & Christina [?]: Niclaus, b. 10/6/1792; bapt. 10/11/1792 (SJC:66). Sponsors: Niclaus Thumm & Elisabeth Thumm.

PINCKNY

1790 Census

Pinckny, Jonathan   [Appendix B]

PINE

1790 Census

Pine, Joshua   [Appendix B]

PINEW

1790 Census

Pinew, Silveneus   [Appendix B]

PIPER (also see PFEIFFER)

Marriage

Piper, Andreas P. m. Elisabeth Fr: Fox, 1/4/1785 (DRGF:201)

Piper, Jacob m. Elisabetha Foltz, 3/16/1763 (RDSA:172)

Piper, Peter Jac: m. Margreth Kleppsattle, 2/8/1791 (DRGF:207)

Birth/Baptism

Piper, Andrew & Elisabeth [?]: Jacob, b. 7/13/1785; bapt. 7/17/1785 (DRGF:99). Sponsors: Johannes Schumacher & Anna Elisabeth Fox.

Piper, Jacob & Elisabetha [?]: Ernestina, b. 10/17/1763, bapt. 11/7/1763 (RDSA:42); Johann Jost, b. 10/18/1765, bapt. 12/4/1765 (RDSA:59); Johann Peter, b. 12/20/1767, bapt. 1/19/1768 (RDSA:83); Andreas, b. 4/15/1770, bapt. 5/25/1770 (RDSA:102); Pieter, b. 1/26/1781, bapt. 3/10/1781 (DRGF:43); Margretha, b. 3/6/1783, bapt. 3/15/1783 (DRGF:69). Sponsors: Ernestina Bellinger & Melchior Foltz (re:1); Jost Foltz & Margretha Bellinger (re:2); Peter Wever & Maria Foltz (re:3); Henrich Harter & Catharina (re:4); Pieter Orndorff & Catharina (re:5); Andreas Pfeiffer & Margreth Vols (re:6).

Piper, Johann Peter & Maria Catharina [?]: Andreas, b. 1/6/1760, bapt. 1/24/1760 (RDSA:18); Elisabetha, b. 3/7/1763, bapt. 3/15/1763 (RDSA:39). Sponsors: Andreas Weber & his wife (re:1); Elisabeth Franck & Johann Jost Schumacher (re:2).

Death Record

Piper, Jacob, (husband), d. 5/17/1819, Germanflats, age 21 years; buried in the cemetery of Andreas Clepsattle (RDH:278)

Tryon County Militia

Piper, Andrew   [Appendix A]
Piper, Jacob
Piper, Jost

COMPENDIUM

Pension Abstract

Piper, Andrew, b. 1/6/1760, son of Peter Piper, German Flatts, N.Y.; m. Elizabeth Fox, 1/4/1785; d. 6/5/1842, Frankfort, Herkimer Co., N.Y. (Elizabeth Piper, b. 1765/6, dau. of Frederick Fox; resident of Frankfort, N.Y. on 7/31/1843.) Children: James, b. 1804/5 [living in 1844]. Andrew enlisted from German Flatts in the summer of 1776 for three months under Capt. Henry Harter; from the spring of 1777, he served for five months under Capt. Frederick Getman in Col. Peter Bellinger's 4th. Regt.; Andrew fought in the battle of Oriskany; he was in the batteau service for ten months from 3/8/1778 under Capt. John Lafler in Col. Christopher Yates' Regt. and was a sergeant for four months in 1779 in Capt. Mark Demuth's Co., Col. Dubois' Regt.; Andrew was captured in 1782 at Little Falls, N.Y. and imprisoned at Montreal on a prison ship and in jail; he was then carried to Quebec and then to Boston where he was exchanged and arrived home a few days after Christmas. (RWPA: #W26893)

1790 Census

Piper, [?]   [Appendix B]
Piper, Jacob

PIPPINGER

1790 Census

Pippinger, Richard   [Appendix B]

PIRE

1790 Census

Pire, Jonah   [Appendix B]

PIXLEY

1790 Census

Pixley, David   [Appendix B]

PLACE

Marriage

Place, Enoch m. Elizabeth Milligan, both of Saratoga Dist., 3/31/1785 (JDR:3)

PLANK

Marriage

Plank, John m. Nelyltje Gardinier, 6/8/1775 (DRC:160)

Birth/Baptism

Plank, Adam & Catrina (Klyn): Johannis, b. 11/9/1774, bapt. 1/8/1775 (DRC:32); Godfry, b. 3/15/1777, bapt. 5/25/1777 (DRC:43). Sponsors: Johannis Bossart & Elizabeth Klyn (re:1); Hendrick Yaney & Elizabeth Yanney (re:2).

Plank, John & Neeltje (Gardinier): Hendrik, b. 5/1/1777; bapt. 6/14/1777 (DRC:43). Sponsors: Samuel Gardinier & Rachel Van Alstyne.

COMPENDIUM

Probate Abstract

Plank, Adam, (of Johnstown), will dated 12/31/1814; codicil dated 1/14/1815; probated 8/17/1815. Legatees: wife [name not given]; sons, Adam, Philip, Frederick, Christian, Godfred (& his wife, Gertrout), Jacob (decd. & his son, Adam), John (& his wife, Mary); dau., Dorothy (wife of Peter Shaver). Executors: Henry Yanney, Jacob Denny. Witnesses: William Shults, Peter Coughnut, Daniel Walker. (WMC 56:395)

Plank, Adam I., [residence not stated], will dated 9/6/1825; probated 9/18/1825. Legatees: wife, Amy; sons, Jacob, James and William; dau., Catherine; mother [not named]. Executors: Frederick Plank, Robert Squires, James Eickenbrack. Witnesses: Frederick Plank, Robert Squires, James Eickenbrack. (WMC 57:184)

Tryon County Militia

Plank, Adam   [Appendix A]
Plank, John

1790 Census

Plank, Adam   [Appendix B]
Plank, Henry
Plank, John

PLANTZ

Birth/Baptism

Planz, Peter & Charlotta [?]: Adam, b. 8/9/1794 (LTSA:85). Sponsors: Johannes Hiegel & Catarina.

Death Record

Plantz, Julia Augusta, (dau. of Nicholas & Sally Plantz), d. 3/13/1845, age 1 year, 2 months; buried sect. 7, Colonial Cemetery, Johnstown (JC:186)

Tryon County Militia

Plantz, Johannes   [Appendix A]

1790 Census

Plants, John   [Appendix B]
Plants, John, Jr.
Plants, Peter

PLAPPER (also see PLUPPER)

Birth/Baptism

Plaper/Plapper, Christian & Maria [?]: Maria, b. 3/25/1790 (LTSA:65); Christian, b. 9/21/1793 (LTSA:80). Sponsors: Jacob Schulz, Maria Hering (re:1); John Frey & Anna (re:2).

Tryon County Militia

Plapper, Christian   [Appendix A]

PLATNER

Death Record

Platner, Henry C., d. 7/14/1848, age 61 years, died in one hour of a Fit; buried Cherry Valley Presbyterian Church cemetery (PCV:89)

1790 Census

Platner, Jacob   [Appendix B]

PLATO

Marriage

Platow, James m. Elizabeth Fletcher, both of
Warrensborough, 7/31/1792 (JDR:#114)

Pletoy, Thomas m. Bally Rodgers, 5/11/1770
(RDSA:189)

Birth/Baptism

Plato, James & Catrina (Van Duisen): Neyltje,
b. 8/11/1775; bapt. 10/6/1775 (DRC:35).
Sponsors: Melchert Van Duisen & Neyltje Van
Duisen.

Plato, Thomas & Mary (Rogers): James, b.
3/6/1773; bapt. 4/4/1773 (DRC:25). Sponsors:
Abraham Davis & Catrina Davis.

Platow, James & Elizabeth (Fletcher),
Warrensborough: Thomas, bapt. 5/12/1793
(JDR:24).

1790 Census

Plato, James   [Appendix B]

PLATTS (also see PLETZ)

1790 Census

Platts, George   [Appendix B]

PLAU

Marriage

Plau, John m. Hannah Munro, 3/20/1800.
Witnesses: [?] Munro (JPC:93)

PLETAU

Birth/Baptism

Pletau, Christian (of Schnellenbusch) &
Catharina [?]: Catharina, bapt. 1/11/1789
(SJC:8); Magdalena, bapt. 6/3/1792 (SJC:59).
Sponsors: Gottlieb Braun & Catharina Schnell
(re:1); Joseph Pikard & Magdalena Pikard
(re:2).

PLETZ (also see PLATTS)

Birth/Baptism

Pletz, Georg & Anna [?]: Elisabeth, b.
2/13/1782, bapt. 2/20/1782 (DRGF:55); Anna,
b. 2/13/1782, bapt. 2/20/1782 (DRGF:55).
Sponsors: Wilhelm Oel & Catharina (re:1);
Adam Jordan & Anna Gilly (re:2).

PLOOGH

Birth/Baptism

Ploogh, Henderick & Neyltje (Wieler): Sophia,
b. 3/11/1774, bapt. 5/1/1774 (DRC:29);
Petrus, b. 5/20/1776, bapt. 6/17/1776
(DRC:37); Annatje, b. 8/18/1778, bapt.
9/1/1778 (DRC:49). Sponsors: Hannis

Dogsteder & Sophia Dennis (re:1); Casper Van Dewerken & Annatje Daksteder (re:2); Adam Evertson & Annatje Philipse (re:3).

1790 Census

Plupper, Christian   [Appendix B]

PLOSS

Death Record

Ploss, Phebe, (a member of Methodist Episcopal Church), d. 7/31/1849, age 22 years, of brain fever; buried Cherry Valley Presbyterian Church cemetery (PCV:89)

PLYMATE

1790 Census

Plymate, Bononi   [Appendix B]

POLDMANN

Marriage

PLUMB

1790 Census

Plumb, Joseph   [Appendix B]

Poldmann, Heinrich m. Catharina Tonner, 2/17/1794 (DFP:51)

POLLARD

PLUMP

1790 Census

Plump, Gerard   [Appendix B]

1790 Census

Pollard, Jeremiah   [Appendix B]

POLLY

PLUMTEAU

1790 Census

Plumteau, John H.   [Appendix B]

1790 Census

Polly, Matthew   [Appendix B]
Polly, Uriah

POMEROY

PLUPPER (also see **PLAPPER**)

COMPENDIUM

Pomeroy, Frederick A., (son of Fredrick A. & Anna S. Pomeroy), d. 1/28/1845, age 3 years, 10 months, 19 days; buried sect. 11, Colonial Cemetery, Johnstown (JC:186)

1790 Census

Pope, Gersham   [Appendix B]
Pope, Ichabod
Pope, Izra

POND

1790 Census

Pond, Barnabas   [Appendix B]
Pond, Timothy
Pond, Timothy, Jr.

POOL

Birth/Baptism

Pool, Charles & Mary (Kinne): Sarah, b. 10/8/1784; bapt. 1/?/1785 (DRC:69). Sponsors: Jacob Bowman & Marinas Flint.

1790 Census

Pool, Simeon   [Appendix B]

POOLER

1790 Census

Pooler, John   [Appendix B]

POPE

PORTEOUS

Birth/Baptism

Portas, John (Herkimer Co.) & [?]: Thomas, bapt. 2/20/1792 (SJC:54); William, bapt. 2/20/1792 (SJC:54). Sponsors: parents themselves (re:1 & 2).

1790 Census

Porteous, John   [Appendix B]

PORTER

Marriage

Porter, William m. Eva Serviss, Warrensbush, 2/2/1790 (JDR:#85)

1790 Census

Porter, Alexander   [Appendix B]
Porter, Ashbel
Porter, Benjlack
Porter, Elijah
Porter, Nathan
Porter, Raphel
Porter, William

POSS

1790 Census

Poss, Nicholas   [Appendix B]

POST

Marriage

Post, Johannis m. Debora Conyne, 10/28/1773 (DRC:158)

Birth/Baptism

Post, Johann Nicolaus & Elisabeth [?]: Anna, b. 3/21/1779, bapt. 3/28/1779 (LTSA:57); Catharina, b. 1/14/1791 (LTSA:67); Elisabetha, b. 9/27/1783, bapt. 11/11/1783 (DRGF:77). Sponsors: Heinrich Krims & Anna (re:1); John Nelles & Anna (re:2); Georg Nelles & Margreth Nelles (re:3).

1790 Census

Post, John   [Appendix B]

POSTLE

1790 Census

Postle, Francis   [Appendix B]

POTTER

Birth/Baptism

Potter, Earl & Margret (Hamil): Margret, b. 1/4/1785; bapt. 5/22/1785 (DRC:72). Sponsors: [none named].

1790 Census

Potter, Aaron   [Appendix B]
Potter, Aseph
Potter, Ephraim
Potter, Jeremiah
Potter, John
Potter, Joseph
Potter, Lemuel
Potter, Michael
Potter, Sheldon
Potter, Stephen
Potter, William

POUIRE

Birth/Baptism

Pouire, Jean Pierre (of Schneidersbusch) & Catharina [?]: Juliana, bapt. 1/1/1790 (SJC:21). Sponsors: Antoine Kaufman & Juliana Kaufman.

POWELL

Birth/Baptism

Powell, [?] & Elizabeth [?]: Joseph, bapt. 5/11/1740 (FH:10). Sponsors: Will. Johnson, Joseph Clement, Anna Clement.

Probate Abstract

Powell, Charles, (of Canajoharie), will dated 1/11/1811; probated 1/17/1812. Legatees: wife,

Mary; sons, John, James and Jacob; daus., Polley Butten, Sally, Lidda Richardson, Elizabeth, Joanna, Caty and Jannechy. Executors: James Knox, Jaben Welch, John Powell. Witnesses: Asa Kimball, William Bartlett, Edward Thompson. (WMC 56:383)

1790 Census

Powell, Charles   [Appendix B]
Powell, Isaac
Powell, Jeremiah

POWERS

1790 Census

Power, Avery   [Appendix B]
Powers, Jacob
Powers, James
Powers, Joseph
Powers, Oliver (2)

PRAG

Marriage

Prag, Ebenezar m. Rebecca Nigason, 1/16/1794 (DRGF:211)

PRAGEL

Birth/Baptism

Pragel, Harpert (Schneidersbusch) & Anna [?]: Johannes, b. 9/15/1791; bapt. 10/9/1791 (SJC:48). Sponsors: Albert Maldon[?] & Anna

Eva Klock.

PRATT

Probate Abstract

Pratt, Darius, (of Stratford), will dated 7/24/1817; probated 3/30/1818. Legatees: wife, Zilpha; sons, Wheeler, Darius, John, Martin, Calvin and Lincoln; daus., Sarepta, Zilpah and Rocksy. Executors: wife; sons, Wheeler and Darius. Witnesses: Levi Bliss, Nathaniel Perkins, Jr., Abiezer, Jr. and Silas Phillips. (WMC 57:167)

1790 Census

Pratt, Chalker   [Appendix B]
Pratt, Izra
Pratt, Jacob
Pratt, Lemuel (2)
Pratt, William

PRAUSS/PREIS/PREUS see PRICE

PRENTICE

Death Record

Prentice, Russell, b. 2/16/1771; d. 12/27/1853; buried sect. 6, Colonial Cemetery, Johnstown (JC:186)

PRENTISS

COMPENDIUM

Death Record

Prentiss, Anna, (wife of Thomas Prentiss), d. 6/?/1822, age [not stated]; buried Cherry Valley Presbyterian Church cemetery (PCV:78)

Prentiss, Thomas, (an old and worthy member of the church), d. 7/24/1849, age 70 years, of Dropsy of heart; buried Cherry Valley Presbyterian Church cemetery (PCV:89)

Prentiss, Willard, (son of Thos. Prentiss), d. 1/12/1828, age 12 years; buried Cherry Valley Presbyterian Church cemetery (PCV:83)

Tryon County Militia

Prentiss, Daniel   [Appendix A]
Prentiss, Joseph

PRESCOTT

Death Record

Prescott, Elizabeth, (wife of [?] Prescott), d. 1/6/1837, age 53 years, of rheumatism; buried Cherry Valley Presbyterian Church cemetery (PCV:87)

PRESSER

1790 Census

Presser, Jonathan   [Appendix B]

PRESTON

1790 Census

Preston, Jacob   [Appendix B]
Preston, John
Preston, Samuel (2)

PRICE

Marriage

Preus, Johannes m. Mary Farmer, 7/24/1785 (DRGF:202)

Birth/Baptism

Prauss, Georg & Elisabeth [?]: Petrus, b. 1/1/1764; bapt. 5/5/1764 (RDSA:46). Sponsors: Peter Kraus & Elisabeth, wife of Nicolaus Serves.

Preis, Hann Niclas & Juliana [?]: Johann Adam, b. 8/15/1752 (LTSA:5); Johann Georg, b. 1/23/1755 (LTSA:10). Sponsors: Adam Schuster, Elisabetha Oehl (re:1); Hans Jerg Wehrli & his wife, Barbara (re:2).

Preis/Preus, Johannes/John & Maria [?]: David, bapt. 1/14/1790 [parents of Palatine] (SJC:22); Abraham, bapt. 7/10/1793 [parents of Sniedersbush] (SJC:77). Sponsors: Jacob C. Klock & Maria Klock (re:1); Joseph Pikard & Anna Eva Pikard (re:2).

Tryon County Militia

Price, John   [Appendix A]

Pension Abstract

COMPENDIUM

Price, John, b. ca. 1746/7, Germany; (brother: Andrew Price, b. 1747/8; resident of Minden, Montgomery Co., N.Y., 1818); came to this country when a small child; (father: [not named] died when John was young); lived with Jacob G. Klock in Palatine through the war years; (mother: [not named] massacred at Fort Walrath in the war); John was a resident of Fairfield, Herkimer Co., N.Y. on 5/6/1824. John enlisted in 1776 and served under Capt. Jacob Seeber in Col. Dayton's Regt.; by order of Col. Van Schaick, John was placed in a mill in Palatine as a miller to grind grain for the soldiers and inhabitants; he remained as a miller for the troops for two years. (RWPA: #R8469)

1790 Census

Price, George   [Appendix B]
Price, Jessu
Price, John

PRIME

Marriage

Prime, Francis m. Anna Wanple [Wemple?], 11/1/1770 (RDSA:190)

Pruim, David m. Elsje MomBrute, 11/25/1772 (DRC:158)

Pruim, Hendk. m. Sara De Freest [DeForest], 8/26/1775 (DRC:161)

Pryme, David m. Catharine Hughes, both of Mohawk Town, 8/26/1792 (JDR:#116)

Birth/Baptism

Prime/Pruim, Frans & Annatje (Davis/Davids): Pieter, bapt. 8/26/1758 (DRC:2); Henderick,

bapt. 3/5/1763 (DRC:8); Elizabeth, b. 2/3/1777, bapt. 2/23/1777 (DRC:41). Sponsors: Lowis Davis & Maria Davis (re:1); Johannes Pootman & Annaatje Pootman (re:2); Hendrik Prime & Sarah Prime (re:3).

Prime, John & Maragrita (Salman): Johan Jacob, b. 8/19/1777, bapt. 9/21/1777 (DRC:44); Anna Mary, b. 10/4/1780, bapt. 10/30/1780 (DRC:57); Catrina, b. 4/2/1783, bapt. 4/5/1783 (DRC:65). Sponsors: John Pickel & Lena Salman (re:1); Hannis Pikkle & Anna Mary Pikkle (re:2); Johannis Salman & Catrina Salman (re:3).

Pruim, David & Lena (Snock): Davy, bapt. 8/26/1758 (DRC:2). Sponsors: Jacob Pootman & Annaatje Pootman.

Pruim, Henderick & Sarah (De Freest): Abram, b. 12/2/1781, bapt. 1/27/1782 (DRC:60); Franciscus, b. 3/11/1785, bapt. 4/1/1785 (DRC:72). Sponsors: Willem Mom Brute & Maria MomBrute (r:1); Peter Prime & Alida Prime (re:2).

Pruim, Henderick & Sarah (Mombrute): David, b. 6/27/1777; bapt. 7/13/1777 (DRC:44).

Tryon County Militia

Prime, David   [Appendix A]
Prime, Henry
Prime, John
Prime, Peter

Pension Abstract

Prime, John, m. Angeline Vrooman, 8/30/1791, Reformed Dutch Church of Caughnawaga by Rev. Romeyn; d. 9/14/1826. (Angeline Prime, b. 1769/70; lived in Johnstown before marriage; resident of Utica,

Oneida Co., N.Y. on 2/5/1841.) Children: William, b. 8/?/1800 [only child of this marriage]. John served as a private in Col. Frederick Fisher's 3rd. Regt., Tryon Co. Militia. (RWPA: #W22017)

1790 Census

Prime, David   [Appendix B]
Prime, Elizabeth
Pryme, Francis
Pryme, Hendrick (2)
Pryme, John
Pryme, Lewis

PRINTUP

Marriage

Printup, William m. Esther Heen, 8/24/1765 (RDSA:176)

Birth/Baptism

Printup, Joseph & Annatye (Franck): Sarah, b. 1/15/1773, bapt. 2/13/1773 (DRC:24); Joannes, b. 11/10/1779, bapt. 11/29/1779 (DRC:54); Jannetje, b. 2/2/1783, bapt. 2/25/1783 (DRC:65). Sponsors: Jerimia Quack[enbush] & Griety M'Graw (re:1); Willem Prentip & Catrina Prentip (re:2); Evert Van Eps & Alida Wemple (re:3).

Printup, William, Jr. & Sarah [?]: William, bapt. 6/19/1735 (FH:2); Alida, bapt. 9/28/1740 (FH:11A); Susannah, bapt. 7/17/1743 (FH:21). Sponsors: Nicolaus Hansen, Engeltie Vrooman (re:1); Cornelius Boen, Alida Boen, Mary Ouderkerk (re:2); John Boen, Cornelia Boen, Anna Potman (re:3).

Tryon County Militia

Printup, Joseph   [Appendix A]
Printup, William

Pension Abstract

Printup, Joseph, b. 1748/9; received a pension on 10/25/1786 which was certified by Philip Schuyler and Abraham Ten Broeck; Joseph was a resident of Montgomery Co., N.Y. on 1/2/1826. Joseph was commissioned a lieutenant in Capt. Robert Yates' Co., Col. Frederick Fisher's 3rd. Regt., Tryon Co. Militia; he was engaged in the battle of Johnstown [10/25/1781] and received a wound in his thigh. (RWPA: #S27345)

1790 Census

Prentup, Joseph   [Appendix B]
Prentup, William

PROAL

Death Record

Proal, Pierre, (son of Rev. Alexis P. & Maria Proal), d. 1/27/1821, age 6 months, 2 days; buried sect. 9, Colonial Cemetery, Johnstown (JC:186)

PROPER

Probate Abstract

Proper, Peter, (of Northampton), will dated 8/25/1818; probated 9/23/1818. Legatees: wife, Mary; daus., Rhoda, Elizabeth, Sally, Sophia,

COMPENDIUM

Polly, Eve and Jerusha; sons, James, Philip, George, Peter and Henry. Executors: son, James; son-in-law, Annanies Gifford. Witnesses: Elkanah Sprague, Richard Chambers, Isaac Wilson. (WMC 57:167)

1790 Census

Proper, Samuel   [Appendix B]

PROVOREE

1790 Census

Provoree, Henry   [Appendix B]

PRUNDER

1790 Census

Prunder, Frederick   [Appendix B]
Prunder, Jacob (2)

PRUYNE

Tryon County Militia

Pruyn, Daniel   [Appendix A]
Pruyn, Francis F.
Pruyn, Henry
Pruyn, John
Pruyn, Lewis

Pension Abstract

Pruyne, Henry, b. 1765, Florida [now in Montgomery Co., N.Y.]; resident of

Bridgewater Twp., Susquehanna Co., Pa. on 4/20/1833. Henry was drafted in the spring of 1781 and served as a private in Capt. Garret Putnam's Co., Col. Marinus Willett's Regt.; he was a participant in the battle of Johnstown; Henry was drafted again the spring of 1782 in the same company and was wounded in the right arm while engaged in the battle of Terlow [Turlock?]; he was discharged from the military one month after the battle. (RWPA: #S14225)

Pruyne, Lewis, b. ca. 1750; (brother: Peter Pruyne [RWPA: #R85081]); resident of Danube, Herkimer Co., N.Y. in 1832. Lewis lived about three miles from Fort Hunter (now Glen, Montgomery Co.) when he enlisted in 1776 and served as a private under Lt. Francis Pruyne in Capt. Harmanus Mabee's Co., Col. Frederick Fisher's 3rd. Regt., Tryon Co. Militia; he performed guard duty at Fort Hunter for various time periods through 1780. (RWPA: #R8507)

Pruyne, Peter, b. [not given]; (brother: Lewis Pruyne [RWPA: #R8507]); m. Maria Vroman, 9/6/1788, Reformed Dutch Church of Caughnawaga; d. 9/30/1819. (Maria Pruyne, b. 1761/2; lived in Johnstown, N.Y. prior to her marriage; resident of Ephratah, Fulton Co., N.Y. on 1/21/1841.) Peter lived about three miles from Fort Hunter when he entered the military as a private in Capt. William Snook's Co., Col. Frederick Fisher's 3rd. Regt., Tryon Co. Militia; Peter was reputed to have been on an expedition to Canada early in the war. (RWPA: #R8508)

PRYOR

COMPENDIUM

1790 Census

Pryor, Azariah   [Appendix B]

1790 Census

Pumpstade, Frederick   [Appendix B]

PUATER

Death Record

Puater, Maria, (dau. of Leonard Puater), d. 12/?/1808, age 5 months, 5 days; buried 12/25/1808 (DFP:92)

PUDDY

1790 Census

Puddy, John   [Appendix B]

PUDNEY

1790 Census

Pudney, Thorne   [Appendix B]

PUFFER

1790 Census

Puffer, Isaac   [Appendix B]
Puffer, Jabez

PUMPSTADE

PURCK

Marriage

Purck, Daniel m. Sara Clarck, 7/10/1765 (RDSA:176)

Purck, John m. Anna Elisabeth Riemensneider, 10/28/1766 (RDSA:179)

Purck, John m. Elisabeth Weber, 4/29/1767 (RDSA:181)

Birth/Baptism

Purck, Edward & Maria [?]: Arndt, b. 11/14/1764, bapt. 2/25/1765 (RDSA:54); Maria, b. 4/5/1766, bapt. 4/24/1766 (RDSA:63). Sponsors: Arndt Brawer & Barbara Dachstaeder (re:1); parents (re:2).

Purck, John & Anna Elisabeth [?]: Anna, b. 7/18/1767, bapt. 7/30/1767 (RDSA:76); Anna Martha, b. 2/18/1778, bapt. 2/26/1778 (DRGF:28). Sponsors: Anna & Pieter Ten Broeck (re:1); Johannes Reimensneider & Anna Dorothea (re:2).

PURDY

1790 Census

Purdy, Daniel   [Appendix B]

COMPENDIUM

PUTMAN

Marriage

Putman, Jacob m. Anna Newkerk, 2/3/1743/4 (FH:22)

Putman, Arendt m. Delia Fox, 11/26/1767 (RDSA:183)

Putman, David, jr. m. Catrina Ledder, 7/24/1774 (DRC:160)

Putman, Frans m. Anna Dens, 5/2/1776 (DRC:161)

Putman, Frans m. Maria Fonda, 12/28/1777 (DRC:161)

Putman, Friedrich m. Catharina Bemer, 8/20/1770 (RDSA:190)

Putman, Geisbert m. Catharina Scholl, 1/1/1795 (RDSA:200)

Putman, Jacob J. m. Elizabeth McCarthy, 5/27/1777 (DRC:161)

Putman, Jurry m. Maria Forks, 5/23/1779 (DRC:162)

Putman, Turck m. Aelje van Braekel, 10/7/1767 (RDSA:182)

Putman, Victor m. Maria Shultes, 11/9/1773 (DRC:158)

Birth/Baptism

Potman, Jacob & Anna (Newkerk): Peter, bapt. 10/7/1744 (FH:25). Sponsors: John Potman, Cornelius Potman, Catharina Potman.

Potman, John & [?]: Margaret, bapt. 4/24/1743 (FH:20); Victor, bapt. 5/26/1745 (FH:27). Sponsors: Isaac Collier, Annatie Collier, Cornelia Boen (re:1); Cornelius Boen, Jacob Pootman, Catharina Pootman (re:2).

Putman, Cobus & Sarah (Oosterhout): Maragriet, bapt. 11/11/1781 at age 7 weeks (DRC:59); Arent, b. 1/17/1786, bapt. 3/6/1786 (DRC:77). Sponsors: Jacob Snook & Maragriet Snook (re:1); Arent Potman & Elizabeth Potman (re:2).

Putman, Cornelius & Elizabeth (Pruyn): Johannes, bapt. 5/6/1759 (DRC:3); Henderick, bapt. 9/12/1761 (DRC:5); Pieter, bapt. 8/14/1764 (DRC:13). Sponsors: Jacob Potman & Anna Potman (re:1); Frans F. Pruyn & Annaatje Pruyn (re:2); Arent Pootman & Elizabeth Pootman (re:3).

Putman, Cornelius A. & Dirkje (Vosburgh): Annatje, b. 8/6/1790; bapt. 9/5/1790 (DRC:89). Sponsors: Barent Vosburgh & Elizabeth Vosburgh.

Putman, David & [?]: Charity, b. 4/5/1787, bapt. 11/18/1792 (JPC:6); Elizabeth, b. 2/23/1790, bapt. 11/18/1792 (JPC:7).

Putman, David & Annatye (Van Antwerpen): Johannis, b. 8/5/1773, bapt. 8/15/1773 (DRC:26); Engeltje, b. 8/24/1775, bapt. 9/?/1775 (DRC:35); Ariaantje, b. 2/12/1780, bapt. 2/27/1780 (DRC:55). Sponsors: Johannis Potman & Annatye Potman (re:1); Petrus Putman & Engeltje Van Antwerpen (re:2); John Hanson & Maragrita Hanson (re:3).

Putman, David & Catharina/Catrina (Lederin): David, b. 5/18/1775, bapt. 6/16/1775 (DRC:34); Elizabeth, b. 12/22/1776, bapt. 1/26/1777 (DRC:41); Johann, b. 3/27/1779,

638

COMPENDIUM

bapt. 3/29/1779 (LTSA:57); Catharina, b. 3/31/1782, bapt. 4/2/1782 (DRGF:56); Maria, b. 7/3/1784, bapt. 7/10/1784 (DRGF:85). Sponsors: Christian Leederin & Elizabeth Potman (re:1); Lodewyk Putman & Catrina Leeder (re:2); Johann Lederer, Catharina Graf (re:3); Thomas Siele & Elisabeth Leder (re:4); Abhm Hergheimer & Maria Leder (re:5).

Putman, David & Elisabeth (Lohr): David, bapt. 2/25/1751 (RDSA:10); Ludwig, bapt. 12/19/1752 (RDSA:13). Sponsors: Peter Louis, Hellena Lehr (re:1); Ludwig Bottmann, Elisabetha [?] (re:2).

Putman, David & Rebecca (Davis): John, b. 10/2/1784; bapt. 3/7/1785 (DRC:71). Sponsors: David Ferguson & Mertje Ferguson.

Putman, Derek & Neyltje (Van Brakelen): Cornelia, b. 12/8/1773, bapt. 1/1/1774 (DRC:27); Gerrit, b. 12/6/1776, bapt. 1/5/1777 (DRC:40); Maria, b. 9/12/1779, bapt. 10/12/1779 (DRC:53); Lewis, b. 4/27/1783, bapt. 5/24/1783 (DRC:66); Johannis, b. 1/19/1786, bapt. 3/6/1786 (DRC:77). Sponsors: Crownage Kinkeid & Cornelia Kinkaid (re:1); Gerrit Van Brakelen & Annatje Van Brakelen (re:2); Gerret Van Braklen & Maria Van Braklen (re:3); John Putman & Anna Putman (re:4); Gerrit S. Van Brakelen & Meretje Van Brakelen (re:5).

Putman, Frans C. & Maria (Fonda): Cornelius, b. 11/31/1778, bapt. 12/20/1778 (DRC:51); Johanis, b. 1/17/1783, bapt. 1/19/1783 (DRC:64); Elisabeth, b. 2/19/1787, bapt. 3/18/1787 (DRC:83). Sponsors: Cornelius [Putman] & Elizabeth Putman (re:1); Cornelis Putman & Elizabeth Putman (re:2); Cornelis Putman & Leyba Putman (re:3).

Putman, Frederick & Catrina (Pennel): Philip, b. 5/16/1772, bapt. 6/28/1772 (DRC:22); Joannes, b. 5/16/1779, bapt. 5/24/1779 (DRC:52); Aaron, b. 11/19/1782, bapt. 1/4/1783 (DRC:64); Eva, b. 3/23/1785, bapt. 5/23/1785 (DRC:73). Sponsors: Arent Putman & Elshe Lewis (re:1); Victor Putman & Cornelia Dienstman (re:2); Aaron Putman & Delila Putman (re:3); Tunis Dienstman & Evan Dienstman (re:4).

Putman, George D. & Meritje (Ferguson): David, bapt. 5/17/1785 at age 8 weeks (DRC:72). Sponsors: Nicolas Van Slyk & Meritje Van Slyk.

Putman, Gerrit & Rebecca (Garrison): Anna, b. 7/1/1782, bapt. 7/15/1782 (DRC:63); Catrina, b. 3/9/1791, bapt. 4/24/1791 (DRC:97). Sponsors: Jacob Putman & Anna Putman (re:1); Willem Snook & Catrina Snook (re:2).

Putman, Jacob & Anna [?]: Wilhelm, b. 12/27/1761, bapt. 2/18/1762 (RDSA:31); Margrithje, b. 6/9/1765, bapt. 6/13/1765 (RDSA:56). Sponsors: Wilhelm Nieukerck & Elisabeth Breum (re:1); Margrithje Pottman & Hermanus Moevi (re:2).

Putman, Jacob & Elisabeth [?]: Annaje, b. 9/27/1781; bapt. 11/7/1781 (DRGF:49). Sponsors: John Davis & Sara.

Putman, Jacob, Jr. & Elizabeth (McCarthy): Victore, b. 8/22/1778, bapt. 9/16/1778 (DRC:49); Josua, b. 2/29/1780, bapt. 3/14/1780 (DRC:55); Frans, b. 4/30/1785, bapt. 5/17/1785 (DRC:72); Timothy, bapt. 6/3/1787 (DRC:85). Sponsors: Frans Putman & Annatje Putman (re:1); Johannis Linkerfelter & Catrina Linkerfelter (re:2); Victoor H. Potman & Maragret Potman (re:3); Johannis

639

COMPENDIUM

Linkerfelter & Catrina Linkerfelter (re:4).

Putman, John A. & Machal (Fisher): Elizabeth, b. 3/5/1791; bapt. 4/10/1791 (DRC:96). Sponsors: [none named].

Putman, Ludwig & Elisabeth [?]: Anna Margretha, bapt. 2/3/1765 (DRC:14). Sponsor: Margretha, wife of Frantz Ruppert.

Putman, Ludwig & Elisabeth (Sutz): Anna Margaretha, bapt. [no date: follows 9/13/1751] (RDSA:11). Sponsors: Johannes Wallrad, Amalia Sutz.

Putman, Ludwig & Margaret [?]: Batche, b. 2/10/1795 (LTSA:89). Sponsors: Wilhelm Forelich, Rebecca Osterhaut.

Putman, Ludwig & Maragrita (Halenbeck): Johannis, b. 7/28/1783, bapt. 8/22/1783 (DRC:68); David, b. 2/21/1785, bapt. 3/9/1785 (DRC:71); Catharina, b. 6/29/1791, bapt. 7/28/1791 (DRC:99). Sponsors: Robert Yates & Dirkje Yates (re:1); Adam Ekker & Dorothea Putman (re:2); Frederick Potman & Catharina Potman (re:3).

Putman, Robert David & Rebeca [?]: David, b. 6/4/1793; bapt. ?/4/1793 (JPC:8).

Putman, Victor & Annatje (Schults): Lodewyk, bapt. 2/17/1787 (DRC:82 & 87). Sponsors: Lodewyk Pu[tman] & Meritje Pu[tman].

Putman, Victor & Maria [?]: Magdalena, b. 5/21/1774, bapt. 6/4/1774 (LTSA:46); Arnd, b. 7/7/1779, bapt. 8/3/1779 (LTSA:57). Sponsors: Nicolaus Wallrath & his wife, Barbara (re:1); Arnd Puttmann & Elisabeth (re:2).

Putman, Victor & Maria (Shell): David, b.

3/1/1783, bapt. 4/14/1783 (DRC:65); Lodewyk, b. 5/1/1785, bapt. 6/6/1785 (DRC:73). Sponsors: Arent D. Putman & Delilah Putman (re:1); Lodewyk Putes & Molly Potes (re:2).

Putman, Victor C. & Annatje (Gerritson): Cornelia, b. 4/29/1785; bapt. 5/17/1785 (DRC:72). Sponsors: [none named].

Putman, Victor H. & Maragrita (Beyer): Cornelis, bapt. 6/29/1786 at age 3 weeks (DRC:80). Sponsors: Peter Byer & Nancy Beyer.

Putman, Victor J. & Marigritje [?]: Annat[je], bapt. 9/15/1790 (DRC:89). Sponsors: [destroyed in record].

Death Record

Putman, John L., d. 11/25/1811, age 52 years; buried sect. 3, Colonial Cemetery, Johnstown (JC:186)

Probate Abstract

Putman, Francis I., (of Tripes Hill), will dated 3/17/1804; probated 10/6/1804. Legatees: wife, Ann. Executrix: wife. Witnesses: Richard Duncan, Jacob Weegar, Alexander Rose. (WMC 56:153).

Putman, Garret, (of the Town of Glen), will dated 12/2/1825; probated 5/2/1826. Legatees: wife, Rebecca; sons, Jacob and William G.; daus., Catharine, Margaret and Elizabeth; grandchildren, Garret P., Margaret and Rebecca Post; my five living daughters; dau., Maria (decd.). Executors: sons, Jacob and Wm. G.; son-in-law, John C. Serviss. Witnesses: John Hanchet, Richard Hoff, Jr., Daniel Reed.

640

COMPENDIUM

(WMC 57:264)

Putman, John L., (of Johnstown), will dated 9/22/1811; probated 12/23/1811. Legatees: wife, Lucy; sons, Lodewick, Ebenezer, John and Peter; daus., Sally, Hannah, Betsy (& her dau., Margaret McVean). Executors: sons, Lodewick and Ebenezer. Witnesses: Aaron Haring, John Yost, John Marsh. (WMC 56:382)

Putman, Victor C., (of Charleston), will dated 11/5/1816; probated 1/22/1817. Legatees: wife, Margaret; sons, Cornelius, Abraham and John. Executors: three sons. Witnesses: Enos Fergason, Elsie Ten Eyck, Benjamin Van Vechten. (WMC 57:164)

Tryon County Militia

Putman, Aaron   [Appendix A]
Putman, Arent
Putman, Cornelius, Jr.
Putman, David
Putman, Francis
Putman, Frederick
Putman, George
Putman, Gerrit
Putman, Hendrik
Putman, Henry
Putman, Jacob
Putman, John
Putman, Lewis
Putman, Ludwig
Putman, Richard
Putman, Victor
Putman, William

Pension Abstract

Putman, Arent, m. Claartje [Catharine/Clara] Vedder, 4/18/1764, Reformed Dutch Chruch of Schenectady, N.Y.; d. "after the war".

(Claartje Putman, b. 1740/1; d. 3/?/1837, Niskayuna, Schenectady Co., N.Y.) Children: Christian, d. soon after father's [Arent] death; Jemima, b. 1773/4 (m. John G. Clute in 1807; resident of Niskayuman, N.Y. in 1850). Arent served in the militia for over two years in the regiments of Cols. Fisher, Wemple and Klock; he was also a butcher in the commissary department at Glen (now Montgomery Co., N.Y.). (RWPA: #R8531)

Putman, Francis, b. 5/4/1753, Johnstown, N.Y.; m. [wife not named]; d. 11/23/1834, Johnstown, Montgomery Co., N.Y. Children: Cornelius F., b. 1805/6 (resident of Amsterdam, N.Y. in 1843). Francis enlisted from Charlestown in 1775 and was a private, ensign and first lieutenant under Capts. Jacob Gardenier and Harmanus Mabee, Col. Frederick Fisher's 3rd. Regt., Tryon Co. Militia; he was at the taking of Burgoyne and participated in the battles of Oriskany, Stone Arabia and Johnstown. (RWPA: #S16231)

Putman, Gerret, b. 2/22/1752; m. Rebecca Garrison, 7/8/1781, Fort Hunter, N.Y.; d. 4/12/1826, Glen, Montgomery Co., N.Y. Gerret was a captain in the N.Y. Continental Troops and marched on the Sullivan expedition in 1779; he served under Col. John Harper in 1780 and under Col. Marinus Willett in 1781; he was engaged in the "Hall Battle" near Johnstown. (RWPA: #W16687)

Putman, Richard, m. Nelly Van Braeklen, 10/17/1767, Reformed Dutch Church of Stone Arabia; d. 4/14/1833, Johnstown, Montgomery Co., N.Y. (Nelly Putman, b. 1749/50; resident of Johnstown, N.Y. on 6/2/1837.) Richard entered the militia in 1775 and served as a private in Capt. John Davis' Co., Col. Frederick Fisher's 3rd. Regt., Tryon Co. Militia; Richard was in the battle of Oriskany, at which time Capt. John Davis was killed, and he [Richard] was appointed ensign under the command of Capt. Abraham Veeder; Richard continued to serve as ensign in the same company for the duration of the war. (RWPA: #W16686)

Putman, Victor, b. 11/18/1754, Tripes Hill, N.Y.; resident of Amsterdam, Montgomery Co., N.Y. on 3/10/1834. Victor volunteered in January 1775 and served under Capt. Emanuel Degraff in Col. Frederick Fisher's 3rd. Regt., Tryon Co. Militia; he was stationed in Johnstown prior to and at the time Sir John Johnson surrendered his forces to Gen. Schuyler and in 1776 Victor went to Herkimer where Gen. Philip Schuyler held a treaty with the Indians; Victor served at various times and places through 1782 and he was a participant in the battle of Oriskany. (RWPA: #S22944)

1790 Census

Putman, Aaron (2)   [Appendix B]
Putman, Adam
Putman, Cornelius
Putman, David
Putman, Derick
Putman, Frederick
Putman, Garrit
Putman, Hendrick
Putman, John
Putman, Lodowick
Putman, Victor
Putman, Victor D.

PUTNAM

Death Record

Putnam, Elizabeth, (widow), d. 12/?/1835, age

90 years, of infirmities of age; buried Cherry Valley Presbyterian Church cemetery (PCV:86)

1790 Census

Putnam, Charles   [Appendix B]
Putnam, David (2)
Putnam, Francis
Putnam, George
Putnam, Jacob
Putnam, Jacob, Jr.
Putnam, Jacobus
Putnam, John
Putnam, Victor

PUTNI

Birth/Baptism

Putni, [?] (of Gaiesberg) & Maria [?]: Georg, bapt. 6/13/1790, age 2 years (SJC:28). Sponsors: Georg Preiss & Catharina Preiss.

———

QUACKENBUSH

Marriage

Quackenbush, Abraham m. Annatje van Deusen, 4/2/1770 (RDSA:189)

Quackenbush, David m. Catrina TerWilliger, 4/?/1775 (DRC:160)

COMPENDIUM

Quackenbush, David m. Catrina Tysen, 4/20/1780 (DRC:163)

Quackenbush, Isaac m. Dirckje van Alstyn, 7/17/1769 (RDSA:186)

Quackenbush, Jeremiah m. Elisabeth van Aalstein, 7/22/1769 (RDSA:186)

Quackenbush, Johannes m. Magdalena Quakenbosh, 3/17/1793 (DFP:49)

Quackenbush, Myndert m. Maria Vroom, [no date: listed in 1773] (DRC:158)

Quackenbush, Nicholas m. Madalena Collier, 4/8/1777 (DRC:161)

Quackenbush, Peter m. Lena Lennerts, 3/9/1767 (RDSA:180)

Quackenbush, Peter P. m. Elizabeth Davids, 8/19/1775 (DRC:161)

Quackenbush, Peter W. m. Elisabeth Valkenbourgh, 7/8/1794 (DFP:52)

Quackenbush, Van Sant m. Janitje van Aalsteen, 2/16/1765 (RDSA:175)

Quackenbush, Wilhelm m. Esther Marines, 9/3/1768 (RDSA:184)

Quackenbush, William m. Catharina von Aalstein, 5/29/1763 (RDSA:172)

Birth/Baptism

Quackenboss, Abraham & Catherine (Hoff), Caughnawaga: Richard, bapt. 6/14/1789 (JDR:22).

Quackenbush, Abraham & Jannitje [?]: Enn, b. 12/3/1763; bapt. 12/27/1763 (RDSA:43). Sponsors: Enn Quackenbosch & David Quackenbosch.

Quackenbush, Abraham & Mary [?]: Rachel, bapt. 6/4/1738 (FH:4). Sponsors: Cornls Bowen, Engeltie Hansen, Susan Bowen.

Quackenbush, Abraham David & Mareitje [?]: Samuel, b. 11/9/1765, bapt. 11/?/1765 (RDSA:58); Enni, b. 3/13/1770, bapt. 3/20/1770 (RDSA:101). Sponsors: Samuel Bratt & Cattlein Bratt (re:1); Enni Quackenbosh & Jeremiah Dav: Qake[?] (re:2).

Quackenbush, Abram D. & Catrina (Wemple): Annatje, b. 11/19/1781, bapt. 12/2/1781 (DRC:59); John Schot, b. 5/4/1786, bapt. 5/22/1786 (DRC:78); Folly, b. 6/5/1791, bapt. 6/29/1791 (DRC:99). Sponsors: Peter Quack & Susanna Quack (re:1); Johannes Van Eps & Rebecca Quack (re:2); John J. Rosa & Folly Wemple (re:3).

Quackenbush, Abram. D. & Maryche (Bradt): John Scot, b. 9/19/1772, bapt. 10/4/1772 (DRC:23); Catelyna, b. 8/3/1775, bapt. 8/19/1775 (DRC:34); David, b. 8/6/1778, bapt. 9/1/1778 (DRC:49). Sponsors: Pieter B. Quack & Anna Quack (re:1); Samuel Bradt & Cummertje Bradt (re:2); Vincent Quackinbus & Jannetje Quackinbus (re:3).

Quackenbush, Abram J. & Catrina (Hoff): Elizabeth, b. 12/25/1786, bapt. 1/10/1787 (DRC:82); Rachel, b. 5/29/1791, bapt. 6/29/1791 (DRC:99). Sponsors: Nicolas Qua[ckenbush] & Lena Quakkenb[ush] (re:1); Francis Statts & Rachel Quackenbos (re:2).

Quackenbush, David & Ann [?]: Jannitie, bapt. 3/15/1740/1 (FH:13). Sponsors: Jeremiah Quackenbos, Gertry Quackenbos, Susanah

643

COMPENDIUM

Boen.

Quackenbush, David & Catrina (Terwilleger): Peter, b. 2/8/1776, bapt. 3/3/1776 (DRC:36); Harmanus, b. 8/25/1778, bapt. 9/1/1778 (DRC:49); Myndert, b. 8/26/1781, bapt. 9/4/1781 (DRC:68); Magdelena, b. 6/10/1791, bapt. 7/3/1791 (DRC:99). Sponsors: Andries Wemple & Lena Wemple (re:1); Harmanus Ter Williger & Lena Ter Williger (re:2); Myndert Quack & Maria Quack (re:3); Simon Veeder & Margarieta Veeder (re:4).

Quackenbush, David & Eva [?]: Nelchie, b. 11/1/1792 (LTSA:77). Sponsors: Hander Quackenbusch & Elisabet.

Quackenbush, David H. & Eva (Van Alstyne): Jacob, b. 10/8/1790; bapt. 11/15/1790 (DRC:91). Sponsors: Cornelius J. V. Alstine & Marigrietje V. Alstyn.

Quackenbush, Hunter & Elisabetha [?]: Adam, b. 9/27/1782; bapt. 1/2/1783 (DRGF:65). Sponsors: Johann Adam Wallrat & Catharina.

Quackenbush, Hunter (Mohawk Dist.) & Elizabeth (Klock): [?], bapt. 4/2/1785 at age 5 weeks (DRC:72); Adam, b. 3/24/1790, bapt. 5/23/1790 (SJC:27). Sponsors: Van Sent Quakkenbosch & Jannetje Quakkenbosch (re:1); Adam Wallrath & Magdalena Wallrath (re:2).

Quackenbush, Hunter & Nelje/Neyltje [?]: [?], b. 9/22/1765, bapt. 11/12/1765 (RDSA:59); Johannes, b. 10/29/17770, bapt. 11/18/1770 (RDSA:107); Peter, b. 6/24/1775, bapt. 8/?/1775 (DRC:34). Sponsors: [none named] (re:1); Martin van Aalstein & Anna (re:2); Peter Quack & Catrina Quack (re:3).

Quackenbush, Isaac & Derkje (Van Alstine): John, b. 10/1/1778, bapt. 11/1/1778 (DRC:50);

Neyltje, b. 8/18/1781, bapt. 9/4/1781 (DRC:68). Sponsors: Jacob Collier & Marytje Collier (re:1); Nicholas V Slyck & Abigail V Slyck (re:2).

Quackenbush, Isaac & Rachel [?]: Susanna, b. 3/23/1782; bapt. 4/21/1782 (DRC:62). Sponsors: Gideon Marlat & Maria Quack.

Quackenbush, James & Nelytje (Colier): Rachel, b. 11/20/1790; bapt. 1/9/1791 (DRC:93). Sponsors: Isaac Colier & Rachel Colier.

Quackenbush, Jeremiah & [?]: William, bapt. 2/19/1743/4 (FH:23). Sponsors: Abraham Quackenbos, Will. Prentop Jr, Mary Quackenbos.

Quackenbush, Jeremiah & Elizabeth (Van Aalstyn): Johannis, b. 4/18/1773, bapt. 5/6/1773 (DRC:25); Catrina, b. 3/13/1779, bapt. 4/11/1779 (DRC:51); Peter, b. 7/12/1782, bapt. 8/4/1782 (DRC:63). Sponsors: Martyn Van Aalstyn & Wynche Van Aalstyn (re:1); Willem Quack & Catrina Quack (re:2); Peter Quack & Elizabeth Quack (re:3).

Quackenbush, Johannes & Rachel [?]: Johannes, b. 11/11/1762; bapt. 12/1/1762 (RDSA:36). Sponsors: Pieter Canein & his wife.

Quackenbush, Johannes W. & Alida (Van Der Veer): Catrina, b. 11/29/1790; bapt. 1/1/1791 (DRC:92). Sponsors: [none named].

Quackenbush, John & Sarah (Stern): Johannis, b. 6/27/1786; bapt. 7/13/1786 (DRC:81). Sponsors: Nicolas Quak & Lena Quak.

Quackenbush, John J. & Annatje (Starn): Rachel, bapt. 8/?/1790 (DRC:89); Elizabeth,

b. 7/29/1790, bapt. 8/?/1790 (DRC:89). Sponsors: Cornelius C. V. Alstine & Rachel Quack (re:1); Abrm. J. Quack & Caty Quack (re:2).

Quackenbush, John Scott & Elsje (Staats): Neeltje, bapt. 9/13/1761 (DRC:6); Gerritje, bapt. 1764 (DRC:12); Rebecca, b. 7/7/1767, bapt. 10/4/1767 (RDSA:78). Sponsors: Melcert Van Deusen & Neeltje Van Deusen (re:1); Jeremias Quakkenbosch & Aaraantje Coneyn (re:2); Nelje Quackenbosh & Isaac Quackenbosh (re:3).

Quackenbush, Peter & Elisabeth [?]: Pieter, b. 2/22/1770; bapt. 3/20/1770 (RDSA:101). Sponsors: John Shott Quaken[bush] & Elsje Qaken[?].

Quack[enbush], Peter & Elizabeth (Stern), near the Little Nose: Elizabeth, bapt. 1/7/1802 (JDR:14).

Quackenbush, Peter & Elizabeth (Davis): Maria, bapt. 2/6/1763 (DRC:9); James, bapt. 1/27/1765 (DRC:13); Lena, b. 12/13/1776, bapt. 1/29/1777 (DRC:41). Sponsors: James Davis & Maria Davis (re:1); James Davis & Molly Davis (re:2); Jacob Van Aalstyn & Wyntje Van Aalstyn (re:3).

Quackenbush, Peter & Lena [?]: Saratje, b. 6/12/1768; bapt. 8/14/1768 (RDSA:88). Sponsors: Saratje Quackenbosh & Lena Quack.

Quackenbush, Peter & Lena (Leenderse): Johannes, bapt. 1/20/1770 (DRC:18). Sponsors: Johannes Leenderse & Lena Leenderse.

Quackenbush, Peter, Jr. & Sarah [?]: Neeltie, bapt. 7/15/1739 (FH:7); Ann, bapt. 10/25/1742 (FH:19); Peter, bapt. 6/3/1744 (FH:24).

Sponsors: Jeremiah Quackenbus, Madelene Collier, Rachel Quackenbus (re:1); Myndert Wemp, Volkie Vrooman (re:2); John Quackenbos, John Quakenbos Jr, Neeltie Quakenbos (re:3).

Quackenbush, Peter J. & Susanna (Bradt): Rachel, b. 2/12/1775, bapt. 2/19/1775 (DRC:32); Catalyna, b. 5/26/1777, bapt. 6/29/1777 (DRC:43); Neeltje, b. 8/20/1779, bapt. 9/6/1779 (DRC:53); John, b. 8/22/1785, bapt. 8/?/1785 (DRC:75). Sponsors: Nicholas Quack & Rachel Quack (re:1); Samul Bradt & Huybertje Bradt (re:2); Cornelius Van Als[tyne] & Neeltje Van Alsty[ne] (re:3); Abraham J. Quack & Catrina Quack (re:4).

Quackenbush, Van Sant [Vincent] & Jannitje [?]: David, b. 2/15/1766, bapt. 3/12/1766 (RDSA:62); Catharina, b. 9/3/1769, bapt. 12/25/1769 (RDSA:99). Sponsors: David Quackenbosh, Enni Quackenbosh (re:1); Catharina Quak & her husband, Wilhelm Quak (re:2).

Quackenbush, Van Sant & Jannetje (Van Alstyn): Johannis, b. 9/23/1775; bapt. 10/17/1775 (DRC:1). Sponsors: Jacob Collier & Maria Collier.

Quackenbush, William & Annatye [?]: Jerimiah, b. 1/3/1773, bapt. 1/28/1773 (DRC:24); Abram, b. 7/19/1777, bapt. 8/4/1777 (DRC:44). Sponsors: Isaac Collier & Rachel Collier (re:1); Abram Quack & Maria Quack (re:2).

Quackenbush, William & Engiltje (Quackenbush): Peter, b. 12/10/1774; bapt. 1/8/1775 (DRC:32). Sponsors: Abram. D. Quack & Elizabeth Quack.

Quackenbush, William A. & Catarina (Van

COMPENDIUM

Aalsteyn): Maria, bapt. 8/26/1758 (DRC:2); Jacob, b. 4/15/1772, bapt. 5/25/1772 (DRC:20); Abram, b. 12/21/1774, bapt. 1/8/1775 (DRC:32); Peter, b. 6/4/1777, bapt. 6/22/1777 (DRC:43). Sponsors: Gerrit Cornelisse Niewkerk & Neeltje Newkerk (re:1); Isaac Collier & Rachel Collier (re:2); Abram Quack & Meritje Quack (re:3); Vincent Quackinbush & Jannetje Quackinbus (re:4).

Probate Abstract

Quackenboss, Nicholas, (of Glen), will dated 4/28/1828; probated 7/26/1830. Legatees: wife, Magdalene; daus., Rachel (wife of William I. Newkirk), Mary (wife of Daniel Berry), Nancy (wife of John Quackenboss) and Katherine; sons, Jacob, John N., Isaac N.; grandson, Peter A. Quackenboss. Executors: Isaiah Depuy, Rynier Gardinear, John C. Van Alstine. Witnesses: Isaac Stanley, Lawton Garner, Abraham W. Quackenboss. (WMC 57:277)

Quackenboss, William, (of Root), will dated 8/25/1828; probated 2/2/1829. Legatees: son, Peter W. Administrator: Peter W. Quackenboss. Witnesses: Andrew Hibbard, James Folinsbee, Jacob Van Valkenburgh. (WMC 57:273)

Quackenbush, Abraham D., (of Charleston), will dated 11/20/1809; probated 5/25/1812. Legatees: wife, Catherine; sons, Samuel, David, John, Barent, Henery, Vincent and Abraham; daus., Folkie, Rebecca, Jennitie, Alida, Mary (wife of John Fry), Effie (wife of James Hugenor), Annatie (wife of Hankinson Lane) and Catalina (wife of John Rosa). Executors: Victor C. Putman, Benjamin Van Vechten, Robert Mitchell. Witnesses: Henry Perrine, Abraham V. Putman, Samuel P. Quackenboss, Robert Mitchell. (WMC 56:384)

Quackenbush, Isaac H., (of Oppenheim), will dated 9/2/1829; probated 9/15/1829. Legatees: daus., Nancy (wife of Christopher Snell), Polly, Eve; two illegitimate daus., Cyrena and Mariann and illegitimate son, David (which I had from the body of Margrate, wife of Henry H. Smith, Jr.); "allow Margrate, wife of Henry H. Smith, Jr., to live in my house as long as she may be considered as bearing my name as my wife." Executors: Jacob H. Failing, Ashbell Loomis, Henry Failing, Jr. Witnesses: Henry Failing, Jr., I. W. Riggs. (WMC 57:275)

Quackenbush, John P., (of Root), will dated 7/20/1830; probated 9/13/1830. Legatees: wife, Magdalene; infant son, John; Margaret Ann Quackenbush; Peter Ansley Quackenbush. Executors: wife; Hugh Mitchell. Witnesses: Levi Lee, Cornelius Van Alstine. (WMC 57:277)

Quackenbush, Peter P., [residence not stated], will dated 3/1/1827; probated 3/22/1827. Legatees: wife and two children. Executors: wife; Charles Mitchell. Witnesses: D. F. Sacia, M. Sanford. (WMC 57:267-268)

Quackenbush, Vincent Scott, (of Charleston), will dated 9/8/1807; probated 10/23/1807. Legatees: wife, Jannetie; son, David V.; dau., Catharine (wife of Lambert Hugenor). Executors: Nicholas and Martin Van Slyk. Witnesses: Abraham D. and William Quackenboss, James Lansing. (WMC 56:156)

Quackenbush, William, (of Charleston), will dated 3/4/1815; probated 1/31/1818. Legatees: sons, Cornelius, Peter and John; daus., Maria, Rachel and Catharine; grandchildren, William, Cornelius and Margaret Putman; granddaughter, Elizabeth (wife of Jacob F. Sternbergh). Executors: son, John; grandson, William Putman. Witnesses: Thomas Ostrom, Benjamin

COMPENDIUM

Van Vechten, Thomas Ostrom. (WMC 57:166)

Tryon County Militia

Quackenbush, Abraham   [Appendix A]
Quackenbush, Abraham, Jr.
Quackenbush, David
Quackenbush, Hunter Scot
Quackenbush, Isaac
Quackenbush, Jeremiah
Quackenbush, John
Quackenbush, John G.
Quackenbush, Myndert W.
Quackenbush, Nicholas
Quackenbush, Peter
Quackenbush, Vincent
Quackenbush, William

Pension Abstract

Quackenbush, Abraham D., m. Catharine Wemple, 3/1/1781, Reformed Dutch Church of Caughnawaga, N.Y.; d. 5/20/1812 (burned to death in his home), Glen, Montgomery Co., N.Y. (Catharine Quackenbush, b. 1761/2; resident of Glen on 11/30/1836.) Children: Jane (m. [?] Rosem; resident of Madison Co., N.Y. on 6/14/1852); John S.; [five other children not named in application]. Abraham D. enlisted early in the Revolution and served under Capt. Jacob Gardenier in Col. Frederick Fisher's 3rd. Regt., Tryon Co. Militia; he was promoted to the rank of lieutenant; Abraham D. continued in the military into 1782 and was stationed for three months on the south side of the Mohawk River where a part of his time was spent in construction of a blockhouse called "Fort Yellow". (RWPA: #W16688)

Quackenbush, Abraham J., b. 1760; m. Catrina Hoff; resident of Glen, Montgomery Co., N.Y. on 9/18/1832. Children: Rachel, bapt. 5/29/1791, Reformed Protestant Dutch Church of Caughnawaga, N.Y. Abraham J. was drafted or enlisted in 1776 and served as a private in Capt. Jacob Gardenier's Co., Col. Frederick Fisher's 3rd. Regt., Tryon Co. Militia; he marched to Johnstown in January 1776 with his company to oppose British forces commanded by Sir John Johnson and the American troops took from the British a large quantity of arms and munitions of war which were conveyed down the Mohawk River to a place near Dachstaeder's and Abraham J. was put on guard over them during the night; he then marched on the next day, under the command of Capt. Van Eps, to Canajoharie where they took a number of guns, ammunition & Indian deer skins from an American Tory by the name of "Cook" who kept a store near Canajoharie; Abraham J. marched with his regiment towards Oriskany in the summer of 1777 and was ordered to remain at a distance where he took charge of the baggage and some army horses which he crossed to the south side of the Mohawk River for pasture; he did not participate in the battle of Oriskany (8/6/1777) and following this engagement, Abraham took one of the horses to search for his captain and about ten miles from where he [Abraham] had been stationed found the wounded Capt. Jacob Gardenier and Gen. Nicholas Herkimer; Abraham J. fought in the battle of Johnstown. (RWPA: #R8537)

Quackenbush, David, b. 1760, Charleston, N.Y.; resident of Marcellus, Onondaga Co., N.Y. in 1832 when he applied for pension. David enlisted in the N.Y. Troops in the summer of 1779 and was a private and corporal in Lt. Col. Marinus Willett's Regt.; he was drafted or volunteered in 1780 for duty in the Tryon Co. Militia as a private in Col. Frederick Fisher's 3rd. Regt.; David was taken prisoner by the enemy in the summer of 1782 after a battle near Canajoharie and sent to Fort Niagara where he remained until his release on 7/16/1784. (RWPA: #S23379)

Quackenbush, Nicholas, b. 1749/50; m. Magdalen Collier, 4/8/1777; d. 4/21/1830, Glen, Montgomery Co., N.Y. (Magdalen Quackenbush, b. 3/19/1761; d. 6/14/1843, Glen, N.Y.) Children: Isaac N., b. 1785; Catharine N., b. 1797; Mary (m. [?] Berry); Nancy, Rachel (m. William I. Newkirk); John N., b. 1784/5. [All children living in 1853.] Nicholas enlisted in 1775 and served as a sergeant at various times in Capt. Jacob Gardenier's Co., Col. Frederick Fisher's 3rd. Regt., Tryon Co. Militia; he was stationed at Forts Plain, Dayton and Hunter; Nicholas fought in the battle of Oriskany; he served as deputy quartermaster in 1782 and at the time of his discharge Nicholas' total time in the military amounted to over two years. (RWPA: #W11096)

Quackenbush, Peter J., b. 1754 [present day Glen, Montgomery Co., N.Y.], "has no record of his age as the same was Burnt in the Revolution when his House was Burnt by the British & Indians"; m. Susanna Bradt, 7/19/1774, Reformed Dutch Church of Caughnawaga, N.Y.; d. 1837, Glen, N.Y. Children: Susan (m. [?] Van Antwerp). Peter J. enlisted in the 3rd. Regt., Tryon Co. Militia and was a private, corporal and sergeant; he was engaged in the battle of Oriskany. (RWPA: #R8538)

1790 Census

Quackenbus, Abraham D. [Appendix B]
Quackenbush, Isaac
Quackenbuss, [?]
Quackenbuss, Abraham
Quackenbuss, Abraham I.
Quackenbuss, David H.

Quackenbuss, David P.
Quackenbuss, Hunter
Quackenbuss, Jeremiah
Quackenbuss, John (2)
Quackenbuss, Nicholas
Quackenbuss, Peter
Quackenbuss, Peter, Sr.
Quackenbuss, Vincent
Quackenbuss, William (2)

QUANT[?]

Birth/Baptism

Quant[?], Nicholas & [?] [?]: Maria, bapt. 6/3/1787 (DRC:84). Sponsors: John Nellis & Neeltje [?].

QUEEN

Marriage

Queen, William m. Balli Frass (widow), 2/16/1762 (RDSA:170)

QUEINAL

Marriage

Queinal, James m. Lena van den Werken, 3/13/1764 (RDSA:186)

Queinal, James m. Machtel Collier, 4/7/1776 (DRC:161)

QUICK

648

1790 Census

Quick, Elijah   [Appendix B]

QUILHOT

Death Record

Quilhot, Elizabeth, (wife of John Quilhot), d. 2/27/1819, age 57 years; buried sect. 5, Colonial Cemetery, Johnstown (JC:186)

Probate Abstract

Quilhot, John, (of Johnstown), will dated 8/23/1810; probated 10/16/1815. Legatees: dau., Mary Callaghan; sons, Stephen, James and Henry; grandsons, John, James and Stephen (of Stephen). Executors: sons, James and Henry. Witnesses: Abijah Lobdell, William Grant, Jr., Silas Wood, John McNaughton. (WMC 56:395)

1790 Census

Quilhot, [?]   [Appendix B]
Quilhot, John
Quilhot, Stephen

RAAB

Marriage

Raab, George m. Christina Keller, 7/15/1792 (DFP:45)

RAAN

Marriage

Raan, Jacob m. Anna Eva Fr: Miller, 1/19/1790 (DRGF:206)

RAAS

Marriage

Raas, Georg m. Anna Huppert, 8/29/1769 (LTSA:280)

RABOLT

Birth/Baptism

Rabolt, George (Palatine) & Margretha [?]: Elisabeth, bapt. 3/2/1794 (SJC:94). Sponsors: Conrad Hellegas & Anna Eva Hellegas.

Tryon County Militia

Rabold, George   [Appendix A]

RADDERFORT

Birth/Baptism

Radderfort, Robert & Rosina [?]: Jacob, b. 3/30/1777; bapt. 6/1/1777 (DRGF:23). Sponsors: Jacob Majer & Margretha.

RADLEY

1790 Census

Radley, John   [Appendix B]

RADLI

Birth/Baptism

Radli, Sever (Palatine) & Susanna (Clas): Anna Catharina, bapt. 4/1?/1791 (SJC:41); Anna, bapt. 11/10/1793 (SJC:84). Sponsors: Jacob Clas & Debora Kruass (re:1); John Clas & Gertrud Clas (re:2).

RADLIFF

Probate Abstract

Radliff, John, (of the town of Florida), will dated 5/18/1810; probated 4/11/1811. Legatees: wife, Mary; sons, John, Jacob and Andries; daus., Geartreuy, Mary (and her son, John Radliff Wildie). Executors: Philip Radliff, Abraham Bronk. Witnesses: William Van Olinda, Charles Patterson and Charles Patterson, Jr. (WMC 56:381)

RADTLY

Probate Abstract

Rattley, Jacobus, (of Palatine), will dated 10/24/1804; probated 1/28/1825. Legatees: wife, Susana; sons, John, William and Peter; daus., Pegge, Caty and Nancy. Executors:

Joseph Nellis, Daniel Scouten. Witnesses: Seth Potter, John P. Sutz, Jacob Snell, Nicholas Claus. (WMC 57:181)

1790 Census

Radtly, Jacobus   [Appendix B]

RAISNER

Tryon County Militia

Raisner, Jacob   [Appendix A]

RAMBOUGH

Birth/Baptism

Rambough, Amos & [?], Jerseybush: Jacob, bapt. 7/19/1776 (JDR:15); William, bapt. 6/3/1781 (JDR:24).

RAMSAY

1790 Census

Ramsay, Ebenezer   [Appendix B]

RAMSEY

Deed Abstract

Ramsey, Thomas and William Ramsey, yeomen, of Cherry Valley, Montgomery Co. to Gabriel Duytzer and John Duytzer, of

Hosick [Hoosick] District, Albany Co. Deed dated 10/3/1784; recorded 8/10/1785. Description: Part of a tract of land situated in Montgomery Co. on the south side of the Mohawk River at a place called Cherry Valley (formerly surveyed, laid out and divided into ninety-two lots). Lots #26 (102$^{1/2}$ acres) and #36 (100 acres). Consideration: L450. Signed: Thomas Ramsey (by Will. Ramsey, his Attorney), and William Ramsey. Witnesses: Zele Snell, Chris. P. Yates. (MVL:27)

1790 Census

Ramsey, Ebenezer   [Appendix B]

RANDALL

Death Record

Randall, Phineas, b. 6/5/1789; d. 4/3/1853; buried Fort Plain Cemetery, Minden (FPC 56:43h)

Randall, Sarah Beach, (wife of Phineas Randall), b. 2/11/1800; d. 3/4/1882; buried Fort Plain Cemetery, Minden (FPC 56:43h)

Probate Abstract

Randel, Benejah, (of Palatine), will dated 12/23/1795; probated 12/16/1796. Legatees: wife, Lydia; sons, Samuel, William & Benajah; dau., Orpha; unborn child. Executors: wife; and William Harris. Witnesses: Cornelius Humfrey, Samuel Nichols, C[?] Gillet. (WMC 56:149)

1790 Census

Randell, Nathaniel   [Appendix B]

RANKIN

Marriage

Rankin, James m. Delia Petri (dau. of Dan Petri), 1/22/1787 (DRGF:204)

Rankin, Thomas m. Catharin Kesslar, 11/22/1791 (DRGF:208)

Birth/Baptism

Rankin, James & Elisabeth [?]: Elisabetha, bapt. 12/4/1765 (RDSA:59); Catharina, b. 3/29/1768, bapt. 4/18/1768 (RDSA:85); Janney, b. 5/31/1776, bapt. 6/5/1776 (DRGF:17). Sponsors: Aerdghi Armstrong & his wife, Elisabeth (re:1); Joh. Jost Teughardt & Catharina Bellinger (re:2); Guy Laky & Jannej (re:3).

Death Record

Rankin, Jacob, (little son of James Rinken), d. 9/14/1823, Germanflats, age [not stated]; buried in the cemetery near the church (RDH:288)

Pension Abstract

Rankin, Thomas, m. Catharine [Kessler], 11/22/1791, German Flatts, N.Y.; d. 2/5/1833, German Flatts, Herkimer Co., N.Y. (Catharine Rankin, b. ca. 1772; resident of Little Falls, Herkimer Co. on 10/2/1838.) Thomas enlisted as a fifer in the fall of 1779 under the command of Capt. John Griggs in Col. Van Schaick's Regt., N.Y. Line; he served at Fort Stanwix for most of the war; Thomas was at Yorktown when Cornwallis was taken; he was discharged at Newburg, N.Y. in June 1783 and his discharge was signed by George Washington [stated that it had since been lost]. (RWPA:

651

#W20012)

1790 Census

Rancan, James   [Appendix B]

RANNEY

1790 Census

Ranney, James   [Appendix B]
Ranney, Seth
Ranney, Willett

RANSFORD

1790 Census

Ransford, Haskil   [Appendix B]

RANSIEUR

Birth/Baptism

Ransieur, Georg & Anna Barbara [?]: Anna Barbara, b. 8/8/1780; bapt. 9/27/1780 (DRGF:40). Sponsors: Pieter Birky & Catharina Ringkel.

RANSOME

1790 Census

Ransome, John   [Appendix B]
Ransome, Samuel
Ransome, Thomas

RAPALTE

Marriage

Rapalte, Isaac m. Margreth Schuyler, 3/25/1788 (DRGF:205)

1790 Census

Rapelyee, Isaac   [Appendix B]

RAPON

Birth/Baptism

Rapon, George (of Palatine) & Elisabeth (Fehling): Anna, bapt. 10/25/1788 (SJC:5). Sponsors: Peter Ocher & Magdalena Fehling.

RAPP

1790 Census

Rapp, George   [Appendix B]

RAPSPEL

Tryon County Militia

Rapspel, Frederick   [Appendix A]

RARITY

1790 Census

COMPENDIUM

Rarity, Timothy   [Appendix B]

RASBEL

1790 Census

Rasbel, Marks   [Appendix B]

RASCHER

Birth/Baptism

Rascher, Frans (Caughnawaga Dist.) & Martha
(Kleyn): Maria, b. 12/25/1791; bapt. 1/11/1792
(SJC:52). Sponsors: William Kleyn & Maria
Kleyn.

RASE

1790 Census

Rase, Daniel   [Appendix B]

RASPACH

Marriage

Raspach, Johannes (son of Fritz Raspach) m.
Margretha Moog, 2/7/1792 (DRGF:209)

Raspach, Johannes m. Anna Moog, 11/8/1785
(DRGF:202)

Raspach, Marcus m. Elisabeth Diefendorfff,
1/31/1796 (DFP:54)

Birth/Baptism

Raspach/Raspe, Friedrich & Catharina [?]:
Maria C[?], b. 1/13/1783, bapt. 1/19/1783
(DRGF:66); Johann Jost, b. 6/11/1785, bapt.
6/19/1785 (DRGF:98). Sponsors: Werner Joh:
Tyghart & Maria Catharina Tyghart (re:1); Joh:
Jost Kajser & Maria (re:2).

Raspach, Johann Marcus & Anna Veronica [?]:
Johannes, b. 10/6/1760, bapt. 11/25/1760
(RDSA:23); Johannes, b. 1/23/1764, bapt.
1/31/1764 (RDSA:44); Johann Friedrich, b.
9/1/1766, bapt. 9/16/1766 (RDSA:68); Marcus,
b. 6/14/1769, bapt. 8/1/1769 (RDSA:95);
Johann Adam, b. 3/3/1778, bapt. 3/12/1778
(DRGF:29). Sponsors: Johannes Rasps & his
wife, Margretha (re:1); Johannes Neer & his
wife, Anna (re:2); Friedrich Raspock &
Elisabeth Foltz (re:3); Marcus D. Petri &
Margretha Raspok (re:4); Adam Stahle &
Catharina (re:5).

Death Record

Raspach, Elisabetha, (dau. of Johannes & Anna
(Mokin) Rasbach), d. 3/4/1804, Herkimer, age
10 months; buried in field of Melchior Thumb
(RDH:251)

Raspach, Eva, (dau. of Johannes Rasbach), d.
1/21/1808, Herkimer, age 13 days; buried in
the cemetery of Melchior Thum, Shellsbush
(RDH:259)

Raspach, Marcus, (honest & esteemed resident
in Herkimer), d. 8/10/1822, Fairfield, age 53
years, 1 month, 21 days; buried in the new
cemetery in town (RDH:284)

Raspach, Margaretha, (wife of Adam Rasbach),
d. 5/6/1814, Herkimer, age 33 years; buried in
the cemetery near the Herkimer church

(RDH:270)

Raspach, Veronica, (widow of Marc Rasbach, from Herkimer), b. Switzerland (as was her brother, [Grates Mock], in Switzerland); d. 5/13/1814, age 82 years, 2 months; buried near her brother [Grates Mock] and her husband in the cemetery of the stone church in Germanflats (RDH:270)

Tryon County Militia

Rasbach, John   [Appendix A]

Pension Abstract

Rasbach, Frederick, b. 1748/9; resident of New York State in 1786. Frederick was certified at Albany, N.Y. on 10/19/1786 by Philip Schuyler and Abraham Ten Broeck to have been a private in Capt. Small's Co., Col. Peter Bellinger's 4th. Regt., Tryon Co. Militia; Frederick participated in the battle of Oriskany on 8/6/1777 and became disabled "in consequence of a wound in the lower jaw"; he was granted a pension of two dollars per month. (RWPA: [RASBERG] #S27349)

1790 Census

Rosback, Frederick   [Appendix B]

RATHBON

1790 Census

Rathbon, Edmund   [Appendix B]
Rathbon, Perry

RATTENAUER

Marriage

Rattenauer, George m. Elisabeth Hess, 11/6/1792 (DFP:46)

Birth/Baptism

Rattenauer, Gottfrid & Catharina [?]: Catharina, b. 8/27/1769 (LTSA:29); Anna, b. 8/18/1771 (LTSA:39). Sponsors: Caspar Jordan & his wife (re:1); Joh: Jordan & his wife (re:2).

Rattenauer, Jacob & Dorothea [?]: Maria Margretha, b. 8/1/1761, bapt. 8/6/1761 (RDSA:28); Christina, b. 10/2/1781, bapt. 10/7/1781 (DRGF:48); Heinrich, b. 1/8/1791 (LTSA:66). Sponsors: Maria Margretha, wife of Johannes Baart (re:1); Henrich Nelles & Christina (re:2); Heinrich Ratenauer, Margaret Jordan (re:3).

Death Record

Rattenauer, [?], (child of [?] Rattenauer), d. 3/?/1810, age 1 year, 10 months; buried 3/3/1810 (DFP:93)

Tryon County Militia

Rattenauer, George   [Appendix A]
Rattenauer, Jacob

Pension Abstract

Rattenauer, George, b. 1760/1; m. Elizabeth Hess, 11/6/1792, Reformed Dutch Church of Fort Plain; d. 5/30/1844, Lenox, Madison Co., N.Y. (Elizabeth Rattenauer, b. 1767/8; d. 5/20/1846, Lenox, N.Y.) Children: George, b. 1/15/1795 (resident of Lenox, N.Y., 1845); Elizabeth, b. 1793 (d. ca. 1800 of small pox);

654

Henry, Lana (m. [?] White); Catharine (m. [?] Hendrickson); Jacob, William, Abraham, Susan (m. [?] Smith); and Barnhardt. [All surviving children over twenty-one years of age in 1847. Surname spelled *RATNOUR* by sons in that year.] George served in 1780 as a private in Capt. Dana's Co., Col. Hays' Regt. of the N.Y. Line; he was a private in Col. Marinus Willett's Regt. from 1781 through 1782; George was engaged in the battles of Sharon and Johnstown. (RWPA: #W11100)

Rattenauer, Jacob, b. 1757/8; resident of the Territory of Michigan on 3/5/1831 where he had recently settled and requested transfer of his pension. Jacob was a private in Capt. Lipe's Co., Col. Samuel Clyde's 1st. Regt., Tryon Co. Militia; Jacob was wounded in his hip in an action with the enemy in 1781 and received a pension for his disability on 9/14/1786, at which time he was a resident of Montgomery Co., N.Y. (RWPA: #S25377)

RAULINS

Marriage

Raulins, Peter m. Mary McArthur, 5/15/1795 (JPC:91)

RAWLENS

Deed Abstract

Rawlins, Michael, Innkeeper, and Ruth, his wife, of Johnstown, Montgomery Co. to George Shea, merchant, of New York City. Deed dated 1/31/1786; recorded 3/4/1786. Description: Land situated at Johnstown, Montgomery Co., known as Lot #9, which lot

has been conveyed to Michael Rawlins by the Commissioners of Forfeiture (together with Lots E#5 and F#6, by an Indenture, dated 6/1/1785). Whereby, the said Lot #9 (5 acres) is the same lot on which Michael Rawlins now has his potash works. Consideration: L70. Witnesses: T. V. [Tunis Van] Wagenen, John Littel. (MVL:27)

1790 Census

Rawlens, Aaron [Appendix B]
Rawlens, Michael

RAYMOND

1790 Census

Raymond, Daniel [Appendix B]

REACHIE

Marriage

Reachie, Andrew (b. 9/?/1743) m. Margaret Adair, 6/22/1774 (UPSC:67)

READ

Death Record

Read, Catharine, (wife of Dr. Thomas Read), d. 11/24/1839, age 77 years; buried sect. 9, Colonial Cemetery, Johnstown (JC:186)

Read, Thomas, (Dr., a surgeon in the Revolutionary War), d. 9/18/1826, age 73

655

COMPENDIUM

years; buried sect. 9, Colonial Cemetery, Johnstown (JC:186)

READY

Tryon County Militia

Ready, Charles   [Appendix A]

REAVER

1790 Census

Reaver, Andrew   [Appendix B]

REBER

Birth/Baptism

Reber, Johannes & Ottilia [?]: Catharina, b. 11/18/1770 (LTSA:34). Sponsors: Philipp Emge, jr., Catharina Engeland.

REDFIELD

1790 Census

Redfield, Jared   [Appendix B]

REDINGTON

1790 Census

Redington, John   [Appendix B]

REDLEY

Birth/Baptism

Redley, Michael & Regina [?]: John, b. 11/1/1780; bapt. 12/17/1780 (DRC:58). Sponsors: John Halenbeck & Maragriet Halenbe[ck].

REDWAY

1790 Census

Redway, Samuel   [Appendix B]

REED (also see REID/RIED)

Marriage

Reed, Abner m. Anna G. Zimmerman, 2/2/1794 (DRGF:211)

Reed, Israel Wm. m. Margretha G: Zimmerman, 2/25/1794 (DRGF:211)

Reed, Johannes m. Dorothea Suz, 10/28/1787 (RDSA:192)

Birth/Baptism

Reed, Conrad & Barbara (Stooner): Michel, b. 3/30/1773; bapt. 5/6/1773 (DRC:25). Sponsors: Michel Warner & Maragriet Warner.

Reed, Isaac & Utilia (Wagner): Johannes, b. 6/2/1753 (LTSA:7); Jacob, b. 7/29/1755 (LTSA:14). Sponsors: Hannes Frey, Margaretha Tillenbach (re:1); Jacob Glock & his wife, [?] (re:2).

656

COMPENDIUM

Reed, Johannes & Dorotea [?]: Peter, b. 3/6/1791 (LTSA:67). Sponsors: Peter Suz & Elisabet.

Reed, John & Anna [?]: Elisabetha, b. 3/21/1756 (LTSA:17); William, b. 12/31/1760, bapt. 1/4/1761 (RDSA:24); Jahn, b. 12/16/1762, bapt. 1/1/1763 (RDSA:37). Sponsors: Robbert Garter & his wife, Elisabetha (re:1); Sem Van Etten & his wife, Maria (re:2); Wilhelm Laux & his wife (re:3).

Tryon County Militia

Reed, Conrad   [Appendix A]
Reed, John

Pension Abstract

Reed, John, b. 1761/2; [both John's mother and father were killed and scalped by the Indians during the war]; resident of Lewis Co., N.Y. on 9/20/1832. John entered the military from Palatine in 1777 and served under Capt. Henry Miller in Col. Jacob Klock's 2nd. Regt. of the Tryon Co. Militia until 1781; he enlisted for nine months in 1781 and served in Col. Willett's Regt.; John was in the battles of Johnstown, Turlock and West Canada Creek. (RWPA: #S14271)

1790 Census

Reed, Curtis   [Appendix B]

REEDENBAKER

1790 Census

Reedenbaker, Baltus   [Appendix B]

REEDER

Tryon County Militia

Reeder, Hendrick   [Appendix A]

REES/REESE see REIS

REEVES

1790 Census

Reeves, Abner   [Appendix B]

REID (also see REED/RIED)

Death Record

Reid, Elizabeth, (dau. of Peter & Susan Reid), d. 3/22/1855, age 29 years, 9 months, 14 days; buried sect. 2, Colonial Cemetery, Johnstown (JC:186)

Reid, James S., (son of Peter & Susan Reid), d. 9/11/1838, age 13 months; buried sect. 2, Colonial Cemetery, Johnstown (JC:186)

Reid, William, (Dr.), d. 8/15/1818, age 58 years; buried sect. 9, Colonial Cemetery, Johnstown (JC:186)

Reid, William, (son of W.[illiam] A. & Jane Reid), d. 12/8/1809, age 1 month, buried sect. 9, Colonial Cemetery, Johnstown (JC:186)

657

REILY

Marriage

Reily, James m. Catharine Jac: Mejer, 9/29/1795 (DRGF:213)

Reily, Jimmy (son of Robert Reily) m. Anna Klok (dau. of Adam Klok, decd.), 2/17/1789 (DFP:39)

Birth/Baptism

Reily, John & Delia [?]: Patrick, b. 2/12/1776; bapt. 3/25/1776 (DRGF:16). Sponsors: Florentz Donnavan & Elisabetha Petri.

Riley, James (of Canajoh. Dist.) & Anna (Klock): Catharina, bapt. 1/25/1790 (SJC:23). Sponsors: Jacob Meyer & Catharina Meyer.

REIN

Birth/Baptism

Rein, Johann Nicol & Maria Elisabeth [?] (New Petersburg): Eva Catharina, b. 6/29/1770; bapt. 7/3/1770 (RDSA:103). Sponsors: Catharina & [?] Gruning [?].

REIS

Marriage

Reis, John (son of Johannes Riess) m. Anna Eppli (dau. of Johannes Eppli of Butler's land), 12/12/1759 (RDSA:166; LTSA:277)

Reis, John (widower) m. Elisabeth Ensly (widow), 2/28/1770 (RDSA:188)

Reis, John m. Catharina Hillegas, 5/29/1784 (DRGF:199)

Reis, Nicholas m. Anna Clyne, 8/17/1767 (RDSA:182)

Birth/Baptism

Rees, John & Margaret (Pettengell), Warrensborough: Nicholas, bapt. 10/16/1791 (JDR:21); Hannah, bapt. 4/27/1794, age 3 months (JDR:15).

Reese, Jacob & [?], Warrensborough: Elizabeth, bapt. 8/29/1779 (JDR:12).

Reis, Adam & Annitje (Bell): Johannis, b. 9/4/1783, bapt. 6/3/1785 (DRC:73); Melchert, b. 5/17/1785, bapt. 6/3/1785 (DRC:73). Sponsors: Samuel Rees & Annatje Rees (re:1); Johannis Yong & Elizabeth Rees (re:2).

Reis, Conrad & Barber [?]: Barent, bapt. 7/25/1779 (DRC:19), bapt. 7/5/1779 (DRC:53); Johan Jurry, b. 4/12/1782, bapt. 5/12/1782 (DRC:62). Sponsors: Barent Fredrik & Dorethea Fredrik (re:1); Jurry Cratsenberg & Elizabeth Shoop[?] (re:2).

Reis, Henry & Anna (Crossit): Caty, b. 10/7/1786; bapt. 3/16/1787 (DRC:83). Sponsors: [none named].

Reis, Jacob & Catrina (Daksteder): Marks, b. 3/29/1777, bapt. 4/15/1777 (DRC:42); Lena, b. 8/1/1783, bapt. 9/6/1783 (DRC:68); Nicholas, b. 1/21/1786, bapt. 2/17/1786 (DRC:76). Sponsors: Jurry Doxteder & Lena Ries (re:1); Matthew Young & Eliz. Rees (re:2); Nicholas Rees & Annatje Rees (re:3).

COMPENDIUM

Reis, Johann Friderich & Anna Margareth (Dillenbach): Margaretha, b. 6/1/1755 (LTSA:14); Magdalena, b. 3/18/1757 (LTSA:21). Sponsors: Henrich Tillenbach & his wife, Anna Margaretha (re:1); Johannes Schulz & his wife, Magdalena (re:2).

Reis, Johannes & Anna [?]: Elisabeth, b. 2/?/1766; bapt. 8/17/1769 (RDSA:95). Sponsors: Eva Coppernoll & Jacob Eppli.

Reis, Johannes (of Palatine) & Catharina [?]: Anna, bapt. 1/1/1791 (SJC:36); Maria, bapt. 12/16/1792 (SJC:68). Sponsors: Rudolf Koch & Anna Koch (re:1); Wilhelm Wallrath & Margretha Hellegas (re:2).

Reis, Jonas & Anna Maria [?]: Jacob, b. 5/19/1791 (LTSA:68); Johannes, b. 2/23/1794 (LTSA:82); Daniel, b. 4/12/1796 (LTSA:94). Sponsors: Jacob Neher, Maria Loscher (re:1); John Merkel & Anna (re:2); Nicolaus Copernoll & Maria (re:3).

Reis, Nicholas & Anna (Klyne): Adam, b. 12/6/1779, bapt. 12/23/1779 (DRC:54); Madalena, b. 2/9/1782, bapt. 3/3/1782 (DRC:61); Catrina, b. 1/2/1786, bapt. 5/22/1786 (DRC:80). Sponsors: Hendrik Snook & Christina Snook (re:1); Jurry Doxteder & Madalena Doxteder (re:2); William Snook & Catrina Snook (re:3).

Reis, Peter & Margaret [?]: Johannes, b. 10/4/1793 (LTSA:80); Friderich, b. 2/9/1795 (LTSA:88); Catarina, b. 10/101/796 (LTSA:97). Sponsors: Josua Ries, Maria Graf (re:1); Friderich Ries, Magdalena Loescher (re:2); Heinrich Dachstetter & Catarina (re:3).

Reis, Samuel & Anna (Doxteder): Marks, b. 4/4/1779, bapt. 5/25/1779 (DRC:52); Catrina, b. 1/7/1781, bapt. 2/6/1781 (DRC:58);

Nichlas, b. 11/13/1782, bapt. 12/1/1782 (DRC:64). Sponsors: Lenard Doxteder & Anna Doxteder (re:1); Daniel Service & Catrina Service (re:2); Hannikel Doxteder & Dorothea Doxteder (re:3).

Ries, Gideon & Barbara [?]: Margareta, b. 8/16/1792 (LTSA:75). Sponsors: Martin Nestel & Elisabet.

Ries, Martin & Maria [?]: Johannes, b. 8/8/1784; bapt. 8/18/1784 (DRGF:86). Sponsors: Johannes Glock, Junr. & [?].

Death Record

Reis, Samuel, d. 9/?/1809, age 52 years, 6 months; buried 9/5/1809 (DFP:93)

Probate Abstract

Rees, Nicholas, (of Florida), will dated 3/17/1829; probated 6/11/1829. Legatees: wife [not named] (decd.); sons, Marks, John, Jacob, Adam, Martin, William, Samuel, Henry and Nicholas; daus., Magdalen (wife of Henry Disbrow) and Betsy; grandson, Cornelius (of Betsy); granddaus., Caty and Peggy (of Nicholas). Executor: son, Nicholas, Jr. Witnesses: Platt Potter, Ira Vaughan, George Young. (WMC 57:274)

Reese, Samuel, (of Canajoharie), will dated 8/15/1809; probated 11/6/1809. Legatees: sons, Frederick, Samuel, Jacob, Henry, Nicholas, John and George; dau., Catherine Waggoner; grandson, Samuel M. Reese; granddaughter, Hannah Quackenboss. Executors: son, Henry; Jonathan Eights, George Lasher. Witnesses: Jeremiah McCarney, Niclas P. Herter, Abraham Mower, Jr. (WMC 56:160)

Tryon County Militia

Rees, Samuel   [Appendix A]

1790 Census

Rees, Jonas   [Appendix B]
Rees, Nicholas
Rees, Peter
Reese, Adam
Reese, Jacob

REIST

Birth/Baptism

Reist, Humphry (of Gaesberg) & Johanna [?]: Jacob, bapt. 12/19/1790 (SJC:35). Sponsors: Jacob Reist & Elisabeth Reist.

REITER

Birth/Baptism

Reitter, Georg & Maria [?]: Anna Maria, b. 2/7/1770 (LTSA:30). Sponsors: Andraeas Heinz, Anna Maria Gre.

Death Record

Reiter, George, d. 9/?/1809, age 81 years; buried 9/9/1809 (DFP:93)

REMSEN

1790 Census

Remsen, Jonathan (2)   [Appendix B]

RENNALDS

1790 Census

Rennalds, George   [Appendix B]

RENNO

Birth/Baptism

Renno, Frantz & Elisabeth [?]: Catharina, b. 12/1/1777; bapt. 12/7/1777 (LTSA:51). Sponsors: Johann Joseph Wagner, Catarina Renno.

RENNORS

Marriage

Rennors, Sam m. Denglas Devis, 10/22/1765 (RDSA:177)

RENOLDS

1790 Census

Renolds, Eli   [Appendix B]
Renolds, Eli, Jr.

RENOUARD

COMPENDIUM

1790 Census

Renouard, Andrew   [Appendix B]

RESNER

Deed Abstract

Resner, George and George Countryman (by Samuel Clyde, Sheriff of Montgomery Co. [by Writ of Fieri Facias] against the aforementioned individuals for their debt of L360 and damages of L4.18.0 to the estate of Tobias Ten Eyck, deceased, through the Executrix, Rachel Ten Eyck and Myndert S. Ten Eyck, Henry Ten Eyck, John D. P. Ten Eyck, Jacob Ten Eyck, and Barent Ten Eyck, Executors of said estate) to Abraham Copeman, of Canajoharie, Montgomery Co. Instrument dated 3/13/1786; recorded 8/17/1786. Description: Land situated at Canajoharie District in a patent granted on 6/20/1723 to Peter Waggoner, Johannes Lawyer and Conrad Weiser. About 20 acres of Lot #5, so much of Lot #6 as will make up the same quantity of acres Jacobus Resner had in Lot #6, together with the one-half part of 100 acres in Lot #8 of a patent granted to Jacob Lansing, Abraham Lansing and others. By virtue of the Writ the said lots were purchased by Abraham Copeman as the highest bidder. Consideration: L212. Witnesses: William Haskin, Rudolph Diefendorff. (MVL:8-9)

RESSEGUIE

Probate Abstract

Resseguie, Daniel, (of Northampton), will dated 1/24/1825; probated 3/23/1825. Legatees:

wife, Mary; sons, David, Daniel, Charles, Jacob, Samuel and Belding; daus., Esther Scott, Polly Chrouch and Minerva; granddau., Mary Fields. Executors: wife and sons, David and Daniel. Witnesses: Joseph Spier, Isaac Betts, Samuel Storee. (WMC 57:181-182)

REUT

Birth/Baptism

Reut, Jacob & Elisabeth [?]: Maria, b. 3/22/1779; bapt. 4/1/1779 (LTSA:57). Sponsors: Johann Joseph Nelles, Maria Wagner.

REYNER

Tryon County Militia

Reyner, Francis   [Appendix A]

RHEEL

1790 Census

Rheel, Frederick   [Appendix B]

RHEINHOLTZ

Birth/Baptism

Rheinholtz, Johann & Maria Magdalena [?]: Catharina, b. 6/13/1779; bapt. 10/25/1779 (LTSA:58). Sponsors: Theobald Delert,

Catharina von Peltz.

RHEINUH

Birth/Baptism

Rheinuh, Joh. Nicel & Maria Elisabeth [?]: Jacobus, b. 8/17/1767; bapt. 10/23/1767 (RDSA:79). Sponsors: Jacob Dinges, Michel Seitzer & Sussanna Marg.

RHIMA (also see **RIEMAU**)

Marriage

Rima, Johan Friedr: m. Maria Bekker, 3/17/1795 (DRGF:212)

Rima, Peter m. Catharina Hofstatter (dau. of Christian Hofstatter), 12/31/1793 (DRGF:210)

Rima, Theobald m. Margretha Breitenbacher, 3/3/1795 (DRGF:212)

Birth/Baptism

Rhima, Johannes & Catharina [?]: Johann Christian, b. 8/14/1767, bapt. 10/23/1767 (RDSA:79); Johann Deobald, b. 12/12/1770, bapt. 1/26/1771 (RDSA:108). Sponsors: Jacob Mohr, Jacob Hiller & Cath. Rank (re:1); George Schiff, Maria Groonhard & George B[?] (re:2).

Rima, George (of New Deutschland) & Sara [?]: Johannes, bapt. 1/9/1791 (SJC:38). Sponsors: Christian Rima & Margretha Rima.

Rima, Jacob (of New Deutschland) & Dorothea

[?]: Catharina, bapt. 9/13/1789 (SJC:17); Elisabeth, b. 7/18/1791, bapt. 10/2/1791 (SJC:47). Sponsors: Georg Rima & Sara Lenzia (re:1); Friederich Rima & Elisabeth Mayer (re:2).

Tryon County Militia

Rimah, George   [Appendix A]
Rimah, John
Rimah, John, Jr.

RICE

Birth/Baptism

Rice, James & Elizabeth [?]: Mary, b. 1/29/1791; bapt. 2/26/1792 (JPC:6).

1790 Census

Rice, Amaziah   [Appendix B]
Rice, Hezekiah (2)
Rice, James
Rice, John (2)
Rice, John, Jr.
Rice, Pebetiah
Rice, Seth
Rice, William

RICH

1790 Census

Rich, Calvin   [Appendix B]
Rich, Luther
Rich, Moses
Rich, Simon

RICHARDS

<u>1790 Census</u>

Richards, Moses   [Appendix B]

RICHARDSON

<u>Marriage</u>

Richardson, Bill m. Christina Nelles (widow of Henrich Nelles), 3/24/1784 (DRGF:199)

<u>Birth/Baptism</u>

Richardson, Wiliam & Christina [?]: David, b. 10/28/1784; bapt. 11/7/1784 (DRGF:88). Sponsors: David Mabee & Sally Sneider.

<u>Tryon County Militia</u>

Richardson, Jonathan   [Appendix A]

<u>1790 Census</u>

Richardson, Daniel, Sr.   [Appendix B]
Richardson, Jonathan
Richardson, William

RICHEL

<u>1790 Census</u>

Richel, Christian   [Appendix B]

RICHMAN

<u>Marriage</u>

Richman, Peter m. Lydy Eaten, [no date: precedes 2/2/1790] (DRGF:207)

RICHMOND

<u>1790 Census</u>

Richmond, Daniel   [Appendix B]
Richmond, Edward

RICHTER

<u>Probate Abstract</u>

Richter, Nicholas, (of Palatine), Captain & late a U.S. invalid pensioner; will dated 3/16/1820; probated 9/1/1823. Legatees: all my children; son-in-law, Peter Fox. Executor: Philip R. Frey. Administrator: Peter Getman. Witnesses: John Fink, Lany Fox and William W. Fox, Jr. (WMC 57:176)

<u>Tryon County Militia</u>

Richter, Nicholas   [Appendix A]

<u>Pension Abstract</u>

Richter, Nicholas, m. [wife not named; d. prior to 1855]; resident of Montgomery Co., N.Y. on 9/15/1788; d. 11/25/1820. Children: Peter; [one other not named and both living in 1820]. There is no data concerning Nicholas' military service in the pension application file. However, the roster of Col. Jacob Klock's 2nd. Regt., Tryon Co. Militia enumerates Nicholas as a captain. (RWPA: #S27372)

1790 Census

Richter, Nicholas [Appendix B]

RICKEL

Tryon County Militia

Rickel, Christian [Appendix A]

RICKER

Birth/Baptism

Ricker, Henry & Rachel (Hardendolf): Peter, bapt. 4/15/1787 (JDR:21)

1790 Census

Ricker, Peter [Appendix B]

RICKERT

Marriage

Rickart, Henrich Conr: m. Catharin Seuffer, 5/24/1791 (DRGF:208)

Rickert, Ludwig m. Maria Seuffer, 3/19/1787 (DRGF:204)

Rickert, Nicolaus m. Barba Stamm, 1/29/1792 (RDSA:196)

Rickert, Peter m. Elisabeta Gerlach, 4/28/1767 (RDSA:182)

Birth/Baptism

Rickert, George (Canajoharie) & Catharina [?]: Samuel, bapt. 5/20/1793 (SJC:76)

Rickert, Henderick & Christina [?]: [not named], bapt. 10/18/1778 (DRC:50). Sponsors: Jacob Gardinier & Derkje Gardinier.

Rickert, Henrich (Schneidersbusch) & Catharina [?]: Conrad, bapt. 12/25/1791 (SJC:52). Sponsors: Conrad Rikard & Elisabeth Rikard.

Rickert, Johannes (Sneidersbush) & Catharina [?]: Catharina, b. 8/5/1793; bapt. 8/12/1793 (SJC:79). Sponsors: John Payeux & Catharina Payeux.

Rickert, Ludwig & Catharina [?]: Johannes, b. 10/7/1783; bapt. 10/9/1783 (DRGF:76). Sponsors: Johannes Koch & Anna Eva Gettmann.

Rickert, Ludwig (of Schneidersbusch) & Maria [?]: Anna, bapt. 9/20/1789 (SJC:18); Conrad, b. 8/30/1791, bapt. 10/9/1791 (SJC:48); Peter, b. 8/3/1793, bapt. 8/12/1793 (SJC:79). Sponsors: Johannes Seufer & Maria Seufer (re:1); Conrad Rikard (re:2); Peter Louks & Anna Louks (re:3).

Rickert, Marx & Elisabetha [?]: Marcus, b. 7/26/1770 (LTSA:33). Sponsors: Peter Sommer, Margaretha Greisler.

Rickert, Peter & Elisabeth [?]: Jacobus, b. 4/14/1769, bapt. 4/23/1769 (RDSA:94); Eva, b. 12/23/1775, bapt. 1/12/1776 (DRGF:15). Sponsors: Jacob Rikkert & Margretha Gerlach (re:1); Joh: Riemensneider & Eva (re:2).

Death Record

Rickert, [?], (wife of Conrad Rickert), d. 3/?/1813, age 51 years, 6 months; buried 3/15/1813 (DFP:96)

Probate Abstract

Rickerts, Ludwig, (of Palatine), will dated 3/20/1817; probated 3/20/1819. Legatees: brother, Jacob; sons, John, George, Ludwig and Frederick; daus., Naomi, Anna Eve (wife of Caspar C. Cook), Catharine (wife of George Adam Blanck), Elizabeth (wife of Joseph Getman), Maria (wife of William H. Shults) and Delia (wife of George Williamson). Bequest: Large German bible. Executors: son, George; Jacob Getman, Adam Blanck (of Johnstown). Witnesses: Richard Young, Lewis and John A. Beck. (WMC 57:168)

Tryon County Militia

Rickert, Bartholomew   [Appendix A]
Rickert, Jacob
Rickert, John
Rickert, Ludwig
Rickert, Nicholas

Pension Abstract

Rickert, John, b. 1749/50; m. [wife not named]; b. 1769/70]; resident of Danube, Herkimer Co., N.Y. on 12/14/1820. John enlisted at Hoosack, N.Y. in April 1778 as a private and served for nine months or more under Capt. Tunis Fisher in Col. Hay's Regt.; he was honorably discharged at Fishkill, Dutchess Co., N.Y. (RWPA: #R8795)

Deed Abstract

Rickert, Marcus [by Samuel Clyde, Sheriff of Montgomery Co. (by a Writ of Fieri Facias) against the estate of Marcus Rickert, deceased, through Elizabeth Rickert, Administratrix of the said estate for a debt of L60 and damages of L4.2.0. owed to Ludowic Rickert] to Christopher P. Yates, Attorney, of Canajoharie, Montgomery Co. Instrument dated 3/1/1786; recorded 7/10/1786. Description: All of Marcus Rickert's land situated on the south side of the Mohawk River in Canajoharie District, in a patent granted to James Alexander and others. Lot #1 (100 acres), by virtue of the aforesaid Writ was purchased by Christopher P. Yates as the highest bidder for the said land of Marcus Rickert, decd. Consideration: L80. Witnesses: Rudolph Diefendorf, Jacob Snyder. (MVL:8)

1790 Census

Rickart, Conradt (2)   [Appendix B]
Rickart, Ludwick
Rickhart, George
Rickhart, John

RICKEY

1790 Census

Rickey, Andrew   [Appendix B]

RIDDLE

Probate Abstract

Riddle, Samuel, (of Mayfield), will dated 3/12/1825; probated 4/20/1825. Legatees: wife, Sally; sister, Nancy; dau., Nancy; sons, George, John and Joseph. Executors: Samuel A. Gilbert and Nathan Dauchy[?] (of Troy). Witnesses: Daniel Baldwin, Russel Weller, Lucian A. Gilbert. (WMC 57:182)

1790 Census

Riddle, Robert   [Appendix B]

RIDER

1790 Census

Rider, George   [Appendix B]

RIEBSAMEN

Birth/Baptism

Riebsamen, Matthias & [?]: Conrad, b. 4/22/1766; bapt. 5/4/1766 (RDSA:63). Sponsors: Conrad Zimmermann & his wife.

Tryon County Militia

Riebsamen, Matthew   [Appendix A]
Riebsamen, William

RIECHEL

1790 Census

Riechel, Godfrey   [Appendix B]

RIED (also see **REED/REID**)

1790 Census

Ried, Abner   [Appendix B]
Ried, Conradt
Ried, Daniel

Ried, Ebenezer
Ried, John
Ried, Thomas

RIEGEL

Marriage

Riegel, Adam m. Catharina Huyser, 1/19/1796 (DRGF:213)

Riegel, Christian m. Margretha Helmer, 3/15/1763 (RDSA:172)

Riegel, Frederick (of Little Falls, son of Gottfried, decd.) m. Catharine Helmers (dau. of Adam Helmers), 12/26/1759 (RDSA:166; LTSA:277)

Riegel, Gottfried m. Gertraut Th: Folmer, 11/24/1789 (DRGF:206)

Birth/Baptism

Riegel, Christian & Anna Margretha [?]: Friederich, b. 1/1/1764, bapt. 1/10/1764 (RDSA:44); Maria Elisabetha, b. 11/13/1765, bapt. 1/7/1766 (RDSA:60); Gottfried, b. 8/1/1767, bapt. 8/11/1767 (RDSA:76). Sponsors: Friederich Riegel & his wife, Catharina (re:1); Maria Helmer & Gottfried Hultz (re:2); Gottfried Hieltz & Catharina Foltz (re:3).

Riegel, Joh. Friedrich & Catharina [?]: Anna Margretha, b. 10/16/1760, bapt. 11/26/1760 (RDSA:23); Christian, b. 1/27/1763, bapt. 2/4/1763 (RDSA:37); Gottfried, b. 11/26/1764, bapt. 12/4/1764 (RDSA:52); Catharina, b. 2/7/1767, bapt. 4/29/1767 (RDSA:75); Friedrich, b. 6/15/1769, bapt. 8/1/1769 (RDSA:95). Sponsors: Anna Margreth (dau. of

Adam Helmer) & Timotheus (son of Conrad Franck) (re:1); Christian Riegel & [?] (re:2); Johannes Helmer & Margretha Bellinger (re:3); Maria Hieltz & Henrich Helmer (re:4); Friederich Helm[er] & Philippina (re:5).

Tryon County Militia

Rigel, Frederick   [Appendix A]
Rigel, Godfrey

1790 Census

Riegel, Cornelius   [Appendix B]

RIEMAU (also see RHIMA)

1790 Census

Riemau, Christian   [Appendix B]
Riemau, Jacob
Riemau, John

RIEMENSNYDER

Birth/Baptism

Riemensnyder, Henrich & Anna Dorodea [?]: [?], b. 12/7/1755 (LTSA:16). Sponsors: Rudolph Koch & his wife, Elisabeth.

Riemensnyder, Johannes (of Schneidersbusch) & Eva (Bitley): Anna, b. 10/12/1782 (DRC:64); Adam, bapt. 9/5/1790 (SJC:32). Sponsors: [none named] (re:1); Heinrich [?] & Susanna [?] (re:2).

Tryon County Militia

Riemensnyder, John   [Appendix A]

1790 Census

Riemensnider, John   [Appendix B]

RIENHART

1790 Census

Rienhart, William   [Appendix B]

RIENSIER

1790 Census

Riensier, George   [Appendix B]

RIGHTMIRE

Marriage

Rightmire, Hendrik m. Maria Schever, 12/?/1784 (DRC:164)

Birth/Baptism

Rightmire, Johannes & Gertruy (Coonraet): Johannes, bapt. 1/27/1765 (DRC:13); Elizabeth, b. 5/9/1774, bapt. 8/13/1774 (DRC:30); Maria, bapt. 8/13/1774 [Note: There is some doubt as to whether she is the child of the above; there were no parents listed.] (DRC:30). Sponsors: Jeremia Quakkenbosch & Jannetje Quakkenbosch (re:1); Johannis Starn & Catrina Dogsteder (re:2); John Carl & Mary McDonnel (re:3).

COMPENDIUM

1790 Census

Ritmier, Henry   [Appendix B]
Ritmier, John

RIKER

1790 Census

Riker, Charles Sedam   [Appendix B]
Riker, Henry

RIMS

1790 Census

Rims, Christopher   [Appendix B]

RINKEL

Birth/Baptism

Rinkel, Lorentz & Catharina [?]: Maria Sybilla, b. 11/4/1770, bapt. 11/24/1770 (RDSA:107); Lorentz, b. 12/8/1777, bapt. 12/20/1777 [decd.] (DRGF:27). Sponsors: Jacob Dines & Maria Sybilla (re:1); Johannes Dinges & Barbara Birck (re:2).

RIPLEY

Death Record

Ripley, John, (son of Mr. Horace Ripley), d. 11/6/1829, age 12 years, by a kick from a horse; buried Cherry Valley Presbyterian Church cemetery (PCV:84)

RIPSOME

1790 Census

Riepsome, Conradt   [Appendix B]
Ripsome, Elizabeth
Ripsome, Peter
Ripsome, William

RISE

Marriage

Rise, John m. Margaretha Daevis, 11/4/1792 (DFP:46)

RISLEY

1790 Census

Risley, Allen   [Appendix B]
Risley, Elijah

RISS

Marriage

Riss, John m. N[?] N[?], 11/14/1771 (LTSA:282)

RITCHSER

Birth/Baptism

Ritchser, John & Elsje [?]: Jacobeina, b.

COMPENDIUM

4/30/1762; bapt. 5/19/1762 (RDSA:33). Sponsors: Jahn Boon Jun: & Christina Bottmann.

RITSCH

Birth/Baptism

Ritsch, Michael & Anna Maria [?]: Jacob, b. 10/7/1770 (LTSA:34). Sponsors: Jacob Kielmann, Catharina Ergezniger.

RITTER

Marriage

Ritter, Friedrich m. Elisabeth Seuffer, 4/11/1787 (DRGF:204)

Ritter, Henrich m. Maria Petri, 1/1/1786 (DRGF:202)

Ritter, Matthew Joh: m. Anna Glock (dau. of Joh: Adam Glock), 1/19/1792 (DRGF:208)

Birth/Baptism

Ritter, Frederick (of Schneidersbusch) & Elisabeth [?]: Johannes, bapt. 6/15/1790 (SJC:29); Catharina, b. 7/6/1792, bapt. 7/12/1792 (SJC:60). Sponsors: Matheus Ritter & Catharina Seufer (re:1); Baldes Strauch & Catharina Strauch (re:2).

Ritter, Henrich (Sneidersbush) & Margretha [?]: Margretha, bapt. 12/30/1792 (SJC:69). Sponsors: Johannes Bayer & Margretha Bayer.

Ritter, Johannes & Anna Barbara [?]: Henrious,

b. 12/28/1759, bapt. 1/1/1760 (RDSA:18); Maria Catharina, bapt. 2/14/1765 (RDSA:54); Anna Elisabeth, b. 4/7/1767, bapt. 4/28/1767 (RDSA:74); Anna Maria, b. 1/30/1775, bapt. 1/31/1775 (LTSA:48). Sponsors: Henrich Riemensneider & his wife, Anna Dorothea (re:1); Catharina Petri & George Helmer (re:2); Anna Elisabeth & Johannes Porck (re:3); Joh. Schmid & his wife, Maria (re:4).

Ritter, Matthew (Royal Grant) & Anna Eva [?]: Catharina, bapt. 2/22/1793 (SJC:73). Sponsors: Adam Klock & Catharina Klock.

Tryon County Militia

Ritter, Johannes   [Appendix A]

Pension Abstract

Ritter, Frederick, b. 1764, Herkimer, N.Y.; (brother: Henry Ritter [RWPA: #S19499]); m. Elizabeth Seuffer, 4/11/1787, Germanflatts, N.Y.; resident of Salisbury, Herkimer Co. on 10/12/1833; d. 1/21/1840, Salisbury, N.Y. Frederick enlisted as a substitute for his brother, Henry, in 1780 under Capt. Phelps in the N.Y. Line; he joined Capt. Moody's Co. of Artillery and went to West Point where he [Frederick] remained on duty in the garrison until 10/8/1780; Frederick enlisted into Capt. Moody's Co. and remained at West Point for the next three years; he was discharged from military service on 10/8/1783. (RWPA: #W20026)

Ritter, Henry, b. 1759, Stone Arabia, N.Y.; [stated that his mother and father died at Oriskany]; (brother: Frederick Ritter [RWPA: #W20026]); resident of Manheim, Herkimer Co., N.Y. on 4/5/1833. Henry enlisted in the winter of 1775 and served as a ranger in Capt.

669

Damewood's Co. until 1776; he was drafted to serve from 1776 until 1777 as a ranger under command of Capt. Gertman; he enlisted in 1777 as a private in Col. Peter Gansevoort's Regt.; he continued service in 1779 for about one year and in 1780 enlisted under the command of Capt. Phelps [at which time his brother, Frederick Ritter, continued his (Henry's) service as a substitute]. (RWPA: #S19449)

1790 Census

Ritter, Frederick   [Appendix B]
Ritter, Henry

RITZMA

Marriage

Ritzma, Johannes m. Barbara Knautz, 3/31/1761 (RDSA:169)

Tryon County Militia

Ritzman, Johannes   [Appendix A]

RIVERSON

1790 Census

Riverson, John Peter   [Appendix B]

RIX

1790 Census

Rix, Michael   [Appendix B]

ROACH

Marriage

Roach, Isaac m. Gertrydt Herkemer, 10/28/1794 (DFP:52)

ROATH

Probate Abstract

Roath, Charles B., (of Florida), will dated 7/24/1827; probated 8/15/1827. Legatees: Mary Stanton; second brother, Alexander (residing in Connecticut). Executor: Gerret B. Van De Veer. Witnesses: Isaac Jackson, William Griffith, Jr. (WMC 57:269)

ROB

Probate Abstract

Rob, George, (of Florida), will dated 11/11/1829; probated 6/14/1830. Legatees: daus., Jane (wife of George Murray), Margaret (wife of Angus Campbell); step dau., Isabella (wife of William Lauder); sons, James and Alexander. Executors: two sons. Witnesses: Platt Potter, William Murray, Cornelius Van Housen. (WMC 57:277)

Tryon County Militia

Rob, George   [Appendix A]
Rob, John

ROBBERSON

COMPENDIUM

Birth/Baptism

Robberson, Robert & Rebecca [?]: Robbert, b. 9/1/1776; bapt. 9/17/1776 (DRGF:20). Sponsors: Johannes Smidt & Eva.

Tryon County Militia

Roberson, Robert   [Appendix A]

ROBBETSON

Marriage

Robbetson, Peter m. Catharina Rattenauer (widow), 5/5/1783 (DRGF:197)

ROBBINS

Probate Abstract

Robbins, Thomas, (of Johnstown), will dated 1/15/1825; probated 2/27/1828. Legatees: wife, Rosannah; grandsons, Thomas and Asa Robbins (sons of Amasa); two youngest sons, [not named]; dau., Sally; sons, Alvin, Amasa and William. Executors: wife and son, William. Witnesses: William McConnell, Duncan Robertson, John Robertson. (WMC 57:270)

ROBENS

1790 Census

Robens, Ephraim   [Appendix B]

ROBERTS

Birth/Baptism

Roberts, Sally & [husband's name not stated]: Betsey Hannah, bapt. 9/22/1799 (JPC:16).

1790 Census

Roberts, James   [Appendix B]
Roberts, John
Roberts, Peter

ROBERTSON

Marriage

Robertson, Danil m. Christy Clark, 7/5/1799. Witnesses: John McVean, James Mitchell (JPC:92)

Robertson, Joseph m. Cornelia Quenald, 1/1/1794 (DFP:51)

Robertson, Robert m. Margrith Bealy, 10/16/1768 (RDSA:184)

Birth/Baptism

Robertson, Daniel & [?]: [?], bapt. 3/13/1801 (JPC:19).

Robertson, Jisheis & Sarah (Smith): Jisheis, b. 3/21/1785; bapt. 4/19/1785 (DRC:72). Sponsors: [none named].

Robertson, John & [?], (Breadalbane) [Broadalbin]): Ann, b. 1/13/1791; bapt. 2/6/1791 (JPC:4).

Robertson, John & Bally [?]: Daniel, b.

1/4/1778; bapt. 9/13/1778 (DRGF:32). Sponsors: Nicolas Varrbos & Sara.

Robertson, Robert & Christian [?]: Duncan, b. 6/1/1789 (JPC:13); Catharine, b. 5/23/1791 (JPC:13); Jannet, bapt. 6/2/1793 (JPC:13); John, b. 1/28/1797 (JPC:13).

Robertson, Robert & Jane (McMartin): Catharine, b. 5/22/1791; bapt. 6/26/1791 (DRC:99). Sponsors: [none named].

Robertson, Robert & Margaret (White): John, b. 9/26/1777; bapt. 10/19/1777 (DRC:45). Sponsors: John Shaver & Maria Hartell.

Death Record

Robertson, Jane, (wife of Robert Robertson), d. 1/21/1821, age 71 years; buried sect. 3, Colonial Cemetery, Johnstown (JC:186)

Robertson, Robert, d. 8/28/1825, age 81 years; buried sect. 3, Colonial Cemetery, Johnstown (JC:186)

Probate Abstract

Robertson, Catharine, (of Broadalbin), will dated 9/29/1819; probated 3/5/1821. Legatees: grandsons of late brother, John (Hugh, John and Duncan McCallum). Executors: Duncan McMartin (of Galway), John McMartin (of Charlton). Witnesses: Duncan McMartin, Duncan McMartin, Jr. (WMC 57:171)

Robertson, John, [residence not stated], will dated 6/27/1812; probated 12/20/1815. Legatees: Alexander Robertson (of Broadalbin & his brother, John); Janet (wife of James Stuart Taylor, of Johnstown); Thomas Stuart (my nephew by marriage, of Johnstown); Christiana (wife of John McBeth, of Broadalbin). Executors: Daniel McKercher, Duncan and John McMartin. Witnesses: Andrew Thatcher, Daniel Stewart, Daniel Walker. (WMC 56:396)

Robertson, Robert, (of Johnstown), will dated 5/11/1816; probated 2/4/1826. Legatees: wife, Jean; sons, Duncan, John and Daniel; daus., Catherine, Jane, Christian McNaughton and Sarah Smith. Executors: Daniel McMartin, Jr., Duncan McMartin, Jr. (of Broadalbin). Witnesses: Flora McMartin, Peter McMartin, Jr., Daniel Robertson. (WMC 57:185)

1790 Census

Robertson, Alexander (2)   [Appendix B]
Robertson, John

ROBESON

Birth/Baptism

Robeson, John & [?], Schenectady: Duncan, bapt. 4/22/1783 (JDR:11).

ROBINSON

Marriage

Robinson, Robert m. Maragrita White, 11/19/1775 (DRC:161)

Birth/Baptism

Robinson, James & Fannecy [?]: Esabell, b. 9/6/1762; bapt. 3/3/1763 (RDSA:38). Sponsors: Cptn. Robt. Gray, William Queen, Mrs. Brown & Mary Queen.

Robinson, Richard & Maria (Service): Richard, b. 8/11/1774; bapt. 9/18/1774 (DRC:31). Sponsors: John Service & Caty Service.

Death Record

Robinson, [?], (dau. of Elder Hugh Robinson), d. 6/18/1833, age 35 years, of Fits; buried Cherry Valley Presbyterian Church cemetery (PCV:85)

1790 Census

Robinson, Hugh   [Appendix B]
Robinson, John
Robinson, Matthew
Robinson, Peter (2)
Robinson, Robert
Robinson, Samuel

ROBISON

Tryon County Militia

Robison, George   [Appendix A]
Robison, Joseph

ROCHELLE

Marriage

Rochelle, Sam m. Gertraud M: Demuth, 1/11/1791 (DRGF:207)

ROCK

1790 Census

Rock, Jonathan   [Appendix B]

ROCKWELL

1790 Census

Rockwell, Silas   [Appendix B]

RODENHOUR

1790 Census

Rodenhour, Jacob   [Appendix B]

RODT

Birth/Baptism

Rodt, Carl & Christina [?]: Carl, b. 10/15/1794 (LTSA:86). Sponsors: Abraham Hees, Maria Straub.

ROE

1790 Census

Roe, William   [Appendix B]

ROELOFSON

Birth/Baptism

Roelefson/Roelfse, Abraham/Abram & Catrina

(Service/Souse): Harmanis, b. 1/13/1773, bapt. 2/7/1773 (DRC:24); Elizabeth, b. 5/4/1774, bapt. 6/19/1774 (DRC:29); Maragrita, b. ?/17/1776[?], bapt. 1/5/1777 (DRC:41). Sponsors: William Van Brute & Meryche Van Brute (re:1); Wiliam Mom brute & Maria Mom brute (re:2) [Note: It would appear that the first sponsors were also Mom brute.]; Arent Burrens & Maria Sarvis (re:3).

Roelefson, Lawrence & Elizabeth (Bernhart): Morya, b. 5/10/1775; bapt. 5/27/1775 (DRC:3). Sponsors: [none named].

Probate Abstract

Roelofson, Abraham, (of Charleston), will dated 9/12/1815; probated 9/20/1815. Legatees: sons, Harman, Ruluf, Abraham and Frederick; daus., Elizabeth, Margaret, Mary, Catherine (& her eldest son). Executors: sons, Harman, Ruluf, Abraham. Witnesses: George Northup, Alvah Gardner, Nathaniel B. Gardner. (WMC 56:395)

Tryon County Militia

Roelofson, Abraham   [Appendix A]

1790 Census

Ruluffson, Lawrence   [Appendix B]
Rulufson, Samuel

ROGER

Death Record

Roger, Joh. Frederick, (son of Benjamin & Margaretha Rodger), d. 5/10/1803, age 6 months, 3 days (died of putrid fever); buried

in cemetery at Germanflats (RDH:250)

Roger, Johannes, (from Schenectady), d. 12/18/1803, Germanflats, age 27 years (died of consumption); buried in the Germanflats cemetery near the church in the same place (RDH:251)

ROGERS

Marriage

Rogers, Jacob m. Sarah Dikenson, both of Saratoga, 3/25/1784 (JDR:2)

Rogers, John m. Mary Williams, 7/22/1767 (RDSA:182)

Birth/Baptism

Rogers, Cornelius & Christina (Putman): William, b. 2/3/1775; bapt. 2/19/1775 (DRC:32). Sponsors: Willem Rogers & Jannetje Rogers.

Rogers, Frances & [?], Mohawk River: Hester, [no birth or baptism date given] (JDR:15).

Rogers/Rodgers, Samuel & Neeltje/Neylche (Philipse/Philpse): Philip, bapt. 10/20/1769 (DRC:17); Maragriet Sarah, b. 2/2/1773, bapt. 2/28/1773 (DRC:24). Sponsors: Willem Monbrut & Maria Monbrut (re:1); Jonathan Ronyen & Catrina Runyen (re:2).

Tryon County Militia

Rogers, John   [Appendix A]
Rogers, Samuel

COMPENDIUM

Pension Abstract

Rogers, Jacob, b. 4/6/1765; m. Sarah [?],
3/25/1784; d. 1/9/1830. (Sarah Rogers, b.
8/25/1768; resident of Warren Twp., Bradford
Co., Pa. on 5/22/1840.) Children: Zebulon, b.
1/12/1785, d. 4/15/1823; William, b.
6/29/1786, d. 9/11/1823; Elizabeth, b.
6/9/1788; James, b. 3/4/1790, d. 7/30/1791;
Alaxandria, b. 4/10/1792; Dickerson, b.
4/17/1795; Philip, b. 5/22/1797; Nancy, b.
4/17/1799; Hanah, b. 2/22/1801; Jacob, b.
5/22/1803; Abrazina, b. 3/12/1805; Phebe, b.
3/4/1807; Sarah M., b. 5/18/1809; Hezekiah,
b. 9/16/1811. Jacob was listed on the military
payroll as having served as a private in Capt.
Abram Fonda's Co., Col. Marinus Willett's
Regt. of the N.Y. Line in 1781; [no further
record of his duties was given]. (RWPA:
#W4574)

1790 Census

Rogers, Francis   [Appendix B]
Rogers, Simeon

ROHRBACH

Marriage

Rohrbach, Johannes m. Lena Snell (widow),
[no date: follows 10/31/1786] (DRGF:204)

1790 Census

Roorback, John   [Appendix B]

ROHRIG

Marriage

Rohrig, Henrich m. Anna Nortmenn, 6/12/1770
(LTSA:282)

ROLINGS

Marriage

Rolings, Coloph m. Catharina Beas, 8/24/1784
(DRGF:200)

Birth/Baptism

Rolings, Caloph & Catharina [?]: Catharina, b.
1/22/1785; bapt. 1/22/1785 (DRGF:92).
Sponsors: Joh: Jost Beas & Elisabetha Barbara.

ROLLER (also see ROLLERUND)

Birth/Baptism

Roller, Andreas & Rebecca [?]: Margretha, b.
10/19/1763, bapt. 10/30/1763 (RDSA:42);
Dorothea, b. 6/3/1766, bapt. 6/15/1766
(RDSA:65). Sponsors: Margretha, wife of
Johannes Kajser (re:1); Dorothea Elisabetha &
Michael Kayser (re:2).

Tryon County Militia

Roller, Andrew   [Appendix A]

ROLLERUND (also see ROLLER)

Birth/Baptism

Rollerund, Andreas & Rebecca [?]: Elisabetha,
b. 6/19/1761; bapt. 6/28/1761 (RDSA:27).
Sponsor: Dorothea Elisabetha, wife of Michael

675

Kayser.

Romine, Nicholas
Romine, Theodorus F.

ROMEYN

Birth/Baptism

Romyne, Abraham   [Appendix B]
Romyne, Thomas

Romeyn, Abraham & Mary (Moore): Susanna,
b. 8/1/1785, bapt. 8/21/1785 (DRC:75);
Agnes, b. 2/1/1787, bapt. 3/4/1787 (DRC:83
& 87); Maria, b. 1/28/1791, bapt. 3/13/1791
(DRC:96). Sponsors: [none named] (re: 1-3).

RONNEN

Romeyn, Thomas & Susanna (Van Campen):
Benjamin, b. 8/4/1774, bapt. 8/13/1774
(DRC:30); Thomas, b. 2/22/1777, bapt.
3/2/1777 (DRC:41). Sponsors: Douw Fonda &
Rebecca Conyne (re:1); Jellis Fonda & Jannetje
Fonda (re:2).

Marriage

Ronnen, Israel m. Dorothea Nelles (dau. of
Andr. Nelles), 11/3/1782 (DRGF:196)

Birth/Baptism

Death Record

Ronnen/Ronnels, Israel (of Palatine) &
Dorothea (Nelles): Dorothea, bapt. 1/2/1790
(SJC:21). Sponsors: John Frederic Hess &
Catharina Hess.

Romeyne, Thomas, Rev. Dr. ("was 40 years a
faithful servant of Christ; and served for 23
years the Congregation at Cagnawagha, where
he has been buried in the Church"), d.
10/23/1794, age 65 years, 7 months; buried
10/25/1794 (RDSA:235)

ROOF

Birth/Baptism

Probate Abstract

Roof, Christian & Elisabetha [?]: Catharina, b.
10/27/1756 (LTSA:20); Johannes, b.
8/26/1761, bapt. 8/30/1761 (RDSA:28); Anna,
b. 4/11/1764, bapt. 4/23/1764 (RDSA:46);
Christian, b. 1/11/1767, bapt. 2/1/1767
(RDSA:72). Sponsors: Martin Tillenbach,
Catharina Rosner (re:1); Balthasar Dillenbach
& Catharina Finck (re:2); Anna Maria, wife of
Johann Christ Dillenbach (re:3); Christian [?]
& Barbara Schultz (re:4).

Romeyn, Thomas, (of Caughnawaga), will
dated 8/20/1792; probated 5/24/1797. Legatees:
wife, Susannah; sons, Abraham, Nicholas,
Jacobus, John, Benjamin & Thomas. Executors:
wife; sons, Abraham, Nicholas, Jacobus, John;
& Abraham Van Vechten. Witnesses: James
Lansing, [?] Fonda. (WMC 56:149)

Tryon County Militia

Roof, Christian, Jr. & Eva [?]: Abraham, b.
8/24/1797 (LTSA:99). Sponsors: Jacob

Romine, Abraham   [Appendix A]

COMPENDIUM

Dillebach & Jannetche.

Roof, Henrich & Catharina [?]: Elisabetha, b. 3/12/1766; bapt. 4/6/1766 (RDSA:62). Sponsors: Raachel Gardinier & Jacob Sternberger.

Roof, John & Maria [?]: Nicolaus, b. 8/28/1762, bapt. 3/3/1763 (RDSA:38); Maria, b. 3/23/1777, bapt. 8/4/1777 (DRGF:25); Daniel, b. 3/4/1779, bapt. 5/6/1779 (DRGF:35); Margretha, b. 1/17/1781, bapt. 3/4/1781 (DRGF:43); Martin, b. 4/5/1783, bapt. 4/22/1783 (DRGF:70). Sponsors: Nicolaus Hercheimer & his wife, Maria (re:1); Maria, wife of Genl. Hergheimer (re:2); Stophel Yates, Major & Maria (re:3); Margretha Cox & Matthaeus Gerhard (re:4); Christian Laemm & Anna Elisabeth (re:5).

Probate Abstract

Roof, Johannis, (of Canajoharie), will dated 4/18/1798; probated 12/26/1798. Legatees: wife, Mary; sons, John, Adam, Daniel, Andrew, Martin (land in Dorlach, Schoharie County & Cherry Valley, Otsego County); daus., Susanna, Barbara and Mary. Executors: wife; John Jacob Diefendorf, George Kraus, Christopher Yates. Witnesses: Nicholas Van Slyke, Jacob Burhart, James McEakeran[?]. (WMC 56:150)

Roof, Martin, [residence not stated], will dated 1/22/1827; probated 5/22/1827. Legatees: wife, Elizabeth; sons, George L., Philip, Adam L., Garret L.; daus., Anna Maria and Elizabeth. Executor: brother, Andrew. Witnesses: N. I./[J.] Keller, E. Kane Roof, James D. Hilton. Codicil dated 3/26/1827. Witnesses: D. F. Sacia, John Atwater, N. I./[J.] Keller. (WMC 57:268)

Tryon County Militia

Roof, John   [Appendix A]
Roof, Michael

Pension Abstract

Roof, John, b. 9/3/1762, Fort Stanwix (now Rome, Oneida Co., N.Y.); resident of Canajoharie, Montgomery Co., N.Y. on 9/19/1832. John's father and family lived at Fort Stanwix until shortly before the battle of Oriskany when they moved down the Mohawk River and were taken into General Nicholas Herkimer's home. During the remainder of the war the family lived at one of the forts in the Mohawk Valley. [John's father was a captain of a company in the Tryon Co. Militia and also served as a member of the Committee of Safety.] John enrolled in Capt. Adam Lipe's Co., Col. Samuel Clyde's 1st. Regt., Tryon Co. Militia in 1778 at the age of sixteen years; he marched on the Sullivan expedition and fought at the battle of Johnstown; John's entire service time amounted to more than two years. Following the war, John was appointed captain of a company of light infantry and served some years until he received the appointment of colonel of the same regiment. He was also elected to be a member of the State Legislature of New York. (RWPA: #S14371)

1790 Census

Rooff, John   [Appendix B]

ROOS

Birth/Baptism

Roos, Callso & Jenny [?]: Danil, b. 6/17/1774;

bapt. 7/9/1774 (DRC:30). Sponsors: [none named].

Roos, Heinrich & Anna Margaretha [?]: Susanna, b. 8/7/1778; bapt. 9/7/1778 (LTSA:54). Sponsors: Carl Simon, Maria Wuth.

ROOT

Tryon County Militia

Root, Christian   [Appendix A]

1790 Census

Root, Daniel   [Appendix B]
Root, Joseph, Sr.
Root, Josiah
Root, Moses
Root, Simeon

ROSA

Probate Abstract

Rosa, Henry P., (of Mayfield), will dated 4/20/1829; probated 7/1/1829. Legatees: sister, Catharine Ann Rosa; brothers, James and Isaac R.; mother, Nancy Rosa. Executors: brothers, James and Isaac R. Witnesses: A. McFarlan, Ahasuerus G. Marselis, Gabriel Gunsalus. (WMC 57:274)

Rosa, Richard, (of Mayfield), will dated 4/20/1809; probated 10/23/1809. Legatees: wife, Anna; sons, Henry, Isaac, John and James; daus., Maria, Elizabeth and Caty Ann. Executors: wife, Ashbell Cornwell, Sr., Peter Thompson. Witnesses: Coenrod Ten Eick,

Roswell Churchill, Ashbell Cornwell, Jr. (WMC 56:160)

ROSE

Marriage

Rose, Benjamin m. Jude Conner, 3/12/1795 (DFP:53)

Birth/Baptism

Rose, John & Christina (Valkenburg): Maria, b. 8/13/1773; bapt. 8/29/1773 (DRC:26). Sponsors: Daniel Smith & Maria Smith.

Death Record

Rose, [?], (Mr.), d. 1/29/1810, age 82 years (DFP:93)

Probate Abstract

Rose, Charles, [residence not stated], will dated 12/25/1829; probated 3/21/1831. Legatees: wife, Rhoda; sons, William and Charles; daus., Rhoda, Mary and Sally; grandchildren, Willard, Charles and Rhoda Wilson. Bequest: Land in Rensselaer Co. to his daughters. Executors: wife; son, Charles. Witnesses: John and Daniel McEwen, A. Haring. (WMC 57:278-279)

1790 Census

Rose, Jacob   [Appendix B]
Rose, William

COMPENDIUM

ROSEBOOM

Death Record

Roseboom, Abraham, (town of Roseboom
resident), b. 1777, Schenectady; moved to
Cherry Valley ca. 1800, owned large tract of
land upon which he settled and lived until his
death; d. 1/3/1867, age 89 years; removed to
Cherry Valley Cemetery (CVC:2)

Roseboom, Cornelia, (dau. of Henry &
Cornelia Roseboom), d. [not stated]; removed
to Cherry Valley Cemetery (CVC:2)

Roseboom, Henry M., d. 6/28/1824, age 25
years; buried Cherry Valley Presbyterian
Church cemetery (PCV:81)

Roseboom, Henry Myndert, (son of [?]
Roseboom), d. 6/29/1824, age 24 years; buried
in Old Cemetery & removed ca. 1864 to Cherry
Valley Cemetery (CVC:2) [Note: The deaths
noted for Henry M. Roseboom in the preceding
entry and this entry for Henry Myndert
Roseboom are for the same individual.]

Roseboom, John I., (son of John Roseboom &
brother of Abraham Roseboom), d. 3/15/1829,
age 55 years; removed ca. 1864 to Cherry
Valley Cemetery (CVC:2)

Roseboom, John, (son of Abraham Roseboom),
d. 5/16/1839, age 58 years; buried in Old
Cemetery & removed ca. 1864 to Cherry Valley
Cemetery (CVC:2)

Roseboom, Ruth, (wife of Abraham Roseboom,
town of Roseboom), d. 3/2/1864, age 84 years;
removed to Cherry Valley Cemetery (CVC:2)

Deed Abstract

Roseboom, Myndert, merchant, of the City of
Albany, to William Cook, of Cherry Valley,
Montgomery Co. Deed dated 2/23/1786;
recorded 5/26/1786. Description: Lot #16 (64
acres) situated in Newtown Martin (which said
land Peter Martin leased on 1/3/1786 to Elisha
Marsh, who has since assigned said lot to said
Myndert Roseboom and another transfer by
Peter Martin and his wife, Molly, to said
Myndert Roseboom). Consideration: L62.10.0.
Witnesses: Volkert Oothout, John Roseboom.
(MVL:28)

1790 Census

Roseboom, John   [Appendix B]
Roseboom, Robert

ROSEL

Marriage

Rosel, Daniel m. Anna Dorothea Schmid,
12/13/1768 (LTSA:279)

ROSEN

1790 Census

Rosen, Silas   [Appendix B]

ROSENCRANTZ

Marriage

Rosencrantz, Georg m. Anna Schnell (dau. of
Jacob Schnell), 5/6/1792 (DRGF:209)

679

Birth/Baptism

Rosencrantz, Abraham & Anna Maria [?]: Nicolaus, b. 8/25/1760, bapt. 9/7/1760 (RDSA:22); Margretha, b. 4/26/1762, bapt. 5/2/1762 (RDSA:33); Georgius, b. 3/15/1764, bapt. 3/20/1764 (RDSA:46); Henricus Jacobus, b. 5/13/1766, bapt. 5/21/1766 (RDSA:64); Catharina, b. 7/23/1768, bapt. 7/27/1768 (RDSA:88); Johann Jost Hergheimer, b. 7/26/1778, bapt. 7/29/1778 (DRGF:31). Sponsors: Johann Nicolaus Hergheimer & his wife, Maria (re:1); Cptn. Henrich Frey & Elisabetha (re:2); Johann Jost Schumacher & Elisabeth, wife of Esq. Henrich Frey (re:3); Henrich Frej, Esqr. & Elisabetha (re:4); Catharina, wife of Mr. Andreas Finck (re:5); Georg Hergheimer, Cptn. & Alita (re:6).

Death Record

Rosencrantz, [not named], (infant dau. of Henry Rosencrantz, of Fall Hill, Germanflats), d. 2/28/1816, Germanflats, age [not given]; buried in the field of Judge George Rosencrantz (RDH:272)

Rosencrantz, Peggy, (dau. of Henry Rosencrantz), d. 11/10/1808, Germanflats, age 1 month, 28 days (died of whooping cough); buried on brother's land at Fall Hill (RDH:261)

Tryon County Militia

Rosecrantz, George   [Appendix A]
Rosecrantz, Nicholas

Deed Abstract

Rosencrantz, Abraham, Minister, of Canajoharie, Tryon Co. to John Rooff, yeoman, of the same place. Deed dated 2/2/1782; recorded 2/16/1782. Description: A lot situated at Burnetsfield on the south side of the Mohawk River and known by the name Lot #43 (as by a certain certificate bearing date 3/28/1723 is more fully described) containing (100 acres). Consideration: L400. Witnesses: John Frey, Chris. P. Yates. (MVL:28)

Rosencrantz, Nicholas, yeoman, of German Flats District, Montgomery Co. to Harmanus H. Van Slyck and Garret Van Schaick, yeomen, of Schenectady Township, Albany Co. Deed dated 3/15/1787; recorded 4/26/1787. Description: Land situated in a patent granted to Hans Dederick Staley, Hanjost Herkimer, Jr. and others, known as Lot #50 (200 acres of woodland). Consideration: L50. Witnesses: Peter Marsh, Severenus Deygart. (MVL:28)

1790 Census

Rosegrants, Abraham   [Appendix B]

ROSNER

Birth/Baptism

Rosner, Georg & Maria Catharina (Wagner): Jacobus, b. 3/28/1752 (LTSA:5); Johann Georg, b. 4/17/1755 (LTSA:13). Sponsors: Jacobus Siz, Margaretha Tillenbach (re:1); Han Jerg Haus & his wife, Sophia (r:2).

ROSS

Marriage

Ross, David m. Ann Barlass, ca. 1817 (UPSC:70)

COMPENDIUM

Birth/Baptism

Ross, Benjamin (Canajoharie) & Maria [?]; Susanna, bapt. 2/3/1793 (SJC:71). Sponsors: Jonas Krankheit & Maria Krankheit.

Ross, Christian (Canajoharie) & Elisabeth [?]: Jacob, bapt. 6/12/1791 (SJC:43). Sponsors: Jacob Young & Eva Young.

Ross, Samuel & Annatje (Doxteder): Elizabeth, b. 9/2/1777; bapt. 9/25/1777 (DRC:44). Sponsors: Adam Ross & Elizabeth Doxteder.

Ross, Thomas & Elizabeth [?]: Nancy, b. 12/29/1774; bapt. 2/26/1775 (DRC:32). Sponsors: [none named].

Death Record

Ross, Alexander, d. 11/6/1823, age 76 years; buried Cherry Valley Presbyterian Church cemetery (PCV:80)

ROTE

1790 Census

Rote, Charles   [Appendix B]

ROTH

Tryon County Militia

Roth, John   [Appendix A]

Pension Abstract

Roth, John, b. 1751/2; m. Elizabeth Nellis,

11/15/1774 by Rev. Gros at Minden, N.Y.; d. 7/5/1816, Minden, Montgomery Co., N.Y. (Elizabeth Roth, b. 1755/6; remarried in 1824 to Thomas Cradle.) John and Elizabeth Roth took their family to Fort Plank during the war for protection and while there one of their children, a four or five year old daughter, was killed by the Indians when she was outside the fort gathering apples in an orchard. John Roth served as a private in the 1st. Regt., Tryon Co. Militia and performed garrison duty at Fort Plank for several tours "a number of months each season"; he was a participant in the battle of Johnstown. (RWPA: #W16936)

1790 Census

Roth, John   [Appendix B]

ROTHBONE

1790 Census

Rothbone, Benjamin   [Appendix B]

ROUND

1790 Census

Round, John   [Appendix B]
Round, Samuel

ROUREY

Marriage

Rourey, William (Justice) m. Margaret Becker,

681

COMPENDIUM

Warrensbush, 7/4/1787 (JDR:#67)

Birth/Baptism

Roury, Henry & [?] (Nortman), Warrensborough: Frederick, bapt. ?/?/1788 (JDR:14).

Rurey, Justice Wm. & Mary/Marg. (Becker), Warrensborough: Elizabeth, bapt. 3/9/1788 (JDR:13); Henry, bapt. 3/4/1796, age 4 days, of Shelottsbush (JDR:15); Fredrick, bapt. 8/28/1801 (JDR:14).

Tryon County Militia

Rury, Henry   [Appendix A]
Rury, William

1790 Census

Rury, Henry   [Appendix B]
Rury, William

ROUSE

Death Record

Rouse, Andrew, d. 3/?/1813, age 66 years, 1 month, 13 days; buried 3/18/1813 (DFP:96)

ROWLAND

1790 Census

Rowland, Henry   [Appendix B]

ROWLEY

1790 Census

Rowley, William   [Appendix B]
Rowly, Daniel
Rowly, Joe
Rowly, Seth

ROWN

1790 Census

Rown, Nicholas   [Appendix B]

ROXFORD

1790 Census

Roxford, Ensign   [Appendix B]

RUBY

1790 Census

Reuby, Christopher   [Appendix B]
Ruby, John

RUCKERT

Birth/Baptism

Ruckert, Ludwig & Catharina (Goedmann): Friedrich, b. 8/5/1787; bapt. 8/12/1787 (RDSA:114). Sponsors: Friedrich Goedmann & his wife.

682

COMPENDIUM

RUDO

Marriage

Rudo, Elias m. Catharine Wohlgemuth, 4/18/1790 (RDSA:195)

RUFF

Probate Abstract

Ruff, Sarah, (of Florida), will dated 7/23/1829; probated 10/26/1829. Legatees: mother, Sarah Ruff; brothers, Benjamin Franklin, Thomas J. Ruff and Jesse Ruff; sisters, Nancy Cady and Priscilla Frisbee. Executor: Ebenezer Cady. Witnesses: Nancy Corhan[?], Ruth Patterson, Janet Adair. (WMC 57:275)

RULESON

Birth/Baptism

Ruleson, Laurance & Elizabeth (Barnhart), Warrensborough: Catarine, bapt. 4/1/1781 (JDR:10).

RUMERFIELD

1790 Census

Rumerfield, Anthony   [Appendix B]

RUMMER

1790 Census

Rummer, John   [Appendix B]

RUNELS

Probate Abstract

Runels, Benjamin, (of Mayfield), will dated 10/13/1814; probated 1/19/1815. Legatees: wife, Anne; sons and daughters. Executors: wife; Isaac Bogert, Jr., David Knapp. Witnesses: Francis Gurnee, Abraham Wells, Harman F. Van Buren. (WMC 56:393)

1790 Census

Runnelds, Jarid   [Appendix B]
Runnells, Stephen
Runnels, Elijah
Runnils, [?]l

RUNKEL

Probate Abstract

Runkel, John, (of Canajoharie), will [undated]; probated 6/30/1810. Legatees: wife; sons, Cornelius, Henry, John and Daniel; daus., Mary (married), Elizabeth, Catharine and Gitty. Executors: wife and son, Cornelius. Witnesses: Daniel Cuck, Aaron Clement, John Keller. (WMC 56:380)

RUNYON

COMPENDIUM

Birth/Baptism

Runyon, Benjamin & Annatje (Evertse): John, b. 2/14/1785; bapt. 2/14/1785 (DRC:70). Sponsors: Jacob Evertse & Neyltje van Deusen.

Runyon, Jonathan & Elizabeth (Mc[?]): Elizabeth, b. 2/11/1785; bapt. 5/22/1785 (DRC:73). Sponsors: Adolf Walradt & his wife.

Runyon, Samuel & [?]: [?], bapt. 6/1/1786 (DRC:80). Sponsors: [none named].

Runyon, Samuel & Anges/Tangulus (Davis): Richard, b. 6/17/1782, bapt. 7/20/1782 (DRC:63); Meritje, b. 2/27/1786, bapt. 3/12/1786 (DRC:77). Sponsors: Timothy Leonardse Jun. & Mary Runyens (re:1); [?] Huger & Meritje Helmer (re:2).

Tryon County Militia

Runyons, Henry   [Appendix A]
Runyons, John
Runyons, Samuel

1790 Census

Runyan, Benjamin   [Appendix B]
Runyan, Henry
Runyan, John
Runyan, Jonathan
Runyan, Samuel

RUPERT

Marriage

Rupert, Frantz m. Elisabeth Kochenath, 3/11/1794 (RDSA:199)

Birth/Baptism

Rupert/Ruppert, Johann Adam & Anna Barbara [?]: Peter, b. 3/21/1764, bapt. 5/5/1764 (RDSA:46); Johannes, b. 2/16/1766, bapt. 4/19/1766 (RDSA:62); Margreth, b. 3/3/1768, bapt. 7/4/1768 (RDSA:87); Anna Maria, b. 7/21/1770 (LTSA:32). Sponsors: Peter Hooman (re:1); Johannes Ruppert (re:2); Margretha, wife of Frantz Ruppert (re:3); Cunrad Schneider, Maria Altbrand (re:4).

RUPULSON

1790 Census

Rupulson, John   [Appendix B]

RUSE

Tryon County Militia

Ruse, Jacob   [Appendix A]

RUSS

Tryon County Militia

Russ, Johannes   [Appendix A]
Russ, John

RUSSELL

Marriage

684

Russel, William m. Margaret Morgan, 6/30/1795 (JPC:91)

Russell, Samuel m. Dorothea Durell, [no date: follows 5/12/1789] (DRGF:206)

Birth/Baptism

Russell, James & Ann [?]: Alexander, b. 9/9/1800; bapt. 12/7/1800 (JPC:18).

Russell, John & Sarah (Cheesecox): Margerita, b. 12/12/1790; bapt. 1/21/1791 (DRC:93). Sponsors: [none named].

Russell, William & Margaret [?]: Jane Ann, b. 7/31/1800; bapt. 12/7/1800 (JPC:18).

Death Record

Russel, Margaret, (wife of Alexander Russel), d. 8/8/1793, age 57 years; buried sect. 1, Colonial Cemetery, Johnstown (JC:186)

1790 Census

Russel, Samuel   [Appendix B]
Russell, Alexander
Russell, Daniel
Russell, John
Russell, Nathan

RUST

Birth/Baptism

Rust, Amazia & Catrina (Quackenbush): Maria, b. 7/6/1785; bapt. 8/16/1785 (DRC:75). Sponsors: Myndert Quack & Maria Quack.

Death Record

Rust, Amaziah, (Captain, a soldier in the Revolution), d. 7/8/1801, age 69 years; buried sect. 9, Colonial Cemetery, Johnstown (JC:186)

Rust, Frances, (Mrs.; dau. of Clement & Rebecca Sadleir), d. 6/21/1820, age 36 years; buried sect. 9, Colonial Cemetery, Johnstown (JC:186)

Rust, Frances Mandeville, (granddaughter of Clement & Rebecca Sadleir), d. 11/17/1844, age 27 years; buried sect. 9, Colonial Cemetery, Johnstown (JC:186)

Rust, Mary, (widow of Capt. Amaziah Rust), d. 3/7/1814, age 79 years, 2 months, 14 days; buried sect. 9, Colonial Cemetry, Johnstown (JC:186)

Rust, Prudence, (Cherry Valley resident), d. 9/12/1820, age 75 years, 6 months; buried in Old Cemetery & removed to Cherry Valley Cemetery; buried on lot owned by James A. Whitaker (CVC:2)

Tryon County Militia

Rust, George   [Appendix A]

1790 Census

Rust, Amaziah   [Appendix B]
Rust, Elijah
Rust, Samuel

RUYENS

Birth/Baptism

685

Ruyens, Samuel & Agnes [?]: Anna Catharina, b. 10/4/1770 (LTSA:34). Sponsors: Philipp Runiel, Catharina Veter.

RYAN

Marriage

Ryan, John m. Lena Miller (widow of Hen. Miller), 1/2/1784 (DRGF:198)

Birth/Baptism

Ryan, Lawrence (of Geisberg) & Anna Dieter [?]: Cornelia, bapt. 7/5/1789 (SJC:16). Sponsors: Johannes Wollever & Catharina Wollever.

Ryon, John & Lena [?]: Margretha, b. 11/8/1784; bapt. 11/9/1784 (DRGF:89). Sponsors: Joh: Dieterich Petri & Elisabeth.

Tryon County Militia

Ryan, John   [Appendix A]

1790 Census

Ryan, Magdalin   [Appendix B]

RYE

Birth/Baptism

Rye, John (of Caughnawaga) & Elisabeth [?]: Salomon, bapt. 2/9/1792, age 6 years (SJC:53); Jacob, bapt. 2/9/1792, age 4 years (SJC:53); John, bapt. 2/9/1792, age 18 months (SJC:53). Sponsors: John Mengis & Catharina Mengis

(re:1); John Mengis & Catharina Kleyn (re:2); Michael Kiener & Margretha Rascher (re:3).

RYKER

Birth/Baptism

Ryker, Henderick & Christiana (Barmoor): Jacob, b. 1/22/1774, bapt. 3/13/1774 (DRC:28); Rachel, b. 4/7/1776, bapt. 4/27/1776 (DRC:37). Sponsors: [none named] (re:1); Nicholas Quack & Rachel Gardinier (re:2).

RYNE

1790 Census

Ryne, Lawrence   [Appendix B]

RYNES

1790 Census

Rynes, John   [Appendix B]

SABINS

1790 Census

Sabins, Walter   [Appendix B]

SABLE

1790 Census

Sable, William   [Appendix B]

SADLEIR

Death Record

Sadleir, Clement, Jr., (Late Captain in 6th Regiment of the U.S. Infantry; he was wounded at Little York, Upper Canada, 4/27/1813), d. 3/26/1823, age 36 years; buried sect. 9, Colonial Cemetery, Johnstown (JC:187)

Sadleir, Rebecca Carlton, (wife of Clement Sadleir), d. 12/5/1817, age 56 years; buried sect. 9, Colonial Cemetery, Johnstown (JC:187)

Sadleir, Richard, (son of Clement & Rebecca Sadleir), d. 11/26/1827, age 39 years; buried sect. 9, Colonial Cemetery, Johnstown (JC:187)

SAEGER

Birth/Baptism

Saeger, Henrich & Anna (Saeger): Maria, b. 12/13/1787; bapt. 12/16/1787 (RDSA:115). Sponsors: Jacob Schnell & Maria (born: Merckel).

SAFFORD

1790 Census

Safford, Darius   [Appendix B]

SAGE

1790 Census

Sage, Silah   [Appendix B]

SAGNER

1790 Census

Sagner, Conradt   [Appendix B]
Sagner, Paul

SAILS

1790 Census

Sails, Darius   [Appendix B]
Sails, George
Sails, Jeremiah

SALER

1790 Census

Saler, Gasper   [Appendix B]

SALISBURY

Marriage

Salsburry, Harmanus m. Susanna Dely[ne], 5/10/1773 (DRC:158)

Tryon County Militia

Salisbury, John   [Appendix A]

1790 Census

Salisbury, Richard   [Appendix B]

SALLIE

Birth/Baptism

Sallie, Henry (Herkimer Co.) & Catharina [?]: Margretha, b. 9/20/1793; bapt. 11/3/1793 (SJC:84). Sponsors: Adam Sallie & Elisabeth Stahli.

SALTS

Marriage

Salts, Frans m. Mary Cash, 8/26/1778 (DRC:162)

SALTSMAN

Birth/Baptism

Saltsman, Georg & Catharina Elisabetha [?]: Maria Elisabetha, b. 9/25/1743 (LTSA:43),

bapt. 10/23/1743 (RDSA:6); Anna Margaretha, b. 11/14/1748 (LTSA:43); Johannes, b. 7/13/1750 (LTSA:43); Anna Barbara, b. 6/16/1752 (LTSA:5); Magdalena, b. 5/11/1754 (LTSA:9); Jacob, b. 7/22/1756 (LTSA:19); Peter, b. 2/8/1758 (LTSA:43); Elisabetha, b. 7/6/1762 (LTSA:43), bapt. 7/18/1762 (RDSA:34). Sponsors: Hennrich Salzmann & his wife (re:1); Peter Wagner, Anna Marg Haus (re:2); Johannes Schulz & his wife (re:3); Jacob Schulz & his wife, Anna Barbara (re:4); Joh. Schulz & his wife, Magdalena (re:5); Jacob Schulz & his wife, Dorodea (re:6); Peter Haus, Barbara Knaus (re:7); Joh: Schulz, Elisabetha Laux (re:8). [Note: Sponsors: (re:1; RDSA:6) Hendrich Salzman, Maria Lisabet Wagner; (re:8; RDSA:34) Elisabetha (dau. of Adam Laux) & Johannes (son of Stophel Schultz)]

Saltsman, Henrich & Maria Elisabetha (Wagner): Georg, b. 12/6/1752 (LTSA:6); Henrich, b. 12/6/1752 (LTSA:6); Anna Margaretha, b. 5/14/1755 (LTSA:14); Catharina, b. 9/3/1757 (LTSA:22). Sponsors: Jerg Salzmann (re:1); Henrich Tillenbach (re:2); Maria Tillenbach, Margaretha Crims, Henrich Nellis (re:3); Peter Haus, Catharina Rosner, Catharina Wallrath (re:4).

Saltsman, Jerg & Sabina [?]: Maria, b. 3/3/1791 (LTSA:67); Anna, b. 3/15/1795 (LTSA:89). Sponsors: John Empie, Maria Streher (re:1); Heinrich Salzmann & Frena (re:2).

Saltsman, Johann & Susanna Maria [?]: George, b. 1/9/1779, bapt. 1/17/1779 (LTSA:56); Jacob, b. 3/27/1780, bapt. 4/9/1780 (LTSA:60); Maria, b. 12/20/1782, bapt. 1/1/1783 (DRGF:65). Sponsors: George Schultz, Delila Saltzmann (re:1); Jacob Schnell, Maria Schnell (re:2); Georg Salsmann & Elisabeth (re:3).

Saltsman, John & Elisabet [?]: Margaret, b. 11/4/1793 (LTSA:80); Daniel, b. 2/12/1795 (LTSA:88). Sponsors: Friz Getman & Anna Eva (re:1); Friderich Getman, Catarina Getman (re:2).

Saltsman, Michael & Anna Maria [?]: Elisabeth, b. 9/17/1754 (LTSA:10); Maria, b. 4/28/1757 (LTSA:21); Johann Georg, b. 12/13/1763, bapt. 12/25/1763 (RDSA:43); Wilhelm, b. 7/18/1766, bapt. 7/27/1766 (RDSA:66). Sponsors: Peter Wagener & his wife, Barbara Elisabetha (re:1); Wilm Nellis & his wife, Wina (re:2); Johannes Schultz & his wife, Mar. Lena (re:3); Johannes Nelles & Maria Magdalena (re:4).

Saltsman, Wilhelm & Catarina [?]: Michael, b. 12/21/1788 (LTSA:62); Friderich, b. 7/24/1791 (LTSA:62); Peter W., b. 5/19/1794 (LTSA:83); Catarina, b. 7/8/1796 (LTSA:96). Sponsors: Jerg Salzman & Sabina (re:1); Frid. Gettmann & Anneb (re:2); Peter Wagner & Anna (re:3); John Schulz & Catarina (re:4).

Probate Abstract

Saltsman, John, (of Palatine), will dated 7/5/1822; probated 3/8/1827. Legatees: wife, Elisabeth; sons, Peter and Daniel; daus., Margaret and Fanny. Executors: son, Peter; Peter G. Getman. Witnesses: Christopher Getman, Peter G. Getman, Solomon Cummings. (WMC 57:267)

Tryon County Militia

Saltsman, George   [Appendix A]
Saltsman, Henry
Saltsman, John

Pension Abstract

Saltsman, George, b. 12/13/1763, son of Michael Salzman of Palatine, N.Y.; m. Catharine Lepper, 2/20/1787 in Palatine; d. 2/14/1838, Palatine, Montgomery Co., N.Y. Children: [not named]. (Son-in-law: William Gray, b. 1790/1; resident of Palatine in 1838.) George enlisted in 1779 and served at various times under Cols. Klock, Harper, Brown, Willett and Wagner; he fought in the battles of Stone Arabia and Johnstown; George served in the military until 1783. (RWPA: #W22152)

Saltsman, Peter, b. 1756/7; m. Sophia [?] (b. 1759/60); resident of Lenox, Madison Co., N.Y. on 10/5/1820. Children: John, b. 1804/5. Peter served in Capt. John Bleecker's Co., Col. Goose Van Schaick's Regt. of the N.Y. Line during the war. (RWPA: #S42239)

1790 Census

Saltsman, George   [Appendix B]
Saltsman, Henry
Saltsman, John
Saltsman, William

SALTZBERG

Marriage

Saltzberg, Hermanus m. Maria Magdalena Mejer, 1/20/1763 (RDSA:172)

Birth/Baptism

Saltzberg, Hermanus & Lena [?]: Johannes, b. 3/24/1764, bapt. 5/7/1764 (RDSA:47); Maria, b. 10/30/1766, bapt. 12/12/1766 (RDSA:71); Adam, b. 7/14/1768, bapt. 8/7/1768 (RDSA:88). Sponsors: Pieter (son of Henrich Laux, sen.) & Elisabeth (dau. of Georg Ecker) (re:1); Lena & Gerret Taimsen (re:2); Ulrich Bader & Elisabeth (re:3).

SAMMONS (also see SIMMONS)

Birth/Baptism

Sammon/Sammons, Frederick & Ruth (Shutinkirk): Lydia, b. 9/16/1790, bapt. 10/17/1790 (DRC:90); Rachel, bapt. 6/3/1792 (JPC:6). Sponsors: [none named] (re:1; re:2).

Sammons, Jacob & Cornelia (Baker), Newtown: Peter, bapt. 7/31/1785 (JDR:21).

Tryon County Militia

Sammons, Frederick   [Appendix A]
Sammons, Thomas

Pension Abstract

Sammons, Benjamin, b. 12/5/1758, son of Sampson and Rachel Sammons, Shawngunck, Ulster Co., N.Y.; resident of Johnstown, Montgomery Co., N.Y. on 9/19/1832. [Cousin: Cornelius Sammons, resident of Springfield, Otsego Co., N.Y. on 8/29/1832.] Benjamin enlisted in 1775 and served through 1777 under Capts. John Davis and Nicholas Marselius, Major Jelles Fonda, and Cols. Frederick Fisher & Abraham Cuyler in the N.Y. Troops; he enlisted as a private in March/April 1779 in Capt. Robert Hunter's Co., Col. Albert Pawling's Regt. of the N.Y. Line; he again served in Col. Cuyler's Regt. and was in a small engagement at Col. Jacob Klock's place (later called Oppenheim, Montgomery Co.). (RWPA: #S11345)

Sammons, Frederick, b. 1759/60; (brother:

Thomas Sammons [RWPA: #W19000]); m. [wife not named]; d. 5/22/1838. Children: Lydia (widow of John Van Wagenen); Rachel (m. Joseph Wert); Mary (m. Horace Foote); Elizabeth (m. William Nicholas); Ruth Ann (m. Timothy Johnson); Jane (m. William Sammons); Catharine (m. Thomas Sammons); Hester (m. James Davis); Angeline (m. John Spraker). [All of these children were living in 1838.] Frederick served as a sergeant in Capt. Abraham Veeder's Co. under command of Col. Frederick Fisher in the 3rd. Regt., Tryon Co. Militia; Frederick was taken prisoner [along with his brother, Thomas Sammons] on 5/22/1780 by the enemy and transported to Chambley in Lower Canada; he escaped from Chambley but was soon retaken and kept a prisoner at "prison Island" for more than two years "the most part of the time in Irons"; Frederick made his final escape with another prisoner named McMullen and traveled through the wilderness to home in about two weeks. On 2/2/1838 a bill was passed in the U.S. Congress [H.R. 515] "For the relief of Frederick Sammons" in which he was granted a pension for the rest of "his natural life". (RWPA: #S11350)

Sammons, Thomas, b. 10/29/1762, son of Sampson and Rachel Sammons, Shawngunck, Ulster Co., N.Y.; m. Maria Wood, 12/16/1792, Caughnawaga, N.Y. by Rev. Thomas Romeyn; d. 11/20/1838, Johnstown, Montgomery Co., N.Y. (Maria Sammons, b. 1773/4; resident of Mohawk, Montgomery Co., N.Y. on 1/25/1843.) Children: [none were named in the application file]. Thomas enlisted from his home in Johnstown in 1778 and served as a private in Capt. Abraham Veeder's Co., Col. Frederick Fisher's 3rd. Regt., Tryon Co. Militia; Thomas "was taken prisoner together with his father & his two brothers [on 5/22/1780] by a party of the enemy about 600 strong under Sir John Johnson-- the same day he succeeded in effecting his escape & returned to the village of Johnstown"; (Thomas' parents "removed to the town of Marbletown in said County of Ulster, [in the latter part of 1780] they being obliged to abandon their residence in said town of Johnstown in consequence of the enemy who destroyed their dwelling house & other property"); Thomas was in the military for a total period of thirteen months and eight days. (RWPA: #W19000)

Deed Abstract

Sammons, Samson, farmer, of the Mohawk District, Tryon Co. to Reverend Thomas Romien [Romeyn], Gentleman, of the same place. Deed dated 7/2/1778; recorded 8/3/1787. Description: The equal undivided half moiety of a certain lot, being part of a tract of land granted by patent on 1/16/1770 to Alexander McKee and others, situated near Cherry Valley on the south side of the Mohawk River in Tryon Co. Said lot (1,000 acres) is bounded by Lot #5 beginning at the northeast corner of Lot #14, thence east along the south bounds of Lot #4, thence to the southeast corner on the west bounds of land granted to Stephen Skinner and others, thence south to the northeast corner of Lot #6, thence west along the north bounds of Lot #6, thence north along the east bounds of Lot #14 to the place where this lot began. Consideration: L50. Witnesses: John Fonda, Robt. S. Butcher. (MVL:29)

SAMPLE (also see SEMPLE)

Marriage

Sampell, James m. Anne Vensisco, both of Warrensbush, 11/4/1790 (JDR: #90)

Sample, John m. Nansy Hill, both of Warrensborough, 12/10/1791 (JDR: #102)

Sample, Robert m. Angela Davis, both of Warrensborough, 3/28/1792 (JDR: #113)

Sample, William m. Olive Hobbs, both of Warrensborough, 3/5/1792 (JDR: #111)

Birth/Baptism

Sampell, John & Nancy (Hill), both of Florida: Sarah, bapt. 7/21/1793 (JDR:23); Peggy, bapt. 5/26/1799 (JDR:22).

Sampell/Sample, Hugh & [?] (Crull): Frederick, bapt. 9/6/1789 [Warrensborough] (JDR:14); Samuel, bapt. 2/26/1792 [Sharlattsbush] (JDR:23); Evah, bapt. 11/12/1794, age 6 wks. old [Warrensborough] (JDR:13); John, b. 4/4/1797, bapt. 6/4/1797 [of Florida] (JDR:18); Peter, bapt. 6/29/1800 [Florida] (JDR:22); Annah, bapt. 8/29/1802 [Florida] (JDR:10).

Sample, Samuel & Sarah (Lenix): Sarah, b. 4/14/1777, bapt. 4/16/1777 (DRC:42); Solomon, bapt. 9/7/1779 (JDR:23); Elizabeth, bapt. 1/9/1786 (JDR:13). [Note: baptisms #2 & #3, the parents were of Warrensborough & Samuel was listed as Sr.]. Sponsors: [none named for #1-3].

1790 Census

Sample, Samuel   [Appendix B]

SANDER

Marriage

691

COMPENDIUM

Sander, Henrich m. [?] Majer, 10/30/1764 (RDSA:175)

Birth/Baptism

Sander, Henrich & Elisabeth [?]: Barbara, b. 3/2/1782, bapt. 8/24/1782 (DRGF:60); Maria, b. 12/17/1783, bapt. 12/20/1783 (DRGF:78). Sponsors: Corneles van Campen & Barbara (re:1); Jacob Dieffendorff & Margreth Guntermann (re:2).

Death Record

Sanders, [?], (wife of Henry Sanders), b. 3/?/1744; d. 7/28/1808, age 64 years, 4 months; buried 7/30/1808 (DFP:92)

1790 Census

Sanders, Hendrick　　　　[Appendix B]

SANFORD

1790 Census

Sanford, Jonah　　　　[Appendix B]

SANGOR

1790 Census

Sangor, Jedediah　　　　[Appendix B]

SARLES

1790 Census

Sarles, Lemuel　　　　[Appendix B]
Sarles, Reuben

SARTEL

1790 Census

Sartel, John　　　　[Appendix B]

SASHY

1790 Census

Sashy, Abraham　　　　[Appendix B]

SATCHEL

1790 Census

Satchel, William　　　　[Appendix B]

SATERLY

1790 Census

Saterly, Selah　　　　[Appendix B]

SATTERLES

Death Record

Satterles, Caroline, (dau. of Elisha & Martha Satterles), d. [not given], age 11 years; buried

692

sect. 6, Colonial Cemetery, Johnstown (JC:187)

Satterles, Mary, (dau. of Elisha & Martha Satterles), d. 11/4/1806, age 4 months; buried sect. 6, Colonial Cemetery, Johnstown (JC:187)

SAUFFER

Marriage

Sauffer, Johannes m. Maria Bettli, 12/2/1765 (RDSA:177)

SAUNDERS

1790 Census

Saunders, Henry   [Appendix B]

SAUSELIN

Birth/Baptism

Sauselin, Joh. Michael & Maria Catharina [?]: Maria Catharina, b. 8/10/1753 (LTSA:7). Sponsors: Andreas Rheber & his wife, Anna Maria.

SAVAGE

1790 Census

Savage, Gideon   [Appendix B]

SAWYER

Marriage

Sawyer, Humphray m. Mary Hoag (from Marlattsbush), 12/29/1791 (JDR:#103)

SCARBURY

Tryon County Militia

Scarbury, William   [Appendix A]

SCHAAB

Birth/Baptism

Schaab, Micael & Dorothea [?]: Dorothea, b. 5/18/1778; bapt. 1/31/1779 (LTSA:56). Sponsors: Heinrich Gallinger, Susanna Hickert.

SCHAFER (also see SHAVER)

Marriage

Schafer, Henrich m. Anna Snell, 4/2/1782 (DRGF:196)

Schafer, Jacob m. Engelge van Slyk, 6/11/1782 (DRGF:196)

Schafer, Johannes (son of Adam Schafer) m. Anna Osteroth (dau. of John Osteroth), 3/16/1794 (DRGF:211)

Schafer, Johannes m. Dorothea Stamm, 4/5/1795 (RDSA:201)

Schafer, John m. Margarete Loucks (dau. of

693

Henrich Loucks), 12/4/1759 (RDSA:166; LTSA:277)

Birth/Baptism

Schafer, Adam & Susanna [?]: Anna, b. 8/4/1792 (LTSA:73). Sponsors: John Jenkens & Margaret.

Schafer, Andrew (Palatine) & Anna [?]: Johann Friderich, bapt. 7/17/1791 (SJC:44); Abraham, bapt. 7/21/1793 (SJC:78). Sponsors: J. Friderich Bellinger & Catharina Bellinger (re:1); Abraham Keller & Elisabeth Keller (re:2).

Schafer, Bartholomeus & Anna Dorothea (Haine): Johannes, b. 3/24/1779, bapt. 3/28/1779 (LTSA:57); Johann Peter, b. 12/3/1780, bapt. 12/8/1780 (DRGF:41); Friedrich, b. 3/25/1787, bapt. 3/31/1787 (RDSA:112). Sponsors: Johann Casselmann & Anna Eva (re:1); Georg Heiny & Anna Emgie (re:2); Friedrich Goedmann & his wife [?] Fro[?] (re:3).

Schafer, Bernt & Dorotea [?]: Margaret, b. 4/13/1796 (LTSA:93). Sponsors: Samuel Cree & Catarina.

Schafer, Henrich & Anna (Schnell): Casparus, b. 6/22/1783, bapt. 6/30/1783 (DRGF:73); Petrus, b. 3/10/1785, bapt. 3/13/1785 (DRGF:94); Magdalena, bapt. 1/11/1789 (SJC:8); Jacob, bapt. 4/10/1791 (SJC:40); Heinrich, bapt. 6/9/1793 (SJC:76)[Note: Last three baptisms; parents of Schnellenbusch & Royal Grant]. Sponsors: Nicolas Schaffer & Anna Eva Snell (re:1); Pieter Laux & Sussanna (re:2); Conrad Zimmerman & Magdalena (re:3); Johannes Scheffer & Margretha Scheffer (re:4); Johannes Snell & Anna Snell (re:5).

Schafer, Jacob & Engelge/Angelica [?]: Johannes, b. 3/[5 or 7]/1783, bapt. 3/16/1783 (DRGF:69); Eva, b. 3/[5 or 7]/1783, bapt. 3/16/1783 (DRGF:69); Jacob, bapt. 9/26/1790 (SJC:33); Magdalena, bapt. 8/26/1792 (SJC:63) [Note: Parents of Canajoharie for last two baptisms]. Sponsors: Johannes Schaffer & Veronica (re:1); Martinus van Slyck & Maria Schaffer (re:2); Heinrich Krankheit & Anna Krankheit (re:3); John Hauss & Magdalena Hauss (re:4).

Schafer, Joh. Conrad (Lieut.) & Dorothea [?]: Gertraut, b. 2/18/1784; bapt. 3/7/1784 (DRGF:81). Sponsors: Gertraut Grimm & Georg Haussmann.

Schafer, Johannes & Anna Margretha [?]: Henrich, b. 7/1/1760, bapt. 7/13/1760 (RDSA:20); Casper, b. 7/24/1762, bapt. 8/1/1762(RDSA:34); Nicolaus, b. 12/28/1764, bapt. 12/30/1764 (RDSA:53); Andreas, bapt. 4/8/1767 (RDSA:74); Petrus, b. 4/27/1769, bapt. 4/30/1769 (RDSA:94); Anna Eva, b. 11/3/1775, bapt. 11/15/1775 (LTSA:50); Gertraut, b. 2/25/1782, bapt. 3/3/1782 (DRGF:55); Georg, bapt. 11/10/1784 (DRGF:89). Sponsors: Henrich Laux & his wife, Anna Elisabetha (re:1); Casper Keller & Barbara Laux (re:2); Nicolas Schaeffer & his wife, Elisabeth (re:3); Adam Foore & Catharina Laux (re:4); Pieter H. Laux & Margretha Arnhold Sielebach (re:5); Jerg Schnell & his wife, Anna Eva (re:6); Wilhelm Father & Gertraut Schaffer (re:7); Georg Stamm & [?] (re:8).

Schafer, Johannes & Maria [?]: Anna Maria, b. 9/28/1781; bapt. 10/15/1781 (DRGF:49). Sponsors: Jacob Schafer & Catharina Albrandt.

Schafer, Nicholas (of Palatine) & Anna (Schall) (Snellenbush): Johannes, bapt. 1/17/1790

(SJC:22); Wilhelm, bapt. 12/25/1791 (SJC:51); Margretha, bapt. 7/7/1793 (SJC:78). Sponsors: Peter Scheffer & Magdalena Schnell (re:1); Wilhelm Schall & Anna Eva Scheffer (re:2); Joh: Jost Snell & Margretha Scheffer (re:3).

Schafer, Niclas & Elisabetha [?]: Jerg Adam, b. 2/29/1756 (LTSA:17); Elisabetha, b. 2/6/1764, bapt. 3/18/1764 (RDSA:45); Jacobus, b. 12/12/1765, bapt. 1/4/1766 (RDSA:60). Sponsors: Jerg Adam Dagstetter, Eva Berlot (re:1); Elisabeth, wife of Friederich Dachstaeder (re:2); Jacob Sever & Maria Esther (re:3).

Schafer, Philipp & Elisabeth [?]: Conrad, b. 4/21/1766; bapt. 5/25/1766 (RDSA:64). Sponsors: Jacob Boshardt & Margretha.

Tryon County Militia

Schaffer, James   [Appendix A]
Schaffer, John
Schefer, Adam
Schefer, Bartholomew
Schefer, Henrich
Schefer, Henry
Schefer, John
Schefer, Nicholas

Pension Abstract

Schefer, Henry, b. 1758/9, son of Henrich Schaefer, Schoharie, N.Y.; m. Elizabeth Warner, 11/23/1777 at St. Paul's Lutheran Church, Schoharie, N.Y.; d. 4/15/1839, Cobleskill, N.Y. (Elizabeth Schefer, b. 1758/9; resident of Cobleskill, N.Y. on 6/4/1839.) Henry enlisted in the fall of 1775 and was a sergeant under Capts. John Bank and George Mann's Cos. in Col. Peter Vrooman's Regt.; he was wounded in the battle of Cobleskill and assisted in the building of Fort Dubois at the same place; Henry was stationed in 1781 at "the lower fort" in Schoharie to protect the inhabitants; he continued serving various tours of duty into 1782. (RWPA: #W19355)

Schefer, Henry, b. 5/20/1764, Cobleskill, Schoharie, Co., N.Y.; m. Susannah Appleton, 3/?/1803 by Rev. John D. Shafer at Cobleskill, N.Y.; d. 9/29/1851, Richmondville, Schoharie Co., N.Y. (Susannah Schefer, b. ca. 1776; resident of Richmondville, N.Y. on 3/20/1855.) Henry was a private under Capts. Gray and Harrison in Col. Marinus Willett's Regt. of the N.Y. Line; he also served in the Schoharie Militia during the war. (RWPA: #W6002)

Schefer, Henry, m. Sophia Hiltz, 12/14/1780; d. 8/27/1832, Schoharie, Schoharie Co., N.Y. (Sophia Schefer, b. 1759/60, dau. of George Hiltz; d. 6/3/1840, Schoharie, N.Y.) Children: [one not named and living in 1840]. Henry enlisted from Schoharie in 1776 and served various tours of duty into 1782; he was under command of Capts. Mann, George Rechtmyer and Stubrach in the regiments of Cols. Sternberg and Vrooman. (RWPA: #W16397)

1790 Census

Shaffer, Adam   [Appendix B]
Shaffer, Henry
Shaffer, Jacob
Shaffer, John (2)
Sheaffer, Henry

SCHAKO

Marriage

Schako, Jacob m. Catharina Heering, 1/29/1792

695

COMPENDIUM

(RDSA:196)

Schako, Nicholas m. Anna Betsinger, 12/19/1790 (RDSA:195)

Birth/Baptism

Schako, Georg Adam & Anna Margretha [?]: Maria Elisabetha, b. 11/8/1763, bapt. 11/20/1763 (RDSA:43); Catharina, b. 5/22/1766, bapt. 6/8/1766 (RDSA:64); Nicolaus, b. 6/25/1768, bapt. 7/10/1768 (RDSA:87); Jacob, b. 3/4/1770, bapt. 3/11/1770 (RDSA:101). Sponsors: Elisabetha Christmann & Johannes Schultz (re:1); Catharina Elisabetha & Adam Laux (re:2); Henrich Fritsher & Maria Eva (re:3); Jacob Christman & [?] (re:4).

Schako, Jacob & Catarina [?]: Eva, b. 1/5/1793 (LTSA:77). Sponsors: Jerg Schako, Lena Hering.

Schako, Nicolaus & Anna [?]: Catarina, b. 11/7/1792 (LTSA:70); Maria, b. 9/29/1795 (LTSA:91). Abraham Hasch & Catarina (re:1); Johannes von de Werke, Maria Tschako (re:2).

SCHALL

Marriage

Schall, Henrich m. Catharina Brunner, 12/7/1784 (DRGF:200)

Schall, Johannes m. Elisabeth Brunner, 10/26/1784 (DRGF:200)

Birth/Baptism

Schall, Georg & Maria [?]: Georg, b. 7/18/1780; bapt. 7/23/1780 (DRGF:39).

Sponsors: Georg Snell & Anna Eva.

Schall, Joh. & [?]: Matheus, b. 8/10/1755 (LTSA:15). Sponsors: Matheus Schafer, Eva Contrimann.

Schall, Johann Jost & Anna Eva [?]: Joh. Jost, b. 10/25/1790 (LTSA:66). Sponsors: Ludwig Rekert & Catharina.

Schall, Labees (Canajoharie) & Maria [?]: Isaack, bapt. 8/28/1791 (SJC:46); Jacob, bapt. 8/28/1791 (SJC:46). Sponsors: Frans Schemel & Elisabeth Schemel (re:1); Sebastian Schall & Magdalena Schall (re:2).

Schall, Matthew (of Gaiesberg) & Maria [?]: Johannes, bapt. 3/1/1789 (SJC:11). Sponsors: Johannes Schall & Margretha Schall.

Schall, William (Canajoharie) & Eva [?]: Lea, bapt. 9/1/1793 (SJC:80). Sponsors: Peter Knieskern & Lea Knieskern.

Tryon County Militia

Schall, George   [Appendix A]
Schall, Johannes Jost
Schall, John
Shall, Frederick

Pension Abstract

Schall, John, b. 2/18/1760; (brothers: Henry, b. 1757/8; Sebastian, and Mattice Shaul); m. Elizabeth Bronner, 10/11/1784; resident of Stark, Herkimer Co., N.Y. on 10/9/1832; d. 6/8/1844, Stark, N.Y. (Elizabeth Schall, b. 12/25/1761; resident of Stark, N.Y. on 10/7/1844.) John lived at a settlement called the "Osquago" about ten miles south of the Mohawk River, where he was enrolled at the age of sixteen years in Capt. Henry Eckler's

Co., Col. Peter Bellinger's 4th. Regt., Tryon Co. Militia; John was ordered to remain at German Flatts, at the time of the battle of Oriskany, to guard the fort and that Walter Butler "was then a prisoner at that fort" and John was on duty "as a sentinel at the door of the room where he [Walter Butler] was confined"; John and his brother, Sebastian Shaul were taken prisoners in November 1778 by the Indians at Osquago when "they were surprised in the house at Osquago by a party of seven indians headed by Joseph Brant" who burned the entire settlement and took their prisoners to Niagara; John was kept a prisoner until his release at the close of the war. (RWPA: #W11441)

SCHARMAN

Birth/Baptism

Scharman, Jacob & Maria (Gundel): Maria Elisabeth, b. 9/?/1758; bapt. 12/8/1765 (RDSA:59). Sponsors: Maria Elisabeth & Henrich Saltzmann.

SCHATT

Birth/Baptism

Schatt, Thomas & [?]: Johannes, b. 7/13/1771 (LTSA:37). Sponsors: Johannes Bender, Maria Lenk.

SCHAUFFLIN

Death Record

Schaufflin, Johann Jacob, (widower), b. 10/16/1734, Switzerland; (arrived in America, 8/7/1794); d. 9/20/1794, age 63 years, 11 months, less 4 days [Note: Age does not agree with birth]; buried 9/22/1794 (DFP:85)

Scheufflin, Johann Jacob, (son of Johann Jacob Scheufflin), b. 6/24/1791; d. 4/21/1795; buried 4/23/1795 (DFP:87)

SCHECOKA

Birth/Baptism

Schecoka, David & Margretha [?]: Sara, b. 11/29/1769; bapt. 1/14/1770 (RDSA:99). Sponsors: Benjamin Atch[?] & Sara.

SCHEEL

Birth/Baptism

Scheel, Friederick Ludwig (Royal Grant) & Elisabeth [?]: Johann Gottfried, bapt. 8/21/1791 (SJC:46). Sponsors: Johann Jost Schnell & Susanna Staring.

SCHELL (also see SHELL)

Marriage

Schell, Christian m. Elisabeth P. Segner, 4/6/1794 (DRGF:211)

Schell, Christian Joh: m. Catharina H: Hauser, 8/8/1786 (DRGF:204)

Schell, Fritz Chr: m. Catharina Staring, [no date: follows 7/1/1788] (DRGF:205)

Schell, Henrich (son of Chr: Schell) m. Maria Gerlach Majer, 4/13/1794 (DRGF:211)

Schell, Johannes (of Little Falls) m. Barbara Raspe (dau. of Johannes Raspe), 2/16/1762 (RDSA:170)

Schell, Johannes (widower) m. Anna Eva Kesslar (dau. of Jac: Kesslar), 8/5/1794 (DRGF:211)

Schell, Johannes Joh: m. Margreth Thum (dau. of Melchior Thum), 1/31/1792 (DRGF:208)

Schell, Marcus Chr. m. Delia Kesslar, 10/19/1794 (DRGF:211)

Schell, Marcus Joh: m. Catharina Elisabeth Raan (dau. of Joh: Nic: Raan), 3/25/1788 (DRGF:205)

Schell, Peter Joh: m. Catharina G: Hielz, 1/19/1790 (DRGF:206)

Birth/Baptism

Schell, Johann Christian & Elisabeth [?]: Augustin, b. 4/17/1763, bapt. 4/26/1763 (RDSA:39); Friedericus, b. 12/16/1764, bapt. 12/18/1764 (RDSA:52); Anna Maria, b. 2/16/1767, bapt. 4/29/1767 (RDSA:74); Maria Catharina, b. 12/1/1777, bapt. 12/25/1777 (DRGF:27). Sponsors: Augustinus Hess & his wife (re:1); Friderich Mayer & [?] Petri (re:2); Anna Maria & Johannes Heering (re:3); Christian Hess & Elisabeth (re:4).

Schell, Johann Christian & Maria Elisabetha [?]: Maria Elisabetha, b. 9/21/1760, bapt.

9/26/1760 (RDSA:22); Eva, b. 11/7/1768, bapt. 11/15/1768 (RDSA:91); Johann Henrich, b. 9/22/1770, bapt. 10/10/1770 (RDSA:106); Marcus, b. 9/22/1770, bapt. 10/10/1770 (RDSA:106). Sponsors: Maria Elisabeth (dau. of Marcus Petri) & Dieterich (son of Johan Jost Petri) (re:1); Catharina Petri & Diedrich Petri (re:2); Joh: Henrich Widderstein & Magdalena (re:3); Jacob Nic: Kesslar & Cordelia (re:4).

Schell, Johannes & Maria Barbara [?]: Johann Christian, bapt. 1/6/1763 (RDSA:37); Johannes Marcus, b. 6/11/1764, bapt. 7/5/1764 (RDSA:48); Anna Catharina, b. 4/12/1766, bapt. 5/5/1766 (RDSA:63); Johannes, b. 9/17/1767, bapt. 10/24/1767 (RDSA:79); Peter, b. 3/24/1769 (LTSA:27). Sponsors: Johan Christ Schell & Elisabeth (re:1); Johann Marcus Raspe & Veronica (re:2); Anna Catharina Bentz & Joh. Friedrich Rasbock (re:3); Johannes Hess & Margretha Raspock (re:4); Peter Volz, Elisabetha Rasbach (re:5).

Death Record

Schell, Catharina, (wife of Christian Schell; born: Haeuser), d. 5/9/1822, Herkimer, age 53 years; buried in the cemetery near the church in town (RDH:283)

Schell, Catharina, (wife of Peter Schell; born: Hilts), d. 9/6/1822, Herkimer, age 52 years; buried in the cemetery near the church (RDH:285)

Schell, Elisabeth, (dau. of Peter & Catharina Schell), d. 2/10/1802, Herkimer, age 7 years, 9 months, 6 days; buried Herkimer cemetery (RDH:245)

Schell, John, b. 1734, Principality of Nassau-Dillenburg, Germany; d. 8/1/1802, Herkimer,

698

COMPENDIUM

age 68; (John Schell came to Philadelphia in 1752, died at Schell's bush, from whom it acquired the name from clearing the woods; he died suddenly of suffocation caused by disease); buried Herkimer cemetery (RDH:248)

Schell, Maria Catharina, (dau.[?] of Peter J. Schell), d. 9/22/1822, Herkimer, age 1 year; buried near the church (RDH:285)

Tryon County Militia

Schell, Christian   [Appendix A]
Schell, Johannes

Pension Abstract

Schell, Christian, b. 1757/8, Palatine, N.Y.; m. [wife not named]; d. 1841, Vaughan Twp., Privince of Upper Canada. Children: Henry C., b. 1795/6 (eldest son and resident[?] of Erie Co., N.Y. in 1853). Christian enlisted in 1775 into a company of rangers commanded by Capt. Mark Demuth and was ordered to march to Ticonderoga where he [Christian] was engaged "in assisting to build a Bridge across Lake Champlain, from Fort Ticonderoga"; he enlisted in 1777 at Fort Herkimer as a continental soldier under the command of Capt. Thomas DeWitt. [Christian Schell's claim for pension on 1/18/1833 was rejected "because he deserted".] (RWPA: #R9253)

Schell, Johannes, b. [no information given on his birth, marriage or death]. Johannes was a private in Col. Peter Bellinger's 4th. Regt., Tryon Co. Militia and fought in the battle of Oriskany where he was wounded in his left side. [There are no papers on file due to the destruction of such papers when the War Office was burned in 1800.] (American State Papers: Class 9, p.94; application for invalid pension, returned by the District Court of N.Y. to the

Secretary of War in 1794.)

SCHEMBLE

Birth/Baptism

Schemble, Francs & Elisabeth [?]: Elisabeth, b. 1/7/1763; bapt. 3/3/1763 (RDSA:38). Sponsors: Elisabeth, wife of Conrad Franck & Elisabeth, wife of John Burgis.

SCHENHOLZ

Birth/Baptism

Schenholz, Frederick (Gaiseberg) & Elisabeth [?]: Margaretha, bapt. 8/8/1790 (SJC:31). Sponsors: Friderich Countermann & Gertrud Counterman.

1790 Census

Sheanhults, Frederick   [Appendix B]

SCHENK

Marriage

Schenk, Georg m. Dorothea Wirt, 10/8/1771 (LTSA:282)

Birth/Baptism

Schenk, George & Magdalena (Spendeler): Johannes, bapt. 1/27/1765 (DRC:14). Sponsors: Johannes Smith & Anna Pikler.

Tryon County Militia

Schenck, George   [Appendix A]

Deed Abstract

Schenck, Ralph, and Ann, his wife, of Montgomery Co. to Rulef P. Schenck, of Monmouth County, New Jersey. Deed dated 12/1/1786; recorded 7/16/1787. Description: Land situated in Montgomery Co. on the north side of the Mohawk River in a patent granted to the late Sir William Johnson, known as Kingsland or Royal Grant. Lot #15 (200 acres) in the second allotment of said patent and forfeited to the State of N.Y. by the attainder of Sir John Johnson, late of Tryon Co., Knight and Baronet. Consideration: L160. Witnesses: rd. Throckmorton, Robert Coombs. (MVL:29)

SCHEPPERMAN

Birth/Baptism

Schepperman, Christian & Dorothea [?]: Peter, b. 7/6/1790 (LTSA:65). Sponsors: Peter Fuchs, Dorothea Feder.

Death Record

Schepperman, Catharina (maiden name: Bellinger), b. 3/25/1754; m. 12/10/1787; d. 8/30/1788; buried 9/1/1788 (RDSA:230)

SCHERER

Marriage

Scherer, Christian m. Anna Margretha Bellinger, 3/2/1767 (RDSA:180)

Birth/Baptism

Scherer, Joh. Christian & Anna Margreth [?]: Anna Margretha, b. 9/23/1767; bapt. 10/24/1767 (RDSA:79). Sponsors: Anna Margretha & Pieter Bellinger.

SCHERMERHORN

Birth/Baptism

Schermerhorn, Jacob H. & Aeltje [?]: Hendrick, b. 1/25/1791; bapt. 3/6/1791 (DRC:95). Sponsors: [none named].

1790 Census

Schermerhorn, Jacob H.   [Appendix B]
Schermerhorn, John

SCHERP

Death Record

Scherp, Susannna (wife of Johannes Scherp), b. 3/17/1772; d. 9/24/1793, (in child birth); buried 9/24/1793 (DFP:84)

SCHERREB

Marriage

Scherreb, John (son of Jacob Scherreb) m. Susanna Falkenburg (dau. of Peter Falkenburg, decd.), 10/1/1791 (DFP:44)

SCHEUERMAN

Birth/Baptism

Scheuerman, Georg & Maria [married to Benjamin Makkis]: Margrtha, b. [?]; bapt. 2/27/1781 (DRGF:43). Sponsors: Nicholas Wohleben & Margretha.

SCHEURMAN

Birth/Baptism

Scheurman, Johannes & Anna Elisabeth [?]: Georg, b. 1/2/1782; bapt. 1/22/1782 (DRGF:54). Sponsors: Georg Hergheimer, Esqr. & Alita.

SCHIB

Birth/Baptism

Schib, Jerg Frid. & Anna Christina [?]: John Tobias, b. 11/2/1792 (LTSA:76). Sponsors: John Feicks, Maria Kochner.

SCHIELIE (also see SCHILE)

Marriage

Schielie, Wilhelm (son of Martin Schielie) m. Margaretha Jung (dau. of Johann Jung, decd.), 11/3/1789 (DFP:41)

SCHIFF

Marriage

Schiff, Hans Georg m. Christina Verbos, 1/13/1784 (DRGF:199)

Birth/Baptism

Schiff, Georg & Christina [?]: Jacob, b. 3/29/1785, bapt. 4/2/1785 (DRGF:94); Alida, bapt. 8/15/1790 [parents of Fallberg] (SJC:31). Sponsors: Jacob Forbes & Maria Margreth Schiff (re:1); Johannes Meyer & Alida Meyer (re:2).

Schiff, Georg & Maria Catharina [?]: Christian, b. 3/22/1767; bapt. 4/29/1767 (RDSA:75). Sponsors: Georg Hieltz & Maria Elisabetha.

Tryon County Militia

Schiff, George   [Appendix A]

Pension Abstract

Schiff, George, b. 1756/7; (sister: Mary, wife of [Jacob?] Multer; living in Oneida Co., N.Y. in 1818); m. Christina Vorbos; d. 4/9/1820, Deerfield, Oneida Co., N.Y. (Christina Schiff, d. 9/23/1842 or 9/25/1842, Deerfield, N.Y.) Children: George, b. 6/27/1788; Olive, b. 8/9/1790; Eve, b. 5/1/1793 (m. Abraham Weaver); Conrad, b. 4/18/1795; Margareta, b. 2/4/1801 (m. Stephen Luther; resident of Clayton, N.Y. in 1846); Mary, b. ca. 1804 (m. [?] Finster; resident of Ellisburg, N.Y. in 1846). [All other children residents of Deerfield, N.Y. in 1846.] George took his father's place in the military in 1776 at Fort Stanwix and served in Capt. Swarthout's Co.., Col. Peter Gansevoort's 3rd. N.Y. Regt.; he was in the siege of Fort Stanwix and marched on the Sullivan expedition; he also served in Col. Van Schaick's Regt. of the N.Y. Line; George's father, while at work in the field, was scalped by the Indians and died in the spring of

1781; George was granted a furlough to return hone; he enlisted again in 1782 and served for nearly eight months as a corporal in Capt. Abner French's Co., Col. Marinus Willett's Regt. (RWPA: #W19029)

his wife.

Tryon County Militia

Schimmel, Dieterich   [Appendix A]
Schimmel, Francis

SCHILE (also see SCHIELIE)

Birth/Baptism

Schile, Martin & Catharina [?]: Maria Elisabetha, b. 5/18/1769 (LTSA:26). Sponsors: Mattaeus Warmoth, Catharina Seber.

Tryon County Militia

Shiele, Mantus   [Appendix A]

SCHILL

Marriage

Schill, Jacob m. Elisabeth Smidt, 9/9/1781 (DRGF:195)

Birth/Baptism

Schill, Jacob & Elisabet [?]: Anna, b. 8/14/1790 (LTSA:63). Sponsors: Jacob Schnell, Anna Merten.

SCHIMMEL

Birth/Baptism

Schimmel, Franz & Elisabetha [?]: Sophia, b. 11/2/1771 (LTSA:40). Sponsors: Jost Haus &

SCHMANN

Birth/Baptism

Schmann, John & Catharina [?]: John Friderich, b. 7/26/1788 (LTSA:61). Sponsors: Jost Nelles, Maria Nelles.

SCHNAUTZ

Marriage

Schnautz, John m. Catharina Klok, 4/16/1793 (DFP:49)

SCHNEID

Birth/Baptism

Schneid, Hannes & [?]: Joannes, b. 1/10[?]/1755 (LTSA:10). Sponsors: Jacob Roth & his wife.

SCHNEIDER

Marriage

Schneider, Ludwig m. Margretha Klock,

702

COMPENDIUM

11/13/1764 (RDSA:175)

Birth/Baptism

Schneider, Michael & Elisabetha [?]: Anna Maria, b. 5/28/1771 (LTSA:38). Sponsors: Gottlieb Schneider, Ottilia Resner.

Probate Abstract

Schneider, Michael, (of Minden), will dated 5/28/1810; probated 2/6/1813. Legatees: sons, Jacob M., John and John George; daus., Margaret, Magdalena and Elizabeth. Executors: Godfrey Young, Rev. John Waek. Witnesses: Marcus Kasslar, John Hooke, John Waek. (WMC 56:385)

Tryon County Militia

Schneider, Jacob   [Appendix A]
Schneider, Michael

SCHNEK

Marriage

Schnek, Johann Friedrich m. Lea Sits, 11/27/1792 (DFP:47)

Birth/Baptism

Schnek, Hans Georg & Maria Barbara [?]: Margretha, b. 11/15/1767, bapt. 1/19/1768 (RDSA:83); Johann Jacob, b. 5/15/1770, bapt. 5/25/1770 (RDSA:102). Sponsors: Margretha Frank & Johannes Smith (re:1); Jacob Hiller & Elisabeth (re:2).

Tryon County Militia

Schneck, George   [Appendix A]

SCHNELL (also see SNELL)

Probate Abstract

Schnell, Adam, (of Canajoharie), will dated 11/18/1828; probated 1/12/1829. Legatees: wife, Elizabeth; children of my four brothers (Peter, Joseph, Jacob and George). Executors: Abial Bingham, Squeir Hill. Witnesses: P. Randell, Oliver C. Chase, Ebenezer Tillotson. (WMC 57:273)

SCHOBE

Birth/Baptism

Schobe, James & Catrina (Brown): Timotheus, b. 2/23/1787; bapt. 4/30/1787 (DRC:84). Sponsors: [none named].

SCHOCH

Birth/Baptism

Schoch/Schock/Shok, Andreas & Catharina [?]: Jacob, b. 8/10/1767, bapt. 9/25/1767 (RDSA:78); Andreas, b. 3/19/1769 (LTSA:26); Catharina, b. 5/9/1771 (LTSA:38). Sponsors: Jacob Alcajer & Catharina (re:1); Jacob Algaier & his wife (re:2); Mother & Father (re:3).

Schoch, Gottfried & Catharina [?]: Maria Elisabetha, b. 8/6/1765; bapt. 9/13/1765 (RDSA:57). Sponsors: Elisabetha & Johannes Dorn.

1790 Census

Shok, Zachariah   [Appendix B]

SCHOLL (also see SCHOOL)

Marriage

Scholl, Joh. Jost (widower of N. Dillenburg) m. Anna Eva Godmann (dau. of Christian Godmann), 7/8/1788 (RDSA:192)

Scholl, Johannes m. Rachel Hurtig, 6/14/1795 (RDSA:201)

Scholl, Sebastian m. Magdalena Cuntermann, 2/9/1789 (RDSA:194)

Birth/Baptism

Scholl, Joh. & Rahel [?]: Nicolaus, b. 2/28/1796 (LTSA:93); Anna, b. 2.28/1796 (LTSA:93). Sponsors: Nicolaus Streter & Margaret (re:1); Philip Dehas & Anna (re:2). Scholl, Johannes & Maria [?]: Jacob, b. 3/13/1791 (LTSA:67). Sponsors: Isaac Seber, Catharina Scholl.

Scholl, Joh: Jost & Elisabeth [?]: Maria, b. 9/22/1783, bapt. 10/19/1783 (DRGF:76); Elisabetha, b. 9/22/1783, bapt. 10/19/1783 (DRGF:76). Sponsors: John Scholl & Maria (re:1); Leonhard Kratzer & Elisabeth Kuhl (re:2).

Death Record

Scholl, Maria Sabina, (wife of Johannes Scholl), d. 9/28/1794, age 45 & some months; buried 9/30/1794 (RDSA:235)

Tryon County Militia

Scholl, Han Yost   [Appendix A]

Pension Abstract

Scholl, John Jost, b. 1751, Nassau Dillenburg, Principality of Prince of Orange, Germany; m. Anna Eva Godman, 7/8/1788, Reformed Dutch Church of Stone Arabia [John Jost was a widower at the time of their marriage]; d. 1/10/1837. (Anna Eva Scholl, d. 3/4/1841.) Children: Joseph, Jacob, John, Catharine (m. Peter Smith) [all of Danube, Herkimer Co., N.Y.]; Nancy (widow of Jacob Getman; resident of Frankfort, Herkimer Co.); Delia (m. Peter Dillenbach); Lany (m. Abraham Smith) [both of Orleans, Jefferson Co., N.Y.]. John Jost entered the military in 1775 and served at various times until the end of the war; he held the ranks of corporal, ensign and lieutenant during the war. (RWPA: #W16396)

1790 Census

Scholl, George   [Appendix B]
Sholl, Bastian
Sholl, Hendrick
Sholl, Honyost
Sholl, John (2)
Sholl, John, Sr.
Sholl, Matice

SCHOOL (also see SCHOLL)

Marriage

School, Johannes m. Maria Sabina Smidt, 9/18/1770 (RDSA:190)

COMPENDIUM

SCHOONMAKER

Probate Abstract

Schoonmaker, Cherick, (of Florida), will dated 11/21/1823; probated 2/20/1824. Legatees: wife [not named]; sons, Peter, Samuel, Charles, Christian and Egbert; daus., Dinah and Dolly; several children [not named]. Executors: sons, Egbert and Peter. Witnesses: Amler[?] Cady, Peter Covenhoven, James Greenman. (WMC 57:178)

Tryon County Militia

Schoonmaker, Thomas   [Appendix A]

SCHOONOVER

Death Record

Schoonover, William, d. 3/31/1833, age 21 years, of Dysentery; buried Cherry Valley Presbyterian Church cemetery (PCV:85)

SCHOT

Tryon County Militia

Schot, Joseph   [Appendix A]

SCHOWTEN (also see SCOWTEN)

Birth/Baptism

Schowten, Jesajas & Margretha [?]: Benjamin, b. 11/11/1781; bapt. 11/18/1781 (DRGF:50). Sponsors: Benjamin Elwoeth & Elisabeth.

1790 Census

Schoten, Isaiah   [Appendix B]

SCHRAM

Birth/Baptism

Schram, Peter (Tillenburg) & Anna [?]: Peter, b. 7/8/1792; bapt. 7/15/1792 (SJC:61). Sponsors: Leonhard Krauss & Magdalena Krauss.

SCHREMLING

Marriage

Schremling, Henrich m. Engel Merckel (widow), 10/25/1782 (DRGF:196)

Schremling, Henrich m. Rachel Lennerts, 11/19/1763 (RDSA:173)

Schremling, Henrich m. Sara Lennerts, 12/27/1763 (RDSA:173)

Schremling, John m. Rebecca Marinus, 7/14/1793 (DFP:49)

Birth/Baptism

Schremling, David (Otsego Co.) & Susanna [?]: Andreas, b. 7/19/1793; bapt. 2/1/1794 (SJC:90). Sponsors: Johannes Keller & Elisabeth Keller.

Schremling, Henderick & Rachel (Leenderse): Cornelis, b. 11/9/1771; bapt. 12/?/1771

705

(DRC:20). Sponsors: John Van Everen & Cornelia Van Everen.

Schremling, Peter (Otsego Co.) & Catharina [?]: Sara, b. 12/9/1793; bapt. 2/1/1794 (SJC:90). Sponsors: Johannes F. Hess & Catharina Schremling.

Tryon County Militia

Schremling, Dewald   [Appendix A]
Schremling, Henry

Pension Abstract

Schremling, George, b. ca. 7/?/1761, Canajoharie, N.Y.; (nephew: David Scrambling, resident of Washtenaw Co., Michigan in 1837); George moved from Otsego, Otsego Co., N.Y. in 1833 to Pitt Twp., Washtenaw Co., Mich. where he applied for pension on 2/3/1837. George enlisted in 1778/1779 for nine months as a private in Capt. Gros' Co., Col. Gansevoort's N.Y. Regt.; he again enlisted in the same regiment and company for another nine months and was stationed at Fort Plain and along the frontiers of the Mohawk River in Tryon Co.; he also served tours of duty in Capt. Saben's Co., Col. Wayne's Regt. and in Capt. Mabie's Co., Col. Veeder's N.Y. Regt.; George fought in the battle of Johnstown, marched on an expedition against Oswego Fort under Col. Willett and was in an engagement at Turlock (now Sharon); he served until the close of the war under Col. Willett. (RWPA: #R9323 SCRAMBLING)

Deed Abstract

Schremling, Catharina, (widow of the late George Schremling, decd.), Hendrick Schremling (eldest son and heir-at-law of George Schremling, decd.), and Sarah, his

wife, and John Winn, and Elizabeth, his wife, to Melgert Batter [Bader]. Deed dated 2/17/1787; recorded 3/6/1787. Description: Land situated at Stone Arabia, Montgomery Co., being part of a tract of land granted by patent on 10/19/1723 to Johannes Lawyer, Ludowick Casselman and others, known as Lot #34 (100 acres). Consideration: L300. Witnesses: Fredk. Fisher, Ab. Van Vechten. (MVL:29)

Schremling, George, of Canajoharie, Tryon Co. to John Rooff, of the same place. Deed dated 5/1/1778; recorded 11/14/1783. Description: Two lots of land situated on the south side of the Mohawk River in Tryon Co. and are part of a larger tract of land granted by Letters Patent on 6/20/1723 to Lewis Morris, Abraham Van Horne, Cadwallader Colden, James Alexander and Margaret Vedder. The first lot begins on the Mohawk River in the division line of Lots #5 and #6 of the said patent and runs to the Canajoharie or Schremling Kill or Creek, down through the middle of the creek to the said river and up the river to the place of beginning (325 acres). The second lot begins on the said Kill or Creek above the third or great fall on the said Creek (334 acres). Also parcels of land on the south side of the Mohawk River in a Patent granted on 2/10/1762 to Philip Livingston, Rudolph Keller and others. The north half of Lot #48 in the first tract (100 acres), the northeast equal quarter of Lot #56 in said tract (50 acres), the south half part of Lot #25 in the second tract (200 acres), the north half of Lot #34 in the same tract (200 acres). In addition the equal northwest fourth part of Lot #54 in the said first tract (50 acres and bounded on the east by land granted to Margaret Hess; south by that of Hendrick Klock; north and west by parts of Lot #53 & #35). Also the one-half of Lot #58 in the second tract (150 acres). Lastly, all the undivided right which George Schremling has to a patent on the south side of the Mohawk River granted to Peter DuBois, Adam Young, Frederick Young and Company comprehending several thousand acres of upland. Consideration: L3000. Witnesses: Jacob Klock, Chris. P. Yates. (MVL:29-30)

1790 Census

Scramlin, David [Appendix B]
Scramlin, George
Scramlin, Henry
Scramling, Henry

SCHULF

Birth/Baptism

Schulf, Christian & Elizabeth (Bierman): Maragriet, bapt. 7/4/1762 (DRC:7). Sponsors: Willem Snock & Catarina Snock.

SCHULER

Tryon County Militia

Schuler, Lorentz [Appendix A]

SCHULL

Birth/Baptism

Schull, Johannes & Maria [?]: Elisabetha, b. 3/2/1771 (LTSA:36); Johann, b. 8/13/1778, bapt. 8/16/1778 (LTSA:54). Sponsors: Fridrich Heine & his wife (re:1); Johann Hess & Eva

(re:2).

SCHULTZ

Marriage

Schultz, Henrich m. Anna Barbara Empie (widow of Jacob Empie), 4/20/1783 (RDSA:191; DRGF:197)

Schultz, Johannes m. Elisabeth Sutz, 9/9/1781 (DRGF:195)

Birth/Baptism

Schultz, Johann Jac:, Jr. & Catharina [?]: Benjamin, b. 11/15/1778, bapt. 11/22/1778 (LTSA:55); Catharina, b. 1/9/1783, bapt. 1/191/1783 (DRGF:66). Sponsors: Benjamin Engelland, Anna Empie (re:1); Growndetsh Kingets & Catharina (re:2).

Schultz/Schulz, Johannes & Anna [?]: Elisabeth, b. 2/22/1780, bapt. 2/26/1780 (LTSA:59); Anna, b. 9/16/1783, bapt. 10/9/1783 (DRGF:76); Catarina, b. 10/2/1792 (LTSA:70). Sponsors: Willhelm Schultz, Elisabeth Landmann (re:1); Pieter Lampmann & Elisabeth (re:2); John Nelles, Elisabet Lampmann (re:3).

Schultz, Johannes & Elisabeth (Sutz): Catharina, b. 4/1/1782, bapt. 4/7/1782 (DRGF:56); Elisabeth, b. 6/13/1787, bapt. 6/17/1787 (RDSA:113). Sponsors: Georg Schultz & Catharina (re:1); Peter P. Suz & his wife, Elisabeth (born: Gerster) (re:2).

Schultz, Johannes & Maria Magdalena [?]: Henricus, b. 2/21/1766; bapt. 3/2/1766 (RDSA:61). Sponsors: Henrich Saltzmann & Maria Elisabetha.

COMPENDIUM

Schulz, Christoph & Margaretha (Emig/Emgie): Wilhelmus, b. ?/?/1751 (LTSA:5). Sponsors: Wilhelm Emige, Maria Margaretha.

Schulz, Heinrich & Anna Barbara [?]: Catharina, b. 10/23/1790 (LTSA:66); Petrus, b. 5/25/1792 (LTSA:73); Margareta, b. 9/9/1794 (LTSA:85). Sponsors: Heinrich Dachstetter & Catharina (re:1); Peter Koch & Anna Eva (re:2); Peter Ries & Margareta (re:3).

Schulz, Henry & Sara [?]: Magdalena, b. 12/23/1790 (LTSA:66); Michel, b. 2/2/1793 (LTSA:77); Maria, b. 9/10/1795 (LTSA:91). Sponsors: Michel Bader & Magdalena (re:1); Michel Mohr & Margaret (re:2); Georg Schulz & Catarina (re:3).

Schulz, Jacob & [?]: Johannes, b. 2/21/1754 (LTSA:9). Sponsors: Hanes Schulz & his wife, Magdalena.

Schulz, Jacob & Catharina [?]: Margareta, b. 5/1/1791 (LTSA:67); Maria, b. 1/23/1793 (LTSA:77); Anna, b. 6/24/1795 (LTSA:90). Sponsors: Henry Kaiser & Margareta (re:1); Johannes Streher & Maria (re:2); Christophel Schulz, Anna Streher (re:3).

Schulz, Johannes, Jr. & Catharina [?]: Jacob, b. 9/26/1773 (LTSA:45). Sponsors: Jacob Schulz & Thoroadea [?].

Schulz, Johannes J. & Elisabet [?]: Anna, b. 5/?/1790 (LTSA:65); Maria, b. 2/2/1792 (LTSA:71); Peter, b. 4/10/1795 (LTSA:89); Nichoaus, b. 3/7/1796 (LTSA:93). Sponsors: Peter Suz & Elisabet (re:1); Johannes Nelles & Anna (re:1); Peter Merkel & Elisabet (re:3); Nicolaus Ekert & Barbara (re:4).

Tryon County Militia

Schultz, Hendrick   [Appendix A]
Schultz, Jacob
Schultz, John

Pension Abstract

Schultz, Jacob, b. 1760, Palatine, N.Y.; (uncle: General Nicholas Herkimer); resident of Martinsburg, Lewis Co., N.Y. on 9/21/1832. Jacob enlisted from Palatine in the summer of 1777 and served on various tours of duty, as a private, in the regiments of Cols. Klock and Waggoner, Tryon Co. Militia, into 1782; he was a participant in the battles of Oriskany and Palatine. (RWPA: #S11387)

Shults, George, b. 1758/9; resident of Onondaga Co., N.Y. in 1832. George enlisted from his home in Stone Arabia in 1775 as a private in Col. Jacob Klock's 2nd. Regt., Tryon Co. Militia; he served at various times into 1782; George was engaged in the battles of Oriskany, Stone Arabia, Turlock, Johnstown and West Canada Creek. (RWPA: #S14432)

Shults, Henry, b. 4/1/1750, Palatine, N.Y.; (brothers: John [older] and William [younger]); resident of Palatine, Montgomery Co., N.Y. on 9/6/1838. Henry enlisted in 1775 and served at various times until July 1782; he was a private in the regiments of Cols. Klock, Brown, Willett and Harper; he fought in the battles of Oriskany, Stone Arabia, Klock's Field, Landman's [Lampman's], and Johnstown; Henry and his two brothers, John and William, were working in a meadow, about three miles from Fort Paris, in July 1782 when they were captured by Indians and taken to Canada where they were held for one year and five months. (RWPA: #S14453)

1790 Census

708

Shoults, Henry   [Appendix B]
Shoults, John
Shoults, John Jacob
Shoultz, George
Shoultz, Henry I.
Shoultz, John I.

SCHUMANN

Birth/Baptism

Schumann, Johannes & [?]: Anna Gertraut, b. 5/9/1779; bapt. 6/15/1779 (DRGF:36). Sponsors: Johannes Bierhaussen & Anna Elisabeth.

Schumann, Wilhelm & Margretha [?]: Catharina, b. 11/29/1767, bapt. 1/10/1768 (RDSA:82); Catharina, b. 9/16/1769 (LTSA:29); Martin, b. 3/27/1771 (LTSA:35). Sponsors: Jacob Aallcajer & Catharina (re:1); Martinus Algaier & his wife (re:2); Martin Leffler, Catharina Ergeziner (r:3).

SCHUNK

Marriage

Schunk, John Nicol: m. Magdalena Fehling, 10/23/1792 (DFP:46)

SCHUPP

Tryon County Militia

Schupp, Nicholas   [Appendix A]

SCHUTT

Marriage

Schutt, Peter m. Elisabeth Gerlogh, 9/8/1795 (DFP:54)

Schutt, Wilhelm m. Catharina Harter (Little Falls), 10/20/1764 (RDSA:175)

Birth/Baptism

Schutt, Friederich & Elisabetha [?]: Maria, b. 4/8/1761, bapt. 4/23/1761 (RDSA:26); Johann Wilhelm, b. 3/27/1763, bapt. 4/26/1763 (RDSA:39); Johann Friedrich, b. 9/16/1764, bapt. 10/17/1764 (RDSA:51); Catharina, b. 3/11/1768, bapt. 4/17/1768 (RDSA:84); Nicolaus, b. 5/5/1776, bapt. 5/12/1776 (DRGF:17); Sussanna, b. 8/16/1778, bapt. 8/23/1778 (DRGF:32). Sponsors: Anna Maria Wehleben & Johann Werner Spaan (re:1); Wilhelm Schott & Elisabeth Hess (re:2); Joh. Friedr. Schumacher & Catharina (re:3); Catharina & P[?] Wohleben (re:4); Joh: Nicol Weber & Catharina (re:5); Thomas Schumacher & Susanna Flagg (re:6).

Schutt, Jacob & [?]: Johann Georg, bapt. 3/9/1767 (RDSA:73). Sponsors: [none named].

Schutt, Petrus & Catharina [?]: Abraham, b. 7/6/1778; bapt. 7/12/1778 (LTSA:53). Sponsors: Johann Joseph Finck & Elisabeth.

Schutt, Wilhelm & Catharina [?]: Maria Catharina, b. 6/20/1766, bapt. 6/21/1766 (RDSA:65); Appollonia, b. 6/20/1766, bapt. 6/21/1766 (RDSA:65); Johann Friedrich, b. 3/17/1768, bapt. 4/17/1768 (RDSA:84). Sponsors: Anna Maria & Johann Nicol Harter (re:1); Elisabeth & Friedr. Schutt (re:2); Friedrich Franck & Maria Elisabe[?] (re:3).

709

Schutt, Wilhelm & Margretha [?]: Elisabeth, b. 7/13/1769; bapt. 8/2/1769 (RDSA:95). Sponsors: Sophia Wohlebe[n] & Friedrich Hes[s].

Schutt, William & Susanna (Hover): Rebecca, b. 5/17/1787; bapt. 6/29/1787 (DRC:85). Sponsors: Fredrik Lewis & Rachel Lewis.

Death Record

Schutt, Catharina, (from Florida [Montgomery Co., N.Y.]), d. 8/18/1816, age 23 years; buried in the cemetery near the new church in the town of Herkimer (RDH:273)

1790 Census

Schut, William   [Appendix B]

SCHUTZ

Marriage

Schutz, Christian m. Maria Engel Fridrichsin, 1/12/1772 (LTSA:282)

Tryon County Militia

Schuts, Joseph   [Appendix A]

SCHUYLER

Marriage

Schuyler, David m. Hilletje Smidt, 10/31/1790 (DRGF:207)

Schuyler, David Ph. m. Margretha Kesslar

(widow of Peter Kesslar), 5/12/1784 (DRGF:199)

Schuyler, James N. (of Danube) m. Eliza Seber (of Canajoharie), 3/17/1833 (PCB:52)

Schuyler, Johann Jost m. Anna Schyler (widow of Phil. Schyler), 11/14/1784 (DRGF:200)

Schuyler, Nicholas P. m. Elisabeth H. Hergheimer, 11/14/1784 (DRGF:200)

Schuyler, Peter (son of Anton Schuyler, decd.) m. Catharina Weil (dau. of Franz Weil, Decd.), 4/20/1790 (DFP:41)

Birth/Baptism

Schuyler, David A. (of Canajoh. Castle) & Margretha (Wollever): Niclaus, bapt. 4/5/1790 (SJC:25); Lea, bapt. 7/29/1792 (SJC:62). Sponsors: John Wollever & Catharina Wollever (re:1); Peter Wollever & Catharina Wollever (re:2).

Schuyler, David Ph. (Canajoharie) & Hellstay [?]: Maria, bapt. 10/28/1792 (SJC:66). Sponsors: Johannes Schuyler & Maria Smith.

Schuyler, Jacob & Delia [?]: Margretha, b. 12/10/1775, bapt. 1/1/1776 (DRGF:15); Johannes, b. 9/3/1778, bapt. 9/4/1778 (DRGF:32); Philippus, b. 3/11/1781, bapt. 3/21/1781 (DRGF:43); Jacobus, b. 5/31/1785, bapt. 6/3/1785 (DRGF:97). Sponsors: Joh: Jost D: Petri & Maria J. Petri (re:1); Joh: Adam Stahle & Catharina (re:2); Joseph Maevi & Catharina (re:3); Georg Hergheimer, Esqr. & Alita (re:4).

Schuyler, Nicholas & Elisabetha [?]: Pieter David, b. 8/19/1785; bapt. 8/20/1785 (DRGF:100). Sponsors: Pieter Schyler, Jun: &

710

Catharin & Anna Schyler.

Schuyler, Nicholas P. (of Canajoh. Castle) & Elisabeth (Herchimer): Heinrich, bapt. 4/26/1789 (SJC:15); Johann Jost, bapt. 5/22/1791 (SJC:43); Margretha, b. 6/9/1793, bapt. 8/4/1793 (SJC:79). Sponsors: Severinus Deyggert & Magdalena Herchimer (re:1); John Herchimer & Anna Herchimer (re:2); Niclaus Herkemer & Margretha Herkemer (re:3).

Schuyler, Peter, Jr. & Catharina [?]: Elisabeth, b. 4/7/1777, bapt. 6/8/1777 (DRGF:23); Anna, b. 6/190/1779, bapt. 6/15/1779 (DRGF:36); Pieter, b. 7/3/1784, bapt. 9/5/1784 (DRGF:87). Sponsors: Margretha Rosencrantz & Nicolas Schyler (re:1); Georg Hergheimer Esqr. & Alita (re:2); Pieter Schyler & Elisabeth Barbara (re:3).

Schuyler, Peter A. (of Canajoharie Castle) & Catharina (Freymaurer): Abraham, b. 3/29/1789, bapt. 4/10/1789 (SJC:14); Johann Jost, b. 7/3/1792, bapt. 7/6/1792 (SJC:60); Anna, bapt. 11/24/1793 (SJC:85). Sponsors: Abraham Mebie & Margaretha Freymaurer (re:1); Joh. Jost Deygert & Gnelia Deygert (re:2); Heinrich Keller & Anna Wild (re:3).

Probate Abstract

Schuyler, Jacob, (of Florida), will dated 3/8/1825; probated 6/7/1825. Legatees: wife, Martha; daus., Effy Taylor, Sally Covenhoven, Rachel Covenhoven, Anna, Polly and Caty; sons, Richard, Jacob, John J., Jeremiah and Thomas. Executors: sons, John J. and Richard. Witnesses: George Bradshaw, Jesse Van Slyke, Daniel N. Heath. (WMC 57:183)

Schuyler, Jacob, [residence not stated], will dated 5/19/1806; probated 10/7/1807. Legatees: wife, Sarah; sons, William, Daniel, John,

Jacob, Philip and Samuel; daus., Elizabeth, Christena, Caty, Margred, Anna, Eva (wife of Israel Luce), and Dorado (wife of John Wiley). Executors: son, John; son-in-law, Richerd Fansher. Witnesses: Christian, William and John Servos, Jr. (WMC 56:156)

Schuyler, Peter, (of Palatine), will dated 11/24/1786; probated 1/9/1792. Legatees: Gertruy. Executrix: wife. Witnesses: Charles Newkerck, Douw Fonda, John Diell. (WMC 56:147)

Schuyler, Philip, II, (of Canajoharie), will dated 11/28/1806; probated 7/20/1807. Legatees: wife, Eve; sons, Philip (III) and Samuel; daus., Elizabeth, Anne, Eve, Mary and Margaret. Executors: two sons; John Schuiler (son-in-law). Witnesses: Ebenezer Hebberd, Samuel Bailey, John C. Toll. (WMC 56:156)

Tryon County Militia

Schuyler, David   [Appendix A]
Schuyler, Jacob
Schuyler, John Jost
Schuyler, Nicholas
Schuyler, Peter P.

Pension Abstract

Schuyler, David A., b. ca. 1761; resident of Herkimer Co., N.Y. in 1832. David volunteered from Fort Plain in January 1779 and served as a private in regiments commanded by Cols. Yates, Schuyler, and Willett; he served various tours of duty for a total service time of fourteen months. (RWPA: #S14423)

Schuyler, John S., m. Catharina Cuyler, 2/21/1793, Reformed Protestant Dutch Church, Schenectady, N.Y.; d. 12/2/1834,

711

Westmoreland, Oneida Co., N.Y. (Catharine Schuyler, b. 1772/3; resident of New Hartford, Oneida Co., N.Y. in 1846.) Children: Stephen, b. 11/2?/1793; Abram, b. 6/14/179?; Stephen, b. 6/30/1797; Cuyler, b. 11/26/1799; Katlin, b. 1/16/180?; Eycke, b. 7/?/180?; Margret, b. 1/?/1806; John, b. 5/2?/1809. John S. was a private in companies commanded by Capt. Sharp in Col. H.K. Van Rensselaer's Regt. and Capt. Thomas Skinner's Co., Col. Marinus Willett's Regt.; he served in the military for more than two years. (RWPA: #R9277)

Schuyler, Nicholas, m. [wite not named]; d. 2/20/1837, Herkimer Co., N.Y. Children: Peter N., b. 1786/7; Nicholas, Jr., Henry, George N., Philip, Daniel, James, Margaret (m. [?] Knieskern); Elizabeth Schuyler [all over the age of twenty-one years on 2/4/1846.] Nicholas was alleged to have been taken a prisoner during the war and carried to Canada where "he was kept several years in prison". (RWPA: #R9278)

Schuyler, Peter S., b. 5/12/1758, Watervliet, Albany Co., N.Y.; m. Catharine Cuyler, 12/5/1789; d. 11/1/1832, Watervliet, N.Y. (Catharine Schuyler, b. 4/17/1764; d. 9/28/1855.) Children: Engelica, b. 9/8/1790, d. 9/24/1793; Susanna, b. 4/17/1793, d. 9/17/1793; Engelica, b. 1/25/1795, d. 7/16/1796; [dau. not named], b. 7/18/1797, d. same day; Engelica, b. 10/7/1798; John Cuyler, b. 12/1/1804. Peter S. was elected in 1776 to be a lieutenant in Capt. Ostrom's Co., Col. Philip P. Schuyler's N.Y. Regt.; he marched in the expedition against Sir John Johnson and was present when he [Johnson] surrendered to Col. Schuyler; Peter S. was appointed a member of a Court Martial held in Albany for the trial of Tories; he was stationed near Lake George in the fall of 1776; Peter S. fought in the battle of Saratoga and was present when

Gen. John Burgoyne surrendered; he continued to serve as a lieutenant at various times in the same company and regiment until the end of the war; Peter S. was in several expeditions against the Indians and Tories in the Mohawk Valley and was stationed at Forts Herkimer and Hunter for a period of about two years. (RWPA: #W17778)

1790 Census

Schuyler, Cimon	[Appendix B]
Schuyler, David A.	
Schuyler, David P.	
Schuyler, Jacob	
Schuyler, John	
Schuyler, Lear	
Schuyler, Nicholas	
Schuyler, Peter	
Schuyler, Peter D.	
Schuyler, Peter P.	

SCHWARM

Birth/Baptism

Schwarm, Georg & Catharina [?]: Elisabetha, b. 5/26/1771 (LTSA:38). Sposors: Philipp Helmer & his wife.

SCHWARTZWALD

Birth/Baptism

Schwartzwald, Albert & Sophia [?]: Anna, b. 4/22/1770; bapt. 4/30/1770 (RDSA:102). Sponsors: Anna Zimmermann & Carl Bischoph.

COMPENDIUM

SCOTT

Marriage

Scott, [?] m. Christian Fisher, 10/29/1798 (JPC:92)

Scott, Thomas m. Maria Bender, 8/14/1766 (RDSA:179)

Birth/Baptism

Scott, John & Maria [?]: Sander, b. 2/11/1782; bapt. 2/17/1782; d. 2/18/1782 (DRGF:54). Sponsors: Sander Martin & Margretha.

Scott, Joseph & Cornelia (Oosterhout): Jannetje, b. 4/16/1778; bapt. 5/3/1778 (DRC:47). Sponsors: Hannes Flipse & Jannetje Delyne.

Scott, Thomas & Maria [?]: David, b. 8/12/1767, bapt. 8/16/1767 (RDSA:77); Anna, b. 1/16/1769, bapt. 1/22/1769 (RDSA:93); Andreas, b. 3/4/1783, bapt. 3/11/1783 (DRGF:69). Sponsors: Pieter Hauss & wife, Maria (re:1); Eva Coppernole & Johannes Emg[ie] (re:2); Andreas Reeber & Maria (re:3).

Scott, William & Sary (Snyder): Mary, b. 9/30/1790; bapt. 12/8/1790 (DRC:91). Sponsors: [?] Snyder & Elizabeth Scot.

Death Record

Scott, Catharina, b. 1/11/1763, (did live with her husband two years and seven months, has one child); d. 8/11/1791 (RDSA:232)

Scott, Jane, (widow), d. 4/12/1837, age 64 years, of consumption; buried Cherry Valley Presbyterian Church cemetery (PCV:87)

Probate Abstract

Scott, Barent, (of Minden), will dated 8/13/1828; probated 1/1/1829. Legatees: wife, Nelly; dau., Mary Catharine. Executors: wife; Abraham Devendorff. Witnesses: John D. Lipe, James Post/Port[?], Henry Cook. (WMC 57:273)

Tryon County Militia

Scott, James   [Appendix A]
Scott, Joseph

1790 Census

Scott, [?]   [Appendix B]
Scott, David
Scott, Elijah
Scott, Henry
Scott, James
Scott, John (2)
Scott, Joseph
Scott, Thomas

SCOVILLE

Death Record

Scoville, Daniel, (son of Lyman & Elizabeth Scoville), d. 2/13/1834, age 19 years; buried sect. 6, Colonial Cemetery, Johnstown (JC:187)

Scoville, Daniel, b. 5/25/1756; d. 1/9/1813; buried just north of Elizabeth, wife of Lyman Scovill, in the Colonial Cemetery, Johnstown (JC:190) [Daniel Scoville, private, belonged to Capt. Daniel Hand's Company, Connecticut Militia that assisted in fortifying Brooklyn Heights in the spring of 1776.]

713

COMPENDIUM

Scoville, Eliza, (dau. of Lyman & Elizabeth Scoville), d. 1/21/1811, age 26 years; buried sect. 6, Colonial Cemetery, Johnstown (JC:187)

Scoville, Elizabeth, (wife of Lyman Scoville), d. 2/13/1840, age 54 years, 3 months; buried sect. 6, Colonial Cemetery, Johnstown (JC:187)

Scoville, Lyman, d. 7/25/1840, age 59 years, 5 months; buried sect. 6, Colonial Cemetery, Johnstown (JC:187)

Scoville, Mary, (dau. of Lyman & Elizabeth Scoville), d. 7/27/1811, age 1 year, 6 months, 8 days; buried sect. 6, Colonial Cemetery, Johnstown (JC:187)

Scoville, Sarah Coffin, (dau. of John & Marissa Clarissa Scoville), d. 1/20/1832, age 1 year, 1 month; buried sect. 6, Colonial Cemetery, Johnstown (JC:187)

SCOWTEN (also see SCHOWTEN)

Birth/Baptism

Scowten, Jesajas & Margretha [?]: Abraham, b. 2/20/1785; bapt. 3/6/1785 (DRGF:94). Sponsors: Jacob J. Dieffendorff & Anna Dieffendorff.

Scowten, Jesjas & Maria [?]: Catharina, b. 1/11/1783; bapt. 1/19/1783 (DRGF:66). Sponsors: Johannes Dachstaeder & Catharina Glock.

Death Record

Scouten, John, b. 6/17/1775; d. 4/13/1794; buried 4/15/1794 (DFP:85)

SCRIBNER

1790 Census

Scribner, Aaron   [Appendix B]

SCRIVER

Death Record

Scriver, Catharine, d. 4/12/1818, age 47 years; buried sect. 8, Colonial Cemetery, Johnstown (JC:187)

Scriver, Simeon, d. 5/4/1814, age 43 years; buried sect. 8, Colonial Cemetery, Johnstown (JC:187)

SEAHOUSE

1790 Census

Seahouse, Yost   [Appendix B]

SEAMORE

1790 Census

Seamore, Ebenezer   [Appendix B]
Seamore, Enos
Seamore, Sarah
Seamore, Uriah

SEARS

COMPENDIUM

1790 Census

Sears, Allen   [Appendix B]

SEBOR

1790 Census

Sebor, Henry   [Appendix B]

SECKLER

Birth/Baptism

Seckler, John (Canajoharie) & Anna [?]: Charlotta, bapt. 5/5/1793, age 2 years (SJC:75); Mary, bapt. 5/5/1793, age 4 months (SJC:75). Sponsors: Conrad Counterman & Margretha Counterman (re:1); Adam Bellinger & Elisabeth Bellinger (re:2).

SEDAND

Birth/Baptism

Sedand, Charles & Fanny (Britton): Nelly, bapt. [date not stated] (JDR:21)

SEEBER (also see SEEVER)

Marriage

Seeber, Gottfrid m. Elisabeth Lauchs, 11/16/1769 (RDSA:188)

Seeber, Henrich (son of Wilhelm Seeber) m. Anna Eva Kessler (dau. of Tomas Kessler), 5/9/1790 (DFP:41)

Seeber, Henrich m. Veronica Berleth, 5/7/1767 (RDSA:182)

Seeber, Isaac m. Christina Harth, 1/19/1792 (DFP:45)

Seeber, Jacob m. Elisabeth Barbara Laux, 3/18/1766 (RDSA:179)

Seeber, Johannes (son of Wilh: Seeber, decd.) m. Margaretha Diel (dau. of John Diel, decd.), 1/9/1791 (DFP:43)

Seeber, Johannes m. Maria Wohlgemuth, 11/8/1768 (RDSA:184)

Seeber, Wilhelm J: m. Elisabeth Schnerr, 10/2/1764 (RDSA:175)

Birth/Baptism

Seeber, Henrich & Elisabetha [?]: Marines Willet, b. 8/10/1782; bapt. 8/25/1782 (DRGF:60). Sponsors: Marines Willet, Colln. [Colonel] & Elisabeth Davis.

Seeber, Henrich & Veronica [?]: Margretha, b. 7/22/1768, bapt. 8/1/1768 (RDSA:88); Wilhelmus, b. 3/22/1770, bapt. 4/1/1770 (RDSA:101). Sponsors: Maria Elisabeth & Johannes Berlet (re:1); Friedrich Emgie & Maria Elisabeth (re:2).

Seeber, Jacob & Barbara Elisabetha [?]: Maria Elisabetha, b. 12/24/1766, bapt. 12/28/1766 (RDSA:71); Margretha, b. 1/6/1772, bapt. 1/19/1772 (RDSA:110). Sponsors: Maria Elisabeth Sever & Pieter Laux (re:1); Severines Seeber & Margreth Wohl[?] (re:2).

715

COMPENDIUM

Seeber, Jacob & Elizabeth (Tyger [Dygert]): Willem, b. 1/22/1779, bapt. 6/27/1779 (DRC:53); Sepherinus, bapt. 10/20/1781 at age 3 weeks (DRC:59); Lena, b. 8/26/1783, bapt. 9/27/1783 (DRC:68); Thiobolt, bapt. 3/12/1786 at age 4 weeks (DRC:77). Sponsors: Cobus Seeber & Maragriet Tyger (re:1); Peter Schremling & Anna Mari Tulbach (re:2); Hendk. Tyger & Anna Maria Tyger (re:3); Thiobolt Tygert & Congunda Tygert (re:4).

Seeber, Jacob & Maria Esther [?]: Jacob, b. 5/2/1760; bapt. 5/8/1760 (RDSA:20). Sponsors: Jacob (son of Jacob Sever) & Anna Maria (dau. of Henrich Dillenbach).

Seeber, Johannes & Mary (Harts): Mari-herter, b. 2/21/1780; bapt. 3/6/1780 (DRC:55). Sponsors: Christiaan Wilkley & Mari herter Seever.

Seeber, Wilhelm & Elisabeth [?]: Elisabetha, b. 9/16/1782; bapt. 9/29/1782 (DRGF:63). Sponsors: Georg Gerlach & [?].

Seeber, Wilhelm, Jr. & Elisabeth [?]: Isaacus, b. 2/4/1765, bapt. 2/11/1765 (RDSA:53); Maria, b. 9/21/1767, bapt. 10/6/1767 (RDSA:78). Sponsors: Isaac Paris & his wife, Catharina (re:1); Maria Smidt & Conrad Seever (re:2).

Seeber, William & [?]: Eva, bapt. 9/27/1791 (DRC:100). Sponsors: Jacob [?] & [?].

Death Record

Seeber, [?], (child of Wm. H. Seeber), d. 11/20/1812, 26 days (DFP:95)

Seeber, Anna Maria, (widow), b. 11/1/1712; d. 11/25/1789; buried 11/26/1789 (left behind 8 children, 28 grandchildren, 13 great-grandchildren) (DFP:78-79)

Seeber, Catharina, (legitimate dau. of Wilhelm Seeber), b. 9/17/1787; d. 8/12/1788 (at 7 A.M. from the worm sickness & waste); buried 8/13/1788 (DFP:78-79)

Seeber, Conrad, d. 9/?/1812, age 63 years, 4 months, 29 days; buried 9/2/1812 (DFP:95)

Seeber, Elizabeth, (wife of Jacob Seeber), d. 6/18/1834, age 51 years, 5 months (stone inscription: "A friend, a wife and mother sleeps"); buried in the Seeber Cemetery, located on the former Seeber Copley farm, Clinton Road, near Sprout Brook, Minden (SC 243:71)

Seeber, Henry, d. 9/?/1830, age 73 years; buried Seeber Cemetery, located on the former Seeber Copley farm, Clinton Road, near Sprout Brook, Minden (SC 243:71)

Seeber, Jacob, d. 12/23/1854, age 77 years, 4 months, 17 days (stone inscription: "Gone but not lost"); buried in the Seeber Cemetery, located on the former Seeber Copley farm, Clinton Road, near Sprout Brook, Minden (SC 243:71)

Seeber, Johannes, (son of the deceased Johannes Seeber), d. 7/10/1795, age 23 years, 5 months, less 2 days; buried 7/12/1795 (RDSA:236)

Seeber, Maria, (wife of Conrad Seeber), d. 4/?/1813, age 60 years, 8 months; buried 4/23/1813 (DFP:96)

Seeber, Maria, (wife of Jacobus Seeber & born: Keller); b. 3/1/1766; m. 7/20/1784; d. 4/3/1791 (left 3 children); buried 4/5/1791 (DFP:82)

Seeber, Maria Elisa, (dau. of Adam Seeber), d.

716

COMPENDIUM

1/?/1808, age 4 years, 2 months, 2 days; buried 1/30/1808 (DFP:91)

Seeber, (legitimate son of Isaac Seeber), d. 12/5/1793, age 2 months, less one day; buried 12/7/1793 (RDSA:234)

Probate Abstract

Seeber, William, [residence not stated], will dated 9/23/1810; codicil dated 7/28/1821; probated 6/2/1828. Legatees: wife, Elizabeth; sons, John, Henry (decd. & his Margaret and William H.), Adolphus; daus., Mary Elizabeth, Elizabeth and Maria. Codicil: Wife now dead and John moved away. Executors: wife; brother, John. Witnesses: Silas Adsit, James Adsit, Eliza Seeber (to the will); David and John R. Failing, Jacob Wendell (to the codicil). New Executors: [1828] John Warner, Lawrence Gros. (WMC 57:271)

Tryon County Militia

Seeber, Conrad   [Appendix A]
Seeber, Jacob
Seeber, John
Seeber, John W.
Seeber, William

Pension Abstract

Seeber, Henry, b. 1745/6; m. [wife not named]; resident of Johnstown, Montgomery Co., N.Y. on 11/25/1786 when he received an invalid pension. Children: Suffrenes (resident of Warren, Herkimer Co., N.Y. on 2/17/1858). Henry was a private in the 1st. Regt., Tryon Co. Militia and served in Capt. Rynier Van Everen's Co.; particpated in the battle of Oriskany on 8/6/1777 and received "two gunshot wounds in the right thigh, one near the hip joint the other alittle below and one in the

left thigh-- and further that the degree of disability under which he now labours is total". (RWPA: #S27469)

Deed Abstract

Seeber, Henry William, yeoman, of Tryon Co. to Conrad Seeber, of the same place. Deed dated 7/24/1783; recorded 8/23/1783. Description: Henry William Seeber sold all his crops on the ground, eleven hogs small and great, all bonds, notes and debts due to him, and all his moveable household goods. Signed and sealed on 7/24/1783 by Henry William Seeber at Fort Rensselaer. Consideration: no payment recorded. Witnesses: Lawrence Gros, William Robertson. (MVL:30)

1790 Census

Seeber, Conradt   [Appendix B]
Seeber, James
Seeber, John
Seeber, William

SEEGER

Birth/Baptism

Seeger, Johannes & Rebecca (Baus): Rebecca, b. 2/25/1785 (RDSA:111); Henrich, b. 4/13/1787, bapt. 4/15/1787 (RDSA:113). Jacob Wallrad, jr. & Rebecca von Schleick (re:1); Peter Wallrad & Anna Eva Hellekas (re:2).

Seeger, Johannes & Sarah (Vander Roof): Maryche, b. 8/25/1772; bapt. 9/13/1772 (DRC:23). Sponsors: Thomas Seeger & Polly Weever.

Seger, Johann & Engel (Bradt): Susanna, b.

717

2/26/1780; bapt. 4/6/1780 (LTSA:60). Sponsors: Johann Bradt & Susanna.

1790 Census

Segar, Thomas   [Appendix B]

SEELBACH

Birth/Baptism

Seelbach, Arnold & Anna Sybilla [?]: Maria Elisabetha, b. 9/30/1763, bapt. 10/9/1763 (RDSA:42); Anna, b. 3/8/1765, bapt. 3/24/1765 (RDSA:54). Sponsors: Johann Georg Densman & Anna Maria, wife of Georg Exen (re:1); Anna Margretha & Johannes Schaffer (re:2).

Tryon County Militia

Seelbach, Johannes   [Appendix A]

1790 Census

Selleback, John   [Appendix B]

SEELY

Death Record

Seely, Theoda H., d. 7/6/1828, age 44 years; buried Cherry Valley Presbyterian Church cemetery (PCV:83)

Seely, William Henry, (son of Isaac & Julia Seelye), d. 1822, age 14 years; buried Cherry Valley Presbyterian Church cemetery (PCV:78)

Seelye, Isaac, d. 3/15/1833, age 54 years, of "a Paralytick stroke"; buried Cherry Valley Presbyterian Church cemetery (PCV:85)

1790 Census

Seeley, James   [Appendix B]
Seeley, Nathaniel
Seeley, Nathaniel, Jr.
Seeley, Samuel
Seely, Bezeliel
Seley, David
Seley, John

SEERVERSTEEN

Birth/Baptism

Seerversteen, Jacob & Sarah (Bernhart): Elizabeth, b. 4/25/1775; bapt. 5/27/1775 (DRC:33). Sponsors: [none named].

SEEVER (also see SEEBER)

Birth/Baptism

Seever, Henderick & Pryna (Berlet): Maria Magdalena, b. 11/18/1773; bapt. 12/5/1773 (DRC:27). Sponsors: Hendrick Dogsteder Junr. & Magdalena Dogsteder.

Seever, Jacob & Engeltje (Van Slyk): Maragrita, bapt. 12/17/1784 at age 7 weeks (DRC:69). Sponsors: Thomas Zeele & Maragrita Funda.

Seever, Martin (Canajoharie) & Maria [?]: Catharina, bapt. 12/23/1792 (SJC:68). Sponsors: James Siever & Catharina Siever.

COMPENDIUM

SEGNER

Seldon, Benjamin   [Appendix B]

Marriage

Segner, Conrad m. Margreth P. Pfeiffer,
5/23/1786 (DRGF:203)

Segner, Johann Paul m. Eisabetha Eisemann (of
Little Falls), 3/12/1762 (RDSA:171)

Birth/Baptism

Seghner, Paul & Maria Elisabeth [?]: Johann
Antoni, bapt. 1/6/1763 (RDSA:37); Conradus,
b. 11/23/1764, bapt. 12/5/1764 (RDSA:52);
Maria Magdalena, b. 3/1/1767, bapt. 4/30/1767
(RDSA:75); Anna, b. 6/17/1769, bapt.
8/1/1769 (RDSA:95); Antony, b. 8/19/1776,
bapt. 9/9/1776 (DRGF:20); Jannitje, b.
3/16/1779, bapt. 4/9/1779 (DRGF:35); [?], b.
1/19/1782, bapt. 1/22/1782 (DRGF:54).
Sponsors: Johann Antoni Eisenman & Jannetje
(re:1); Conrad Franck, esqr. & his wife (re:2);
Maria Orhrndorff & Joh. Stephan Eisenman
(re:3); Cptn. Johann Jost Hergheimer &
Marg[?] (re:4); Johann Jost Bell & Maria
Bekker (re:5); Johannes Eisenmann & Jannitje
(re:6); Pieter Wohleben & Bally Niers (re:7).

SEIMER

Tryon County Militia

Seimer, Isaac   [Appendix A]

SELDON

1790 Census

SELMSER

Marriage

Selmser, Hendk. m. Anna Maria Ehanisin,
3/13/1776 (DRC:161)

SELNAAR

Birth/Baptism

Selnaar, Ambrosus & Margarita (Schefin):
Elizabeth, bapt. 1/27/1765 (DRC:14); Maria,
bapt. 9/14/1765 (DRC:15). Sponsors: Philip
Philipse & Elizabeth Wanner (re:1); Jacob
Alkajer & Maria Wals (re:2).

SELTER

Probate Abstract

Selter, Henry, (of Oppenheim), will dated
3/28/1813; probated 7/11/1816. Legatees: sons,
Calvin, Jonathan and Henry; dau., Zerujah.
Executors: son, Jonathan; William Lasscells.
Witnesses: Jesse Dayton, John Leek, William
Steward. (WMC 57:163)

SEMPLE (also see SAMPLE)

Tryon County Militia

Semple, Hugh   [Appendix A]

719

COMPENDIUM

Semple, Samuel

SERENIAS

1790 Census

Serenias, Christopher [Appendix B]

SERVICE

Marriage

Service, Daniel m. Catharina Dachstatter, 2/21/1771 (RDSA:190)

Service, Johannes m. Catharina Schenck, 10/1/1769 (RDSA:187)

Service, Philip m. Maria Catharina Seever (dau. of Jac: Seever), 9/6/1769 (RDSA:187)

Servis, John m. Catharine Pettengall, both of Warrensbush, 1/29/1789 (JDR:#79)

Birth/Baptism

Service, Christian & Catrina (Overback): Maria, b. 10/9/1778, bapt. 1/17/1779 (DRC:51); Peter, b. 10/10/1780, bapt. 10/29/1780 (DRC:57); Annatje, b. 5/22/1785, bapt. 1/21/1786 (DRC:75). Sponsors: [none named] (re:1-3).

Service, Christopher & Clara (Crief): Christiaan, bapt. 1758 (DRC:1). Sponsors: Johannes Winkel & Catarina Winkel.

Service, Daniel & Cattrien (Dogsteder): Catrina, b. 11/13/1772; bapt. 11/8/1772 [Note: Either the birth or baptismal date is incorrect in the record] (DRC:23). Sponsors: Hendrick Dogsteder & Cattrina Dogsteder.

Service, Frederick & Appollonia (Johnson): Catrina, b. 6/29/1777; bapt. 7/6/1777 (DRC:43). Sponsors: Richard Service & Elizabeth Service.

Service, Frederick & Efje (Janson): John, b. 9/23/1779, bapt. 12/19/1779 (DRC:54); Aaron, b. 7/29/1783, bapt. 7/27/1783 [Note: Either the birth or baptismal date is incorrect in the record] (DRC:67). Sponsors: Frans Cosaadt & Nancy Janson (re:1); [none named] (re:2).

Service, George & Maria (Overback): Lena, b. 12/6/1780, bapt. 1/15/1781 (DRC:59); Wilhelmus, b. 1/18/1785, bapt. 2/19/1785 (DRC:70). Sponsors: Laurence Shever & Sarah Seber (re:1); [none named] (re:2).

Service, Peter & Lena (Miller): Philip, b. 2/8/1775, bapt. 4/16/1775 (DRC:33); Thomas, b. 11/27/1777, bapt. 1/8/1778 (DRC:46); Alida, b. 4/1/1786, bapt. 6/5/1786 (DRC:80). Sponsors: John Service & Catrina Service (re:1); Adam Klyne & Helena Kitts (re:2); Hendrik Visbak & Maria Visbak (re:3).

Service, Petrus & Helena [?]: Willhelm, b. 2/13/1780; bapt. 3/5/1780 (LTSA:60). Sponsors: Adam Ruppert & Barbara.

Service, Philip & Catrina (Shaver): Johan Jacob, b. 2/13/1773, bapt. 2/17/1773 (DRC:24); Catrina, b. 3/18/1775, bapt. 3/26/1775 (DRC:33); Mari Ester, b. 6/8/1777, bapt. 7/6/1777 (DRC:43); Joannis, b. 3/14/1780, bapt. 3/28/1780 (DRC:56). Sponsors: Hannis Sever & Anna Service (re:1);

720

COMPENDIUM

Johannis Service & Catrina Service (re:2); Johannis Shaver & Maria Shaver (re:3); Johannis Emer & Maria Service (re:4).

Service, Philipp & Catharina [?]: Magdalena, b. 6/25/1770 (LTSA:32). Sponsors: Peter Serves & his wife.

Service, William & Sophia (Young): Willem, b. 3/12/1777, bapt. 4/25/1777 (DRC:42); Maragrita, b. 12/13/1783, bapt. 5/11/1784 (DRC:69). Sponsors: Peter Yong & Eva Yong (re:1); Peter Young & Maragrita Young (re:2).

Probate Abstract

Service, George, (of the town of Florida), will dated 5/10/1811; probated 6/15/1812. Legatees: wife, Mary; sons, Solomon, George, Philip, Lawrence, Wilhelmus, John and David; daus., Sophia, Mary and Sarah. Executors: son, Lawrence; son-in-law, Peter P. Young. Witnesses: Winslow Paige, Jacob Staley, Benjamin Ovarbagh. (WMC 56:384)

Serviss, Christian, (of Florida), will dated 10/18/1821; probated 3/15/1826. Legatees: sons, John, William, Peter and Jacob; daus., Mary (wife of William Schuyler), Sarah (decd. & her Caty, Elizabeth and Daniel Campbell), Caty (decd. & her Elizabeth and Caty Thomas). Executors: son, John C.; son-in-law, William William [sic.] Schuyler. Witnesses: Rachel Liswell, Maria and Jane Lansing. (WMC 57:185-186)

Tryon County Militia

Service, Christian   [Appendix A]
Service, Frederick
Service, George
Service, John
Service, Philip

Service, Richard

Pension Abstract

Service, John, b. 12/25/1760, Johnstown, N.Y.; (brother: Philip, b. 1766/7; living in Florida, Montgomery Co., N.Y. in 1832; cousin: Christian Service); resident of Florida, N.Y. on 9/19/1832. John enlisted in April 1778 and served as a private and sergeant under Capts. David McMaster, Solomon Woodworth, and Garret Putnam in the regiments of Cols. Frederick Fisher and Marinus Willett; John served in the summer of 1779 as a substitute for his cousin, Christian Servoss. (RWPA: #S22971 *SERVOSS*)

Deed Abstract

Servis, Frederick, farmer, of Tryon Co., to his brother, Richard Servis, tailor, of the same place. Deed dated 4/7/1783; recorded 3/28/1786. Description: Frederick Servis' equal share of land (147 acres) on Charlotte River in Tryon Co., willed to him by his brother, Henry Servis, decd., jobber, late of the said county, in his Last Will and Testament, dated 1/13/1775. (Henry Servis purchased the said land from Sir William Johnson on 2/6/1773 for the sum of L67.1/8). Consideration: L5. Witnesses: William Schuyler, Elizabeth Servis. (MVL:30)

1790 Census

Service, Christian (2)   [Appendix B]
Service, Frederick
Service, George
Service, John
Service, Peter
Service, William

721

COMPENDIUM

SETTEL

Marriage

Settel, Sam m. Maria Kamer, 3/9/1767 (RDSA:181)

SEUFFER

Birth/Baptism

Seuffer, Johannes & Maria [?]: Anna Maria, b. 5/19/1766, bapt. 6/23/1766 (RDSA:65); Johannes, b. 6/19/1768, bapt. 7/14/1768 (RDSA:88); Elisabetha, b. 3/16/1770, bapt. 3/22/1770 (RDSA:101); Maria Catharina, b. 9/4/1777, bapt. 9/6/1777 (DRGF:26); Margretha, b. 9/17/1779, bapt. 9/26/1779 (DRGF:37). Sponsors: Maria & Johann Nicolas Hergheimer (re:1); Werner Teychart & his wife, Lena (re:2); Mr. Joh: Nicolas Hergheimer & his wife, Maria (re:3); Maria Hergheimer & Joh: Jost Schyler (re:4); John van Sleik & Margretha (re:5).

Seuffer, Johannes (of Schneidersbusch) & Anna Maria [?]: Gertrud, bapt. 3/10/1789 (SJC:11). Sponsors: Georg Louks & Gertrud Louks.

SEVERT

1790 Census

Severt, Jacob   [Appendix B]

SEWARD

1790 Census

Seward, Nathan   [Appendix B]

SEXTON

1790 Census

Sexton, James   [Appendix B]

SEYDELMAN

Marriage

Seydelman, Johannes m. Anna Maria [?], 8/4/1761 (RDSA:169)

SEYMORE

Birth/Baptism

Saymoure/Seymour, James & [?]: Sarah, b. 4/7/1798, bapt. 2/17/1798 (JPC:14); Catharine, bapt. 8/24/1800 (JPC:18).

Death Record

Seymore, Sarah, (wife of James Seymore), d. 5/24/1795, age 40 years, 14 days; buried sect. 3, Colonial Cemetery, Johnstown (JC:187)

SHADDOCK

COMPENDIUM

Tryon County Militia

Shaddock, James   [Appendix A]
Shaddock, Thomas

Pension Abstract

Shaddock, Thomas, m. Evelina Frank, 6/22/1771; d. 8/18/1815. (Evelina Shaddock, b. 1752/3; [brothers: Albert and Andrew Frank]; resident of Albany, N.Y. on 6/4/1839.) Thomas served in Col. Frederick Fisher's 3rd. Regt., Tryon Co. Militia and in Col. Marinus Willett's Regt. of the N.Y. Line; "Thomas Shaddock was a favorite in said regiment being of a lively disposition and always disposed to frolic. He was nick named 'Tommy Jigger' in consequence of his excellence in dancing jigs"; Thomas marched on an expedition in 1777 to Sacondaga under the command of Capt. Gardinier. (RWPA: #W19027)

SHAFFEE

1790 Census

Shaffee, Joseph   [Appendix B]

SHALLOP

Marriage

Shellup, Henry m. Catharine Connelly, Warrensbush, 10/13/1778 (JDR:1)

Shillop, Christian m. Jenny Truman, ?/?/1786 (JDR:3)

Birth/Baptism

Shellip, Henrick & Catharine (Connelly), Warrensborough: Patrick, bapt. 10/18/1786 (JDR:21); Henrick, b. 7/31/1789, bapt. 10/25/1789 (JDR:15).

Probate Abstract

Shallop, Henry, Sr., (of Charleston), will dated 3/26/1818 [should be 1817, according to probate date]; probated 10/4/1817. Legatees: wife, Catharine; sons, Henry, John, Patrick, William, Christian, Hugh (& his son, Henry); daus., Polly and Elizabeth. Executors: wife; Henry Shallop, John Merrell. Witnesses: Christian Wyckoff, William Putman, Samuel Tallmadge. (WMC 57:165)

Tryon County Militia

Shilip, Christian   [Appendix A]
Shilip, Frederick

1790 Census

Shallup, Hendrick   [Appendix B]
Shalop, Christian

SHANKCLING

1790 Census

Shankcling, Alexander   [Appendix B]

SHANLEY

Birth/Baptism

Shanley, Laurence & Charity (Pinkeny), Florida: Daniel, bapt. 1/9/1803 (JDR:12).

COMPENDIUM

SHARE

Birth/Baptism

Share, Lodowick & Margaret (Gauncy), Half
Moon: Susanna, bapt. 7/9/1786 (JDR:23).

SHARES

1790 Census

Shares, Lenox   [Appendix B]

SHARPENSTINE

Probate Abstract

Sharpenstine, Jacob, (of the town of Florida),
will dated 5/16/1821; probated 4/15/1822.
Legatees: wife, Mary; sons, John, Mathias,
Samuel, Benjamin and Peter; daus., Sarah,
Gertrude, Rebecca, Anna, and Mary Staley
(decd. & her daus., Anna and Lydia);
grandsons, Martin, John and Barnhardt
Buskark. Executors: son, John; John C.
Serviss. Witnesses: William Johnson, Joseph
and Harmanus R. Staley. (WMC 57:173)

Tryon County Militia

Sharpenstine, Jacob   [Appendix A]

1790 Census

Sharpenstine, Jacob   [Appendix B]

SHASHA

Tryon County Militia

Shasha, Abraham   [Appendix A]
Shasha, William

SHAUL see SCHALL

SHAUT

Probate Abstract

Shaut, Theodarus, (of Minden), will dated
12/9/1801; probated 3/11/1806. Legatees: wife,
Mary; sons, John, George and Jacob; dau.,
Hannah (wife of Peter C. House & her dau.,
Mary). Executors: Christopher Monk, Abraham
Coopman. Witnesses: Christopher Monk,
Christiana Monk, Adam Oliver. (WMC 56:155)

SHAVER (also see SCHAFER)

Birth/Baptism

Shaver, Hendrick & Catrina (Barlet): Barber,
b. 3/6/1787; bapt. 3/29/1787 (DRC:83).
Sponsors: Jacob Fredrik & Margrita Fredrik.

Shaver, John & Maria (Harts): Anna, bapt.
8/18/1778 [Note: 4 weeks old] (DRC:49).
Sponsors: Hendrik Haan & Anna Haan.

Shaver, Philip & Elizabeth (Angst): Jacob,
bapt. 1764 (DRC:12); Philip, bapt. 6/17/1769
(DRC:17); Barbara, b., [not stated], bapt.
5/25/1772 (DRC:20); Marrigrita, b. 4/21/1772,
bapt. 5/25/1772 (DRC:20); Hendrick, bapt.

724

6/19/1774 (DRC:29); Peter, b. 9/27/1776, bapt. 10/29/1776 (DRC:39). Sponsors: Jacob Neef & Catarina Neef (re:1); Jacob Kits & Eva Kits (re:2); Hans Neef & Anna Neef (re:3); Hendrick Bussart & Elizabeth Bussart (re:4); Hendrick Jane & Christina Bosart (re:5); John Kitts & Annatje Kitts (re:6).

Probate Abstract

Shaver, Bartholomew, (of Palatine), will dated 8/15/1805; probated 3/7/1817. Legatees: wife, Dorothy; sons, George, John, Harmanus, Henry and Frederic; dau., Margaret (unmarried). Executrix: wife. Witnesses: Stephen Coggswell, John Groff, Abraham Mabie. (WMC 57:164)

Shaver, George, (of Palatine), will dated 2/26/1807; probated 2/27/1808. Legatees: wife, Betsey; unborn child; brothers, Andrew, Henry, Nicholas, Peter and John. Executors: brothers, Nicholas and John; Jacob J. Failing. Witnesses: James Parker, Michael V. Panter, John C. House. (WMC 56:157)

Pension Abstract

Shaver, Henry, b. 1/15/1760, near Fort Plain, N.Y.; (father: [not named] was killed by Indians early in the Revolution); resident of Stark, Herimer Co., N.Y. on 10/10/1832. Henry entered the military from Fort Plank in Canajoharie [where his mother and family had moved following the death of his father] and served as a private in Capt. Ehle's Co., Col. Peter Gansevoort's Regt. of the N.Y. Line from 1778 through 1779; he entered Col. Hay's Regt. in the spring of 1780 and served for nine months or one year; he served for another nine months starting in the spring of 1781, in Capt. Lawrence Gross' Co., Col. Marinus Willett's Regt.; Henry was in the battle of Johnstown

and "the morning after the battle he was among forty white men and several Indians who were selected by Col. Willett to go in pursuit of the Indians and Tories who were under Walter Butler, they killed Butler on West Canada Creek and an Indian scalped him and they took fourteen prisoners"; he enlisted again in the spring of 1782 for nine months service in Capt. Abner French's Co. of the same regiment. (RWPA: #S11376)

1790 Census

Shaver, Adam   [Appendix B]
Shaver, Henry

SHAVES

1790 Census

Shaves, John   [Appendix B]

SHAW

Probate Abstract

Shaw, William, (of Johnstown), will dated 6/8/1826; probated 8/24/1826. Legatees: wife, Sally; son, Marvel; daus., Susan and Caroline. Executors: wife and son; Solomon Jeffers. Witnesses: Robert Weaver, Richard Shaw, William Lowry. (WMC 57:266)

1790 Census

Shaw, Comfort   [Appendix B]
Shaw, Samuel

COMPENDIUM

SHEADELL

Probate Abstract

Sheadell, Ezra, (of Oppenheim), will dated 12/1/1829; probated 12/18/1829. Legatees: wife, Polly; sons, Daniel and Rufus; daus., Sophia (wife of John Greenfield) and Mary Cross. Executors: two sons. Witnesses: Joseph Hewit, Samuel M. Slawson, Nicholas H. Cool. (WMC 57:276)

SHEAPY

Marriage

Sheapy, Henry m. Anna Forbes (widow of John Forbes), 2/1/1795 (DRGF:212)

SHEARMAN

1790 Census

Shearman, James   [Appendix B]
Shearman, Levy
Shearman, Solomon

SHEEIN

Birth/Baptism

Sheein, William & Elizabeth (Comerson): John, b. 11/22/1774; bapt. 12/25/1774 (DRC:31). Sponsors: [none named].

SHEHAM

Tryon County Militia

Sheham, Butler   [Appendix A]

SHEEP

1790 Census

Sheep, George F.   [Appendix B]

SHEER

1790 Census

Sheer, Ludowick   [Appendix B]
Sheer, Manassa

SHELDON

1790 Census

Sheldon, Asa   [Appendix B]
Sheldon, Elickim
Sheldon, Elisha
Sheldon, Stephen

SHELEY

1790 Census

Sheley, Martin   [Appendix B]
Sheley, Martin, Jr.

COMPENDIUM

SHELL (also see SCHELL)

1790 Census

Shell, Frederick   [Appendix B]
Shell, John
Shell, Marks
Shell, Marks, Sr.

SHEMELL

1790 Census

Shemell, Conradt   [Appendix B]
Shemell, Francis

SHEPPARD

Death Record

Shepherd, Elizabeth, (wife of Mather Shepherd), d. 4/6/1840, age 18 years; buried sect. 6, Colonial Cemetery, Johnstown (JC:187)

Probate Abstract

Sheppard, Thomas, (of Charleston), will dated 8/10/1811; probated [date not given]. Legatees: wife, Margaret; daus., Sall[y], Katharine, Polly, Hannah and Eleanor; sons, John, Rulif and Cornelius. Executors: Andrew Crawford, Elijah Mount, Rulif Schanck. Witnesses: Jael Edson, Hendrick Vunck, William Jamison. (WMC 56:382)

1790 Census

Shepperd, Henry   [Appendix B]

SHEPPERMAN

1790 Census

Shepperman, Christian   [Appendix B]

SHERBURG

Birth/Baptism

Sherburg, William & Anna (Mason): Nichlas, b. 12/1/1781; bapt. 7/19/1782 (DRC:63). Sponsors: [none named].

SHERMAN

Death Record

Sherman, Margaretha, (wife of N. Sherman), d. 2/23/1806, Oneida County, age 69 years, 8 months, 13 days; buried in the new cemetery in the town of Herkimer (RDH:256)

SHERWOOD

Marriage

Sherwood, Thomas (of Fort Edward) m. Elizabeth Mitts (of Schenectady), 9/26/1784 (JDR:2)

Probate Abstract

Sherwood, David, (of Johnstown), will dated 2/15/1813; probated 11/20/1813. Legatees: wife, Helena; son, Reuben. Executrix: wife. Witnesses: Sarah and Helena Leroy, John

727

Palen. (WMC 56:390)

SHEUER

Marriage

Sheuer, Henry m. Barbara Harbey (widow), 4/24/1796, both from New York (DFP:55)

SHEVER

SHEW

Marriage

Shew, Henry m. Anna Cassity, 3/10/1785 (DRC:164)

Birth/Baptism

Shew, Godfrey & Catrina (Fry): Godfrey, b. 3/9/1771, bapt. 1/16/1782 (DRC:60); Sarah, b. 6/8/1776, bapt. 1/16/1782 (DRC:60). Sponsors: Isaac Davis & Catrina Davis (re:1); [none named] (re:2).

Shew, Stephen & Rachel (Simmons): Eva, b. 3/4/1791; bapt. 4/10/1791 (DRC:96). Sponsors: [none named].

Probate Abstract

Shew, Godfrey, (of Northampton), will dated 2/20/1805; probated 10/16/1805. Legatees: sons, Godfrey (& his wife Catharine & their eldest dau., Susanar), Jacob (& his eldest son, Godfrey), Stephen, Heneary; daus., Mary Jackson, Sarah Jackson. Executors: Jacob and Godfrey Shew. Witnesses: Caleb Watson, Prudence Park, Samuel Scribner. (WMC 56:154)

Tryon County Militia

Shew, Godfrey   [Appendix A]
Shew, Henry
Shew, Jacob
Shew, John
Shew, Stephen

Pension Abstract

Shew, Henry, b. 3/9/1759, near Philadelphia, Pa.; his father moved the family to Albany, N.Y. when Henry was two or three years old and about a year later they removed to Johnstown, N.Y.; subsequently Henry and his family settled in Northampton, N.Y. when he was about eleven years old; Henry was a resident of Monroe Co., Michigan on 10/17/1832. Henry enlisted at Schenectady, N.Y. in February 1776 for ten months service in Capt. John Clute's Co. of batteaumen; he was stationed at Fort Miller and traveled between said fort and Fort Edward; he enlisted again under the same captain for ten months on 3/1/1777; he was assigned to remove the military stores and those taken from the British army following the surrender of Gen. Burgoyne at Saratoga; Henry was discharged and returned home to Northampton on 6/4/1778 to learn that "the Indians came & took this Deponent's Father and brothers prisoners and burned the home and barn and killed all the stock except three horses which they took away"' Henry enlisted in Capt. Garret Putman's Co., Col.

728

John Harper's Regt. on 4/1/1780 and was appointed sergeant; he served for nine months and was stationed at Johnstown, Forts Plain and Herkimer. (RWPA: #S29448)

Shew, Jacob, b. 4/15/1763, son of Godfrey Shew, Johnstown, N.Y.; (brothers: Stephen [RWPA: #W1090]; John, Godfrey, Jr. [b. 1770/1]); m. [wife not named]; resident of Northampton, Montgomery Co., N.Y. on 8/22/1828 and of Broadalbin, N.Y. in 1848; d. 1/23/1853. Children: Godfrey (resident of Jefferson Co., N.Y. in 1848). Jacob's father moved the family from Johnstown to Sacondaga, N.Y. about eight years before the Revolution and it was there on 6/2/1778 that Jacob, with his father and brothers, Stephen, John and Godfrey, Jr. were ordered out by Sgt. Solomon Woodworth of Col. Fisher's 3rd. Regt., Tryon Co. Militia on an alarm in pursuit of Indians; they were captured by Indians, their home was burned and their mother was driven back to Johnstown; Jacob and the other members of his family were taken to Canada and kept on a prison ship which moved from Montreal to Quebec and Halifax; Jacob was sent to Boston about December 1778 where he was exchanged; he contracted small pox and upon reaching Sudbury (about twenty miles from Boston) remained there until his health improved and reached Johnstown on 3/17/1779; Jacob returned to his regiment in the fall of 1779 and continued to serve as a private and corporal until the end of the war. (RWPA: #S22985)

Shew, Stephen, b. 1760/1; m. Susannah Wells, summer of 1802/3 at Providence, Saratoga Co., N.Y.; resident of Rutland, Jefferson Co., N.Y. on 9/4/1832; d. 3/27/1841, Wilna, Jefferson Co., N.Y. (Susannah Shew, b. 1776/7; [brother: Job Wells]; resident of Wilna, N.Y. on 9/6/1853.) Stephen was called out on an

alarm on 6/3/1778 by Solomon Woodworth of Col. Frederick Fisher's 3rd. Regt., Tryon Co. Militia; he marched to an area fifteen miles east of Johnstown to guard agains an impending attack by the enemy; Stephen and other members of the company were captured by the enemy; he was taken to Canada and while there "encouraging proposals were made to them to enlist in the British Army which the claimant, and the others rejected with disdain"; he was exchanged at Boston the following December and returned to Johnstown; Stephen enrolled in Capt. Little's Co. on 1/1/1779 and served at the garrison in Johnstown; he was in the battle of "Hall field, a little below the village [Johnstown]". (RWPA: #W1090)

1790 Census

Shoe, Henry	[Appendix B]
Shoe, Jacob	
Shoe, Stephen	

SHIER

Birth/Baptism

Shier, Manassah & Mary (Lance): Anna, b. 11/29/1789; bapt. 10/24/1790 (DRC:90). Sponsors: Lambert Hugener & Catrina Hugener.

SHILL

Probate Abstract

Shill, Jacob, (of Palatine), will dated 7/22/1818; probated 3/10/1829. Legatees: wife, Elizabeth; sons, William, John and Jacob;

COMPENDIUM

daus., Nancy and Gertrout. Executors: sons, William and John; Jacob Eaker. Witnesses: Jacob Hees, Alva Fuller, Boltes Cook. (WMC 57:273-274)

1790 Census

Shill, Jacob   [Appendix B]

SHILLING

1790 Census

Shilling, James   [Appendix B]

SHIPMAN

1790 Census

Shipman, David   [Appendix B]
Shipman, Samuel

SHIPPEY

1790 Census

Shippey, Ashkenius   [Appendix B]

SHIREMAN

1790 Census

Shireman, Elizabeth   [Appendix B]

SHITE

Pension Abstract

Shite, Peter, b. [date not stated], Long Island, N.Y.; resident of Ephratah, Montgomery Co., N.Y. for sixty years on 7/22/1830. Peter served as a private in Capt. Nicholas Richter's Co., Col. Jacob Klock's 2nd. Regt., Tryon Co. Militia on various tours of duty from the spring of 1777; [Elsie Getman, dau. of Capt. Nicholas Richter, deceased, and wife of Peter Getman, gave the following deposition in Montgomery Co., N.Y. on 12/31/1828], to wit.: "on the 20th day of April [1778] at or near the house of said Capt. Richter in the then County of Tryon, .. That Peter Shite was one of said party of Militia under the command of said Capt. Richter [which] was in a Skirmish [which] took place between a party of Indians and Tories on one side and a party of Militia on the other side [Peter Shite] was wounded in the right arm by a ball passing through the same, that the Father [Capt. Richter) of this deponent received a wound in the same Skirimish [and] that her mother also received a wound in the leg at the same time by a ball"; Peter also fought in the battle of Oriskany. (RWPA: #S11375)

SHOAF

1790 Census

Shoaf, Michael   [Appendix B]

SHOEMAKER

Marriage

730

Shoemaker, Friedrich Joh: m. Elisabeth P. Wohleben, 12/19/1786 (DRGF:204)

Shoemaker, Joh. Thomas m. Dorothea Sitz[?], 12/23/1783 (DRGF:198)

Shoemaker, Johann Thomas m. Elisabeth Herder, 11/16/1762 (RDSA:171)

Shoemaker, Johannes Joh: m. Anna Elisabeth Fox (dau. of Fr. Fox), 11/2/1785 (DRGF:202)

Shoemaker, Lorentz Th: m. Catharina M. J: Petri, 6/26/1787 (DRGF:204)

Shoemaker, Rudolph Joh: m. Margretha Iddig dau. of Christ: Iddig), 12/20/1795 DRGF:213)

Shoemaker, Rudolph R. m. Margretha Rosencrantz, 6/26/1785 (DRGF:201)

Shoemaker, Stophel J: Thom: m. Maria Catharin Bellinger, 5/20/1794 (DRGF:211)

Birth/Baptism

Shoemaker, Christopher & Elisabeth [?]: Margretha, b. 9/20/1780, bapt. 9/27/1780 (DRGF:40); [?], b. 6/31/1783 & 7/23/1783 [Note: both given as the date of birth]; bapt. 7/24/1783 (DRGF:73). Sponsors: Joh: Thomas Schumacher & Maria Franck (re:1); Conrad Ittig & Dorothea Schumacher (re:2).

Shoemaker, Joh: Jost & Maria [?]: Rudolph, b. 8/19/1776, bapt. 8/25/1776 (DRGF:20); Johann Jost, b. 10/13/1779 (DRGF:37); Robbert, b. 10/14/1782, bapt. 10/15/1782 (DRGF:63). Sponsors: Rudolph Schumacher Esqr. & Gertraut (re:1); Rudolph Schumacher Esqr. & Gertraut (re:2); Jost Stahl & Maria (re:3).

Shoemaker, Joh: Thomas & Dorothea [?]: Catharina, b. 9/24/1784; bapt. 10/3/1784 (DRGF:87). Sponsors: Lorentz Schumacher & Anna Elisabeth Fox.

Shoemaker, Johan Thomas & Elisabetha [?]: Johann Thomas, b. 8/15/1763, bapt. 9/5/1763 (RDSA:41); Laurentz, b. 5/28/1767, bapt. 6/17/1767 (RDSA:76); Friedrich, b. 4/10/1776, bapt. 4/14/1776 (DRGF:16); Nicolaus, b. 8/24/1778, bapt. 8/25/1778 (DRGF:32); Elisabetha, b. 3/5/1783, bapt. 3/15/1783 (DRGF:69). Sponsors: Thomas Schumacher & his wife, Dorothea (re:1); Lorentz Herder & Elisabeth Schumacher (re:2); Friedrich Harter & Dorothea Bellinger (re:3); Joh: Nicol Harter & Maria (re:4); Friedrich Franck & Elisabeth (re:5).

Shoemaker, Johannes & Catharina [?]: Johann Georg, b. 1/301/1756 (LTSA:16); Catharina, b. 1/23/1761, bapt. 2/1/1761 (RDSA:25); Dorothea, b. 2/?/1763, bapt. 3/6/1763 (RDSA:38); Johannes, b. 9/19/1765, bapt. 9/29/1765 (RDSA:58); Johann Friedrich, b. 7/7/1768, bapt. 7/17/1768 (RDSA:88). Sponsors: Jerg Gettman & his wife, Utilia (re:1); Catharina (dau. of Wilhelm Laux) & Johannes Gettman (re:2); Johannes Deighert & his wife, Dorothea (re:3); Johannes Klock & his wife, Anna Margretha (re:4); Friedrich Gettmann & Anna Maria Bell (re:5).

Shoemaker, Rudolph & Gertraud [?]: Rudolphus, b. 10/9/1762; bapt. 10/27/1762 (RDSA:36). Sponsors: John Friederich Schumacher & his wife.

Shoemaker, Thomas & Anna Eva (Orendorf): Friedrich, b. 11/25/1780, bapt. 1/6/1781 (DRGF:42); Joannes, b. 3/27/1782, bapt. 4/1/1782 (DRC:61); Anna Eva, b. 11/25/1783, bapt. 1/4/1784 (DRGF:79). Sponsors: Fritz

COMPENDIUM

Orndorff & Barbara (re:1); Jurry Steel & Dorothea Steel (re:2); Joh: Jacob Petri & Maria (re:3).

Death Record

Shoemaker, Benjamin, (infant son of Johannes Nicholas Schumacher, from Warren), d. 1/15/1814, age 6 months; buried in the same place in the field of Henry Grim (RDH:269)

Shoemaker, Catharina, (wife of Johannes Schumacher), d. 6/23/1806, Germanflats, age 69 years, several months; buried in the stone church cemetery (RDH:256)

Shoemaker, Christopher, (from Germanflats), d. 9/24/1811, age 39 years, 10 months (Died of a burning fever, which he contracted in the constant performance of his duties of son, husband, father of a family, deacon of this church for four years and elder for five years, a venerable example to this whole congregation for good, a pillar not to be shaken, a true Israelite in whom there was no guile.); buried near the stone church at the western corner (RDH:264)

Shoemaker, Christopher, (son of Christopher T. Schumacher), d. 8/23/1814, Germanflats, age 19 years, 6 months, 17 days; buried in the cemetery near the stone church (RDH:270)

Shoemaker, David, (little son of Thomas L. Shoemaker), d. 11/2/1818, Germanflats, age 1 year, 1 month; buried in the cemetery near the stone church (RDH:276)

Shoemaker, Dorothea, (wife of Thomas T. Schumacher), d. 1/4/1817, Germanflats, age 54; buried in the cemetery of the church in the same place (RDH:274)

Shoemaker, Elisabetha, (wife of Joh. Thomas Schumacher), d. 6/1/1805, Germanflats, age 68 years, minus 59 days; buried near the stone church of the same place (RDH:254)

Shoemaker, Frederick, (son of Joh. Thomas & Dorothea Schumacher), b. 3/27/1786; d. 6/20/1803, Germanflats, age 17 years, 3 months, 3 days (body consumption); buried Germanflats Church cemetery (RDH:250)

Shoemaker, George, (son of Johannes Schumacher), d. 5/10/1808, Germanflats, age 1 year, 1 month, 16 days; buried in the Germanflats church cemetery (RDH:260)

Shoemaker, Gertrude, (widow of Rudolph Schumacher), d. 2/12/1806, age 84 years; buried in cemetery near her home in Germanflats (RDH:256)

Shoemaker, Han Thomas, d. 12/11/1824, Columbia, age 67 years, 5 months, 2 days; buried in the family field towards the south from the house (RDH:290)

Shoemaker, Henry, (son of Joh. Thomas Schumacher), d. 5/20/1806, Warrentown, age 19 years, 6 months, 15 days; buried in cemetery near the church in Warren (RDH:256)

Shoemaker, Johannes, (widower), d. 1/13/1808, Germanflats, age 81 years, etc.; buried in the cemetery of the stone church (RDH:259)

Shoemaker, Johannes Thomas, (widower from Germanflats), d. 8/24/1813, age 82 years, 4 months; :erat maritus 30 gesimi anni aetat"; buried near the stone church in the same place (RDH:268)

Shoemaker, Margaretha, (dau. of Christopher

732

COMPENDIUM

Schumacher), d. 1/27/1802, Germanflats, age 21 years, 5 months, 5 days (of uterine disease); buried Germanflats Church cemetery (RDH:245)

Shoemaker, Moses, (little son of Thomas L. Shoemaker), d. 7/30/1819, Germanflats, age 3 years; buried near the stone church (RDH:278)

Shoemaker, Peter, (little son of Thomas L. Shoemaker), d. 8/31/1822, Germanflats, age 3 months; buried in the cemetery near the stone church in the same place (RDH:285)

Shoemaker, Phoebe, (dau. of Rudolph, Esqr. & Margaretha (Clepsattle) Schumacher), d. 3/21/1813, age 2 years, 2 months; buried in the Schumacher cemetery (RDH:267)

Probate Abstract

Shoemaker, Abraham, (of Canajoharie), will dated 8/24/1818; probated 2/14/1825. Legatees: wife, Maria; sons, Peter and Jacob; daus., Anna, Elizabeth, Catharine, Sally, Peggy and Maria. Executors: Albert Lintner, George Goertner. Witnesses: Philip Failing, George Wohlgemuth, Benjamin Diffendorff. (WMC 57:181)

Tryon County Militia

Shoemaker, Christopher   [Appendix A]
Shoemaker, Frederick
Shoemaker, Hanjost
Shoemaker, John
Shoemaker, Jost
Shoemaker, Rudolph
Shoemaker, Thomas

Pension Abstract

Shoemaker, Christopher, b. Germanflats, N.Y.,

son of John Shoemaker; m. Elisabeth Ittig, spring of 1779 in German Flatts; d. 3/19/1831, German Flatts, N.Y. (Elisabeth Shoemaker, b. 12/?/1758, dau. of Christian Ittig; [brother: Conrad Ittig, b. 1761/2; resident of Frankfort, Herkimer Co., N.Y. in 1837]; d. 2/8/1846.) Children: [first not named, stillborn in fall of 1779]; Margretha, b. 9/20/1780, bapt. 9/27/1780, (sponsors: John Thomas Shoemaker and Maria Frank [b. 1764/5, dau. of Timothy Frank and widow of Conrad Getman]). [Twelve other children not named in application file]. Christopher enlisted on 2/19/1777 and served for three months as a private in Capt. Michael Ittig's Co., Col. Peter Bellinger's 4th. Regt., Tryon Co. Militia; he enlisted in the spring of 1778 as a private for nine months duty in a company of rangers; he again volunteered in the spring of 1779 for nine months in the batteau service under Capt. Samuel Gray, Col. Christopher Yates' Regt.; Christopher was on the Sullivan expedition and he was in an engagement at Fort Herkimer in 1782 when it was attacked by the enemy; he continued in the military until the end of the war. (RWPA: #W19031)

Shoemaker, John, b. [not given], son of John Shoemaker; (grandfather: Thomas Shoemaker); m. Anna Elizabeth Fox; d. ca. 1841. Children: John, Jr., b. ca. 1785. John enlisted from his home in German Flatts, situated near Fort Herkimer, and served as a private in Col. Peter Bellinger's 4th. Regt., Tryon Co. Militia; John was taken prisoner, [as was his cousin, Thomas Shoemaker], while serving in Capt. Frederick Frank's Co. near Fort Herkimer and transported to Canada where he remained in captivity until the close of the war when he was allowed to return to his home in German Flatts. (RWPA: #S29452)

Shoemaker, Thomas T., b. 8/8/1764, German

733

Flatts, N.Y.; resident of his birthplace on 10/21/1832 when he applied for pension. Thomas T. was drafted into the militia in 1778 and served as a private under the command of Captains Harter, Frank and Staring in Col. Peter Bellinger's 4th. Regt., Tryon Co. Militia for the duration of the war; he was on duty at Fort Herkimer about May 1782 when he was sent to the Little Falls as a guard of the boats which were transporting wheat and other grain "to be ground into flour at a Grist Mill at the Little Falls"; Thomas and eleven others, including Andrew Piper, were attacked by the enemy and taken to Oswegatchie (now Ogdensburgh) on the St. Lawrence River; from there they were moved to Montreal and about six miles from the city, Thomas "was compelled by the Indians to run the gauntlet"; he was imprisoned in Montreal for about six months, then sent to Quebec and from there to Boston where he was exchanged and sent home to German Flatts arriving there "about Christmas of the same year". (RWPA:#R9525)

<u>1790 Census</u>

Shoemaker, [?], Sr.   [Appendix B]
Shoemaker, Cartroudt
Shoemaker, Christopher
Shoemaker, Frederick
Shoemaker, Frederick, Sr.
Shoemaker, Rudolph
Shoemaker, Samuel
Shoemaker, Thomas
Shoemaker, Yost

SHOOTS (also see **SHUTE**)

<u>Marriage</u>

Shoots, William m. Anne Pettengal, both of Warrensbush, 12/2/1788 (JDR:#76)

<u>Birth/Baptism</u>

Shoots, Frederick & [?], Charlottsbush & Warrensborough: Ketty, bapt. 4/14/1793 (JDR:18); Rachel, bapt. 2/22/1795 (JDR:22).

SHORT

<u>1790 Census</u>

Short, Dorus   [Appendix B]

SHOTTENKIRK

<u>Marriage</u>

Shottenkirk, George (of Johnstown) m. Hester Leach (of Marlattsbush), 3/11/1792 (JDR:#112)

<u>Death Record</u>

Shottenkirk, Lydia, d. 8/29/1814, age 78 years; buried sect. 8, Colonial Cemetery, Johnstown (JC:187)

<u>1790 Census</u>

Shotenkirk, Lydia   [Appendix B]

SHOUTZ

<u>1790 Census</u>

Shoutz, Jacob   [Appendix B]

SHUETLIFF

Birth/Baptism

Shuetliff/Shurliff, Joseph & Olive (Ripley/Riploy), Schenectady: Clark, bapt. 6/25/1788 (DJR:11); Polly, bapt. 6/25/1788 (JDR:21).

SHULER

Marriage

Shuler, Soloman m. Lydia Wood, both of Remsonbush, 1/27/1789 (JDR:#78)

Probate Abstract

Shuler, George, (of the town of Amsterdam), will dated 5/27/1806; probated 6/17/1816. Legatees: wife, Margaret; all my sons; all my daughters [names Anna and Elizabeth]. Executors: Aaron Marselus; sons, Frederick and John. Witnesses: Lowrentz Schuler, Russell Persons, David Cady. (WMC 57:163)

Shuler, John J., (of Palatine), will dated 4/17/1820; probated 10/21/1828. Legatees: wife, Margareth; sons, John, Nicholas, Philip and Solomon; daus., Beade, Margareth (wife of Frederick Shaver); my seven daughters. Executors: son, John; Rudolph C. Cook, Jacob J. Snell, Jr. Witnesses: Frederick Saltsman, Martinus Nestell, John Cook, Adam Wofle. (WMC 57:272)

Shuler, Lawrence, (of the town of Florida), will dated 6/1/1808; probated 3/22/1813. Legatees: wife, Lena; dau., Anna (wife of David Cady); my children [not named]. Executors: son, John; brother-in-law, George

Serviss. Witnesses: John Van Vleck, William Ventin, Jr., Jellis Swart. (WMC 56:386)

1790 Census

Shuler, Jacob   [Appendix B]
Shuler, John
Shuler, Lawrence
Shuler, Solomon

SHULTHEIS (also see **SHULTYS**)

Tryon County Militia

Shultheis, George   [Appendix A]
Shultheis, Johannes

SHULTS see **SCHULTZ**

SHULTYS (also see **SHULTHEIS**)

Deed Abstract

Shultys, John I. and Elizabeth, his wife, of Stone Arabia, Montgomery Co. to George Shultys, yeoman, of the same place. Deed dated 3/12/1785; recorded 4/8/1785. Description: A parcel of land, being the half part of one hundred acres in a larger Lot #2 situated on the north side of the Mohawk River in Montgomery Co., in a patent granted to Francis Harrison, Colonel Peter Schuyler and others. This said parcel of land was bequeathed to John I. Shultys by the Last Will and Testament of his father, Johannes Shultys, decd., bearing date of 9/19/1771, and also conveyed to him by Hendrick Loucks and Elizabeth, his wife, deed dated 1/4/1774. The parcel of land is bounded

735

on the east by the lands of John Broadbake [Breadbake], on the north by the lands of Jacob Walradt, on the west by the lands of George Eaker, Jr., and on the south by thirty acres of land conveyed to George Eaker, Jr., by the said John I. Shultys. This part of Lot #2 sold to George Shultys contains (20 acres). Consideration: L112. Witnesses: Andrew Finck, Jr., George Eaker, Jr., Jacob Yoran. (MVL:30-31)

SHURLIFF see **SHUETLIFF**

SHURMAN

1790 Census

Shurman, Jedediah   [Appendix B]
Shurman, Palmer
Shurman, Samuel

SHUTE (also see **SHOOTS**)

Tryon County Militia

Shute, Frederick   [Appendix A]
Shute, William

Pension Abstract

Shute, William, m. [wife not named]; d. 11/24/1839, Herkimer Co., N.Y. Children: Olive (m. Nicholas F. Smith); Nancy (m. Nicholas G. Hilts and resident of Herkimer); Eve (m. Philip Daly and resident of Butternuts, Otsego Co., N.Y.); William, Mary (both unmarried and living in Michigan) [all children

over the age of twenty-one years in 1840]. William served as a private in Capt. Garret Putman's Co., Col. Marinus Willett's Regt. for a total period of eleven months and three days. (RWPA: #S10012)

1790 Census

Shutes, William   [Appendix B]

SHUTTS

1790 Census

Shutts, Christian   [Appendix B]

SICE

1790 Census

Sice, Gilbert   [Appendix B]

SICKLE

Birth/Baptism

Sickle, Abraham & Elizabeth (Johnston), Schenectady: Stephen, bapt. 4/27/1802 (JDR:24).

SIELE (also see **ZIELE**)

Birth/Baptism

Siele, John & Catharina [?]: Elisabetha, b.

736

10/14/1781; bapt. 10/21/1781 (DRGF:49). Sponsors: Johann Jost Fink & Maria.

SILAH

1790 Census

Silah, Josiah   [Appendix B]

SILES

1790 Census

Siles, Jobe   [Appendix B]

SILI

Birth/Baptism

Sili, Johann & [?]: Ege, b. 10/30/1777; bapt. 12/11/1777 (LTSA:51). Sponsors: Jacob Kroetz, Elisabeth Sili.

SILL

1790 Census

Sill, Andrew   [Appendix B]

SILLEBACH (also see ZILLEBACH)

Birth/Baptism

Sillebach, Joh. Gerret & Sussanna [?]: Catharina, b. 3/16/1783; bapt. 3/19/1783 (DRGF:69). Sponsors: Pieter Giels & Elisabetha Sillebach.

Sillebach, Johannes & Elisabeth (Dygert): Severinus, b. 6/1/1780 (RDSA:111). Sponsors: Severinus Tyghert & his wife, Gertraudt.

Sillenbach, Christian (Herkimer Co.) & Elisabeth [?]: Johannes, b. 8/16/1792; bapt. 9/9/1792 (SJC:64). Sponsors: Johannes Inhof & Anna Weber.

Probate Abstract

Silbach, John, (of Palatine), will dated 11/5/1818; probated 12/25/1824. Legatees: wife, Susannah; son, Severanus; daus., Catharina (wife of Samuel Rees) and Margareth (wife of Peter M. Ehle). Bequest: Large Bible to son, Severanus. Executors: Jacob Snell, Peter N. Kilts; sons, Severnus. Witnesses: J. Cook, Aaron Vedder, Richard P. Suts. (WMC 57:181)

Tryon County Militia

Sillebach, Christian   [Appendix A]
Sillebach, John

1790 Census

Sillebach, Christian   [Appendix B]

SILLIMAN

Probate Abstract

Silliman, Ebenezer H., (of Amsterdam), will dated 9/22/1815; probated 11/21/1815. Legatees: wife, Mary. Executrix: wife.

COMPENDIUM

Witnesses: Amy Johnson, Benedict Arnold, J. W. Phillips. (WMC 56:396)

SILSBURG (also see SILSBURY)

Death Record

Silsburg, Abigail, (wife of Jonathan Silsburg), d. 5/13/1860, age 87 years, 6 months; buried Ames Rural Cemetery, Canajoharie (ARC:13)

Silsburg, Jonathan, d. 10/21/1840, age 78 years; buried Ames Rural Cemetery, Canajoharie (ARC:13)

SILSBURY (also see SILSBURG)

1790 Census

Silsbury, Jonathan [Appendix B]
Silsbury, Jonathan, Jr.

SIMMONN

Birth/Baptism

Simmonn, Isaac & Maria Margaretha [?]: Stephanus, b. 8/29/1778; bapt. 9/7/1778 [in Albany] (LTSA:54).

SIMMONS (also see SAMMONS)

Marriage

Simmons, Jacob m. Eva Veeder, 7/2/1777

(DRC:161)

Birth/Baptism

Simmons, Jacob & Eva (Veeder): Rachel, b. 8/11/1779, bapt. 8/23/1779 (DRC:19 & 53); Johanis, bapt. 1/5/1787 at age 3 weeks (DRC:82). Sponsors: Fredrik Simmons & Rachel Simmons (re:1); John J. Veeder & Catrina Davis (re:2).

1790 Census

Simmons, Abraham [Appendix B]
Simmons, Benjamin
Simmons, Frederick
Simmons, Isaac
Simmons, Jacob
Simmons, John
Simmons, Martin

SIMON

Marriage

Simon, Martin m. Maria Adamy, 11/13/1792 (DFP:46)

SIMPSON

Birth/Baptism

Simpson, John & Mary (Schenk): William, b. 4/9/1789; bapt. 8/23/1789 (JPC:3).

Simson, John & Catharina [?]: Johannes, b. 2/27/1766; bapt. 6/18/1766 (RDSA:65). Sponsors: Johannes Gemmel & Margretha Bellinger.

Simson, John & Elisabeth [?]: Elisabetha, b. 5/18/1760, bapt. 5/29/1760 (RDSA:20); Lena, bapt. 4/3/1762 (RDSA:33); Maria, b. 2/25/1764, bapt. 5/22/1764 (RDSA:47). Sponsors: Maria Dorothea, wife of Jacob Kessler (re:1); Lena, wife of Werner Deighert (re:2); Elisabeth Kessler & Johann Jost Petri (re:3).

Simson, Nicholas & Maragrita (Beemer): Philip, b. 12/29/1782; bapt. 1/10/1783 (DRC:64). Sponsors: Martin Simson & Elizabeth Simson.

Tryon County Militia

Simpson, Henry   [Appendix A]
Simpson, Nicholas

1790 Census

Simpson, John   [Appendix B]
Simpson, Joseph
Simpson, Robert

SIMS

1790 Census

Sims, William   [Appendix B]

SIMSER

Marriage

Simser, Nicholas m. Maragrita Emer, 4/26/1779 (DRC:162)

SINES

1790 Census

Sines, Peter   [Appendix B]

SISER

1790 Census

Siser, Samuel   [Appendix B]

SITEMORE

1790 Census

Sitemore, John   [Appendix B]
Sitemore, John, Jr.

SITZ

Marriage

Sitz, Balthasar m. Anna Haus, 9/10/1771 (LTSA:282)

Sitz, George (son of Peter Sitz, decd.) m. Anna Meyer (dau. of Henry Meyer), 8/2/1791 (DFP:44)

Sitz, Henrich m. Elisabeth Gerlach (dau. of Carl Gerlach), 12/21/1783 (DRGF:198)

Birth/Baptism

Sitz, Balthes & Anna [?]: Henrich, b. 12/10/1784; bapt. 1/2/1785 (DRGF:91).

Sponsors: Pieter Walls & Anna Davis.

Sitz, Johannes & Anna Margretha [m. to (?) Wanner]: Johannes, b. 12/19/1765; bapt. 12/7/1766 (RDSA:71). Sponsors: Christian Graff & Barbara.

Sitz, Peter & [?]: Joann Georg, b. 4/14/1770 (LTSA:31). Sponsors: Joann Georg Wagner, Christina Warmuth.

Sitz, Peter & Juliana [?]: Henrich, b. 8/29/1754 (LTSA:9); Anna, b. 9/13/1767, bapt. 10/4/1767 (RDSA:78); Magdalena, b. 8/23/1772 (LTSA:44); Lea, b. 11/24/1774, bapt. 12/26/1774 (LTSA:47). Sponsors: Henrich Schiz & his wife, [?] (re:1); Anna Barbara Schultz & Balthes Sitz (re:2); Joh: Salzmann, Margaretha Nellis (re:3); Joh. Nellis, Magdalena (re:3).

Tryon County Militia

Sits, Baltes   [Appendix A]
Sits, George
Sits, Hendrick
Sits, John
Sits, Nicholas
Sits, Peter
Sitz, Peter

Pension Abstract

Sitts, Henry, b. 8/29/1754, son of Peter Sitts; m. [wife not named; d. 6/?/1823]; resident of Minden, Montgomery Co., N.Y. in 1843. Children: nine daus. and five sons [not named in application file]. Henry enlisted in the spring of 1776 and served in Capt. Christian Getman's Co., Col. Peter Gansevoort's Regt.; he was engaged in the battles of Oriskany, Stone Arabia and Johnstown; Henry was on active military duty for a total period of seventeen

months. (RWPA: #S42297)

Sitts, Peter, b. ca. 1759-1762; m. Margaret Thumb, 2/10/1799; d. 5/12/1844, Minden, Montgomery Co., N.Y. (Margaret Sitts, b. ca. 1769; [brother: Adam Thumb, b. 1775/6; resident of Oppenheim, Fulton Co., N.Y. in 1851].) Children: Susanna, b. 10/15/1800; Adam, b. 10/20/1802; James, b. 1806/7; Maria (m. Robert Nellis. Children: David, b. 1817/8; Fanny, b. 1821/2; James, b. 1824/5). In 1821 Peter Sitts referred to his orphan niece, Eve Dum, aged twenty-one years. Peter served as a private in Capt. Gray's Co., Col. Gansevoort's Regt. of the N.Y. Line from 1779 through 1780; he was allowed a pension on 9/4/1818 and was living in Danube, Herkimer Co., N.Y. (RWPA: #W6056)

1790 Census

Siets, Henry   [Appendix B]
Siets, Peter
Sits, Baltus

SIVER

Probate Abstract

Siver, Robert, (of the town of Florida), will dated 3/29/1825; probated 6/19/1826. Legatees: wife, Elizabeth; sons, David and William; daus., Margaret, Eleanor and Mary. Executors: Bethuel Dean, Phillip Phillips. Witnesses: Andrew Frank, Peter M. Becker, Samuel Servoss. (WMC 57:265)

SIXBURY

COMPENDIUM

Birth/Baptism

Sixbury, [?] & [?]: William, bapt. 2/14/1791 (DRC:94). Sponsors: William [?] & [portion of record destroyed].

Sixbury, Adam & Annaatje (Olin): Willem, bapt. 8/26/1758 (DRC:2); Catrina, b. 4/10/1772, bapt. 5/31/1772 (DRC:20). Sponsors: Willem Boin & Jannetje Boin (re:1); Frederick de Graaf & Sarah Degraaf (re:2).

Sixbury, Will & Mary [?]: Cornelius, bapt. 1/26/1734/5 (FH:1). Sponsors: John Hough, Mary Phillipse.

Tryon County Militia

Sixberry, Adam   [Appendix A]
Sixberry, Bangnen
Sixberry, Cornelius
Sixberry, Cornelius, Jr.

1790 Census

Sixbury, Adam   [Appendix B]
Sixbury, Cornelius
Sixbury, Hendrick

SKEAL

1790 Census

Skeal, Nathan   [Appendix B]
Skeal, Niram
Skeal, Thomas

SKEILING

Marriage

Skeiling, Robert m. Cornelia Zealy, 6/28/1789 (RDSA:194)

SKIFF

1790 Census

Skiff, Benjamin   [Appendix B]
Skiff, Stephen

SKINNER

Marriage

Skinner, Gersasm m. Margretha Gettmann, 9/30/1783 (DRGF:198)

Birth/Baptism

Skinner, Gerason & Margreth [?]: Margretha, b. 2/18/1784; bapt. 3/7/1784 (DRGF:81). Sponsors: Fritz Gettmann & Chatarina.

Tryon County Militia

Skinner, John   [Appendix A]
Skinner, Thomas

1790 Census

Skinner, David   [Appendix B]
Skinner, Gershom
Skinner, Jessee
Skinner, Jonathan
Skinner, Josiah
Skinner, Levy
Skinner, Nathaniel

SKIPPERD

1790 Census

Skipperd, Samuel   [Appendix B]

SKULGRAFT

1790 Census

Skulgraft, Richard   [Appendix B]

SLACK

Probate Abstract

Slack, Beneagal, (of the town of Amsterdam), will dated 5/7/1818; probated 9/1/1818. Legatees: wife, Elizabeth; sons, William, Nathan, Joseph, Beneajah, Bengaman, Roswell (& his sons, Roswell and Nethan); dau., Elizabeth; grandson, Beneagh Fauls; granddaus., Marey and Ann Fauls. Executors: William Rob, Peter Van Nist. Witnesses: George Van Neste, David S. Wells, Samuel Case. (WMC 57:167)

Tryon County Militia

Slack, Martin   [Appendix A]

SLATER

Death Record

Slater, Mary, (wife of Samuel Slater), d. 10/31/1839, age 53 years, 10 months; buried

sect. 6, Colonial Cemetery, Johnstown (JC:187)

SLATTERY

Probate Abstract

Slattery, Andrew, tallow chandler, late of New York City, (now of Johnstown), will dated 2/12/1808; probated 4/5/1808. Legatees: brother, James; and father, John. Executors: brother, James; John McKiernen. Witnesses: Clement Sadlier, Sr. and Jr., Conrad Smith. (WMC 56:157-158)

Slattery, John, merchant & Episcopalian, (of Johnstown), will dated 7/8/1807; probated 1/13/1808. Legatees: wife, Ann; sons, John, Edmund, James, Joseph, Andrew and Jeremiah (all religious books); daus., Ellen and Elizabeth Ann. Executors: wife; John McCarthy, John McKernon, William Conway (of Louisiana). Witnesses: Henry F. Yates, Jonathan Judd, Peter Brooks, Jr. (WMC 56:157)

SLEEPER

1790 Census

Sleeper, John, Sr.   [Appendix B]
Sleeper, Joseph, Sr.
Sleeper, Samuel

SLITER

1790 Census

Sliter, Cornelius   [Appendix B]

742

Sliter, Jonas
Sliter, Peter

SLOAN

Marriage

Slone, Hugh m. Hester Hersy, Stillwater, 7/29/1784 (JDR:2)

Death Record

Sloan, Samuel, b. 2/26/1782; d. 12/19/1844; buried sect. 6, Colonial Cemetery, Johnstown (JC:187)

Sloan, William, d. 4/19/1848, age 38 years; buried sect. 6, Colonial Cemetery, Johnstown (JC:187)

1790 Census

Sloan, Hugh   [Appendix B]
Sloan, John
Sloan, Peter

SLOCUM

Probate Abstract

Slocum, Elezer, (of Northampton), will dated 8/29/1826; probated 12/11/1826. Legatees: wife, Ausutus[?]. Executors: Elezer Slocum, Jr.; dau., Sarah Hodge. Witnesses: Lemuel D. Sabin, Samuel Downing, Eli Stone. (WMC 57:266)

SLOSON

Marriage

Sloson, John m. Cloe Dotty, both of Warrensborough, Montgomery Co., 8/17/1786 (JDR:3)

SMALL

Birth/Baptism

Small, Jacob & Susanna [?]: Jacob, b. 1/11/1779; bapt. 2/14/1779 (LTSA:56). Sponsors: Melchior Thum & Elisabeth.

Small, John & [?]: Jacob, b. 1/28/17777; bapt. 2/9/1777 (DRGF:22). Sponsors: Jacob Petri & Maria.

Death Record

Small, David, (legitimate son of Frederich & Margaretha (Schmitt) Schmall), d. 12/13/1807, Herkimer, age 2 months, 4 days (RDH:259)

Small, Louisa, (infant dau. of Frederick Small), d. 4/4/1819, Herkimer, age 7 months, 22 days; buried in the cemetery near the church in the town of Herkimer (RDH:277)

Tryon County Militia

Small, Jacob   [Appendix A]

SMEALLE

Marriage

COMPENDIUM

Smealle, James (b. 4/10/1786) m. Mary (b. 12/8/1796, dau. of John Smealle), 10/1/1812 (UPSC:70)

Smealle, John m. Jean Biggam, 4/13/1789 (UPSC:68)

SMILEY

1790 Census

Smiley, William   [Appendix B]

SMITH

Marriage

Smith, [?] (at the German Flatts) m. [?] Bohm, 8/25/1795 (DFP:54)

Smith, Adam m. Sara Hultz, 12/4/1764 (RDSA:175)

Smith, Andrew (son of Johann Schmidt) m. Magdalena Bettinger (dau. of Martin Bettinger), 2/11/1790 (DFP:41)

Smith, Caseam m. Helena Ries (Osquaak), 1/31/1792 (DRGF:208)

Smith, Corneles m. Arriana Cone, 8/9/1766 (RDSA:179)

Smith, Cornelis (widower) m. Catharina Schultz (widow), 1/30/1785 (DRGF:201)

Smith, Fredrich (widower) m. Christina Majer (widow of Henrich Majer), 11/20/1791 (DRGF:208)

Smith, Fredrich m. Catharina Hiels (widow), 9/8/1782 (DRGF:196)

Smith, Heinrich m. Elisabeth Jordan, 3/13/1796 (DFP:54)

Smith, Henrich m. Anna Rieth, 2/8/1783 (DRGF:197)

Smith, Isaac m. Maria Catharina Koch, 9/9/1792 (RDSA:197)

Smith, Jacob (of Canajoharie) m. Elizabeth Wiles (of Canajoharie), 8/?/1832 (PCBC:52)

Smith, Jacob m. Margretha Helmer (dau. of H: Helmer), 5/5/1795 (DRGF:212)

Smith, James m. Mary Mason, 5/1/1792 (JPC:89)

Smith, Johann Conrad m. Catharina Adami, 9/25/1783 (DRGF:198)

Smith, Johann Nicol m. Margretha Bellinger, 11/21/1769 (RDSA:188)

Smith, Johannes m. Margaretha Jordan, 2/19/1793 (DFP:49)

Smith, John (widower) m. Barbara Elisabeth Gimel (widow), 12/25/1792 (DRGF:209)

Smith, Nichol m. Elisabeth Van Yveren, 12/25/1792 (DFP:47)

Smith, Peter (of Herkimer Co.) m. Elizabeth Livingston (of Johnstown), 2/5/1792 (JDR:#106)

Smith, Peter (son of Martin Schmidt) m. Maria Mundlein (dau. of Johannes Mundlein), 7/26/1788 (DFP:38)

744

Smith, Simon m. Annatje Van Eabern, 11/10/1795 (DFP:54)

Smith, Wilhelm m. Anna Ursula Spanneknebel, 4/26/1789 (RDSA:194)

Birth/Baptism

Smith, Aaron/Arent & Catrina (Veeling/Veling): Eva, b. 6/1/1765, bapt. 6/13/1765 (RDSA:56); William, b. 1/25/1773, bapt. 2/7/1773 (DRC:24); Harmanis, b. 5/25/1775, bapt. 6/4/1775 (DRC:34); Arent, b. 11/3/1778, bapt. 12/?/1778 (DRC:50). Sponsors: Debora & Cornelis Feeling (re:1); Johanis Veeder & Catrina Veeder (re:2); Harmanis Smith & Moria Smith (re:3); Aaron Brouwer & Elizabeth Brouwer (re:4).

Smith, Abraham & Elisabet [?]: Elisabet, b. 7/17/1792 (LTSA:73); Abraham, b. 5/29/1796 (LTSA:95). Sponsors: Nicolaus Smit & Elisabet (re:1); Peter Smit & Jannetche (re:2).

Smith, Adam & Sara [?]: Anna Elisabeth, b. 3/8/1766, bapt. 5/5/1766 (RDSA:63); Anna, b. 1/1/1768, bapt. 1/19/1768 (RDSA:82); Jacob, b. 11/9/1769, bapt. 11/19/1769 (RDSA:98); Adamus, b. 8/7/1779, bapt. 8/16/1779 (DRGF:36); Magdalena, b. 12/5/1782, bapt. 1/8/1783 (DRGF:65). Sponsors: Catharina Hultz & Joh. Jost Smidt (re:1); Anna Weber & Peter Smith (re:2); Friedrich Smidt & Catharina Baumann (re:3); Joh: Georg Hiels & Catharina (re:4); Adam Baumann & Lena Mac Koom (re:5).

Smith, Baltas & Christina [?]: Johannes, b. 3/14/1791 (LTSA:67); Elisabet, b. 10/12/1792 (LTSA:76); Anna, b. 8/12/1794 (LTSA:85); Christina, b. 4/4/1796 (LTSA:94). Sponsors: Joh. Schulz & Anna (re:1); Heinrich William, Elisabet Smit (re:2); Georg Smith & Anna (re:3); Jerg Heinel & Sophia (re:4).

Smith, Carl & Kati [?]: John, b. 1/16/1795 (LTSA:88). Sponsors: parents.

Smith, Cornelius & Catharina (Loux): Adam, b. 4/27/1791; bapt. 5/1/1791 (DRC:97). Sponsors: Arent Smith & Chatarina Smith.

Smith, Ephraim & [?], Marlattsbush: Legonier, bapt. 2/20/1791 (JDR:19).

Smith, Friederich & Catharina [?]: Catharina, b. 4/5/1783, bapt. 5/18/1783 (DRGF:71); Maria, b. 4/1/1785, bapt. 4/6/1785 (DRGF:95). Sponsors: Johannes Smidt & Catharina (re:1); Jacob Weaver & Elisabeth Smidt (re:2).

Smith, Georg & Anna [?]: Thomas, b. 1/25/1781, bapt. 1/30/1781 (DRGF:42); Elisabetha, b. 2/8/1783, bapt. 2/16/1783 (DRGF:67). Sponsors: Jacob Christmann & Anna (re:1); Jacob Schill & Elisabeth (re:2).

Smith, Georg & Maria [?]: Pieter, b. 3/29/1779, bapt. 4/6/1779 (DRGF:35); Maria Margretha, b. 10/1/1781, bapt. 12/31/1781 (DRGF:52); Elisabeth, b. 10/1/1781, bapt. 12/31/1781 (DRGF:52); Maria, b. 10/15/1783, bapt. 11/26/1783 (DRGF:78). Sponsors: Adam Smidt & Sara (re:1); Marcus Petri & Margretha (re:2); Adam Baumann & Elisabeth Smidt (re:3); Joh: Nicol Harter & Maria Franck (re:4).

Smith, George & Meretje [?]: Abram, b. 2/12/1785; bapt. 3/9/1785 (DRC:71). Sponsors: Abram Vosburg & Debora Vosburg.

Smith, George Adam (of Canajoh. Castle) & Anna [?]: Rodolph, bapt. 10/18/1789 (SJC:18); Gastina, bapt. 2/17/1793 (SJC:73). Sponsors:

Joseph Smith & Elizabeth Clark (re:1); Heinrich Richtmajer & his wife (re:2).

Smith, George M. (of Tillenberg) & Anna [?]: Maria, bapt. 4/3/1791 (SJC:40). Sponsors: Georg Schmid & Janike Schmid.

Smith, Harmanus & Maria (Wemple): Sarah, b. 3/29/1774, bapt. 4/25/1774 (DRC:29); Barent, b. 8/3/1776, bapt. 9/1/1776 (DRC:39); Arent, b. 2/13/1779, bapt. 3/14/1779 (DRC:51). Sponsors: Folkert Veeder & Elizabeth Veeder (re:1); Barent Wemp & Sarah Wemple (re:2); Arent Smith & Catrina Smith (re:3).

Smith, Henrich (of Tillenburg) & Elisabeth [?]: Maria, bapt. 12/31/1790 (SJC:36). Sponsors: Peter Schram & Maria Harti.

Smith, Henry & Anna [?]: Christina, b. 1/1/1783, bapt. 2/8/1783 (DRGF:67); Johannes, b. 7/25/1792 (LTSA:75). Sponsors: Jerg Smit & Anna (re:1); Johannes Miller & Maria (re:2).

Smith, Henry & Elisabet [?]: Heinrich, b. 11/4/1788 (LTSA:61); Anna, b. 4/11/1796 (LTSA:94). Sponsors: Henry Hering & Eva (re:1); Ludwig Hering, Anna Smit (re:2).

Smith, Hermanus & Catrina (Frits): Maria, b. 11/18/1784; bapt. 12/19/1784 (DRC:69). Sponsors: Johan Wemple & Maria Wemple.

Smith, Jeremias & Jannetche [?]: Nicolas, b. 10/24/1784, bapt. 11/18/1784 (DRGF:89); Anna, b. 8/27/1788 (LTSA:61); Jeremias, b. 9/8/1790 (LTSA:65); Maria, b. 3/23/1793 (LTSA:78); Catarina, b. 2/20/1796 (LTSA:92); Elisabet, b. 9/12/1797 (LTSA:99). Sponsors: Nicolas Smidt & Elisabeth (re:1); Wilhelm Schram, Anna Smit (re:2); Philip Empie &

Elisabet (re:3); Wilhelm Smit, Elisabet Smit (re:4); Nicolaus Smit, Maria Brandau (re:5); Abraham Smit & Elisabet (re:6).

Smith, Jerg & Anna [?]: Heinrich, b. 4/10/1793 (LTSA:78); Catarina, b. 10/24/1795 (LTSA:91); Christina, b. 10/24/1795 (LTSA:91). Sponsors: Heinrich Smit, Elisabet v. Lunen (re:1); Maria Christman, Heinrich Williams (re:2); Friderich Getman & Anna Eva (re:3).

Smith, Joh. Adam (Canajoh. Castle) & Anna [?]: Eva, bapt. 11/20/1791 (SJC:51). Sponsors: Heinrich Rechtmeyer & Maria Richmayer.

Smith, Joh: Jost & Appollonia [?]: Johann Georg, b. 5/14/1777, bapt. 5/17/1777 (DRGF:23); Appolonia, b. 2/5/1781, bapt. 2/13/1781 (DRGF:42); [?], bapt. 6/14/1783 (DRGF:72). Sponsors: Joh: Georg Smidt & [?] (re:1); Lorentz Herder & Appollonia Herder (re:2); [sponsors names obliterated in record] (re:3).

Smith, Joh. Rudolph (Canajoharie) & Catharina [?]: Daniel, bapt. 2/5/1792 (SJC:53). Sponsors: parents themselves.

Smith, Johann & Abiel [?]: Regina, b. 9/17/1768 (LTSA:25). Sponsors: Hennrich Seber & his wife.

Smith, Johann & Catharina [?]: Adam, b. 7/29/1776, bapt. 8/4/1776 (DRGF:19); Johannes, b. 8/14/1778, bapt. 8/16/1778 (DRGF:31). Sponsors: Georg Smidt & Maria (re:1); Johannes Bellinger & Elisabeth Harter (re:2).

Smith, Johann Conrad & Catharina [?]: Petrus, b. 11/26/1784; bapt. 12/1/1784 (DRGF:90). Sponsors: Henrich Adams & [?] Seeber.

COMPENDIUM

Smith, Johannes & Anna [?]: Conrad, b. 2/5/1764, bapt. 5/6/1764 (RDSA:46); Dorothea, b. 5/30/1770 (LTSA:32). Sponsors: Conrad Schmidt & his wife, Catharina (re:1); Michael Rossel & his wife (re:2).

Smith, Johannes & Anna Eva [?]: Maria Catharina, b. 7/28/1776, bapt. 8/4/1776 (DRGF:19); Nicolas, b. 6/24/1781, bapt. 6/29/1781 (DRGF:45); John, b. 6/16/1785, bapt. 7/3/1785 (DRGF:98). Sponsors: Georg Hauss & Maria (re:1); Nicolas Tyghart & Engelje Van Slyk (re:2); Johannes Hauss & Lena (re:3).

Smith, John & [?] (Dingman): John, bapt. 8/11/1799 (JDR:18).

Smith, John & Anna (Picking): Catrina, b. 8/29/1776; bapt. 10/13/1776 (DRC:39). Sponsors: Jacob Pikkle & Moria Pikkle.

Smith, John & Elisabeth Perdrich (of Tillenburg) [unmarried]: Anna Maria, bapt. 4/23/1790 (SJC:26). Sponsors: Gottlieb Bottiger & Anna Maria Bottiger.

Smith, John & Maria [?]: Isaacus, b. 10/19/1766, bapt. 10/30/1766, d. 10/31/1766 (RDSA:69); Catharina, b. 9/10/1770, bapt. 9/30/1770 (RDSA:106). Sponsors: Isaac Paris & his wife, Catharina (re:1); Catharina & Mr. Isaac Paris (re:2).

Smith, John (Esqr.) & Maria Elisabeth [?]: Margrtha, b. 6/16/1784; bapt. 6/26/1784 (DRGF:84). Sponsors: Joh: Jost Hesse & Catharina Nelles.

Smith, John (Lieut.) & Maria Elisabeth [?]: Maria Elisabetha, b. 7/?/1777, bapt. 7/13/1777 (DRGF:24); Georg, b. 4/2/1780, bapt. 4/10/1780 (DRGF:38); Alita, b. 10/9/1784,

bapt. 3/5/1784 (DRGF:81). Sponsors: Joh: Friedr: Helmer & Elisabeth (re:1); Georg Hergheimer Esqr. & Alita (re:2); Georg Hergheimer, Esqr. & Alita (re:3).

Smith, John & Nyeche (Kittle): Richard, b. 10/10/1790; bapt. 12/23/1790 (DRC:91). Sponsors: [none named].

Smith, Nicolaus & Elisabet [?]: Georg, b. 10/9/1794 (LTSA:86); Georg, b. 10/20/1796 (LTSA:98). Sponsors: Conrad Sprecher & Ali. (re:1); Isaac Bogert, Christina Sprecher (re:2).

Smith, Peter & Jannetche/Jannike [?]: Peter, bapt. 9/24/1791 [parents of Tillenburg] (SJC:47); Anna, b. 5/27/1794 (LTSA:83); Nicolaus, b. 9/26/1797 (LTSA:100). Sponsors: Abraham Schmid & Elisabeth Muller (re:1); Jacob Hertung, Margaret Muller (re:2); Nicolaus Smit, Maria Muller (re:3).

Smith, Peter & Maria (Hurler): Elizabeth, b. 12/28/1790; bapt. 1/23/1791 (DRC:94). Sponsors: [none named].

Smith, Philip & Anna Elisabeth [?]: Johannes, b. 4/6/1769; bapt. 4/16/1769 (RDSA:94). Sponsors: Johannes School & Christina Helmer.

Smith, Robert & Grace [?]: Johannes, b. 10/30/1777; bapt. 12/7/1777 (DRGF:27). Sponsors: Pieter Bellinger, Col. [Colonel] & Delia.

Smith, Wilhelm & Anna [?]: Henrich, b. 6/9/1794 (LTSA:84); Anna, b. 4/17/1796 (LTSA:94). Sponsors: Ludwig Crem & Maria (re:1); Heinrich Kuhl & Anna (re:2).

Death Record

Smith, [?], (dau. of Rev. J. Smith), d.

11/?/1834, age 8 years (sore throat); buried Presbyterian Church cemetery, Cherry Valley (PCV:86)

Smith, [?], (widow), d. 3/6/1813, age 71 years, 5 months (DFP:95)

Smith, Adam, d. 5/21/1824, Herkimer, age 84 years, less 3 months & 10 days; buried in the cemetery near the church (RDH:289)

Smith, Almira P., (dau. of John & Caroline Smith), d. 8/16/1813, age 20 years; buried sect. 1, Colonial Cemetery, Johnstown (JC:187)

Smith, Benjamin E., (son of John & Caroline Smith), d. 8/2/1813, age 16 months, 7 days; buried sect. 1, Colonial Cemetery, Johnstown (JC:187)

Smith, Catharina, (born: Koch), d. 9/10/1793, age 24 years, 1 month, 8 days; buried 9/12/1793 (RDSA:233)

Smith, Conrad, d. 11/27/1831, age 22 years, 6 days; buried sect. 2, Colonial Cemetery, Johnstown (JC:187)

Smith, Delos, d. 4/7/1824, age 12 years; buried Cherry Valley Presbyterian Church cemetery (PCV:81)

Smith, Doratha, (wife of Isaac Smith), d. 3/17/1838, age 64 years; buried sect. 2, Colonial Cemetery, Johnstown (JC:187)

Smith, George, (son of Peter & Dorothea Schmitt), d. 12/16/1809, Herkimer, age 4 years, 6 months, 3 days; buried near the church in Herkimer (RDH:261)

Smith, George, d. 3/29/1809, Herkimer, age 65 years; buried in the cemetery near the new

church in the same place (RDH:261)

Smith, Henry E., (son of John & Caroline Smith), d. 8/25/1813, age 16 months, 3 days; buried sect. 1, Colonial Cemetery, Johnstown (JC:187)

Smith, Johannes, (son of Peter Smith), d. 2/4/1818, Herkimer age 14 years, 9 months, 2 days; buried in the cemetery of the Herkimer church (RDH:275)

Smith, Johannes Josephus, (from Herkimer), d. 5/19/1811, age 68 years; buried in the cemetery of the church in Herkimer (RDH:263)

Smith, Johannes M., (farmer), d. 3/12/1822, Herkimer, age 74 years; buried in the cemetery near the church (RDH:283)

Smith, Margaretha, (dau. of Jacob Schmitt), d. 5/17/1816, Herkimer, age 1 year, 8 months; buried in the cemetery near the new church (RDH:272)

Smith, Mary, (dau. of Calvin & Margaret Smith), d. 2/10/1840, age 1 year; buried sect. 3, Colonial Cemetery, Johnstown (JC:187)

Smith, Matthew, d. 2/?/1813, age 88 years; buried 2/28/1813 (DFP:95)

Smith, Peter, (unmarried from Herkimer), d. 12/30/1813, age 79 years, 2 months, 2 days; buried near the new church in Herkimer (RDH:269)

Smith, Robert, (from Yorkshire, England), d. 6/12/1822, Germanflats, age 95 years, 6 months; buried in the cemetery of the Schumacher family (RDH:283)

Smith, Sarah, (wife of Adam Schmitt), d.

COMPENDIUM

1/3/1802, Herkimer age 58 years, 7 months, 10 days; buried Herkimer Cemetery [Sarah Smith, along with Elisabeth, Anna, & Catharina Foltz, died from "dry quinsey" from drinking the same deadly water flowing from the lake (or cistern?) nearby.] (RDH:245)

Smith, Solomon, d. 12/21/1825, age [not stated]; buried sect. 1, Colonial Cemetery, Johnstown (JC:187)

Probate Abstract

Smith, Abraham, (of Palatine), will dated 9/28/1825; probated 12/11/1826. Legatees: wife, Elizabeth; sons, Abraham and Peter; dau., Elizabeth Gray (decd. & her son, Peter). Executors: two sons. Witnesses: Christopher Getman, Peter Schram, Asa Catlin. (WMC 57:266)

Smith, Anna, (formerly Anna Cady; now wife of George Smith, of the town of Florida), will dated 9/26/1823; probated 6/16/1824. Legatees: mother; sister, Sarah (decd.); brothers, Jay, David, John W.; brother John W.'s wife (Maria C. and infant dau.); Sarah (dau. of James Smith); Sarah (dau. of Adam Smith); Sarah (dau. of Jay Cady); my step-children (David Cady Smith and Charlotte Smith, children of George). Executor: husband. Witnesses: L. Carlisle, Peter P. Rouse. (WMC 57:179)

Smith, Benjamin, (of Johnstown), will dated 8/2/1815; probated 6/17/1816. Legatees: wife, Catherine; sons, Henry and Jacob; daus., Catharine, Elizabeth and Mary. Executors: wife; brothers, Cornelius A. and Hermanus A. Witnesses: Cornelius Smith, James Williamson, Deborah Veeder. (WMC 56:397)

Smith, Frederick, (of Palatine), will dated 3/19/1825; probated 7/11/1831. Legatees: wife,

Eve. Executors: wife; Andrew Dillenbeck, John Bauder. Witnesses: John Bauder, Peter P. Nellis, Daniel Dillibaugh. (WMC 57:279)

Smith, Frederick, a tailor, (of Kingsborough), will dated 5/6/1806; probated 6/30/1806. Legatees: father, Gerrard; sons, Elias (a cooper), Gerrard (a farmer). Executors: the two sons. Witnesses: Jonathan and Thomas Carpenter, Salmon Bard. (WMC 56:155)

Smith, Harmanus, (of Johnstown), will dated 2/12/1813; probated 4/7/1813. Legatees: wife; sons, Cornelius H. and Barent; grandson, Harmanus (of Cornelius H.); daus., Mary (wife of John Dockstader) and Deborah (wife of John V. Veeder). Bequest: a large bible. Executors: John V. Veeder, Abraham N. Veeder, James Lansing. Witnesses: Cornelius and Catharine Smith, John Bradt. (WMC 56:387)

Smith, Hendrick, (of New Dillenburgh), will dated 1/24/1789; probated 12/12/1803. Legatees: wife, Anna Mary; sons, William and Philip; daus., Elizabeth, Mary Suviena, Mary (wife of John Wolkamuth), Mary Elizabeth. Executors: Andrew Finck, Adam Laucks. Witnesses: Henry Cook, Samuel Billington, Magdalena Laucks. (WMC 56:153)

Smith, Henry N., (of Minden), will dated 10/19/1812; probated 2/10/1817. Legatees: wife, Catherine; sons, Martaise, Jacob, John, George and Henry; dau., Margrate. Executors: friend, Jacob Smith; George Dievendorf. Witnesses: Daniel Ayres, Marcus Garber, Cornelius C. Beeckman. (WMC 57:164)

Smith, John, (of Mohawk Town), will dated 3/1/1791; probated 6/6/1791. Legatees: wife, Eytie; son, Jury; dau., Sophia Smith. Executors: brother, Jeremiah; Chas. R. Sedarn[?], Richard Smith. Witnesses: Thomas

749

Ostrom, Joshua Ostrom, John Smith. (WMC 56:146)

Smith, Solomon, (of Johnstown), will dated 12/18/1825; probated 12/24/1825. Legatees: wife, Elizabeth (& her child, or children, should another be born after my decease); father, John. Executrix: wife. Witnesses: H. Cunningham, Oran Johnson, George T. Wells. (WMC 57:185)

Tryon County Militia

Smith, Adam	[Appendix A]
Smith, Baltus	
Smith, Baltus S.	
Smith, Frederick	
Smith, George	
Smith, Harmanus	
Smith, Henry	
Smith, James	
Smith, John	
Smith, Jost	
Smith, Matthew	
Smith, Nicholas	
Smith, Nicholas, Jr.	
Smith, Peter	
Smith, Philip	
Smith, William	

Pension Abstract

Smith, Cornelius, b. 8/19/1743; resident of Mohawk, Montgomery Co., N.Y. in 1838. Cornelius was a private in Capt. Jelles Fonda's Co. of Associated Exempts, Col. Frederick Fisher's 3rd. Regt., Tryon Co. Militia; his total military service amounted to six months and twenty-three days; Cornelius was also a member of the Tryon County Committee of Safety for one year. (RWPA: #S22996)

Smith, Frederick, m. Christina [?], 11/20/1791

by Rev. Abraham Rosencrantz [both were widowed at the time of their marriage]; d. 6/11/1828, Herkimer, Herkimer Co., N.Y. (Christina Smith, b. 1758/9; m. 1st. Henrich Mayer; was declared mentally incompetent in 1855 when she was past the age of ninety-six years.) Children: Matthew (resident of Herkimer in 1855); Nicholas F. (d. 6/?/1854). Frederick served for nine months in the batteau service under the command of Capt. Samuel Gray; he was a participant in the battle of Oriskany. (RWPA: #W25015)

Smith, George, b. [not given]; (brother: Henry [RWPA: #W6126]); m. Hannah Hall, 1777/8 in Palatine, N.Y. by Rev. Abraham Rosencrantz; d. ca. 1812. (Hannah Smith, dau. of Shower Hall.) Children: Benjamin (petitioned for mother's pension on 3/2/1848 from Steuben, Oneida Co., N.Y.). George enlisted in 1775 for one year under Capts. Andrew A. Fink and Christopher P. Yates and went "on the campaign to Canada"; he was appointed acting sergeant of his company in 1776 and continued with this rank for four years; George was engaged in the battle of Oriskany in 1777 while under the command of Capt. Nicholas Richter. (RWPA: #R9741)

Smith, George, b. [not given]; m. Anna Maria Bellinger, ca. 1771 in Herkimer by Rev. Abraham Rosencrantz; d. 3/29/1809. (Anna Maria Smith, b. ca. 1751; resident of Herkimer, Herkimer Co., N.Y. on 11/5/1841.) Children: Peter, b. 3/29/1779. George served in the regiments of Cols. Bellinger and Klock; he attained the rank of sergeant and was stationed at Fort Dayton in Herkimer; he also served in the batteau service for a period of time with John Campbell and John House; George fought in the battle of Oriskany. (RWPA: #W19064)

Smith, Henry, b. 3/31/1764, Catskill, Green Co., N.Y.; (brother: George [RWPA: #R9741]); m. Nancy Shults, 9/1/1809; d. 5/3/1840, Ephratah, Fulton Co., N.Y. (Nancy Smith, b. ca. 1780; resident of Ephratah, N.Y. on 3/12/1855.) Henry enrolled at the age of fourteen years as a volunteer in Capt. Nicholas Richter's Co., Col. Jacob Klock's 2nd. Regt., Tryon Co. Militia; he was in frequent skirmishes with "marauding parties of Indians and Tories" and during his two year tour of duty was wounded; Henry enlisted on 4/1/1780 into a company of rangers under Capt. John Casselman for nine months; he again enlisted for nine months on 4/1/1781 in Capt. Lawrence Gross' Co., Col. Marinus Willett's Regt.; he was a participant in the battle of Johnstown and was discharged from the military at Fort Plain on 1/1/1782. (RWPA: #W6126)

Smith, William, b. 5/19/1763, Canajoharie, N.Y.; resident of Ephratah, Montgomery Co., N.Y. on 9/20/1832. William enlisted from his home in Palatine in May 1779 and was a private in Capt. Nicholas Richter's Co., Col. Jacob Klock's 2nd. Regt., Tryon Co. Militia; he enlisted in April 1780 into a company of rangers commanded by Capt. John Casselman; he volunteered for nine months duty in 1781 under Capt. Skinner and again in 1782 for nine months in Capt. French's Co., William was engaged in the battle of Johnstown and received his discharge from the military at Fort Herkimer on 1/1/1783. (RWPA: #S11420)

Deed Abstract

Smith, Arent, and Catharine, his wife, and Sarah Smith, widow & relict of Cornelius Smith, decd., all of Caughnawaga District, Montgomery Co. to Cornelius Hardenbergh, farmer, of the same place. Deed dated 4/28/1786; recorded 12/9/1786. Description:

Two lots of land situated in Caughnawaga District, known and distinguished as Lots #2 and #5 (139$^{1/4}$ acres) in the subdivision of Lot #3 in a patent granted to James Alexander and Andrew Coeymans, Esqs., and are the same lots marked on a map made by John R. Bleecker in 1768. (Exception: Allow Timothy Leendersen and Philip Flipse the privilege of cutting wood and timber on the unenclosed portions of the aforesaid lots.) Consideration: L600. Witnesses: Marx Dachstetter, Cornelius Smith. (MVL:31)

Smith, Cornelius Are., trader, of Schenectady, Albany Co. to William Barrett and John Leenderse, of the same place. Deed dated 1.10/1737/38; recorded 3/17/1774. Description: (Whereas, Rip Van Dam, Esq., of New York City by deed dated 10/29/1735 granted unto Cornelius Are. Smith Lot #3, situated on the north side of the Mohawk River, about five miles above Fort Hunter in Albany Co., containing nearly 38 acres, 22 perches, $^{2/9}$ of 2 square perches of lowland and 850 acres, 3 rods of upland.) All that tract of upland within the bounds of Lot #3, allotted and divided unto Rip Van Dam, which lies on the north side of the Stone Arabia road, about two miles above the house of Capt. Hendk. Vroman is known by the name of [*het groote stucks*], and begins in the center of a muddy place called [*Plaase Key Kuyl*]. This tract of land contains (202 acres). Consideration: L200. Witnesses: Robt. Sanders, Caleb Beck. (MVL:31)

Smith, John and Frederick Smith, farmers, of Kingsland District, Montgomery Co. to Hezekia Talcot, farmer, of the same place. Deed dated 1/29/1787; recorded 3/8/1787. Description: Lot #9 upland (70 acres), being woodland, commonly called a Homestead place in Kingsland District. Consideration: L200. Witnesses: Wm. Petry, Johannes Phillip.

(MVL:32)

<u>1790 Census</u>

Smith, Aaron   [Appendix B]
Smith, Adam
Smith, Alexander
Smith, Amos
Smith, Andrew
Smith, Asa
Smith, Baltus
Smith, Benjamin
Smith, Bill
Smith, Christopher
Smith, Clark
Smith, Conradt (2)
Smith, Cornelius
Smith, David
Smith, Ebenezer
Smith, Edmund
Smith, Edward
Smith, Elijah
Smith, Ephraim
Smith, Frederick
Smith, George (3)
Smith, Gerard
Smith, Gershom (2)
Smith, Gilbert
Smith, Hendrick
Smith, Hendrick, Jr.
Smith, Henry (2)
Smith, Hermanus
Smith, Isaac
Smith, Israel
Smith, Israel, Jr.
Smith, Jacobala
Smith, James (6)
Smith, James, Jr.
Smith, Jeremiah (2)
Smith, Jessee
Smith, John (10)
Smith, John M.
Smith, Joseph

Smith, Joshua
Smith, Matthew
Smith, Nathan
Smith, Nathaniel
Smith, Nicholas
Smith, Noah
Smith, Peter (3)
Smith, Philip
Smith, Recompence
Smith, Reuben
Smith, Rosel
Smith, Samuel
Smith, Shederick
Smith, Stephen, Jr.
Smith, Stephen, Sr.
Smith, Teunis
Smith, Thomas
Smith, Yost

SMOCK

<u>Birth/Baptism</u>

Smock, Matthew & Hannah (Stout): Margarit, b. 5/10/1790; bapt. 8/1/1790 (DRC:88). Sponsors: [none named].

SNAKE

<u>1790 Census</u>

Snake, Frederick   [Appendix B]

SNEAF

<u>1790 Census</u>

COMPENDIUM

Sneaf, Lucas [Appendix B]

SNELL (also see SCHNELL)

Marriage

Snell, Adam m. Elisabetha Bellinger, 11/10/1763 (RDSA:173)

Snell, Friedrich m. Catharina Zimmermann, 3/4/1766 (RDSA:179)

Snell, Friedrich m. Maria Heering, 3/18/1792 (RDSA:197)

Snell, Jacob (son of J: Snell) m. Margretha Snell (dau. of Joh: Snell, jr.), 11/2/1769 (RDSA:188)

Snell, Jacob (son of Johann Jost Schnell) m. Gertrude Matthews (dau. of Nicel Matthews, Schoharie), 10/7/1760 (RDSA:168; LTSA:278)

Snell, Jacob m. Anna Margaretha Van Netten, 4/19/1795 (RDSA:201)

Snell, Jacob G. m. Maria D. Markell (dau. of Teobald Markell), 1/16/1783 (RDSA:191; DRGF:197)

Snell, Joh. Nicol (widower) m. Lena Tyghart (widow), 10/20/1782 (DRGF:196)

Snell, Johann (son of Joh. Schnell) m. Elisabeth Scholl (dau. of Joh. Scholl), 10/18/1788 (RDSA:193)

Snell, Johann Jost m. Margaretha Nestel (widow), 6/9/1793 (RDSA:198)

Snell, Johann Nicol m. Elisabeth [?], 5/7/1771

(RDSA:190)

Snell, Johannes m. Catharina Schnell, 11/14/1765 (RDSA:177)

Snell, Johannes m. Elisabeth Dussler, 5/18/1783 (DRGF:197)

Snell, Jost m. Maria Sophia Lepper, 3/6/1766 (RDSA:179)

Snell, Peter (son of Georg Schnell) m. Maria Kills (dau. of Joh. Adam Kills), 7/26/1788 (RDSA:193)

Snell, Peter m. Anna Kieltz, 3/10/1768 (RDSA:184)

Birth/Baptism

Snell, Friederich & Anna Maria [?]: Petrus, b. 10/13/1755 (LTSA:15). Sponsors: Peter Deigert, Peter Schnell, Maria Emig.

Snell, Friderich & Maria [?]: Eva, b. 11/10/1794 (LTSA:86). Sponsors: Johannes Schnell & Lena.

Snell, Jacob & Catharina [?]: Friedrich, b. 12/30/1766; bapt. 1/4/1767 (RDSA:71). Sponsors: Friedrich Snell & Catharina.

Snell, Jacob (Schnellenbush) & Elisabeth [?]: Catharina, bapt. 5/22/1791 (SJC:42); Margretha, bapt. 12/30/1792 (SJC:68). Sponsors: Peter Wollever & Catharina Wollever (re:1); Jost Snell & Rosina Zimmerman (re:2).

Snell, Jacob & Gertraud [?]: Johannes, b. 9/23/1761, bapt. 9/27/1761 (RDSA:28); Catharina, b. 7/1/1763, bapt. 7/3/1763 (RDSA:41); Sara, b. 4/7/1765, bapt. 5/5/1765 (RDSA:55). Sponsors: Georg Schnell & his wife, Anna Eva (re:1); Catharina Snell & Johannes Snell (re:2); Sara & Peter Teughert (re:3).

Snell, Jacob & Margaret [?]: Benjamin, b. 4/23/1796 (LTSA:94). Sponsors: Johannes Schnell & Elisabet.

Snell, Jacob & Margretha [?]: Friedricus, b. 11/21/1770; bapt. 11/29/1770 (RDSA:107). Sponsors: Friedrich Snell & Cathari[?].

Snell, Jacob & Maria [?]: Maria, b. 7/25/1783, bapt. 8/10/1783 (DRGF:73); Johann Georg, b. 5/24/1785, bapt. 6/10/1785 (DRGF:97). Sponsors: Pieter Merckel & Maria Snell (re:1); Georg A: Laux & Maria Joh: Snell widow (re:2).

Snell, Joh. Friedrich & Catharina [?]: Adamus, b. 1/31/1767, bapt. 2/8/1767 (RDSA:73); Anna Maria, b. 11/10/1768, bapt. 11/12/1768 (RDSA:91); Catharina, b. 8/19/1770, bapt. 8/26/1770 (RDSA:106). Sponsors: Jacob Snell, Jun. & Elisabeth Emgie (re:1); Elisabeth Helmer & John Nichol. Snell (re:2); Catharina & her husband, Johan[?] Snell (re:3).

Snell, Joh. Nicholas (Tillenberg) & Elisabeth [?]: Johannes, b. 1/12/1792; bapt. 1/21/1792 (SJC:52). Sponsors: John Schnell & Catharina Frey.

Snell, Joh: Nicolas Friedr: & Elisabeth [?]: Anna Elisabeth, b. 10/26/1784; bapt. 11/1/17/1784 (DRGF:89). Sponsors: Johannes Sutz & Anna Elisabeth.

Snell, Johann & Catharina [?]: Nickolaus, b. 4/27/1778, bapt. 5/10/1778 (LTSA:52); Anna Maria, b. 3/30/1783, bapt. 4/7/1783 (DRGF:70); Jerg, b. 10/10/1792 (LTSA:70). Sponsors: Ludwig Rickert, Anna Schnell (re:1);

Henrich Kuhl & Anna Dussler (re:2); Jacob Schnell & Maria (re:3).

Snell, Johann Adam & Elisabeth [?]: Appollonia, b. 3/26/1770; bapt. 4/1/1770 (RDSA:101). Sponsors: Felix Majer & Appollonia.

Snell, Johann Georg & Anna Eva [?]: Johann Jost, b. 12/25/1756 (LTSA:20); Adam, b. 9/15/1762, bapt. 9/19/1762 (RDSA:35); Johannes, b. 5/11/1764, bapt. 5/20/1764 (RDSA:47); Petrus, b. 3/16/1766, bapt. 3/23/1766 (RDSA:62); Elisabeth, b. 4/?/1768, bapt. 5/?/1768 (RDSA:85); Anna Maria, b. 9/16/1769, bapt. 9/24/1769 (RDSA:97). Sponsors: Jost Schnell & his wife, Maria Catharina (re:1); Adam Schnell & Elisabeth Bellinger (re:2); Johannes Teughard & his wife, Dorothea (re:3); Pieter Schnell & Anna Kieltz (re:4); Elisabeth Laux & Gottfridrich Seyber (re:5); Anna Maria & her husband, Pieter Gieltz (re:6).

Snell, Johann Georg & Maria [?]: Johannes, b. 5/30/1757, bapt. 6/12/1757 (RDSA:16); Anna Margretha, b. 12/3/1759, bapt. 12/16/1759 (RDSA:18); Jacobus, b. 12/15/1761, bapt. 12/27/1761 (RDSA:29); Anna Margretha, b. 12/20/1763, bapt. 1/8/1764 (RDSA:43); Catharina, b. 5/18/1766, bapt. 6/1/1766 (RDSA:64); Anna Maria, b. 10/17/1768, bapt. 10/30/1768 (RDSA:91); Anna Elisabeth, b. 10/2/1770, bapt. 10/14/1770 (RDSA:106). Sponsors: Johannes Schnell & his wife (re:1); Anna Margretha, wife of Wilhelm Fox (re:2); Dieterich (son of Adam Laux) & Anna Margretha (dau. of George Ecker) (re:3); Margretha Finck & Stophel Fox, jun. (re:4); Catharina Elisabetha & Adam Laux (re:5); Maria Nelles & Georg Ecker, jr. (re:6); Gottfried Seiffer & Elisabeth (re:7).

Snell, Johann Nicholas & Elisabeth [?]: Jacob, b. 7/28/1778; bapt. 8/2/1778 (LTSA:53). Sponsors: Andreas Weimar & Friederica.

Snell, Johannes & Anna [?]: Jacob, b. 9/18/1782, bapt. 9/22/1782 (DRGF:62); Severinus, b. 11/29/1784, bapt. 11/30/1784 (DRGF:90). Sponsors: Jost Kayser & Maria (re:1); Severines Snell & Anna Eva (re:2).

Snell, Johannes (of Schnellenbusch) & Anna [?]: Magdalena, bapt. 11/7/1790 (SJC:34); Maria, bapt. 2/23/1794 (SJC:94). Sponsors: Conrad Zimmermann & Magdalena Zimmermann (re:1); Johannes Stoll & Maria Stoll (re:2).

Snell, Johannes & Elisabeth [?]: Maria, b. 8/4/1783, bapt. 8/10/1783 (DRGF:73); Jacob, b. 5/11/1785, bapt. 5/29/1785 (DRGF:97). Sponsors: Andrees Finck, Mjr. & Maria (re:1); Jacob Dussler & Sara Snell (re:2).

Snell, Johannes (of Schnellenbusch) & Elisabeth [?]: Johann Jost, bapt. 12/26/1789 (SJC:20). Sponsors: Frideric Meyer & Catharina Mayer.

Snell, Johannes & Frena [?]: Anna, b. 12/17/1755 (LTSA:16). Sponsors: Jerg Schnell & his wife, Anna Eva.

Snell, Johannes & Gertraud [?]: Johann Nicolaus, b. 12/30/1766; bapt. 1/4/1767 (RDSA:72). Sponsors: Johann Nicol Snell & Maria Margretha.

Snell, Johannes (in Palatine) & Magdalena [?]: Magdalena, bapt. 2/4/1792 (SJC:53). Sponsors: Jacob Yuker & Magdalena Yuker.

Snell, Johannes & Margaretha (Fink): Anna Margaretha, bapt. 5/2/1751 (RDSA:10). Sponsors: Willhelm Finck & his wife, Anna

Margaretha.

Snell, Johannes Sev: & Maria [?]: Anna, b. 8/22/1780 (DRGF:39). Sponsors: Jost Snell & Anna Snell.

Snell, Nicholas & [?]: Johann Nicolas, b. 5/31/1780; bapt. 7/6/1780 (DRGF:39). Sponsors: Nicolas Jost Snell & [?].

Snell, Niclas & Margaretha [?]: Anna Maria, b. 6/11/1757 (LTSA:21). Sponsors: Severinus Deigert & his wife, Anna Maria.

Snell, Peter & Anna [?]: Georg, b. 3/23/1782, bapt. 3/25/1782 (DRGF:56); Severinus, b. 6/26/1784 (DRGF:85). Sponsors: Georg Snell & Anna Eva (re:1); Severines Snell & Anna Eva (re:2).

Snell, Peter G. (Schnellenbusch) & Maria [?] (Palatine): Anna Eva, bapt. 11/1/1791 (SJC:50); Georg, bapt. 2/17/1793 (SJC:73). Sponsors: Georg Schnell & Anna Eva Kiles (re:1); Jacob Snell & Susanna Killes (re:2).

Death Record

Snell, [?], (child of Joseph Snell), d. 3/?/1813, age [?]; buried 3/28/1813 (DFP:96)

Snell, [?], (wife of Silus Schnell), d. 3/5/1793; buried 3/6/1793 (DFP:83)

Snell, [?], (child of Joseph Snell), d. 3/28/1813, age [not given] (DFP:96)

Snell, Anna, (wife of Johannes Snell), d. 2/?/1813, age 52 years, 1 month, 27 days; buried 2/24/1813 (DFP:95)

Snell, Betsy, (Mrs.), d. 6/12/1823, age 28 years; buried Cherry Valley Presbyterian

Church cemetery (PCV:80)

Snell, Jacob, (son of Friedrich Snell), d. 7/22/1794, age 1 year, 4 months; buried 7/24/1794 (RDSA:234)

Snell, Johannes, b. 1696, in the Pfalz in Europe, nearly 92 years old; d. 9/12/1787; left 3 daus., 26 grandchildren; 72 great-grandchildren; 3 great-great grandchildren (RDSA:230)

Snell, Maria, (legitimate dau. of Jacob Schnell), b. 1783; d. 9/20/1790; buried 9/22/1790 (RDSA:232)

Tryon County Militia

Snell, Adam	[Appendix A]
Snell, George	
Snell, Jacob	
Snell, John	
Snell, John F.	
Snell, John J.	
Snell, John P.	
Snell, John, Jr.	
Snell, Nicholas	
Snell, Peter	
Snell, Severines	
Snell, Thomas Jacob	

Pension Abstract

Snell, Hanyost, b. 1758/9, Manheim, N.Y.; d. 7/28/1832, in the town of his birth. Hanyost was a private in Capt. Cogh's [Cook] Co., Col. Jacob Klock's 2nd. Regt., Tryon Co. Militia; he was wounded in October 1781 [battle of Johnstown?] while on duty and received two injuries, one through his side and the other in his foot; Hanyost was allowed a disability pension for his wounds on 9/15/1786. (RWPA: #S28607)

Snell, Jacob, b. 12/15/1761, Stone Arabia, N.Y.; resident of Palatine, Montgomery Co. on 2/18/1832; d. 8/28/1838. (Grandfather: [not named] built the fort at Stone Arabia in the "French War"; father: [not named] and Jacob's only brother, John G. Snell, were both killed in the battle of Oriskany.) Jacob enlisted in 1776 and served at various times for over two years until 1782; he was a private, drummer and sergeant under Capts. Fox, Miller, Getman, Seeber and Nellis in the regiments of Cols. Klock, Waggoner, Harper, Brown and Willett; Jacob fought in the battle of Stone Arabia where he was wounded by a ball which penetrated through his back into his right shoulder and following the battle Jacob's home & all its contents were destroyed and his mother & sisters made homeless; he was also engaged in the battles of Landman's [Lampman's] and Johnstown. After the war Jacob held a number of civil and military positions. (RWPA: #S2429 & #S28608)

Snell, John, b. 8/2/1755, Stone Arabia, N.Y.; moved to Manheim, Herkimer Co., N.Y. in March 1784 where he remained for thirty-three years; resident of Shelby, Orleans Co., N.Y. on 2/5/1834. John volunteered and served for six months in 1775 as a sergeant in Capt. Christian House's Co., Col. Jacob Klock's 2nd. Regt., Tryon Co. Militia; John enlisted in the batteau service in 1776 and served for six months under Capt. Van Eps and for one month in Capt. Garrit Lansing's Co.; John continued to serve on various tours of duty until the end of the war; he was a participant in the battle of Stone Arabia. (RWPA: #S10021)

Snell, Peter, b. ca. 1720; (brothers: [two not named] both killed in the battle of Oriskany); m. Susannah Kilts, 3/10/1768, Reformed Dutch Church of Stone Arabia; d. 7/24/1804. (Susannah Snell, b. 1749/50, dau. of Peter

COMPENDIUM

Kilts; resident of Manheim, N.Y. on 12/26/1838.) Peter served as a sergeant from 1775 until the fall of 1780 under Capts. Christian House and Henry Miller in Col. Jacob Klock's 2nd. Regt., Tryon Co. Militia; he fought in the battle of Oriskany. (RWPA: #R9897)

1790 Census

Snell, Adam   [Appendix B]
Snell, Eve
Snell, Jacob
Snell, John
Snell, John J.
Snell, John S.
Snell, Nicholas
Snell, Peter
Snell, Peter G.
Snell, Severinius
Snell, Zeely

SNIKERBRACKER

1790 Census

Snikerbacker, Francis   [Appendix B]

SNOOK

Marriage

Snoock, Jacob m. Margaret Pottman, 10/15/1762 (RDSA:171)

Birth/Baptism

Snock, Mary & [?]: Jacobus, bapt. 10/12/1740 (FH:12). Sponsors: Henderick Snock, Helena Snock.

Snock, William & Catarina (Kleyn): Christina, bapt. 9/12/1761 (DRC:5). Sponsors: Johanes Kleyn & Christina Kleyn.

Snoock, John & Agnes (McGraw): Mary, b. 11/7/1790; bapt. 1/6/1791 (DRC:92). Sponsors: [none named].

Snook, Henderick & Sophia (Oosterman): William, b. 3/19/1787; bapt. 4/16/1787 (DRC:84). Sponsors: William Snook & Catrina Van Jevertse [Evertse?].

Probate Abstract

Snoeck, William, (of the town of Florida), will dated 1/17/1812; probated 2/6/1815. Legatees: wife, Catharine; sons, Henry, John, Jacob and Peter; daus., Christianah (& her children, Eve Visher, Margret Frank and Mary Pettingell). Executors: Garret Putman, Barny Martin, Nicholas Hill. Witnesses: Nicholas and Ellenor Hill, John Bartholomew. (WMC 56:393)

Snook, Jacob, (of the town of Amsterdam), will dated 12/14/1806, Johnstown, N.Y.; probated 1/28/1818. Legatees: wife, Margaret; brother, William's (sons, John, Henry, Jacob and Peter). Executors: Frances and Victor J. Putman (of Johnstown and Amsterdam). Witnesses: Cornelius Phillips, William Bowen, Peter Bowen, Jr. (WMc 57:166)

Tryon County Militia

Snook, Henry   [Appendix A]
Snook, William

Pension Abstract

Snook, Henry, b. 1760, son of William Snook,

757

Florida, N.Y.; resident of his birthplace on 9/19/1832. Henry entered the military in 1776 and was a private in Capt. Samuel Pettingell's Co., Col. Frederick Fisher's 3rd. Regt., Tryon Co. Militia; he was stationed at a fort near the Johnstown jail in 1777 as a guard and was always "in readiness as a minute man during the whole war when called upon either by draft or as a volunteer". [Henry Snook stated that his father, William Snook, was made captain of his company after the death of Samuel Pettingell in the battle of Oriskany. He also said that John Pettingell, James Phillips, Peter Putman and Stephen Tuttle had been killed at Oriskany.] (RWPA: #S11435)

1790 Census

Snook, Jacob   [Appendix B]
Snuke, Henry
Snuke, William

SNOW

1790 Census

Snow, Elijah   [Appendix B]
Snow, Joseph

SNYDER

Birth/Baptism

Snyder, Adam & Maria (Link): Caty, bapt. 12/20/1778 (DRC:50). Sponsors: Nicholas Alt & Caty Link.

Snyder, Jacob & Maria [?]: Gertraut, b. 9/6/1783; bapt. 9/8/1783 (DRGF:75). Sponsors: Conrad Walls & Gertraut.

Snyder, Ludwig & Margretha [?]: Jacob, b. 12/7/1766; bapt. 12/21/1766 (RDSA:71).

Death Record

Snyder, [?], (Mr.), d. 1/21/1849, age 76 years, of an accident; buried Cherry Valley Presbyterian Church cemetery (PCV:89)

Probate Abstract

Snyder, Andrew, (of Johnson's Bush), will dated 8/2/1783; probated 1/12/1795. Legatees: wife, Dorothy; son-in-law, James Warner. Executors: James Warner, Mathias Lynk, Johannis Walter. Witnesses: Mathias Lynk, Johannis Walter, James Livingston. (WMC 56:148)

Snyder, Jacob, (of Minden), will dated 2/9/1816; probated 2/16/1816. Legatees: wife, Maria; daus., Lena, Maria, Rachel, Margretha, Elizabeth, Gertrud and Anna. Executors: my friend Isaac (of Isaac) Elwood. Witnesses: Gottlib Snyder, Jacob B. Sitts, Abraham Arndt. (WMC 56:396)

Snyder, John, (of Minden), will dated 9/12/1825; probated 3/27/1829. Legatees: wife, Margaret; sons, Daniel, Benjamin, Jacob, John and Abram; daus., Susanna, Caty, Margaret and Mary. Executors: wife; Williams Jenkins. Witnesses: Adam and Daniel Seiber, Solomon Countryman. (WMC 57:274)

Tryon County Militia

Snyder, Adam   [Appendix A]

1790 Census

758

Snider, Cutlip   [Appendix B]
Snider, Jacob
Snider, John
Snider, Michael
Snider, William

SOAP

1790 Census

Soap, Michael   [Appendix B]

SOBEL

Marriage

Sobel, Willem m. Maria Nukirk, 7/30/1779 (DRC:162)

Birth/Baptism

Sobel, William & Maria (Nukirk): Barber, b. 5/12/1783; bapt. 6/1/1783 (DRC:66). Sponsors: Matthew Young & Sarah Nukirk.

SODORE

1790 Census

Sodore, Isaac   [Appendix B]

SOUCH (also see **SOUTCH**)

1790 Census

Souch, Peter   [Appendix B]

SOUL

1790 Census

Soul, Jonathan   [Appendix B]
Soul, Joseph
Souls, Moses

SOUTCH (also see **SOUCH**)

1790 Census

Soutch, George   [Appendix B]
Soutch, John (2)
Soutch, John P.
Soutch, Peter P.

SOUTEL

1790 Census

Soutel, Peter, Sr.   [Appendix B]

SOUTHWARD

Birth/Baptism

Soutwerst, William & Sussanna [?]: Echje, b. 2/2/1765; bapt. 2/24/1765 (RDSA:54). Sponsors: Catharina van den Werken & Marteines Gardinier.

Tryon County Militia

Southworth, William [Appendix A]

1790 Census

Southward, William [Appendix B]
Southward, William, Jr.

SOX

Birth/Baptism

Sox, Jacob & Catherine (Reis), Stillwater: Roseana, bapt. 2/22/1783 (JDR:22).

SPAAN see SPOHN

SPAANENBURG

Marriage

Spaanenburg, Hendrik m. Maragrita Veder, 11.10/1785 (DRC:164)

Birth/Baptism

Spannenberg, Henderick & Maragrita (Veeder): Catrina, b. 1/20/1787; bapt. 2/25/1787 (DRC:83, 87). Sponsors: Philip Plank & Dorethea Plank.

Probate Abstract

Sponenbargh, Adam, (of Johnstown), will dated 4/12/1817; probated 4/18/1817. Legatees: wife, Catharine; father, Henry; brothers, Lucas and Henry; sisters, Catharine (widow of Volkert Van Antwerp & their children, John, Margaret

and Henry), and Agnes (wife of Aaron Smith & their son, Adam). Executors: father, Henry; uncle, Adam Plank; James Williamson. Witnesses: Richard Van Meter, William Van Meter, John M. Devoe. (WMC 57:165)

1790 Census

Sponenbarack, George [Appendix B]

SPAFFORD

Probate Abstract

Spafford, Thomas, (of Manheim), will dated 12/29/1809; probated 2/2/1801. Legatees: wife, Buly (nee Ransom); sons, John, Thomas, Calvin and Luke; dau., Susana; Calvin Ransom. Executors: father-in-law, Jonathan Ransom; Jacob Markel. Witnesses: Anthony Kaufman, Calvin Moffet, Calvin Ransom. (WMC 56:160)

SPALTSBERGER (also see SPAULSBERRY)

Marriage

Spalsberger, Jacob m. Margretha Wallrath, 6/17/1793 (DFP:49)

Spaltsberger, Johannes m. Anna Margreth Sutz, 6/1/1766 (RDSA:179)

Birth/Baptism

Spaltzberger/Spalzberger, Johannes & Margretha [?]: Johannes, b. 3/12/1767, bapt. 3/22/1767 (RDSA:74); Catharina, b. 3/1/1771 (LTSA:35); Maria, b. 12/15/1780, bapt. 12/26/1780 (DRGF:41); Anna, b. 10/4/1783, bapt. 10/10/1783 (DRGF:76). Sponsors: Dietrich Coppernoll & Catharina Coppernoll (re:1); Dewald Deigert & his wife (re:2); Johann Jost Fink & Maria (re:3); Johannes Sutz & Catharina (re:4).

Tryon County Militia

Spalsberger, John   [Appendix A]

SPANKNABLE

Birth/Baptism

Spanknebel, Johannes & Elisabeth [?]: Herman, b. 6/7/1782; bapt. 6/9/1782 (DRGF:58). Sponsors: Joh: Ludw: Kring & Maria.

Death Record

Spanneknebel, Christopher, d. 6/12/1792, age 1 year, 2 months, 3 days; buried 6/14/1792 (RDSA:233)

Probate Abstract

Spanknable, Johannes, (of Palatine), will dated 9/8/1825; probated 12/26/1827. Legatees: wife, Elisabeth; sons, Philip, John (decd. & his heirs), Henry, Harmanus (decd. & his Henry H., Philip, John, Catharine and Harriet); daus., Ursula (wife of William Smith & her daus.), Elizabeth (wife of Jacob Youker) and Maria (wife of Philip Cool, Jr.). Executors: son, Philip; son-in-law, Jacob Youker; Christoper Getman. (WMC 57:270)

Tryon County Militia

Spanknable, John   [Appendix A]

Pension Abstract

Spanknable, John, m. Elizabeth [?], 2/9/1770; d. 12/20/1825. (Elizabeth Spanknable, b. 1751/2; resident of Ephratah, Montgomery Co., N.Y. on 10/11/1836.) John enlisted and served as a private in Capt. Nicholas Richter's Co., Col. Jacob Klock's 2nd. Regt., Tryon Co. Militia; he fought in the battle of Oriskany and was captured by the enemy; John was taken to Canada where he remained a prisoner for upwards of four years. (RWPA: #W11519)

SPARBEK

Birth/Baptism

Sparbek, Martinus & Anna Margaretha [?]: Joannes, b. 10/14/1768 (LTSA:25). Sponsors: Jacob Rother & his wife.

Sperbeck, Gabriel & Margaretha [?]: Anna Margaretha, b. 1/21/1757 (LTSA:21). Sponsors: Johannes Jung & his wife, Margaretha.

SPARKS

1790 Census

Sparks, Pearl   [Appendix B]

SPAULDING

1790 Census

COMPENDIUM

Spaulding, Amasa   [Appendix B]
Spaulding, Edward
Spaulding, Nehemiah

SPAULSBERRY (also see SPALTSBERGER)

1790 Census

Spaulsberry, John   [Appendix B]

SPECK

Birth/Baptism

Speck, Rachel & [?]: Claes, bapt. 2/18/1738/9 (FH:6). Sponsors: Will Sixbury and his wife.

SPENCER

Marriage

Spencer, Daniel (son of Georg Spinster, decd.) m. Catharina Cremer (dau. of Johannes Cremer), 3/13/1791 (DFP:43; RDSA:196)

Spencer, Robert (son of Michael Spenster) m. Catharina Sternberger (dau. of Adam Sternberger), 12/3/1761 (RDSA:170)

Birth/Baptism

Spencer, Robert & Catharina (Sternberg): Appollonia, b. 10/4/1762, bapt. 10/24/1762 (RDSA:36); Elisabeth, b. 10/30/1764, bapt. 12/7/1764 (RDSA:52); Jacobus, b. 11/16/1766, bapt. 1/17/1767 (RDSA:72); Robert, b.

8/10/1772, bapt. 8/30/1772 (DRC:23). Sponsors: Rachel Quackenbusch & Wilhelm Quackenbusch (re:1); Elisabeth, wife of Johannes Evertsen (re:2); Jacob Sternberger & Lena von Aaale (re:3); Jacob Gardinier & Derkey Gardinier (re:4).

Tryon County Militia

Spencer, Aaron   [Appendix A]
Spencer, Jonathan
Spencer, Nathan

1790 Census

Spencer, John   [Appendix B]
Spencer, Jonathan
Spencer, Orange
Spencer, Rufus
Spencer, William

SPENGLE

Birth/Baptism

Spengle, Georg (Dr.) & Anna Dorothea [?]: Anna Catharina, b. 12/9/1783; bapt. 1/25/1784 (DRGF:80). Sponsors: Pieter Waggoner & Anna.

SPIES

Birth/Baptism

Spies, Heironymus & Barbara [?]: Maria, b. 7/1/1767; bapt. 8/11/1767 (RDSA:77). Sponsors: Elisabeth & Wilhelm Teughard.

SPONDABLE

1790 Census

Spondable, John   [Appendix B]

SPOHN

Marriage

Spaan, Joha. Nicol m. Catharina Giels (dau. of J. Nic. Giels), 6/20/1786 (DRGF:203)

Spoon, Henrich m. Margret Hiller (dau. of Joh: Hiller), 5/10/1791 (DRGF:208)

Birth/Baptism

Spohn, Johann Nicolaus & Elisabeth [?]: Anna Eva, b. 5/18/1761, bapt. 5/31/1761 (RDSA:26); Johann Niclas, b. 8/27/1762, bapt. 9/7/1762 (RDSA:35); Johannes, b. 1/26/1765, bapt. 2/14/1765 (RDSA:53); Johann Henrich, b. 6/8/1766, bapt. 6/22/1766 (RDSA:65); Sussanna, bapt. 5/25/1770 (RDSA:103). Sponsors: Anna Eva (dau. of Joseph Staring) & Jacob Dieffendorff (re:1); Werner Spaan & Elisabeth Foltz (re:2); Johannes Dieffendorff & Catharina Hess (re:3); Johannes Miller & his wife, Elisabeth (re:4); Johann Friedrich Fr[?] & his wife, Sussanna (re:5).

Death Record

Spohn, Elisabeth (Deifendorff), (widow of Nicholas Spoon, from Herkimer), d. 8/30/1817, age 84 years; buried in the cemetery of the stone church in Germanflats (RDH:274)

Tryon County Militia

Spohn, Nicholas   [Appendix A]
Spohn, Werner

Pension Abstract

Spohn, Nicholas, m. Catharine Kills, 6/?/1786, at the home of Nicholas Spohn's father [not named] in Herkimer, N.Y. by Rev. Abraham Rosencrantz; d. 4/27/1830. (Catharine Spohn, b. 3/20/1767; [brother: Peter N. Kills, b. 5/27/1763; m. [?], 6/20/1786]; resident of Herkimer, Herkimer Co. on 2/6/1839.) Grandchild: John F. Spoon (resident of Little Falls, Herkimer Co. on 5/31/1839). Nicholas enlisted from his home in Fort Plain and served for at least one year in Col. Brown's Regt. of the N.Y. Line; he was a participant in the battle of Johnstown. (RWPA: #W17861 *SPOON*)

1790 Census

Spoon, Nicholas   [Appendix B]
Spoon, Warner

SPOHR

Marriage

Spohr, Abraham m. Jeannetje Gallier, 8/11/1793 (DFP:50)

Probate Abstract

Spoore, Mary, (of Charleston), will dated 2/26/1798; probated 3/13/1802. Legatees: sons, John and Nicholas; daus., Eva Van Olinder, Leona Hogoboom, Mary Cotton, Sarah Spoore and Catrine Spoore. Executors: Dirck Van Vechten, John Spoore. Witnesses: Nathaniel Campbell, Mary Van Vaughten, Rachel Van Veghten. (WMC 56:151)

Tryon County Militia

Spoor, John   [Appendix A]
Spoor, Nicholas

Pension Abstract

Spoor, John, b. 1749/50; m. Rachel Fries, 3/8/1781, Claverack, Columbia Co., N.Y.; resident of Pompey, Onondaga Co., N.Y. on 5/8/1818; d. 7/1/1834. (Rachel Spoor, b. 1751/2; resident of Lafayette, Onondaga Co. on 12/7/1838.) Children: Polly (living in 1838). John enlisted on 11/21/1776 and served as an ensign in Capt. Thomas Dewitt's Co., Col. Peter Gansevoort's Regt. of the N.Y. Line; he was taken prisoner by the enemy at Fort Stanwix in July 1777 and kept captive for about six months; John marched on Sullivan's expedition; he was discharged from the military in March 1780. (RWPA: #W25065)

1790 Census

Spoore, John   [Appendix B]
Spore, Henry
Spore, John
Spore, Nicholas

SPOTTON

Marriage

Spotton, James m. Thankful Baker, 7/13/1738, Schenectady (FH:4)

SPRAIG

1790 Census

Spraig, Jonathan   [Appendix B]

SPRAKER see SPRECHER

SPRECHER

Marriage

Sprecher, Georg (son of Georg Sprecher) m. Batje Mekie (dau. of Johann Mekie), 6/30/1789 (DFP:39)

Sprecher, Johann Jost m. Catharina Fraser, 6/17/1787 (RDSA:192)

Sprecher, Johannes m. Margretha [?], 11/6/1781 (DRGF:195)

Birth/Baptism

Sprecher, Conrad & Alita [?]: Christina, b. 1/18/1796 (LTSA:93); Beata, b. 5/25/1797 (LTSA:99). Sponsors: John Dillebach, Christina Sprecher (re:1); Jerg Sprecher & Maria (re:2).

Sprecher, Conrad & Philippina [?]: Johannes, b. 11/14/1760; bapt. 11/23/1760 [deceased] (RDSA:23). Sponsors: Johann Taber & Maria Elisabetha (dau. of Henrich Crems).

Sprecher, Georg [b. 8/25/1736] (LTSA:43) & Anna Maria [?]: Anna Maria, b. 8/11/1769 (LTSA:29); Gertrudis, b. 11/1/1771 (LTSA:39); Christina, b. 12/17/1778, bapt. 1/4/1779 (LTSA:56); Anna, b. 12/10/1781, bapt. 12/28/1781 (DRGF:52). Sponsors: Jo. Christian Dillenbach, Margaretha Wik (re:1); Jost Haus, Gertrudis Sprecher (re:2); Martin Nistel & Elisabeth (re:3); Johannes Kasselmann & Anna Snell (re:4).

764

COMPENDIUM

Sprecher, Jerg & Batche [?]: Catarina, b. 1/10/1795 (LTSA:88). Sponsors: Jost Sprecher & Catarina.

Sprecher, Johannes & Margaret [?]: Maria, b. 6/30/1782, bapt. 8/18/1782 (DRGF:60); Elisabet, b. 5/3/1790 (LTSA:65); Lydia, b. 3/12/1793 (LTSA:78); Magdalena, b. 6/24/1795 (LTSA:90); Anna, b. 6/24/1795 (LTSA:90). Sponsors: Andreas Finck, Mjr. & Maria Sprecher (re:1); Philip Empie & Elisabet (re:2); Wilhelm Wolgemuth & Maria (re:3); Jost Sprecher & Catarina (re:4); Andreas Dillebach, Anna Sprecher (re:5).

Sprecher, Jost & Catarina [?]: Elisabet, b. 3/12/1794 (LTSA:83); Georg, b. 8/16/1796 (LTSA:97). Sponsors: Jerg Sprecher & Bada (re:1); Georg Sprecher & Maria (re:2).

Probate Abstract

Spracker, George, (of Palatine), will dated 8/12/1807; probated 1/29/1823. Legatees: wife, Maria; sons, Jost, Johannis, George and Conradt; daus., Maris (wife of James Frasod), Rachel (wife of George Counderman, Jr.), Christiana (wife of David I. Zielly), Anna (wife of Jacob I. Lawyer) and Elizabeth (wife of Martin Van Beuren). Executors: wife and son, Jost. Witnesses: Jon'n Eights, Jacob P. Wever, Aaron Taft. (WMC 57:175)

Spraker, George, (of Canajoharie), will dated 4/21/1828; probated 9/5/1828. Legatees: wife, Nancy; sons, Peter and George Wieting; "each of my three daughters". Executors: wife; Delos White, Peter L. Nellis. Witnesses: Delos White, Simon Smith, John Le Baron. (WMC 57:271)

Spraker, George, Jr., (of Canajoharie), will dated 12/26/1806; probated 9/10/1807.

Legatees: wife, Eva; son, George; daus., Maria and Cady; wife's son, Peter Nellis. Executors: brother, Joseph; Mathias Lane, John Seeber. Witnesses: Jacob and Johanes Kramer, Margaret Seeber. (WMC 56:156)

Tryon County Militia

Spracher, Conrad   [Appendix A]
Spracher, George
Spracher, George, Jr.
Spracher, John

Pension Abstract

Spracher, John, b. 7/9/1756, Palatine, N.Y.; resident of his birthplace on 9/19/1832. John entered the military in the spring of 1776 and served at various times until the close of the war; he was a private and batteauman under Capts. Jacob W. Seeber, John Breadbake, John Leffeller, Samuel Gray in the regiments of Cols. Dayton, Cox, Klock, Lewis, Harper, Waggoner, Brown and Willett; John was at the surrender of Gen. Burgoyne and he fought in the battles of Oriskany, Stone Arabia, Turlock and Johnstown; his total period of service in the military amounted to three years and twenty-seven days. (RWPA: #S14555)

1790 Census

Spraker, Conradt   [Appendix B]
Spraker, George
Spraker, John
Spraker, Joseph

SPRIG

1790 Census

Sprig, Alexander   [Appendix B]

765

SPRINGSTEEL

Springsteel, Jacob   [Appendix B]
Springsteel, John

SQUIRE

1790 Census

Squire, John   [Appendix B]
Squire, John, Jr.
Squire, Zachariah
Squires, Ichabod

STAAL

Birth/Baptism

Staal, Jacob & Dorothea [?]: Abram, b. 8/26/1783; bapt. 8/28/1783 (DRC:68). Sponsors: Abram Nukirk & Eliz. Staal.

Staal/Stall, Joseph & Maria/Polly (Grant): Catrina, b. 6/3/1778, bapt. 6/21/1778 (DRC:48); Rachel, b. 2/13/1780, bapt. 2/27/1780 (DRC:55); Maria, b. 12/17/1781, bapt. 1/1/1782 (DRC:59); Margerieta, b. 1/1/1791, bapt. 1/30/1791 (DRC:94). Sponsors: Hendrik Staal & Annatje Staal (re:1); Arent Burns & Maragrita Hall (re:2); Volkert Veeder & Elizabeth Veeder (re:3); John Yates & his wife (re:4).

Stall, Anthony & [Eliza]beth (Holder): Anatje, b. 12/4/1790; bapt. 3/6/1791 (DRC:95). Sponsors: [none named].

Stall, [?drik] & Annatje (Kelder): Catrina, b. 1/22/1791; bapt. 2/23/1791 (DRC:95). Sponsors: [none named].

Stall, Peter & Gertruy (Beccor): Marrigrietje, b. 12/19/1790; bapt. 1/1/1791 (DRC:92). Sponsors: Jost Stall & Polly Stall.

Tryon County Militia

Stall, Rudolph   [Appendix A]

1790 Census

Staals, Garret   [Appendix B]
Stall, Anthony, Jr.
Stall, Joseph

STAATS

Death Record

Staats, Catherine Van Santford, (wife of Henry W. Staats), d. 1/6/1835, age 42 years; buried sect. 9, Colonial Cemetery, Johnstown (JC:187)

1790 Census

Staats, Francis   [Appendix B]

STABITZ

Tryon County Militia

Stabitz, Michael   [Appendix A]

STACKWEATHER

1790 Census

Stackweather, Elijah   [Appendix B]

STACY

1790 Census

Stacy, Isaac   [Appendix B]

STALEY

Birth/Baptism

Staley, George (of Fald) & Dorothea (Schumacher) (Germanflats, Herkimer Co.): Delia, bapt. 9/13/1789 (SJC:17); Johannes, bapt. 6/19/1791 (SJC:43); Niclaus, b. 12/1/1792, bapt. 1/27/1793 (SJC:70). Sponsors: Marx Kesseler & Delia Kesseler (re:1); John Stahli & Catharina Stahli (re:2); Niclaus Stahli & Eva Bayer (re:3).

Staley, Johannes & Maria Elisabeth [?]: Johann Georg, b. 10/27/1784, bapt. 12/7/1784 (DRGF:90); Heinrich, bapt. 11/11/1792 [parents of Royal Grant] (SJC:66). Sponsors: Henrich Mejer & Gertraud (re:1); Heinrich Scheffer & Anna Scheffer (re:2).

Probate Abstract

Staley, Jacob, (of the town of Florida), will dated 2/16/1824; probated 5/21/1824. Legatees: wife, Susanna; sons, Henry, Valentine and Oliver; daus., Ann, Susanna and Elizabeth. Executors: Robert Blood, Henry I. and Valentine Staley. Witnesses: Robert Blood, Shuler Cady, William Bunn. (WMC 57:178)

Staley, Rulof, (of Florida), will dated 11/26/1828; probated 7/18/1831. Legatees: sons, Henry, Joseph and Harmonus; daus., Barbara Post, Ann Smith, Margaret Quilhot (& her Elizabeth), Mary Robb, Catherine Staley. Executors: son, Harmonus Staley; son-in-law, James Post. Witnesses: Peter Milroy, Andrew Johnson, Andrew McClyman. (WMC 57:279)

Stalley, Harmanus, (of [not stated]), will dated 8/3/1793; probated 10/3/1797. Legatees: wife, Mary; my children; brothers, Hendrick & George. Executors: Hendrick & George. Witnesses: Nathaniel Campbell, John Taylor, Jacob Bodine. (WMC 56:149)

Tryon County Militia

Staley, George   [Appendix A]
Staley, Henry
Staley, Joseph
Staley, Rudolph

Pension Abstract

Staley, George, b. 7/6/1753, Truxberry [Tewksbury?], Hunterdon Co., N.J.; m. Janette McCall, 1/?/1775, Schenectady, N.Y.; d. 3/26/1839 or 3/27/1839, Princetown, Schenectady Co., N.Y. (Janette Staley, b. 8/21/1753; d. 7/5/1846, Rotterdam, Schenectady Co., N.Y.) Children: Ann, b. 9/21/1775; Henry, b. 5/13/1777, bapt. 6/19/1777; Oliver, b. 7/1/1781 (resident of Princetown, N.Y. in 1846); Jacob, b. 8/16/1783; Janet, b. 1/15/1785 (m. [?] Dunce and resident of Madison Co., N.Y. in 1846); Mary, b. 6/12/1788 (m. [?] Chambers and resident of Schoharie Co., N.Y. in 1846); Betsy, b. 3/18/1791 (m. [?] McCarley and resident of Michigan in 1846); Susan, b. 8/4/1793 (m. [?] Swart and resident of Florida, N.Y. in 1846); George, b. 1/13/1796. George enlisted from Corriesbush (later called Princetown, Schenectady District) early in 1775 and was called out in 1776 when he served over one month as a private in Capt. Thomas Wasson's Co., Col. Abraham Wemple's Regt.; George enlisted again in 1777 and was sent on the northern campaign to Ticonderoga; he served again in 1778 and assisted in bringing cannon and ammunition from Ticonderoga to Albany; George was on several tours of duty in 1779 and was stationed at Forts Paris, Plain, Schoharie, and Plank; he was a participant in the battle of Saratoga. (RWPA: #W19123)

Staley, Henry, b. 2/15/1746, son of Matthias Staley [RWPA: #S23440] of Raritan, N.J.; resident of Florida, Montgomery Co., N.Y. on 8/30/1832. Henry entered the military in May 1776 and served as a private in Capt. David McMaster's Co., Col. Frederick Fisher's 3rd. Regt., Tryon Co. Militia; he continued to serve in this company until the close of the war; Henry fought in the battle of Oriskany. (RWPA: #S11490)

Staley, Matthias, b. 1737, Hunterdon Co., N.Y.; m. [wife not named]; resident of Blenheim, Schoharie Co., N.Y. on 9/8/1832 where he had lived for the past twenty-eight years. Children: Henry, b. 1763/4 [RWPA: #S11490]. Matthias enlisted from Schenectady in 1776 for three months under Capt. Minard Wemple in Col. Cortland's Regt.; he served for six months in 1777 under Capt. Thomas Wasson and was at the taking of Burgoyne; he enlisted in 1778 for six months in the batteau service on the North River and helped to transport cannon south from Ticonderoga; Matthias was drafted in 1779 and stationed at Stone Arabia under Lt. John Thornton.

(RWPA: #S23440)

1790 Census

Stally, Job   [Appendix B]
Staly, Hendrick
Staly, Jacob
Staly, John
Staly, Ruloof
Staly, Silvanus

STALL see STAAL

STALLER

Birth/Baptism

Staller, Michael & Dorothea [?]: Adam, bapt. 3/9/1767 (RDSA:73); Charlotta, b. 4/15/1769 (LTSA:28); Magdalena, b. 3/11/1771 (LTSA:35). Sponsors: [none named] (re:1); J. Georg Hoch & his wife (re:2); Balthasar Ergezinger, Magdalena Morin (re:3).

STAMM

Marriage

Stamm, Bastiane m. Catharina Snell (widow of Friedr. Snell), 6/6/1786 (DRGF:203)

Stamm, Georg m. Catharina Kills, 4/18/1790 (RDSA:195)

Stamm, Georg m. Eva Bell (of Sir Williams

COMPENDIUM

Bush), 12/11/1765 (RDSA:177)

Stamm, Lorentz m. Anna Wohlgemuth,
1/8/1792 (RDSA:196)

Birth/Baptism

Stamm, George & Anna Eva [?]: Georgius, b.
4/19/1769, bapt. 4/23/1769 (RDSA:94);
Lorentz, b. 5/2/1771, bapt. 5/4/1771
(RDSA:109); Johannes, b. 6/2/1775, bapt.
6/7/1775 (LTSA:49); Maria Elisabeth, b.
4/10/1780, bapt. 4/16/1780 (LTSA:60);
Margretha, b. 5/13/1783, bapt. 5/19/1783
(DRGF:72); Johann Jost, b. 7/13/1785, bapt.
7/21/1785 (DRGF:99); Anna, b. 3/3/1791
(LTSA:67). Sponsors: Georg Stamm & Maria
Magdalena (re:1); Lorentz Stamm & Elisabeth
(re:2); Johannes Deichert & his wife, Dorothea
(re:3); Willhelm Feder, Elisabeth Stamm (re:4);
Pieter Giels & Margretha Kayser (re:5); John
Mac Garan & Margretha Kayser (re:6); Wilh.
Wabel & Elisabet (re:7).

Stamm, Jerg & Catharina [?]: Catharina, b.
11/27/1790 (LTSA:66); Jerg, b. 3/4/1794
(LTSA:82). Sponsors: Adam Kils & Catharina
(re:1); Peter Kils & Lena (re:2).

Stamm, Lorentz & Elisabetha [?]: Barbar, bapt.
1764 (DRC:12); Anna Eva, b. 3/16/1768, bapt.
3/20/1768 (RDSA:84); Severines, b.
10/28/1769, bapt. 11/5/1769 (RDSA:98);
Dorothea, b. 11/5/1775, bapt. 11/15/1775
(LTSA:50); Lorentz, b. 4/30/1781, bapt.
5/3/1781 [posthumously] (DRGF:45).
Sponsors: George Stam & Barbar Stam (re:1);
Anna Eva & Georg Snell (re:2); Severines
Tyghart, sen. & his wife, Maria (re:3);
Johannes Deichert & his wife, Dorothea (re:4);
Georg Snell & Anna Eva (re:5).

Stamm, Lorenz & Anna [?]: Maria, b.

11/10/1794 (LTSA:86). Sponsors: Wilhelm
Wolgemut & Maria.

Death Record

Stam, Henry, d. 5/3/1872, age 74 years, 3
months; buried in a private cemetery on the
Bowman farm, about two miles from the town
of Hessville; about one-half mile from the road
on a knoll (BFC 41:1)

Tryon County Militia

Stamm, George   [Appendix A]
Stamm, Jacob
Stamm, Lawrence

1790 Census

Stam, Elizabeth   [Appendix B]

STAN

Birth/Baptism

Stan, Philip & Elizabeth (Reddefort): Nichs.,
b. 9/20/1784; bapt. 11/12/1784 (DRC:70).
Sponsors: Hendk. Rigtmyer & Maria Shever.

STANCLIFF

Birth/Baptism

Stancliff, Stambrough P. (Palatine Town) &
Sybille [?]: Mary, b. 2/15/1786; Thomas, b.
8/22/1788; Betsi, b. 10/8/1790; Perry, b.
8/20/1792 [all baptized on 12/30/1792] (all
noted in SJC:69). Sponsors: J. Jost Snell &
Maria Snell (re:1); Johannes Snell & Anna
Snell (re:2); Johannes Mayer & Catharina

769

Mayer (re:3); Conrad Zimmerman & Margretha Zimmerman (re:4).

STANDARD

1790 Census

Standard, Oliver   [Appendix B]

STANDRING

Death Record

Standring, Benjamin, d. 2/22/1814, age 52 years; buried sect. 7, Colonial Cemetery, Johnstown (JC:187)

Standring, Emma, (wife of Benjamin Standring), d. 7/10/1829, age 55 years; buried sect. 7, Colonial Cemetery, Johnstown (JC:187)

STANLY

1790 Census

Stanly, John   [Appendix B]

STANSIL

Birth/Baptism

Stanzel, Wilhelm & Elisabetha [?]: Niclas, b. ?/?/1756 (LTSA:20). Sponsors: Friderich Emige, Maria Elisabeth Schulz.

Tryon County Militia

Stansil, George   [Appendix A]
Stansil, Nicholas
Stansil, William

Pension Abstract

Stansil, George, b. 1759/60; resident of Canajoharie, Montgomery Co., N.Y. in 1824. George enlisted and served in Capt. Cogh's Co., Col. Jacob Klock's 2nd. Regt., Tryon Co. Militia as a private; he was wounded through his shoulder in the battle of Johnstown on 10/25/1781; George was allowed a pension on 9/22/1786 for disability resulting from his wound. (RWPA: #S27536)

STANSON

1790 Census

Stanson, George   [Appendix B]
Stanson, John

STANTON

1790 Census

Stanton, Daniel   [Appendix B]
Stanton, Elijah
Stanton, John
Stanton, Rosel

STANZEL see STANSIL

STAPLES

1790 Census

Staples, George [Appendix B]

STARENBURG

1790 Census

Starenbarack, Adam [Appendix B]
Starenburg, Joseph, Jr.
Starnbarack, Adam

STARING

Marriage

Staring, Adam m. Catharina MacGinnes, 7/3/1770 (RDSA:189)

Staring, Adam m. Catharina Weber, 11/8/1768 (RDSA:185)

Staring, Conrad m. Sussanna Staring (dau. of Jac: Staring), 8/30/1795 (DRGF:212)

Staring, Georg (son of Ad: Staring) m. Anna Wohleben, 5/10/1795 (DRGF:212)

Staring, Georg (son of H: Staring) m. Catharina Dachstaeder, 2/10/1795 (DRGF:212)

Staring, Georg Ad: m. Margretha Hagedorn, 6/29/1792 (DRGF:209)

Staring, Georg m. Anna Zimmermann (dau. of Henr: Zimmermann), 6/6/1786 (DRGF:202)

Staring, Henrich m. Elisabeth Hess (Little Falls), 10/2/1764 (RDSA:173)

Staring, Jacob V: m. Elisabeth G. Laux, 1/10/1786 (DRGF:203)

Staring, Joh. Adam m. Ernestina Herter, 7/25/1784 (DRGF:200)

Staring, Nicholas m. Catharina Singer, 2/26/1789 (DRGF:206)

Staring, Nicholas m. Cunigunda Tygert, 9/22/1793 (DFP:50)

Staring, Peter, Adam m. Sabina Helmer (dau. of Fried: Helmer), 2/5/1792 (DRGF:209)

Birth/Baptism

Staren, Frederick & Elizabeth (France): Johannis, b. 1/6/1774; bapt. 6/26/1774 (DRC:27). Sponsors: Johannis Frank & Maria Grand.

Staring, Adam & Anna Elisabeth [?]: Catharina, b. 8/31/1784; bapt. 9/26/1784 (DRGF:87). Sponsors: Jacob Staring & Elisabeth Huber.

Staring, Adam & Catharina [?]: Maria Barbara, b. 3/22/1762, bapt. 4/3/1762 (RDSA:33); Johann Georg, b. 7/18/1764, bapt. 8/8/1764 (RDSA:49); Johann Peter, b. 8/20/1766, bapt. 9/16/1766 (RDSA:68); Johann Nicolaus, b. 2/27/1770, bapt. 3/8/1770 (RDSA:101); Friedrich, b. 6/16/1776, bapt. 6/17/1776 (DRGF:18); Jacob, b. 7/16/1778, bapt. 7/18/1778 (DRGF:31); Friedrich, b. 12/13/1781, bapt. 12/31/1781 (DRGF:52). Sponsors: Elisabeth (dau. of Peter Foltz) & Philipp (son of Friederich Helmer) (re:1); Johann Georg Helmer & Catharina Hess (re:2); Peter Hajer & Anna Maria (re:3); Johann

Nicolas Weber & Catharina (re:4); Friedrich Bell & his wife (re:5); Johann Adam Stahle & Catharina (re:6); Joh: Fredr. Helmer & Barbara (re:7).

Staring, Adam (of [?]) & Catharina [?]: Elisabeth, bapt. 3/9/1789 (SJC:11). Sponsors: Friderich Gemmer & Catharina Staring.

Staring, Adam (of [Burnets]field Dist.) & Christina (Herter): Maria Elisabeth, bapt. 4/11/1790 (SJC:25). Sponsors: Ludwig Bersch & Margretha Bersch.

Staring, Adam & Elisabeth [?]: Anna, b. 3/3/1779; bapt. 3/6/1779 (DRGF:34). Sponsors: Conrad Staring & Lena.

Staring, Conrad & Lena [?]: Delia, b. 12/25/1777; bapt. 1/1/1778 (DRGF:28). Sponsors: Henrich Keller & Adelheit.

Staring, Conrad (Royal Grant) & Magdalena [?]: Magdalena, bapt. 1/17/1794 (SJC:88). Sponsors: Valentin Bayer & Margretha Bayer.

Staring, Conrad (Royal Grant) & Margretha [?]: Benjamin, bapt. 5/8/1791 (SJC:42). Sponsors: Martin Von Schleyk & Maria Von Schleyk.

Staring, George (of Schnellenbusch) & Anna [?] (Royal Grant): Dorothea, bapt. 9/20/1788 (SJC:4); Anna, bapt. 5/8/1791 (SJC:42); Jacob, bapt. 10/13/1793 (SJC:82). Sponsors: Johannes Staring & Dorothea Zimmerman (re:1); Adam Zimmerman & Maria Von Schleyk (re:2); Jacob H. Zimmerman & Maria Zimmerman (re:3).

Staring, Henrich J: & Elisabeth [?]: Henricus, b. 7/9/1765, bapt. 7/10/1765 (RDSA:56); Johannes Nicolaus, b. 3/24/1767, bapt. 4/29/1767 (RDSA:74); Georg, b. 9/11/1768, bapt. 9/24/1768 (RDSA:90); Catharina, b. 3/7/1770, bapt. 3/22/1770 (RDSA:101); Augustinus, b. 5/2/1776, bapt. 5/23/1776 (DRGF:17); Henrich, b. 2/25/1778, bapt. 5/23/1778 (DRGF:30); Gertraut, b. 11/18/1779, bapt. 12/26/1779 (DRGF:37); Johann Adam, b. 8/27/1781, bapt. 8/28/1781 (DRGF:47). Sponsors: Adam Staring & Catharina Hess (re:1); Johann Nicel Staring & his wife, Anna (re:2); Hans Georg Kass & Geertruid (re:3); Maria Staring & Friedrich Hess (re:4); Augustin Klepsattel & Barbara (re:5); Joseph Staring & Maria (re:6); Henrich Nic: Staring & Elisabeth (re:7); Leonhard Dachstader & Anna (re:8).

Staring, Henrich Nic: & Elisabeth [?]: Maria Catharina, b. 2/7/1780, bapt. 2/13/1780 (DRGF:38); [?], b. 8/10/1783, bapt. 8/13/1783 (DRGF:74); Johann Nicolas, b. 2/26/1785, bapt. 3/6/1785 (DRGF:93). Sponsors: Adam Staring & Catharina (re:1); Nicolas Staring & Maria Barbara (re:2); Joh Nicol Nic: Staring & Margretha Pfeiffer (re:3).

Staring, Jacob & Catharina [?]: Jacobus, b. 7/30/1761, bapt. 8/2/1761 (RDSA:27); Johann Georg, b. 5/29/1763, bapt. 6/6/1763 (RDSA:40); Anna, b. 3/28/1765, bapt. 4/21/1765 (RDSA:54); Lena, b. 8/30/1766, bapt. 9/6/1766 (RDSA:67); Elisabeth, b. 4/4/1768, bapt. 5/1/1768 (RDSA:85); Johannes, b. 8/29/1771 (LTSA:38). Sponsors: Jacob Christmann & Elisabetha Laux (re:1); [none named] (re:2); Catharina & Dieterich Sutz (re:3); Lena & Henrich Dachstaeder (re:4); Elisabeth & James Bellington (re:5); Johannes Dachstetter, Eva Copernoll (re:6).

Staring, Jacob (Schneidersbusch) & Elisabeth [?]: Elisabeth, bapt. 3/4/1792 (SJC:56). Sponsors: Georg Louks & Elisabeth Staring.

Staring, Joh. Adam & Ernestina [?]: Anna, b.

6/30/1785; bapt. 7/5/1785 (DRGF:98). Sponsors: Pieter Peiffer & Barbara Harter.

Staring, Joh: Nicol & Bally [?]: Johann Nicolas, b. 7/30/1776, bapt. 8/4/1776 (DRGF:19); Johann Adam, b. 4/4/1780, bapt. 4/9/1780 (DRGF:38). Sponsors: Henrich Staring & Maria J: Staring (re:1); Joh: Adam Staring & Catharina (re:2).

Staring, Joh. Valentin & Anna Elisabetha (Muller): Johann Valentin, bapt. 6/25/1752 (RDSA:12); Jacobus, b. 5/18/1764, bapt. 5/27/1764 (RDSA:47); Anna Elisabetha, b. 9/22/1767, bapt. 9/27/1767 (RDSA:78); Catharina, b. 1/30/1770, bapt. 2/20/1770 (RDSA:100). Sponsors: Dieterich Lauchs, jr. & Maria Margaretha [?] (re:1); Jacob Staring & his wife, Catharina (re:2); Anna Elisabeth & Peter Sutz (re:3); Johann Adam Staring & his wife, Catharina (re:4).

Staring, Johann Adam & Catharina [?]: Anna, b. 10/3/1776, bapt. 10/6/1776 (DRGF:21); Timotheus, b. 5/17/1778, bapt. 6/14/1778 (DRGF:30); Adam, bapt. 2/22/1782 (DRGF:55); Anna, b. 7/27/1784, bapt. 8/1/1784 (DRGF:85); Johann Nicol, b. 3/6/1785, bapt. 5/10/1785 (DRGF:95). Sponsors: Henrich Staring & Elisabeth (re:1); Henrich Staring & Elisabetha (re:2); Joh: Nic: Staring & Maria (re:3); Joh: Dieterich Stahle & Anna Cunnigham (re:4); Joh: Nicol H: Staring & Catharina Kinket (re:5).

Staring, Peter & Maria [?]: Anna, b. 2/13/1779, bapt. 2/14/1779 (DRGF:34); Margretha, b. 6/10/1783, bapt. 6/14/1783 (DRGF:72). Sponsors: Henrich Staring & Maria Staring (re:1); Debald Dieterich & Margretha (re:2).

Staring, Peter Joseph & Maria [?]: Maria, b.

12/26/1784; bapt. 1/23/1785 (DRGF:92). Sponsors: Lorentz Schumacher & Maria Catharin Stahli.

Staring, Philipp & Elisabetha [?]: Anna Margretha, b. 12/8/1759, bapt. 1/18/1760 (RDSA:18); Elisabetha Catharina, b. 4/20/1763, bapt. 5/25/1763 (RDSA:40); Sara, b. 4/20/1763, bapt. 5/25/1763 (RDSA:40); Johann Wilhelm, b. 10/5/1765, bapt. 1/15/1766 (RDSA:61). Sponsors: Anna Margretha (dau. of Philipp Crommel) & Henrich (son of Jacob Muller) (re:1); Elisabetha, wife of Johannes Ebert (re:2); Sara Dachstaeder & Jacob Sternberger (re:3); Willem Brentup & Catharina (re:4).

Staring, Valentin & Margretha [?]: Marcus, b. 11/28/1775; bapt. 12/24/1775 (DRGF:15). Sponsors: Marcus Raspach & Veronica.

Death Record

Staring, Adam, d. 11/4/1815, Germanflats, age 63 years; buried in the cemetery of the stone church (RDH:272)

Staring, Catharina, (dau. of Joh. Nicholas & Maria (Mayer) Stahring), d. 6/12/1803, Skeilertown, age 5 months, 3 days; buried in the garden of her uncle, Judge Stahring (RDH:250)

Staring, Catharina, (sister of Marx Staring who d. 10/23/1823), d. 10/29/1823, Germanflats, age 18 years; buried next to her brother [near the church in Germanflats] (RDH:288)

Staring, Elisabeth, (little dau. of Johannes & Catharina (Fuchs) Stahring), d. 7/28/1819, Germanflats, age [not stated]; buried near the stone church in the same place (RDH:278)

Staring, Henry, d. 5/27/1808, Shylertown, age 65 years; buried on his land (RDH:26)

Staring, Jacob, (legitimate son of Adam & Ernestina Stahring), d. 5/27/1807, Germanflats, age 6 years, 1 month (RDH:258)

Staring, James Henry, (son of Henry Stahring, Jr., from Germanflats), d. 1/7/1813, age 3 years, 3 months, 5 days; buried in the cemetery near the stone church (RDH:266)

Staring, Johannes Nicholas, (resident in Germanflats), d. 11/12/1816, age 63 years; buried in the cemetery of the stone church (RDH:273)

Staring, Marx, (brother of Catharina Staring, who d. 10/29/1823), d. 10/23/1823, Germanflats, age 14 years; buried next to his sister [near the church in Germanflats] (RDH:288)

Staring, Nicholas, (from Shylertown), d. 2/11/1813, (died on a trip to Albany), age 46 years, 10 months, 18 days; buried in the family cemetery in Shylertown (RDH:266)

Probate Abstract

Starin, Deborah, [residence not stated], will dated 5/23/1826; probated 11/11/1826. Legatees: granddau., Deborah Vandeusen; son, Adam; daus., Jenny van Deusen (wife of Abraham, Jr.), Elizabeth (wife of Isaac Maxwell). Executors: John Printup, Jacob I. Fraleigh. Witnesses: John Leonardson, Jr., Nicholas Starin. (WMC 57:266)

Starin, Jacob F., (of Glen), will dated 4/7/1828; probated 6/23/1828. Legatees: wife, Harriet; sons, John, Frederick and Henry; brother, John F. Executors: brother, John F.;

nephew, Abraham Starin. Witnesses: Peter Fonda, Solomon Ostrander, James Lansing. Codicil dated 4/19/1828. Witnesses: Harman De Graff, William Halliday. Ralph Putman. (WMC 57:271)

Staring, Adam, (of Oppenheim), will dated 6/4/1812; probated 6/16/1814. Legatees: wife, Nelly; sons, Frederick, Phillip, John and Harry; daus., Betsey (wife of Jacob Fishbach), Elly (wife of John Fishbach), Peggy and Caty. Executrix: wife. Witnesses: John Starin, Luther Pardee, Reuben Ford. (WMC 56:392)

Tryon County Militia

Staring, Adam   [Appendix A]
Staring, Adam A.
Staring, Adam J.
Staring, Adam, Sr.
Staring, Conrad
Staring, Frederick
Staring, George
Staring, Henrich
Staring, Jacob
Staring, John
Staring, Joseph
Staring, Margred
Staring, Nicholas
Staring, Nicholas N.
Staring, Peter
Staring, Philip

Pension Abstract

Staring, Adam, m. Nelly Quackenboss, 1777; d. 6/6/1812. (Nelly Staring, b. 1758/9; resident of Oppenheim, Montgomery Co., N.Y. on 4/14/1837.) Children: Margaret, John, b. 1788/9; and Philip. Adam enlisted from his home in Charlestown in 1777 and served for nineteen months and twelve days as a private, batteauman, and sergeant in the regiments of

COMPENDIUM

Cols. Marinus Willett and Frederick Fisher; he was a participant in the battle of Oriskany. (RWPA: #W19106)

Staring, John, m. Jane Wemple, 2/18/1781, Caughnawaga, N.Y.; d. 2/19/1832. (Jane Staring, b. 1758; resident of Glen, Montgomery Co., N.Y. on 5/2/1837.) John served as a private in Col. Frederick Fisher's 3rd. Regt., Tryon Co. Militia; he fought in the battle of Oriskany and in that same year [1777] John spent forty-two days at Saratoga before Gen. Burgoyne surrendered; John enlisted in the batteau service for nine months and his wife [Jane] stated that she "was present when he enlisted and saw him pass & repass the place where they lived in boats during the war". (RWPA: #W16741)

Staring, Nicholas, b. 1738/9; m. Catharine Rightmeyer, 12/2/1776 in Charlestown, N.Y. at the home of her [Catharine's] father; d. 6/22/1823 or 6/23/1823, Charlestown, Montgomery Co., N.Y. (Catharine Staring, b. 1746/7; d. 12/4/1843, Fultonville, Montgomery Co., N.Y.) Children: Maria (m. [?] Dockstader and resident of Glen, N.Y. in 1845. She was the only surviving child in the same year.) Nicholas enlisted from Caughnawaga in 1776 and served for one year in a company of batteaumen under Capt. Evert Van Eps; he also served at various times under Capt. Gardinier and Cols. Veeder, Fisher and Bellinger; Nicholas was in the battles of Oriskany, Fort Stanwix and at the burning of Caughnawaga. (RWPA: #W19124)

1790 Census

Staring, Adam (3)   [Appendix B]
Staring, Adam A.
Staring, Adam N.
Staring, Adam, Sr.

Staring, Conradt
Staring, Falatine
Staring, Frederick
Staring, George
Staring, Henry
Staring, Henry N.
Staring, Jacob (2)
Staring, John
Staring, Joseph
Staring, Nicholas
Staring, Philip
Staring, William

STARR

1790 Census

Starr, Ebenezer   [Appendix B]

STATE

Tryon County Militia

State, George   [Appendix A]

1790 Census

State, Anthony, Jr.   [Appendix B]

STEBBINS

1790 Census

Stebbins, Judah   [Appendix B]
Stebbins, Judah, Jr.

775

COMPENDIUM

STEDT

Birth/Baptism

Stedt, Johann & Anna Maria [?]: Johannes, b. 1/8/1780; bapt. 2/27/1780 (LTSA:59)

STEELE

Marriage

Steele, Adam (son of Rudolph Stahle) m. Anna Eva Staring (dau. of Joseph Staring), 3/9/1764 (RDSA:173)

Steele, Adam m. Catharina Krantz, 1/29/1771 (RDSA:190)

Steele, Johann Dieterich m. Anna Cunnigham (dau. of Joh. Cunnigham), 1/3/1785 (DRGF:202)

Steele, Jost m. Polly Grant, 7/24/1777 (DRC:161)

Steele, Rudolph m. Anna Maria Wentz, 11/6/1770 (RDSA:190)

Death Record

Steele, Anna, (wife of Dederick Stahl), d. 11/20/1815, Germanflats, age 52 years; buried in the cemetery of the stone church (RDH:272)

Steele, Catharina Crantz [maiden name], (widow of Adam Steele, from Germanflats), d. 5/19/1813, age 63 years; buried in the cemetery near the Germanflats church (RDH:268)

Steele, Dorothea, (widow of George Stehle), d. 11/28/1809, Germanflats, age 56 years, (she had 15 children, of whom 14 are still living); buried in the Clepsattle cemetery in Germanflats (RDH:261)

Steele, Elisabetha, (wife of Adam Steel; born: Dygert), d. 5/29/1822, Germanflats, age 39 years; buried at Frankfort in the Folts' field (RDH:283)

Steele, George, (legitimate son of Johannes Stehle), d. 7/29/1803, Germanflats, age 6 months, 11 days; buried Germanflats Church cemetery (RDH:250)

Steele, George, d. 11/23/1803, Germanflats, age 53 years, 1 month, 7 days; buried in the garden cemetery of Andreas Clepsattle in the same place (RDH:251)

Steele, Margaretha, (wife of Rudolph Steel; born: Wenz), d. 6/20/1820, Germanflats, age 72 years, 11 months, 12 days; buried near her home on the hill towards the east (RDH:279)

Steele, Peter, (son of Joh. Nicholas Steele, a builder), d. 1/11/1808, Germanflats, age 4 months; buried in the cemetery of Andreas Clepsattle (RDH:259)

Probate Abstract

Steel, Justus, (of Broadalbin), will dated 3/7/1810; probated 7/22/1815. Legatees: wife, Thankful; sons, John and Harvey. Executors: wife; Reuben Lilly, Duncan McMartin, Jr. Witnesses: Nell Whitaker [a man], Samuel Clarke, Jr., Duncan McMartin, Jr. (WMC 56:395)

Tryon County Militia

Steele, Adam [Appendix A]
Steele, Deterich

776

COMPENDIUM

Pension Abstract

Steele, Rudolph, b. 5/1/1745, German Flatts, N.Y.; resident of German Flatts, Herkimer Co., N.Y. on 10/10/1832. Rudolph was appointed quartermaster in Col. Peter Bellinger's 4th. Regt., Tryon Co. Militia in the spring of 1776 and served there until the spring of 1780; Rudolph "had charge of the guard in Protecting the Baggage and Waggons at the Battle of Oriskany in August 1777"; he was also "out at the Unadilla River when Genl. Herkimer Visited Brandt to make a treaty with him"; Rudolph stated that he "was in pursuit of [Walter] Butler in 1781 at which time he [Rudolph] resided at Schenectady"; he moved to Schenectady in the spring of 1780 where he was quartermaster in Col. Peake's Regt. and he [Rudolph] was "furnished with a horse & saddle & bridle"; Rudolph remained in this regiment until the end of 1783. (RWPA: #R10099)

1790 Census

Stale, Adam	[Appendix B]
Stale, Dedrick	
Stale, George	
Stale, Rudolph	
Steel, Hezekiah	
Steel, James	
Steel, Nathaniel	
Steel, Seth	

STEEN

Birth/Baptism

Steen, Conrad & Efje (Werdt): Annatje, b. 3/17/1784; bapt. 5/11/1784 (DRC:69). Sponsors: Marks Werdt & Jane Werdt.

STEER

Birth/Baptism

Steer, James & Gertrudie [?]: Christina, b. 2/23/1770 (LTSA:31). Sponsors: Jacob Klein & his wife.

STEINBACH

Birth/Baptism

Steinbach, Joh. Arendt & Maria Catharina [?]: Catharina, b. 12/5/1765; bapt. 1/7/1766 (RDSA:61). Sponsors: Catharina Dachstaeder & Christian Hen. Berkoff.

STEINMAN

Birth/Baptism

Steinman, Ludwig (of Canajoh. Castle) & Catharina [?]: Friderich, bapt. 9/20/1789 (SJC:17); Rachel, bapt. 5/10/1792 (SJC:58). Sponsors: Friderich Bonstetter & Maria Bonstatter (re:1); John Wynsi & Rachel Wynsi (re:2).

STEINMETZ

Birth/Baptism

Steinmetz, Philip & Maria [?]: Maria Elisabeth, b. 6/3/1780, bapt. 9/26/1780 (DRGF:39); Maria, b. 3/14/1782, bapt. 6/26/1782 (DRGF:58). Sponsors: Johanes Bierhausen & Anna Elisabeth (re:1); Matthias Bekker &

Maria Schaffer (re:2).

STEINWACHS

Birth/Baptism

Steinwachs, Adam & Maria Gertraud [?]: Johann Caspar, b. 9/17/1767; bapt. 10/23/1767 (RDSA:79). Sponsors: Joh. Caspar Hassenkleber, Joh. Schaad & Maria Catharin Bender.

STELLER

Birth/Baptism

Steller, Peter & Elisabet [?]: Elisabet, b. 10/30/1795 (LTSA:92). Sponsors: parents.

STEMPLER

1790 Census

Stempler, [?]   [Appendix B]

STENTOR

Death Record

Stentor, James Nash, d. 9/10/1823, Germanflats, age 69 years; buried in the church cemetery (RDH:288)

STENTZEL

Birth/Baptism

Stentzel, Nicholas & Margretha [?]: Johannes, b. 3/29/1781, bapt. 4/8/1781 (DRGF:44); Wilhelm, b. 10/19/1782, bapt. 10/27/1782 (DRGF:63); Nicolas, b. 10/26/1784, bapt. 11/16/1784 (DRGF:89). Sponsors: Johannes Veterle & Elisabeth (re:1); Henrich Sitz & Elisabeth Vetterle (re:2); Johannes Vatterle & Maria (re:3).

Stenzel, Wilhelm & Elisabetha [?]: Wilhelm, b. 1/27/1755 (LTSA:11); Catharina, b. 2/10/1770 (LTSA:30). Sponsors: Wilhelm Nellis & his wife, Maria Dorthea (re:1); Joannes Schulz, Barbara Schulz (re:2).

STEPHAN

Marriage

Stephan, Johannes m. Maria Jung, 1/12/1767 (RDSA:180)

Birth/Baptism

Stephan, John & Anna Maria [?]: Johann Peter, b. 2/18/1768; bapt. 4/17/1768 (RDSA:85). Sponsors: Peter Foltz & his wife, Anna Elisabeth.

STEPHENS (also see STEVENS)

Probate Abstract

Stephens, John, (of Canajoharie), will dated 6/19/1798; probated 8/29/1798. Legatees: sons,

COMPENDIUM

John, Joseph, Septimeus, William and James; daus., Unis & Polly; brother, James. Executors: brother, James; William Barlett, Jr., Benjamin Burton. Witnesses: Charles Powell, Cornelius Lane, Caleb Clark. (WMC 56:149)

Tryon County Militia

Stephens, Amasa   [Appendix A]

1790 Census

Stephens, Adam   [Appendix B]

STEPHSON

Birth/Baptism

Stephson, John & Calva (Beove), Stillwater: John, bapt. 6/15/1783 (JDR:16)

STERMAN

Tryon County Militia

Sterman, Christian   [Appendix A]

STERN

Marriage

Stern, John m. Jane Wemple, Caughnawaga, 2/18/1781 (JDR:1)

Stern, Nicholas m. Catrina Rightmyer, 12/2/1776 (DRC:161)

Birth/Baptism

Stern, Adam & Neltje (Quackenbush): Frederic, b. 12/2/1776, bapt. 12/28/1776 (DRC:40); Elsje, b. 9/13/1781, bapt. 10/20/1781 (DRC:59); Philip, b. 3/1/1783, bapt. 4/18/1783 (DRC:65); Elizabeth, b. 1/20/1787, bapt. 2/10/1787 at age 3 weeks (DRC:82, 86); Maragreita, b. 1/1/1791, bapt. 1/30/1791 (DRC:94). Sponsors: Frederick Stern & Elizabeth Stern (re:1); Abram Quack & Gerritje Quack (re:2); Jacob Shever & Eliz. Shever (re:3); Philip [Stern] & [Eliz]abeth Stern (re:4); Ahasuerus Van Ant[werp?] & Marrigritje Van Antwerp (re:5).

Stern, Frederick & Elizabeth (Frans): Philip, b. 5/12/1776, bapt. 5/26/1776 (DRC:37); Jacob, b. 7/20/1785, bapt. 7/?/1785 (DRC:74). Sponsors: Robert Hillborn & Maria Hillborn (re:1); Johannes Stern & Jannetje Stern (re:2).

Stern, Johannes & Jannetje (Wemph): Myndert, b. 5/31/1786; bapt. 7/2/1786 (DRC:80). Sponsors: Myndert H. Wemph & Catrina Wemph.

Stern, William & Debora (Philips): Meritje, b. 3/11/1787, bapt. 4/16/1787 (DRC:84); Susana, b. 11/24/1790, bapt. 1/16/1791 (DRC:93). Sponsors: Johannis [?.] Vanalstyne & Sarah Van alstyne (re:1); [none named] (re:2).

William & Maragrita (Bekker): Maria, b. 11/9/1784; bapt. 2/19/1785 (DRC:70). Sponsors: Antony Lassey & Catrina Lassey.

Tryon County Militia

Stern, Nicholas   [Appendix A]

COMPENDIUM

STERNBERGER (also see STARENBURG)

Marriage

Sternberger, Adam (son of Adam Sternberger) m. Anna Margreth Brentop, [no date: follows 10/4/1768] (RDSA:184)

Sternberger, Jacob m. Margretha Moog, 6/13/1767 (RDSA:182)

Sternberger, Jost m. Catharine Dachstaedter, 3/6/1794 (DFP:51)

Birth/Baptism

Sternberger, Adam & Elisabetha (Rikert): Jacob, bapt. 1742 (RDSA:5); Johann Jost, bapt. 1/13/1751 (RDSA:9). Sponsors: Jacob Sternberg, Margreta Wis (re:1); Johann Jost Schnell, Maria Catherina Krafft (re:2).

Sternberger, Adam & Maragriet (Printup): Elizabeth, b. 10/16/1772, bapt. 11/2/1772 (DRC:23); Willem, b. 6/9/1775, bapt. 7/9/1775 (DRC:34); Maria, b. 4/26/1777, bapt. 5/11/1777 (DRC:43); Jannetje, b. 10/13/1781, bapt. 11/11/1781 (DRC:59). Sponsors: Hans Everse & Elizabeth Eversen (re:1); Willem Prentip & Catrina Prentip (re:2); Adam Everse & Anna Shaver (re:3); Jeremiah Van Alstine & Maragriet Sternburg (re:4).

Death Record

Sternberger, [?], (widow), d. 3/21/1795, age 85 years & some months; buried 3/23/1795 (DFP:87)

Probate Abstract

Sternberg, Jacob, (of Marlit's bush), will dated 9/4/1793; probated 10/26/1793. Legatees: wife,

Elizabeth; dau., Eve; son, Jacob Frederick; Jacob Enders, Sr. Executors: Jacob Enders, Sr., Jacob Campbell. Witnesses: Samuel De Riemer, Matthew V. Valkenburgh, Jacob Enders, Jr. (WMC 56:147)

Tryon County Militia

Sternbergh, Christian   [Appendix A]
Sternbergh, Jacob
Sternbergh, Joseph

Pension Abstract

Sternbergh, Joseph, b. 1/24/1751, Charleston, N.Y.; resident of Cambria, Niagara Co., N.Y. on 5/9/1833. Joseph served as a guard to Col. Philip Schuyler in 1775 during the treaty proceedings with the Indians at German Flats; he continued to serve from 1777 until the close of the war on various tours of duty as a private and orderly sergeant under command of Capt. Peter Yates and Cols. Volkert Veeder and Newkirk; Joseph fought in the battle of Oriskany. (RWPA: #S14579)

1790 Census

Sternbarack, Nicholas   [Appendix B]

STERNS

Death Record

Sterns, Barnabas, (son of Josiah & Elizabeth Sterns, residents of Cherry Valley), d. 12/11/1859, age 26 years; buried in Old Cemetery & removed 1865 to Cherry Valley Cemetery (CVC:1)

Sterns, Elizabeth, (wife of Josiah Sterns, resident of Cherry Valley), d. 2/4/1860, age 75

780

years; buried in Old Cemetery & removed ca. 1864 to Cherry Valley Cemetery (CVC:1)

Sterns, Josiah, (Cherry Valley resident), d. 4/30/1852, age 82[?] years; buried on farm & removed ca. 1864 to lot in Cherry Valley Cemetery owned by son, Daniel Sterns (CVC:1)

Sterns, Willard, (son of Josiah & Elizabeth Sterns, residents of Cherry Valley), d. 7/3/1837, age 29 years; buried in Old Cemetery & removed to Cherry Valley Cemetery in 1865 (CVC:1)

Sterns, William, (son of Barnabas Sterns), d. 12/?/1861, age 26 years; buried in Old Cemetery & removed ca. 1865 to Cherry Valley Cemetery (CVC:1)

STERRITT

1790 Census

Sterritt, Henry   [Appendix B]

STEVENS (also see STEPHENS)

Birth/Baptism

Stevens, Amasa & Maragriet (Putman): Lodewyk, b. 7/24/1777; bapt. 9/4/1777 (DRC:44). Sponsors: John Putman & Sarah Putman.

Stevens, Arent & Mary [?]: Jacobus, bapt. 1/3/1739/40 (FH:8). Sponsors: Ephraim Smith, Annatie Smith.

Probate Abstract

Stevens, Ira, (of Mayfield), will dated 9/25/1831; probated 10/31/1831. Legatees: wife (decd.) [not named]; only son, Ira Henry; daus., Sarah Mathews Stevens, Lucy Maria Stevens and Hannah Elizabeth Stevens; Darius Clark (guardian to Sarah M. and Ira Henry); Collins Odell (guardian to Lucy M. and Hannah E.). Executors: Darius Clark, Collins Odell. Witnesses: William McConnell, Alinos Mathews, Benjamin Berry. (WMC 57:281)

1790 Census

Stevens, Daniel   [Appendix B]
Stevens, James
Stevens, Jeremiah
Stevens, Josiah
Stevens, William

STEVENSON

1790 Census

Stevenson, John   [Appendix B]

STEVES

1790 Census

Steves, Jeremiah   [Appendix B]

STEWART

Birth/Baptism

Stewart, Allan & Christian [?]: Mary, b. 2/21/1793; bapt. 2/9/1794 (JPC:8).

Stewart, Daniel & [?], Stillwater: Jannet, bapt. 2/7/1783 (JDR:16).

Stewart, Duncan & Janet [?]: Isabell, b. 1/12/1800; bapt. 2/23/1800 (JPC:16).

Stewart, James & Margaret [?]: John, b. 8/5/1801; bapt. 8/23/1801 (JPC:20).

Stuart, Daniel & Elizabeth [?]: Elizabeth, b. 5/10/1792, bapt. 7/15/1792 (JPC:6); Margaret, b. 9/28/1794, bapt. 10/19/1794 (JPC:9).

Stuart, Donald & [?]: [?], [birth & bapt. not stated; listed in the 1793 period] (JPC:8)

Stuart, Robert & Jean/Jane (Wilson): Christian [dau.], bapt. 8/10/1788 (JPC:2); Jane, b. 2/1/1791, bapt. 5/22/1791 (JPC:4); [?], bapt. 5/19/1793 (JPC:8); William, bapt. 7/7/1799 (JPC:14).

Stuart, Thomas & Catharine [?]: Isobel, b. 11/29/1791, bapt. 2/26/1792 (JPC:6); [?] dau., b. 9/12/1793, bapt. 2/16/1794 (JPC:9); John, b. 8/3/1801, bapt. 1/23/1801 (JPC:20).

Death Record

Stewart, Ann, (wife of John Stewart, Sr.), d. 11/20/1817, age 71 years; buried sect. 4, Colonial Cemetery, Johnstown (JC:188)

Stewart, Ann Sarah, (dau. of Thomas & Catherine Stewart), d. 6/7/1839, age 8 months [Catherine, mother, had been dead for 18 years]; buried sect. 3, Colonial Cemetery, Johnstown (JC:188)

Stewart, Catharine, (eldest child of Mr. A. Stewart), d. 4/4/1830, age 10 years, died of Scarlet fever; buried Cherry Valley Presbyterian Church cemetery (PCV:84)

Stewart, Catherine, (dau. of Thomas & Catherine Stewart), d. 7/27/1840, age [not stated]; buried sect. 3, Colonial Cemetery, Johnstown (JC:188)

Stewart, Catherine, (wife of Thomas Stewart), d. 5/29/1821, age 51 years, 10 months; buried sect. 3, Colonial Cemetery, Johnstown (JC:188)

Stewart, Charles, d. 7/24/1840, age 57 years; buried sect. 4, Colonial Cemetery, Johnstown (JC:188)

Stewart, Donald, d. 2/28/1847, age 86 years; buried sect. 3, Colonial Cemetery, Johnstown (JC:188)

Stewart, Dougal, d. 9/23/1839, age 72 years; buried sect. 11, Colonial Cemetery, Johnstown (JC:188)

Stewart, Elizabeth, (3rd child of Mr. A. Stewart), d. 3/17/1830, age 5 years, of Scarlet fever; buried Cherry Valley Presbyterian Church cemetery (PCV:84)

Stewart, Elizabeth, (dau. of Douglad & Elizabeth Stewart), b. 4/2/1814; d. 9/3/1848; buried sect. 11, Colonial Cemetery, Johnstown (JC:188)

Stewart, Isabella, (dau. of Douglad & Elizabeth Stewart), d. 8/8/1834, age 10 years, 4 months, 3 days; buried sect. 11, Colonial Cemetery, Johnstown (JC:188)

Stewart, James A., (son of Thomas & Catherine Stewart), d. 3/17/1841, age 30 years; buried sect. 3, Colonial Cemetery, Johnstown (JC:188)

Stewart, Jane, (wife of Robert Stewart), d. 10/12/1837, age 83 years; buried sect. 4, Colonial Cemetery, Johnstown (JC:188)

Stewart, John, d. 7/19/1832, age 76 years; buried sect. 3, Colonial Cemetery, Johnstown (JC:188)

Stewart, John, Jr., d. 7/2/1853, age 35 years; buried sect. 3, Colonial Cemetery, Johnstown (JC:188)

Stewart, Margaret, (dau. of Douglad & Elizabeth Stewart), d. 8/20/1839, age 30 years; buried sect. 11, Colonial Cemetery, Johnstown (JC:188)

Stewart, Mary, (dau. of John & Jane Stewart), d. 9/18/1847, age 21 years, 7 months; buried sect. 1, Colonial Cemetery, Johnstown (JC:188)

Stewart, Mary, (wife of Donald Stewart), d. 11/3/1832, age 61 years; buried sect. 3, Colonial Cemetery, Johnstown (JC:188)

Stewart, McIntyre, (son of John & Jane Stewart), d. 5/12/1862, age 3 years, 1 month, 10 days; buried sect. 1, Colonial Cemetery, Johnstown (JC:188)

Stewart, Robert, d. 6/23/1837, age 88 years; buried sect. 4, Colonial Cemetery, Johnstown (JC:188)

Stewart, Sarah, (wife of John Stewart), d. 8/20/1821, age 28 years, 6 months; buried sect. 3, Colonial Cemetery, Johnstown (JC:188)

Stewart, Simeon Peter, (son of Douglad & Elizabeth Stewart), d. 12/20/1828; age 10 months, 1 day; buried sect. 11, Colonial Cemetery, Johnstown (JC:188)

Stewart, Thomas, d. 4/9/1836, age 61 years; buried sect. 3, Colonial Cemetery, Johnstown (JC:188)

Stewart, William C., (son of Charles & Lena Stewart), d. 11/1/1840, age 26 years, 6 months, 6 days; buried sect. 4, Colonial Cemetery, Johnstown (JC:188)

Probate Abstract

Stewart, Duncan, (of the town of Amsterdam), will dated 7/14/1811; probated 8/23/1811. Legatees: wife, Betsy; daus., Betsy, Jean, Ann, and Catherine; sons, Archibald, Duncan and John. Executors: George Bell, Finlay McMartin, Daniel Stewart. Witnesses: Robert Brown, Duncan McMartin, John Thomson, Jr. (WMC 56:382)

Stewart, Thomas, (of Johnstown), will dated 3/25/1826; probated 4/17/1826. Legatees: sons, Duncan and James Alexander; daus., Catherine Guilick and Jennet. Executors: Eleazer Wells, Dougal Stewart. Witnesses: Simeon Oaks, John and Donald Stewart. (WMC 57:186)

Tryon County Militia

Stuart, William   [Appendix A]

1790 Census

Stewart, Aaron   [Appendix B]
Stewart, Allen
Stewart, Anna
Stewart, Duncan
Stewart, Ebenezer
Stewart, James (3)
Stewart, Jessee
Stewart, John (2)

COMPENDIUM

Stewart, Robert
Stewart, William (2)

STICHAVIL

Birth/Baptism

Stichavil, Gustavus & [?], New Amsterdam: Gustavus Hamilton, bapt. 7/22/1798 (JDR:14)

STICKNY

1790 Census

Stickny, Joseph   [Appendix B]

STIEN

Marriage

Stien, Conrad m. Evah Whart, Warrens, 11/3/1778 (JDR:1)

Birth/Baptism

Stien, Conrad & Evah (Wert), Warrensborough: John, bapt. 11/26/1779 (JDR:15); Matthias, bapt. 10/15/1781 (JDR:19); Evah, bapt. 11/20/1790 (JDR:13); Philip, bapt. 8/30/1794, aged 2 months (JDR:22).

Tryon County Militia

Stine, William   [Appendix A]

1790 Census

Stien, Ludweek   [Appendix B]
Stine, George
Stine, John
Stine, William

STIFFORD

1790 Census

Stifford, David   [Appendix B]
Stifford, Jacob
Stifford, Richard
Stifford, Samuel

STILLMAN

1790 Census

Stillman, Benjamin   [Appendix B]
Stilman, John
Stilman, Samuel

STILTSON

1790 Census

Stiltson, Amos   [Appendix B]

STINBERG

Birth/Baptism

Stinberg, Jerem. & Elisabet [?]: Anna, b.

4/31/1794 (LTSA:83); Catarina, b. 2/24/1796 (LTSA:93). Sponsors: Jerem. Smit & Jannetche (re:1); Nicolaus Streter & Margaret (re:2).

STIRLING

Birth/Baptism

Stirling, William & Elizabeth (Miller), Warrensborough: Peter, b. 3/1/1788; bapt. 7/27/1788 (JDR:22).

STIVER

1790 Census

Stiver, Henry   [Appendix B]

STIVERSANT

1790 Census

Stiversant, John   [Appendix B]
Stiversant, Samuel

ST. JOHN

Death Record

St. John, John, (Captain), b. 12/8/1768; d. 12/4/1814; buried Ames Rural Cemetery, Canajoharie (ARC:19)

St. John, John, d. 12/1/1814, age 16 years, 19 days; buried Ames Rural Cemetery, Canajoharie (ARC:19)

St. John, John L., b. 7/7/1796; d. 2/13/1846; buried Ames Rural Cemetery, Canajoharie (ARC:19)

St. John, Lois, (dau. of Rev. Aaron Drake; wife of Capt. John St. John), b. 12/21/1768; d. 11/10/1854, age 85 years, 11 months, 8 days; buried Ames Rural Cemetery, Canajoharie (ARC:19)

St. John, Sylvanus, b. 10/8/1790; d. 3/5/1861; buried Ames Rural Cemetery, Canajoharie (ARC:19)

St. John, Sylvester, b. 1/31/1792; d. 2/4/1815; buried Ames Rural Cemetery, Canajoharie (ARC:19)

1790 Census

St. John, David   [Appendix B]

STOCKER

1790 Census

Stocker, William   [Appendix B]

STODDARD

1790 Census

Stoddard, Orange   [Appendix B]

STOEL

1790 Census

Stoel, Asa   [Appendix B]
Stoel, Israel (2)
Stoell, Hezekiah
Stoll, Jacob

STOHLEN

Birth/Baptism

Stohlen, Georg Jacob & Anna Christina [?]: Elisabet, b. 3/15/1793 (LTSA:78). Sponsors: Peter Getmann & his wife, Elisabeth.

STONE

Death Record

Stone, [?], (child of Mr. Stone), d. ?/?/1823; buried Cherry Valley Presbyterian Church cemetery (PCV:80)

Tryon County Militia

Stone, Conrad   [Appendix A]
Stone, George

1790 Census

Stone, Charles   [Appendix B]
Stone, Eaton
Stone, George
Stone, Seth
Stone, Squire

STONEMACH

Birth/Baptism

Stonematch, Philip & Mary (Becker), Florida:

Anne, bapt. 10/23/1796 (JDR:10).

1790 Census

Stonemach, Philip   [Appendix B]

STONER

Marriage

Stoner, Nicholas m. Nancy Munson (widow), 12/11/1784 (DRC:164)

Birth/Baptism

Stoner, John & Susanna (Philes): John, b. 10/4/1790; bapt. 11/7/1790 (DRC:91). Sponsors: Jacob Philes & Peggy Ackerman.

1790 Census

Stoner, John   [Appendix B]
Stoner, Nicholas

STORES

1790 Census

Stores, Nathaniel   [Appendix B]

STORM

Birth/Baptism

Storm, Isaac & Rebecca (Willsen), Johnstown: Nicholas, bapt. 10/28/1784 (JDR:21).

STORNBURY

Stornbury, Jacob   [Appendix B]

STORY

Death Record

Story, Livey, (dau. of Jacob Sisum; wife of Robert Story, Jr.), d. [not stated]; removed to Cherry Valley Cemetery (CVC:2)

Story, Robert, (son of Robert & Elizabeth Story), d. [not given], from wound received at Gettysburg; removed to Cherry Valley Cemetery (CVC:2)

Story, Robert, Sr., (Cherry Valley resident), d. [not stated]; removed ca. 1864 to Cherry Valley Cemetery (CVC:2)

Story, Willie, (son of Robert & Elizabeth Story), d. [not stated], no remains; removed as a matter of record to Cherry Valley Cemetery (CVC:2)

1790 Census

Story, Benjamin   [Appendix B]
Story, Oliver

STOUGTON

1790 Census

Stougton, Amaziah   [Appendix B]

STOUT

1790 Census

Stout, James   [Appendix B]

STOUTENBURGH

Death Record

Stoutenburgh, Abraham M., (son of Tobias A. & P. Stoutenburgh), d. 2/23/1813, age 5 months, 25 days; buried sect. 4, Colonial Cemetery, Johnstown (JC:188)

Stoutenburgh, Amelia, (wife of Tobias A. Stoutenburgh), d. 9/26/1828, age [not given]; buried sect. 4, Colonial Cemetery, Johnstown (JC:189)

Stoutenburgh, Catharina A., (dau. of T. A. & A. Stoutenburgh), d. 10/3/1831, age 3 years, 2 months, 19 days; buried sect. 4, Colonial Cemetery (JC:189)

Stoutenburgh, Gideon, (son of Tobias A. & Amelia Stoutenburgh), d. 5/7/1827, age 1 year, 1 month, 2 days; buried sect. 4, Colonial Cemetery, Johnstown (JC:189)

Stoutenburgh, Levina A., (dau. of T.A. & Emily Stoutenburgh), d. 3/5/1843, age 10 weeks; buried sect. 4, Colonial Cemetery, Johnstown (JC:189)

Stoutenburgh, Mary, (dau. of Tobias A. & Emily Stoutenburgh), d. 10/7/1836, age 11 months, 3 days; buried sect. 4, Colonial Cemetery, Johnstown (JC:189)

Stoutenburgh, Phebe, (wife of Tobias A.

Stoutenburgh), d. 1/26/1821, age 31 years; buried sect. 4, Colonial Cemetery, Johnstown (JC:188)

Stoutenburgh, Thankful Ann, (dau. of Tobias A. & P. Stoutenburgh), d. 5/13/1820, age 1 year, 7 months, 6 days; buried sect. 4, Colonial Cemetery, Johnstown (JC:188)

Stoutenburgh, Tobias Abraham, (son of T.A. & A. Stoutenburgh), d. 10/2/1828, age 1 month, 2 days; buried sect. 4, Colonial Cemetery, Johnstown (JC:189)

STOUTINGER

1790 Census

Stoutinger, George   [Appendix B]

STOW

1790 Census

Stow, Daniel   [Appendix B]
Stow, David
Stow, Josiah

STOWARTT

Birth/Baptism

Stowartt, Murdock & [?]: William, bapt. 3/4/1783 (JDR:24).

STOWITZ

Marriage

Stowitz, Michael (son of Philipp Stowitz) m. Maria Elisabeth Bellinger (dau. of John Bellinger, decd.), 2/16/1790 (DFP:41)

Birth/Baptism

Stowits, Michael & Marilis (Pellinger): Philip, b. 11/22/1790; bapt. 12/26/1790 (DRC:92). Sponsors: Jury Stowits & Margaret Stowits.

Probate Abstract

Stowits, George, (of Root), will dated 11/9/1830; probated 9/15/1831. Legatees: wife [not named]; sons, Philip, Henry and Jacob; dau., Mary (wife of John Runkle). Executors: three sons. Witnesses: David Eacker, Charles Mc Vean, J. Wentworth (all of Canajoharie). (WMC 57:280)

1790 Census

Stowids, George   [Appendix B]
Stowids, Samuel

STOYLE

1790 Census

Stoyle, Stephen   [Appendix B]

STRABACK (also see STROBECK)

1790 Census

Straback, Frederick   [Appendix B]

STRADER

Tryon County Militia

Strader, Nicholas   [Appendix A]

Pension Abstract

Strader, Nicholas, b. 1750/1; m. Margaret [?], 9/22/1775, by Rev. Daniel Gros; d. 4/21/1833, Martinsburgh, Lewis Co., N.Y. (Margaret Strader, b. 1755/6; resident of Martinsburgh, N.Y. on 5/11/1833.) Nicholas entered the military from Palatine in 1775 and served through the summer of 1777 in Col. Jacob Klock's 2nd. Regt., Tryon Co. Militia; he enlisted in the summer of 1777 and served for one year in Capt. Christian Kitman's Co., Col. Marinus Willett's Regt.; he again enlisted in 1778 for four years, until his discharge in the fall of 1782, in Capt. John Castleman's Co., Col. Brown's Regt. of the N.Y. Line; Nicholas was engaged in the battles of Oriskany, Palatine, Johnstown and West Canada Creek. (RWPA: #W16742)

1790 Census

Strader, Nicholas   [Appendix B]

STRAHER

Marriage

Streher, Johann Burkhard m. Maria Schulz, 7/8/1770 (LTSA:282)

Birth/Baptism

Streher/Stroeher, Johannes & Maria [?]: Elisabetha, b. 7/28/1782, bapt. 8/4/1782 (DRGF:59); Margaret, b. 4/5/1793 (LTSA:79). Sponsors: Marcus Dachstaeder & Elisabeth (re:1); Johannes Schulz & Catarina (re:2).

Streher, Burkhard & Catharina [?]: Catharina, b. 10/2/1770 [Mother: Catharina] (LTSA:45); Anna, b. 5/31/1773 [Mother: Maria] (LTSA:45). Sponsors: Georg Dachstetter & his wife (re:1); Peter Lauks & his wife (re:2).

Tryon County Militia

Straher, John   [Appendix A]

1790 Census

Strayer, Jacob   [Appendix B]

STRAIL

1790 Census

Strail, John   [Appendix B]

STRAIN

1790 Census

Strain, James   [Appendix B]
Strain, James, Jr.

STRANG

Marriage

Strang, Joel m. Luisa Gahe, 12/8/1793

789

(DRGF:210)

STRAUS

Birth/Baptism

STRAUB

Marriage

Straus, Thomas & Catarina [?]: Wilhelm, b. 3/9/1797 (LTSA:98). Sponsors: Adam Kuns & Magdalena.

Straub, Heinrich m. Rachel Schmidt, 7/6/1794 (RDSA:199)

STREET

Birth/Baptism

1790 Census

Straub, Wilhelm & Maria [?]: Wilhelm, b. 4/11/1791 (LTSA:67); Anna, b. 4/1/1793 (LTSA:78); Daniel, b. 8/14/1795 (LTSA:91). Sponsors: John Salzmann, Catharina Horlich (re:1); Johannes Schulz & his wife, Anna (re:2); Dieterich Suz, Cat. Elis. Hording (re:3).

Street, Robert   [Appendix B]

STRICKLAND

Tryon County Militia

1790 Census

Straub, William   [Appendix A]

Strickland, John   [Appendix B]
Strickland, Noah

STRAUCH (also see **STRAUPE**)

Marriage

STROBECK (also see **STRABACK**)

Strauch, Balthazer m. Maria Catharina Ritter, 9/28/1784 (DRGF:200)

Marriage

Strobeck, Fridrich m. Anna Maria Gross, 7/29/1770 (LTSA:282)

Birth/Baptism

STRAUPE (also see **STRAUCH**)

Strobeck, Friedrich & Anna Maria [?]: Johann Fridrich, b. 5/1/1771 (LTSA:37); Henrich, b. 10/18/1784, bapt. 11/16/1784 (DRGF:89). Sponsors: J. Fridrich Strohbek, Anna Elisabetha Gros (re:1); Henrich Joh: Fheling & Catharina (re:2).

Birth/Baptism

Straupe, Balthazar & Maria Catharina [?]: Henrich, b. 7/17/1785; bapt. 7/19/1785 (DRGF:99). Sponsors: Henrich Ritter & Maria Petri.

COMPENDIUM

Death Record

Strobeck, [?], (widow), d. 9/?/1807, age 99 years, 3 months, 13 days; buried 9/18/1807 (DFP:91)

Pension Abstract

Strobeck, Adam, b. 9/7/1763, Canajoharie, N.Y.; resident of Sharon, Schoharie Co., N.Y. from 12/19/1786 through 1833 when he was allowed pension. Adam volunteered from Sharon on 4/1/1781 and was a private in Capt. Lawrence Gros' Co., Col. Marinus Willett's N.Y. Regt.; he was in the battle of Turlock where he received wounds in the small of his back and in the arm; he rejoined his regiment and company in October of the same year [1781] and fought in the battle of Johnstown; Adam was discharged at the end of December 1781 and reenlisted in April 1782 for nine months service in Capt. French's Co. of the same regiment. (RWPA: #S14584 & #S26759)

1790 Census

Strowback, Adam   [Appendix B]
Strowback, Jacob

STRODER

Birth/Baptism

Stroder, Nicholas & Anna Margreth [?]: Henrich, b. 10/28/1782; bapt. 11/10/1782 (DRGF:64). Sponsors: Henrich Krembs & Anna Nolles.

STRONG

1790 Census

Strong, Asher   [Appendix B]

STROUD

1790 Census

Stroud, Thomas   [Appendix B]

STROUP

1790 Census

Stroup, William   [Appendix B]
Stroup, William, Jr.

STROW

1790 Census

Strow, Baltus   [Appendix B]

STROWBRIDGE

1790 Census

Strowbridge, Philo   [Appendix B]

STRUBLE

COMPENDIUM

Tryon County Militia

Straubel, Christopher   [Appendix A]
Strubel, Christian
Strubel, Christopher

1790 Census

Struble, Christopher   [Appendix B]

STRUEL

Marriage

Struel, Stophel m. Elisabeth Weber, 4/29/1767 (RDSA:182)

STRUNCK

1790 Census

Strunck, Henry   [Appendix B]

STUART see STEWART

STUDDERT

Birth/Baptism

Studdert, William & [?] (Hallenbek): William, b. 5/1/1787; bapt. 8/7/1787 (DRC:85). Sponsors: [none named].

STULEY

1790 Census

Stuley, Robert   [Appendix B]

STUTSON

1790 Census

Stutson, Timothy   [Appendix B]

STUTTS

Birth/Baptism

Stutts, Michael & Dorothea (Klyne): Elizabeth, b. 3/21/1780; bapt. 4/9/1780 (DRC:56). Sponsors: Hendk. Yauney & Elizabeth Yauney.

STUYVESANT

Marriage

Stuyvesant, John m. Agnis Jones, 3/11/1792 (DRGF:209)

STYLES

1790 Census

Styles, Asel   [Appendix B]

SUITS (also see SUTZ)

Pension Abstract

Suits, Peter J., m. Mary Magdalene Fraley, 1786; resident of Palatine, Montgomery Co., N.Y. (Mary Magdalene Suits, dau. of Jacob Fraley; [brother: John Fraley, b. 1775/6]; living on 1/26/1847.) Peter J. enlisted for nine months in 1780 and was a private in Capt. Samuel Gray's Co. of batteaumen transporting materials between Fort Stanwix and Schenectady on the Mohawk River; Peter J. fought in the battles of Oriskany and Johnstown. (RWPA: #W19128)

Sutz, Peter, b. 1732/3; m. Elizabeth (Laucks) Epply, 6/?/1780, by Rev. Joh. Daniel Gross; d. 5/14/1824, Palatine, Montgomery Co., N.Y. (Elizabeth Sutz, b. 1747/8, dau. of William Laucks; m. 1st. Jacob Epply (killed on 4/?/1779 by Indians while on military duty); [sister: Magdalena (Laucks), b. 5/11/1755; m. Adam A. Laucks]; resident of Ephratah, Montgomery Co. on 12/12/1836.) Children: Peter, Moses, b. 3/?/1791 (resident of Ephratah, Fulton Co., N.Y. on 10/26/1847). Peter entered the militia in 1775 and was a private and sergeant in Capt. Christopher W. Fox's Co., Col. Jacob Klock's 2nd. Regt., Tryon Co. Militia; he served at various times until the end of the war; Peter fought in the battle of Oriskany where his captain, Christopher W. Fox, was seriously wounded. Following the war, Peter Sutz served as a magistrate and was "a highly respectable man". (RWPA: #W13941 *SUITS*)

SULLIVAN

Marriage

Sullivan, J. Edward m. Magdalena Gerlach, 10/22/1782 (DRGF:196)

Birth/Baptism

Sullivan, Edward & Magdalena (Garlock): John Haver, b. 3/24/1783, bapt. 4/1/1783 (DRC:65); Peter, b. 2/6/1785, bapt. 3/1/1785 (DRC:71). Sponsors: Jacobus VC. Romine & Jannetje Van Eps (re:1); Michael Hikky & Maria Hikky (re:2).

SUMMERS

1790 Census

Summers, John   [Appendix B]
Summers, Nicholas
Summers, Peter N.
Summers, William

SUTPHEN (also see ZUTPHIN)

Marriage

Sutphen, James m. Catharine VanDeVear, Marlattsbush, 1/30/1791 (JDR:#92)

Death Record

Sutphen, Sarah, (Mrs.), d. 11/21/1823, age 70 years; buried Cherry Valley Presbyterian Church cemetery (PCV:80)

SUTZ (also see SUITS)

Marriage

Sutz, Adam (son of Joh. Stuz) m. Elisabeth

Franck (dau. of Conrad Franck), 1/11/1789 (RDSA:193)

Sutz, Adam (widower) m. Delia Fox, 3/15/1795 (RDSA:201)

Sutz, Dieterich (son of Peter Sutz) m. Catharina Coppernoll (dau. of Georg Coppernoll), 7/14/1761 (RDSA:169)

Sutz, John (1st son of Johann Sutz) m. Catharina Wabel (1st dau. of George Wabel), 8/16/1778, both of Stone Arabia (LTSA:285)

Birth/Baptism

Sutz, Benjamin & Catarina [?]: Maria, b. 9/13/1794 (LTSA:85). Sponsors: Georg Smit & Anna.

Sutz, Diedrich/Dieterich & Catharina [?]: Johannes, b. 3/31/1762, bapt. 4/9/1762 (RDSA:33); Georg, b. 12/29/1763, bapt. 1/1/1764 (RDSA:43); Margretha, b. 7/10/1766, bapt. 7/13/1766 (RDSA:66); Elisabeth, b. 11/19/1768, bapt. 11/25/1768 (RDSA:91); Petrus, b. 8/22/1771, bapt. 9/28/1771 (RDSA:109). Sponsors: Wilhelm Coppernoll & Engelge Sutz (re:1); Georg Coppernoll & his wife, Elisabeth (re:2); Eva Coppernoll & Andreas Finck (re:3); Elisabeth Laux & Diedrich Coppernoll (re:4); Peter Sutz & Anna Elisabeth (re:5).

Sutz, Dieterich & Catarina [?]: Thomas, b. 4/23/1796 (LTSA:94). Sponsors: Thomas Getmann & Elisabet.

Sutz, Jacob & Margaret [?]: Catarina, b. 2/10/1793 (LTSA:77). Sponsors: Heinrich Suz, Catarina Kils.

Sutz, Johann & Catharina [?]: Johann, b. 1/30/1780, bapt. 2/5/1780 (LTSA:59); Maria, b. 3/5/1782, bapt. 3/17/1782 (DRGF:56) Sponsors: Johann Sutz & Anna Elisabeth (re:1 Georg Wabel & Maria Esther (re:2).

Sutz, Johannes & Anna [?]: Anna, b 11/30/1780, bapt. 12/8/1780 (DRGF:40) Elisabetha, b. 8/16/1783, bapt. 8/31/178 (DRGF:74). Sponsors: Pieter Sutz & Elisabet (re:1); Ludwig Nelles & Margretha Sutz (re:2)

Sutz, Johannes & Anna Elisabetha [?]: Anna b. 4/12/1762, bapt. 4/25/1762 (RDSA:33) Anna Barbara, b. 2/20/1764, bapt. 3/4/176 (RDSA:45); Adam, b. 12/14/1766, bapt 12/25/1766 (RDSA:71); Jacobus, b. 10/5/1768 bapt. 10/16/1768 (RDSA:91); Henrich, b 9/21/1770, bapt. 10/7/1770 (RDSA:106) Sponsors: Anna Merckle & Johannes Walra (re:1); Elisabeth & Georg Coppernoll (re:2) Martin Nestel & Elisabetha (re:3); Jaco Walrath & his wife, Lena (re:4); Henric Lauchs & Maria Elisabeth (re:5).

Sutz, Peter & Anna Elisabetha [?]: Margretha b. 12/1/1760, bapt. 12/7/1760 (RDSA:23) Anna Elisabetha, b. 5/26/1762, bapt. 5/31/176 (RDSA:33); Johann Peter, b. 3/3/1764, bapt 3/11/1764 (RDSA:45); Catharina, b 8/15/1766, bapt. 8/24/1766 (RDSA:67) Dorothea, b. 4/6/1769, bapt. 4/16/176 (RDSA:94); Dieterich, b. 8/6/1771, bapt 9/28/1771 (RDSA:109). Sponsors: Catharina wife of Isaac Barry (re:1); Sophia Lepper & Johannes Snell (re:2); Wilhelm Laux & Mari Magdalena (re:3); Catharina Walrath & Wian Lepper (re:4); Dorothea & Philipps Fox (re:5) Dieterich Sutz & Catharina (re:6).

Sutz, Peter & Margreta (Borckert): Engelge bapt. 1740 (RDSA:3). Sponsors: Willian KoberNoll & his wife.

utz, Peter P. Esqr. & Elisabet (Gerster): Wilhelm, b. 5/28/1782, bapt. 6/2/1782 (RGF:58); Adam, b. 2/19/1788, bapt. /24/1788 (RDSA:116); Moses, b. 3/21/1791 (LTSA:67); Daniel, b. 8/6/1796 (LTSA:96). ponsors: Pieter Sutz & Anna Sev: Koch (re:1); r. Johann Georg Vach & Ottilia (born: Gerster) (re:2); Johannes Hess & Eva (re:3); Heinrich Schulz & Sara (re:4).

Death Record

utz, Adam, (legitimate son of Peter Sutz), b. /6/1788; d. 1/8/1788; buried 1/10/1788 (RDSA:230)

utz, Dieterich, d. 12/8/1794, age 65 years, 5 months (left besides his wife, 8 children & 7 grandchildren); buried 12/11/1794 (RDSA:235)

utz, Elisabeth, (born: Frank), d. 9/13/1792, ge 20 years, 4 days; buried 9/15/1792 (RDSA:233)

Probate Abstract

Suts, Adam, (of Johnstown), will dated 10/21/1821; probated 1/8/1825. Legatees: wife, Deliah; sons, Adam, William, Jacob, Solomon, Daniel, Jost, Benjamin and John; daus., Maria and Hertia/Kertia[?]. Executors: sons, Adam and Jacob. Witnesses: Martinus Nestell, Erastus P. Jones, John I. Cook. (WMC 57:181)

Suts, Peter, (of Palatine), will dated 2/11/1819; probated 5/31/1824. Legatees: wife, Elizabeth; sons, Daniel, Henry, Peter and Moses; daus., Dorothea (wife of John Reid), Mary (wife of Solomon Longshore), Nancy (wife of Jacob Boshart) and Caty (wife of Matthias Gunn, decd.). Executors: Christopher C. Fox, Charles Waggoner, William Shultis. Witnesses: Jacob Snell, Jacob Snell, Jr., Benjamin Loucks.

(WMC 57:179)

Suts, Richard, (of Palatine), will dated 6/9/1826; probated 3/8/1827. Legatees: wife, Catherine; sons, Thomas and Christopher; dau., Catherine. Executors: Peter G. Getman, Peter I. Saltsman. Witnesses: Peter G. Getman, C. Getman, Samuel Packer. (WMC 57:267)

Sutz, John, (of Palatine), will dated 9/2/1794; probated 6/28/1823. Legatees: wife, Elizabeth; sons, John, Henry, Jacob, Peter and Adam; daus., Margaret, Elizabeth, Molly, Catharine, Maria, Anne and Barbara. Bequest: Large German Bible to son, John. Executors: Henry Keyser, Nathan Christie. Witnesses: Noadiah Child, Andrew Dillenbach, William Gayner. (WMC 57:176)

Tryon County Militia

Sutz, Derick   [Appendix A]
Sutz, John
Sutz, John P.
Sutz, Peter
Sutz, Peter P.

Pension Abstract

Sutz, John I., son of John Suts; (uncles: Peter and Richard Suts; cousins: John Suts & John P. Suts [RWPA: #W25171; m. Nancy, dau. of Andrew Nellis]); m. Catharine Wauffel, 8/31/1778, Evangelical Lutheran Church, Stone Arabia, N.Y.; d. 1/31/1817. (Catharine Sutz, b. 1759/60; resident of Steuben, Oneida Co., N.Y. in 1838; d. prior to 1852.) John I. enlisted in the spring of 1775 and served for eighteen months under Capts. Andrew Dillenbach and Severines Cook in Col. Jacob Klock's 2nd. Regt., Tryon Co. Militia; he was also a batteauman under the command of Capt. Samuel Gray; John I. fought in the battles of

Oriskany, Brown's, Klock's Field and Johnstown. (RWPA: #W16747)

Sutz, John P., b. 12/25/1758, son of Peter Sutz, Palatine, N.Y.; m. Nancy Nellis; d. 1/8/1836, Ephratah, N.Y. (Nancy Sutz, b. 1758/9; d. 10/17/1839, Oppenheim, N.Y.) Children: son [not named]; Mary, b. 1779; Nancy, b. 11/29/1780 (m. Christopher Fox, 11/15/1801); Elizabeth (m. Daniel Hess); Catherine (m. John Radley). John P. enlisted in May 1775 from Palatine and served for two years and eight months as a fifer in the regiments of Cols. Cox, Gansevoort, Klock, Waggoner, Willett and Dubois; he fought in the battles of Stone Arabia, Lampman's and Johnstown. (RWPA: #W25171)

Sutz, Peter P., b. 1763/4; resident of Harrisburgh, Lewis Co., N.Y. on 9/20/1832. Peter P. enlisted from Palatine in October 1780 for fifteen days in Capt. Henry Miller's Co., Col. Jacob Klock's 2nd. Regt., Tryon Co. Militia; he served again in the spring of 1781 for two months in the same company and regiment; he enlisted for four months in August 1781 in Capt. Skinner's Co., Col. Marinus Willett's Regt.; he was on garrison duty at the fort in Palatine for more than one year and fought in the battle of Johnstown. (RWPA: #S14630)

1790 Census

Sutch, Derick   [Appendix B]

SWAIN

1790 Census

Swain, John   [Appendix B]

SWAN

Probate Abstract

Swan, Lyman, (of Florida), will dated 11/?/1826; probated 6/6/1828. Legatees: son, Freeman Stanton Swan; Mansfield Hunt and wife Mary (parents of my late wife, Sally). Executors: Reuben Howe, Joseph Braman. Witnesses: Anson Knibloe, Nathan Barlow, 2nd., Schuyler Fancher. (WMC 57:271)

SWART

Marriage

Swart, Wouter m. Eva Quackinbush, 3/8/1778 (DRC:162)

Birth/Baptism

Swart, Wouter & Elizabeth [?]: Teunis, bapt. 8/18/1738 (FH:4). Sponsors: Terrey Thickston, Teunis Swart, Christina Swart.

Probate Abstract

Swart, Benjamin, (of Florida), will dated 4/24/1815; probated 12/30/1815. Legatees: sons, Jeremiah B., Isaac B., Josias B., Ryer B., Walter B. and John B.; granddaughter (of Ryer B.); dau., Elizabeth Staley. Executors: John, John B. and Josias Swart. Witnesses: David Campbell, Martin and Nicholas Van O. Linda. (WMC 56:396)

Swart, Elias, (of the town of Florida), will dated 6/14/1817; probated 10/8/1817. Legatees: mother; brothers, Jeremiah and William; sisters, Anna and Eleanor. Executors: Walter, John and William Swart. Witnesses: John,

COMPENDIUM

William and Josias B. Swart. (WMC 57:165)

Swart, Isaiah, (of the town of Florida), will dated 7/13/1816; probated 10/8/1817. Legatees: wife, Sussanna; sons, Jeremiah, Elias and William; daus., Anna and Eleanor. Executors: Walter, William and John Swart. Witnesses: John I., Jeremiah W. and Josias B. Swart. (WMC 57:165)

Swart, Jeremiah, (of the Willigas on the Mohawk River, Tryon County), will dated 10/4/1780; probated 10/12/1813. Legatees: wife, Mary; sons, Josias, Benjamin, Walter, John and William; dau., Nancy (wife of Simon Groat); brother, William. Administrator: Isaiah Swart. Witnesses: Isaac Marselis, Marte Ve Olynde, Jacobus Cloet. (WMC 56:389)

Swart, John, (of Amsterdam), will dated 3/2/1826; probated 3/26/1829. Legatees: wife, Eleanor; son, John; dau., Maria (& her Eleanor, Andrew, Maria and Catharine). Executor: [none named]. Witnesses: John C. Searle, Abraham Shaver, John I. [J.?] Snell. (WMC 57:274)

Swart, John B., (of Florida), will dated 9/4/1826; probated 11/22/1827. Legatees: Rebecca, wife of brother, Josias B. Swart & their William, Benjamin, Ann, Maria and John; Uncle Walter. Executor: Dr. John Swart. Witnesses: William Van Olinda, Walter and John W. Swart. (WMC 57:269)

Swart, Tunis, (of the town of Florida), will dated 12/11/1811; probated 4/26/1813. Legatees: sons, Walter, Josiah, Jeremiah, Jelles, John Baptist (decd. & his five children); daus., Catherine Van Vleck and Elizabeth. Executors: William Van Olinde, Thomas Campbell. Witnesses: Nathaniel Campbell, Cornelius Wample, John Van Wormer. (WMC 56:387)

Tryon County Militia

Swart, Benjamin	[Appendix A]
Swart, Isias J.	
Swart, Jeremiah	
Swart, John	
Swart, Tunis	
Swart, Walter	
Swart, William	

Pension Abstract

Swart, Tunis, m. Margaret Mynderse prior to the Revolution; d. 2/21/1830 or 2/24/1830. (Margaret Swart, d. before 1830; [brother: Harmon Mynderse]. Children: Jacob (resident of Rotterdam, Schenectady Co., N.Y. in 1848); Barney (resident of Charlton, Saratoga Co., N.Y. in 1848). Tunis was commissioned a lieutenant in Capt. John Van Petten's Co., Col. Abraham Wemple's Regt. in Albany Co. on 6/20/1778 and served in all the principal expeditions on the Mohawk River; Tunis commanded the advance guard under Col. Willett in 1781 at the battle at West Canada Creek in which Walter Butler was killed and fourteen of the enemy were taken prisoner. This pension claim filed on 6/15/1848 was not allowed as there was no provision in the law under which children of soldiers in the Revolutionary War were entitled to a pension. (RWPA: #R10342)

1790 Census

Swart, (Widdow)	[Appendix B]
Swart, Benjamin	
Swart, John	
Swart, Josiah	
Swart, Teunis	
Swart, Walter	

797

COMPENDIUM

Swart, William
Swart, William, Sr.

Sweep, Jacob   [Appendix B]
Sweep, William

SWARTOUT

1790 Census

Swartout, Moses   [Appendix B]

SWEET

Birth/Baptism

Sweet, Caleb & Geritje (Newkirk): Elizabeth, b. 11/28/1790; bapt. 1/16/1791 (DRC:93). Sponsors: [none named].

SWAT

1790 Census

1790 Census

Swat, Daniel   [Appendix B]

Sweet, Caleb   [Appendix B]
Sweet, Jonathan
Sweet, William

SWEAT

1790 Census

Sweat, Isaac   [Appendix B]

SWEETMAN

Birth/Baptism

Sweetman, John & [?], Schenectady: Thomas, bapt. 2/22/1782 (JDR:24).

SWEATMAN

Birth/Baptism

Sweatman, Isaac & Sarah (Smith): Nicholas, b. 9/12/1790; bapt. 1/18/1791 (DRC:93). Sponsors: Nicholas S[?] & Christina S[?].

SWIER

Birth/Baptism

Swier, Lambertus Ernestus & Eva (Fitcher): Willem, b. 1/25/1783, bapt. 2/26/1783 (DRC:65); Annatje, b. 4/20/1785, bapt. 6/19/1785 (DRC:74). Sponsors: John Van Eps & Alida Van Eps (re:1); Isaac Sweir & Catrina Wilson (re:2).

SWEEP

COMPENDIUM

SWIFT

1790 Census

Swift, Ambross   [Appendix B]

SWITS

Birth/Baptism

Swits, Jacob & Helena [?]: Ariyaentie, bapt. 9/27/1739 (FH:7). Sponsors: Isaack Wimple, Elizabeth Wimple.

SWOOP

1790 Census

Swoop, Michael   [Appendix B]

SYDELMAN

Birth/Baptism

Sydelman, Johannes & Anna Maria [?]: Anna Elisabeth, b. 2/25/1769; bapt. 2/28/1769 (RDSA:93). Sponsors: Anna Foltz, Elisabet & Debald Tygert.

SYLLEBACK

1790 Census

Sylleback, Garrit   [Appendix B]

SYMERS

Marriage

Symers, Robert m. Margaret Fery, 11/26/1792 (UPSC:69)

SYMONS

1790 Census

Symons, Anthony   [Appendix B]

SYNN

Marriage

Synn, Aron m. Mary Tuttle, Schenectady, 1/9/1782 (JDR:1)

SYPHERT

Tryon County Militia

Syphert, Godfrey   [Appendix A]

1790 Census

Syphert, John   [Appendix B]

COMPENDIUM

SYTEX

1790 Census

Sytez, George   [Appendix B]

Margaret; sisters, Hannah Kline, Elizabeth, Gertruyd's (grandson, Aaron Bradt); brother, David. Executor: Simeon Dennis (of East Town, Washington County). Witnesses: Christopher Long, Jr., Polly Brower, Robert Mitchell. (WMC 57:165)

TAEGER

Death Record

Taeger, George Frederick, (son of Joh. Andreas & Anna (Muller) Taeger), d. 10/5/1804, Herkimer, age 3 years, 10 months, 15 days; buried in the new cemetery in Herkimer (RDH:253)

TALBOT

1790 Census

Talbot, Silas   [Appendix B]

TALCOT

1790 Census

Talcot, Hesekiah   [Appendix B]

TALLHAMMER

Probate Abstract

Tallhammer, Andrew, (of Mayfield), will dated 7/9/1817; probated 8/4/1817. Legatees: wife,

TALMAGE

Birth/Baptism

Talmage, Samuel & [?]: William Hilton, b. 3/15/1791; bapt. 5/1/1791 (JPC:4).

1790 Census

Talmage, Samuel   [Appendix B]

TANNER

Marriage

Tanner, Jacob m. Maria Luis, 7/24/1773 (DRC:158)

Birth/Baptism

Tanner, Jacob & Meritje (Lewis): Catrina, b. 2/12/1774, bapt. 3/1/1774 (DRC:28); Petrus, b. 9/23/1775, bapt. 10/30/1775 (DRC:35); Lena, b. 8/6/1777, bapt. 9/1/1777 (DRC:44); Echje, bapt. 9/9/1779 (DRC:53); Maragrita, b. 3/6/1786, bapt. 4/21/1786 (DRC:78). Sponsors: William Lewis & Catrina Lewis (re:1); David Lewis & Meritje Lewis (re:2); Hannes Luis & Sarah Luis (re:3); Adam Luis & Echje Luis (re:4); William Lewis & Elizabeth Lewis (re:5).

COMPENDIUM

Tryon County Militia

Tanner, Jacob   [Appendix A]

Pension Abstract

Tanner, Jacob, b. 12/?/1745, Lancaster, Pa.; resident of Sharon, Schoharie Co., N.Y. on 4/18/1833. Jacob enlisted from Currytown (later called Root, Montgomery Co., N.Y.) in August 1776 as a private under Capt. Robert Yates and Col. Volkert Veeder for a period of ten months; he was appointed sergeant on 6/1/1781 in Capt. Garret Putnam's Co., Col. Marinus Willett's Regt. and served for one year and six months; Jacob and his neighbor, Frederick Olman [RWPA: #S14743 Ulman], together with Olman's father and mother, were captured by Indians at Currytown and taken to Fort Hunter on 10/24/1781; they were then transported to and imprisoned at "Fort Niagara, Sackett's Harbor, Island of Despair in the St. Lawrence and Montreal"; Jacob, released with John Lewis (deceased in 1833) and others at Boston, walked home a distance of "240 miles", and found his [Jacob's] home burned by the Indians. (RWPA: #S11513)

1790 Census

Tanner, Jacob   [Appendix B]

TAPPAN

Death Record

Tappan, Charles, d. 7/9/1853, age 61 years, 25 days; buried Fort Plain Cemetery, Minden (FPC 56:43i)

TAROGE

Marriage

Taroge, David m. Agnes Yool, both of Schenectady, 5/12/1783 (JDR:2)

TASTE

1790 Census

Taste, Stephen   [Appendix B]

TAYLOR

Marriage

Taylor, Daniel m. Christian McPherson, 11/?/1798 (JPC:92)

Taylor, Elisha m. Genny Van Ebern, 12/8/1792 (DFP:47)

Birth/Baptism

Tayler, Daniel & Christian [?]: Mary, b. 11/12/1799, bapt. 1/26/1800 (JPC:16); Janet, b. 3/18/1801, bapt. 5/17/1801 (JPC:20).

Tayler, Stephen & Lena (Grigs), Newtown: Elijah, bapt. 7/31/1783 (JDR:13).

Death Record

Taylor, Ann, (dau. of Elisha Taylor), d. 8/4/1830, age 13 years; buried Cherry Valley Presbyterian Church cemetery (PCV:84)

Taylor, James Edwin, (of Charlton, New

York), d. 4/10/1830, age 23 years, of Consumption; buried Cherry Valley Presbyterian Church cemetery (PCV:84)

Taylor, Margaret, (Mrs.), d. 6/5/1823, age 45 years; buried Cherry Valley Presbyterian Church cemetery (PCV:80)

Deed Abstract

Tayler, John, merchant, and Margaret, his wife, of the City of Albany, to Lemuel Leavenworth, and Margaret, his wife, of Montgomery Co. Deed dated 2/24/1785; recorded 3/19/1785. Description: Land situated above Burnetsfield in Montgomery Co. on the south side of the Mohawk River to the west of the lands or Manor of the late Governor Crosby. Being a tract of land (441 acres) in the Sedachqueda Patent lying on the south side of the Mohawk River and conveyed by the Commissioners of Forfeitures of the Western District to John Taylor by Deed dated 1/3/1784. Consideration: L600. Witnesses: Stephen Lush, Jeremiah Lansing. (MVL:32)

1790 Census

Tayler, Ebenezer   [Appendix B]
Taylor, Aaron
Taylor, Israil
Taylor, John
Taylor, John, Jr.
Taylor, John, Sr.
Taylor, Joseph
Taylor, Niles
Taylor, Philip
Taylor, Silas
Taylor, Thomas
Taylor, William

TEAL

1790 Census

Teal, Joseph   [Appendix B]

TEEL

1790 Census

Teel, Timothy   [Appendix B]

TEHURST

1790 Census

Tehurst, Abraham   [Appendix B]
Tehurst, Martin
Tehurst, Philip

TEMPLE

Birth/Baptism

Temple, Joh. Lorenz & Ellinot [?]: Dieterich, b. 9/1/1795 (LTSA:91). Sponsors: Dieterich Coppernoll & Elisabet.

1790 Census

Temple, Joseph   [Appendix B]

TEN BROECK

COMPENDIUM

Marriage

Ten Broeck, Nicholas m. Delia Bellinger, 12/23/1792 (DRGF:209)

Tenbrook, John C. m. Anne Tenbrook (of Cravorick [Claverack?]), 12/30/1784; pubd. by Henry Miller, Minister of the Gospel at Albany and Loonenbourgh (JDR:2)

Birth/Baptism

Ten Broeck, Peter & Anna [?]: Jacobus, b. 12/?/1761, bapt. 1/5/1762 (RDSA:30); Johannes, b. 10/26/1764, bapt. 12/5/1764 (RDSA:52); Anna Gertraut, bapt. 2/7/1769 (RDSA:93); Joh: Nicolaus Hergheimer, b. 1/10/1771, bapt. 1/27/1771 (RDSA:108). Sponsors: Jost Hercheimer & his wife, Catharina (re:1); Johannes Hergheimer & Maria (dau. of Werner Teughert) (re:2); Gertraut & Rudolph Schum (re:3); Esqr. Joh: Nicolaus Hergheimer & Maria (re:4).

TEN EYCK

Birth/Baptism

Ten Eyck, Andrew & Sarah (Brugen): Jesper Burgen, b. 6/8/1790; bapt. 8/1/1790 (DRC:88). Sponsors: [none named].

Death Record

Ten Eyck, Margaret (Peggy), b. 9/10/1801; d. 6/21/1806, age 4 years, 9 months, 11 days (DFP:91)

Deed Abstract

Ten Eyck, Abraham, Gentleman, and Anna, his wife, of the City of Albany, to Joseph Tucker, of York Co., Massachusetts. Deed dated 5/21/1784; recorded 4/1/1785. Description: All the estate of John Jost Herkimer, yeoman, late of Tryon Co., forfeited to New York State. Land situated at Burnetsfield in said County on the south side of the Mohawk River in a patent granted to John Jost Petri and others. Lot #44 (100 acres) begins at a stake on the bank of the south side of the river three yards to the west of an apple tree in the division line of said John Jost Herkimer and Johannis Ruff. Consideration: L550. Witnesses: Marte Beeckman, Catharine Ten Eyck. (MVL:32)

Ten Eyck, John H. and Abrm., Loan Officers of the City & County of Albany to Abraham Arndt, of Montgomery Co. Deed dated 1/26/1786; recorded 11/25/1786. Description: Land situated on the south side of the Mohawk River, being part of Lot #2 (105 acres) in a patent granted to Rutger Bleecker and others. Consideration: L112. Witnesses: Jacob G. Lansing, John Tillman, Sr. (MVL:33)

1790 Census

Ten Eyck, Andrew (2)   [Appendix B]

TENNANT

1790 Census

Tenant, John   [Appendix B]
Tennant, Thomas

TENUS

803

COMPENDIUM

1790 Census

Tenus, Jacob (2)   [Appendix B]

TERA

Birth/Baptism

Tera, Matthew & Maragrita (Heveling): Catrina, b. 2/23/1777; bapt. 6/1/1777 (DRC:43). Sponsors: [none named].

TERRELL

1790 Census

Terrell, Hezekiah   [Appendix B]

TERRY

1790 Census

Terry, [?]   [Appendix B]
Terry, Gamaliel

TERWILLIGER

Tryon County Militia

Terwilliger, Hermanus   [Appendix A]
Terwilliger, James

1790 Census

Tewilleger, Isaac   [Appendix B]

Tirwilleger, Hermanus

THARP

1790 Census

Tharp, Daniel   [Appendix B]
Tharp, Nathan

THAYER

Probate Abstract

Thayer, Ezra, (of Florida), will dated 9/6/1824; probated 10/17/1831. Legatees: daus., Joanna, Lydia, Lucinda, Eliza Jane, Sally and Lois; sons, Samuel, Solomon, Ezra, William, Benjamin Cummins and Lorenzo; James Neff. Executors: William Reid, Bethuel Dean. Witnesses: Benedict Arnold, Mathias J. Bovee, Abraham Pulling, William G. Lewis. (WMC 57:280)

1790 Census

Thare, Ezra   [Appendix B]
Thare, John
Thare, Pheneas

THOMAS

1790 Census

Thomas, Henry   [Appendix B]
Thomas, Lewis
Thomas, Samuel

COMPENDIUM

THOMPSON

Marriage

Thompson, Alexander m. Elizabeth Thompson, 10/2/1798 (JPC:91)

Thompson, James m. Elizabeth Gollinger, 1/20/1785 (DRC:164)

Thompson, John m. Gertraud Philipps (dau. of Hen. Philipps), 11/11/1787 (DRGF:205)

Thomson, Thomas m. Charity Van Slyken, 6/24/1794 (DFP:52)

Birth/Baptism

Thompson, [?] & [?]: Gredia Margretha, bapt. 8/4/1793, age 9 years (SJC:79). Sponsors: Niclaus Herkemer & Margretha Herkemer.

Thompson, James & Elisabeth (Gill): Samuel, b. 2/9/1787; bapt. 6/10/1787 (DRC:85). Sponsors: [none named].

Thompson, John & Dorothea [?]: Margretha, b. 8/23/1761, bapt. 8/30/1761 (RDSA:28); Timothy, b. 7/23/1763, bapt. 7/24/1763 (RDSA:41). Sponsors: Sara, wife of Pieter Deighert (re:1); Wilhelm Lauchs & his wife, Margretha (re:2).

Thompson, John (of Palatine) & Gertrud (Philipson): Maria, bapt. 3/14/1790 (SJC:24). Sponsors: Heinrich Philips & Minna Philips.

Thompson, William (of Canajoharie) & Rosina (Wild): Daniel, bapt. 6/13/1790 (SJC:28). Sponsors: Georg Wild & Dorothea Wild.

Death Record

Thompson, Allan B., (son of Michael & Julia Thompson), d. 2/21/1844, age 1 year, 2 months, 25 days; buried sect. 6, Colonial Cemetery, Johnstown (JC:189)

Thompson, Else, (dau. of Squire Briggs; wife of David Thompson), d. 5/5/1837, age 37 years, 11 months; buried on Whitbeck farm and removed ca. 1864 to Cherry Valley Cemetery; buried beside her father on lot of Ralph Rudd, Sr. (CVC:2)

Thompson, Gertrude, (wife of Ward Thompson), d. 4/16/1822, age 43 years; buried sect. 6, Colonial Cemetery, Johnstown (JC:189)

Thompson, John, d. 10/15/1824, age 31 years; buried Cherry Valley Presbyterian Church cemetery (PCV:82)

Thompson, Polly, (wife of Ward Thompson), d. 11/11/1859, age 74 years; buried sect. 6, Colonial Cemetery, Johnstown (JC:189)

Thompson, Robert, d. 11/23/1828, age 56 years; buried Cherry Valley Presbyterian Church cemetery (PCV:83)

Thompson, Ward, d. 5/13/1847, age 79 years; buried sect. 6, Colonial Cemetery, Johnstown (JC:189)

Probate Abstract

Thompson, Ichabod, (of Minden), will dated 3/14/1816; probated 3/23/1816. Legatees: wife, Elizabeth; sons, Joseph M., Jonathan B. and Ichabod; daus., Sarah, Elizabeth and Emily. Executors: Benjamin Hillaker, Nathan Wilcox. Witnesses: Caleb Easterbrooks, John Holmes, John Atwater. (WMC 56:396)

Thompson, John, (of Broadalbin), will dated

3/21/1820; probated 6/24/1820. Legatees: my sons; my daus. Executors: Peter Van Nest, Jane and Isaac Thompson. Witnesses: Newcombe Bassett, Mary and Betsey Thomson. (WMC 57:170)

Thomson, John, Jr., [residence not stated], will dated 1/26/1818; probated 2/11/1818. Legatees: sons, Mathew Perrine and Thomas Lyle. Bequest: Left his two sons, "all my medical library and military uniforms". Executors: son, Thomas; wife, Mary; Peter Van Ness (of Amsterdam). Witnesses: Daniel Stewart, John Tallman, Coenrad Ten Eick. (WMC 57:166)

Tryon County Militia

Thompson, Aaron   [Appendix A]
Thompson, James
Thompson, John
Thompson, Thomas
Thompson, William

Pension Abstract

Thompson, William, b. 4/12/1758, Cherry Valley, Albany Co., N.Y.; m. [wife not named]; resident of Pendleton, Niagara Co., N.Y.; d. 10/7/1841. Children: Jennie (m. [?] R. Smead). Grandson: William L. Thompson. William enlisted from Cherry Valley in March 1776 and served as a private under Capt. Robert McKean in Cols. Wynkoop and Nichols' Regts. of the N. Y. Line; he enlisted in December 1776 as a private in Capt. Thomas Whittaker's Co., Col. Ebenezer Cox's 1st. Regt., Tryon Co. Militia; William marched against the Tories and Indians at Harpersfield & Unadilla and was at the burning of Cherry Valley; he transferred to Capt. Ballard's Co. in the summer of 1778 where he served for ten months; he then moved to the Mohawk River where he enlisted in the spring of 1779 in Capt.

Van Eaver's Co., Col. Marinus Willett's Regt and was stationed at Forts Herkimer and Ehle William fought in the battle of Johnstown an continued in the military until the close of th war. (RWPA: #S14677)

1790 Census

Thompson, Aaron   [Appendix B
Thompson, Alexander
Thompson, Alpheus
Thompson, Hugh
Thompson, James (2)
Thompson, John
Thompson, Jonathan
Thompson, Nathan
Thompson, Phenius
Thompson, Thomas
Thompson, William (3)
Thompson, Zebulan

THORNE

1790 Census

Thorne, Samuel   [Appendix B]

THORP

1790 Census

Thorp, Joseph   [Appendix B]

THRALL

Probate Abstract

COMPENDIUM

Thrall, Isaac, (of Johnstown), will dated 2/18/1814; probated 3/5/1814. Legatees: wife, Rhoda; sons, Isaac, John and Friend; daus., Rhoda, Lynda and Patty; granddaughter, Hannah Polly Enos. Executors: sons, Isaac and John. Witnesses: Gurdon Parsons, Flavel Enos, Ali'h Cheadel. (WMC 56:391)

Fisk. Witnesses: Michael Lusk, George R. Bass, Robert Mitchell. (WMC 56:391)

1790 Census

Throup, George   [Appendix B]
Throup, George B.
Throup, Josiah

THRASHER

1790 Census

Thrasher, George   [Appendix B]
Thrasher, Stephen

THROOP

Birth/Baptism

Throop, George B. & Abia [?]: Enos Thompson, b. 8/21/1784, bapt. 7/24/1791 (JPC:5); Mehitabel, b. 8/3/1786, bapt. 7/24/1791 (JPC:5); Mary Ann, b. 10/18/1790, bapt. 7/24/1791 (JPC:5); George, bapt. 5/5/1793 (JPC:8).

Death Record

Throop, George Bliss, d. 11/13/1794, age 54 years, 27 days; buried sect. 7, Colonial Cemetery, Johnstown (JC:189)

Probate Abstract

Throop, John, (of Mayfield), will dated 2/23/1814; probated 3/18/1814. Legatees: wife, Bathsheba; daus., Polly, Loranda, Eliza and Preemala; sons, John and William Lothrop. Executors: wife; Robert Mitchell, Jonathan

THUM (also see DUM)

Birth/Baptism

Thum, Adam & Christina [?]: Conrad Melchior, b. 11/19/1761, bapt. 1/5/1762 (RDSA:30); Adam, b. 8/26/1775, bapt. 8/27/1775 (LTSA:50). Sponsors: Conrad Franck & his wife, Elisabetha; Friderich Hess & his wife, Catharina (re:2).

Thum, Conrad (of Palatine) & Anna (Haus): Adam, bapt. 5/1/1790 (SJC:26); Jacob, bapt. 6/17/1792 (SJC:60). Sponsors: Adam Thumm & Christina Thumm (re:1); Johannes Hellmer & Magdalena Hellmer (re:2).

Thum, Conrad Melchior & Anna [?]: Johannes, b. 11/21/1784; bapt. 12/7/1784 (DRGF:90). Sponsors: Joh: Joh: Hauss & Margreth Thumm.

Thum, Joh. Nicholas (Palatine) & Elisabeth [?]: Magdalena, bapt. 2/9/1794 (SJC:92). Sponsors: Christian Fink & Elisabeth Deyggert.

Thum, Joh: Nicolaus & Elisabetha (Dygert): Elisabetha, b. 6/27/1767 (LTSA:24); Margaretha, b. 11/16/1768 (LTSA:24); Johann Nicolaus, b. 9/2/1769 (LTSA:38); Christina, b. 1/11/1770 (LTSA:30: Anna, b. 1/18/1773 (LTSA:45); Barbara, b. 12/10/1777, bapt. 12/14/1777 (LTSA:51); Melchior, b.

10/3/1779, bapt. 10/101/1779 (LTSA:57); Margretha, b. 5/3/1781, bapt. 5/6/1781 (DRGF:45); Maria, b. 2/17/1783, bapt. 2/20/1783 (DRGF:67); Delia, b. 3/6/1787, bapt. 3/8/1787 (RDSA:112). Sponsors: Elisabetha Wagner, Peter Deigert (re:1 & 2); Johannes Reber & his wife (re:3); Adam Dumm & his wife (re:4); Hennrich Salzmann, jr., Margaretha Wallrad (re:5); Johann Finck, Anna Hufnagel (re:6); Heinrich Wallrath & Catharina (re:7); Catharina Smidt & Christian Hufnagel (re:8); Severines Koch & Catharina (re:9); Captain John Bigbr[ead] & his wife, Anna (born: Merckel) (re:10).

Thum, Melchior & [?]: [?], b. 10/?/1770; bapt. 11/6/1770 (RDSA:107). Sponsors: Pieter Krembs & Anna Margreth.

Thum, Melchior & Elisabeth [?]: Maria, b. 3/14/1778, bapt. 4/19/1778 (DRGF:30); Catharina, b. 5/4/1782, bapt. 5/5/1782 (DRGF:58); Maria, b. 1/1/1785, bapt. 1/2/1785 (DRGF:91). Sponsors: Godfried Hiels & Maria (re:1); Wilhelm Tyghart & Agnes (re:2); Pieter S: Tyghart & Anna Huffnagel (re:3).

Thum, Theobald (Palatine) & Eva [?]: Johannes, bapt. 9/23/1792 (SJC:65). Sponsors: Adam Thumm & Maria Kringg.

1790 Census

Tum, Adam   [Appendix B]
Tum, Conradt

THURSTEN

1790 Census

Thursten, Amos   [Appendix B]
Thursten, Daniel
Thursten, Edward
Thursten, Increase
Thursten, John
Thursten, Moses

TICE

1790 Census

Tice, [?]   [Appendix B]

TICKNER

Marriage

Tickner, Jonathan m. Demas Eton, Warrensbush, 9/6/1787 (JDR:#68)

Birth/Baptism

Tickner, Benjamin & Elizabeth (Serviss), Jerseybush: Rode, bapt. 7/12/1788 (JDR:22).

1790 Census

Tickner, Benjamin   [Appendix B]
Tickner, Jonathan

TICKNEY

1790 Census

Tickney, Jonathan   [Appendix B]

808

COMPENDIUM

TIDD

<u>1790 Census</u>

Tidd, Samuel [Appendix B]

TIFFANY

<u>Marriage</u>

Tiffany, Charles G. (of Canajoharie) m. Corally C. Powell (of Canajoharie), 12/31/1832 (PCBC:52)

<u>1790 Census</u>

Tiffiny, Recompence [Appendix B]

TIGMEL

<u>1790 Census</u>

Tigmel, Asel [Appendix B]

TILLEBACK (also see **DILLENBACH**)

<u>1790 Census</u>

Tilleback, Martinus [Appendix B]
Tilleback, William

TILLOTSON

<u>1790 Census</u>

Tillotson, John [Appendix B]

TILMAN

<u>Birth/Baptism</u>

Tilman, Johann Ludwig & Dorotea [?]: Johann Antonius, b. [no date: between May/June 1795] (LTSA:90). Sponsors: Joh. Ant. Bek & Maria.

TILTON

<u>Birth/Baptism</u>

Tilton, Peter & Margaret (Youl), Newtown: Mary, bapt. 7/17/1785 (JDR:19).

TIMESON

<u>1790 Census</u>

Timeson, Garret [Appendix B]

TIMMERMAN (also see **ZIMMERMAN**)

<u>Probate Abstract</u>

Timerman, Henry, (of Oppenheim), will dated 6/3/1829; probated 8/28/1830. Legatees: wife, Anna; sons, John H., Andrew and Jacob H.; daus., Mary (wife of Benjamin van Allen) and Catharine; mother, Elizabeth Timerman. Executors: three sons. Witnesses: Ashbel Loomis, Jonas Snell, Peter Moyer. (WMC 57:277)

COMPENDIUM

Timerman, John I. [J.?], (of Oppenheim), will dated 7/4/1814; probated 11/28/1814. Legatees: brother, Henry I. [J.?]; mother. Administrator: brother, Henry. Witnesses: Jacob and Nicholas Timerman, David Anderson, Jr. (WMC 56:392)

Timmerman, Adam, (of Minden), will dated 7/3/1808; probated 7/5/1814. Legatees: wife, Anna Margretha; daus., Elizabeth, Anna and Maria; son, Abraham. Executors: wife; brothers, Thomas and John. Witnesses: Thomas Timerman, John D. Timerman, John Mettise. (WMC 56:392)

Tryon County Militia

Timmerman, Christian   [Appendix A]
Timmerman, Conrad
Timmerman, Hendrick
Timmerman, John

Pension Abstract

Timmerman, Henry, b. 1/1/1750, Manheim, Albany Co., N.Y.; m. [wife not named; b. 1764/5]; resident of Le Roy, Jefferson Co., N.Y. on 12/4/1832. Henry enlisted from Manheim in the spring/summer of 1775 and was a private for eleven months in Capt. Christopher P. Yates' Co., Col. Goose Van Schaick's 3rd. Regt. of the N.Y. Line; he went on Gen. Montgomery's campaign to Canada where he participated in the taking of St. Johns and fought in the battle of Chambley; he marched in 1776 with his company in the same regiment to Ticonderoga; he enlisted in 1777 and served under his uncle, Lt. Henry Timmerman, for six months; Henry fought in the battle of Oriskany and was a member of Sullivan's expedition to "Wyoming"; he continued his military service through 1779.

(RWPA: #S14701)

Timmerman, John, b. 4/17/1760, Palatine, N.Y.; resident of Shelby, Orleans Co., N.Y. on 2/5/1834. John was drafted into the military in the spring of 1777 and served in Capt. Christian House's Co., Col. Jacob Klock's 2nd. Regt., Tryon Co. Militia; he was made a corporal and remained in the militia until the end of the war; John fought in the battle of Oriskany and participated in the skirmish at West Canada Creek. (RWPA: #R21795)

1790 Census

Timmerman, Adam   [Appendix B]
Timmerman, Christian
Timmerman, George
Timmerman, Henry (2)
Timmerman, Jacob
Timmerman, Lawrence
Timmerman, William

TIMS

Tryon County Militia

Tims, Michael   [Appendix A]

TINIS

Tryon County Militia

Tinis, Jacob   [Appendix A]
Tinis, John

COMPENDIUM

TIPPET

Marriage

Tippet, James m. Jane Bradford, both of Warrensborough, 7/6/1791 (JDR:#98)

1790 Census

Tippet, Henry   [Appendix B]

TOBY

1790 Census

Toby, Ephraim   [Appendix B]

TONN

Birth/Baptism

Tonn, Johann & Maria [?]: Maria, b. 8/14/1778; bapt. 8/24/1778 (LTSA:54). Sponsors: George Adam Dachstedter, Elisabeth Jucker.

TOOBY

Marriage

Tooby, Emmanuel, Ensign m. Dorothea Peiffer, 8/28/1782 (DRGF:196)

Birth/Baptism

Tooby, Emanuel & Dorothea [?]: Maria Catharina, b. 12/20/1782; bapt. 1/9/1783

(DRGF:66). Sponsors: Lorontz Schumacher & Margretha Peiffer.

TOOL

Marriage

Tool, Immanuel m. Elisabeth Kesslar (dau. of Joh. Thomas Kesslar), 11/18/1784 (DRGF:200)

TOPPING

Probate Abstract

Topping, Hetty, (of Charleston), will dated 9/30/1814; probated 2/9/1815. Legatees: mother, Jemima Topping; son, Edward Topping; sisters, Statira Peckham and Polly Sutton; niece Hetty Peckham; cousin, Robert Hudson (of Schenectady). Executors: brother, Jared Topping; brother-in-law, Perry Peckham. Witnesses: Thomas Leek, Beriah Crocker, William Clark. (WMC 56:393)

TOURNBALL

Marriage

Tournball, George m. Mary Phillips, both of Warrensborough, 1/11/1792 (JDR:#104)

TOWER

Birth/Baptism

COMPENDIUM

Tower, Rudolph & Elisabetha Barbara [?]: Maria Elisabeth, b. 2/2/1757 (LTSA:21). Sponsors: Jerg Ecker & his wife, Maria Elis.

1790 Census

Tower, Lidia   [Appendix B]

TOWN

Death Record

Town, Phebe, (wife of John Town), d. 11/26/1828, age 52 years; buried Cherry Valley Presbyterian Church cemetery (PCV:83)

TOWNSEND

Probate Abstract

Townsend, John (of Saulsbery), will dated 5/20/1812; probated 4/17/1813. Legatees: wife, Jane; sons, Elijah and John; grandsons (of Elijah); daus. [not named]. Executors: wife, Joseph Penny, Allen Irwin. Witnesses: Joseph Drake, Jeremiah Coons. (WMC 56:387)

1790 Census

Townsend, Absolem   [Appendix B]
Townshend, Gerdeus (2)
Townshend, John
Townshend, Nathaniel
Townshend, Platt

TRACY

1790 Census

Tracy, Christopher   [Appendix B]
Tracy, Jonathan
Tracy, Nathan

TRAVER

1790 Census

Traver, Peter   [Appendix B]

TRAVIS

1790 Census

Travis, James   [Appendix B]

TREMBACH

Birth/Baptism

Trembach, Jacob & Christiana [?]: Maria, b. 9/24/1792 (LTSA:70). Sponsors: Peter Schnell, Catarina Frei.

TREMPAW

1790 Census

Trempaw, Jacob   [Appendix B]

812

COMPENDIUM

TRIES

Birth/Baptism

Tries, Johann & Catharina [?]: Anna, b. 12/22/1778; bapt. 1/17/1779 (LTSA:56). Sponsors: Christian Lederer, Elisabeth Kaas.

TRIP

1790 Census

Trip, Jaba   [Appendix B]

TROTTS

1790 Census

Trotts, John   [Appendix B]

TROWBRIDGE

Marriage

Trowbridge, John m. Rachel Gould, both of Warrensborough, 10/7/1792 (JDR:#117)

Death Record

Trowbridge, Betsy, (dau. of Daniel Trowbridge), d. 12/9/1813, age 28 years; buried sect. 7, Colonial Cemetery, Johnstown (JC:189)

Trowbridge, Mary, (dau. of Daniel Trowbridge), d. 1/30/1814, age 24 years;

buried sect. 7, Colonial Cemetery, Johnstown (JC:189)

1790 Census

Trowbridge, Samuel   [Appendix B]

TRUAX

Marriage

Truax, Jacob m. Catrina Doxteder, 3/5/1775 (DRC:160)

Birth/Baptism

Truax, Jacob & Catrina (Doxteder): Jacob, b. 1/8/1780; bapt. 1/24/1780 (DRC:55). Sponsors: Jacob Doxteder & Catrina Doxteder.

Truax, Joh. Wyngard & Magdalena [?]: Petrus Hayser, b. 8/28/1782; bapt. 9/19/1782 (DRGF:62). Sponsors: Petrus Truax & Cathleina Truax.

Truax, Johann & Anna [?]: Maria, b. 11/28/1778; bapt. 11/30/1778 (LTSA:55). Sponsors: Johann Schmidt & Maria.

TRULL

1790 Census

Trull, John   [Appendix B]

TRUSDELL

813

COMPENDIUM

1790 Census

Trusdell, Justice   [Appendix B]

TRYON

1790 Census

Tryon, Thomas   [Appendix B]

TUBBS

1790 Census

Tubbs, Enos   [Appendix B]
Tubbs, Ezekiel
Tubbs, Lebeus
Tubbs, Samuel

TUBENDORF

Birth/Baptism

Tubendorf, Jacob & Barbara [?]: Jacob, bapt. 9/28/1740 (FH:11A). Sponsors: Peter Young, Matthias Shalamon, Eliz. Tubendorf.

TUCKER

Death Record

Tucker, Caleb, d. 11/15/1828, age 48 years; buried Cherry Valley Presbyterian Church cemetery (PCV:83)

Tucker, Hannah, (wife of Joshua Tucker), d. 10/22/1828, age 50 years; buried Cherry Valley Presbyterian Church cemetery (PCV:83)

Tucker, Joshua, Sr. (elder of the church), d. 4/17/1822, age 82 years; buried Cherry Valley Presbyterian Church cemetery (PCV:78)

Tryon County Militia

Tucker, George   [Appendix A]
Tucker, Jacob
Tucker, Johannes

1790 Census

Tucker, Moses   [Appendix B]

TULLER

1790 Census

Tuller, James   [Appendix B]

TUNN

1790 Census

Tunn, Nicholas   [Appendix B]

TUNNECLIFF

1790 Census

Tunnecliff, John   [Appendix B]

TURNER

Turner, Asa   [Appendix B]
Turner, Nathan
Turner, William

TUSSLER (also see DUSSLER)

Tusler, Mark   [Appendix B]
Tussler, John

TUTTLE

Birth/Baptism

Tuttle, Ezra & Hanna (Mc Graw): David McGra[w], bapt. 5/17/1785 at age 4 weeks (DRC:72); Jeremiah Schuyler, b. 6/30/1791, bapt. 8/7/1791 (DRC:100). Sponsors: David Mc Gra[w] & his wife (re:1); Jeremiah Schuyler & Mary Martin (re:2).

Tuttle, Solomon & [?]: Stephen, bapt. 4/13/1781 (JDR:23).

Tuttle, William Young & Nancy (Whitaker): William Henry, b. 11/20/178[?]; bapt. 1/11/1789 (JPC:2).

Death Record

Tuttle, Anna, (wife of William Y. Tuttle), d. 1/1/1822, Herkimer, age 80 years; buried near the Episcopal [*litturgiam*] in the new cemetery in town (RDH:282)

1790 Census

Tutle, William Y.   [Appendix B]
Tuttle, Ezra
Tuttle, Samuel
Tuttle, Timothy

TWEEDIE

Probate Abstract

Tweedie, James, (of Florida), will dated 10/11/1828; probated 11/18/1829. Legatees: wife, Janet; daus., Jane, Margaret, Mary Eliza, Anna and Jennet; sons, John and James. Executrix: wife. Witnesses: Platt Potter, Washington Love, Robert Arnot. (WMC 57:275-276)

TYGERT (also see DYGERT)

Tyger, Angrew   [Appendix B]
Tygert, David
Tygert, Henry
Tygert, Nicholas
Tygert, Peter H.
Tygert, Peter S.

TYLER

Tyler, Ashbel   [Appendix B]
Tyler, Benjamin
Tyler, Ephraim

Tyler, Silas

TYMENSON

Birth/Baptism

Tymenson, Gerrit & Madalena (Sybergen): Emilia, b. 3/16/1782; bapt. 6/9/1782 (DRC:62). Sponsors: Lodewyk Pater & Anna Emilia [?].

TZINTS

Birth/Baptism

Tzints, Casper & Elizabeth (Heychet): Philip, bapt. 1758 (DRC:1). Sponsors: Philip Cool & Catarina Winkel.

UHLY

Marriage

Uhly, Henrich m. Lena Tyghart (dau. of Werner Tyghart), 9/9/1784 (DRGF:200)

Birth/Baptism

Uhly, Henrich & Lena [?]: Dorothea, b. 12/1/1784; bapt. 12/25/1784 (DRGF:91). Sponsors: Severines W: Tyghart & Dorothea P: Tyghart.

ULENDORFF (also see OLENDORPH)

Birth/Baptism

Ulendorff, Daniel & Catharina [?]: Elisabeth, b. 9/3/1783; bapt. 10/5/1783 (DRGF:75). Sponsors: Anna Elisabeth Haber & Friedrich Jung.

ULMAN (also see OOLMAN)

Marriage

Uhlmann, Frederick m. Lena Weber (widow), 11/10/1794 (DFP:52)

Birth/Baptism

Ulman, Friderich & Maria [?]: Catarina, b. 3/3/1794 (LTSA:83). Sponsors: Heinrich Muller & Margaret.

Ulman, Jacob & Elizabeth (Spenser): Philip, b. 5/18/1785; bapt. 5/29/1785 (DRC:73). Sponsors: Michal O'Cotter & Anna O'Cotter.

Tryon County Militia

Ulman, Barent   [Appendix A]
Ulman, Johannes
Ulman, Leonard

Pension Abstract

Ulman, Frederick, b. 6/?/1755, Lancaster, Pa.; m. Laney Keller, 11/10/1794 at Fort Plain, Montgomery Co., N.Y.; d. 8/14/1841, Carlisle, Schoharie Co., N.Y. (Laney Ulman, d. 2/10/1845.) Children: David, b. 1804/5; Susan (m. [?] Sailsbury/Salsburg); Abram, Peter, Elizabeth (m. [?] Read). [All children were residents of Carlisle, Schoharie, N.Y. in 1845.] Frederick enlisted from his home in Lancaster, Pa. in March 1776 and served for one year and nine months as a private in Capt. Matthias Weidman's Co., Col. Samuel Atlee's Pennsylvania Regt.; he was in the battle of Long Island where he was taken prisoner but escaped in the night; he enlisted from Tryon Co., N.Y. in March 1779 and served for nine months in Col. Dubois' Regt. of the N.Y. Line; Frederick served for one month in 1780 as a member of Capt. Garret Putman's Co., Col. Marinus Willett's Regt. of the N.Y. Line and enlisted again in the same company in April 1781; he was taken prisoner while on a scouting mission on 11/24/1781 and held until peace was confirmed. (RWPA: #S14743)

ULSHEVER (also see OULTSAVER)

Birth/Baptism

Ulsheffer, Sebastian & Elisabeth [?]: Anna, b. 9/23/1782; bapt. 9/29/1782 (DRGF:62). Sponsors: Wilhelm Riebsamen & Philippina Ulsheffer.

Ulshever, Stephan & Magdalena [?]: Maria Magdalena, b. 6/21/1781; bapt. 6/27/1781 (DRGF:46). Sponsors: Frantz Baater & Maria Magdalena.

Death Record

Ulshoefer, George, d. 4/21/1796, age 7 years; buried 4/23/1796 (DFP:89)

Ulshoefer, Magdalena, (wife of Stephan Ulshoefer); d. 12/22/1794, age 41 years; buried 12/24/1794 (DFP:86)

Tryon County Militia

Ulshever, Bastian   [Appendix A]
Ulshever, Stephen

ULTARMARK

Death Record

Ultarmark, Angelica, d. 3/24/1863, age 90 years; buried Fort Plain Cemetery, Minden (FPC 56:43i)

UNDERHILL

1790 Census

Underhill, David   [Appendix B]

UNDERWOOD

1790 Census

Underwood, Elias   [Appendix B]
Underwood, Joseph
Underwood, Parker

[UNKNOWN ?]

Birth/Baptism

[Unknown] & [?]: Eva, b. [unknown, but between Oct./Nov. 1757] (LTSA:22). Sponsors: Conrad Windecker & his wife, Egie.

[Unknown] & [?]: Maria, b. 1/18/1779; bapt. 1/25/1779 (LTSA:56). Sponsors: Heinrich Saltzmann & Maria Elisabeth.

[Unknown] & Anna (dau. of Friederich Lepper): Anna Maria, bapt. 5/11/1761 (RDSA:26). Sponsors: Anna Maria, wife of Hans Michael Ittig.

[Unknown] & Margretha [?]: [?], b. 4/5/1763; bapt. 5/9/1763 (RDSA:39). Sponsors: George Hauss & [?].

[Unknown] & Rosina (Veix): Elisabetha Maria, b. 9/3/1771 (LTSA:40). Sponsors: Georg Veix, Elis: Marg Klein.

[Unknown: soldier] & [?]: Johannes Adamus, b. 4/16/1762; bapt. 8/18/1762 (RDSA:35). Sponsors: Adam Contermann & Anna Margretha.

[Unknown] & Sophia Eleonora [?]: Fridrick, b. 5/22/1769 (LTSA:26). Sponsors: Christian Lemm & his wife.

[Unknown] & [?]: Jonas, b. 8/18/1789 (LTSA:68). Sponsors: Conrad Loscher & Lena.

[Unknown], Thomas & Maria [?]: Anna Eva, b. 1/20/1791 (LTSA:67). Sponsors: John Casselman & Anna Eva.

URGET

Birth/Baptism

Urget, William & Jenny [?]: Catrina, b. 1/6/1780; bapt. 2/3/1780 (DRC:55). Sponsors: [none named].

USNER

Tryon County Militia

Usner, Peter George   [Appendix A]

UTT

Tryon County Militia

Utt, Francis   [Appendix A]

VACH

Birth/Baptism

Vach, Johann Georg (Doctor) & Delia [?]: Margaretha Christiana, b. 10/15/1780 (LTSA:60; RDSA:110); Henrietta, b. 1/10/1783, bapt. 1/16/1783 (LTSA:60; DRGF:66). Sponsors: Christian Senff, Cornel., Margaretha Paris (re:1); Jacob Schultz & Elisabetha Gerster (re:2).

Death Record

Vach, [?], (son of the deceased Dr. Vach), d. 8/15/1794, age 6 years, [?] months, 21 days; buried 8/17/1794 (RDSA:235)

COMPENDIUM

Tryon County Militia

Vach, Johann George [Appendix A]

VAGER

Birth/Baptism

Vager, John & [?] (Deal), Amsterdam: Thomas, bapt. 7/22/1795 (JDR:24).

VALENTINE

1790 Census

Valentine, James [Appendix B]

VAN ALLEN

Marriage

Van Alen, Jacob m. Rachel Quackenbush, 1/25/1742 (FH:19)

Birth/Baptism

Van Alen, Jacob & Rachel (Quackenbush): Sarah, bapt. 6/5/1743 (FH:20); Peter, bapt. 1/12/1745/6 (FH:29). Sponsors: John Collier, Magdalene Collier, Sarah Quackenbos (re:1); Peter Quackenbos, Ann Quackenbos (re:2).

Van Allen, Peter & Maria [?]: Jacobus, b. 8/30/1771 (LTSA:39). Sponsors: Jacob von Alen, Ana Margaretha Albert.

Probate Abstract

Van Alen, Adam E., (of Johnstown), will dated 5/23/1807; probated 9/26/1808. Legatees: wife, Eve; daus., Hannah, Peggy and Lydia Maria; sons, John Evart and Austin. Executors: Lawrence E. Van Alen (& his son, Evart); Garret Ten Broock; wife, Eve; son, John. Witnesses: Daniel Cady, William Vosburgh, Trustem Dunham. (WMC 56:158-159)

Van Alen, Lourence E., (of the town of Amsterdam), will dated 4/8/1819; probated 11/8/1819. Legatees: sons, Cornelius, Stephen, Evart (decd.); daus., Alida, Polly (wife of Daniel Winne); brother, John (decd.); grandchildren, Rachel and Lawrence (of Evart). Executors: son, Cornelius; James Cushney. Witnesses: James Cushney, Victor and Abraham I. Vosburgh. (WMC 57:169)

Tryon County Militia

Van Allen, Jacob [Appendix A]

VAN ALSTYNE

Marriage

Vanalstine, John m. Rachel Vandewerker, 11/4/1800. Witnesses: [?] Vanderwerker, [?] Vanalstine (JPC:93)

Van Alstyne, Abraham m. Marlena van Deuysen, 9/16/1770 (RDSA:190)

Van Alstyne, Corneles m. Jacomyntje Pottmann, 10/7/1769 (RDSA:188)

Van Alstyne, Corneles m. Jannitje Quakenbosh, 3/1/1765 (RDSA:175)

819

COMPENDIUM

Van Alstyne, Gysbert m. Lemmitje
Quack[enbush], 12/11/1772 (DRC:158)

Van Alstyne, Jacob (widower) m. Elisabeth von
den Wercken (dau. of Marteines von den
Wercken), 2/5/1762 (RDSA:170)

Van Alstyne, Johannes M. m. Sarah Wemple,
6/?/1785 (DRC:164)

Van Alstyne, Martin m. Annatje
Quack[enbush], 9/25/1761 (RDSA:170)

Van Alstyne, Martinus m. Margaretha Zealy,
2/1/1789 (RDSA:194)

Van Alstyne, Nicholas m. Cornelia Van
Alstine, [no date: follows 1/20/1777]
(DRC:161)

Van Alstyne, Peter m. Agnitje Van Alstyne,
11/14/1793 (DFP:50)

Van Alstyne, Peter A. m. Alida Mabe,
4/?/1785 (DRC:164)

Van Alstyne, Philip m. Barbara Ruff, 7/8/1792
(DFP:45)

Van Alstyne, Philip m. Maria Davis, 8/?/1785
(DRC:164)

Birth/Baptism

Van Alstine, Johann & Elisabeth [?]: Johannes,
b. 4/14/1778; bapt. 5/17/1778 (LTSA:53).
Sponsors: Jacobus von Schleick, Margaretha v.
Schleick.

Van Alstyne, Abraham & Gertruid
(Quackenbush): Peter, bapt. 1/28/1746/7
(RDSA:9). Sponsors: Jacob van Alstyn,
Catharina van Aalstyn.

Van Alstyne, Abraham G. & Helena (Van
Deusen): Cornelis, b. 5/14/1772, bapt.
5/31/1772 (DRC:20); Neyltje, b. 1/7/1774,
bapt. 2/20/1774 (DRC:28); Catrina, b.
12/16/1775, bapt. 1/22/1775 (DRC:36).
Sponsors: Cornelis Van Alstyn & Neylche Van
Alstyn (re:1); Melgert Van Deusen & Nyltje
Van Deusen (re:2); Cornelius Van Aalstyn &
Jannetje Van Aalstyn (re:3).

Van Alstyne, Abram & Catye (Vallac):
Elizabeth, b. 12/23/1771; bapt. 12/?/1771
(DRC:20). Sponsors: Gose Van Alstyn &
Elizabeth Van Alstyn.

Van Alstyne, Abram A. & Jannetje
(Quackenbush): Abram, b. 11/6/1775, bapt.
11/25/1775 (DRC:35); John, b. 9/13/1781,
bapt. 10/20/1781 (DRC:59); Peter, b.
5/3/1783, bapt. 6/8/1783 (DRC:66); Annatje,
b. 5/10/1787, bapt. 6/26/1787 (DRC:85);
Anatje, b. 12/21/1790, bapt. 1/23/1791
(DRC:94). Sponsors: Abram Van Aalstyn &
Geertruy Van Aalstyn (re:1); Gysbert Van
Alstyne & Lemmitje Van Alstine (re:2); Jacob
V. Alstine & Nancy V. Alstine (re:3); Abram
Potman & Rebecca Quak (re:4); [destroyed]
(re:5).

Van Alstyne, Cornelius & Deunge (Fort):
Geretge, bapt. 1740 (RDSA:3). Sponsor:
Daniell Fortt.

Van Alstyne, Cornelius & Jannitje
(Quackenbush): Corneles, bapt. 9/29/1765
(RDSA:58); Abraham, b. 4/30/1770, bapt.
6/3/1770 (RDSA:103); Hunter, b. 5/8/1772,
bapt. 6/7/1772 (DRC:22); Catrina, b.
6/12/1774, bapt. 7/10/1774 (DRC:30); David,
b. 7/4/1776, bapt. 8/4/1776 (DRC:38); Maria,
b. 9/7/1777, bapt. 10/19/1777 (DRC:45).
Sponsors: Corneles van Aalsteen & Neelje
(re:1); Abraham [?] & Lena V[?] (re:2); Hunter

Quackenbush & Neylche Quackenbush (re:3); Nicholas Quack[enbush] & Jannetje Quack[enbush] (re:4); Abram Quack & Moria Quack (re:5); Cornelius Van Everen & Jannetje Van Everen (re:6).

Van Alstyne, Cornelius J. & Marigrieta (Lenardson): Wyntje, b. 8/13/1790; bapt. 9/14/1790 (DRC:89). Sponsors: Albt. Cainal & Mary V. Alstine.

Van Alstyne, Cornelius, 3rd. & Mareitje (Corey): Gosen, b. 11/25/1790; bapt. 2/6/1791 (DRC:94). Sponsors: [none named].

Van Alstyne, Eva & [?]: Mary, bapt. 2/8/1739/40 (FH:9). Sponsors: Joseph Dans, Mary Butler, Issabella Wilson.

Van Alstyne, Goose & Elisabeth [?]: Philippus, b. 12/7/1762; bapt. 1/9/1763 (RDSA:37). Sponsors: Henrich Schremling & Gerretje van Aalstein.

Van Alstyne, Gysbert & Annatie (Gardenier): Niclaas, bapt. 1/28/1746/7 (RDSA:9); Martinus, b. 3/23/1765, bapt. 4/21/1765 (RDSA:55). Sponsors: Johannes van Aalstyn & his wife, Catharina (re:1); Martin van Aalstein & Cornelia Van Alstein (re:2).

Van Alstyne, Gysbert & Linetje/Lemmitje (Quackinbush): Abram, b. 9/19/1773, bapt. 10/3/1773 (DRC:26); John, b. 6/27/1775, bapt. 7/16/1775 (DRC:34); Cornelis, b. 12/5/1780, bapt. 12/31/1780 (DRC:58). Sponsors: Abram Van Aalstyn & Geertruy Van Alstyn (re:1); Jeremiah Quack & Elizabeth Quack (re:2); Cornelis Van Alstine & Neeltje Van Alstine (re:3).

Van Alstyne, Gysbert A. & Janneke (Quackenbush): Meritje, b. 6/1/1785; bapt.

6/19/1785 (DRC:74). Sponsors: Samuel Gardenir & Meritje Gardenir.

Van Alstyne, Harmanus & Elizabeth (Flint): Maria, b. 2/26/1782; bapt. 3/16/1782 (DRC:61). Sponsors: Robert Flint & Maragrita Hornet [Horning].

Van Alstyne, Jacob & Annatje (Cirle): Mareitje, b. 2/2/1791; bapt. 3/6/1791 (DRC:95). Sponsors: John Cirle & his wife.

Van Alstyne, Jacob & Eva (Neps): Cornelius, bapt. 3/4/1751 (RDSA:10). Sponsors: Cornelius van Alstein, Janie van Nufveren.

Van Alstyne, Jacob & Nancy (Carrel): Abram, b. 5/12/1782, bapt. 6/16/1782 (DRC:63); Gertruy, b. 1/12/1786, bapt. 2/?/1786 (DRC:76). Sponsors: Cornelis Van Alstine & Neeltje Van Alstine (re:1); [none named] (re:2).

Van Alstyne, Jacob & Wyntje [?]: Eva, b. 2/5/1765; bapt. 2/24/1765 (RDSA:54). Sponsors: Nelje & Reinier van Ivern.

Van Alstyne, Jacob & Wyntye (Leenderse): Maria, b. 8/13/1773; bapt. 8/22/1773 (DRC:26). Sponsors: William Merinus & Maria Merinus.

Van Alstyne, Jeremiah & Catrina (Gardenier): Gertruy, b. 4/5/1787; bapt. 4/16/1787 (DRC:84). Sponsors: John Carl & Meritje Carl.

Van Alstyne, Johannes & Catterina (Schremling): Cornelia, bapt. 1741 (RDSA:4). Sponsors: Mardines von allStein & his wife, Cornelia.

Van Alstyne, Johannes & Maragrita (Loux): Jacob, b. 2/3/1783; bapt. 2/25/1783 (DRC:65). Sponsors: John Carroll & Maria Carroll.

COMPENDIUM

Van Alstyne, Johannes & Maragrita (Price): Maria, b. 12/9/1784, bapt. 1/27/1785 (DRC:70); Johanis, b. 8/9/1791, bapt. 9/17/1791 (DRC:100). Sponsors: Joseph Prentip & Annatje Prentip (re:1); John Loux & Eva, his wife (re:2).

Van Alstyne, Martin & Anna (Quack[enbush]): Abram, b. 2/25/1773, bapt. 3/31/1773 (DRC:24); Jurry, b. 8/12/1778, bapt. 10/6/1778 (DRC:50); Leonard Bronk, b. 4/23/1782, bapt. 5/20/1782 (DRC:62); Neyltje, b. 1/29/1786, bapt. 7/9/1786 (DRC:81). Sponsors: David Quack[enbush] & Annatye Quack[enbush] (re:1); Mattheus Schremling & Annatje Schremling (re:2); [none named] (re:3); Hunter Quak & Sarah Quak (re:4).

Van Alstyne, Martin & Annatje [?]: Elisabeth, b. 5/16/1763; bapt. 6/29/1763 (RDSA:40). Sponsors: Henrich Schremling & Cornelia.

Van Alstyne, Martin C. & Elisabeth (Van Slyk): Cornelia, b. 6/7/1787; bapt. 6/12/1787 (DRC:85). Sponsors: Nicolas Van alstyn & Cornelia Van alstyn.

Van Alstyne, Martin G. & Marigrietje (Schremling): Caty, b. 10/29/1785; bapt. 1/3/1786 (DRC:75). Sponsors: Philip V. Alstyn & Maria V. Alstyn.

Van Alstyne, Nicholas & Cornelia [?]: Corneles, b. 3/4/1781; bapt. 5/6/1781 (DRGF:45). Sponsors: Nicolas van Slyk & Gertraud.

Van Alstyne, Nicholas G. & Cornelia (Van Alstine): Gysbert, b. 10/17/1778, bapt. 12/19/1778 (DRC:50); Jennetje, b. 12/26/1785, bapt. 3/12/1786 (DRC:77). Sponsors: Gysbert Van Alstine & Annatje Van Alstine (re:1); Cornelis Van Yveren & Jennetje Van Yveren (re:2).

Van Alstyne, Peter & Gerritje (Van Aalstyn): Neyltje, b. 8/6/1774, bapt. 9/4/1776 (DRC:30); Cornelia, b. 9/3/1777, bapt. 9/28/1777 (DRC:44); Geertruy, b. 4/8/1780, bapt. 5/14/1780 (DRC:56). Sponsors: Abram Van Aalstyn & Geertruy Van Aalstyn (re:1); Martha G.V. Alstyne & Cornelia Van Alstyne (re:2); Abram V. Alstyne & Jannetje V. Alstyne (re:3).

Van Alstyne, Philip G. & Maria (Davis): Annatje, b. 5/12/1786; bapt. 6/20/1786 (DRC:80). Sponsors: Martin Van Alstyn & Maragrita Van Alstyn.

Death Record

Van Alstyne, [?], (son of Mart G. Van Alstyne), d. 4/10/1796; buried 4/12/1796 (DFP:88)

Van Alstyne, [?], (son of Mart G. Van Alstyne), d. 4/12/1796; buried 4/14/1796 (DFP:88)

Van Alstyne, [?], (widow of Goshen Van Alstein), d. 7/?/1808, age 88 years; buried 7/28/1808 (DFP:92)

Van Alstyne, [?], d. 12/?/1811, age 29 years; buried 12/28/1811 (DFP:94)

Van Alstyne, Gilbert, (settled in Cherry Valley, ca. 1800), d. 1/21/18[?], age 90 years, 11 months; removed to Cherry Valley Cemetery (CVC:2)

Van Alstyne, Gysbert, (son of Johannes Van Alstyne), b. 1788; d. 4/12/1796; buried 4/14/1796 (DFP:88)

COMPENDIUM

Van Alstyne, Maria, (wife of Philip Van Alstine & born: Davis), b. 11/1/1768; m. 8/7/1785; d. 11/1/1790, (left 2 children); buried 11/3/1790 (DFP:81)

Van Alstyne, Philip, Esqr., d. 3/29/1806, age [?] (DFP:91)

Probate Abstract

Van Alstine, Abraham C., (of the town of Canajoharie), will dated 10/25/1824; probated 6/13/1826. Legatees: dau., Nelly (wife of Martin Davis); grandsons, Abraham A., John and Henry Davis (of Nelly); granddaus., Jane, Magdalen, Maria, Catharine, Sarah Margaret, Alida and Elizabeth Davis; granddau., Maria Warner. Executors: dau., Nelly Davis; Henry I. Frey. Witnesses: Herman I. Ehle, George S. Zielley, Henry Johnson. (WMC 57:265)

Van Alstine, Cornelius, III, (of Canajoharie), will dated 6/9/1824; probated 4/20/1825. Legatees: wife, Maria; sons, Cornelius, Benjamin, John, Martin C., Solomon, Garret and Gorhen/Goshen [?]; heirs of son, Daniel; dau., Charity Rogers. Executors: wife; sons, Benjamin and Solomon. Witnesses: Charles Mitchell, John and Solomon Hamilton. (WMC 57:182)

Van Alstine, Martin I., (of Canajoharie), will [undated]; probated 10/3/1827. Legatees: wife, Alida; children; brother, Jacob; father, John. Executors: wife; Jacob Van Alstine, William Cretsinger. Witnesses: D.F. Sacia, Thomas B. Mitchell, Jacob Van Alstine. (WMC 57:269)

Van Alstyne, Cornelius, Jr., (of Minden), will dated 2/22/1813; probated 7/22/1813. Legatees: wife, Marea; Fanny Dunigan; Cornelius (son of Abraham A. Mabie). Bequest: my dutch bible. Executors: wife; Conrad Kilts, Peter P.

Bellinger. Witnesses: Samuel Tucker, Jacob Smith, Nicholas G. House. (WMC 56:388)

Van Alstyne, Cornelius J., (of Charleston), will dated 8/22/1800; probated 1/12/1801. Legatees: wife, Annatie; son, John; daus., Eve, Nancy and Wyntie; step-mother, Wyntie; sister Neeltie. Executors: Nicholas H. Gardinier, Isaiah Depuy, Abraham C. Van Alstine. Witnesses: John Starin, John C. Van Eps, James Lansing. (WMC 56:150)

Van Alstyne, Cornelius M., (of Canajoharie), will dated 7/12/1787; probated 4/14/1792. Legatees: wife; sons, Martin, Cornelius C., Daniel (land in Half Moon), Peter; Daniel's uncle (Johanis Fort); dau., Cornelia (wife of Nichless Van Allstine); granddaus., Cornallas, Gartrrute, Nelly (all of Peter). Executors: Rynier Vaneverin[?], & sons. Witnesses: James Platto & Cornalus Vancoren (of Canajoharie), John Vancoren. (WMC 56:147)

Tryon County Militia

Van Alstyne, Abraham	[Appendix A]
Van Alstyne, Abraham C.	
Van Alstyne, Cornelius	
Van Alstyne, Cornelius C.	
Van Alstyne, Cornelius J.	
Van Alstyne, Gilbert	
Van Alstyne, Harmanus	
Van Alstyne, Isaac	
Van Alstyne, Jacob	
Van Alstyne, John	
Van Alstyne, John G.	
Van Alstyne, John M.	
Van Alstyne, Martin	
Van Alstyne, Martin A.	
Van Alstyne, Martin C.	
Van Alstyne, Martin G.	
Van Alstyne, Nicholas	
Van Alstyne, Peter	

COMPENDIUM

Van Alstyne, Philip

Pension Abstract

Van Alstyne, Jacob, b. 6/4/1749, Albany,
N.Y.; m. [wife not named; d. ca. 5/?/1844];
resident of Mohawk, Montgomery Co., N.Y.
in 1842 and died there on 5/11/1844. Children:
Catlyna (m. [?] Wemple and resident of
Cambridge, Mass. on 4/17/1850. She was the
only surviving child). Jacob was a resident of
Greenbush (now in Rensselaer Co., N.Y.) on
10/20/1775 when he was appointed
quartermaster in the Sixth Regt. of Militia of
Foot in Albany Co., commanded by Col.
Stephen J. Schuyler; he began active duty in
May 1776 and served as quartermaster until his
appointment as adjutant on 5/28/1778; Jacob
was in the battle of Stillwater and at the
surrender of Burgoyne at Saratoga; he
continued to serve in the military until late
1782. (RWPA: #S28923)

Van Alstyne, John, b. 1759/60, Canajoharie,
N.Y.; resident of his birthplace in Montgomery
Co. on 7/30/1833. John enlisted in the 1st.
Regt., Tryon Co. Militia and was a private
under Capt. Van Every and Cols. Cox,
Campbell, Clyde and Willett; he marched to
Unadilla, Forts Dayton, Plank, Ehle, Plain and
Stanwix; John fought in the battle of Johnstown
and his total military service amounted to over
two years. (RWPA: #S9501)

Van Alstyne, Martin A., b. 3/7/1753; resident
of Root, Montgomery Co., N.Y. on 3/12/1835
when he applied for a pension. Martin A.
enlisted from Canajoharie in the spring of 1775
and was a private in the 1st. Regt., Tryon Co.
Militia; he fought in the battles of Stone
Arabia, Sharon and Johnstown. (RWPA:
#S23036)

Van Alstyne, Nicholas, b. 1746/7; m. [wife not
named]; (brother: John Van Alstyne [RWPA:
#S9501]); resident of Montgomery Co., N.Y.
in 1832; d. 8/20/1836. Children: Gilbert N.,
Cornelius N., John N., Charity, Nancy (m. [?]
St. John); Abraham N. (Administrator of his
father's estate). Nicholas was drafted from
Canajoharie in 1776 and commissioned a
lieutenant in Capt. Demuth's Co., Col.
Ebenezer Cox's 1st. Regt., Tryon Co. Militia;
he fought in the battle of Turlock and remained
in the military through 1781. (RWPA:
#S23982)

Van Alstyne, Peter, b. 1/17/1760, Canajoharie,
Albany Co., N.Y.; (brother: John Van Alstyne
[RWPA: #S9501]); resident of Wooster,
Oswego Co., N.Y. from 1784 until 1786 when
he moved to Middleburgh, Schoharie Co, N.Y.
where he remained through 1831; lived in
Glen, Montgomery Co., N.Y. in 1832. Peter
enrolled as a private in Col. Ebenezer Cox's
1st. Regt., Tryon Co. Militia in January 1776;
he was made an orderly sergeant in the same
regiment in 1779; Peter was a participant in the
battle of Johnstown in 1781. (RWPA: #S14762)

Deed Abstract

Van Alstyn, Marten Johannes, of Canajoharie,
Tryon Co. to Hunter Scot Quackenbous, of the
same place, blacksmith. Deed dated 3/13/1773;
recorded 3/17/1773. Description: Three parcels
of land in Canajoharie on the south side of the
Mohawk River. The first begins on the south
bank of the river at the division line between
Marten J. Van Alstyn and Hendrick Schrimling
(2 morgen). The second is situated to the
southwest from the above and adjoins land
formerly owned by Jacob Muller (2 morgen).
The third is one-half of an island in the
Mohawk River above the house of Marten J.
Van Alstyn (5 acres). Consideration: L85.

COMPENDIUM

Witnesses: Chris'r. Yates, Claus Hendrickson. (MVL:34)

1790 Census

Van Alstine, Abraham (2)   [Appendix B]
Van Alstine, Abraham C.
Van Alstine, Cornelius
Van Alstine, Cornelius C.
Van Alstine, Cornelius I.
Van Alstine, Elizabeth
Van Alstine, Gilbert
Van Alstine, Jacob
Van Alstine, Jeremiah
Van Alstine, John (4)
VAn Alstine, Martin
Van Alstine, Martin A.
Van Alstine, Martin C.
Van Alstine, Martin G.
Van Alstine, Nicholas
Van Alstine, Peter (2)
Van Alstine, Philip

VAN ANTWERP

Birth/Baptism

Van Antwerp/Antwerpen, John & Annache/Annatje (Veeder): Volkert, b. 12/10/1771, bapt. 12/15/1771 (DRC:20); Daniel, b. 9/19/1774, bapt. 9/25/1774 (DRC:31); Jannetje, bapt. 4/23/1780 at age 5 weeks (DRC:56). Sponsors: John Wemp & Maria Wemp (re:1); Symon Veeder & Neyltje Van Antwerp (re:2); Symon Veeder & Grietje Veeder (re:3).

Van Antwerpen, Johannes & Annatje (Davis): Catarina, bapt. 3/5/1763 (DRC:8). Sponsors: Abraham Veder & Jannetje Veder.

Van Antwerpen, John & Annatje [?]: Elisabeth, b. 5/16/1765; bapt. 6/13/1765 (RDSA:56). Sponsors: Elisabetha & Volckert Veeder.

Van Antwerpen, John, Jr. & Rachel (Allen): Hester, b. 10/19/1784, bapt. 11/12/1784 (DRC:70); Johannis, bapt. 7/16/1786 at age 3 weeks (DRC:81); Johannis, b. 5/17/1787, bapt. 6/17/1787 (DRC:85); [?], bapt. 11/7/1790 (DRC:91). Sponsors: John Veeder & Catrina Van Antwerpen (re:1); John Van Antwerpen & Annatje Van Antwerpen (re:2); John Van Antwerpen & Annatje Vanantwerpen (re:3); [destroyed] (re:4).

Probate Abstract

Van Antwerp, John, (of Johnstown), will dated 3/28/1827; probated 6/4/1827. Legatees: wife, Rachel; sons, Abraham, Tunis and Daniel; daus., Caty, Hester, Nelly, Polly, Rachel and Jane. Executors: sons, Daniel and Tunis. Witnesses: Barent H. Vrooman, Richard Horning, Hars. Van Dusen. (WMC 57:268)

Van Antwerp, Simon, (of Charleston), will dated 6/11/1808; probated 10/11/1808. Legatees: wife, Rebecca; sons, Peter, John and Abraham; daus., Margaret, Susannah, Annatie and Sarah; sister, Neltie. Executors: 3 sons. Witnesses: Benjamin Van Vechten, Joseph Bratt, John Van Patten. (WMC 56:159)

Tryon County Militia

Van Antwerp, John, Jr.   [Appendix A]
Van Antwerp, John, Sr.

Pension Abstract

Van Antwerp, John, m. Rachel Allen, 11/22/1783, in the home of John V. Veeder's

825

father [Rachel had lived there for about six years during the war], by Rev. Thomas Romeyn; d. 4/10/1827, Johnstown, Montgomery Co., N.Y. (Rachel Van Antwerp, b. 1762/3; resident of Johnstown on 10/31/1838.) Children: Catharine, b. 1805/6 (m. [?] Coughnut and resident of Johnstown in 1839). John enlisted as a private in 1775 and served in Col. Frederick Fisher's 3rd. Regt., Tryon Co. Militia; he was in the siege of Fort Stanwix and fought in the battles of Oriskany [where he was wounded in the left heel] and Cherry Valley; John was taken prisoner by a band of Tories and Indians under Sir John Johnson on 5/22/1780 and taken to Canada where he remained until his escape in the following autumn. (RWPA: #W19897)

1790 Census

Van Antwerp, [?]   [Appendix B]
Van Antwerp, Asmarius
Van Antwerp, John, Jr.

VAN ARNUM

Death Record

Van Arnum, Rhoda, (wife of John Van Arnum), d. 10/2/1844, age 47 years; buried sect. 10, Colonial Cemetery, Johnstown (JC:189)

VAN ATER (also see VAN ETTEN)

1790 Census

Van Ater, Samuel   [Appendix B]

VAN AUKEN

Birth/Baptism

Van Auken, Johannes & Maria (Mastin) Gertruy, bapt. 3/26/1785 at age 6 weeks (DRC:71). Sponsors: Jacob Winne & Gertruy Winn.

1790 Census

Van Awken, John   [Appendix B]

VAN BRAKELEN

Marriage

Van Brakelen, Gysbert, Jr. m. Polly W[ilson], 10/9/1773 (DRC:158)

Birth/Baptism

Van Brakelen, Gerrit & Anna (Kitts): Simon, bapt. 6/16/1769 (DRC:17); Johannis, b. 1/7/1772, bapt. 1/11/1772 (DRC:20); Johannis, b. 4/9/1774, bapt. 4/22/1774 (DRC:28); Sander, b. 10/4/1776, bapt. 11/4/1776 (DRC:40); Maria, b. 3/2/1782, bapt. 3/10/1782 (DRC:61). Sponsors: Gerrit S. Van Brakelen & Maria Van Brakelen (re:1); Johannis Kitts & Sara Van Brakelen (re:2); Johannis Kitts Junr. & Anna Kitts (re:3); Claas Van Brakelen (re:4); Cobus Davis & Rebecca Davis (re:5).

Van Brakelen, Gerrit G. & Maria (Van Brakelen): Catarina, bapt. 10/16/1763 (DRC:10); Lena, bapt. 10/21/1769 (DRC:17); Marytie, b. 6/17/1773, bapt. 7/11/1773 (DRC:26); Gysbert, b. 4/?/1777, bapt. 5/18/1777 (DRC:43). Sponsors: Gerrit Van Brakelen & Rebecca Van Brakelen (re:1);

COMPENDIUM

Harpert Van Brakelen & Sarah Van Brakelen (re:2); Gysbert Van Brawkly & Meryche Van Brawkley (re:3); Cobus Davis & Rebecca Davis (re:4).

Van Brakelen, Gysbert S. & Polly [Maria/Barbara] (Wilson): Engeltje, b. 5/11/1774, bapt. 5/15/1774 (DRC:29); Barbara, b. 1/17/1777, bapt. 2/16/1777 (DRC:41); Sander, b. 11/6[?]/1778, bapt. 12/20/1778 (DRC:50); John, b. 9/5/1781, bapt. 11/11/1781 (DRC:59); Catrina, bapt. 7/2/1786 (DRC:80); Nicolas, b. 5/26/1786, bapt. 7/2/1786 (DRC:80); Margarieta, b. 5/1/1791, bapt. 6/12/1791 (DRC:98). Sponsors: Melchert Van Brawkley & Engeltje Van Brawkley (re:1); John Wilson & Barbar Wilson (re:2); Gerrit S. Van Brakele & Maria Van Brakele (re:3); [none named] (re:4); [none named] (re:5); Claas Van Brakelen & Weyntje Van Dusen (re:6); Arent Crommel & his wife (re:7).

Probate Abstract

Van Brocklen, Gysbert, (of Johnstown), will dated 2/18/1817; probated 11/17/1817. Legatees: wife, Barbara; sons, Alexander and Nicholas; daus., Angelike, Margret, Hannah (wife of Gilbert G. Van Brocklen) and Cathrine (wife of Jellis Van Veghten); heirs of Abraham Sheley. Executors: wife and son, Allix. Witnesses: James Williamson, Margret Crummell, Jacob Claurwater. (WMC 57:166)

Tryon County Militia

Van Brakelen, Alexander   [Appendix A]
Van Brakelen, Garett S.
Van Brakelen, Garret G.
Van Brakelen, Garrett G.
Van Brakelen, Gysbert
Van Brakelen, Melchior

Deed Abstract

Van Brakelen, Garret, yeoman, of Schenectady Twp., Albany Co. and Geysbert Van Brakelen, yeoman, of the Mohawks land, Albany Co. to Sander Van Brakelen (son of Garret Van Brakelen and brother of Geysbert Van Brakelen), yeoman, of the Mohawks land, Albany Co. Deed dated 6/1/1741; recorded 3/9/1773. Description: Land situated within the bounds of a patent and known as Lot $4 (allotted to John Dunbar, Johan. Mynders, Lawrence Vander Vollegon and by them conveyed to Geysbert Van Brakelen and by him conveyed to his father, Garret Van Brakelen) which lies on both sides of the Stone Arabia road, about two miles above the house of Myndert Wimpel, in the Mohawks country of Albany County (300 acres). Consideration: L50. Witnesses: John Sanders, Barent Sanders. (MVL:34)

Van Brakel[en], Gysbert, yeoman, of Albany Co. to Hendrick Brower, shoemaker, of Schenectady, Albany Co. Deed dated 12/26/1744; recorded 3/2/1774. Description: (Whereas by Letters Patent bearing date 5/6/1725 did grant to James Alexander, Andries Coeymans for himself, Andries Coeymans for the heirs of Samuel Staats, Esq., decd., Robert Walter, Esq., Rip Van Dam, Peter Hansen and Richard Hansen, Abraham Gouverneur, John Dunbar, Johannis Myndertse and Lawrence Claese, land situated in Albany Co. on the north side of the Mohawk River about five miles above Fort Hunter and beginning at the westerly bounds of lands granted to John Collins and at the north side of Canada Creek (called in the Indian language *Teodondariegoe*). And the patentees did on 3/1/1725 partition the lands into a lot called #4, which was divided between John Dunbar, Johannis Myndertse and Lawrence Claese. And these three owners on

827

COMPENDIUM

3/2/1733 did sell the said Lot #4 to Gysbert Van Brakel[en]. And Gysbert Van Brakel[en] on 5/1/1741 did sell to Gerrit Van Brakel[en] all the half of land marked #4.) Now this indenture witnesses that Gysbet Van Brakel[en] sold to Hendrick Brower the one-half part of Lot #4 (excepting the 300 acres of woodland sold to Sander Van Brakel[en]) containing nearly 38 acres, 2 perches, and 2/9 of a square perch of lowland and 850 acres, 3 rods of upland. Consideration: L200. Witnesses: Ja. Stevenson, Hen. Holland. On 3/2/1744, John Stevenson swore to the veracity of his father's [James Stevenson, decd.] handwriting as a witness to the deed in 1744. (MVL:34-35)

1790 Census

Vanbrackel, Garrit   [Appendix B]
Van Brackle, Herbert
Van Brockle, Garrit
Van Brockle, Gisebert

VAN BRUTE

1790 Census

Van Brute, William   [Appendix B]

VANBURA

Marriage

Vanbura, Mathew m. Nanse Nowell, both of Saratoga Dist., ?/?/1784 (JDR:2)

VAN BUREN

Marriage

Van Buren, William m. Catrina Putman, 11/8/1785 (DRC:164)

Birth/Baptism

Van Buren, Tobias & Ann [?]: Ephraim, bapt. 3/4/1742, Kinderhook Church (FH:17). Sponsors: Cornelius V Buren, Eytie Vosburg.

Probate Abstract

Van Buren, Harmon, (of Mayfield), will dated 8/20/1807; codicil dated 5/29/1819; probated 11/4/1819. Legatees: wife, Elizabeth; sons, Barent and Francis H.; dau., Mariah Eston (probably wife of Phineas Eston). Executor: son, Francis. Witnesses: Abraham Wells, Samuel and Mathew Van Den Berck (to the will); Pete Vandberck, John Becker, A. Wells (to the codicil). (WMC 57:169)

1790 Census

Van Buren, Cornelius   [Appendix B]
Van Buren, Francis
Van Buren, Gosha
Van Buren, Peter

VAN CAMP

Marriage

Van Camp, Isaac m. Elisabeth Klock, 1/13/1794 (DFP:51)

Van Campen, Moses m. Elisabeth H: Wallrath, 1/11/1785 (DRGF:201)

COMPENDIUM

Birth/Baptism

Van Camp/Van Campen, Isaac & Jane/Jannike [?]: Elisabeth, bapt. 1/11/1785 (DRGF:92); Sara, bapt. 10/12/1788 (SJC:5). Sponsors: Ciems [James] Wilson & Elisabeth (re:1); Moses Von Camp & Elisabeth Von Camp (re:2).

Death Record

Van Camp, Jenny, (wife of Isaac Van Camp), b. 7/25/1752; d. 7/20/1789; buried 7/21/1789 (DFP:78-79)

Tryon County Militia

Van Camp, Cornelius   [Appendix A]
Van Camp, Isaac

Pension Abstract

Van Camp, Cornelius, b. 11/?/1761, Wawarsing, Ulster Co., N.Y.; m. Barbara Dieffendorf, 1/31/1781 or 2/1/1781 at Fort Willett, Canajoharie, N.Y.; d. 11/21/1839, Minden, Montgomery Co., N.Y. (Barbara Van Camp, b. 1763/4, dau. of Henry and Rosina Diefendorff [Capt. Henry Diefendorff was killed in the battle of Oriskany]; d. 1/24/1847, Minden, N.Y.) Children: Anna, b. 9/17/1785 (m. David Devendorf of German Flatts, Herkimer Co., N.Y.); Catharine, b. 9/1/1788; Elizabeth, b. 3/17/1791 (m. [?] Elwood of Minden, N.Y.); Henry D., b. 10/3/1794 (resident of Clayton, Jefferson Co., N.Y.); Cornelius, b. 10/2/1796. [All children named above were living in 1847.] Cornelius enlisted from Canajoharie in 1777 and served in Capt. Henry Diefendorff's Co., Col. Ebenezer Cox's 1st. Regt., Tryon Co. Militia through 1778; he enlisted into Capt. Jacob Diefendorff's Co. of the same regiment in 1779 and was made a

sergeant; Cornelius fought in the battle of Johnstown. (RWPA: #W19569)

Van Camp, Isaac, b. 1759, Wawarsing, Ulster Co., N.Y.; m. [wife not named]; d. 4/20/1843, Hanover, Chautauqua Co., N.Y. Children: Ann (m. Elias Maxfield); Jane (m. Joseph Sweetland); Rachel (m. Phineas Biggs); Mary (m. Amos Smith); Joseph Van Camp. [All children named in application file were living in 1843.] Isaac volunteered for duty from his home in Canajoharie in the spring of 1776 and served in the batteau service under the command of Capts. Evert Van Eps and Garret Lansing; he enlisted again in February 1777 and was a boatman on the Mohawk and Hudson Rivers; Isaac was appointed sergeant in Capt. John Bradbick's Co., Col. Van Rensselaer's Regt. in 1778 and continued in the military until his discharge on 1/1/1780. (RWPA: #S11603)

1790 Census

Van Camp, Cornelius   [Appendix B]
Van Camp, Isaac
Van Camp, Moses

VAN CLICK

Birth/Baptism

Van Click, Henry & Anne (Brower), Stillwater: Elizabeth, bapt. 1/6/1784 (JDR:12)

VAN DAULSON

1790 Census

Van Daulson, Henry   [Appendix B]

VANDER BELT

1790 Census

Vander Belt, Henry   [Appendix B]

VANDERBERGH

Marriage

Vanderbergh, Phillip m. Hanah Yates, both of Scaghtecough, 1/16/1785 (JDR:3)

VANDERBILT

Probate Abstract

Vanderbilt, Catharine, (late of Stony Point, Bergen Co., N.J.), will dated 8/7/1792; probated 7/3/1800. Legatees: daus., Cornelia (widow of Daniel Mushroe), Catharine (wife of John Veghte); sons, John and his children (Catharine, Beilaby, John and Aaron), Jacob; granddau., Sarah Price. Executors: Jacob Vanderbilt, John Veghte. Witnesses: Abraham Veghte, John and Daniel Walker. (WMC 56:150)

Vanderbilt, Douw, (of Mayfield), will dated 7/27/1797; probated 9/6/1797. Legatees: wife, Maria; my children. Executrix: wife. Witnesses: Cornelius & Daniel D. Haring, Woodhul Sarneur [?]. (WMC 56:149)

VAN DERHOOF

Probate Abstract

Van Derhoof, Gilbert, (of the Town of Wells), will dated 2/26/1825; probated 5/12/1826. Legatees: sons, Henry (eldest), Giles, Listel[?] (under age 21), Joel and Gilbert, Jr.; all my daus. [not named]. Executors: sons, Gilbert, Jr., Joe; John L. Francisco. Witnesses: John L. Francisco, Washington Craig, Stephen Francisco. (WMC 57:264-265)

VANDER MATER

1790 Census

Vander Mater, John   [Appendix B]

VANDERPOOL

Birth/Baptism

Vanderpool, Abraham & Elizabeth [?]: Catharina, bapt. 8/27/1739 (FH:7); Peter Coieman, bapt. 6/14/1740 (FH:11). Sponsors: Melkert Van der Pool, Ariyaentie van der Pool, Maike Witbeek (re:1); Peter Coieman, Andries Widbeek, Charlotta Amelia Coieman (re:2).

VANDERVEER

Probate Abstract

Vanderveer, Jacob, (of the town of Florida), will dated 10/17/1805; probated 9/3/1806. [His signature was V: D: Veear.] Legatees: wife,

Anna; dau., Nelly; sons, Garret, John and Samuel; my first wife's children; Tunas [probably a son]; granddau., Lydia Stillwell; last wife's children (son, Asher; daus., Polly and Sally). Executors: son, Samuel; Albert Covenhoven, Tunis Vanderveer. Witnesses: David Cady, Charles and John Hubbs. (WMC 56:155)

1790 Census

Vanderveer, Henry   [Appendix B]

VANDER VEET

1790 Census

Vander Veet, Garret   [Appendix B]
Vander Veet, Jacob

VANDERWERKEN

Marriage

Vanderwerken, Albert m. Barbara Dachstaeder, 12/8/1767 (RDSA:183)

Vanderwerken, Henrich m. Saritje von Ale, 3/31/1764 (RDSA:173)

Vanderwerken, Hermanus m. [?] [?], 11/28/1782 (DRGF:197)

Vanderwerken, Jacob m. Catharina Hauss, 11/9/1794 (RDSA:200)

Vanderwerken, Ruloph m. Cornelia Gallier (widow of Pieter Gallier), 9/17/1763 (RDSA:172)

Vanderwerken, Thomas (son of Johannes von der Wercke) m. Anna Kiltz (dau. of Johannes Kiltz), 1/20/1778, both from Schwejatzche (LTSA:285)

Vanderwerken, Wilhelm m. Margretha van Sleuck, 2/6/1767 (RDSA:180)

Vanderwerkin, John m. Mary Launsing, 2/12/1786 (JDR:3)

Birth/Baptism

Vanderwerken, Abraham & Maria (Defy): Albert, bapt. 1741 (RDSA:4). Sponsors: Albert Vonder Werken & his wife, Derkjes.

Vanderwerken, Albert & [?], Johnstown: Henry, bapt. 8/1/1779 (JDR:14)

Vanderwerken, Albert & Barbara F.[?] (Dogsteder): Catharina, b. & bapt. [obliterated: 1770 period] (RDSA:104); Annatye, b. 11/2/1772, bapt. 11/8/1772 (DRC:23); Jacob, b. 3/13/1777, bapt. 5/18/1777 (DRC:43). Sponsors: Nicolas Dachstaeder & his wife, Catharina (re:1); Hans Dogsteder & Annatie Dogsteder (re:2); Casper Van De Werken & Elizabeth Daxteder (re:3).

Vanderwerken, Albert & Catarina [?]: Sara, b. 3/2/1796 (LTSA:93). Sponsors: Henry v. de Werke & Sara.

Vanderwerken, Albert & Maria [?]: Maria, b. 1/31/1780; bapt. 2/6/1780 (LTSA:59). Sponsors: Joh: v der Wercke & Helena.

Vanderwerken, Albert & Maria (Kills): Jannetje, b. 3/15/1777, bapt. 3/22/1777 (DRC:42); Hendk., b. 5/19/1782, bapt. 6/16/1782 (DRC:62); Adam, b. 7/4/1783, bapt. 7/13/1783 (DRC:66). Sponsors: Michel

Eeel & Jannitje Eel (re:1); Hendk. Van De Werken & Sarah Van De Werken (re:2); Godfrey Condy[?] & Eliz. Tilleback (re:3).

Vanderwerken, Albert & Salome [?]: Johannes, b. 11/10/1771 (LTSA:39). Sponsors: Johannes Devis, Johannes Casselmann & his wife.

Vanderwerken, Casper & Elizabeth (Hover): Jacob, b. 11/5/1780, bapt. 11/12/1780 (DRC:57); Elizabeth, b. 6/31/1782, bapt. 7/21/1782 (DRC:63); Catrina, b. 6/15/1790, bapt. 8/1/1790 (DRC:88). Sponsors: Jacob Van De Werke & Maria Van De Werke (re:1); Johannis Hover & Elizabeth Hover (re:2); John Docksteder & Catrina V.D. Werken (re:3).

Vanderwerken, Cobus J. & Catrina (Auck): Derkye, b. 4/1/1786; bapt. 7/2/1786 (DRC:80). Sponsors: William Pellinger & Annatje Pellinger.

Vanderwerken, Hannes Marteines & Turckje [?]: Hermanus, b. 2/22/1762; bapt. 3/14/1762 (RDSA:32). Sponsors: Johannes van der Wercken & his wife, Christina.

Vanderwerken, Henderick & Sarah (Van Aalen): Peter, b. 10/12/1776, bapt. 10/26/1776 (DRC:39); Peter, b. 5/27/1778, bapt. 7/7/1778 (DRC:48); Rachel, b. 8/22/1782, bapt. 8/30/1782 (DRC:63). Sponsors: Nicholas Dogsteder & Catrina Dogsteder (re:1); Michael Eel & Jannetje Eel (re:2); Johannis Antony Mondt & Maragrita Mondt (re:3).

Vanderwerken, Henrich & Sara [?]: Johannes, b. 11/2/1764, bapt. 11/16/1764 (RDSA:52); Jacob, b. 1/1/1767, bapt. 1/4/1767 (RDSA:72); Jacobus, b. 6/24/1769, bapt. 6/30/1769 (RDSA:95). Sponsors: Johannes von den Wercken & his wife (re:1); Hannes Schauer & Rachel (re:2); Harpert van Deuse[n] & Lena

van Aal[stein] (re:3).

Vanderwerken, Jacob & Anna Maria [?]: Jacobus, b. 4/13/1760, bapt. 4/17/1760 (RDSA:19); Turckje, b. 7/25/1762, bapt. 8/1/1762 (RDSA:34); Anna, b. 7/27/1766, bapt. 8/10/1766 (RDSA:67). Sponsors: [none named] (re:1); Elisabeth, wife of Cptn. Henrich Frey (re:2); Anna Leip & Johannes Frej (re:3).

Vanderwerken, Jochem & Elisabeth [?]: Elisabeth, b. 9/26/1781; bapt. 1/28/1782 (DRGF:54). Sponsors: Jahn vonden Wercken & Turkje.

Vanderwerken, Johann & Magdalena [?]: Juliana, b. 7/12/1778, bapt. 8/2/1778 (LTSA:53); Maria, b. 3/4/1781, bapt. 3/5/1781 (DRGF:43). Sponsors: Michael Oehl & Juliana (re:1); Albert van den Wercken & Maria (re:2).

Vanderwerken, John & Derkje (Van Aalstyn): Maragriet, b. 4/17/1774; bapt. 6/19/1774 (DRC:29). Sponsors: Jacob Gardinier & Rachel Gardinier.

Vanderwerken, John J. & Leentje (Van Aalen): Peter, b. 2/9/1776, bapt. 2/12/1776 (DRC:36); Lena, bapt. 1/21/1786 [Note: Mother not named & therefore may not be child of above] (DRC:75). Sponsors: Peter Eel & Rachel Van Aalen (re:1); [none named] (re:2).

Vanderwerken, Martinus & Maria Margaretha (Ojons): Isack, bapt. 2/1/1751 (RDSA:10). Sponsors: Adam Venegardenier & Janie [?].

Vanderwerken, Rulof & Cornelia (Van Alstyne): Peter, b. 3/30/1774, bapt. 5/1/1774 (DRC:29); Elizabeth, b. 9/23/1776, bapt. 10/26/1776 (DRC:39). Sponsors: Jacob Gardinier & Derkje Gardinier (re:1); Ma[r]tinus Gardinier & Rachel Gardinier (re:2).

Vanderwerken, Thomas & Anna [?]: Maria, b. 3/21/1779, bapt. 3/29/1779 (LTSA:57); Johannes, b. 8/8/1781, bapt. 8/18/1781 (DRGF:46). Sponsors: Joh: Nicolaus Dachstedter & Dorothea (re:1); Johannes Gieltz & Elisabeth (re:2).

Vanderwerken, Wilhelm & Margrith [?]: Elisabeth, b. 8/7/1767; bapt. 8/30/1767 (RDSA:77). Sponsors: Christina & Johannes van den Wercken.

Vanderwerken, William & Geertruy (Van Slyck): Geertruy, b. 4/2/1783; bapt. 5/4/1783 (DRC:66). Sponsors: Adam & Geertruy Van Slyck.

Vanderwerken, William & Maragrita (Van Slyk): Mertynes, b. 3/29/1772, bapt. 5/25/1772 (DRC:20); Petrus, b. 5/25/1774, bapt. 8/6/1774 (DRC:30); Maragrite, b. 5/16/1776, bapt. 7/7/1776 (DRC:38); Catrina, b. 10/15[?]/1778, bapt. 11/8/1778 (DRC:50); Maria, b. 11/17/1780, bapt. 1/15/1781 (DRC:58). Sponsors: Jacob Gardinier & Derkye Gardinier (re:1); Adam Brown & Elizabeth Van Slyk (re:2); Hendrick B. Vrooman & Maragriet Vrooman (re:3); Peter Eel & Elizabeth (re:4); Aaron S. Bradt & Maria Bradt (re:5).

Probate Abstract

Van Derwerken, John R., (of Broadalbin), will dated 7/13/1822; probated 5/1/1828. Legatees: son, Rolif; dau., Gitty Fox (& her children). Executors: son, Rolif; son-in-law, William Fox; James Sumner. Witnesses: Samuel Putney, James Sumner, Elisha Cotton. (WMC 57:271)

Tryon County Militia

Vanderwerken, Casper   [Appendix A]
Vanderwerken, Harmanus

Vanderwerken, John
Vanderwerken, Joshua
Vanderwerken, Thomas
Vanderwerken, William

Pension Abstract

Vanderwerken, Albert, b. 1746/7, Tryon Co., N.Y.; resident of Salina, Onondaga Co., N.Y. when he applied for pension on 4/24/1818. Albert was commissioned a lieutenant in February 1776 by the Continental Congress of New York and served until his discharge on 12/31/1776 in Capt. Robert McKean's Co., Col. Wynkoop's Regt. of the N.Y. Line where he "was engaged in the erection of Fort Stanwix on the Mohawk River & was never in any action with the enemy". Albert Vanderwerken's pension was "stopt in September 1820 and remained suspended until November last, on account of information from Mr. John Sammons, who resides in Salina". John Sammons stated that Albert Vanderwerken "deserted his country Joined the enemy headed their Indian Allys conducted them amongst our Defenceless frontier inhabitants, ..., he was at the massacre at Cherry Valley". Myndert Vrooman deposed on 9/22/1823 that he and Albert Vanderwerken both went & joined the British at the same time in 1778. John Van Antwerp gave a deposition on the same date [9/22/1823] that he was a prisoner of the British at Montreal in 1780 and saw Albert Vanderwerken "walking about at large in the streets". William Wallace, Nicholas Stoner and James Williamson gave sworn testimony on 9/5/1823 at Johnstown, Montgomery Co. that "about the year 1779 the said Albert [Vanderwerken] quit the American Standard and went to Canada to Join & did Join the British forces and Indians in the British service, ..., that about the year 1782, ..., Albert returned to this County and in this Town [Johnstown] and at the Stone Gaol there yet standing surrendered himself a prisoner at War to Captain John Little the then Commandant of said Gaol". William Wallace further stated that in the year 1779 he was present when John Quackenbush was examined under oath by a Tryon County Justice of the Peace and testified that he "swore that this same Albert Van De Werker had killed & scalped one William Stansel, ..., while he the said Albert was with the British & savages on an expedition against the Mohawk & Springfield settlements". (RWPA: #S42590)

Vanderwerken, Martin, m. Anna Maria [?], 4/27/1780, Canajoharie, Montgomery Co., N.Y.; d. 1787. (Anna Maria Vanderwerkin, d. 1/10/1843 at the residence of William Weller in Kalamazoo, Kalamazoo Co., Michigan.) Children: [first child not named], b. 1781; William, b. 4/17/1783 (resident of Kalamazoo Co., Michigan on 1/4/1848). Martin was reputed to have served in the military for a period of three years and was discharged in 1781. (RWPA: #R10854)

Deed Abstract

Vanderwerken, John M., yeoman, of Warrensburgh, Tryon Co. to Hermanus H. Wendell, merchant, of Schenectady, Albany Co. Deed dated 4/27/1774; recorded 7/2/1774. Description: Two lots in Warrensburgh (whereon he now lives), Tryon Co. and distinguished by the names, Lots #34 & #35 (204 acres). Together with all the cattle, horses, and farmers utensils hereinafter mentioned, viz.: five cows, two geldings, one mare, two heifers (of about a year old), eight calves (of this year), one new iron bound wagon, one new plough, one new square harrow, one new iron bound slay [sleigh]. Consideration: L224.5.4. Witnesses: Matthew Lyne, Henry Glen.

(MVL:35)

1790 Census

Vanderwerker, Gersham   [Appendix B]
Vanderwerker, John
Vanderworker, Albert I.
Vander Worker, Casper
Vanderworker, Henry
Vanderworker, Jacobus
Vanderworker, John
Vanderworker, Thomas
Vandeworker, William

VANDERWORMER

1790 Census

Vanderwormer, John   [Appendix B]

VAN DEURSEN

Birth/Baptism

Van Deursen, Peter (Palatine) & Anna [?]: Johann Jost Schuyler, b. 12/6/1793; bapt. 12/15/1793 (SJC:85). Sponsors: Niclaus Schuyler & Elisabeth Schuyler.

VAN DE WAATERS

Marriage

Van De Waaters, Samuel m. Elisabeth Neer, 10/7/1794 (DFP:52)

COMPENDIUM

VAN DOREN

Probate Abstract

Van Doren, Cornelius I.[J.?], (of Charleston), will dated 5/2/1829; probated 5/2/1831. Legatees: wife, Alida Van Doren; nephew, Joseph Van Doren. Executors: James Ingersoll, Jr., William Carlisle. Witnesses: Samuel P. Schuyler, Letty Schuyler, Jennett Ingersoll. (WMC 57:279)

VAN DORN

Birth/Baptism

Van Dorn, Christian & Nelly [?]: Caty, b. 10/9/1785; bapt. 1/21/1786 (DRC:75). Sponsors: [none named].

1790 Census

Van Dorne, Christian   [Appendix B]
Van Dorne, William

VAN DRIESEN

Birth/Baptism

Van Driesen, Peter & Engeltie [?]: Maria, bapt. 6/16/1741 (FH:14). Sponsors: Barent Vroman, Maria Vroman.

Van Driesen, Peter (Palatine) & Anna [?]: John, bapt. 4/20/1792 (SJC:58). Sponsors: John Van Driesen & Margretha Van Driesen.

Probate Abstract

Van Driesen, John, (of Minden), will dated 8/21/1804; probated 6/27/1809. Legatees: wife, Margaret. Executors: Felix Green, John H. Failing, John Stafford. Witnesses: Cornelius H. Waldron, Henry Van Driesen, John Schuyler, Jr. (WMC 56:159)

VAN DRUSEN

1790 Census

Van Drusen, John   [Appendix B]

VAN DRUSER

1790 Census

Van Druser, John   [Appendix B]

VAN DUSA

Birth/Baptism

Vandusa, Garet & Margaret (Fosburry), Florida: John, bapt. 1/30/1803 (JDR:18).

Van Dusa, Gilbert & [?], Schenectady: John, bapt. 3/7/1782 (JDR:16).

VAN DUSEN (also see VAN DUSER)

Marriage

Van Dusen, Abram m. Annatje Van Sicol, [no date: follows 6/?/1785] (DRC:164)

Van Dusen, Gilbert m. Neeltje Van Antwerpen, 10/9/1775 (DRC:161)

Van Dusen, Harport m. Rebecca Brewer, 10/11/1795 (RDSA:202)

Van Dusen, Melchior (4th son of Melchior van Dusen) m. Maria Pfilips, 12/8/1778, both of Caughnawaga (LTSA:285)

Birth/Baptism

Van Dusen, Abram & Annatje (Van Zeyel): Cornelis, b. 3/17/1786, bapt. 3/26/1786 (DRC:78); Maria, b. 6/10/1787, bapt. 6/17/1787 (DRC:85); Abraham, b. 10/30/1790, bapt. 11/28/1790 (DRC:91). Sponsors: Cornelis Van Zeyel & Meritje Van Duisen (re:1); Adam Copernol & Elisabeth Copernol (re:2); [none named] (re:3).

Van Dusen, Gilbert & Neyltje (Van Antwerpen): Annatje, b. 3/7/1776, bapt. 4/9/1776 (DRC:37); Andries, b. 12/7/1777, bapt. 12/23/1777 (DRC:46); Elizabeth, b. 11/23/1779, bapt. 12/19/1779 (DRC:54); Harmanus, b. 5/17/1787, bapt. 6/22/1787 (DRC:85); Arent, b. 8/21/1791, bapt. 9/18/1791 (DRC:100). Sponsors: John Van Antwerpen & Annatje Van Antwerpen (re:1); Abram Veeder & Annatje Veeder (re:2); Joannes Van Antwerp & Catrina Van Antwerp (re:3); Volkert Veeder & Elisabeth Veeder (re:4); [none named] (re:5).

Van Dusen, Marcus & Nelje [?]: Rahel, bapt. 2/11/1770 (RDSA:99). Sponsors: Pieter Quack[enbush] & Rahel Q[uackenbush].

Van Dusen, Matthew & Maria (Philips): Neeltje, bapt. 5/29/1783 at 4 weeks (DRC:66). Sponsors: David V. Deusen & Neeltje V. Deusen.

Van Dusen, Melchior & Nelge (Quackenbush): Anna, bapt. 8/31/1750 (RDSA:11); Catharina, b. 7/9/1753, bapt. 8/5/1753 (RDSA:14); Engelgen, b. 3/7/1761, bapt. 6/7/1761 (RDSA:27); Jantje, b. 1/16/1763, bapt. 1/30/1763 (RDSA:37); Maria, b. 3/18/1765, bapt. 4/19/1765 (RDSA:54); Nelje, b. 11/4/1766, bapt. 12/14/1766 (RDSA:71). Sponsors: Annatge Daniels, Peter Quackenbusch (re:1); Debus V. deusen, Catharina Winne (re:2); Engelgen Van Praackel & Sander van Praackel (re:3); Janitje Quack & Jeremiah Quack (re:4); Maria & Gerret van Braakel (re:5); Rachel Gallier & Isaac Gallier (re:6).

Probate Abstract

Van Deusen, Harpert, (of Johnstown), will dated 11/29/1826; probated 1/5/1828. Legatees: wife, Rebecca; daus., Nancy, Margaret and Gitty; son, Harpert. Bequest: Land in Rensselaer Co. to dau., Nancy. Executors: son, Harpert; Harman W. Brown, Aaron Haring, Abraham Van Deusen, George F. Dockstater. (WMC 57:270)

Van Deusen, Melchior, (of Caughnawaga), will dated 9/9/1788; probated 8/16/1789. Legatees: wife, Nelly. Sole executrix: wife. Witnesses: Richard Atkins, John Thompson, Joseph Vansice. (WMC 56:145)

Van Dusen, Barrent, (of Palatine), will dated 8/15/1825; probated 10/25/1825. Legatees: wife [not named]; daus., Sarah and Ginny; sons, Robert, Minard (& his wife and son, Barent); Benjamin Viely. Executors: Benjamin Vieley and grandson, Barent Van Dusen. Witnesses: David Sager and Nicholas Gee. (WMC 57:184)

Tryon County Militia

Van Dusen, Abraham [Appendix A]
Van Dusen, Gilbert
Van Dusen, Harpert
Van Dusen, Matthew

Van Elter, Peter [Appendix B]

VAN EPS

1790 Census

Van Dusen, Abraham [Appendix B]
Van Dusen, Gilbert
Van Dusen, Harpert
Van Dusen, Matthew

Birth/Baptism

Van Eps, Carol Hanse/Karel & Catharina/Catrina (Winne/Winner): Johannes, bapt. 11/29/1759 (DRC:3); Efje, b. 9/13/1774, bapt. 9/18/1774 (DRC:31). Sponsors: Evert van Eps & Maria van Eps (re:1); Evert Van Eps & Alida Wemp (re:2).

VAN DUSER (also see VAN DUSEN)

Probate Abstract

Van Deuser, Nelly, (of Johnstown), will dated 2/27/1797; probated 9/21/1804. Legatees: all to son, David; he to give any of it to his brothers or sisters as he may see fit. Executor: son, David. Witnesses: Matthew Van Deuser, Gershom Kittle, William Carrol. (WMC 56:153)

Van Eps, Evert & Mary (Minthorne): Lucy, b. 3/11/1791; bapt. 4/17/1791 (DRC:96). Sponsors: [none named].

Van Eps, John & Alida (Funda): Carol Hanse, b. 6/11/1786; bapt. 7/9/1786 (DRC:81). Sponsors: Carol Van Eps & Catrina Van Eps.

Van Eps, John C. & Alida (Wemple): Evert, b. 12/27/1781, bapt. 1/20/1782 (DRC:60); Catharina, b. 4/1/1791, bapt. 5/1/1791 (DRC:97). Sponsors: Joannes Van Eps & Jannetje Van Eps (re:1); Charles Van Eps & Catharina V. Eps (re:2).

VAN EHR

Marriage

Van Ehr, Peter m. Catty Stephany, 1/20/1793 (DFP:47)

Probate Abstract

Van Eps, Evert, (of Charleston), will dated 11/29/1813; probated 2/3/1814. Legatees: daus., Lucy, Hannah, Eve and Jane. Executors: dau., Jane; Frederick Starin. Witnesses: Hannah Starin, Susannah Coenradt, Adam Eacker, Jr. (WMC 56:390)

VAN ELTER

Tryon County Militia

1790 Census

Van Eps, John [Appendix A]

Pension Abstract

Van Eps, Evert, b. ca. 1740; m. Polly Minthorne, 6/12/1787 at the Reformed Dutch Church of Caughnawaga by Rev. Thomas Romeyn; d. 12/19/1813, Montgomery Co., N.Y. (Polly Van Eps, d. 10/10/1839.) Children: John E., b. 1787/8 (resident of Glen, Montgomery Co. in 1844); Jane (m. Richard Hugeman); Hannah (m. David P. Quackenbush); Eveline (m. Luke Wessels); Lucy (m. Eli Crampton). Evert entered the military from his home in Charleston, Tryon Co. in 1776 and served for one year as captain of batteaumen and laborers in the quartermaster's department at Lake George; he also served as a private and sergeant in Capt. Jellis Fonda's Co., Col. Frederick Fisher's 3rd. Regt., Tryon Co. Militia between 1778 and 1782; Evert fought in the battles of Oriskany [where he was wounded in the left leg] and Johnstown [in which he was captured and held prisoner in Canada for eighteen months]. (RWPA: #W15969)

1790 Census

Van Eps, Charles   [Appendix B]
Van Eps, Evert
Van Eps, John
Van Eps, John E.

VAN ETTEN

Marriage

Van Ette, Samuel m. Catharina Schnell, 12/16/1790 (RDSA:195)

Van Netten, Samuel (widower) m. Elisabeth Bekker, 10/1/1769 (RDSA:187)

Birth/Baptism

Van Etten, Peter & Margareta (Froelich): Elisabeth, b. 11/28/1787, bapt. 12/11/1787 (RDSA:115); Jacob, b. 10/13/1792 (LTSA:70); Catarina, b. 12/18/1793 (LTSA:81). Sponsors: Conrad Franz & Salome (born: Bezzinger) (re:1); Jacob Nier, Maria Heess (re:2); Johannes Froelich, Catarina Kerter (re:3).

Van Etten/Van Netten, Samuel & Elisabeth [?]: Samuel, b. 7/?1/1770, bapt. 7/?5/1770 (RDSA:104); Johannes, b. 10/11/1781, bapt. 10/21/1781 (DRGF:49). Sponsors: Friedrich G. Gettmann & Elisabeth Lauchs (re:1); Johannes Empie & Anna Eva Gettmann (re:2).

Van Etten, Samuel & Maria [?]: Samuel, b. 12/12/1760, bapt. 12/17/1760 [deceased] (RDSA:24); Aarii, b. 3/5/1762, bapt. 3/14/1762 (RDSA:32); Jacobus, b. 4/14/1764, bapt. 4/23/1764 (RDSA:46); Elisabetha, b. 6/6/1766, bapt. 6/15/1766 (RDSA:65). Sponsors: Roppert Gerder & Catharina Coppernoll (re:1); Dieterich (son of Adam Laux) & Rebecca Gerder (re:2); Wilhelm Emgie & his wife (re:3); Elisabetha & Ludolph Koch (re:4).

Tryon County Militia

Van Etten, Jacob   [Appendix A]
Van Etten, Samuel

Pension Abstract

Van Etten, Samuel, m. Elizabeth Bekker, 10/?/1769, Reformed Dutch Chruch of Stone Arabia, N.Y.; d. 1815. (Elizabeth Van Etten, b. ca. 1747; d. 5/17/1837, Watson, Lewis Co., N.Y.) Children: Jacob and Peter. [These were the only surviving children on 9/15/1842 and they had changed the spelling of their surname to Van Atta and Van Netter.] Samuel was appointed ensign of a company in Col. Jacob Klock's 2nd. Regt., Tryon Co. Militia on 6/25/1778; he received promotions in the same company and regiment to the rank of 2nd. lieutenant on 3/4/1780 and to 1st. lieutenant on 9/29/1780. (RWPA: #W18193 *VANNETTER*)

VAN EVERY

Marriage

Van Ivern, Corneles m. Cornelia von Aalstein, 10/29/1762 (RDSA:171)

Van Ivern, Johannis m. Eva Mabe, [no date: follows 4/?/1785] (DRC:164)

Van Ivern, John (son of Jahn Van Ivern) m. Cornelia van Aalstein (dau. of Cosen van Aalstein), 12/12/1766 (RDSA:179)

Birth/Baptism

Van Every, Cornelius & Cornelia (Van Aalstyn): Johannes, b. 6/13/1763, bapt. 7/1/1763 (RDSA:41); Geisbert, b. 12/9/1765 (RDSA:60); Jannetye, b. 3/4/1773, bapt. 3/21/1773 (DRC:24). Sponsors: Samuel Gardenier & Maria (re:1); Geisbort van Alstein & Annatje (re:2); Jacob VanAalstyn & Janneche Van Everen (re:3).

Van Every/Van Ivern, John & Cornelia (Van Alstyn): Johannes, b. 12/20/1768, bapt. 1/29/1769 (RDSA:93); Elisabeth, b. 1/28/1771, bapt. 3/10/1771 (RDSA:109); Maria, b. 5/29/1787, bapt. 6/26/1787 (DRC:85). Sponsors: Nicolas van Yvern & Nelje (re:1); Goose van Aalstein & Elisabeth (re:2); Samuel Gard[enier] & Maria Garden[ier] (re:3).

Van Every, John & Jannetje (Smith): Cornelia, b. 1/25/1791; bapt. 2/13/1791 (DRC:94). Sponsors: Marten v'Alstine & Marrigrethia [?].

Van Every, Renier & Nelje/Neylche (Van Eps): Abraham, b. 7/28/1765, bapt. 8/18/1765 (RDSA:57); Janitje, b. 8/10/1766, bapt. 8/17/1766 (RDSA:67); Neylche, b. 12/10/1771, bapt. 12/?/1771 (DRC:20); Renier, b. 3/31/1774, bapt. 4/25/1774 (DRC:28). Sponsors: Abraham van Eps & Catharina Veeder (re:1); Cornelia & Cornels van Ivern (re:2); Cornelius Van Alstyn & Gerritche Van Alstyn (re:3); Samuel Gardinier & Meritje Gardinier (re:4).

Probate Abstract

Van Everer, Rynere, (of Canajoharie), will dated 6/29/1824; probated 6/16/1825. Legatees: wife, Catherine; sons, John, James and Cornelius; daus., Jane, Eliza, Catherine (all unmarried) and Cornelia & Sally (both married). Executors: son, Cornelius; friend, Cornelius N. Van Evera. Witnesses: Cornelius N. and John N. Van Everer, John Taylor. (WMC 57:183)

Van Every, Rinear, (of Canajoharie), will dated 10/22/1806; probated 5/28/1812. Legatees: wife, Elizabeth; sons, Rinear R. and John R.; daus., Elizabeth, Maria, Jane (decd., and her children), and Nelly (decd., and her children). Executors: wife; James Knox, Cornelius Wynkoop. Witnesses: Abram C. Van Alstine, Aron Brower, John Van Slyke. (WMC 56:384)

Tryon County Militia

Van Every, Cornelius   [Appendix A]
Van Every, John
Van Every, Ryner

1790 Census

Van Ever, Cornelius   [Appendix B]
Van Ever, John
Van Ever, John, Jr.
Van Ever, Renier

VAN GEISLING

Tryon County Militia

Van Geisling, Peter   [Appendix A]

VAN GORDER

1790 Census

Van Gorder, Samuel   [Appendix B]

VAN HORN

Marriage

Van Horn, Thomas m. Maria Fredrick, 10/21/1779 (DRC:162)

Birth/Baptism

Van Horn, Abraham & Anna (Hoff): Hanna, b. 1/18/1778, bapt. 5/10/1778 (DRC:47); Abraham, b. 6/26/1783, bapt. 7/27/1783 (DRC:67). Sponsors: [none named] (re:1 & 2).

Van Horn, Cornelius & Eva (Fredrick): Elizabeth, b. 4/21/1785; bapt. 6/6/1785 (DRC:73). Sponsors: John Carl & Sophia Cary.

Van Horn, Henderick & Elizabeth (Van Horn): Jacobus, b. 5/2/1774; bapt. 6/26/1774 (DRC:29). Sponsors: Frans Van Hoorn & Elizabeth Vanhoorn.

Van Horn, Thomas & Maria (Fredrick): Lea, b. 12/25/1781; bapt. 1/27/1782 (DRC:60). Sponsors: Hendk. Van Horen & Orietje Fredrick.

Probate Abstract

Van Horne, Cornelius, (of Charleston), will dated 1/9/1818; probated 3/12/1823. Legatees: wife [not named]; youngest son, Cornelius C.; my other children. Executors: son, Cornelius C.; Cornelius H. Putman, Peter Hall/Hale[?]. Witnesses: Howland Fish, David Eacker, Daniel S. Bell. (WMC 57:176)

Van Horne, Cornelius, (of Florida), will dated 5/31/1831; probated 9/10/1831. Legatees: wife [name not given]; sons, Peter, Daniel (& his John and Cornelius), David and Levi; daus., Hannah and Margaret; "son Levi to maintain Ruluff Van Horne in decent manner." Executors: John G. Sweet, Col. Peter Young; sons, Daniel, David and Levi. Witnesses: Lawrence Serviss, Steward Blood, George Howe. (WMC 57:281)

Van Horne, Hannah, (widow of Abraham), [residence not stated], will dated 1/5/1811; probated 4/27/1816. Legatees: son, Cornelius. Executor: son, Cornelius. Witnesses: Cholett Cady, Joseph Earl, Thomas Vanderveer. (WMC 56:396)

Tryon County Militia

Van Horn, Abraham   [Appendix A]
Van Horn, Cornelius
Van Horn, Henry

COMPENDIUM

Van Horn, John
Van Horn, Thomas

Pension Abstract

Van Horn, John, b. 10/5/1756; m. Sarah [?], 12/15/1774 at Lebanon, N.J.; d. 5/27/1820, Hannibal, Oswego Co., N.Y. (Sarah Van Horn, resident of Sterling, Oswego Co., N.Y. on 6/5/1837.) Children: Jesse, b. 1776/7 (resident of Sterling, N.Y. in 1837); [another child not named in the application file]. John enlisted from his home in Charleston, Tryon Co. in August 1778 and was a private in Capt. Norton's Co., Col. Weisenfel's Regt. of the N.Y. Line; he fought in the battle of Monmouth and was in the siege of Yorktown; John served in the military until the end of the war. (RWPA: #W16771)

Van Horn, Thomas, b. 1745, Hunterdon Co., N.J.; m. Maria Frederick, 10/21/1779, at her father's home in Caughnawaga, Tryon Co., N.Y. by Rev. Thomas Romeyn; d. 2/26/1841, Springfield Otsego Co., N.Y. (Maria Van Horn, b. 1757/8, dau. of Philip Frederick; resident of Springfield, N.Y. on 6/29/1841.) Children: Philip, b. 1783/4 (resident of Springfield, N.Y. in 1841); Leah (m. [?] Davis and resident of Ontario Co., N.Y. in 1853). Thomas entered the military from his home in Warrensbush (later Florida, Montgomery Co., N.Y.) in 1775 and served under Capts. Mabie, Yeomans and Pettingell in Col. Frederick Fisher's 3rd. Regt., Tryon Co. Militia; he was engaged in the battle of Oriskany; Thomas received his commission as 1st. lieutenant on 3/8/1781 and continued in military service until the close of the Revolution. (RWPA: #W18210)

Deed Abstract

Van Horne, Abraham, Sheriff of Montgomery

Co. (by a Writ of Fieri Facias against Jacob G. Klock for debt of L2478 to Harme Gansevoort) to Christopher Fox. Instrument dated 1/22/1784; recorded 1/11/1788. Description: The Supreme Court of Judicature of New York State commanded that the goods, chattels, lands and tenements of Jacob G. Klock be seized for a Judgement to be paid to Harme Gansevoort amounting to L2478 of debt and L15.2.0 for damages. Land situated in Palatine District, on the north side of the Mohawk River, in a patent granted to George Klock, William Nellis, Lenerd Helmer and known as Lot #13 (100 acres). Consideration: L147.4.0, bid by Christopher Fox at public vendue. Witnesses: John Hess, Anna X Hess. (MVL:36)

Van Horne, Abraham, Sheriff of Tryon Co. (by a Writ of Fieri Facias against Nicholas Oxner for debt of L220.10.4 to Rosina Diefendorf, Executrix of the Will of Henry Diefendorf, decd.) to Adam Bellinger, of said County. Instrument dated 5/16/1783; recorded 4/26/1787. Description: The Inferior Court of Common Pleas, Tryon Co. commanded that the goods, chattels, lands and tenements of Nicholas Oxner be seized for a Judgement to be paid to Rosina Diefendorf amounting to L220.10.4 for a debt and L6.17.6 for damages. Lot #20 (about 100 acres) situated at Riemensnyder's Bush on the north side of the Mohawk River about two English miles from the said river in a patent granted to Jacob Glen. Consideration: L226, bid at public vendue. Witnesses: Gerhard Walrad, Hendrick Kyser. (MVL:35-36)

1790 Census

Van Horn, [?]   [Appendix B]
Van Horn, Abraham
Van Horn, Cornelius
Van Horn, Cornelius, Jr.

841

COMPENDIUM

Van Horn, Hendrick
Van Horn, Thomas

Van Husen, Albert   [Appendix B]
Van Husen, Jacob

VAN HUSEN

Probate Abstract

Van Hoesen, Jacob, (of the town of Florida), will dated 11/14/1804; probated 3/11/1812. Legatees: sons, Albert and John; daus., Mary Bodine and Rachel Staley; grandson, Isaac Bodine. Executors: son, John; Nathaniel Campbell. Witnesses: George Robb, Thomas and Mary Campbell. (WMC 56:383)

Van Housen, John, (of the town of Florida), will dated 4/5/1826; probated 2/7/1827. Legatees: only living son, John; son, Jacob (decd. & his John and Benjamin). Executor: son, John. Witnesses: Andrew Johnson, John V. Wemple, Lawrence Vosburgh. (WMC 57:267)

Tryon County Militia

Van Heusen, Albert   [Appendix A]

Pension Abstract

Van Heusen, Albert, b. 10/15/1750, Lunenburgh, Albany Co. (now Athens, Greene Co., N.Y.); resident of Florida, Montgomery Co., N.Y. on 8/30/1832. Albert volunteered for military service in 1776 and was a private in Capt. David McMaster's Co., Col. Frederick Fisher's 3rd. Regt., Tryon Co. Militia; he served on various tours of duty until the close of the war. (RWPA: #S28925)

1790 Census

VAN INGER

1790 Census

Van Inger, Joseph   [Appendix B]

VAN LOON

Marriage

Van Loon, John m. Elizabeth Fye, 8/20/1776 (DRC:161)

Birth/Baptism

Van Loon, John & Elizabeth (Fye): Jurry, b. 4/12/1778; bapt. 5/18/1778 (DRC:48). Sponsors: Jelis Fonda & Jannetje Fonda.

Tryon County Miiltia

Van Loon, John   [Appendix A]

Pension Abstract

Van Loon, John, m. Elizabeth Fry [Fye?], 8/20/1776, at Caughnawaga, N.Y.; d. 10/27/1786. (Elizabeth Van Loon, b. 1760/1; m. 2nd. Peter Steller [d. pre 1839], 1/5/1827; resident of Wheeler, Steuben Co., N.Y. on 5/9/1839.) Children: Peter (resident of Montgomery Co., N.Y. on 5/30/1839.) John entered the Tryon Co. Militia in 1776 as a private under Capt. Jacob Seeber in Col. Ebenezer Cox's 1st. Regt. and was stationed at Fort Stanwix for a period of six months.

842

(RWPA: #W19089)

VAN NAST

Probate Abstract

Van Nast, Abraham G., (of Glen), will dated 8/24/1824; probated 10/1/1824. Legatees: wife, Elizabeth; father-in-law, Matthew Van Valkenburgh; brother, John; children of sister Sarah (wife of John J. Skeanck). Executors: wife; James Voorhees, Cornelius H. Putman. Witnesses: Peter Shults, David Lyon, Cornelius H. Putman. (WMC 57:180)

VAN NEER

1790 Census

Van Neer, Peter   [Appendix B]

VAN NESS (also see VAN NESTE)

Birth/Baptism

Van Ess, Wilhelm & Maria [?]: Maria, b. 11/5/1792 (LTSA:72); Annatche, b. 8/5/1793 (LTSA:79). Sponsors: Jacob Majer & Eva (re:1); Henrich Fitscher & Elisabet (re:2).

Van Est, George & Jenny (Jacobson): Jacob, b. 9/16/1790; bapt. 1/13/1791 (DRC:93). Sponsors: [none named].

Van Est, Henderick & Maria (Ten Eyke): Gerritje, b. 3/10/1791; bapt. 4/10/1791 (DRC:96). Sponsors: [none named].

1790 Census

Van Ness, George   [Appendix B]
Van Ness, Henry
Van Ness, William

VAN NESTE (also see VAN NESS)

Probate Abstract

Van Neste, John, (of Montgomery County), will dated 8/13/1788; probated 10/27/1788. Legatees: sons, Hendrick and George; dau., Sarah Ten Eick; grandson, Gerrit Ten Broeck; John Vorehase and Jacob Vorehase. Executors: son, Hendrick; Robert Roseboom, Peter P. Dumont. Witnesses: Andrew Ten Eick, Thomas Burnside, Robert Roseboom. (WMC 56:145)

VAN NIER

Birth/Baptism

Van Nier, Peter, (Canajoharie) & Catharina [?]: Peter, bapt. 9/29/1793 (SJC:81). Sponsors: Johannes Ehle & Delia Ehle.

VAN NORMAN

1790 Census

Van Norman, Joseph   [Appendix B]

VAN OLINDA

Probate Abstract

Van O'Linda, Martin, (of the Willigers on Mohawk River, Tryon County), will dated 6/2/1781; probated 8/9/1813. Legatees: wife, Cornelia; sons, Jacob, Peter Benjamin, William and Tunis; daus., Catherine and Eve. Executors: Frederick Clute, Henry Brewer. Witnesses: John and Isaias Swart, Isaac Marselis. (WMC 56:389)

Van Olinda, Tunis, (of Florida), will dated 9/2/1825; probated 11/26/1825. Legatees: wife, Tiney/Liney[?]; dau., Caty Ann. Executors: wife and dau., and Samuel Bant (of Broadalbin). Witnesses: John Peck, Caty Bant and Tunis I. Swart. (WMC 57:184-185)

Tryon County Militia

Van Olinda, Benjamin   [Appendix A]
Van Olinda, Jacob
Van Olinda, Peter

1790 Census

Van Olenda, Benjamin   [Appendix B]
Van Olenda, Jacob
Van Olenda, Martin
Van Olenda, Peter

VAN OSTRANDER

1790 Census

Van Ostrander, John   [Appendix B]

VAN PRAKEL

Marriage

Van Praakel, Gerrit m. Anna Gotz, 11/7/1765 (RDSA:177)

Birth/Baptism

Van Prakel, Gerrit Gysbert & Anna [?]: Anna, b. 2/21/1768; bapt. 3/21/1768 (RDSA:84). Spnsors: Anna & Johannes Goetz.

VAN RENSSELAER

Marriage

Van Rensselaer, Stephen m. Margaret Schuyler (dau. of Genl. [Philip] Schuyler of Saratoga), 6/6/1783 (JDR:2)

Deed Abstract

Van Rensselaer, Jeremiah, and Henry Oathoudt, Esqrs., two of the Commissioners of Forfeiture for the Western District to Conrad Seber, yeoman, of Canajoharie, Montgomery Co. Deed dated 9/16/1785; recorded 10/5/1785. Description: Land situated on the north side of the Mohawk River in Caughnawaga District, Montgomery Co. Lot #1 (19 acres of lowland) begins at the northwest corner of a lot belonging to George Adam Dockstader and Lot #4 (97 acres) which begins at the northwest corner of Lot #1. The said land deemed to have been forfeited by the conviction of John Dachsteder, farmer, late of Caughnawaga District. Consideration: L1400. Witnesses: Peter Ball, Abrm. Romine. (MVL:36)

VAN SCHAICK

844

Probate Abstract

Van Schaick, John, (of Glen), will dated 3/30/1827; probated 6/23/1827. Legatees: wife, Hannah; sons, William, John, Thomas, Keort[?] and Henry; daus., Patience, Betsey and Ann. Executors: Abraham V. Putman, Thomas Vanderveer. Witnesses: Abraham Aurnoch, Cornelius H. Putman, James [?]. (WMC 57:269)

1790 Census

Van Schaack, William   [Appendix B]

VAN SICE

Tryon County Militia

Van Sice, Cornelius   [Appendix A]

VAN SICKLE

Marriage

Van Sikkelen, Renier m. Engenietje Philipse, [no date: follows 12/16/1784] (DRC:164)

Birth/Baptism

Van Sickle, Adrian & Rebecca [?]: Reinier, b. 8/27/1764, bapt. 9/23/1764 (RDSA:51); Cornelius, b. 7/27/1769, bapt. 8/14/1769 (RDSA:96). Sponsors: Jeremias Quackenboosh & Janitje Quackenboosh (re:1); Moses Abbet & Abigail van Breston (re:2).

Van Sikkelen, Renier & Angenietje (Philipse): Rebecca, b. 4/20/1785; bapt. 7/11/1785

(DRC:74). Sponsors: Fredrick Lewis & Rachel Lewis.

Tryon County Militia

Van Sickle, Ryner   [Appendix A]

1790 Census

Van Sickle, Renier   [Appendix B]
Van Sickler, Rebecca

VAN SLYCK

Marriage

Van Slyck, Adam m. Margaretha Seeber, 2/26/1793 (DFP:48)

Van Slyck, Georg m. Margreth Bikkert, 4/11/1784 (DRGF:199)

Van Slyck, Gerrit (son of John) m. Catharin Wohleben (dau. of Pieter Wohleben), 1/22/1793 (DRGF:209)

Van Slyck, Johannes m. Gertruyd Marines, 8/29/1767 (RDSA:182)

Van Slyck, Martinus m. Anna Bikkert, 4/25/1784 (DRGF:199)

Van Slyck, Martinus m. Maria Stern, [no date: follows 8/13/1774] (DRC:160)

Van Slyck, Nicholas m. Elisabeth Leder (dau. of Johan. Leder), 2/23/1783 (DRGF:197)

Van Slyck, Nicholas m. Geertruy Fisher, 9/27/1778 (DRC:162)

COMPENDIUM

Birth/Baptism

Van Slyck, Cobus, & [?]: Jacobus, b. 11/12/1783; bapt. 1/11/1784 (DRGF:79). Sponsors: Georg Van Slyk & Margretha Bekker.

Van Slyck, Cornelius, Jr. & Jannitie [?]: Christina, b. 9/21/1739; bapt. 9/27/1739 (FH:7). Sponsors: Abraham & Christina Truax.

Van Slyck, George & Margretha (Pikard): Margretha, b. 4/8/1785, bapt. 4/11/1785 (DRGF:95); Gerret, bapt. 10/11/1789 [parents of Canajoh. Castle] (SJC:18). Sponsors: Jost Laux & Margretha (re:1); Gerret Von Schleyk & Anna Von Schleyk (re:2).

Van Slyck/Van Schlaick, George (of Canajoh. Castle) & Anna (Mabie/Mebie): Elizabeth, bapt. 8/10/1788 (SJC:3); Johann Jost, bapt. 6/6/1790 (SJC:28); Eva, bapt. 5/28/1792 (SJC:59). Sponsors: David F. Schuyler & Elizabeth Mabie (re:1); David Freymaurer & Gadlyn Mebie (re:2); [none named] (re:3).

Van Slyck, Gerrit & Echje [?]: Nicolaus, b. 10/20/1764, bapt. 10/24/1764 (RDSA:51); Gerrit, b. 8/30/1767, bapt. 9/14/1767 (RDSA:77). Sponsors: Cptn. Joh. Nicolaus Hercheimer & Maria (re:1); Georg Henrich Bell & his wife, Catharina (re:2).

Van Slyck, Hermanus & Elisabeth [?]: Harme, b. 7/3/1760, bapt. 7/20/1760 (RDSA:21); Rebecca, b. 12/17/1762, bapt. 1/9/1763 (RDSA:37); Engelge, b. 9/20/1766, bapt. 10/5/1766 (RDSA:69); Hermanus, b. 12/1/1769, bapt. 12/24/1769 (RDSA:99). Sponsors: Harme Brauer & Sartie Brauer (re:1); Cathrina, wife of Arent Sath (re:2); Elisabetha Brauwer & Arendt Brauer (re:3); Harme Browe[r] & his wife, Itie (re:4).

Van Slyck, Jacob & Gertraut [?]: Margretha, b. 7/14/1785, bapt. 7/24/1785 (DRGF:99); Catharina, bapt. 6/15/1790 [parents of Schneidersbush] (SJC:29). Sponsors: Johannes Windekker & Eva Windekker (re:1); John Dieterich Petri & Catharina Wendeker (re:2).

Van Slyck, Johannes & Geertruid/Geertruy (Merines): Margretha, b. 9/11/1768, bapt. 9/29/1768 (RDSA:91); Gertruyt, b. 12/22/1770, bapt. 1/5/1771 (RDSA:109); Johannis, b. 3/23/1773, bapt. 4/10/1773 (DRC:25); Batje, b. 6/2/1775, bapt. 7/2/1775 (DRC:34); Maria, b. 2/28/1781, bapt. 3/18/1781 (DRGF:43). Sponsors: Johannis Van Slyck, Jr. & Maragritje (re:1); David Merines & Gertruyt (re:2); William Van de Werken & Marregriet Van de werken (re:3); Tyme Leenderson & Baatje Leenderson (re:4); Samuel van Slyck & Gertraud Marines (re:5).

Van Slyck, Martin & Anna [?]: Eva, b. 3/16/1785, bapt. 3/24/1785 (DRGF:94); Catharina, bapt. 8/15/1790 (SJC:31); Niclaus, bapt. 8/5/1792 (SJC:62) [Note: parents of Canajoharie for 2nd. & 3rd. bapts.]. Sponsors: Nicolas Windekker & Bally (re:1); Ebert Vosberk & Catharina Vosberk (re:2); Niclaus Haus & Catharina Van Alstyne (re:3).

Van Slyck, Martin & Maria (Stern): Meritje, b. 12/15/1774, bapt. 1/13/1775 (DRC:32); Catrina, bapt. 9/8/1776 (DRC:39); Aron, b. 5/22/1778, bapt. 6/21/1778 (DRC:48). Sponsors: Nicholas Van Slyk & Grietje Staarn (re:1); Joost Van Slyck & Geertruy Van Slyck (re:2); [none named] (re:3).

Van Slyck, Nicholas & Elisabeth (Leder): Marteines, b. 8/14/1783, bapt. 8/24/1783 (DRGF:74); Eva, bapt. 11/26/1789 [parents of Canajoh. Castle] (SJC:20). Sponsors: Marteines von Slyck & Maria (re:1); Niclaus Haus & Eva

COMPENDIUM

Knieskern (re:2).

Van Slyck, Sever (Schneidersbusch) & Gertrud [?]: Friderich, b. 7/1/1792; bapt. 7/12/1792 (SJC:61). Sponsors: Friderich Wendeker & Maria Dolder.

Van Slyck, William & Magdelena (Merines): Johannis, b. 5/12/1785; bapt. 6/18/1785 (DRC:74). Sponsors: Samuel Van Slyk & Gertruy Van Slyk.

Probate Abstract

Van Slyke, Nicholas A., (of the town of Glen), will dated 3/30/1826; probated 7/22/1826. Legatees: wife, Abigail; Abigail (wife of Richard Hudson); Magdalen (wife of Cornelius Hanson). Executors: John C. Van Alstine, Richard Hudson. Witnesses: Peter Sidnigh, Joseph Miller, Joseph Applegate. (WMC 57:265)

Tryon County Militia

Van Slyck, Adam   [Appendix A]
Van Slyck, Garret
Van Slyck, George
Van Slyck, Jacob
Van Slyck, John
Van Slyck, Nicholas
Van Slyck, Nicholas G.
Van Slyck, Samuel
Van Slyck, William

Pension Abstract

Van Slyck, Nicholas, m. Abigail Wood, 4/25/1779, at Stone Arabia, N.Y.; (brother-in-law: John Barlat); d. 5/28/1826, Glen, Montgomery Co., N.Y. (Abigail Van Slyck, b. 1760/1; resident of Glen, N.Y. on 6/1/1837.) Nicholas served from 1775 through 1777 in

Capt. Jacob Gardenier's Co., Col. Frederick Fisher's 3rd. Regt., Tryon Co. Militia; he enlisted again in 1778 as a batteauman under the command of Capt. Simon Degraff; Nicholas fought in the battle of Oriskany. (RWPA: #W18199)

Van Slyck, William, b. 2/26/1759, Schoharie, N.Y.; m. 1st. Magdalena [?], 1780, at Canajoharie, N.Y.; m. 2nd., Elizabeth Adair, 7/10/1825, Pike, Wyoming Co., N.Y. (Magdalena Van Slyck, d. 1823, Montgomery Co., N.Y. Elizabeth (Adair) Van Slyck, b. 1777/8; resident of Pike, N.Y. on 2/26/1853.) Children: [1st. wife], John W., b. 1784/5 (resident of Wyoming Co., N.Y. in 1852). William enlisted from Canajoharie in July 1776 and served in Col. Jacob Klock's 2nd. Regt., Tryon Co. Militia as a private under Capts. Fox and Breadbake; he entered the batteau service for duty on the Hudson River in the spring of 1777 under Capt. Lefler; he also served as a carpenter under Capt. Snyder constructing boats at Saratoga; William continued in the military until his discharge on 1/1/1780. (RWPA: #W2461)

1790 Census

Van Slyk, Jacobus   [Appendix B]
Van Slyk, Martin
Van Slyk, Nicholas
Van Slyk, Sylvanus
Van Slyke, Adam
Van Slyke, Elizabeth
Van Slyke, Eve
Van Slyke, George
Van Slyke, Jacobus
Van Slyke, John
Van Slyke, Martenus
Van Slyke, Nicholas
Van Slyke, Peter
Van Slyke, Samuel

847

Van Slyke, William

VAN VECHTEN

Marriage

VAN[?] STINBERG see V. STINBERG

Van Vechten, Anthony m. Mary Fonda
7/21/1770 (RDSA:189)

Birth/Baptism

VAN VALKENBURG

Birth/Baptism

Van Valkenburg, Lambert & Anna (Head):
Hendrik, b. 2/14/1791; bapt. 3/20/1791
(DRC:96). Sponsors: Jacobus Quilh[ot] &
Catrina Quilhot.

Probate Abstract

Van Valkenburgh, Henry F., (of Mayfield),
will dated 5/9/1808; probated 1/25/1814.
Legatees: sons, Lambert, Francis and Malgert.
Executors: sons, Lambert and Francis.
Witnesses: Daniel McLaren, William and
Francis H. Van Beuren. (WMC 56:390)

Van Valkenburgh, John, (of Canajoharie), will
dated 2/25/1813; probated 9/18/1813. Legatees:
wife, Hannah; sons, Richard, Jacob and Peter;
daus., Catherine, Caity and Margaret.
Executors: wife; Abram Wessels, James
Folmsbee. Witnesses: William Newton, Peter
Colyar, Jacob Wessels. (WMC 56:389)

VAN VAUGHN

Tryon County Militia

Van Vaughn, Teunis   [Appendix A]

Van Vechten, Abraham & Cathrine (Schuyler)
Elizabeth, b. 5/10/1791; bapt. 6/4/1791
(DRC:98). Sponsors: [none named].

Van Vechten, Antony & Maria (Fonda): Jellis
Fonda, b. 5/27/1774, bapt. 6/26/1774
(DRC:29); Annatje, b. 6/10/1776, bapt.
6/17/1776 (DRC:37); Jannetje, b. 7/9/1779,
bapt. 7/?/1779 (DRC:19 & 53); Douw, b.
2/16/1785, bapt. 3/13/1785 (DRC:71).
Sponsors: Jellis Fonda & Jannetje Fonda (re:1);
Peter De Wandelaer & Annatje De Wandelaer
(re:2); Jelles Funda & Jannetje Funda (re:3);
Douw Funda & Peggy Funda (re:4).

Van Vechten, John & Catrina (Van Der Volt):
Elionora, b. 5/2/1782; bapt. 7/19/1782
(DRC:63). Sponsors: [none named].

Tryon County Militia

Van Vechten, Derick   [Appendix A]
Van Vechten, John

Pension Abstract

Van Vechten, Derick, b. 10/24/1753, Catskill,
Albany Co., N.Y.; m. [wife not named];
resident of Florida, Montgomery Co., N.Y. on
9/19/1832. Grandchild: George R. Milmine
(resident of Fonda, Wisconsin in 1850). Derick
was elected ensign in Capt. Emanuel Degraff's
Co., Col. Frederick Fisher's 3rd. Regt., Tryon
Co. Militia and received his commission on

'22/1778; he fought in the battles of Oriskany
ad Klock's Field and was called out when
herry Valley was burned; Derick remained in
iilitary service into 1783. (RWPA: #S23047)

Deed Abstract

'an Vechten, Teunis, Gentleman, of Katts Kill
Catskill], Albany Co. to Gutlis Nastle [Gotlieb
estle], yeoman, of Tryon Co. Deed dated
'3/1783; recorded 11/14/1783. Description:
and situated in Tryon Co., being part of a
act of land granted by Letters Patent on
'1/1716 to Harmen Van Slyck and others. This
and is known by the name Lot #3 ($105^{1/2}$
cres). Consideration: L260. Witnesses: Saml.
llen, Abm. Vn. Vechten. (MVL:39)

1790 Census

an Vechten, Abraham   [Appendix B]
'an Vechten, Anthony
'an Vechten, Dirick

'AN VEE

1790 Census

'an Vee, Andrew   [Appendix B]
'an Vee, John

'AN VLEECK

1790 Census

'an Vleeck, Benjamin   [Appendix B]
'an Vleeck, John

VAN VLEET

Death Record

Van Vleet, Amos M., d. 10/10/1830, age 2
years, 7 months, 10 days; buried sect. 10,
Colonial Cemetery, Johnstown (JC:189)

Van Vleet, Evart, d. 2/10/1831, age 37 years;
buried sect. 10, Colonial Cemetery, Johnstown
(JC:189)

Van Vleet, James William, (son of J. & T. Van
Vleet), d. 8/5/1854, age 5 months, 24 days;
buried sect. 10, Colonial Cemetery, Johnstown
(JC:189)

1790 Census

Van Vleet, Dury   [Appendix B]
Van Vleet, John

VAN VORST

Tryon County Militia

Van Vorst, Jelles   [Appendix A]

Pension Abstract

Van Vorst, Jellis Jno. Baptist, m. Catharine
Swart, 2/18/1780, at Schenectady, N.Y. by
Rev. Barent Vrooman; (sister: Maria [m. [?]
Putman]); d. 12/16/1813. (Catharine Van
Vorst, b. ca. 1761, dau. of Josias Swart;
(sister: Rachel [m. John Lewis]); m. 2nd. John
Van Vleet [d. 3/14/1832]; resident of
Johnstown, Montgomery Co., N.Y. on
10/28/1837.) Children: Catharine, b.
1/16/1781, bapt. 2/12/1781; Annatie, b.
9/11/1782. Jellis served as a private in 1778

under the command of Capt. Jacobus Peck in a company of batteaumen in the department of the quartermaster general; he moved to Warrensbush (now Florida, Montgomery Co.) in 1779 and enrolled in Capt. McMaster's Co., Col. Frederick Fisher's 3rd. Regt., Tryon Co. Militia for various periods of duty into 1782. (RWPA: #W26614)

VAN VOSEN

1790 Census

Van Vosen, Henry   [Appendix B]

VAN VOST

1790 Census

Van Vost, Ellis   [Appendix B]
Van Vost, John

VAN VRONKER

1790 Census

Van Vronker, Dirick   [Appendix B]
Van Vroonker, Richard

VAN VRONKIN

1790 Census

Van Vronkin, Garrit   [Appendix B]

VAN VUVER

1790 Census

Van Vuver, Cornelius   [Appendix B]

VAN WAGNER

Birth/Baptism

Van Wagner/Van Wagonon, Tunis [Note: Firs name, Jacob, given incorrectly in bapt (DRC:73)] & Maria (Newkirk): Jacob, b 3/10/1785, bapt. 6/6/1785 (DRC:73); Maria bapt. 5/16/1787 (DRC:84); Tunis, bapt 12/28/1789 [parents of Johnstown] (JDR:24) Sponsors: [none named] (re:1-3).

1790 Census

Van Waganer, Henry   [Appendix B
Van Wagener, Teunis

VAN WIE

Birth/Baptism

Van Wie, Andres & Margaret [?]: Annatche b. 12/1/1792 (LTSA:76). Sponsors: John V Wie & Annatche.

Van Wie, Johannes H. & Agnetje (Winne) Hendrik, b. 12/14/1784; bapt. 2/13/178 (DRC:70). Sponsors: Hendrik Van [?] & Annatje Van [?].

Death Record

Van Wie, [?], (widow), d. 2/23/1813, age 59

years, 2 months (DFP:95)

Probate Abstract

Van Wie, John H., (of Palatine), will dated 1/20/1821; probated 5/8/1821. Legatees: sons, Henry (eldest), John, Andrew, Daniel and Arie; daus., Catharine, Nancy (wife of George L. Schumniel[?]). Bequest: Land in Norway, Herkimer County [N.Y.] to son, Henry. Executors: sons, Andrew, John and Daniel. Witnesses: Adam Van Slyck, Henry Dillenbach, David I. Zieley. (WMC 57:171)

VAN WINGER

Marriage

Van Winger, Joseph m. Nyltje van Alstyne, 3/13/1785 (DRC:164)

VAN WORMER

Probate Abstract

Van Wormer, John, (of Florida), will dated 2/28/1805; probated 10/2/1813. Legatees: wife, Rachel; sons, John, Lawrence, Egbert and Jacob; daus., Elizabeth Spoore, Judith Vosburgh, Rachel Staley, Mary Degraff. Executors: sons, Lawrence and Egbert. Witnesses: William Clover, Nathaniel Campbell, Conrad Schelhemmer. (WMC 56:389)

Van Wormer, Peter, (of Amsterdam), will dated 3/1/1808; probated 7/2/1808. Legatees: wife, Rachel (she was a Van Hoesen); sons, Casper, Lawrence and John; daus., Judith (wife of Matthew Holliday), Mary (wife of Ire Puffer),

Elizabeth (wife of Jeremiah Groot) and Rachel. Executors: John and William Swart. Witnesses: John and William Swart, Philip Fairchild. (WMC 56:158)

1790 Census

Van Wormer, Peter　　　　[Appendix B]

VAN WYL

Birth/Baptism

Van Wyl, Johannes & Catryna (Nykman): Annatie, b. 6/15/1773; bapt. 7/11/1773 (DRC:26). Sponsors: Joseph Prent & Annatie Prent.

VAN ZELAN

1790 Census

Van Zelan, Johannes　　　　[Appendix B]

VARRBOS (also see FORBUSH)

Marriage

Vorbos, James m. Margreth Nelles, 2/2/1784 (DRGF:199)

Vorbush, Jacob m. Margaretha Erhard, 7/17/1763 (RDSA:172)

Birth/Baptism

Varbus/Varrbos, John & Anna [?]: Johannes,

COMPENDIUM

b. 9/9/1780, bapt. 9/26/1780 (DRGF:39); Georg, b. 9/26/1783, bapt. 10/5/1783 (DRGF:75). Sponsors: Johannes Haus & Lena (re:1); Hans Georg Schiff & Christian Varbes (re:2).

Varrbos, Bartholomew & Catharina [?]: David, b. 8/17/1784; bapt. 8/22/1784 (DRGF:86). Sponsors: David Mavis & Elisabeth Hergheimer.

Varrbos, John & Margretha [?]: Alita, b. 2/16/1781, bapt. 3/21/1781 (DRGF:43); Alexander, b. 10/19/1784, bapt. 11/9/1784 (DRGF:89). Sponsors: Georg Hergheimer Esqr. & Alita (re:1); Barthomeus Vorbes & Catharina (re:2).

Varrbos, Nicholas & Sara [?]: Marcy, b. 9/26/1780, bapt. 9/26/1780 (DRGF:39); Bartholomeus, b. 8/26/1784, bapt. 9/30/1784 (DRGF:87). Sponsors: Jacob Varrbos & Margretha (re:1); Bartholomeus Vorbes & Catharina (re:2).

VAUGHAN

1790 Census

Vaughan, John   [Appendix B]
Vaughan, John, Jr.
Vaughan, Micajah
Vaughn, Joseph

VEAL

1790 Census

Veal, David   [Appendix B]

Veal, Stephen

VECHTA

1790 Census

Vechta, John   [Appendix B]

VEDDER see **VEEDER**

VEEDER

Marriage

Vedder, Adam m. Anna Van Vleck, of Remsonsbush, 11/6/1792 (JDR:#119)

Vedder, Arent, Jr. m. Sarah Van den Bogaert, 6/24/1738, Schenectady (FH:4)

Veeder, Arnout m. Arriana Wemp[le], 5/27/1769 (RDSA:186)

Veeder, Simon m. Maragrita Putman, 6/1/1777 (DRC:161)

Veeder, Simon m. Maragrita Terwillig[er], 10/30/1774 (DRC:160)

Veeder, Volckert (son of Hanage Veeder) m. Elisabeth Smidt (dau. of Cornelies Smidt), 3/4/1762 (RDSA:171)

Veeder, Wilhelm m. Elisabeth Bellinger, 4/31/1782 (DRGF:196)

COMPENDIUM

Birth/Baptism

Veeder, Abram & Annatje (Fonda): Johannis, b. 7/6/1774, bapt. 7/10/1774 (DRC:30); Catrina, b. 5/9/1776, bapt. 5/19/1776 (DRC:37). Sponsors: Johannis Veeder & Catrina Veeder (re:1); Johannis Fonda Junr. & Eva Veeder (re:2).

Veeder, Arnold/Arnout & Arriaantje/Arriana (Wemp[le]): Marytje, b. 5/14/1770, bapt. 5/24/1770 (RDSA:102); Ephraim, b. 10/10/1771, bapt. 10/15/1771 (RDSA:109); Angenitje, b. 4/2/1775, bapt. 4/30/1775 (DRC:33); Annaje, b. 4/?/1783, bapt. 4/27/1783 (DRGF:70); Johannes, b. 6/20/1785, bapt. 7/5/1785 (DRGF:98). Sponsors: Arendt Vetter & Annatje Vetter (re:1); Ephraim Wemple & Agnitje (re:2); Arent Brower & Rebecca Wemple (re:3); Nicolas van Slyk & Gertruyd (re:4); Joh: Vedder & Margrithje Vischar (re:5).

Veeder, Harman & Mary [?]: Arent, bapt. 2/16/1739/40 (FH:9). Sponsors: Arent Vedder Senr, Simon Vedder, Mary Vedder.

Veeder, Johannes & Catarina (Mebie): Eva, bapt. 4/2/1761 (DRC:16). Sponsors: Johannes Leentartje jun. & Anna Leendertje.

Veeder, Lucas & Agnes [?]: Wilhelm, b. 1/6/1756 (LTSA:16). Sponsors: Wilhelm Zobel, Catharina Copernoll.

Veeder, Lucas & Maria (Bellinger): Philip, bapt. 11/10/1777 (DRC:45). Sponsors: Jacob Bushart & Maragriet Bushart.

Veeder, Lucas & Maria Eva [?]: Anna, b. 8/27/1767; bapt. 9/24/1767 (RDSA:78). Sponsors: Lena & Peter Serves.

Veeder, Lucas & Maria Eva (Bel): Elizabeth, bapt. 1/24/1765 (DRC:13). Sponsors: Adam Colbilich & Anna Maria Colbilich.

Veeder, Peter S. & Marytje [?]: Nicolas, b. 11/5/1784; bapt. 12/7/1784 (DRGF:90). Sponsors: Stophel Fox & Catharina.

Veeder, Simon & Maragrita (Putman): Maria, b. 12/20/1778, bapt. 1/17/1779 (DRC:51); Cornelis, b. 10/19/1781, bapt. 11/28/1781 (DRC:59). Sponsors: Harmanis Vedder & Annatje Vedder (re:1); Cornelis Putman & Elizabeth Putman (re:2).

Veeder, Simon & Margrita (Terwilliger): Catrina, b. 4/16/1776, bapt. 4/21/1776 (DRC:37); Harmanus, b. 9/30[?]/1777, bapt. 10/7/1777 (DRC:45); Johannis, b. 3/3/1780, bapt. 3/12/1780 (DRC:55); Volkert, b. 2/10/1782, bapt. 3/10/1782 (DRC:61); Abram, b. 4/1/1786, bapt. 4/23/1786 (DRC:78). Sponsors: Johannis Veeder & Catrina Veeder (re:1); Harmanus Ter Williger & Lena Ter Willige (re:2); Johannis Veeder & Catrina Veeder (re:3); Volkert Veeder & Elizabeth Veeder (re:4); Abram Veder & Annatje Veder (re:5).

Veeder, Volkert & Elizabeth (Smith): Cornelius, bapt. 10/21/1764 (DRC:13); Annatye, b. 3/23/1773, bapt. 4/10/1773 (DRC:25); Sarah, b. 8/29/1775, bapt. 9/?/1775 (DRC:35); Janntje, b. 3/2/1778, bapt. 3/8/1778 (DRC:47); Arent, b. 4/22/1780, bapt. 4/26/1780 (DRC:56); Maria, b. 11/24/1782, bapt. 12/8/1782 (DRC:64); Elizabeth, b. 6/20/1785, bapt. 7/13/1785 (DRC:74). Sponsors: Cornelis Smit & Sarah Smit (re:1); Barent Hansen & Annatie Hansen (re:2); Barent Wemple & Sarah Wemple (re:3); Symon Veeder & Jannetje Davids (re:4); Arent Smith & Catrina Smith (re:5); John Wemple & Maria

Wemple (re:6); Johannes M. Van Alstyn & Sarah Van Alstyn (re:7).

Veeder, Wilhelm/William & Elisabeth (Bellinger): Adam, b. 10/30/1782, bapt. 11/4/1782 (DRGF:64); George Heinrich, bapt. 3/20/1789 [parents of Schneidersbusch] (SJC:12). Sponsors: Adam Bellinger & Magdalena (re:1); Georg Heinrich Bell & Catharina Bell (re:2).

Death Record

Veeder, [?], (sister-in-law of Ephraim Vedder), d. 9/3/1811, age 27 years, 9 months, 3 days (DFP:94)

Probate Abstract

Vedder, John A., (of Charleston), will dated 3/26/1816; probated 11/30/1818. Legatees: wife, Eve; daus., Hester, Elizabeth, Rachel, Mary and Tanneken; sons, John, Jacob, France and Albert. Executors: wife; Cornelius Veeder, Joseph Yates Bratt. Witnesses: Harmonus Peek, Benjamin Van Vechten, Jacob C. Van Dord. (WMC 57:167)

Veeder, Abraham, (of Johnstown), will dated 11/27/1801; probated 2/7/1814. Legatees: wife, Anachie; sons, Henry, Albert and John; daus., Catherine, Sarah, Alida, Nancy and Elizabeth. Executors: brother, John; Douw Wemple, Henry A. Fonda. Witnesses: John S. Veeder, Volkert S. Veeder, William Carrol. (WMC 56:390)

Veeder, Johannis, (of Johnstown), will dated 5/16/1798; probated 1/18/1803. Legatees: wife, Elisebeth; sons, Simon (& his dau., Elisebeth), John Volkert, and Abraham; daus., Eve Simmons, Annatie Van Antwerp, Maria, (John Wemp's children), Jannetie, (John Davis'

children); John W. Wallace. Executors: son, Simon; Jacob H. Schermerhorn. Witnesses: Cornelius Haring, William Goetz, Christopher Shuttis. (WMC 56:152)

Veeder, Volkert, (of Johnstown), will dated 8/7/1811; probated 8/2/1813. Legatees: wife, Maria; daus., Elizabeth (wife of Henry I. [or J.] Fonda), Mary (wife of Jacob N. Gardennier), Nancy (wife of Barent H. Vrooman), Caty (wife of Mindert Wemple), Jenney (wife of Jacob Hardenbergh), Sarah (wife of David Brightman); sons, John, Abraham, Cornelius and Aaron. Bequest: willed daus. land in Galen, Cayuga Co., and Manlius and Virgil, Onondaga Co. Executors: wife; son, Cornelius; brother, Simon. Witnesses: John and Abbey Morrell, Jacob Empie. (WMC 56:389)

Tryon County Militia

Veeder, Abraham	[Appendix A]
Veeder, Albert	
Veeder, Arnout	
Veeder, Cornelius	
Veeder, Isaac	
Veeder, John	
Veeder, John J.	
Veeder, Simon	
Veeder, Volkert	

Pension Abstract

Veeder, Cornelius, b. 9/14/1764; m. Harriet Zielly, 10/18/1789 by Rev. Thomas Romeyn; d. 11/9/1848, Glen, Montgomery Co., N.Y. (Harriet Veeder, b. 7/18/1770; resident of Glen, N.Y. on 9/13/1855.) Cornelius served as a private under Capt. Veeder in Col. Frederick Fisher's 3rd. Regt., Tryon Co. Militia for "fourteen days". (RWPA: #R10946)

Veeder, Frederick, b. 4/28/1761, son of Arent and Catrina (Van Patten) Vedder, in a town later called Glenville, Schenectady Co., N.Y.; bapt. 5/3/1761, Protestant Reformed Dutch Church, Schenectady; lived in Broadalbin, Montgomery Co. [time not specified] and resident of Duanesburg, Schenectady Co. on 4/30/1834. Frederick enlisted in September 1779 and served as a sergeant on various tours of duty until 1781 in Capt. Outhout's Co., Col. Wemple's Regt.; he was stationed in the areas of Stone Arabia, Fort Clyde and Fort Hunter. (RWPA: #S21547 *VEDDER*)

Veeder, John, m. Sarah Vedder, 1/28/1786, Reformed Dutch Church of Schenectady, N.Y.; d. 12/23/1823. John enlisted in the summer/fall of 1776 as a private in a company of rangers under the command of Capt. John A. Bradt in the Continental Line; he was stationed at Fort Paris in Stone Arabia, Tryon Co. in October 1779 under the command of Capt. John Mynderse in Col. Abraham Wemple's Regt. (RWPA: #W18219)

Veeder, Simon, b. 5/31/1748, Schenectady, N.Y.; m. [wife not named]; d. 12/18/1836, Mohawk, Montgomery Co., N.Y. Children: Simon, John S., Magdalen (m. [?] Wemple). [These children all lived in Mohawk, N.Y. in 1850.] Simon enlisted at Caughnawaga in 1775 into Capt. John Davis' Co., Col. Frederick Fisher's 3rd. Regt., Tryon Co. Militia; he was appointed quartermaster of the 3rd. Regt. in the spring of 1781 and held this rank until the end of the war; Simon was at the taking of Burgoyne and fought in the battle of Johnstown. (RWPA: #S19494)

Deed Abstract

Veeder, Johannes, yeoman, of Caughnawaga, Montgomery Co. to John Glen, Esq., of Schenectady, Albany Co. Deed dated 8/14/1786; recorded 8/17/1786. Description: Land situated on the south side of the Mohawk River at a place called Aries Kill in Montgomery Co. One-third part of Lot #15, one-third part of Lot #16, one-third part of Lot #17. These three parcels contain (292 acres). Consideration: L365. Witnesses: Peter Schuyler, Douw Fonda. (MVL:39)

Veeder, Johannes, of Caughnawaga District, Montgomery Co. to Lucas W. Veeder, Volkert S. Veeder of Norman's Kill and John Glen, of Schenectady, Albany Co. Deed dated 9/27/1786; recorded 12/15/1786. Description: All that undivided third part of land on the south side of the Mohawk River at Aries Kill in Montgomery Co., known as Lot #10 (182 acres). Consideration: L117.10.0. Witnesses: Dirk Van Ingen, Elizabeth Van Ingen. (MVL:39)

1790 Census

Veder, John	[Appendix B]
Veeder, [?] (2)	
Veeder, Abraham, Jr.	
Veeder, Albert H.	
Veeder, Arnold	
Veeder, Isaac	
Veeder, Peter	
Veeder, Peter V.	
Veeder, Simon (2)	
Veeder, Volkert	

VEITH see VEIX

VEIX

855

Marriage

Veith, Daniel m. Anna Ruppert, 3/9/1767 (RDSA:181)

Birth/Baptism

Veix, Daniel & Anna [?]: Franciscus, b. 7/17/1771 (LTSA:40). Sponsors: Franz Altbrand, Anna Barbara Rubert.

Veix, Philipp & Anna Margaretha [?]: Johannes, b. 6/16/1771 (LTSA:37); Peter, b. 12/25/1772 (LTSA:44). Sponsors: Johannes Wik & his wife (re:1); Peter Veix, Catharina Leder (re:2).

VENTIN

Probate Abstract

Ventin, William, (of Florida), will dated 4/11/1823; probated 6/17/1823. Legatees: wife, Gitty; Polly Shanly; Minerva Carlisle; James (of Daniel/David[?] Starks; Cornelius (of Andrew Radley). Executors: wife and Daniel/David[?] Starks. Witnesses: Lewis Carlisle, Abram D. Vanantwerp, Rachel McGee. (WMC 57:176)

1790 Census

Venton, William   [Appendix B]

VERGIL

1790 Census

Vergil, James   [Appendix B]

VERMYLIA

Death Record

Vermylia, William, d. 8/24/1823, age 36 years; buried Cherry Valley Presbyterian Church cemetery (PCV:80)

VERNOR

1790 Census

Vernor, Andress   [Appendix B]

VER PLANK

Birth/Baptism

Ver Plank, Galyne & Annaetje (Deforest): Alida, b. 6/15/1791; bapt. 7/3/1791 (DRC:99). Sponsors: [none named].

Probate Abstract

Ver Planck, William, (of Canajoharie), will dated 10/21/1817; probated 6/29/1825. Legatees: wife [not named]; son, Guillian; grandchildren, Lidia, Christopher and William Lansing; grandchildren, William Denis, Ryneir Rayme[?]. Executors: son and Nicholas Gros. Witnesses: John Loucks, Sarah Curtis, William Bach. (WMC 57:183)

VETTERLIE

Marriage

Vetterlie, Georg (son of John Vetterlie) m. Anna Peggy Dygert (dau. of Henry Dygert), 12/21/1791 (DFP:44)

Vetterlie, Henrich m. Eva Hitshmann, 6/3/1792 (DRGF:209)

Vetterlie, Robert m. Anna Rattenauer, 1/27/1793 (DFP:48)

Vetterlie, Thomas m. Marigreth Schiff, 1/10/1786 (DRGF:203)

Birth/Baptism

Vetterle, Johannes & Maria [?]: Johannes, b. 7/?/1782 (DRGF:59). Sponsors: Wilhelm Wohlgemuth & Maria Veterle.

Vetterle, John & Gertraut [?]: Eva, b. 8/15/1784; bapt. 8/16/1784 (DRGF:86). Sponsors: John Bickert & Rahel Vatterle.

VETTERMANN

Birth/Baptism

Vettermann, Johann Bartholomaus & Anna [?]: Catharina, b. 8/31/1771 (LTSA:38). Sponsors: Caspar Jordan & his wife.

VICORY

1790 Census

Vicory, Thomas   [Appendix B]

VINEGAR

1790 Census

Vinegar, Jacob   [Appendix B]
Vinegar, Samuel

VININGS

1790 Census

Vinings, Jonas   [Appendix B]

VINTON

1790 Census

Vinton, Benoni   [Appendix B]

VISBACK (also see FISHBACK)

Birth/Baptism

Visback, Jacob & Meritje (Freeman): Freeman, b. 9/13/1786, bapt. 1/10/1787 (DRC:82 & 86); Annaetje, b. 12/25/1790, bapt. 3/20/1791 (DRC:96). Sponsors: Gerrit Van Frank & Meritje Van Frank (re:1); Michel Wert & Annaetje Miller (re:2).

VISE

1790 Census

Vise, Samuel   [Appendix B]

857

VISGER

Visger, John   [Appendix B]

VISSCHER (also see FISHER)

Probate Abstract

Visscher, Gazena, (widow of Frederick, of Johnstown), will dated 1/26/1811; probated 9/12/1815. Legatees: dau., Catharine (wife of Jacob S. Glen); granddaus., Gazena and Alida Mabie (of Simon and Gazena). Executors: son, Daniel; son-in-law, Jacob S. Glen; Simon Mabie. Witnesses: Andrew Wemple, Stephen Dykeman, Benjamin Van Vechten. (WMC 56:395)

Vissher/Nissher[?], John, (of Johnstown), will dated 7/14/1821; probated 4/11/1827. Legatees: wife, Maria; son, Abraham; daus., Margaret, Katharine, Maria, Elizabeth, Rebecca and Nelly; grandsons, George and Ira Haveman; granddau., Katharine Haveman (all three of Susannah, decd.). Executors: wife; son, Abraham; Robert Squire. Witnesses: William, Philip and Jacob Frederick. (WMC 57:268)

Pension Abstract

Visscher, John I., m. Annatie Ehl, 12/?/1783, by Rev. Barent Vrooman, Reformed Dutch Church of Schenectady, N.Y.; d. 12/15/1806. (Annatie Visscher lived in Palatine, Montgomery Co., N.Y. on 8/27/1839.) Children: Susanna, bapt. 1/11/1784, Reformed Dutch Church of Schenectady. John I. was a private in Capt. Jelles Fonda's Co., Col. Abraham Wemple's Regt. and was stationed at

Saratoga, the Schoharie Fort and Stone Arabia; he was engaged at Stillwater and was present at the capture of Burgoyne. (RWPA: #R10956)

Visscher, John T., b. 1744/5; m. Annatie Pearce; resident of Glen, Montgomery Co., N.Y. on 9/15/1832; d. 9/18/1834. (Annatie Visscher, d. pre 1834.) Children: Matilda (eldest child; m. [?] Putnam and living in 1832); Alida (m. [?] McDaniels and living in 1850); Elizabeth (m. [?] Voorhees and alive in 1850); Isaac, b. 4/19/1793. [Additional data on Isaac Visscher given by his great granddaughter, Eleanor (Visscher) Wendel (Mrs. John H.), on 1/22/1911: James, son of Isaac Visscher, m. Mary Williamson (b. 1824).] John T. entered the military from his home in Albany, N.Y. on 8/8/1777 and was appointed assistant commissary in the General Hospital in the Northern Department; he was commissioned a 1st. lieutenant in Capt. William Hun's Co., Col. Abraham Cuyler's Regt. on 4/17/1781. (RWPA: #S28929)

1790 Census

Visscher, John T.   [Appendix B]

VLIPCHE

Birth/Baptism

Vlipche, Abraham & Sara [?]: Elisabet, b. 7/4/1796 (LTSA:96). Sponsors: Friderich Strohbek & Maria.

VOGEL

COMPENDIUM

Birth/Baptism

ogel, Joh. Henrich (of Tillenberg) & Maria ?]: Daniel, bapt. 5/6/1792 (SJC:58). Sponsors: ♦aniel Weber & Debora Krauss.

˹OLKENBURGH

1790 Census

˹olkenburgh, [?]   [Appendix B]
˹olkenburgh, Hendrick

˹ON KECHLOR

Birth/Baptism

˹on Kechlor, Micael & [?]: Johannes, b. /14/1778; bapt. 1/17/1778 (LTSA:51). ♭ponsors: Jacob Hellebrand & Catharina.

˅ON KOCHNAT

Marriage

˅on Kochnat, Jacob Eberhard m. Cath. Deixin, /10/1770 (LTSA:281)

˅on Kochnat, Joseph m. Anna Catharina Alt, ?/20/1771 (LTSA:282)

Birth/Baptism

˅on Kochnat, Jacob Eberhard & Catharina [?]: ˹o[h]ann Peter, b. 1/26/1771 (LTSA:35). ♭ponsors: Michael v. Kochnat, Peter Vei, ♭ophia Alt.

Von Kochnat, Joh. Eberh. & Elisabeth [?]: Jacob, b. 1/22/1780; bapt. 2/2/1780 (LTSA:59). Sponsors: Jacob von Kochnat & Elisabeth.

Von Kochnat, Johannes & Elisabetha [?]: Joseph, bapt. 4/20/1766 (RDSA:63). Sponsors: Joseph Kachnat & Anna Ruppert.

VON WISHE

Birth/Baptism

Von Wishe, Johannes & Agnete (Wenne): Daniel, b. 9/8/1787; bapt. 9/16/1787 (RDSA:114). Sponsors: Daniel Wenne & Catharina (born: Hochdeling).

VOORHEES

Marriage

Voorhees, Cornelius (of Canajoharie) m. Catherine Putman (of Canajoharie), 1/26/1826 (PCBC:51)

Voorhees, Daniel (of Cherry Valley) m. Jane Winne (of Cherry Valley), 10/31/1826 (PCBC:51)

Death Record

Voorhees, Hannah, (Mrs.), d. 5/20/1823, age 37 years; buried Cherry Valley Presbyterian Church cemetery (PCV:80)

Probate Abstract

Voorhees, Henry, (of Glen), will dated

859

COMPENDIUM

3/24/1826; probated 3/3/1828. Legatees: son, James; granddau., Rachel (of Peter De Groff); my other children. Executor: son, James. Witnesses: Horatio N. and Henry V. Voorhees, Cornelius H. Putman. (WMC 57:270)

Voorus, Gerret, (of Florida), will dated 3/17/1828; probated 9/26/1831. Legatees: wife, Lavina; sons, Andrew, John, Gerret G., Eleazer and Peter; daus., Mary (wife of Eleazer Peck), Ann (wife of Daniel Francisco) and Keziah (wife of Jacob S. Pulver). Executors: wife; sons, John and Peter. Witnesses: Platt Potter, David Cay, Mark Covenhoven. (WMC 57:281-282)

1790 Census

Voorhees, Andrew   [Appendix B]
Voorhees, Garrit
Voorhees, George
Voorhees, Hendrick
Voorhees, Henry
Voorhees, James
Voorhees, Peter

VOSBURGH

Marriage

Vosburgh, Nicholaus m. Lena Dillenbach, 1/17/1796 (RDSA:203)

Birth/Baptism

Vosburg/Vosburgh, Abraham/Abram & Hendrickje/Henrica (Van Iveren): Gerrit, b. 3/22/1791, bapt. 5/8/1791 (DRC:97); Elisabet, b. 2/11/1794 (LTSA:82). Sponsors: Myndert Van Iveren & Sister Adriaentie (re:1); Peter Vosburg, Elisabet Vosburg (re:2).

Vosburgh, Evan (Canajoh. Castle) & Catharina [?]: Elisabeth, bapt. 5/28/1791 (SJC:43) Sponsors: Johannes Eker & Elisabeth Eker.

Vosburgh, Henderick & Maria (Hanson) Barent, b. 7/6/1790; bapt. 8/1/1790 (DRC:88) Sponsors: Barent Vosburgh & Engeltje Hanson

Death Record

Vosburgh, Charles Mair, (son of Myndert & Elizabeth Vosburgh), d. 4/30/1841, age 1 year 16 days; buried sect. 11, Colonial Cemetery Johnstown (JC:189)

Probate Abstract

Vosburgh, Abraham B., (of Johnstown), will dated 1/21/1825; probated 8/29/1826. Legatees: wife; Hannah; daus., Caty, Betsy and Dorothy; sons, Peter, Barent, Myndert and Harry Executors: son, Barent; Peter B. Vosburgh James Fraser[?]. Witnesses: James Fraser, Peter Mix, Abraham Lake. (WMC 57:266)

Vosburgh, Myndert, (of Johnstown), will dated 1/21/1819; probated 1/21/1824. Legatees: brother, Barent (& his sons, Henry and Myndert). Administrator: Myndert Vosburgh. Witnesses: Volkert C. and John C. Douw, Lawrence Van Allen, Barent M. Vosburgh. (WMC 57:177)

1790 Census

Vosburgh, Abraham   [Appendix B]
Vosburgh, Evert
Vosburgh, Isaac

VOSSBURY

860

COMPENDIUM

Vossbury, Henry, (of Canajoharie), will dated 6/7/1810; probated 5/21/1811. Legatees: wife [not named]; sons, Richard, Isick, Mattey, Abraham, Lambert, James, John and Peater; daus., Mary and Ginney. Executors: John T. Lenardson, John Vosbury. Witnesses: Andrew Tine, Peter Phillips. (WMC 56:381)

VOSSELER

Probate Abstract

Vosseler, Peter, (of Charleston), will dated 5/6/1813; probated 6/30/1813. Legatees: wife, Elizabeth; sons, George, Elias, Jacob and Luke; daus., Anne, Elizabeth, Polly (& her children), Charlotte (& her children). Executors: sons, George and Elias. Witnesses: Francis Carey, John Vanatta, George Folmsbee. (WMC 56:388)

VROOMAN

Marriage

Vrooman, Hendk. H. m. Elizabeth Simmons, 7/23/1779 (DRC:162)

Vrooman, Johannes m. Anna Schafer, 10/15/1781 (DRGF:195)

Vrooman, John m. Maretjie [?] (of Schoharie), 11/29/1762 (RDSA:172)

Vrooman, Martin m. Nancy Van Vechten, 1/31/1795 (RDSA:200)

Vrooman, Barent & Volkie [?]: Mary, bapt. 1/18/1739/40, d. soon after (FH:9); Hendrick, bapt. 5/16/1742 (FH:17). Sponsors: [private: no spon.] (re:1); Barent Vrooman Jr., John Vrooman, Engeltie Van Driesen (re:2).

Vrooman, Barent & Volke (Wimpel): Meyndert, bapt. 1/7/1759 (DRC:3). Sponsors: Henderk Wimpel & Aefje Wimpel.

Vrooman, Bartholomew & Catharina [?]: Geeshie, bapt. 2/15/1739/40 (FH:9). Sponsors: Simon Vrooman, Eytie Vrooman.

Vrooman, Hendrick & Engeltie [?]: Simon, bapt. 1/10/1739/40 (FH:8). Sponsors: Simon Vrooman, Andries Bratt, Eytie Vrooman.

Vrooman, Henderick & Neeltje (Veeder): Hendrick, bapt. [no date: follows 3/3/1754] (RDSA:14); Angeltje, bapt. 2/25/1760 (DRC:4); Barent, bapt. 1764 (DRC:12); Engelje, bapt. 10/21/1769 (DRC:18); Jannetje, b. 10/1/1775, bapt. 10/31/1775 (DRC:35). Sponsors: Barent Vroman, Volckjie Wemp (re:1); Petrus Van Drissen & Engeltje Van Drissen (re:2); Barent Vrooman & Volkje Vrooman (re:3); Jellis Fonda & Jannetje Fonda (re:4); Anthony Van Veghten & Maria Van Veghten (re:5).

Vrooman, Henderick B. & Alida (Coneyn): Peter Coneyn, b. 4/11/1785; bapt. 5/22/1785 (DRC:73). Sponsors: Petrus Coneyn & Susanna Coneyn.

Vrooman, Henderick B. & Maragrita (Vanderwerken): Maragrita, b. 2/20/1773, bapt. 3/15/1773 (DRC:24); Martinus, b. 11/22/1774, bapt. 12/25/1774 (DRC:31); Hendrick, b. 3/7/1776, bapt. 4/7/1776

(DRC:37); Maria, bapt. 1/9/1782 (DRC:60). Sponsors: Jacob Gardinier & Derkye Gardinier (re:1); Nicholas Dogsteder & Catrina Dogsteder (re:2); Hendrick Vrooman & Neyltje Vrooman (re:3); Mynd. Quack & Maria Quack (re:4).

Vrooman, Henderick H. & Elizabeth (Sammons): Hendk., b. 3/7/1780, bapt. 3/18/1780 (DRC:55); Rachel, b. 1/4/1782, bapt. 1/20/1782 (DRC:60); Neyltje, bapt. 6/3/1786 at age 3 weeks (DRC:80); Maria, b. 8/1/1790, bapt. 8/28/1790 (DRC:89). Sponsors: Hendk. A. Vrooman & Maria Vrooman (re:1); Sampson Simmons & Rachel Simmons (re:2); Thomas Simmons & Jannetje Simmons (re:3); [none named] (re:4).

Vrooman, Henk. & [?] [?]: Annatje, b. 7/4/1769; bapt. 7/6/1769 (RDSA:95). Sponsors: Vockje & her husband Bare[nt] Vroomann.

Vrooman, John & Annatje (Sheffler): Jacob, b. 1/20/1782, bapt. 2/9/1782 (DRC:61); Folke, b. 2/1/1787, bapt. 2/17/1787 (DRC:82 & 87). Sponsors: Abram Vrooman & Catrina Vrooman (re:1); Symon Vroom[an] & Susanna Vroo[man] (re:2).

Vrooman, Jno. & [?] (Shuffler): Joseph, bapt. 10/21/1798 (JDR:18).

Vrooman, Peter & Sarah (Van Brakelen): Gysbert, b. 5/17/1786; bapt. 6/3/1786 (DRC:80). Sponsors: Cobus Davis & Rebecca Davis.

Vrooman, Simon & Elisabeth Sitz [not married]: Seimon, b. 8/8/1782; bapt. 9/1/1782 (DRGF:61). Sponsors: Jacob Wright & Elisabeth.

Vrooman, Simon & Susanna (Keller): John, b. 3/23/1787, bapt. 4/30/1787 (DRC:84); Jacob, b. 10/18/1790, bapt. 12/25/1790 (DRC:92). Sponsors: John Kelder & Barber Kelder (re:1); John Vrooman & Annatje Vrooman (re:2).

Probate Abstract

Vrooman, Henry B., (of Johnstown), will dated 10/19/1812; probated 11/27/1813. Legatees: Helena and Margaret (my 2 youngest daus.); son, Barent H. Executors: son, Barent H.; Douw Wemple. Witnesses: Douw Wemple, Barney D. Wemple, Christopher Dockstader. (WMC 56:390)

Tryon County Militia

Vrooman, Henry B.   [Appendix A]
Vrooman, Henry H.
Vrooman, Isaac
Vrooman, John J.
Vrooman, Peter
Vrooman, Simon

Pension Abstract

Vrooman, Adam, b. 4/30/1760, son of Isaac and Dorothea (Boschkirk) Vrooman; bapt. 5/25/1760, Protestant Reformed Dutch Church, Schenectady, N.Y.; m. Englica Van Slyck, 1/5/1789, at Palatine, N.Y. by Rev. Thomas Romeyn, Pastor of the Reformed Dutch Church; d. 5/6/1836, Schenectady. (Engelica Vrooman, b. 9/14/1767; resident of Schenectady, N.Y. in 1843.) Adam enlisted from his home in Schenectady in the fall of 1776 and was a private, corporal and sergeant at various times in Capts. John Mynderse and Jellis Fonda's Cos.; he was in the battle in which Burgoyne was taken; Adam also performed garrison duty at Fort Edward, Stone Arabia, Fort Herkimer, and Schoharie; he remained in the military until the end of the war and his total service amounted to about two years. (RWPA: #W20109)

Vrooman, John J., b. 4/5/1763, Schenectady Twp., Albany Co., N.Y.; m. Amy Rowe, 11/5/1815; d. 11/10/1841, Schenectady, N.Y. (Amy Vrooman, b. 7/28/1778; resident of Schenectady in the fall of 1779 and served a one month tour of duty at Fort Paris in Stone Arabia under Capt. John Mynderse in Col. Abraham Wemple's Regt.; he enlisted again as a private on 1/1/1780 in Capt. Joseph Peek's Co. of batteaumen and was discharged on 12/24/1780; John J. entered the military once more in 1781 and was then stationed at Johnstown. (RWPA: #W25843)

Vrooman, Peter, b. 5/12/1763, Schoharie, N.Y.; m. Angelica [?], 7/12/1784, at Schoharie; d. 11/23/1838, Glen, Montgomery Co., N.Y. (Angelica Vrooman, b. 1765/6; resident of Glen, N.Y. on 4/18/1839.) Children: Adam (resident of Schoharie, N.Y. in 1852); Gilbert (resident of Jefferson Co., N.Y. in 1851 or 1857). Peter volunteered in 1778 as a private in Capt. Stubrach's Co., Col. Vrooman's Regt. and served into 1783. (RWPA: #W18673)

1790 Census

Vrooman, Abraham (2)	[Appendix B]
Vrooman, Cimon	
Vrooman, Henry B.	
Vrooman, John	
Vrooman, Martin	
Vrooman, Peter	
Vrooman, Simon I.	

V. STINBERG

Birth/Baptism

V. Stinberg, John & Maria [?]: Daniel, b. 9/16/1794 (LTSA:85). Sponsors: Daniel Weis & Elisabet.

VTTERMARK

Marriage

Vttermark, Johannes m. Margaretha Jordan, 12/10/1793 (DFP:50)

WABEL see WAFLE

WABURN

1790 Census

Waburn, Samuel	[Appendix B]

WACHTEL

Birth/Baptism

Wachtel, Johannes & Catharina [?]: Johannes,

b. 1/20/1755 (LTSA:10). Sponsors: Johannes Schauman, Anna Jordan, Elisabetha Klock.

1790 Census

Waeres, John   [Appendix B]

WAD

Birth/Baptism

Wad, Francis (Mjr.) & Lena [?]: Francis Dieterich, b. 8/20/1783; bapt. 3/6/1784 (DRGF:81). Sponsors: Nicolas P. Tyghart & Maria.

WADE

1790 Census

Wade, Edward   [Appendix B]

WADHAM

1790 Census

Wadham, Ichabod   [Appendix B]

WADSWORTH

1790 Census

Wadsworth, Israel   [Appendix B]

WAERES

WAFLE

Marriage

Wafel, Georg m. Maragretha Sprecher, 11/?/1769 (LTSA:280)

Wafel, Georg m. Maria Tygert, 2/3/1789 (RDSA:194)

Wafel, Severinus m. Dorothea Ulshoefer, 10/11/1795 (DFP:54)

Birth/ Baptism

Wabel, Han Georg & Maria Esther [?]: Joh. Henrich, b. 12/30/1757 (LTSA:22); Catharina, b. 4/7/1760, bapt. 4/13/1760 (RDSA:19); Adam, b. 7/28/1762, bapt. 8/8/1762 (RDSA:35); Wlhelm, b. 9/15/1764, bapt. 9/30/1764 (RDSA:51); Johann Georg, b. 2/?/1767, bapt. 3/1/1767 (RDSA:73); Anna Maria, b. 4/12/1769, bapt. 4/23/1769 (RDSA:94); Severinus, b. 3/3/1770, bapt. 3/4/1770 (RDSA:100). Sponsors: Henrich Baum & his wife, Anna Maria (re:1); Catharina (dau. of Henrich Dillenbach) & Henrich (son of Wilhelm Sever) (re:2); Adam Schnell & Maria Elisabeth Sever (re:3); Severinus Seeber & Elisabeth Sutz (re:4); [none named] (re:5); Anna Maria Seever & Johannes Wabel (re:6); Severinus Kasselman & Anna Maria (re:7).

Wabel, Johann Henrich & Margretha (Warmuth): Georg, b. 2/18/1783, bapt. 3/2/1783 (DRGF:68); Johann Henrich, b. 7/5/1787, bapt. 7/22/1787 (RDSA:114).

Sponsors: Georg Wabel & Maria Esther (re:1); Severinus Wabel & Catharina Noestel (re:2).

Wabel, Johannes & Margaretha [?]: Johannes, b. 9/24/1770 (LTSA:33); Johann Georg, b. 4/8/1772 (LTSA:42); Conrad, b. 6/8/1775, bapt. 6/18/1775 (LTSA:49); Catharina, b. 3/22/1778, bapt. 4/16/1778 (LTSA:52); Philip, b. 11/30/1779, bapt. 12/19/1779 (LTSA:58). Sponsors: Johannes Dillenbach & his wife (re:1); Georg Wabel & his wife (re:2); Bernhardus Kaiser, Gertraut Sprecher (re:3); Heinrich Wabel, Catharina Sprecher (re:4); Johann Casselmann, Maria Roller (re:5).

Wabel, Wilhelm & Elisabeth (Dornberger): Wilhelm, b. 1/23/1787; bapt. 2/18/1787 (RDSA:112). Sponsors: George Wabel & his wife, Esther (born: Seeber).

Death Record

Wafel, Catharina, (legitimate dau. of Wilhelm Wafel), d. 9/24/1794, age 2 years, 4 months, 24 days; buried 9/26/1794 (RDSA:235)

Probate Abstract

Wafle, John, (of Palatine), will dated 2/21/1815; probated 5/5/1819. Legatees: wife, Margaret; sons, Conradt, Adam, John, Philip, Frederick, Andrew, George and Henry; daus., Caty, Eve and Regeenam; grandson, John & granddaughter, Eve ("living with me"). Executors: son, Conradt; Andrew Dillenback. Witnesses: Jacob Eacker, Ebenezer Wentworth, Casper I. Cook. (WMC 57:168)

Tryon County Militia

Wafle, Adam   [Appendix A]
Wafle, George
Wafle, Hendrick

Wafle, Henry
Wafle, John
Wafle, William

Pension Abstract

Wafle, Henry, b. 1/1/1758; bapt. [date not given] by Rev. Ehle and "Named John Henry, When Baptized"; m. Margaret Wormuth, 4/2/1782, at Oswegatchie by Rev. Abraham Rosencrantz; d. 5/24/1841. (Margaret Wafle, b. 1762/3; resident of Canajoharie, Montgomery Co., N.Y. on 3/30/1843.) Henry enrolled in the militia at the age of seventeen years in 1775 and served as a private under Capt. John Breadbake in Col. Jacob Klock's 2nd. Regt., Tryon Co. Militia; he enlisted again in 1776 for a nine month tour of duty under Capt. Jacob W. Seeber; he fought in the battles of Oriskany and Johnstown; Henry stated that his tours of duty in the eight year war were "five years as a Militia Soldier, 9 months under Capt. Seeber as an Enlisted Soldier, and 9 months in the boat service". (RWPA: #W22526)

1790 Census

Waffle, George   [Appendix B]
Waffle, Henry
Waffle, John
Wafle, George

WAGAR

Probate Abstract

Wagar, Peter, (of Broadalbin), will dated 10/28/1795; probated 1/18/1796. Legatees: wife, Lucy; sons, Mars & Hiror; brother, Daniel; father, Nicholas. Executor: father. Witnesses: William Thompson, David Wagar,

COMPENDIUM

Daniel Wagar. (WMC 56:148)

WAGER

1790 Census

Wager, Henry   [Appendix B]

WAGGONER see WAGNER

WAGNER

Marriage

Wagner, Abraham m. Anna Billington, 2/12/1793 (DFP:48)

Wagner, Andreas m. Anna Rosina Diefendorff, 3/15/1796 (DFP:54)

Wagner, Isaac (son of Engelhardt Wagner) m. Margaretha Hauss (dau. of Adam Hauss), 5/16/1790 (DFP:42)

Wagner, Peter m. Anna Bell, 8/27/1782 (DRGF:196)

Birth/Baptism

Wagner, Fridrich & Maria Marg. [?]: Maria Elisabetha, b. 1/5/1772 (LTSA:41). Sponsors: Mich Harp, jr. & his wife; Maria Margaretha Harp.

Wagner, Friedrich & [?]: Johann Michael, bapt. 3/9/1767 (RDSA:73). Sponsors: [none named].
Wagner, Georg & [?]: Annatje, bapt. 8/10/1781

(DRGF:46). Sponsors: [?] Phleppsen & Annaje.

Wagner, Georg & Elisabeth [?]: Elisabeth, b. 10/7/1781, bapt. 10/10/1781 (DRGF:48); Anna, b. 11/6/1783, bapt. 11/12/1783 (DRGF:77). Sponsors: Pieter Wagener & Barbara Elisabeth (re:1); Pieter Nelles & Anna Waggoner (re:2).

Wagner, Jacob & Anna [?]: Hennrich, b. 6/20/1771 (LTSA:38). Sponsors: Hennrich Hasen & his wife.

Wagner, Jacob & Salome [?]: Christina, b. 2/23/1785; bapt. 3/6/1785 (DRGF:94). Sponsors: Johannes Kramer & Christina.

Wagner, Joh. Peter & Barbara Elizabetha (Dachstaeder): Johann Peter, b. 11/6/1750 (LTSA:4); Johann Georg, b. 1/17/1752 (LTSA:5); Elisabeth, b. 12/9/1753 (LTSA:8); Maria Margaretha, b. 1/26/1755 (LTSA:11); William, b. 9/22/1770 (LTSA:33). Sponsors: Peter Wagener, Sr. & his wife, Maria Margaretha (re:1); Johan Georg Becker, Catharina Dagstetter (re:2); Henrich Salzman & his wife, Maria Elisabeth (re:3); Andreas Tillenbach, Margaretha Rosner (re:4); William Nelles, jr., Catharina Engeland (re:5).

Wagner, Johann & Elisabeth [?]: Susanna, b. 3/24/1780, bapt. 4/6/1780 (LTSA:60); John, b. 4/9/1784 (LTSA:71); Elisabet, b. 5/1/1785 (LTSA:71); Peter Philip, b. 10/11/1788 (LTSA:71). Sponsors: Joh: Friederich Remai & Rebecca (re:1); Jost Wagner, Maria Lampman (re:2); Peter Lampman & Elisabet (re:3); Philip Jacob Groz, Pf. & Margaret (re:4).

Wagner, Jost & Anna Gress [unmarried widow]: Anna, b. 11/27/1781; bapt. 11/30/1781 (DRGF:50). Sponsors: Johannes

Wallrath & his wife, Anna.

Wagner, Jost & Catarina [?]: Johannes, b. 10/6/1793 (LTSA:80). Sponsors: Johannes Schulz & Catarina.

Wagner, Peter & Anna Margaretha/Maria Margaretha (Laues) [Note: Wife's first name appears both ways as shown above.]: Anna Margaretha, b. 4/15/1712 (LTSA:3); Maria Catharina, b. 8/18/1714 (LTSA:3); Utilia, b. 8/16/1716 (LTSA:3); Catharina Elisabetha, b. 9/10/1718 (LTSA:3); Maria Magdalena, b. 1/4/1720 (LTSA:3); Johann Peter, b. 1/8/1722 (LTSA:3); Maria Elisabetha, b. 1/24/1724 (LTSA:3). Sponsors: Christian Gerlag & his wife, Anna Margaretha (re:1); Jerg Ecker, Maria Catharina Jung, Maria Lies Lauks (re:2); Rudolph Lilof & his wife, Utilia (re:3); Lampert Sternberger, Anna Lies Haus, Catharina Leer (re:4); Peter Gloss & his wife, Maria Magdalena (re:5); Peter Knieskern, Gottfried Fidler, Maria Lies Knieskern (re:6); Henrich Fox[?], Maria Lise Mann (re:7).

Wagner, Peter, Jr. & Anna (Bell) [Note: m. 1782]: Peter, b. 12/11/1782 (LTSA:63), bapt. 12/15/1782 (DRGF:64); Catharina, b. 4/10/1784 (LTSA:63); Johann Jost, b. 8/5/1785 (LTSA:63); William, b. 1/21/1787 (LTSA:63); Magdalena, b. 7/29/1788 (LTSA:63); Jerg Heinrich, b. 4/21/1790 (LTSA:63). Sponsors: Jost Waggoner, Maria Bell (re:1); John W. Nelles, Catharina Wagoner (re:2); George Wagner, Elisabeth Wagner (re:3); William W. Nelles, Maria Nelles (re:4); Wilh. Nelles, Magdalena Waggoner (re:5); Wilhelm Conneham, Catharina Deichert (re:6).

Death Record

Wagner, [?], (child of Engelhard Waggoner), d. 2/18/1811, age 9 months (DFP:94)

Wagner, [?], (widow, lived to see 81 grandchildren & 10 great grandchildren), d. 7/4/1809, age 68 years (DFP:93)

Wagner, Andrew, d. 8/?/1808, age 39 years, 1 month; buried 8/15/1808 (DFP:92)

Wagner, Christina, b. 2/23/1785; d. 9/7/1796; buried 9/9/1796 (DFP:90)

Wagner, Joseph, Jr., d. 6/13/1853, age 63 years; buried Fort Plain Cemetery, Minden (FPC 56:43i)

Wagner, Minerva Riggs, (wife of Joseph Wagner, Jr.), d. 9/21/1842, age 43 years; buried Fort Plain Cemetery, Minden (FPC 56:43i)

Probate Abstract

Waggoner, Andrew, (of Canajoharie), will dated 8/8/1808; probated 3/10/1809. Legatees: wife, Catherine; son, Henry; daus., Anna Rozina, Lany and Mary. Executors: brother, Jacob; Nicholas Rese. Witnesses: Amasa Millard, Henry Burns, George Wagner. (WMC 56:159)

Waggoner, George, (of Palatine), will dated 7/21/1819; probated 2/28/1826. Legatees: wife, Mary; sons, George, William and Peter; daus., Nancy (wife of Peter Lautman), Caty (wife of Charles Waggoner), Mary (wife of Augustus Devendorf) and Peggy (wife of Benjamin Loucks). Executors: children and friends, William Waggoner, George Waggoner, Augustus Devendorf. Witnesses: John W. Ehle, John G. Walruth, Jr., Rudolph Devendorf. (WMC 57:185)

Waggoner, Peter, (of Palatine), will dated

COMPENDIUM

6/5/1816; probated 3/10/1827. Legatees: wife, Anna; sons, Nicholas, Peter, Joseph, William, Henry, John, Jacob and Abraham; brother, Joseph; daus., Cathrina (wife of Han Jost Bell), Magdalena (wife of Wm. I. Walrath). Executors: sons, Peter and Henry; George and Nicholas. Witnesses: William Waggoner, Peter W. Nellis, Peter P. Fox (WMC 57:267)

Waggoner, Peter G., (of Palatine), will dated 8/23/1821; probated 2/27/1822. Legatees: wife, Mary; son, James Henry. Executors: wife; Peter Ehle, Jr., George Waggoner. Witnesses: Philip Knapp, Benjamin Loucks, Joseph Waggoner, Nicholas Gross. (WMC 57:173)

Waggoner, Peter Phillip, (of the town of Palatine), will dated 2/11/1826; probated 6/13/1826. Legatees: wife, Polly; sons, Nathan, Edward and Azariah; daus., Mary (a cripple), Lucinda, Julian and Emelia. Executors: wife; John and William Waggoner. Witnesses: John Nellis, Peter C. Fox, John Waggoner. (WMC 57:265)

Wagner, Peter, (of Palatine), will dated 4/5/1806; codicil dated 5/8/1808; probated 6/15/1813. Legatees: wife, Barbara; sons, Peter, George, Hanjost and John; daus., Elizabeth (wife of Andrew Nellis), Margaret (wife of Henry I. [or J.] Klock), Anna (wife of Casper Leib), Maria (wife of William W. Nellis), Catharine (wife of William Saltsman) and Magdalena (wife of William I. [or J.] Nellis); grandsons, Peter G. and William P. Waggoner, John C. Leib. Executors: sons, Peter and George; Peter Grembs, Jr., Richard Young. Witnesses: John Fyckel, Peter W. Fox, George Barsh. (WMC 56:388)

Tryon County Militia

Wagner, Engelhard   [Appendix A]
Wagner, Englehardt
Wagner, George
Wagner, Isaac
Wagner, Jacob
Wagner, Joseph
Wagner, Peter

Pension Abstract

Waggoner, Jacob, b. 2/21/1762, Lancaster, Pa.; (brother: George Waggoner); m. Salome Cronnern, 7/6/1783 in a blockhouse near the stone church in Palatine, N.Y.; resident of Minden, Montgomery Co., N.Y. where he died 5/5/1833. (Salome Waggoner, b. 4/14/1763; resident of Danube, Herkimer Co., N.Y. on 4/22/1840.) Children: Christina, b. 2/23/1784; Elizabeth, b. 12/25/1786; Maria, b. 10/22/1788; Jacob, b. 4/8/1791; Anna, b. 7/27/1793; Abraham, b. 5/6/1798 (m. 1819; resident of Danube, N.Y. in 1840); Felix, b. 2/25/1802; John, b. 5/22/1804; Nensi, b. 10/25/1806 (m. [?] Hall). Jacob enlisted from Canajoharie in 1778 and was a private under Lts. Godlip Snyder and Jacob Snyder, Capts. Jacob Diefendorff, John Danney, Cols. Clyde, Dayton, Willett and Hay; he fought in the battle of Johnstown and in the skirmish at West Canada Creek. (RWPA: #W22528)

Wagner, George, b. 1760/1, son of Engelhart Wagner; (sister: Elizabeth, b. ca. 1774; m. [?] Casler and living in Oneida Co., N.Y. in 1846); m. Mary [?], 1783-1786; d. 12/30/1834 or 12/31/1834, Western, Oneida Co., N.Y. (Mary Wagner, d. 9/14/1832, Fort Plain, Montgomery Co., N.Y.) Children: John, b. 1787/8 (resident of Montgomery Co., N.Y. in 1852); Daniel, b. 1800/1 (resident of Onondaga Co., N.Y. in 1846); Mary (m. Nicholas Reese and resident of Oneida Co. in 1846); Betsey, Nancy Wagner (both deceased by 1846).

868

George enlisted in July 1777 as a substitute for his father and was a private in Capt. Henry Dieffendorf's Co., Col. Ebenezer Cox's 1st. Regt., Tryon Co. Militia; he fought in the battle of Oriskany and was wounded in the left thigh by a musket ball which fractured the bone, after which he returned home disabled for ten months; George again enlisted in the spring of 1780 for eleven months as a private in Capt. Bigbread's Co. of the same regiment under the command of Col. Samuel Clyde [following the death of Col. Cox at the battle of Oriskany]; he again entered the military in the spring of 1781 for a tour of duty that lasted for nineteen months in Capt. Gerrit Putnam's Co., Col. Willett's Regt.; George also fought in the battle of Johnstown and was in the skirmish at West Canada Creek. (RWPA: #S23989)

Wagner, Joseph, son of Col. Peter Waggoner; m. Catharine Gibson, 9/13/1835, at the residence of Harvey Hyuck in Herkimer by Rev. Spinner [the bride and groom were both residents of Fort Plain, Montgomery Co., N.Y.]; d. on or about 8/15/1848. Joseph served in Col. Marinus Willett's Regt. and in 1781 he was sent in pursuit of the enemy at the time of the "Genl. Conflagration around about Fort Timmerman" and fought in the battles of Lampman's in July and Johnstown on October 25th.; he was also stationed at Fort Snell and "at different Houses at Stonearabia"; George continued to serve on various tours of duty until the end of the war. (RWPA: #W2499)

1790 Census

Waggoner, George (2)	[Appendix B]
Waggoner, Honyost	
Waggoner, Inglehart	
Waggoner, Jacob	
Waggoner, John	

Waggoner, Peter

WAIT

Probate Abstract

Wait, Joseph, (of Broadalbin), will dated 4/18/1828; probated 10/21/1828. Legatees: wife, Abigail; sons, George, Clark, Beriah, Joseph, Jr., Walter, Stephen and Peleg; grandson, Benjamin (of George); sister-in-law, Nancy Clark. Executors: sons, Peleg and Clark. Witnesses: John Kennady, Joseph Blair, Salathiel Cole. (WMC 57:272)

1790 Census

Wait, John	[Appendix B]

WAITON

1790 Census

Waiton, John	[Appendix B]

WALDEN

Birth/Baptism

Walden, Nathaniel & Margreth [?]: John, b. 6/2/1785; bapt. 6/5/1785 (DRGF:97). Sponsors: Arendt Rolings & Catharina.

1790 Census

Walden, Nathaniel	[Appendix B]

WALDER

Birth/Baptism

Walder, Marinus & [?]: Margaret, bapt. 7/8/1778 (JDR:19).

WALDO

Birth/Baptism

Waldo, Horatio & Margaret S. [?] [b. 4/7/1773; bapt. 8/23/1801] (JPC:20): Horatio, b. 3/26/1800; bapt. 8/23/1801 (JPC:20).

Death Record

Waldo, Dwight Ripley, d. 3/23/1824, age 28 years; buried Cherry Valley Presbyterian Church cemetery (PCV:81)

Waldo, Peter, (at St. Augustine, E.F.), d. 2/20/1823, age 17 years; buried Cherry Valley Presbyterian Church cemetery (PCV:79)

Waldo, Peter Orlando, (infant), d. 4/22/1823, age [not stated]; buried Cherry Valley Presbyterian Church cemetery (PCV:79)

WALDON

1790 Census

Waldon, Simon   [Appendix B]

WALDORF

Birth/Baptism

Waldorf/Waldorff, Martin & Margaretha [?]: Maria, b. 4/19/1769, bapt. 10/21/1769 (RDSA:97); Martin, b. 2/27/1772 (LTSA:42). Sponsors: Johannes Gotz & Maria Servus (re:1); Peter Servos, Capt. & his wife (re:2).

Tryon County Militia

Woldorf, Johannes   [Appendix A]

WALKER

Marriage

Walker, Ephraim m. Elisabeth Killey, 10/?/1792 (DFP:46)

Walker, John m. Catharine McIntyre, 3/20/1794 (JPC:90)

Walker, Samuel m. Maria Haas, 12/26/1781 (DRGF:195)

Birth/Baptism

Walker, Daniel & Elizabeth (Robertson): Gilbert, b. 2/25/1788, bapt. 8/10/1788 (JPC:2); John, b. 5/21/1789, bapt. 8/23/1789 (JPC:3); Jean, b. 10/30/1790, bapt. 3/13/1791 (JPC:4); Janet, b. 8/8/1792, bapt. 9/30/1792 (JPC:6); Margaret, b. 1/29/1794, bapt. 3/16/1794 (JPC:9); Catharine, b. 10/18/1799, bapt. 12/8/1799 (JPC:16); Alexander, b. 10/12/1801, bapt. 11/15/1801 (JPC:20).

Walker, David & Elizabeth [?]: William, bapt. 9/26/1779 (JDR:24); Christian, bapt. 11/20/1785 (JDR:10) [Note: parents of Johnstown for the foregoing baptisms]; Ann, bapt. 6/27/1790 (JPC:3); John, b. 6/7/1792, bapt. 8/26/1792 (JPC:6); Elizabeth, b. 4/20/1801, bapt. 6/31/1801 (JPC:20).

Walker [Waker in record], Edward (Lake Otsego) & Gertrud [?]: Anna Eva, bapt. 6/27/1790 (SJC:29). Sponsors: Adam Eker & Margretha Eker.

Walker, John & Catharine [?]: Elizabeth, b. 2/24/1795, bapt. 3/?/1795 (JPC:11); Gilbert, b. 1/14/1797, bapt. 3/?/1797 (JPC:10); Jean, b. 11/23/1798, bapt. 3/3/1799 (JPC:14); Duncan, b. 11/4/1800, bapt. 2/8/1801 (JPC:19).

Walker, Stephen & [?]: William, bapt. 4/7/1793 (JPC:7); Stephen, bapt. 4/7/1793 (JPC:7).

Death Record

Walker, David, d. 8/15/1839, age 87 years, 3 days; buried sect. 3, Colonial Cemetery, Johnstown (JC:189)

Walker, Elizabeth, (wife of David Walker), d. 11/19/1813, age 57 years; buried sect. 3, Colonial Cemetery, Johnstown (JC:189)

1790 Census

Walker, David   [Appendix B]
Walker, Edward
Walker, George
Walker, Jeremiah
Walker, Phineas

WALL

Marriage

Wall, Edward m. Deborah Butler, 7/6/1772 (DRC:158)

Birth/Baptism

Wall, Wilhelm/William & Elisabeth (Keller): Johannes, b. 6/5/1790, bapt. 6/13/1790 (SJC:28); Maria, bapt. 4/29/1792 (SJC:58) [Note: parents of Yukersbusch]; Gottfried, b. 9/18/1794 (LTSA:86). Sponsors: Johannes Scheffer & Catharina Joran (re:1); Michel Keller & Sarah Keller (re:2); Gottfried Khni & Maria (re:3).

WALLACE

Birth/Baptism

Wallace, Jacobus & Catharina (Stenzel): Catharina, bapt. 3/2/1751 (RDSA:10); Jean, bapt. 9/16/1752 (RDSA:13). Sponsors: Georg Schnell, Elisabetha Stensel (re:1); Colonel Wilhelm Jenson, Werner Deigert & his wife, Helena (re:2).

Wallace, William & Catrina (Miller): John, b. 3/7/1783; bapt. 4/5/1783 (DRC:65). Sponsors: [none named].

1790 Census

Wallace, William   [Appendix B]

WALLASON

1790 Census

Wallason, Christian   [Appendix B]

COMPENDIUM

WALLISER

Birth/Baptism

Walliser, Anton & Elisabetha [?]: Antonius, b. 8/4/1770 (LTSA:32). Sponsors: Christian Ruff & his wife.

Walliser, Michael & Anna Maria [?]: Johann Nicolaus, b. 7/13/1768, bapt. 7/17/1768 (RDSA:88); Maria Catharina, b. & bapt. [obliterated: 1770 period] (RDSA:104); Maria Elisabetha, b. 4/12/1773 (LTSA:45). Sponsors: Johann Nicol Kieltz & Catharina (re:1); Johann Nicol Giels & Catharina (re:2); Philip Kils & his wife (re:3).

WALLRATH

Marriage

Wallrath, Adolph m. Anna Fink (widow), 12/26/1781 (DRGF:195)

Wallrath, Adolph m. Elisabeth Pottmann, 3/21/1770 (RDSA:188)

Wallrath, Gerrit m. Anna Zimmermann, 8/5/1770 (RDSA:189)

Wallrath, Henry Johann m. Maria H. Bell (dau. of Geo. H. Bell), 1/14/1783 (RDSA:191; DRGF:197)

Wallrath, Jacob m. Anna Zoller, 10/25/1795 (DFP:54)

Wallrath, Jacob m. Maria Oharon, 4/17/1770 (LTSA:281)

Wallrath, Jacob Adolph m. Elisabeth Fheling

(dau. of Jacob Fheling), 10/26/1784 (DRGF:200)

Wallrath, Jacob H. m. Rebecca Van Slyk (dau. of Harm. Van Slyk), 9/11/1785 (DRGF:202)

Wallrath, Joh: Peter Joh: m. Maria Catharina W: Tyghart, 11/17/1784 (DRGF:200)

Wallrath, Johannes m. Elisabetha Etz, 7/16/1767 (RDSA:182)

Wallrath, Johannes, Jr. m. Maria Nelles, 12/16/1768 (RDSA:186)

Wallrath, John m. Elisabeth Lindner, 6/8/1794 (DFP:52)

Wallrath, John Gerhardt m. Catharina Dygert (from Stonearabia), 5/14/1795 (DFP:53)

Wallrath, Wilhelm m. Margaretha Schunk, 10/23/1792 (DFP:46)

Birth/Baptism

Wallrath, Adam (of Palatine) & Magdalena (Klock): David, bapt. 1/14/1790 (SJC:22); Daniel, bapt. 2/26/1792 (SJC:55). Sponsors: Christoph Fox & Catharina Fox (re:1); Adaolph Wallrath & Maria Wallrath (re:2).

Wallrath, Adolph & Anna (Zimmerman): Elisabeth, b. 12/13/1784, bapt. 12/26/1784 (DRGF:91); Margaretha, bapt. 8/23/1790 (SJC:31); Jacob, bapt. 7/1/1793 (SJC:78) [Note: parents of Palatine for bapts. 2 & 3]. Sponsors: Petrus Wallrath & Elisabeth Zimmermann (re:1); John Adam Nelles & Elisabeth Nelles (re:2); Jacob Zimmerman & Magdalena Zimmerman (re:3).

Wallrath, Adolph & Catharina [?]: Maria, b.

9/2/1783; bapt. 9/8/1783 (DRGF:74). Sponsors: Henrich Nelles & Christina.

Wallrath, Adolph & Catrina (Bronnel): Anna, b. 3/8/1785; bapt. 5/22/1785 (DRC:73). Sponsors: [none named].

Wallrath, Adolph & Elisabetha [?]: Jacob, b. 5/11/1771 (LTSA:36). Sponsors: Jacob Wallrad & his wife.

Wallrath, Adolph (of Palatine) & Maria [?]: Adolph Beckman, bapt. 8/26/1792 (SJC:63). Sponsors: Cornelis & Catharina Beckmann.

Wallrath, Frederick (of Canaj. Castle) & Catharina [?]: Elisabeth, bapt. 7/19/1789 (SJC:16). Sponsors: Conrad & Elisabeth Killes.

Wallrath, Friedrich & Catharina [?]: Georg Friedrich, b. 3/3/1770, bapt. 3/8/1770 (RDSA:101); Anna, b. 8/31/1782, bapt. 9/5/1782 (DRGF:61). Sponsors: George Friedrich Hajer & Margretha (re:1); Georg Wallrath & Anna (re:2).

Wallrath, George (of Canajoh. Castle) & Anna (Leip): Heinrich, bapt. 3/1/1790 (SJC:23); Daniel, bapt. 9/2/1792 (SJC:63). Sponsors: Heinrich Dysalin & Anna Margretha Leip (re:1); Johann Wallrath & Catharina Wallrath (re:2).

Wallrath, Gerhard F. & Anna [?]: William, b. 9/2/1771 (LTSA:38); Catharina, b. 11/11/1781, bapt. 11/11/1781 (DRGF:50); Catharina, b. 11/4/1782, bapt. 11/6/1782 (DRGF:64). Sponsors: William Wallrad & Margaretha (Jacob Jungs dau.) (re:1); Henrich Walrad & Catharina (re:2); Henrich Wallrath & Catharina (re:3).

Wallrath, Henrich & Elisabeth [?]: Johann

Friedrich, b. 7/22/1782; bapt. 8/24/1782; d. 8/24/1782 (DRGF:60). Sponsors: Friedrich Wallrath & Catharina.

Wallrath, Henrich & Elisabetha Catharina [?]: Adolphus, b. 4/4/1761, bapt. 4/4/1761 (RDSA:26); Elisabetha, b. 8/5/1764, bapt. 8/12/1764 (RDSA:49); Petrus, b. 8/6/1766, bapt. 8/17/1766 (RDSA:67); Johannis, b. 10/13/1768, bapt. 10/23/1768 (RDSA:91); Johannes, b. 6/30/1770, bapt. 6/30/1770 (RDSA:103); Henrich, b. 6/26/1771 (LTSA:37). Sponsors: Johannes Walrad & Margaretha Glock (re:1); Johann Jost Klock & Elisabeth Warmuth (re:2); Peter Wagner & Barbara Elisabetha (re:3); Johannis Frey, Christina Finck & Anna Klock (re:4); Hermanus Van [?] & Elisabeth (re:5); Hennrich Frey & his wife (re:6).

Wallrath, Henrich & Maria [?]: Nicolas Bell, b. 11/26/1783; bapt. 11/30/1783 (DRGF:78). Sponsors: Henrich Uhly & Christina Bell, widow.

Wallrath, Henrich & Maria [?]: Pieter, b. 11/4/1783; bapt. 11/9/1783 (DRGF:76). Sponsors: Pieter Knieskern & Lea.

Wallrath, Henry (German Flats) & Anna [?]: Johann Jacob, b. 6/22/1792; bapt. 7/22/1792 (SJC:61). Sponsors: Peter Bauman & Margretha Gerlach.

Wallrath, Isaac & Margaretha (Nellis): Wilhelm, b. 4/12/1787; bapt. 4/15/1787 (RDSA:113). Sponsors: [none named].

Wallrath, Jacob & Gertraud [?]: Johannes, b. 8/26/1782, bapt. 8/28/1782 (DRGF:61); Johann Jost, b. 1/7/1785, bapt. 1/10/1785 (DRGF:92). Sponsors: Johannes Wallrath & Maria (re:1); Jost Hauss & Elisabeth (re:2).

Wallrath, Jacob & Magdalena [?]: Isaac, b. 10/5/1754 (LTSA:10); Lea, b. ?/26/1756 [between entries in Oct.] (LTSA:20); Rahel, b. 9/3/1760, bapt. 9/14/1760 (RDSA:22); Magdalena, b. 2/8/1762, bapt. 2/21/1762 (RDSA:32); Petrus, b. 6/9/1764, bapt. 6/14/1764 (RDSA:38); Jonas, b. 2/8/1766, bapt. 2/16/1766 (RDSA:61); Amalia, b. 9/29/1767, bapt. 10/4/1767 (RDSA:78). Sponsors: Isaac Barri, Rahel Pickert (re:1); Isaac Berri, Lea Pickert (re:2); Eva (dau. of Dam Devi) & Johannes (son of Johannes Walrad) (re:3); Magdalena Walrad & Wilhelm Sever (re:4); Johannes Wallrad & Amalia (re:5); Wilhelm Teughard & Elisabeth Ecker (re:6); Georg Hickki & Maria Sutz (re:7).

Wallrath, Jacob & Maria [?]: Jacob, b. 5/12/1783, bapt. 5/13/1783 (DRGF:71); Maria Elisabetha, b. 5/12/1783, bapt. 5/13/1783 (DRGF:71); Georg, b. 9/6/1784, bapt. 12/25/1784 (DRGF:91); Adolph, b. 8/4/1791 (LTSA:69). Sponsors: Jerg Ekert & Catharina (re:1); Jacob Jung & Maria (re:2); Pieter Westerman & Maria Elisabetha (re:3); Georg Wallrath & Anna (re:4).

Wallrath, Jacob (of Geisberg) & Maria [?]: Margaretha, bapt. 5/17/1789 (SJC:15). Sponsors: Niclaus Dachstetter & Margretha Dachstetter.

Wallrath, Jacob, Jr. & Rebecca [?]: Andreas Reber, b. 6/10/1791 (LTSA:68). Sponsors: Andreas Reber & his wife.

Wallrath, Joh. Adam & Lena [?]: Georg, b. 2/4/1782, bapt. 2/10/1782 (DRGF:54); Christian, b. 7/29/1784, bapt. 8/9/1784 (DRGF:86). Sponsors: Georg Glock & Catharina (re:1); Joh: Christ Aetsch & Dorothea (re:2).

Wallrath, Johannes & Amalia (Sutz): Adolph, bapt. 5/20/1752 (RDSA:12); Johann Peter, b. 4/23/1757 (LTSA:21); Henrious, b. 4/3/1760, bapt. 4/13/1760 (RDSA:19); Isaacus, b. 11/15/1762, bapt. 12/5/1762 (RDSA:36). Sponsors: Adam Wallrad & his wife, Anna Barbara (re:1); Joh. Peter Suz, Dorodea Crims (re:2); Henrich Walrad & his wife, Catharina (re:3); Isaac Paris & his wife (re:4).

Wallrath, Johannes & Elisabeth [?]: Christian, b. 1/20/1784; bapt. 1/25/1784 (DRGF:79). Sponsors: Christian [?] & Maria [?].

Wallrath, Nicholas & Anna Barbara [?]: Maria, b. 7/18/1772 (LTSA:44); Margaretha, b. 1/1/1775, bapt. 1/8/1775 (LTSA:48); Catharina, b. 6/28/1778, bapt. 7/5/1778 (LTSA:53); Anna, b. 2/9/1780, bapt. 2/19/1780 (LTSA:60); Rachel, b. 4/6/1782, bapt. 4/7/1782 (DRGF:56); Johannes, b. 9/11/1783, bapt. 10/9/1783 (DRGF:75); Georg, b. 6/2/1796 (LTSA:97). Sponsors: Nicolaus Weser, Maria Schulz (re:1); Isaac Wallrath, Margaretha Siz (re:2); Johan Schulz, jr., Rahel Wallrath (re:3); George Schultz & Catharina (re:4); Henrich Schultz & Catharina Walrath (re:5); Magdalena, widow of Johannes Schultz (re:6); Georg Schulz & Catarina (re:7).

Wallrath, Petrus H. & Eva [?]: Petrus, b. 9/18/1793 (LTSA:80). Sponsors: Peter Hillegas & Catarina.

Wallrath, R[u]dolph & Elisabeth [?]: Elisabetha, b. 11/24/1778; bapt. 12/2/1778 (DRGF:33). Sponsors: John Smidt & Elisabeth.

Wallrath, Wilhelm & [?]: Abraham, b. 10/8/1784; bapt. 10/11/1784 (DRGF:88). Sponsors: Georg Waggner & Maria.

Death Record

Wallrath, Amalia, (widow), b. 2/26/1714; d. 3/5/1795, age 81 years, 7 days; (left behind 12 children, 52 grandchildren & 3 great grandchildren); buried 3/7/1795 (DFP:86)

Wallrath, Elisabeth, (dau. of Peter Wallrad), d. 3/?/1811, age 1 year, 10 months, 3 days; buried 3/27/1811 (DFP:94)

Wallrath, Elisabeth, (wife of Henry Wallrath), b. 7/28/1742; d. 11/8/1808, age 66 years, 3 months, 8 days; (had 14 children: 9 sons & 5 daus.; 43 grandchildren); buried 11/9/1809 (DFP:92)

Wallrath, Gerret, d. 7/8/1806, age 39 years (DFP:91)

Wallrath, Heinrich, b. 1737; m. 1758; d. 1/3/1791; buried 1/5/1791 (RDSA:232)

Wallrath, Henry, b. 2/11/1753; d. 2/26/1792; buried 2/28/1792 (DFP:82)

Wallrath, Jacob, (legitimate son of Isaac Wallrath), b. 5/15/1785; d. 8/4/1789; buried 8/6/1789 (RDSA:231)

Wallrath, Jacob, b. 10/29/1794; d. 9/7/1796; buried 9/9/1796 (DFP:90)

Wallrath, Jacob, b. 2/25/1723, [New York]; m. 6/27/1742; d. 2/1/1790 (died suddenly); buried 2/3/1790 (RDSA:231)

Wallrath, Jacob H., d. 12/?/1812, age 68 years (Had 13 children: 6 dead & 7 alive; & 15 grandchildren); buried 12/2/1812 (DFP:95)

Probate Abstract

Wallrath, John J., (of Palatine), will dated 11/11/1806; probated 9/11/1809. Legatees: wife, Maria; dau., Catharine. Executors: wife; George Eaker. Witnesses: Peter Walrad, John Walratt, Jr., John Fikel. (WMC 56:160)

Walradt, Adolph I. [J.?], (of Canajoharie), will dated 8/20/1812; probated 8/18/1814. Legatees: wife, Catherine; sons, Abraham, Peter (& his son, David); daus., Caty, Polly (& her children). Executors: Joseph White, Lester Holt, Delos White. Witnesses: Menzo White, Joel Norton, Printiss Leonard. (WMC 56:392)

Walradt, Garret, (of Minden), will dated 2/18/1819; probated 5/17/1819. Legatees: wife, Lidia; son, Jacob G. Executors: Jacob I., Jacob G. and Honpeter I. Walrath. Witnesses: Jacob Walrath, Peter Walrad, John C. Yordan. (WMC 57:168)

Walradt, Henry, (of Minden), will dated 4/14/1815; probated 1/19/1822. Legatees: sons, Adam, Peter H. and Jacob; daus., Anna (wife of Henry Moyer), Catharine (wife of Henry I. Dollar), Margaret (wife of Solomon Satman), Mary (wife of Stephen Scubee/Scribee[?]), Elizabeth (widow of Moses Van Campen). Executors: sons, Adam and Peter; Peter T. Moyer. Witnesses: Jacob Bonotadt, Adam M. Conterman, Christopher Glazier. (WMC 57:173)

Walradth, William, (of Canajoharie), will dated 8/11/1802; probated 11/19/1802. Legatees: wife, Cathreen; sons, Peter, Abraham and Garret; dau., Elizabeth Seeber. Executors: wife; Adolph Walradth, Peter Walradth. Witnesses: Peeter and Adolph Walrad, Charles Powell. (WMC 56:151-152)

Walrath, Adam A., (of Oppenheim), will dated ?/?/1818; probated 10/19/1822. Legatees: wife,

COMPENDIUM

Lenah; sons, George A., Anthony A., Henry A., Christian A., David A., Adam A., and Jacob A.; dau., Lenah Bellinger. Executors: Jacob H. Failing, John F. Bellinger, Peter Klock. Witnesses: William Brewster, Charles Devoe, George G. Klock, Jr. (WMC 57:174-175)

Walrath, Jacob H., (of Canajoharie), will dated 6/29/1810; probated 4/22/1815. Legatees: wife, Mariah; sons, Gasper, Adolf, George and John; daus., Elizabeth, Caty and Margaret. Executors: Christian Etz, John C. Flack. (WMC 56:394)

Walrath, Peter H., (of Palatine), will dated 3/16/1831; codicil dated 4/16/1831; probated 8/1/1831. Legatees: wife, Eva; sons, Peter P. and William P.; daus., Caty (wife of Gilbert Storms), Eva (wife of Thomas Easton), Betsy (wife of Caleb Davidson), Nancy (wife of Henry Fuller), Margaret (wife of David W. Fuller, decd., & her sons, Alva and Peter and dau., Mary Ann), and Barbara (wife of Jesse Mattoon). Executors: William P.; sons-in-law, Thomas Easton and David W. Fuller. Witnesses: George G. Eacker, Ephraim Vedder, Nicholas N. Coppernoll (for both will and codicil). (WMC 57:279)

Tryon County Militia

Wallrath, Adam   [Appendix A]
Wallrath, Frederick
Wallrath, George
Wallrath, Gerhart
Wallrath, Henrich
Wallrath, Henry
Wallrath, Isaac
Wallrath, Jacob
Wallrath, Jacob H.
Wallrath, Johannes
Wallrath, John

Wallrath, Nicholas
Wallrath, Peter
Wallrath, William

Pension Abstract

Wallrath, Adolph, b. 4/4/1761; m. Anna [widow of Christian Fink who had been killed in the battle of Oriskany], 2/26/1781; resident of Oppenheim, Montgomery Co., N.Y. in 1832; d. 6/15/1837. (Anna Wallrath, b. 1754/5; resident of Pamelia, Jefferson Co., N.Y. on 5/24/1839.) Adolph entered the military from his home in Palatine and served at various times from 1777 to 1782; he was a private under Capts. Breadbake, Miller, Lipe and Zilley in the regiments of Cols. Klock, Wagoner, Clyde, Brown and Willett; Adolph marched on the Sullivan expedition and he fought in the battles of Stone Arabia, Johnstown and West Canada Creek. (RWPA: #W18275)

Wallrath, Isaac, b. 3/14/1757; m. Margretha Nellis, 8/29/1784; d. 10/21/1841. (Margretha Wallrath, b. 1752/3; resident of Palatine, Montgomery Co., N.Y. on 5/22/1843.) Children: Jacob, b. 5/5/1785; William, bapt. 4/12/1787. Isaac enlisted as a private in 1775 and served various tours of duty in Capt. John Hess' Co., Col. Jacob Klock's 2nd. Regt., Tryon Co. Militia; his total service time amounted to about six years. (RWPA: #W18287)

Wallrath, Jacob H., b. 1756 or 11/17/1758, Palatine District, N.Y.; resident of St. Johnsville, Montgomery Co. on 11/8/1842; moved to the State of Illinois in 1845 and was living in Raymond, Racine Co., Wisconsin in 1847. Jacob H. stated that he enlisted in the spring of 1776 as a private in Capt. John Breadbake's Co., Col. Jacob Klock's 2nd.

876

Regt., Tryon Co. Militia and was made a
corporal in 1777, a rank he held through 1778;
he fought in the battle of Oriskany where he
was wounded in the right shoulder by a musket
ball. Jacob H. was denied a pension because he
failed to furnish the required proof of service.
(RWPA: #R11093)

Walrath, Peter, b. 5/30/1756; resident of
Canajoharie, Montgomery Co., N.Y. when he
applied for a pension on 8/18/1832. Peter
enlisted from his home in Palatine in early
1776 and served as a private in Col. Jacob
Klock's 2nd. Regt., Tryon Co. Militia; he was
a participant in the battles of Oriskany, Turlock
and Johnstown. (RWPA: #S11684)

Deed Abstract

Walrath, Catharine, wife of Hendrick Walrath,
and Lena Walrath, wife of Adam A. Walrath,
both of Palatine District, Montgomery Co. to
Jacob G. Klock, Esq., of the same place. Deed
dated 12/16/1786; recorded 12/20/1786.
Description: (Whereas the N.Y. State
Legislature passed an Act on 5/5/1786 making
it lawful for George Klock & Jacob G. Klock
of Montgomery Co., and John Van Sice of
Albany Co., to locate 48,000 acres of land out
of any ungranted lands in Montgomery Co. and
alledged to have been conveyed to them by
deed dated 5/28/1766. And whereas George
Klock on 8/3/1786 conveyed to Catharine
Walrath and Lena Walrath, each 2,286 acres,
being one-seventh part each of his [George
Klock's] share of the said 48,000 acres.) The
said grantors have now sold all the said two-
seventh parts of (4,572 acres) of land above
mentioned. Consideration: L400. Signed:
Catharina X Walrath, Adam A. Walrath, Lena
Walrath. Witnesses: John D. Fort, Jacob
Failing. (MVL:39)

1790 Census

Walradt, Adam   [Appendix B]
Walradt, Adolph (2)
Walradt, Adolph, Jr.
Walradt, Frederick
Walradt, Frederick A.
Walradt, Garrit
Walradt, George
Walradt, Henry W.
Walradt, Isaac
Walradt, Jacob
Walradt, Jacob A.
Walradt, Jacob H.
Walradt, John (2)
Walradt, John H.
Walradt, John Peter
Walradt, John S.
Walradt, Nicholas
Walradt, Peter
Walradt, Peter H.
Walradt, William

WALSWORTH

1790 Census

Walsworth, Elisha   [Appendix B]
Walsworth, Griswell
Walsworth, James
Walsworth, Jessee

WALTENBERGER

Marriage

Waltenberger, Georg m. Sussanna Weiss,
4/21/1768 (RDSA:184)

877

COMPENDIUM

WALTER

Marriage

Walter, Adam m. Elisabeth Hurtig, 8/8/1790 (RDSA:195)

Birth/Baptism

Walter, Adam & Elisabet [?]: Catarina, b. 7/4/1791 (LTSA:68). Sponsors: Wilhelm Fuchs & Anna Eva.

Walter, Christian & [?]: Mary, bapt. 1/13/1744/5 (FH:26). Sponsors: Lieut Burrows, Mrs. Nukerek.

Walter, Christian & Catharina [?]: Jacob, b. 2/14/1789 (LTSA:62). Sponsors: Michel Walter, Lea Siz.

Walter, Jacob & Catharina [?]: Michael, b. 8/20/1771 (LTSA:41). Sponsors: Michael Germann & his wife.

Walter, Jerg & Magdalena [?]: Magdalena, b. 8/25/1791 (LTSA:69); Dorotea, b. 7/2/1795 (LTSA:90); Maria, b. 4/5/1797 (LTSA:98). Sponsors: Christian Walter & Catarina (re:1); John Koch, Dorotea Schwebing (re:2); Michel Walter & Maria (re:3).

Walter, Michel & Maria [?]: John, b. 9/26/1797 (LTSA:100). Sponsors: Johannes Pickel & Magdalena.

Tryon County Militia

Walter, Adam   [Appendix A]
Walter, Christian
Walter, George

Pension Abstract

Walter, Adam, b. 1752/3; (sister: Mary [Walter] Waltz); m. Elisabeth Hurtick, 8/8/1790, Stone Arabia, Montgomery Co., N.Y.; d. 3/13/1834. Adam enlisted in April 1777 for nine months service in Col. Jacob Klock's 2nd. Regt., Tryon Co. Militia; he volunteered for another nine month tour of duty as a private in the same regiment in April 1779. (RWPA: #R11099)

Walter, Christian, b. 7/15/1758; m. Catharine Sitts, 2/3/1787, Minden, Montgomery Co., N.Y.; d. 5/6/1844, Springfield, Otsego Co., N.Y. (Catharine Walter, b. 10/?/1761; [brother: Henry Sitts; sister: Mary (m. Adam Kesler)]; resident of Springfield, N.Y. on 3/7/1845.) Children: Jacob, b. 7/14/1788; Peter, b. 3/30/1790; John, b. 8/5/1792; George, b. 9/?/179?; Benjamin, b. 8/6/1796; Abraham, b. 4/20/[?]; Conrad, b. 5/3/1801. Christian was a private in Col. Jacob Klock's 2nd. Regt., Tryon Co. Militia and served on various tours of duty throughout the war. (RWPA: #W19590)

Walter, George, m. [wife not named]; d. 5/14/1846, Johnstown, Fulton Co., N.Y. Children: George, b. 1800/1 (resident of Johnstown, N.Y. in 1854); Betsey, Mary, Susan (all living in Johnstown); Hannah (m. Robert Donelson and resident near Buffalo, N.Y.); Eve (m. Henry Avery and living in Michigan). George served as a private in Col. Jacob Klock's 2nd. Regt., Tryon Co. Militia; he was also a batteauman for eighteen months under the command of Capt. Samuel Gray; George fought in the battle of Oriskany where he was wounded in the neck and the hip. (RWPA: #S10040)

COMPENDIUM

1790 Census

Walter, Christian   [Appendix B]
Walter, George
Walter, John
Walter, Mary

WALTON

Birth/Baptism

Walton, Nathaniel & Anna Margretha [?]: Elisabeth, b. 2/1/1783; bapt. 2/1/1783 (DRGF:67). Sponsors: Conrad Beas & Elisabeth.

Death Record

Walton, [?], (infant of William Walton), d. 8/13/1824, age 6 months; buried Cherry Valley Presbyterian Church cemetery (PCV:81)

Walton, John, d. 9/24/1827, age 34 years; buried Cherry Valley Presbyterian Church cemetery (PCV:82)

WALTZ

Marriage

Walts, Conrad m. Elisabeth Schneider, 1/4/1789 (DFP:39)

Birth/Baptism

Wals/Walz, Conrad & Gertraut/Gertrudis [?]: Joh[h]annes, b. 6/16/1770 (LTSA:32); Hennrich, b. 8/29/1772 (LTSA:44); Catharina,

b. 9/16/1774, bapt. 9/18/1776 (LTSA:46); Maria, b. 9/9/1776, bapt. 9/21/1776 (DRGF:20). Sponsors: Joannes Lederer & his wife (re:1); Johannes Kaiser, Margaretha Dillenb. (re:2); Joh. Warmuth & his wife (re:3); Barthel Bickkert & Maria Catharina (re:4).

Walz, Jacob & Margareth [?]: Elisabeth, b. 12/11/1788 (LTSA:61). Sponsors: Conrad Walz, Magdalena Sneider.

Walz, Peter (of Canajoharie) & Anna [?]: Catharina, bapt. 7/4/1790 (SJC:29). Sponsors: Heinrich Dewi & Catharina Wals.

Tryon County Militia

Walls, Conrad   [Appendix A]
Walls, Conrad, Jr.
Waltz, Conrad
Waltz, George
Waltz, Jacob

Pension Abstract

Waltz, Jacob, b. 1762/3; m. [wife not named; d. prior to 1820]; resident of Herkimer Co., N.Y. on 4/8/1818. Children: Jacob and Michael Waltz. Jacob enlisted in the spring of 1777 for nine months as a private in Capt. Robert McKean's Co., Col. Van Schaick or Col. Van Rensselaer's Regt. of the N.Y. Line; he also served for seven months in Col. Marinus Willett's Regt. under Capts. Breadbake and Putnam. (RWPA: #S43243 WALS)

1790 Census

Walts, Conradt (2)   [Appendix B]
Walts, Jacob
Walts, Peter

COMPENDIUM

WANGER

1790 Census

Wanger, Isaac   [Appendix B]

WARD

Birth/Baptism

Ward, Johannes & Dorothea (F[?]eman): Anna, bapt. 3/19/1786 (DRC:78); Dorethea, b. 3/19/1786, bapt. 3/19/1786 (DRC:78). Sponsors: Nicolas Ward & Anna Ellkesand[?] (re:1); Johannis Waldorf & Dorethea Schenk (re:2).

Probate Abstract

Ward, John, (of Johnstown), will dated 10/4/1815; probated 10/16/1815. Legatees: wife, Diadamia; son, Francis. Executors: Abraham Ward, Jennison Giles. Witnesses: Isaac and Elizabeth Ward, William Jones. (WMC 56:395)

Ward, William, (of Johnstown), will dated 5/6/1812; probated 6/30/1812. Legatees: wife, Zurviah; sons, John, Henry, Jennison G., William Elias G., Isaac and Abraham; daus., Phebe, Elizabeth, Mary (wife of George Brownell) and Suckey. Executors: son, John; William T. Mills. Witnesses: James and Horace Burr, H. D. Lounsbery. (WMC 56:385)

1790 Census

Ward, John   [Appendix B]
Ward, Joseph
Ward, William

WARDELL

1790 Census

Wardell, William   [Appendix B]

WARMEN

Birth/Baptism

Warmen, Samuel & Catharina [?]: Catharina, b. 2/18/1779; bapt. 3/25/1779 (LTSA:57). Sponsors: Michael Klein & Catharina.

WARMOUTH see WORMOUTH

WARNE

1790 Census

Warne, Richard   [Appendix B]

WARNER

Marriage

Warner, James m. Catrina Snyder, 12/29/1774 (DRC:160)

Birth/Baptism

Warner, James & Catrina (Snyder): James, bapt. 9/4/1777 (DRC:44). Sponsors: John Link & Barbar Albrandt.

COMPENDIUM

Death Record

Warner, John, d. 1847, age 70 years; buried Fort Plain Cemetery, Minden (FPC 44:126)

1790 Census

Warner, George   [Appendix B]
Warner, Henry
Warner, Nicholas

WARREN

Birth/Baptism

Warren, Jeremiah & Martha (Wilkens): Martha, b. 11/12/1775, bapt. 7/19/1775 (DRC:63); Sarah, b. 9/1/1779, bapt. 7/19/1779 (DRC:63). Sponsors: [none named] (re:1 & 2)

Death Record

Warren, Mary, d. 10/12/1817, age 54 years; buried sect. 7, Colonial Cemetery, Johnstown (JC:189)

1790 Census

Warren, Darius   [Appendix B]
Warren, James
Warren, John

WART

Birth/Baptism

Wart, Johannes & Dorothea (Eman): Nichlas, b. 10/28/1782; bapt. 12/28/1782 (DRC:64). Sponsors: Nichlaas Wart & Anna Albrant.

Wart, Muwits & Deborah (Hogeboom): Anna, b. 3/20/1779; bapt. 5/29/1779 (DRC:52). Sponsors: Marks Hun & Anna Wart.

Tryon County Militia

Wart, Andrew   [Appendix A]
Wart, Matthew

1790 Census

Wart, Matthias   [Appendix B]

WARTMAN

Birth/Baptism

Wartman, Abraham & Anna Catharina [Bowman]: Christina, b. 3/15/1756 (LTSA:18). Sponsors: Jacob Bauman, Margaretha Kremer.

WASBROOK

1790 Census

Wasbrook, Samuel, Jr.   [Appendix B]

WASHBURN

Probate Abstract

Washburn, Joel, (of Canajoharie), will dated 1/19/1805; probated 4/27/1805. Legatees: wife, Elizabeth; sons, Isaac and Stephen; daus., Elizabeth (wife of Amasa Tourteloot), Zillah (wife of Conrad Zoller), Patience (wife of Godfrey Ratanour). Executors: wife and Joseph

881

Herkimer. Witnesses: Daniel Washburn, Sr. and Jr., Pheby Bostwick. (WMC 56:154)

WATER

Tryon County Militia

Water, George   [Appendix A]

WATERBURY

1790 Census

Waterbury, [?]   [Appendix B]

WATERHOUSE

1790 Census

Waterhouse, Walter   [Appendix B]

WATERMAN

1790 Census

Waterman, John   [Appendix B]
Waterman, Samuel
Watterman, Adenijah

WATERS

Marriage

Waters, Aaron m. Margaret Davies, 9/19/1793 (JPC:89)

Birth/Baptism

Waters, Aaron & Margaret [?]: Nathaniel Bachraft, b. 1/6/1795; bapt. 2/8/1795 (JPC:18)

Waters, Amazi & Lucy [?] (bapt. 4/27/1800, age 21 yrs.) (JPC:18): Elijah, b. 12/23/1799; bapt. 4/27/1800 (JPC:18).

Waters, Joseph & [?]: Hannah, bapt. 3/30/1799 (JPC:14).

Probate Abstract

Waters, Lucy, (widow of Andreas) [residence not given], will dated 4/10/1819; probated 9/19/1819. Legatees: my three children; Luther Stiles; mother; sisters, Betsey Lovel, Sophrona Pierce, Polly Brainard, Clarissa Stiles, Sally Waters; brothers, Luther Pierce and Henry Pierce; niece, Almira Waters; Theological Seminary of Princeton. Executor: Marcus T. Reynolds. Witnesses: Moses Tichenor, Jonas Stiles, David W. Cande. (WMC 57:168)

1790 Census

Waters, John   [Appendix B]
Waters, Nathaniel
Waters, Samuel

WATSON

Marriage

Watson, Robert m. Abigail Giles, 9/18/1792 (JPC:89)

1790 Census

Watson, Jud   [Appendix B]
Watson, Nathan
Watson, Samuel

WATTLES

1790 Census

Wattles, John   [Appendix B]
Wattles, Nathaniel
Wattles, Sluman

WATTS

Birth/Baptism

Watts, Thomas & Martha (McCrea), Stillwater:
Alexander, bapt. 1/18/1784 (JDR:9)

WAY

Marriage

Way, Daniel m. Jemina Moshere, both of
Nisquanna, Albany Co., 10/8/1782 (JDR:2)

1790 Census

Way, Martin   [Appendix B]

WEAGER

Birth/Baptism

Weager, John & Margaret (Deal),

Warrensborough: Henry, bapt. 2/13/1791, of
Albany Co. (JDR:15); Daniel, bapt. 4/21/1793
(JDR:12).

WEAVER

Marriage

Weaver, Georg Michael m. Catharina Fr:
Herder, 1/16/1787 (DRGF:204)

Weaver, Jacob J: m. Catharina Hess,
11/19/1767 (RDSA:183)

Weaver, Jacob J. N. m. Margretha Boom,
7/24/1786 (DRGF:203)

Weaver, Johannes Jac. m. Maria Mejer (dau.
of John Mejer), 3/28/1785 (DRGF:201)

Weaver, Peter J. m. Maria Catharina Frank,
2/7/1769 (RDSA:186)

Birth/Baptism

Weaver, Friedrich & Gertraud [?]: Johannes,
b. 7/4/1785; bapt. 7/5/1785 (DRGF:98).
Sponsors: Johannes Weaver & Maria.

Weaver, Georg & Margretha [?]: Margretha,
b. 7/14/1782; bapt. 9/7/1782 (DRGF:61).
Sponsors: Pieter Weaver & Maria.

Weaver, Jacob & Margretha [?]: Johannes, b.
6/6/1767, bapt. 6/16/1767 (RDSA:76);
Henrich, b. 11/29/1769, bapt. 11/20/1769
[Note: Error with date of birth or baptism.]
(RDSA:98). Sponsors: Johannes Mayer & Anna
Maria (re:1); Henrich Herder & his wife,
Catharina (re:2).

883

COMPENDIUM

Weaver, Jacob Ge. & [?]: Elisabeth, b. 6/25/1785; bapt. 6/29/1785 (DRGF:98). Sponsors: Philipp Harter & Anna Mac Koom.

Weaver, Jacob H. & Gertraud [?]: Elisabetha, b. 8/26/1784; bapt. 9/5/1784 (DRGF:87). Sponsors: Joh: Friedrich Kast & Elisabeth.

Weaver, Joh. Nic. H. & Lena [?]: Johannes, b. 8/19/1769; bapt. 8/26/1769 (RDSA:96). Sponsors: Johannes Smidt & Anna Eva Majer.

Weaver, Nicholas & Margretha [?]: Catharina, b. 3/19/1781, bapt. 3/25/1781 (DRGF:44); Johann Peter, b. 1/8/1783, bapt. 2/9/1783 (DRGF:67). Sponsors: Jacob Walrath & Catharina (re:1); Johann Peter Walrath & Rachel (re:2).

Weaver, Peter & Maria [?]: Catharina, b. 1/9/1784; bapt. 2/8/1784 (DRGF:80). Sponsors: Fritz Weaver & Catharina.

Weaver, Peter & Maria Catharina [?]: Georg, b. 7/3/1769; bapt. 8/1/1769 (RDSA:95). Sponsors: Georg Webe[r] & Anna Fran[?].

Weaver, Peter & Rosina (Thimes): Lena, b. 9/2/1791; bapt. 9/18/1791 (DRC:100). Sponsors: Harmanus Thimes & Lena Daxteder.

Weaver, Peter Jac: & Maria Catharina [?]: Johannes, b. 3/11/1784; bapt. 3/28/1784 (DRGF:82). Sponsors: Johannes Weaver & Catharina Weaver.

Death Record

Weaver, Harriet, (little dau. of Nicholas N. & Elisabeth (Shoemaker) Weaver), d. 1/15/1823, Germanflats, age 8 months, 7 days; buried in the family cemetery close by the mountain

(RDH:286)

Weaver, Margaretha, (dau. of Jacob P. Weaver, from Herkimer), d. 2/23/1814, age 3 months (RDH:269)

Probate Abstract

Weaver, Daniel, (of Oppenheim), will dated 3/23/1818; probated 5/2/1818. Legatees: wife, Polly; sons, Jacob, Rufus and Joseph; daus., Caty, Nancy and Polly. Executors: Adam A. Nellis, Joseph Kring. Witnesses: Adam A. Nellis, Joseph Kring, Frederick Fox. (WMC 57:167)

Weaver, Henry, (of Canajoharie), will dated 1/26/1816; probated 1/22/1817. Legatees: daus., Elizabeth (& her four sons); Mary (& her five sons); granddau., Elsey; grandsons, Abraham, Hiram and Peter Hilton. Executors: John Bellinger, William Hilton, Cornelius Loucks, Jr. Witnesses: John Malich, Peter Ball and Cornelius Loucks, Jr. (WMC 57:164)

Weaver, John, (of Palatine), will dated 2/27/1813; probated 1/19/1814. Legatees: only son, John; my 3 daus. by Caty Wood (former wife of Dr. Wood), with whom I have and still continue to co-habit; one unborn child: "so long as said Caty Wood remains the wife or widow of said Dr. Wood and lives apart from him or any other living man on earth". Executors: John Cochran, Frederick Fox. Witnesses: Frederick Fox, John Fikel, Henry P. Nellis. (WMC 56:390)

Weaver, Nicholas P., (of Johnstown), will dated 10/23/1824; probated 4/23/1825. Legatees: wife, Elizabeth; sons, Jacob, Adam and Peter; daus., Elizabeth and Katherine. Executors: wife; son, Jacob; Adam J. Plank. Witnesses: Elijah Hayward, James Eichenbreck,

Adam J. Plank, Abraham Niver. (WMC 57:182)

Wever, Frederick, (of Johnstown), will dated 9/20/1826; probated 1/10/1827. Legatees: wife, Margaret; sons, Mathias, Peter, Abraham, Benjamin, Henry and Frederick; daus., Sally, Margaret, Barbara, Caty and Nancy. Executrix: wife. Witnesses: Hars. Van Dusen, John I. Dockstader, Abraham Van Deusen. (WMC 57:267)

Tryon County Militia

Weaver, Frederick   [Appendix A]
Weaver, Frederick G.
Weaver, Frederick, Jr.
Weaver, George
Weaver, George F.
Weaver, George M.
Weaver, George, Jr.
Weaver, Jacob
Weaver, Jacob G.
Weaver, Jacob J.
Weaver, Jacob N.
Weaver, Johannes
Weaver, Michael
Weaver, Nicholas
Weaver, Nicholas G.
Weaver, Nicholas H.
Weaver, Peter

Pension Abstract

Weaver, George Michael, b. 1764; m. Catharina Herder, 1/16/1787 at the Reformed Dutch Church, German Flatts, N.Y.; resident of Deerfield, Oneida Co., N.Y. in 1832. (Catharina Weaver was the daughter of Frederick Herder.) Children: Frederick G. (stated to be "one of the children" and a resident of Deerfield, N.Y. on 11/1/1857). George Michael entered the military in the summer of 1777 and served under Capt. Peter Dygert at Fort Stanwix; he was a fifer in 1777 and 1778 at Fort Dayton under Capt. Henry Herter, at Fort Stanwix under Capt. Dygert and at Fort Widrick under 2nd. Lt. George I. Weaver; he served for nine months in 1779 as a musician at Germantown and Herkimer; George Michael substituted for Rudolph Cook at Stone Arabia for six months; he remained in the military into 1782. (RWPA: #R11237)

Weaver, Jacob, b. 3/17/1760, German Flatts, N.Y.; m. Margaret Boom, 6/2/1781, Herkimer, N.Y.; resident of Rodman, Jefferson Co., N.Y. on 9/11/1832; d. 3/9/1852, Adams, Jefferson Co., N.Y. (Margaret Weaver, b. 4/22/1763; [brother: William Boom, b. 10/?/1783 and resident of Watertown, Jefferson Co., N.Y. in 1853]; resident of Adams, N.Y. on 4/1/1853.) Children: John F., b. 1802/3 (living in Adams, N.Y. in 1853). Jacob lived with his father and brothers in a blockhouse at Fort Dayton during the Revolution; he enlisted during the first year of the war and served on various tours of duty as a private for two or three years under Lt. Peter Weaver and Capt. Henry Harter in Col. Peter Bellinger's 4th. Regt., Tryon Co. Militia; Jacob fought in the battle at German Flatts and in the skirmish at West Canada Creek. (RWPA: #W25951)

Weaver, Johannes N., m. Sarah Clause, 1792; d. 10/?/1853. Children: Jacob b. 12/15/1815, (bapt. 1/1/1816, Reformed Dutch Church at Stone Arabia, sponsors: Jno. and Christina Strobeck); Betsey, John, David, Henry, Frederick, Lawrence, Lany and Nicholas. [The pension file states that there were a total of ten children; nine of whom were named and still living in 1855.] Johannes served as a private in Col. Peter Bellinger's 4th. Regt., Tryon Co. Militia. (RWPA: #W11751)

Weaver, Nicholas, b. 10/8/1765; m. Elizabeth Zullnerin, 6/13/1791; d. 11/15/1824. (Elizabeth Weaver, b. 1764; resident of Johnstown, Fulton Co., N.Y. on 1/18/1841.) Children: Gertraut, b. 6/?/1791; Margretha, b. 5/21/1792; Elisabetha, b. 7/20/1794; Catharina, b. 5/13/1799 (m. [?] Coughnut); Margretha, b. 5/11/1801; Jacob, Adam, Peter, and Frederick. [Gertraut and Margretha Weaver were the only two children not living in 1844.] Nicholas performed his military duty as a private in the Tryon Co. Militia during the war. (RWPA: #W15860)

Weaver, Nicholas G., b. 4/5/1762; m. Gerdrauth [?]. (Gerdrauth Weaver, b. 1/2/1767.) Children: Elisabet, b. 3/13.1787; Jeremais, b. 9/29/1788; Nicholas, b. 7/29/1791; William, b. 10/17/1794; dau. [not named], b. 1/19/1802; Isaac, b. 5/11/1804; Amese [son], b. 11/5/1808. Nicholas G. served as a private in Col. Peter Bellinger's 4th. Regt., Tryon Co. Militia. (RWPA: #W18234)

Deed Abstract

Weaver, Nicholas, of Schenectady, Albany Co. to Hezekia Talcot, of German Flatts/Kingsland District, Montgomery Co. Deed dated 5/16/1786; recorded 3/7/1787. Description: Lot #4 (about 70 acres) bush land, situated in German Flats/Kingsland District, Montgomery Co. Consideration: L186. Witnesses: Duncan McDougall, Isaac Vrooman. (MVL:40)

Weaver, Nicholas, of Schenectady, Albany Co. to Hezekiah Talcott, of German Flatts/Kingsland District, Montgomery County. Deed dated 2/26/1787; recorded 3/8/1787. Description: Land situated in German Flatts/Kingsland District near the Canada Creek. Lot #3 (3/8 part, lowland), Lot #8 (6/8 part, lowland), Lot #8 (70 acres, woodland), and Lot #4 (3/8 part, lowland). Consideration: L695.4.0. Witnesses: Walter Swits, Duncan McDougall. (MVL:40)

1790 Census

Weaver, Adam   [Appendix B]
Weaver, David
Weaver, Frederick G.
Weaver, George
Weaver, George I.
Weaver, George I. N.
Weaver, George Michael
Weaver, Jacob
Weaver, Jacob H.
Weaver, John
Weaver, Nicholas G.
Weaver, Nicholas I.
Weaver, Peter
Weaver, Peter, Jr.

WEBB

Death Record

Webb, Caroline, L., d. 6/14/1836, age 19 years; buried sect. 12, Colonial Cemetery, Johnstown (JC:189)

1790 Census

Webb, John   [Appendix B]

WEBER

Marriage

Weber, Jacob m. Margreth Franck (dau. of Johannes Franck), 11/6/1791 (DRGF:208)

Weber, Jacob Hen: m. Gertraut Kast, 2/17/1782 (DRGF:196)

Weber, Jacob Joh: N. m. Margretha Majer, 4/13/1766 (RDSA:179)

Weber, Nicholas m. Gertraud Demuth, 12/18/1764 (RDSA:175)

Birth/Baptism

Weber, Friedrich & Gertraut [?]: Friedrich, b. 3/4/1779; bapt. 3/10/1779 (DRGF:34). Sponsors: Catharina Bellinger & Johannes Bellinger.

Weber, Fritz & Elisabeth [?]: Elisabeth, b. 5/7/1776; bapt. 5/10/1776 (DRGF:17). Sponsors: Georg Orndorff & Elisabeth.

Weber, George, Jr. (Field Dist.) & Margretha [?]: Apollon, b. 6/11/1791, bapt. 10/2/1791 (SJC:48); Maria, b. 12/11/1792, bapt. 1/27/1793 (SJC:71). Sponsors: Friderich Rigel & Catharina Weber (re:1); Peter J. H. Weber & Maria Weber (re:2).

Weber, Georg Jac: & Catharina [?]: Johannes, b. 5/18/1776, bapt. 5/26/1776 (DRGF:17); Catharina, b. 6/26/1778, bapt. 7/5/1778 (DRGF:31); Catharina, b. 8/26/1779, bapt. 8/29/1779 (DRGF:37). Sponsors: Johannes Weber & Margreth Gettmann (re:1); Pieter Gettmann & Catharina Hergheimer (re:2); Gertraut Bellinger & Pieter Gettmann (re:3).

Weber, Georg Jac: & Margreth [?]: Anna Margretha, b. 9/27/1777, bapt. 10/5/1777 (DRGF:26); Jacobus, b. 6/30/1779, bapt. 7/3/1779 (DRGF:36); Georg, b. 1/4/1781, bapt. 1/5/1781 (DRGF:41). Sponsors: Peter Jac: Weber & Margreth Bellinger (re:1); Jacob Weber & Catharina (re:2); Georg Michael

Weber & Catharina Weber (re:3).

Weber, Henrich Nicholaus & Anna Margretha [?]: Johann Jacob, b. 5/22/1762; bapt. 5/29/1762 (RDSA:34). Sponsors: Georg Ecker & his wife.

Weber, Jacob & Anna Margretha [?]: Pieter, b. 8/17/1776, bapt. 8/25/1776 (DRGF:20); Anna Margretha, b. 7/29/1779, bapt. 9/12/1779 (DRGF:37). Sponsors: Mattheus Majer & Elisabeth Pfeiffer (re:1); Henrich Harter & Catharina (re:2).

Weber, Jacob & Gertraut [?]: Anna Margretha, b. 6/10/1782; bapt. 6/23/1782 (DRGF:58). Sponsors: Joh: Georg Acker & Maria Elisabetha.

Weber, Jacob (of Eaterstown[?]) & Gertrud [?]: Peter, bapt. 7/18/1790 (SJC:30). Sponsors: Peter Meyer[?] & Catharina Kass.

Weber, Jacob & Maria [?]: Maria, b. 7/19/1766, bapt. 8/4/1766 (RDSA:67); Maria Barbara, b. 12/30/1778, bapt. 1/2/1779 (DRGF:33); Catharina, b. 1/8/1780, bapt. 1/16/1780 (DRGF:38); Johann Thomas, b. 2/14/1782, bapt. 2/22/1782 (DRGF:55). Sponsors: Maria & Henrich Majer (re:1); Melchior Foltz & Maria Eva (re:2); Thomas Bell & Catharina Weber (re:3); Jacob Bell & Elisabeth (re:4).

Weber, Jacob G. & Maria [?]: Georg Michael, b. 12/11/1780 (DRGF:41); Conradus, b. 7/7/1783, bapt. 7/24/1783 (DRGF:73). Sponsors: Georg Michael Weber & Lena Mac Kooms (re:1); Conrad Vols & Anna Margretha (re:2).

Weber, Jacob J., Jr. (Herkimer Co.) & Margretha [?]: Peter, b. 2/1/1793; bapt.

3/3/1793 (SJC:73). Sponsors: Peter Weber junr. & Maria Weber.

Weber, Jacob J. N. (of German Flatts) & Margaretha [?]: Abraham, bapt. 3/3/1789 (SJC:11); Lorenz, b. 10/13/1792, bapt. 10/28/1792 (SJC:66). Sponsors: John Deleny & Gertrud Boom (re:1); Lorenz Frank & Margretha Weber (re:2).

Weber, Jacob N. & Catharina [?]: Catharina, b. 1/8/1764, bapt. 1/11/1764 (RDSA:44); Jacob, b. 8/23/1768, bapt. 8/28/1768 (RDSA:89). Sponsors: Catharina Dachsteader & Johann Nicel H. Weber (re:1); Stophel Fox & his wife, Elisabeth (re:2).

Weber, Joh. Georg & Anna Elisabeth [?]: Johann Nicolaus, b. 4/4/1762, bapt. 4/5/1762 (RDSA:33); Georg Michael, b. 2/9/1764, bapt. 3/15/1764 (RDSA:45). Sponsors: Johann Nicolaus (son of Jacob Weber J:) & Catharina (dau. of Lorentz Herder) (re:1); Hans Michael Ittig & his wife (re:2).

Weber, Joh: Nicol & Catharina [?]: Johann Nicolas, b. 7/26/1777, bapt. 8/3/1777 (DRGF:25); Henrich, b. 6/3/1779, bapt. 6/6/1779 (DRGF:36). Sponsors: Joh: Nicol Franck & Margretha (re:1); Henrich Majer & Catharina Weber (re:2).

Weber, Joh. Nicol & Elisabeth [?]: Joseph, b. 2/2/1778; bapt. 2/8/1778 (DRGF:28). Sponsors: Joseph Mayer & Elisabeth Leutz.

Weber, Joh: Nicolas & Helena [?]: Friedrich, b. 1/19/1771; bapt. 1/27/1771 (RDSA:109). Sponsors: Friedrich Meyer & Anna Weber.

Weber, Johann Georg & Elisabeth [?]: [?], bapt. 8/7/1760 (RDSA:21). Sponsors: Elisabeth Frank & [?].

Weber, Johann Georg Nic: & Barbara [?]: Georg Michael, b. 10/7/1760, bapt. 11/25/1760 (RDSA:23). Sponsors: Marcus Ittig & his wife, Maria Margretha.

Weber, Johann Jacob & Anna Margretha [?]: Johannes, b. 12/20/1760, bapt. 1/24/1761 (RDSA:24); Johann Nicolaus, b. 7/27/1768, bapt. 9/1/1768 (RDSA:89). Sponsors: Johannes (son of Stephanus Franck) & Elisabetha (dau. of Nicolaus Rittman) (re:1); Johann Friedr. Weber & Maria (re:2).

Weber, Johann Nicel Jac. & Gertraud [?]: Catharina, b. 8/29/1765, bapt. 9/10/1765 (RDSA:57); Anna Margreth, b. 2/27/1776, bapt. 3/8/1776 (DRGF:16); Gertraut, b. 9/21/1778, bapt. 10/4/1778 (DRGF:32); Johannes, b. 8/3/1781, bapt. 12/31/1781 (DRGF:52). Sponsors: Catharina Dachstaeder & Jacob Weber (re:1); Georg Jacob Nic: Weber & Anna Margr: Weber (re:2); Johannes Bellinger & Anna Margreth Demuth (re:3); Pieter Weber & Maria (re:4).

Weber, Johannes & Ernestina [?]: Nicolaus, b. 6/29/1763, bapt. 7/11/1763 (RDSA:41); Anna, b. 12/17/1765, bapt. 1/7/1766 (RDSA:60). Sponsors: Johan Nicel (son of Jacob Weber) & Ernestina Bellinger (re:1); Anna Weber & Melchior Thumm (re:2).

Weber, Johannes (of the field) & Barbara [?]: Catharina, bapt. 5/30/1790 (SJC:27). Sponsors: Jacob Weber & Catharina Keller.

Weber, Johannes (of Fald) & Magdalena (Keller): Jacob, bapt. 9/13/1789 (SJC:17). Sponsors: Jacob Weber & Elizabeth Meyer.

Weber, John (of the Flatt) & Maria [?]: Anna Margretha, bapt. 1/31/1790 (SJC:23). Sponsors: Georg Weber & Margretha Weber.

COMPENDIUM

Weber, Nicolaus & Elisabet [?]: Margaret, b. 5/22/1792 (LTSA:73). Sponsors: Friederich Weber, Margaret Zeller.

Weber, Peter & Margaretha [?]: Barbara Elisabetha, b. 5/7/1755 (LTSA:14); Margaretha, b. 5/5/1757 (LTSA:21); Petrus, b. 1/14/1764, bapt. 1/27/1764 (RDSA:44); Friedericus, b. 1/28/1766, bapt. 2/2/1766 (RDSA:61); [?], bapt. 9/11/1768 (RDSA:89). Sponsors: Jerg Dagstetter, Barbara Teigert, Maria Elisabetha Nellis (re:1); Wilm Teigert & his wife, Maria Elisab. (re:2); Peter Teughert & his wife, Barbara (re:3); Friedrich Gettmann & Elisabeth Emgie (re:4); Henrich Dachstaeder (re:5).

Weber, Peter & Maria [?]: Jacob, b. 8/29/1781; bapt. 12/31/1781 (DRGF:52). Sponsors: Jacob Weber & Gertraut Demoeth.

Weber, Peter & Maria Catharina [?]: Elisabeth, b. 11/18/1780 (DRGF:41). Sponsors: Johann Nicol. Weber & Gertraut.

Weber, Peter J. (of German Flatts) & Maria [?]: Elisabeth, bapt. 2/15/1789 (SJC:10); Marcus, b. 10/7/1793, bapt. 1/12/1794 (SJC:87). Sponsors: Jacob Ihig & Elisabeth Weber (re:1); Georg Weber & Margretha Weber (re:2).

Weber, Peter Jac: & Anna [?]: Jacob, b. 7/17/1777; bapt. 7/20/1777 (DRGF:25). Sponsors: Fritz Weber, widower & Elisabeth Ittig.

Death Record

Weber, Barbara, (wife of Nicholas Weber, from Frankfort), d. 6/3/1813, age 45 years; buried in the cemetery of the new church [in Herkimer], near her home on the hill

(RDH:268)

Weber, Elisabeth, (dau. of Peter P. & Elisabeth (Bottmann) Weber), d. 8/18/1804, Germanflats, age 13 months; buried in the new cemetery in Herkimer (RDH:253)

Weber, Elisabetha, (dau. of Jacob P. & Catharina Weber), d. 1/28/1805, Herkimer, age 1 year, minus 3 days; buried in the cemetery near the church at Herkimer (RDH:254)

Weber, Frederick, (blacksmith, from Germanflats), d. 6/6/1813, age about 56 years; buried in the cemetery of the new church in Herkimer (RDH:268)

Weber, George, (resident of the country), d. 7/9/1819, Deerfield, age 72 years; buried in the cemetery near the church in the same place (RDH:278)

Weber, Jacob G., (money merchant), d. 11/28/1820, Herkimer, age 69 years, 2 months; (Died of a stoppage and obstruction in the stomach, an Elder of this church, an exceedingly worthy promoter of religion and though austere, very kind to his family and to the whole congregation; under his auspices the churches belonging to both congregations were built and repaired, to wit.: of Herkimer and Germanflats; he died as a Christian with faith in the Lord.); buried in the cemetery near the church (RDH:280)

Weber, Johannes, (son of Peter Weber), d. 12/9/1805, Herkimer, age 21 years, 9 months, less two days; buried near the new church in Herkimer (RDH:255)

Tryon County Militia

Weber, George A.   [Appendix A]

COMPENDIUM

Weber, Peter

1790 Census

Webber, Christopher   [Appendix B]
Weber, Frederick I.
Weber, Jacob G.
Weber, Jacob N.
Weber, Peter I.

WEBSTER

1790 Census

Webster, Daniel   [Appendix B]
Webster, David

WEDERICK

1790 Census

Wederick, Catherine   [Appendix B]
Wederick, George
Wederick, Jacob
Wederick, Michael

WEEMER

Birth/Baptism

Weemer, Philip & Catarina (Lyser): Philip, bapt. 2/6/1763 (DRC:9). Sponsors: Philip Miller & Anna Visbach.

WEETON

1790 Census

Weeton, John   [Appendix B]

WEHRLI

Birth/Baptism

Wehrli, Jerg & Barbara [?]: Eva Gertraut, b. 3/15/1754 (LTSA:9). Sponsors: Conrad Contrimann, Gertraut Windecker.

WEIL

Marriage

Weil, Johannes m. Magdalena Jordan, 7/19/1796 (DFP:55)

Weil, Jost m. Elisabeth Ekker, 6/5/1791, at Durlach (DFP:43)

Weils, Georg m. Dorothea Nelles, 3/9/1785 (DRGF:201)

Weils, Henrich m. Elisabeth Fritsher, 10/4/1768 (RDSA:184)

Birth/Baptism

Weyl, Henrich & Elisabet [?]: Adam, b. 9/17/1781; bapt. 9/26/1781 (DRGF:48). Sponsors: Johannes Seelbach & Elisabeth.

Weyl, Jost Henrich & Margretha [?]: Maria, b. 1/5/1783; bapt. 1/19/1783 (DRGF:6). Sponsors: Georg Noelles & Maria Gilly.

COMPENDIUM

WEIMER

Tryon County Militia

Weimer, Andrew   [Appendix A]

WEISER

Tryon County Militia

Weiser, John   [Appendix A]
Weiser, Nicholas

WEISS

Marriage

Weiss, Johannes m. Elisabeth Margreth Berns, 12/7/1769 (RDSA:188)

Birth/Baptism

Weis/Weiss, Daniel & Elisabetha [?]: Elisabeth, b. 1/25/1782, bapt. 2/3/1782 (DRGF:54); Daniel, b. 3/4/1783, bapt. 3/9/1783 (DRGF:69); Peter, b. 8/8/1790 (LTSA:63); Heinrich, b. 6/26/1792 (LTSA:73); Wilhelm, b. 7/31/1793 (LTSA:79). Sponsors: Georg Salsmann & Magdalena Straub (re:1); Christian Zimmermann & Eva (re:2); Peter Ries, Maria Straub (re:3); Henry Baker & Margareta (re:4); Heinrich Straub, Maria Engelland (re:5).

WEITHEN

Marriage

Weithen, John m. Alita Schyler, 11/25/1783 (DRGF:198)

Birth/Baptism

Weithen, John & Alita [?]: Peter, b. 8/3/1784; bapt. 8/8/1784 (DRGF:86). Sponsors: Pieter Schyler & Catharina.

WEITING

Death Record

Weiting, Mary, (widow of Henry Weiting), b. 2/17/1788; d. 8/13/1865; buried Fort Plain Cemetery, Minden (FPC 56:43j)

WELCH

Marriage

Welch, Eliah m. Mable Sherman, 6/30/1790 (DRGF:207)

Birth/Baptism

Welch, Richard & Margreth [?]: John, b. 9/20/1784; bapt. 10/10/1784 (DRGF:88). Sponsors: Johannes Gruninger & Delia Mabee.

Welch, Sarah & [?]: Amia, bapt. 9/14/1741 (FH:15). Sponsors: William Welch, Sarah Welch, Ann Mills.

Welch, Will. & Sarah [?]: Nicholaus, bapt. 9/16/1739 (FH:7). Sponsors: Will: Mills, Roger James, Ann Mills.

WELCKLE

Birth/Baptism

Welckle/Welke, Christian & Maragriet/Margaretha (Litteridge): Margaretha, b. 1/16/1779, bapt. 1/31/1779 (LTSA:56); Geertruy, bapt. 11/26/1780, at age 7 weeks (DRC:57). Sponsors: Bernhardt Hertz, Margaretha Stalt (re:1); Gerhard Alt & Geertruy Shever (re:2).

WELLS

Birth/Baptism

Wells, David & Ruth [?]: Royzel, b. 7/20/1791; bapt. 11/20/1791 (JPC:5).

Probate Abstract

Wells, David, (of Amsterdam), will dated 3/19/1807; probated 12/1/1807. Legatees: wife, Ruth; sons, Nathan, Daniel, Rosel and David Shulton; daus., Phebe and Sally Ruth. Executors: wife; James Chushney. Witnesses: Hugh Sandford, James Chusney, Peter Randolph. (WMC 56:157)

Wells, George, (of Caughnawaga), will dated 1/29/1794; probated 1/30/1801. Legatees: wife, Eunice; sons, George and William; daus., Charlotte, Polley and Eunice. Executors: wife and Thruston Wells, John Bove. Witnesses: Calvin Young, John Rogers, Asael Park. (WMC 56:150)

Wells, James, (of Johnstown), will dated 6/11/1811; probated 7/23/1811. Legatees: wife, Lydia; son, James and others; daus., Charlotte (wife of John Wallace), Lydia (wife of Alvin

Robbins), and others. Executors: wife and son, James. Witnesses: John Ayres, Ebenezer Leavenworth, Prudence Wells. (WMC 56:382)

Wells, William, (of Mayfield), will dated 5/27/1830; probated 1/31/1831. Legatees: wife, Anna; daus., Lydia and Anna; sons, John, James (decd. & his John and Richard), Peter, Abraham, William and Richard. Executors: sons, Peter and William; Ebenezer Woodworth. Witnesses: John B. Day, Samuel Pettit, Joel S. Wright. (WMC 57:273)

1790 Census

Wells, Abner   [Appendix B]
Wells, Benjamin
Wells, John
Wells, Josiah
Wells, Philip
Wells, Samuel
Wells, Styles

WELSH

Marriage

Welsch, James m. Catharina Tymese, 2/12/1793 (DFP:48)

Welsh, John (of Litchfield) m. Rosetta Pebles (of Half Moon, Albany Co.), 11/8/1784 (JDR:2)

1790 Census

Welsh, David   [Appendix B]
Welsh, Richard

WEMPLE

Marriage

Wemple, Cornelius m. Sarah E. Wemple, 11/20/1784 (DRC:164)

Wemple, Jacob (of Albany) m. Gertrude Lansing (of Saratoga), 8/25/1784 (JDR:2)

Wemple, John (widower) m. Alida Wemple, 12/19/1785 (DRC:164)

Wemple, John V. C. m. Polly Emgie (dau. of Adam Emgie), 6/9/1793 (DRGF:210)

Wemple, Mynart m. Anna Winn, 1/1/1791 (DRGF:207)

Birth/Baptism

Wemple, Andrew & Lena (Bradt): Hendrick, b. 9/7/1775, bapt. 9/?/1775 (DRC:35); Johannis, b. 4/14/1778, bapt. 5/24/1778 (DRC:48). Sponsors: Gerrit Veeder & Catrina Veeder (re:1); John B. Wemple & Marytje Wemple (re:2).

Wemple, Barent & Deborah [?]: Ariyaentie, bapt. 10/15/1743 (FH:21). Sponsors: Henry Barclay, Volkie Vrooman, Mary Wemp.

Wemple, Barent & Margarita/Margretha (Fonda): Alita, b. 6/7/1760, bapt. 7/13/1760 (RDSA:21); Meyndert, bapt. 1764 (DRC:12); Daue/Douwe, b. 7/30/1769, bapt. 9/20/1769 (RDSA:97) & [also recorded] bapt., 10/21/1769 (DRC:18). Sponsors: Sara Quack & Andreas Wembp (re:1); Adam Fonda & his wife, Nelje/Neeltje Fonda (re:2).

Wemple, Barent Baani & Sarah (Smith): Saratje, b. 1/3/1764, bapt. 3/4/1764 (RDSA:45); Sara, b. 8/7/1766, bapt. 8/9/1766

(RDSA:67); Deborah, b. 6/1/1772, bapt. 6/6/1772 (DRC:22); Benjamin, b. 10/19/1774, bapt. 10/23/1774 (DRC:31); Arriaantje, b. 4/17/1777, bapt. 4/25/1777 (DRC:42). Sponsors: Saratje Schmidt & Cornelis Smidt (re:1); Sartje & Corneles Smidt (re:2); Hermanis Smith & Meriche Smith (re:3); Cornelius Smith & Jane Wemple (re:4); Derick Groot & Arriaantje Groot (re:5).

Wemple, Barent, B., Jr. & Eva (Smith): Sara, b. 8/29/1790; bapt. 10/10/1790 (DRC:90). Sponsors: Barent B. Wemp[le] & Sara Wemple.

Wemple, Cornelius & Sarah [?]: Annatje, b. 3/7/1785; bapt. 5/15/1785 (DRC:72). Sponsors: [none named].

Wemple. Ephraim & Agnittje/Anganieta (Brouwer): Debora, bapt. 2/25/1760 (DRC:4); Sarah, bapt. 2/25/1760 (DRC:4); Johannes, bapt. 9/19/1762 (DRC:8); Wilhelm, b. 8/18/1764, bapt. 9/23/1764 (RDSA:51); Elizabeth, b. 11/22/1772, bapt. 12/11/1772 (DRC:23). Sponsors: Douwe Fonda & Debora Fonda (re:1); Arent Brouwer & Sarah Brouwer (re:2); Andreas Wimp & Ariaantje Wimp (re:3); Abraham Garrison & his wife, Marejtje (re:4); Aron Brower & Elizabeth Brower (re:5).

Wemple, Henderick & Aefje [Eva] (Van Eps): Maria, bapt. 12/1/1759 (DRC:4); Catarina, bapt. 3/17/1762 (DRC:6); Meyndert, bapt. 1/27/1765 (DRC:14); Volkje, bapt. 10/20/1769 (DRC:17). Sponsors: Barent Wimpel & Margarita Wimpel (re:1); Carol N. Van Eps & Catarina Van Eps (re:2); Barent Wimpel & Ariaantje Coneyn (re:3); Henderik Vrooman jn. & Volkje Vrooman (re:4).

Wemple, Isaac & Elizabeth [?]: Ariyaentie, bapt. 1/20/1739/40 (FH:9); Gerrit, bapt. 1/10/1741/2 (FH:16); John, bapt. 7/8/1744

(FH:24). Sponsors: John Wemple, Ariaentie Wemple, Rebecca Wemple (re:1); Gerrit Nukerk, Anna Nukerk, Aria Gerse Nukerek (re:2); Barent Wimple, Ephraim Wimple, Deborah Wimple (re:3).

Wemple, John & Maria (Veeder): Susanna, b. 5/6/1773, bapt. 5/15/1773 (DRC:25); Barent, b. 12/31/1775, bapt. 1/1/1776 (DRC:36); Barent, b. 9/12/1778, bapt. 9/28/1778 (DRC:49); Anna, b. 10/24/1780, bapt. 11/3/1780 (DRC:57); Catylnche, b. 4/3/1783, bapt. 4/27/1783 (DRC:66). Sponsors: Barent Wemple & Susanna Wemple (re:1); Barent Wemp & Sara Wemp (re:2); John Bradt & Folkje Bradt (re:3); John Van Antwerpe & Annatje Van Antwerp (re:4); Jacob Simmons & Eva Simmons (re:5).

Wemple, Myndert & Alida [?]: Andreas, bapt. 3/2/1740/1 (FH:13). Sponsors: Peter Mynderse, Sarah Mynderse.

Wemple, Myndert B. & Catrina (Veeder): Barent, b. 8/9/1790; bapt. 9/5/1790 (DRC:89). Sponsors: [none named].

Wemple, Ryer & Deborah [?]: Susanna, bapt. 9/27/1739 (FH:8). Sponsors: Mynder Symonse Veeder, Elizabeth Veeder.

Death Record

Wemple, [?], (child of Abrah. Wimple), d. 3/6/1807, age about 1 year (DFP:91)

Probate Abstract

Wemple, Abraham, (of Canajoharie), will dated 3/24/1814; probated 5/12/1814. Legatees: wife, Maria; my children [not named]. Executors: wife; Henry Frey, Henry I. [or J.] Frey, Henry F. Cox. Witnesses: John Atwater, Isaac Schermerhorn, Henry N. Bleecker. (WMC 56:391)

Wemple, Barent I. [or J.], (of Johnstown), will dated 1/22/1811; probated 5/18/1811. Legatees: wife, Nelly; my children; sister, Catharine (wife of George Voorhis). Executors: John Veeder, John A. Putman. Witnesses: Joseph N. Yates, James Lansing. (WMC 56:381)

Wemple, Cornelius, (of Mohawk), will dated 7/19/1791; probated 3/9/1792. Legatees: wife, Sarah; eldest & only son, Ephraim; daus., Nancy, Agnes; sister, Lany Horn. Executors: William Wemple, Nicholas Hanson. Witnesses: John I. [or J.] Wample, Cornelius Wample, Cornelius Smith, Jr. (WMC 56:147)

Wemple, Cornelius, (of the town of Florida), will dated 1/1/1820; probated 3/25/1820. Legatees: 1st. wife (decd.); present wife, Jane; mother-in-law, Caty Vreeland; sons, John Vreeland, David Demarest, Ephraim and William; daus., Caty and Agnes. Executors: son, William; Jacob Van Olinda. Witnesses: Jacob L. Van Olinda, Henry Peek, Abraham A. Bradt. (WMC 57:170)

Wemple. Egness, (of the town of Florida), will dated 9/3/1804; probated 10/24/1814. Legatees: sons, John E. and William; daus., Arayantie Vedder, Deborah Hansen, Sarah Huganin, Elizabeth Ten Eycks, Catherine Garrot. Executors: grandsons, Harman A. Vedder and Ephraim Hansen. Witnesses: John Ellis, Christian Enders, Benjamin Van Vechten. (WMC 56:392)

Tryon County Militia

Wemple, Abraham [Appendix A]
Wemple, Barent
Wemple, Cornelius

COMPENDIUM

Wemple, Hendrick
Wemple, John
Wemple, John T.
Wemple, Myndert
Wemple, William

Pension Abstract

Wemple, John, b. 10/4/1749, Fort Hunter, Albany Co., N.Y.; resident of Princetown [formerly Norman's Kill], Schenectady Co., N.Y. when he applied for a pension on 10/5/1832. John enlisted in early 1775 as a member of Capt. John Mynderse's Co. of minutemen and in 1777 this same company was attached to Col. Abraham Wemple's Regt. of Militia; John went to "Johnstown in the beginning of the year 1776 about fourteen days, on which occasion a detachment of soldiers were ordered out under Genls. Schuyler & Ten Broeck in consequence of some hostile movements on the part of Sir John Johnson who eventually surrendered himself a prisoner of war and disarmed his tenants and dependants"; John continued to serve in the same company until the end of the war. (RWPA: #S23490)

Wemple, Myndert B., b. 7/7/1763; m. Catharine V. Veeder, 12/20/1790, Dutch Reformed Church of Caughnawaga, Tryon Co., N.Y.; d. 7/10/1838. (Catharine Wemple, b. 1771/2; resident of Mohawk, Montgomery Co., N.Y. on 12/10/1838.) Myndert B. served in a company commanded by Capt. John Wemple in Col. Volkert Veeder's Regt. of Militia; he was "ordered out [in October 1781] and went to Johnstown to bury the dead next morning [after the battle of Johnstown] which battle was called the Hall Battle otherwise called Willet's Battle"; Myndert was on garrison duty for one season at Veeder's blockhouse in Caughnawaga. (RWPA: #W19604)

1790 Census

Wemple, Alida   [Appendix B]
Wemple, Barant
Wemple, Cornelius
Wemple, Cornelius E.
Wemple, Hagernet
Wemple, Hendrick
Wemple, John E.
Wemple, John J.
Wemple, Menert
Wemple, William E.
Wemple, Wyndert

WENDELL

Death Record

Wendell, Jacob, b. 12/12/1778; d. 3/3/1854; buried Fort Plain Cemetery, Minden (FPC 56:43j)

Wendell, Magdalena, (wife of Jacob Wendell), d. 8/17/1822, age 39 years, 2 months, 24 days; buried Fort Plain Cemetery, Minden (FPC 56:43j)

WENTS

Tryon County Militia

Wents, George   [Appendix A]

WENTWORTH

Birth/Baptism

Wentworth, Charles & Polly (Brower), of Canajoharie: Lurnin, bapt. 11/19/1802 (JDR:19).

1790 Census

Wentworth, Alpheus   [Appendix B]
Wentworth, James

WERLYTZ

Probate Abstract

Werlytz, Michael, (of Palatine), will dated 6/25/1795; probated 10/24/1795. Legatees: Christian Shipperman (of Palatine). Executor: Peter Grems, Jr. Witnesses: James Cochran[?], John Hess. (WMC 56:148)

WERN

Birth/Baptism

Wern, Michael & [?]: Maria Margaretha, b. 6/15/1769 (LTSA:27). Sponsors: Jacob Kilmann, Helena Morin.

WERNER

Marriage

Werner, Andreas m. Maria Kirn, 12/24/1769 (LTSA:281)

Werner, Carl Alexander (b. Stuttgart, Wurtemberg, youngest son of Alexander Werner) m. Christina Crims (dau. of Heinrich Crims of Stone Arabia), 11/1/1778 (LTSA:285)

Birth/Baptism

Werner, Andreas & Anna Maria [?]: Hennrich, b. 6/30/1770 (LTSA:32); Anna Eva, b. 2/24/1778, bapt. 3/8/1778 (LTSA:51); Dorothea Elisabetha, b. 5/12/1782, bapt. 5/16/1782 (DRGF:58). Sponsors: Hennrich Baum & his wife & Dorothea Elisabetha Kaiser (re:1); Georg Stamm & wife (re:2); Georg Wentz & Dorothea Elisab: Kayser (re:3).

Werner, Carl Alexander (Fort Plain) & Christina (Crembs): Peter Alexander, bapt. 6/9/1790 (SJC:28). Sponsors: Peter Young & Maria Lise Young.

Werner, Henry & Catharina [?]: Andreas, b. [no date, follows 1/8/1791] (LTSA:66). Sponsors: Andreas Werner & Maria.

Death Record

Werner, Andrew, (born in Saxony & resident of Germanflats), d. 10/30/1818, age 92 years, 6 months; buried near his home (RDH:276)

Werner, Johann George, (Singing-master, born in Manheim, Germany, and educated in Edenkoben in the Palatinate, near the old Reichstadt), d. 11/15/1819, Warren, age 29 years; (Died from exposing himself to imminent danger while felling a tree, by a limb of which he received a terrible fracture of the skull on the 5th of November, about five o'clock in the afternoon. He leaves a wife and one infant daughter. Jacob Hees, the schoolmaster, conducted the funeral services.); buried in the community cemetery in Hayer's field beyond the hill (RDH:278)

COMPENDIUM

Tryon County Militia

Werner, Alexander   [Appendix A]
Werner, Andrew
Werner, Charles Alexander
Werner, Christian

1790 Census

Werner, Christian   [Appendix B]

WERRINGTON

1790 Census

Werrington, Eber   [Appendix B]
Werrington, Stephen

WERT

Marriage

Wert, Johannis m. Maria Dorothea [?],
5/23/1774 (DRC:160)

Birth/Baptism

Wert, Johannes & Maria Dorothe [?]: Johannis,
b. 8/7/1774; bapt. 8/28/1774 (DRC:30).
Sponsors: [?] Schink & Dorothe Schink.

Wert, Nicholas & Annatje (Albrant): Annatje,
bapt. 12/14/1790 at age 6 weeks (DRC:91).
Sponsors: Christiaane Wert & Lena Wert.

1790 Census

Wert, Michael   [Appendix B]
Wert, Morris

Wert, Nicholas

WESER

Birth/Baptism

Weser, Nicolaus & Margaretha [?]: Elisabetha,
b. 9/14/1774, bapt. 9/18/1774 (LTSA:46);
Isaac, b. 2/28/1779, bapt. 3/6/1779 (LTSA:56).
Sponsors: Adolph Heinrich Walrath, Lea
Walrath (re:1); Isaac Wallrath, Helenea Klock
(re:2).

WESLEY

Birth/Baptism

Wesley, Charles & [?], Schenectady: Charles,
bapt. 4/25/1783 (JDR:10).

WESSELS

Birth/Baptism

Wessels, Andrew & Catharina (Collier): Jacob,
b. 12/19/1790; bapt. 1/23/1791 (DRC:94).
Sponsors: Jacob C[?] & Marrigje Co[?].

Probate Abstract

Wessels, Luke, (of Root), will dated 7/6/1824;
probated 11/4/1825. Legatees: sons, Luke L.,
Cornelius, Isaac I. and Abraham; daus.,
Christina Van Valkenberg and Hannah Van
Evra; Polly Van Housen. Executors: son, Luke
L. and David F. Sacia. Witnesses: David Sacia,
George Spraker, B. Van Keuren, David

897

Hugnanin. (WMC 57:184)

Wesselse, Andrew, (of Canajoharie), will dated 1/17/1813; probated 7/18/1817. Legatees: wife, Catharine; sons, Jacob, Peter, Andrew, Nicholas, John, Daniel, Isaac, Luke and Abraham; daus., Jenny, Nancy, Maria, Helen and Nilly. Executors: Peter Collyer, Isaac Collyer, Nicholas Quackenboss. Witnesses: William Newton, James Dey, Richard I. Van Valkenburgh. (WMC 57:165)

Tryon County Militia

Wessel, Adam   [Appendix A]
Wessel, George
Wessel, Henry
Wessel, John
Wessel, William

1790 Census

Westles, Lucas   [Appendix B]

WESTERMAN

Marriage

Westermann, Johann Peter m. Anna Ehl, 7/27/1794 (DFP:52)

Birth/Baptism

Westerman, Peter & Maria Elisabeth [?]: Anna Maria, b. 11/8/1783; bapt. 11/10/1783 (DRGF:76). Sponsors: Andreas Haens & Anna Maria.

Death Record

Westerman, Heinrich, (legitimate son of Peter

Westermann), b. 6/28/1779; d. 7/1/1788 ("at 1 A.M., from the small-pox sickness"); buried 7/2/1788 (DFP:78 & 79)

Westerman, Nicholas, d. 4/?/1813, age 25 years, 4 months, 4 days; buried 4/4/1813 (DFP:96)

Westerman, Peter, b. 1741, Germany; m. 5/15/1767; d. 11/14/1791; buried 11/15/1791 (DFP:82)

1790 Census

Westerman, Peter   [Appendix B]

WESTFORD

1790 Census

Westford, Cornelias   [Appendix B]

WESTON

1790 Census

Weston, Jonathan   [Appendix B]

WETHERBEE

Probate Abstract

Wetherbee, David, (of Broadalbin), will dated 4/21/1823; probated 2/14/1827. Legatees: wife, Polly; sons, Ephraim, David (if he returns), Ira and Luther; daus., Esther (wife of Parris G. Clark), Polly Hammond, Ruba (wife of

Obadiah Hammond), Harriet (wife of Obed Smith), Sally and Cynthia Wetherbee; Abbley Dwight. Executors: William Woodward, Ephraim Wetherbee. Witnesses: William Woodward, Reuben Thayer, Edmd. G. Rawson. (WMC 57:267)

WETMORE

Death Record

Wetmore, [?], (wife of Jesse Whetmore), d. 4/20/1834, age 20 years, feebleness after child; buried Cherry Valley Presbyterian Church cemetery (PCV:85)

Wetmore, Irving, (son of Jesse Wetmore), d. 10/1/1834, age 10 months, of dysentary; buried Cherry Valley Presbyterian Church cemetery (PCV:86)

Wetmore, Lucy, (wife of Seth Wetmore), d. 8/25/1834, age 59 years; buried Ames Rural Cemetery, Canajoharie (ARC:13)

Wetmore, Seth, d. 4/16/1836, age 75 years; buried Ames Rural Cemetery, Canajoharie (ARC:13)

WEYL

Birth/Baptism

Weyl, Jost Henrich & Margretha [?]: Maria, b. 1/5/1783; bapt. 1/19/1783 (DRGF:6). Sponsors: Georg Noelles & Maria Gilly.

WEYMAR

Death Record

Weymar, [?], (wife of Andreas Weymar), b. Germany; d. 12/15/1793, age 69 years, 2 months, 7 days; buried 12/17/1793 (RDSA:234)

WHALEN

Probate Abstract

Whalen, John, (of Johnstown), will dated 12/24/1824; probated 2/1/1826. Legatees: sons, Charles, Joseph; daus., Martha, Elizabeth Carr and Mary (wife of John Fitzgerald, of Ireland); grandson, Morris Whelan (of William). Bequest: Real estate in St. Lawrence Co. to son, Charles. Executors: son, Joseph; Henry Cunningham, William Rob. Witnesses: Jabes Deake, John McVean, Adam W. Snyder. (WMC 57:185)

1790 Census

Whalen, John   [Appendix B]

WHARRY

1790 Census

Wharry, Evens   [Appendix B]

WHEELER

Marriage

Wheeler, Willard R. (of Canajoharie) m. Laura White (of Canajoharie), 4/18/1826 (PCBC:51)

Death Record

Wheeler, Lucy, d. 3/16/1826, age 90 years; buried Ames Rural Cemetry, Canajoharie (ARC:13)

Tryon County Militia

Wheeler, Isaac   [Appendix A]

Pension Abstract

Wheeler, Isaac, b. 1764/5; m. Eleanor [?]; resident of Bradford Co., Pa. on 6/11/1819; moved to Sciota Co., Ohio where he lived in 1825; d. 9/12/1846, Dearborn Co., Indiana. (Eleanor Wheeler, b. 1767/8; living in 1820.) Children: Betsey, b. 1806/7; Richard, b. 1809/10 (only surviving heir on 10/5/1846). [Reference was made to a grandson, Chauncy Wheeler, in a report made to Mrs. L. Hagerman on 2/13/1933.] Isaac enlisted at Johnstown, N.Y. on 11/1/1778 and served as a drummer in Capt. Rensselaer's Co., Col. Goose Van Schaick's Regt. of the N.Y. Line; he was at the siege of Yorktown and was honorably discharged on 6/8/1783. (RWPA:#S40681)

1790 Census

Wheeler, Timothy   [Appendix B]

WHELTZ

Birth/Baptism

Wheltz, Richard & Eva Catharina [?]: [?], b. 1/4/1776; bapt. 2/6/1776 (DRGF:15). Sponsors: [none named].

WHILEING

Birth/Baptism

Whileing, Georg & Nelly [?]: Mary, b. 11/6/1762; bapt. 3/3/1763 (RDSA:38). Sponsors: William Queen, John Cox, Mary Queen & Regan's wife.

WHIPPLE

1790 Census

Whipple, Barnet   [Appendix B]
Whipple, Calvin
Whipple, Israel
Whipple, Levy
Whipple, Nichols
Whipple, William

WHITAKER

Marriage

Whitaker, Thomas m. Sarah Doxteder, 3/7/1773 (DRC:158)

Birth/Baptism

Whittiker/Wittaker, Thomas & Sarah (Doxteder): John Relig, b. 6/?/1778, bapt. 6/30/1778 (DRC:48); Catrina, b. 2/17/1783,

COMPENDIUM

bapt. 4/14/1783 (DRC:65). Sponsors: [none named] (re: 1 & 2).

Death Record

Whitaker, [?], (Mr.), d. 10/20/1830; buried Cherry Valley Presbyterian Church cemetery (PCV:84)

Whitaker, James T., d. 10/20/1830, age 44 years, 3 months; buried in Old Cemetery, Cherry Valley; removed ca. 1864 to Cherry Valley Cemetery; buried on lot owned by James A. Whitaker (CVC:2) [Note: Previous entry is probably the same individual, namely: James T. Whitaker.]

Whitaker, John R., (resident of Cherry Valley), d. 12/16/1820, age 43 years, 6 months; removed ca. 1864 to Cherry Valley Cemetery; buried on lot owned by James A. Whitaker (CVC:2)

Whitaker, Nancy, (dau. of [?] Rust; widow of John R. Whitaker; later married Z. Keyes), d. 7/4/1838, age 52 years; removed ca. 1864 to Cherry Valley Cemetery; buried on lot owned by James A. Whitaker (CVC:2)

Whitaker, Sarah D., (Cherry Valley resident), d. 18[?], age 68 years; buried in Old Cemetery & removed to Cherry Valley Cemetery; buried on lot owned by James A. Whitaker (CVC:2)

Whitaker, Thomas, (Cherry Valley resident), d. [not stated]; removed to Cherry Valley Cemetery; buried on lot owned by James A. Whitaker (CVC:2)

1790 Census

Witacer, Squire   [Appendix B]
Witaker, Christopher

Witaker, James
Witaker, Thomas

WHITE

Marriage

White, Amos (of Canajoharie) m. Jane Ann Poff (of Canajoharie), 2/13/1833 (PCBC:52)

Birth/Baptism

White, Albert (Palatine Town) & Margretha [?]: Sara, bapt. 8/14/1792, age 12 years (SJC:63); Elisabeth, bapt. 8/14/1792, age 4 years (SJC:63); Maria, bapt. 8/14/1792, age 1 year (SJC:63). Sponsors: James Dannels & Gertrud Dannels (re:1); Salomon Yuker & Elisabeth Yuker (re:2); Jacob Palsli & Anna Lise Palsli (re:3).

White, Daniel & [?], Warrensborough: Edward, bapt. 1/23/1780 (JDR:12).

White, Hugh & Mary [?]: Isobel, b. 9/2/1794; bapt. 10/19/1794 (JPC:10).

White, Jerry & Mar Len. [?]: Jahn, b. 10/10/1762; bapt. 1/30/1762 (RDSA:37). Sponsors: Hunter Quack & Nelje Quack.

Death Record

White, Elizabeth, (wife of John White), d. 11/30/1840, age 90 years, 4 months, 2 days; buried Ames Rural Cemetery, Canajoharie (ARC:21)

White, John, d. 11/18/1826, age 78 years, 7 months, 23 days; buried Ames Rural Cemetery, Canajoharie (ARC:21)

White, Relecty, (dau. of Rev. George & Percy Elliot; wife of John White), d. 2/15/1875, age 80 years; buried Ames Rural Cemetery, Canajoharie (ARC:21)

Probate Abstract

White, John, (of Canajoharie), will dated 6/15/1809; codicil dated 9/7/1818; probated 1/9/1827. Legatees: wife, Elizabeth; sons, Asahel, William (sickly), and John; daus., Molly Hubbs and Lucy. Executors: Asahel and John White. Witnesses: Lebbeus Kimball, Rufus and Matilda Morris (for both will and codicil). (WMC 57:266-267)

Tryon County Militia

White, Edward   [Appendix A]

1790 Census

White, Abel   [Appendix B]
White, Abijah
White, Ansel
White, Daniel C.
White, David
White, Edward
White, Henry
White, Hugh, Jr.
White, Isaac
White, Jeremiah
White, John (2)
White, Joseph (2)
White, Lewis
White, Nathan
White, Nathaniel
White, Philo
White, Thomas
White, William

WHITFORD

1790 Census

Whitford, Joseph   [Appendix B]

WHITING

Birth/Baptism

Whiting [spelled: Weytene in record], John (of Canajoh. Castle) & Alida [?]: Margaretha, bapt. 5/16/1790 (SJC:27). Sponsors: Niclaus Herchimer & Margretha Herchimer.

Whiting, John Christ. & Anna Maria [?]: Anna Maria, b. 9/4/1792 (LTSA:75). Sponsors: John Jenkens & Margareta.

1790 Census

Whiting, John   [Appendix B]

WHITLE

Marriage

Whitle, John m. Catrina Lansing, 1/13/1781 (DRC:163)

WHITMAN

1790 Census

Whitman, Allen   [Appendix B]

WHITMORE

Probate Abstract

Whitmore, Peter, (of Johnstown), will dated 10/10/1827; probated 1/8/1828. Legatees: wife, Margaret; sons, John, Jacob and George; daus., Sally, Jane, Hannah, Katharine, Maria, Margaret and Eliza. Executors: Jacob Boshart, Jacob Yost, Frederick Moore. Witnesses: Peter Putman, Elijah Hayward, Samuel O. Hedden, William B. Sammons. (WMC 57:270)

1790 Census

Whitmore, Amos   [Appendix B]
Whitmore, Parsons
Whitmore, Peletiah

WHITNEY

Death Record

Whitney, Laura, (wife of Asakel Whitney), d. 8/13/1833, age 26 years; buried sect. 12, Colonial Cemetery, Johnstown (JC:189)

Probate Abstract

Whitney, Moses, (of Palatine), will dated 5/4/1814; probated 6/21/1814. Legatees: brother, William (& his son, Moses); brother-in-law, Dr. Levi Maxwell (& wife Sally). Executors: Duty Joslin, John Wiley, Rouse Simmonds. Witnesses: Whitman Harrington, Jr., Andrew Dye, John A. Philips. (WMC 56:392)

1790 Census

Witney, Christopher   [Appendix B]

Witney, Joshua
Witney, Martha
Witney, Thomas
Witney, William

WICK

Marriage

Wick, Severinus (son of Joh. Wieck) m. Anna Cremer (dau. of Joh. Cremer), 7/3/1788 (RDSA:192)

Birth/Baptism

Wick, Johannes & Dorothea [?]: Margaretha, b. 9/13/1756 (LTSA:19); Michael, b. 5/24/1761, bapt. 6/7/1761 (RDSA:26); Johannes, b. 12/12/1762, bapt. 12/26/1762 (RDSA:36); Severines, b. 2/27/1765, bapt. 3/10/1765 (RDSA:54). Sponsors: Johannes Bart & his wife, Margaretha (re:1); Michael Saltzmann & his wife (re:2); Johannes Teughert & his wife, Dorothea (re:3); Severines Kock & Veronica Wolff (re:4).

Wik, John & Margaret [?]: Magdalena, b. 1/12/1792 (LTSA:71). Sponsors: Johannes Newhof & Lena.

Wik, Sepherinus & Lena [?]: Sepherinus, b. 4/20/1796 (LTSA:94). Sponsors: Johannes Neuhof & Magdalena.

Wik, Severinus & Anna [?]: Michel, b. 6/7/1790 (LTSA:63); Johannes, b. 4/5/1792 (LTSA:72); Heinrich, b. 4/14/1794 (LTSA:82). Sponsors: Dorothea Wik (the mother) (re:1); Johannes Cremer, Margareta Erben (re:2); Andreas Pfeifer & Catarina (re:3).

COMPENDIUM

Tryon County Militia

Wick, John   [Appendix A]
Wick, Michael
Wicks, Samuel

1790 Census

Wick, John   [Appendix B]

WICKEESER

Birth/Baptism

Wickeeser, Conrad & Rosina [?]: Anna Margretha, b. 6/30/1766; bapt. 7/21/1766 (RDSA:66). Sponsors: Stephanus Hepp & Anna Margretha.

WICKHAM

1790 Census

Wickham, William   [Appendix B]

WIDERSTEIN

Marriage

Witterstein, Henrich m. Maria Hausse (widow), 4/6/1787 (DRGF:204)

Witterstein, Henrich m. Maria Magdalena Hultz, 5/17/1766 (RDSA:179)

Witterstein, Johannes m. Margreth Kesslar (dau. of Melch. Kesslar), 8/1/1785

(DRGF:203)

Birth/Baptism

Widderstein, Henrich & Catharina [?]: Johannes, b. 7/12/1762, bapt. 7/25/1762 (RDSA:34); Anna, b. 7/12/1762, bapt. 7/25/1762 (RDSA:34). Sponsors: Johannes Schell & his wife, Barbara (re:1); Anna, wife of Augustines Hess (re:2).

Death Record

Wiederstein, Anna Eva, (dau. of Johannes Wiederstein from Herkimer), d. 7/11/1812, age 15 years; buried in the cemetery of the church at Herkimer (RDH:265)

Wiederstein, Henry, (from Herkimer), d. 4/5/1811, age 84 years; buried in the cemetery of the church at Germanflats (RDH:263)

Wiederstein, Peter, (son of Johannes Wiederstein, Jr., from Herkimer), d. 1/11/1813, age 6 months (RDH:266)

Tryon County Militia

Widerstein, Henry   [Appendix A]

Pension Abstract

Witderstein, John, b. 7/12/1762; [cousin: John Schell, b. 1765/6; resident of Herkimer, N.Y. in 1839]; m. Margaret Kessler, 8/2/1786, Reformed Dutch Church at German Flatts, N.Y. (Margaret Witderstein, b. 1769/70, dau. of Melchior Casler; d. 6/16/1848, Herkimer, N.Y.) Children: Abraham, b. 1806/7 (resident of Herkimer, N.Y. on 3/2/1849); Catharine (m. [?] Fulmer); Margaret (m. [?] Folts); David, Mary E. (m. [?] Reed); Betsey (m. [?] Stevens); John and Melchert. John enlisted on

904

6/8/1777 and served as a private in Capt. Thomas DeWitt's Co., Col. Peter Gansevoort's Regt. of the N.Y. Line; he also served in Capt. George Sytez's Co., Col. Van Schaick's 1st. Regt.; John was at the siege of Fort Stanwix, marched on Sullivan's expedition against the Indians, participated in the skirmish on Staten Island, and fought in the battle of Yorktown; he was honorably discharged on 6/8/1783. (RWPA: #W18341)

1790 Census

Wederstawn, Henry   [Appendix B]

WIDRIG

Marriage

Wiederich, Jacob m. Catharina Elisabeth Rinckel, 1/31/1786 (DRGF:203)

Tryon County Militia

Widrig, Conrad   [Appendix A]
Widrig, George
Widrig, Jacob
Widrig, Michael

Pension Abstract

Widrig, Conrad, b. 1762/3; (brother: Jacob Widrig [RWPA: #S11839]); resident of Columbia, Herkimer Co., N.Y. in 1832. Conrad enlisted from Schuyler and served at various times for about three and a half years in Capt. Staring's Co., Col. Peter Bellinger's 4th. Regt., Tryon Co. Militia; he was in the battle at Fort Mike. Conrad's application for pension was denied because the necessary papers for authenticating his service were not submitted. (RWPA: #R11498)

Widrig, Jacob, b. 1/?/1754, Germany; came to America with his father's family when he was about two years old and grew up in Schuyler, N.Y.; (brother: Conrad Widrig [RWPA: #R11498]); resident of Schuyler, Herkimer Co., N.Y. in April 1837. Jacob volunteered in the first year of the war and served as a private in Capt. Dygert's Co., Col. Nicholas Herkimer's Regt.; he served for nine months in the second year of the war in Capt. Staring's Co. at which time he was in a battle near his captain's home in Schuyler; Jacob served for nine months in 1778 in Capt. McKean's Co., Col. Peter Bellinger's 4th. Regt., Tryon Co. Militia; he served for two months in 1779 or 1780 in Capt. Demuth's Co. of the same regiment and was in two engagements with the Indians, one at Fort Mike, and the other at Fort Dayton in which he was taken prisoner by the Indians, carried to Fort Niagara and sold to a British officer to whom he served as a waiter during his imprisonment of more than two years. (RWPA: #S11839)

WIDSLOW

1790 Census

Widslow, Stephen   [Appendix B]

WIELER

Birth/Baptism

Wieler, Jacob & Sophia (Starckwetter): Daniel, b. 4/15/1787; bapt. 6/17/1787 (RDSA:113). Sponsors: Johannes Wohlgemuth, jun. & his wife, Maria (born: Schmidt).

WIELTZER

Birth/Baptism

Wieltzer, Johannes & Barbara [?]: Jacob, b. 4/18/1764; bapt. 5/6/1764 (RDSA:47). Sponsors: Jacob Dieffendorff & his wife, Elisabeth.

WIKOFF (also see WYCKOFF)

1790 Census

Wikoff, Christian   [Appendix B]

WILABER

1790 Census

Wilaber, John   [Appendix B]

WILBUR

1790 Census

Wilbur, Peter   [Appendix B]

WILCOCKS (also see WILLCOX)

1790 Census

Wilcocks, [?]   [Appendix B]
Wilcocks, Benjamin (2)
Wilcocks, David (2)
Wilcocks, Isaac
Wilcocks, Jessee
Wilcocks, John (2)
Wilcocks, Joseph
Wilcocks, Oseas
Wilcocks, Peter
Wilcooks, Samuel

WILD

Birth/Baptism

Wild, George (of Palatine) & Dorothea (Nelles): Frans Daniel, bapt. 5/24/1789 (SJC:15); Anna, bapt. 10/30/1791 (SJC:50); Dorothea, bapt. 1/26/1794 (SJC:89). Sponsors: Heinrich Smith & Maria Smith (re:1); Johannes Nelles & Anna Nelles (re:2); Henry Crembs & Anna Crembs (re:3).

WILE

Tryon County Militia

Wile, Christian   [Appendix A]
Wiles, George

WILEY

Birth/Baptism

Wiley, Benjamin & Catrina (Hicky): Maria, b. 10/15/1790; bapt. 12/26/1790 (DRC:92). Sponsors: Felter Freligh & Maria Freligh.

Wiley, David & Lidia (Bangbourn): William, b. 3/26/1791; bapt. 4/17/1791 (DRC:96). Sponsors: John Gardenier & Nealtje Gardenier.

Death Record

Wiley, Jane, (dau. of S. & M. Wiley), d. 1/15/1847, age 24 years; buried sect. 6, Colonial Cemetery, Johnstown (JC:190)

Wiley, Stephen, d. 1/3/1837, age 49 years; buried sect. 6, Colonial Cemetery, Johnstown (JC:190)

Tryon County Militia

Wiley, Nicholas   [Appendix A]

WILKS

Marriage

Wilks, John m. Anna Baardt, 11/23/1790 (DRGF:207)

Birth/Baptism

Wilks, John (Gaiseberg) & Anna [?]: Schim [James?], bapt. 7/31/1791 (SJC:45); Catharina, bapt. 1/5/1794 (SJC:87). Sponsors: Nicolas Barth & Veronica Barth (re:1); Johannes Bart & Catharina Mayer (re:2).

1790 Census

Wilks, John   [Appendix B]

WILLARD

Marriage

Willard, Samuel m. Lena Ryon, [no date: follows 4/9/1791] (DRGF:207)

Birth/Baptism

Willard, Elias & Catherine (Livingston), Stillwater: Sarah Ten Eyck, bapt. 7/6/1783 (JDR:23).

1790 Census

Willard, Lewis   [Appendix B]
Willard, Rufus

WILLCOX (also see WILCOCKS)

Marriage

Willcox, David m. Abigail Heavens, 3/31/1793 (DRGF:210)

WILLIAMS

Marriage

Williams, Georg m. Dina Cottes, 11/26/1789 (DRGF:206)

Williams, Heinrich m. Maria Christman, 11/28/1795 (RDSA:202)

Williams, John m. Anne Durot [Durst in baptismal record], both of Warrensborough, 1/12/1792 (JDR:#105)

Williams, Lewis m. Sarah Naap, both of Saratoga Dist., 6/1/1785 (JDR:3)

COMPENDIUM

Birth/Baptism

Williams, Cornelius & Tanecka (Clute): Fredrick, b. 6/30/1791; bapt. 7/3/1791 (DRC:99). Sponsors: Frederick Clute & wife.

Williams, Daniel & Magdalena (Angenberg or Langbergh): Mary, b. 2/26/1786, bapt. 5/22/1786 (DRC:78); Catharine, bapt. 3/14/1790 [parents of Irishbush] (JDR:11). Sponsors: [none named] (re: 1 & 2).

Williams, Eliesar & Maria [?]: Samuel, b. 5/12/1778; bapt. 7/15/1778 (LTSA:53). Sponsors: Johann Kayser & Margaretha.

Williams, Johann & Catharina [?]: William, b. 4/19/1771 (LTSA:36). Sponsors: Leonhard Koezer & his wife.

Williams, John & Anne (Durst), Warrensborough: Daniel, bapt. 5/26/1793 (JDR:12).

Death Record

William, Isaac, d. 3/30/1794 (met with an accident in the water, March 30th.; found on the bank of the river), age about 10 years; buried 3/31/1794 (DFP:85)

Williams, Charles, d. 11/5/1836, age 68 years, of eating too much opium; buried Cherry Valley Presbyterian Church cemetery (PCV:87)

Williams, George, (legitimate son of Simon & Ernestina (Stahring) Williams), d. 10/20/1807, Germanflats, age 9 months, 9 days; buried in the Herder cemetery in Warren in one grave (RDH:258)

Williams, Sarah, d. 5/20/1831, age 58 years, of a complicated disease; buried Cherry Valley

Presbyterian Church cemetery (PCV:84)

Probate Abstract

Williams, Francis, (of the town of Florida), will dated 4/8/1822; probated 5/11/1822. Legatees: wife, Nancy; son, Charles. Executors: Isaac Visscher, John and Peter I. Enders. Witnesses: Isaac Visscher, John and Peter I. Enders. (WMC 57:173)

Williams, Samuel, (of Charleston), will dated 5/9/1822; probated 7/13/1822. Legatees: wife, Judey; sons, Stephen, James, Alexander, Samuel, Thomas and Jesse. Executors: wife; sons, Samuel and Thomas. Witnesses: Abraham T. Ouderkirk, Samuel and William A. Campbell. (WMC 57:174)

Tryon County Militia

Williams, Daniel   [Appendix A]
Williams, Eliser

1790 Census

Williams, Andress   [Appendix B]
Williams, Cornelius
Williams, Daniel
Williams, David (2)
Williams, Edward
Williams, Elisha
Williams, Ezekel
Williams, George (2)
Williams, Gurden
Williams, Jabez
Williams, Jacob
Williams, Josiah
Williams, Thomas
Williams, William

WILLIAMSON

Marriage

Williamson, Henrich m. Sara Nelson (widow), 12/25/1770 (RDSA:190)

1790 Census

Williamsen, John   [Appendix B]
Williamson, James

WILLIKEN

Marriage

Williken, Robert m. Anna Philipps, 12/10/1768 (RDSA:186)

WILLIS

1790 Census

Willis, Aseph   [Appendix B]
Willis, Caleb

WILLS

Marriage

Wills, Zabulon m. Sylva Lewis, 8/25/1793 (DRGF:210)

Tryon County Militia

Wills, William   [Appendix A]

1790 Census

Wills, Arnold   [Appendix B]

WILLY

1790 Census

Willy, Benjamin   [Appendix B]
Willy, Bezllial

WILSEY

1790 Census

Wilsey, John   [Appendix B]

WILSON

Marriage

Wilson, Henry m. Salvey Schmidt, 5/8/1794 (DFP:51)

Wilson, Samuel m. Eleanor Robeson, Warrensbush, 7/30/1780 (JDR:1)

Birth/Baptism

Wilson, Alexander G. & Prudy (Palmer), Canajoharie: Mary, bapt. 7/5/1801 (JDR:21).

Wilson, Daniel & Jane [?]: John, b. 6/23/1800; bapt. 8/24/1800 (JPC:18).

Wilson, James (Canajoharie) & Elisabeth [?]: Eva, bapt. 7/29/1792 (SJC:62). Sponsors:

COMPENDIUM

Henry Wi[?] & Anna Mayer.

Wilson, Johannes & Judith [?]: John, b. 7/6/1781; bapt. 8/28/1781 (DRGF:47). Sponsors: Geysebert van Brakel & Bally.

Wilson, John & Barbara (Diefendorf): Henderick, bapt. 10/20/1769 (DRC:17); Elizabeth, b. 7/17/1772, bapt. 7/25/1772 (DRC:22). Sponsors: Johannes Veder & Catarina Veder (re:1); Jacob Tiefendorf & Elizabeth Tiefendorf (re:2).

Death Record

Wilson, [?], (dau. of John Wilson), d. 12/6/1808, age 1 year, 1 month, 23 days (DFP:92)

Wilson, Gennet, d. 12/30/1822, age 14 years; buried Cherry Valley Presbyterian Church cemetery (PCV:79)

Wilson, James, d. 1/8/1847, age 70 years; buried Cherry Valley Presbyterian Church cemetery (PCV:88)

Wilson, John, d. 3/8/1828, age 63 years; buried Cherry Valley Presbyterian Church cemetery (PCV:82)

Wilson, Mary E., (dau. of W. & M. Wilson), d. 6/14/1851, age 16 months, 18 days; buried sect. 11, Colonial Cemetery, Johnstown (JC:190)

Probate Abstract

Wilson, James, (of Minden), will dated 9/25/1807; probated 2/15/1808. Legatees: wife, Elizabeth; sons, Jacob and John; daus., Hannah, Eve and Barbara. Executors: friend, Jacob Wilson; Cornelius V. Camp, Jr.

Witnesses: John Jacob Dievendorf, Cornelius V. Camp, Jr., Jonathan Huestis. (WMC 56:157)

Wilson, John, (of Caughnawaga), will dated 11/1/1788; probated 3/13/1789. Legatees: wife, Barbara; sons, Jacob, James, John, Hendrick; daus., Barbara, Catharine, Margaret, Anatie, Alida, & Elizabeth. Executors: son, Jacob and son-in-law, Isaac Davis, both of Caughnawaga. Witnesses: Sampson Sammons, James Davis, Henry Seeber. (WMC 56:145)

Tryon County Militia

Wilson, Abner   [Appendix A]
Wilson, Andrew
Wilson, James
Wilson, Japes
Wilson, John
Wilson, Samuel

Pension Abstract

Wilson, John, b. 2/?/1767, son of [?] and Jane Wilson [b. 1741/2 and living with her son in 1824]; (brother: Charles, b. ca. 1765 and resident of Johnstown, N.Y. in 1818); m. Sarah [?]; resident of Johnstown, Montgomery Co., N.Y. on 4/14/1818. (Sarah Wilson, b. 1765/6.) Children: Victor, b. ca. 1800 (living with his father in 1820). John enlisted in March/April 1778 and served as a musician in Capt. James Gregg's [John's uncle] Co., Cols. Gansevoort and Van Schaick's Regts. of the N.Y. Line; John was honorably discharged on 3/22/1782 and returned to his mother's home in Albany, N.Y. (RWPA: #S44077)

1790 Census

Wilson, Alexander   [Appendix B]
Wilson, Andrew

910

COMPENDIUM

Wilson, James (3)
Wilson, John (4)
Wilson, John, Jr.
Wilson, John, Sr.
Wilson, Phenias
Wilson, Robert
Wilson, Samuel (2)
Wilson, William (2)

WINCH

1790 Census

Winch, Samuel   [Appendix B]

WINCHEL

1790 Census

Winchel, Benjamin   [Appendix B]
Winchel, Ruggles

WINCHY

1790 Census

Winchy, Jabez   [Appendix B]

WINDECKER

Marriage

Windecker, Friedrich m. Elisabeth Joh: Keller,
10/2/1795 (DRGF:213)

Windekker, Johannes m. Catharin Keller,
3/6/1791 (DRGF:208)

Birth/Baptism

Windecker, Friedrich & Barbara [?]: Friedrich,
b. 4/6/1768; bapt. 4/18/1768 (RDSA:85).
Sponsors: Henrich Keller & Adeli.

Windecker, Jacob (Sneidersbush) & Maria [?]:
Conrad, bapt. 3/4/1793 (SJC:74). Sponsors:
Wilhelm Killes & Eva Killes.

Death Record

Windecker, [?] (widow), b. 7/?/1744; d.
5/18/1810, age 65 years, 10 months; buried
5/20/1810 (DFP:93)

Probate Abstract

Windecker, Frederick, (of Manheim), will
dated 3/16/1803; probated 2/11/1809. Legatees:
wife, Barbara; sons, Henry, John and Frederic;
daus., Anna Barbara, Gertrout (wife of Jacobus
Van Slyke) and Catharine (wife of Frederic
Pickert). Executors: John Keller, Anthony
Kaufman. Witnesses: Henrich Keller, John
Pickert, Bartholomew Pickert, Jr. (WMC
56:159)

Windecker, Johannis, (of Canajoharie), will
dated 6/25/1791; probated 11/10/1794.
Legatees: wife, Catharine; George Hann;
George Jacob Diffindorf (& his sons, John and
Henry); Elizabeth House (of Nicholas).
Executrix: wife. Witnesses: John Fox, Jacob G.
Klock, William Cunningham. (WMC 56:148)

Tryon County Militia

Windecker, Frederick   [Appendix A]
Windecker, Jacob

911

Windecker, Johannes
Windecker, Nicholas

1790 Census

Windecker, Conradt   [Appendix B]
Windecker, Frederick
Windecker, John

WING

1790 Census

Wing, Wiliam   [Appendix B]

WINKLE

Tryon County Militia

Winkle, John   [Appendix A]

WINKLER

1790 Census

Winkler, John   [Appendix B]

WINKOOP

1790 Census

Winkoop, William   [Appendix B]

WINN

Marriage

Winn, Jacob m. Susanna Evertse, 1/14/177
(DRC:162)

Winn, John, Esqr. m. Elisabeth Omensetter
6/30/1793 (DFP:49)

Winn, Robert Irving m. Catharina Hauss
1/29/1793 (DFP:48)

Birth/Baptism

Winne, Conrad & Yannitie (Schonmaker):
David, b. 7/27/1791; bapt. 9/13/179
(DRC:100). Sponsors: David Winne & Lena
Wenne.

Winne, Frans & Lena (Flensburg): David, b.
5/5/1787; bapt. 6/3/1787 (DRC:84). Sponsors:
William Winne & Catrina Winne.

Winne, John & Elizabeth (Schremling):
Catrina, b. 4/1/1779, bapt. 5/24/1779
(DRC:52); Gurge, bapt. 3/26/1785 (DRC:71);
Petr [sic], b. 1/4/1785, bapt. 3/26/1785
(DRC:71). Sponsors: [none named] (re:1);
Martin G. van Alstyn & Maragrit van Alstyn
(re:2); George Schremeling & Anna Cayn
(re:3).

Death Record

Winn, [?], (child of Robert Winn), d.
8/30/1811 (DFP:94)

Winn, Catharina, (dau. of Robert Erving
Winn), d. 7/30/1796, age 2 years, 1 month, 26
days; buried 8/1/1796 (DFP:89)

Winn, Elisabeth, (wife of John Winn, Esquire),

912

.. 12/19/1747; m. 2/?/1771; d. 6/31/1790; ▸uried 7/2/1790 (DFP:80)

▸Vinn, Helena, (widow of John Winn), d. ▸/?/1809, age 28 years, 5 months, 16 days; ▸uried 2/4/1809 (DFP:92)

▸Vinn, John, d. 12/?/1809, age 62 years; buried 2/5/1809 (DFP:93)

Probate Abstract

▸Vinne, Hugh, (of Amsterdam), will dated 1/12/1822; probated 10/11/1826. Legatees: ▸vife, Hannah; sons, Francis H. and Killian; ▸laus., Catherine and Betsey. Executors: wife ▸nd son, Francis H. Witnesses: Deodatus ▸Vright, Louisa M. Wright, Mariah Abbot. WMC 57:266)

▸Vinne, Lucas, (of Glen), will dated 5/21/1831; ▸robated 7/11/1831. Legatees: wife, Rachel; ▸ons, James (& his Lucas), Lucas, John, Henry ▸& his Lucas); daus., Mary Ann (wife of John ▸. Clement), Alida (wife of Peter I. Clute). Executors: sons, James and Lucas. Witnesses: Rowland W. Siver, John C. Davis, Jacob R. H. Hasbrouck. (WMC 57:279)

▸Vinne, William C., (of Amsterdam), will dated 10/20/1829; probated 1/25/1830. Legatees: ▸vife, Hanna; three sons, John, William and ▸ames Henry; five daus. [not named]. Executors: wife; William Rob, Nathan Neff. ▸Witnesses: Isaac Major, Fisher Putman, James Cushney. (WMC 57:276)

Tryon County Militia

Winn, John   [Appendix A]

Pension Abstract

Winne, Jacob, m. Susannah Evertse, 1/14/1778, by Rev. Thomas Romeyn, Pastor of the Reformed Dutch Church of Caughnawaga at the home of John Fonda in the same town; d. 6/11/1807. (Susannah Winne, b. 1759/60; resident of Schenectady, Schenectady Co., N.Y. on 12/2/1837.) Jacob was in the military at the time of his marriage in 1778 and was stationed at the Schoharie forts as a commissary or assistant commissary of issues; Jacob was commissioned a lieutenant and continued to serve as commissary until the end of the war; he was primarily on duty at the middle fort of Schoharie "which was located between what is now called 'Middleburgh' & 'Vrooman's land' and that the upper fort was abandoned immediately after the massacres committed there by the enemy". (RWPA: #W18455)

1790 Census

Winn, John   [Appendix B]

WINNER

1790 Census

Winner, Conradt   [Appendix B]
Winner, Francis
Winner, Francis, Jr.

WINTER

Birth/Baptism

Winter, Christian (of Gaiseberg) & Sophia [?]: Thankful, b. 10/?/1785, bapt. 12/19/1790

(SJC:35); Jannike, b. 11/7/1790, bapt.
12/19/1790 (SJC:35). Sponsors: Johannes
Countermann & Elisabeth Counterman (re:1);
Jannike Winter (re:2).

1790 Census

Winter, Isaac   [Appendix B]
Winters, William

WIRT

Birth/Baptism

Wirt, Jo[h]ann Georg & [?]: Christian, b.
2/18/1769 (LTSA:26). Sponsors: Christian
Welkel, Anna Maria Altbrand.

WIRTH

Birth/Baptism

Wirth, Johannes & Dorothea [?]: Andreas, b.
1/15/1755 (LTSA:10); Adam, b. 5/19/1769
(LTSA:27); Christian, b. 4/1/1772 (LTSA:42).
Sponsors: Andreas Tillenbach, Arnd Bottmann
(re:1); Adam Schneider (re:2); Christian Lemm
& his wife (re:3).

WISER

1790 Census

Wiser, Nicholas   [Appendix B]

WISSELFEL

1790 Census

Wisselfel, Aaron   [Appendix B]
Wisselfel, Andrew

WISWELL

1790 Census

Wiswell, Samuel   [Appendix B]

WITBECK

Marriage

Wittbeck, Adam m. Elisabeth Koelach,
9/4/1792 (RDSA:197)

Birth/Baptism

Witbeck, Andrew & Macke [?]: Peter, bapt.
4/16/1744 (FH:23). Sponsors: David Verplank,
Andries Ten Eyk, Elizabeth Vanderpoel.

Witbeck/Wittbek, Gabriel & Maria/Merytje
(Fyne): Georg Adam, b. 1/24/1772 (LTSA:41);
Sarah, bapt. 7/28/1778 (DRC:48); Robert, b.
12/17/1781, bapt. 2/1/1782 (DRC:60).
Sponsors: Georg Adam Dachstetter & his wife
(re:1); Hanjoost Sternburgh & Annatje
Scheffelaer (re:2); Robert Yates & Derickje
Yates (re:3).

Tryon County Militia

Witbeck, Leonard   [Appendix A]

1790 Census

Witbeek, Gabriel   [Appendix B]

WITFORD

1790 Census

Witford, Storsly   [Appendix B]

WITH

Birth/Baptism

With, Joseph & Delia [?]: Joseph, b. 7/7/1782; bapt. ?/20/1782 (DRGF:62). Sponsors: [?] & [?].

WITT

1790 Census

Witt, Moses   [Appendix B]

WITTMER

Birth/Baptism

Wittmer, Peter & Maria Salome [?]: Maria Barbara, b. 1/9/1769 (LTSA:28); Samuel, b. 4/4/1771 (LTSA:37). Sponsors: the parents themselves (re:1 & 2).

WITTMOSER

Death Record

Wittmoser, Jonas, b. 9/20/1773; d. 9/21/1796; buried 9/23/1796 (DFP:90)

WIXEN

1790 Census

Wixen, Barnabas   [Appendix B]

WODDOMS

Probate Abstract

Woddoms, Ichabod, (of Johnstown), will dated 4/20/1802; probated 7/14/1802. Legatees: wife, Lucinda. Executrix: wife. Witnesses: William Throop, Daniel Garfield, Barzillai Tomson. (WMC 56:151)

WOERKER

Birth/Baptism

Woeker, Samuel & Elionora (Beely): Maria, b. 4/1/1776; bapt. 6/30/1776 (DRC:38). Sponsors: John Bowman & Eva Bowman.

COMPENDIUM

WOHLEBEN

Marriage

Wohleben, Johann Dieterich m. Anna Elisabeth Tygart, 3/8/1770 (RDSA:188)

Wohleben, Nicholas P. m. Anna Elisabeth Smaal, 5/19/1793 (DRGF:210)

Wohleben, Peter m. Catharina Flack, 7/17/1765 (RDSA:176)

Wohleben, Peter Henr. m. Catharina Snell (dau. of Jac. Snell), 7/10/1785 (DRGF:202)

Birth/Baptism

Wohleben, Abraham & Dorothea [?]: Abraham, b. 3/23/1783, bapt. 5/18/1783 (DRGF:71); Elisabeth, b. 2/28/1785, bapt. 3/5/1785 (DRGF:93). Sponsors: Abhm Rosencrantz, P. L. & Anna Maria (re:1); Pieter Fox & Elisabeth Wohleben (re:2).

Wohleben, Dieterich & Maria [?]: Kunigunda, b. 1/12/1771; bapt. 1/27/1771 (RDSA:108). Sponsors: Maria Kunigu[nda] & Debald Tygh[art].

Wohleben, Henrich & Magdalena [?]: Johannes, b. 9/13/1760; bapt. 9/21/1760 (RDSA:22). Sponsors: Debald Deighert & his wife, Kunigunda.

Wohleben, Henrich & Margretha [?]: Petrus, b. 11/27/1764, bapt. 12/9/1764 (RDSA:52); Adamus, b. 9/30/1767, bapt. 10/6/1767; d. 10/6/1767 (RDSA:78); Jacobus, b. 9/30/1769, bapt. 10/7/1769 (RDSA:97). Sponsors: Pieter Lauchs & Catharina Lauchs (re:1); Adam Laux & Cathrin Elisabeth (re:2); Jacob Ecker & Margretha Fink (re:3).

Wohleben, Jacob & Sussanna [?]: Catharina, b. 2/12/1783, bapt. 3/15/1783 (DRGF:69); Lena, b. 10/25/1784, bapt. 11/9/1784 (DRGF:89). Sponsors: Thomas Schumacher & Catharina Delene (re:1); Joh: Friedr: Bellinger & Lena (re:2).

Wohleben/Wolever, Johann Peter & Catharina (Vlack): Maria Elisabeth, b. 4/1/1766, bapt. 5/5/1766 (RDSA:63); Catharina, b. 3/28/1768, bapt. 4/17/1768 (RDSA:85); Johann Nicolaus, b. 8/1/1770, bapt. 8/8/1770 (RDSA:104); Anna, b. 1/29/1777, bapt. 2/8/1777 (DRGF:22); Johannes Petrus, b. 4/12/1779, bapt. 5/25/1779 (DRGF:35); Jacob, b. 9/3/1781, bapt. 12/27/1781 (DRC:59). Sponsors: Maria Elisabeth & Johann Nicolas Wohleben (re:1); Catharina & Johann Michael Ittig (re:2); Joh: Nicolaus Wohleben & Mari[?] Flack (re:3); George Feyl & Anna (re:4); Piter Flack & Sophia (re:5); Jacob Berns & Susanna Vlack (re:6).

Wohleben, Johannes & Catharina [?]: Johann Nicolas, b. 9/15/1780, bapt. 9/17/1780 (DRGF:40); Maria, b. 9/16/1783, bapt. 9/21/1783 (DRGF:75). Sponsors: Nicolas Hergheimer & Margretha Snell (re:1); Pieter Wohleben & Christina (re:2).

Wollever, Johannes (Royal Grant) & Catharina [?] (Palatine Town): Daniel, bapt. 10/23/1791, d. 4/?/1792 (SJC:49); Catharina, bapt. 3/3/1793 (SJC:74). Sponsors: David Schuyler & Margretha Schuyler (re:1); John Mayer & Catharina Mayer (re:2).

Wollever, Peter (Canajoh. Castle) & Catharina [?] (Palatine Town): Heinrich, bapt. 8/1/1790 (SJC:30); Elisabeth, bapt. 4/1/1793 (SJC:74). Sponsors: Heinrich Zimmerman & Anna Schnell (re:1); Johannes Snell & Elisabeth Snell (re:2).

Death Record

Wohleber, Abraham, (personally scalped by the Indians at the time of the war for independence), d. 2/6/1819, Columbia, age 62 years, 2 months, 11 days; buried near the church in the same place (RDH:277)

Wohleber, Maria, (unmarried adult), d. 3/7/1816, Germanflats, age 80 years, 5 months, 22 days; buried in the cemetery of the stone church (RDH:272)

Tryon County Militia

Wohleben, Abraham   [Appendix A]
Wohleben, Jacob
Wohleben, Nicholas
Wohleben, Peter
Wohlever, Peter
Wollever, John
Wollever, Nicholas

Pension Abstract

Wohleben, Abraham, b. 12/26/1756, son of Nicholas and Maria Elisabetha Wohleben; (brothers: John and Dederick [both were killed at Oriskany] and Peter; sister: Magdalena, b. 1/7/1755; nephew: Nicholas, b. 8/?/1769, son of Peter Wohleben; niece: Elizabeth Shoemaker, b. 4/1/1776 & resident of German Flatts, N.Y. in 1843); m. Dorothey Bellinger, 1/25/1778, German Flats; d. 2/16/1819, Herkimer Co., N.Y. (Dorothey Wohleben, b. 1754/5, dau. of Peter Bellinger; resident of Truxton, Cortland Co., N.Y. in 1837; d. 1847.) Children: Abraham, b. ?/25/1785, d. pre 1815; Elisabeth, b. 7/1/1803; Niclas, d. 1/6/1788; Jeremiah, b. ca. 1802 (m. Polly [?] and resident of Truxton, N.Y. in 1837). Abraham served as a private under Capts. Michael Ittig and Frederick Frank in Col. Peter

Bellinger's 4th. Regt., Tryon Co. Militia and fought in the battle of Oriskany; he was sent out to collect firewood for the garrison at Fort Herkimer in October 1781 when enemy Indians captured and scalped him; Abraham was left for dead and he was not found for about three days at which time his feet were frozen; he was unable to perform military duties for almost two years from the exposure and hardships of that experience; he later returned to military duty at Fort Herkimer and he also served as a batteauman during the war. (RWPA: #R17772)

Wohleben, Jacob, m. Susanna Flagg, 5/10/1779, near Fort Herkimer at the home of the groom; d. 12/4/1827. (Susanna Wohleben, b. 2/?/1756; resident of Glen, Montgomery Co., N.Y. on 2/1/1837; d. 9/?/1851.) Children: Jacob, b. 1789/90 (resident of Jefferson Co., N.Y. on 6/26/1852). Jacob was a private in Capt. Ittig's Co., Col. Peter Bellinger's 4th. Regt. Tryon Co. Militia from 1777 through 1780 and was stationed at Fort Herkimer as a guard; he served under Col. Willett in 1781 and fought in the skirmish at West Canada Creek. (RWPA: #W18372 WOOLAVER)

Wohleben, John, b. 9/13/1760, Canajoharie, N.Y.; (brothers: Nicholas and Peter [RWPA: #W19659]; resident of Madison Co., N.Y. on 7/28/1837. John enlisted in 1776 as a private in Capt. Henry Dieffendorf's Co., Col. Ebenezer Cox's 1st. Regt., Tryon Co. Militia and fought in the battle of Oriskany on 8/6/1777; he then served in 1778 as a batteauman under the command of Capt. William Patterson; John was a participant in the battle of Johnstown. (RWPA: #R11771)

Wohleben, Peter, b. 11/27/1764, son of Henry Wohleben, Stone Arabia, N.Y.; (brother: John Wohleben [RWPA: #R1171]; m. Catharine

Snell, 7/10/1785; d. 9/13/1843, Manheim, Montgomery Co., N.Y. (Catharine Wohleben, b. 1763/4, dau. of Jacob Snell; resident of Manheim, N.Y. on 12/23/1843.) Children: Margaret, b. 1786 (eldest child: m. [?] Lepper and resident of Manheim, N.Y. in 1845); Nicholas, b. 1799/1800 (fifth child and resident of Manheim, N.Y. in 1847). [There were four more children who were not named in the file.] Peter enlisted in May 1779 and served at various times until the summer of 1781; he was a corporal in Capt. Jost Dygart's Co., Col. Peter Bellinger's 4th. Regt., Tryon Co. Militia and was in the battle of Stone Arabia where he was wounded in the shoulder; Peter was shot in the right thigh when attacked by Indians on 7/18/1781 [Peter's older brother and brother-in-law were both killed at the same time and his younger brother, John, was captured and removed to Montreal]. (RWPA: #W19659 *WOOLAVER*)

1790 Census

Woolever, Abraham   [Appendix B]
Woolever, Jacob
Woolever, Peter (2)
Wooliber, Henry

WOHLGEMUTH

Marriage

Wohlgemuth, Johannes m. Anna Maria Smidt, 10/15/1769 (RDSA:188)

Wohlgemuth, Wilhelm m. Maria Guntermann, 11/18/1783 (DRGF:198)

Birth/Baptism

Wohlgemuth, Johannes & [?]: [?], bap 9/11/1763 (RDSA:42). Sponsors: [not named].

Wohlgemuth, Johannes & Maria [?]: Christina, b. 10/23/1783; bapt. 11/10/1783 (DRGF:77 Sponsors: Wilhelm Wohlgemuth & Mar Guntermann.

Wohlgemuth, Wilhelm & Maria (Countryman Elisabeth, b. 6/4/1787; bapt. 6/17/178 (RDSA:113). Sponsors: Isaac Bickert Elisabeth Gundermann.

Death Record

Wohlgemuth, Johannes, (son of Wilhel Wohlgemuth), b. 9/6/1785; d. 1/19/1788 buried 1/23/1788 (RDSA:230)

Wohlgemuth, Johannes, d. 3/13/1792, age 7 years, 4 months; buried 3/15/1792 (RDSA:233

Wohlgemuth, Salomon, (son of Johanne Wohlgemuth), b. 5/26/1794; d. 8/11/1794 buried 8/12/1794 (RDSA:235)

Wohlgemuth, William, d. 3/?/1813, age 4 years, 6 months, 20 days; buried 3/28/181. (DFP:96)

Probate Abstract

Wohlgemuth, Johannes, (of Palatine), wil dated 7/17/1788; probated 5/31/1792. Legatees sons, Johannes, William. Executors: son William; Abraham Oathout (of Schenectady) Witnesses: Abraham Oathout, Nicholas Hall, Jonas Oothout. (WMC 56:147)

Wohlgemuth, William, (of Canajoharie), wil dated 6/29/1811; probated 6/28/1814. Legatees wife, Maria; sons, George and Henry; daus.

Elizabeth, Margaret, Anna, Maria, Eve and Christina. Executors: wife; John R. Cook; brother-in-law, Isaac Pickard. Witnesses: Jacob and Abraham Shoemaker, John Failing. (WMC 56:392)

Tryon County Militia

Wohlgemuth, John   [Appendix A]
Wohlgemuth, William

WOLFF

Marriage

Wolff, Joh: Michael m. Anna Elisabeth Meer Rauss, 1/19/1767 (RDSA:180)

Birth/Baptism

Wolff, Georg Mich. & Elisabeth [?]: Magdalena, b. 3/31/1772 (LTSA:42). Sponsors: Peter Jung & his wife.

Wolff, Jacob & Maria Margretha [?]: Catharina, b. 6/12/1782, bapt. 6/16/1782 (DRGF:58); Maria, b. 9/27/1784, bapt. 12/7/1784 (DRGF:90). Sponsors: Johannes Guntermann & Barbara Nelles (re:1); Caspar Miller & Maria Magd: (re:2).

Wolff, Joh. Michael & Elisabetha [?]: Margretha Salome, b. 10/19/1767, bapt. 10/23/1767 (RDSA:79); Valentin, b. 8/12/1770, bapt. 8/21/1770 (RDSA:106); Catharina, b. 8/22/1774, bapt. 9/18/1774 (LTSA:46). Sponsors: Margretha Salome & Wilhelm Petri (re:1); Valentin Miller & [?] Maria Miller (re:2); Dieterich Suz & his wife Catharina (re:3).

Wolff, Michael & [?]: [?], bapt. 7/13/1777 (DRGF:24). Sponsors: [none named].

Tryon County Militia

Wolf, Jacob   [Appendix A]
Wolff, Johannes

1790 Census

Wolff, Jacob   [Appendix B]

WON

Tryon County Militia

Won, Nicholas   [Appendix A]

WOOD

Marriage

Wood, David m. Elizabeth van de Werken, 8/11/1793 (DFP:50)

Wood, John m. Drusilla Nickles, 3/8/1787 (DRGF:204)

Wood, Joseph m. Nelly van Eabern, 11/11/1792 (DFP:46)

Birth/Baptism

Wood, James & Sarah [?]: Robert, b. 6/29/1790, bapt. 8/?/1790 (JPC:3); Benjamin, b. 10/25/1792, bapt. 12/20/1792 (JPC:7); Sarah, bapt. 6/7/1795 (JPC:10).

Wood, John & Meritje (Van De Werken):

Uriah, b. 2/22/1786; bapt. 3/12/1786 (DRC:77). Sponsors: David Wood & Lena Wood.

Wood, Uria & Magdalena (Quakkenbosch): David, bapt. 1758 (DRC:1). Sponsors: David Quakkonb[ush?] & Ann Scott.

Probate Abstract

Wood, Abraham, (of Mayfield), will dated 7/14/1819; probated 9/29/1819. Legatees: wife, Mary; sons, Rufus, David, Daniel, Jesiah, John, Asa, Butler; also William and David who are "naturally incapacitated to act prudently and discreetly for themselves"; daus., Esther, Mary, Hanah Cole, Cynthia Brown, Edith Vandebergh. Executors: sons, Rufus and John; son-in-law, Peter Vandebergh. Witnesses: Ichabod Potter, Alexander Kasson, Duncan McMartin, Jr. Referees in dispute: Welcome Capron, Wing Chase, Duncan McMartin, Jr. (WMC 57:168-169)

Wood, Magdalen, (of Charleston), will dated 1/12/1802; probated 9/25/1816. Legatees: sons, John and David; daus., Marey (wife of John Barlet), Abigail (wife of Nicholas Van Slyke) and Magdalin (wife of John H. Quackenboss); granddaughter, Magdalen (of David). Executors: Nicholas Quackenboss, Nicholas Van Slyke. Witnesses: John Barbera, Wm. Wample, John I. Wample. (WMC 57:163)

Tryon County Militia

Wood, William   [Appendix A]

1790 Census

Wood, Caleb   [Appendix B]
Wood, David
Wood, James (2)

Wood, John (3)
Wood, Joseph
Wood, Palmer
Wood, Thomas

WOODBURN

Death Record

Woodburn, John, (Dr.), d. 6/5/1849, age 34 years, of Consumption; buried Cherry Valley Presbyterian Church cemetery (PCV:89)

WOODCOCK

Tryon County Militia

Woodcock, Abraham   [Appendix A]
Woodcock, John
Woodcock, Peter

Pension Abstract

Woodcock, Peter, b. 1759/60; m. [wife not named; living in 1820]; resident of Maryland, Otsego Co., N.Y. on 10/12/1820. Children: William, b. 1804/5; Sarah, b. 1809/10; Julane, b. 1812/3; Maria, b. 1814/5; Nancy, b. 1816/7; Rachel, b. 1820 [age six months on 10/12/1820]. Peter enlisted in 1776 as a private in Capt. Robert McKean's Co., Col. Van Schaick's Regt. of the N.Y. Line and served "faithfully through the war". (RWPA: #S45157)

1790 Census

Woodcock, Nicholas   [Appendix B]

920

COMPENDIUM

WOODERT

Birth/Baptism

Woodert, James (of Schuylers Lake) & Catharina (Haus): Angelique, bapt. 12/26/1790 (SJC:36); Maria, bapt. 2/10/1793 (SJC:72). Sponsors: Conrad Haus & Angelique Haus (re:1); Georg Haus & Mary Lise Haus (re:2).

WOODRUFF

1790 Census

Woodruff, Amasa   [Appendix B]
Woodruff, Stephen

WOODS

1790 Census

Woods, James   [Appendix B]

WOODWARD

1790 Census

Woodward, David   [Appendix B]
Woodward, James
Woodward, John
Woodward, Oliver

WOODWORTH

Probate Abstract

Woodworth, Selah, (of Mayfield), will dated 9/25/1823; probated 12/15/1823. Legatees: wife, Rebecca; each of my children; sons, Rosel, Jacob, John and Ebenezer. Executors: wife and son, Ebenezer. Witnesses: Ebenezer Woodworth, Selah Woodworth, Jr. Dwelly Spalding. (WMC 57:177)

Woodworth, William S., (of Mayfield), will dated 4/7/1812; probated 8/27/1816. Legatees: wife, Nancy; sons, Joel and James; three daughters. Executors: wife and two sons. Witnesses: Selah, Reecah and Nancy Woodworth. (WMC 57:163)

Tryon County Militia

Woodworth, Selah   [Appendix A]
Woodworth, Solomon

1790 Census

Woodworth, Ezekiel   [Appendix B]
Woodworth, Samuel
Woodworth, Selah
Woodworth, Serenius
Woodworth, Solomon

WOOLCOT

1790 Census

Woolcot, William   [Appendix B]

WOOLKINWOOD

1790 Census

Woolkinwood, John   [Appendix B]
Woolkinwood, John, Jr.

WOOLSEY

1790 Census

Woolsey, David   [Appendix B]
Woolsey, John

WORMOUTH

Marriage

Wormuth, Christian m. Maria Ekker, 12/23/1781 (DRGF:195)

Wormuth, Johann (2nd son of Johannis Warmuth of Stone Arabia) m. Lidia Haal (1st dau. of Simonis Haal of New Tallaborough), 3/24/1778 (LTSA:285)

Wormuth, Johannes (widower) m. Johanna Kihn, 4/9/1787 (RDSA:192)

Wormuth, Johannes (widower) m. Sophia Biller (widow of Henrich Biller, soldier), 1/13/1761 (RDSA:169)

Wormuth, Johannes m. Nancy Clark, 3/13/1770 (RDSA:188)

Wormuth, Matthew m. Anna van den Werken, 10/28/1781 (DRGF:195)

Wormuth, Peter m. Anna Fheling, 6/3/1783 (DRGF:198)

Birth/Baptism

Wormouth, Christian & Maria (Eker): Johannes, b. 7/30/1782, bapt. 8/1/1782 (DRGF:59); Christian, bapt. 11/15/1789 [parents of Canajoh. Castle] (SJC:19). Sponsors: Johannes Ekker & Elisabeth (re:1); Wilhelm Fox & Margretha Fox (re:2).

Wormouth, Johann & Elisabeth [?]: Heinrich, b. 1/27/1780; bapt. 2/2/1780 (LTSA:59). Sponsors: Heinrich Keyser & Margaretha.

Wormouth, Johann Henrich & Anna Elisabetha (Empie): Johann Willhelm, bapt. 6/24/1752 (RDSA:12); Anna Margretha, b. 2/24/1756, bapt. 3/7/1756 (RDSA:16); Matthous, b. 12/7/1760, bapt. 12/21/1760 (RDSA:24); Christina Elisabeth, b. 3/3/1763, bapt. 3/20/1763 (RDSA:39); Anna, b. 5/22/1765, bapt. 6/16/1765 (RDSA:56); Anna Eva, b. 10/2/1767, bapt. 11/9/1767 (RDSA:80). Sponsors: Joseph Wermouth & his wife, Catharina (re:1); Anna Margretha, wife of Wilhelm Wermuth (re:2); Matthouse (son of Henrich Crem) & Elisabetha (dau. of Henrich Crem) (re:3); Elisabetha, Ecker, Christina Kasselman & Casper Keller (re:4); Anna Elisabeth Krembs & Johannes Eppli (re:5); Anna Eva Schultz, Anna Eva Emgie & Johannes Krem[?] (re:6).

Wormouth, Johannes & Barbara Elisabetha [?]; m. 2nd. Sophia [?]: Johannes, b. 4/9/1755 [1st. wife] (LTSA:13); Petrus, b. 11/24/1761, bapt. 12/3/1761 [2nd. wife] (RDSA:29); Anna Margretha, b. 7/12/1764, bapt. 8/5/1764 [2nd. wife] (RDSA:49); Johann Henrich, b. 7/18/1767, bapt. 7/26/1767 [2nd. wife] (RDSA:76). Sponsors: Johannes Frey, Maria Elisabetha Nellis, Hann Henrich Schremling (re:1); Mattheus (son of Peter Warmuth) & Margretha (dau. of Andreas Finck) (re:2);

Henrich Sever & Margretha Sutz (re:3); Henrich Kling & Catharina (re:4).

Wormouth, Johannes & Catharina [?]: Andreas, b. 11/25/1765; bapt. 11/25/1765 (RDSA:59). Sponsors: Andreas Finck & Catharine.

Wormouth, Johannes & Nancy (Clark): Elisabetha, b. 6/1/1771 (LTSA:37); Catharina, b. 6/20/1781, bapt. 6/23/1781 (DRGF:46). Sponsors: Georg Wabel & his wife; Elisabetha Bader (re:1); John Sieles & Catharina (re:2).

Wormouth, Johannes & Sophia [?]: Henrich, b. 8/18/1768; bapt. 8/[2]8/1768 (RDSA:89). Sponsors: Johannes Kajser & Elisabeth Vorrer.

Wormouth, John & Anna [?]: Peter, b. 7/12/1793 (LTSA:82). Sponsors: Peter Jerg Laux & Margaret.

Wormouth, Joseph & Catharina (Wies): Willhelm, bapt. 11/7/1751 (RDSA:11); Anna Margareth, bapt. 1/9/1753 (RDSA:13); Johannes, b. 6/27/1761, bapt. 6/28/1761 (RDSA:27); Maria, b. 2/5/1764, bapt. 2/12/1764 (RDSA:45); Maria Catharina, b. 8/13/1766, bapt. 8/17/1766 (RDSA:67). Sponsors: Willhelm Wermouth & his wife, Anna Margaretha (re:1); Johannes von den Wercke, Christina Seche (re:2); Adam Schnel & Janitje von der Wercken (re:3); Margretha & Wilhem Finck (re:4); Anna Margaretha & Nicol Snell (re:5).

Wormouth, Matthew & Salome [?]: Margretha, b. 11/20/1782; bapt. 12/8/1782 (DRGF:64). Sponsors: Henrich Wabel & Margretha.

Wormouth, Willhelm & Regina [?]: Matthes, b. 9/19/1778, bapt. 10/26/1778 (LTSA:54); Martynes, b. 2/11/1785, bapt. 2/13/1785 (DRGF:92). Sponsors: Matthes Warmuth,

Catarina Sprecher (re:1); Nicolas Windekker & Maria (re:2).

Death Record

Wormouth, Peter, d. 5/?/1811, age 55 years, 8 months, 23 days; buried 5/12/1811 (DFP:94)

Wormuth, Matthew, (Lieutenant), b. 8/17/1744, Palatine; d. 5/?/1778 (Shot from his horse, near Cherry Valley in May 1778, by Indians under Brant while carrying dispatches between Fort Plain and Fort Alden.); buried Fort Plain Cemetery, Minden (FPC 56:43j)

Probate Abstract

Wormouth, Peter, (of Canajoharie), will dated 4/6/1811; probated 3/26/1816. Legatees: wife, Anna Eva; wife's dau., Margaret Countriman; David Gray (whom I brought up); brother, Johannes. Executors: brother-in-law, Jacob A. Wallrad, John Failing, wife [Anna Eva]. Witnesses: William Wohlgemuth, Jacob Shoemaker, John Waeck. (WMC 56:383)

Tryon County Militia

Warmouth, Christian   [Appendix A]
Warmouth, John
Warmouth, Matthew
Warmouth, Nathaniel
Warmouth, Peter
Warmouth, Peter J.
Warmouth, William

Pension Abstract

Warmouth, Christian, m. Maria Ekker, 12/23/1781 by Rev. Abraham Rosencrantz; d. ca. 1830, Herkimer Co., N.Y. (Maria Warmouth, dau. of John Ekker of Palatine, N.Y.) Christian enlisted from his home in

923

Palatine and served as a private in Col. Jacob Klock's 2nd. Regt., Tryon Co. Militia; he fought in the battle of Johnstown. (RWPA: #W18279)

Warmouth, John, m. Catharine [?]; d. 2/18/1832, Manlius, Onondaga Co., N.Y. (Catharine Warmouth, b. 1766/7; resident of Manlius, N.Y. in 1844.) Children: John, b. 6/?/1794 (stated to be the fourth child; resident of Huron, Wayne Co., N.Y. on 12/24/1844). John, resident of Palatine, enlisted in the 1st. Regt., Tryon Co. Militia and served as a private from 1780 through 1782. (RWPA: #W26093)

Warmouth, John, m. Hannah Kane, 4/9/1787, Reformed Dutch Church of Stone Arabia; d. 12/17/1799. (Hannah Warmouth, b. 1767/8; m. 2nd. Thomas Rawley [he died 3/25/1814]; she was a resident of Cobleskill, Schoharie Co., N.Y. in 1843 and of Deerfield, Oneida Co., N.Y. in 1848.) Children: Mary (m. [?] Empie and resident of Fulton Co., N.Y. in 1844); John (living in Fulton Co. in 1844). John enlisted on 8/23/1776 and was a private in Capt. Christian Getman's Co. of rangers until 3/27/1777; he fought in the battle of Oriskany and saw Capt. Andrew Dillenback killed; John also served as a batteauman under the command of Capts. Samuel Gray and John Lefler. (RWPA: #W24797)

Warmouth, Matthew, b. 8/23/1749/50; (brother: Peter Warmouth [RWPA: #W226801]); m. [wife not named]; d. 12/11/1836. Children: Margaret (m. [?] Weaver); one other child not named in file. [These were the two surviving children on 12/11/1838.] Matthew enlisted at Stone Arabia on 1/10/1777 for a period of one year and two months in Col. Van Schaick's Regt. of the N.Y. Line and served in the companies of

Capt. Andrew Finck and Capt. Hick; he fought in the battle of Johnstown. (RWPA: #S45459)

Warmouth, Peter, b. ca. 1757-1761; (brother: Matthew Warmouth [RWPA: #S45459]); m. Sarah Putman, 4/19/1786, Caughnawaga, Montgomery Co., N.Y.; resident of Johnstown, N.Y. on 4/9/1818; d. 7/23/1836. (Sarah Warmouth, b. ca. 1757; resident of Glen, Montgomery Co., N.Y. on 1/17/1843.) Children: Eva, b. 1802/3. Peter enlisted at Stone Arabia on 3/5/1782 as a private and matross in Capt. Moodie's Co., Col. John Lamb's Regt. of Artillery and served until the "Peace of 1783"; he was also a member of Col. Jacob Klock's 2nd. Regt., Tryon Co. Militia and fought in the battle of Johnstown where he was "severely wounded in the side". (RWPA: #W22680)

1790 Census

Wormwood, Abraham	[Appendix B]
Wormwood, Christian	
Wormwood, John	
Wormwood, Matthias	
Wormwood, Peter (2)	
Wormwood, Ryena	

WREITH

Birth/Baptism

Wrieth, Jacob & Elisabeth [?]: Isaac, b. 3/18/1784; bapt. 3/30/1784 (DRGF:83). Sponsors: Marcus Dussler & Catharina Hausse.

WRIGHT

Probate Abstract

Wright, Jacob, (of Minden), will dated 10/19/1810; probated 3/6/1811. Legatees: daus., Maria, Catherine and Elizabeth; sons, Isaac and Jacob. Executors: son, Isaac; Abraham House, Peter P. Wagner. Witnesses: Abraham Arndt, Isaac Wright, Jacob Wright, Jr. (WMC 56:381)

Tryon County Militia

Wright, David   [Appendix A]

1790 Census

Wright, Daniel   [Appendix B]
Wright, Earl
Wright, Ebenezer
Wright, Gabriel
Wright, Humphry
Wright, Jacob (2)
Wright, John
Wright, Luther
Wright, Samuel
Wright, Solomon
Wright, Thomas

WUTERICH

Birth/Baptism

Wuterich, Georg & Maria Elisabeth [?]: Catharina, b. 6/17/1777, bapt. 6/22/1777 (DRGF:24); Maria Elisabetha, b. 9/10/1782, bapt. 6/22/1783 (DRGF:72); Johannes, b. 9/12/1784, bapt. 10/7/1784 (DRGF:88). Sponsors: Hans Adam Hartmann & Maria Catharina (re:1); Christian Hochstatter & Maria Elisabeth (re:2); Johannes Fenster & Maria Shneck (re:3).

Wuterich, Michael & [?]: Elisabeth, b. 3/15/1783; bapt. 5/6/1783 (DRGF:71). Sponsors: Jacob Guntermann & Elisabeth Walrath.

Wuterich, Michael & Elisabeth [?]: Michael, b. 11/12/1780 (DRGF:41); Elisabeth, bapt. 3/3/1789 [parents of New Deutschland] (SJC:11). Sponsors: Christian Hochstader & Maria Catharina (re:1); Jacob Lenz & Elisabeth Hofstatter (re:2).

Wuterich, Michael & Magdalena [?]: Eva Catharina, b. 1/2/1771; bapt. 1/26/1771 (RDSA:108). Sponsors: Lorentz Ranckel & Margretha Keller.

Wuterich, Michael & Maria Catharina [?]: Maria Sybilla, b. 10/21/1779; bapt. 11/6/1779 (DRGF:37). Sponsors: Jacob Dunches & Maria Sybilla.

Death Record

Wuterich, Hiob, (legitimate son of George Wiederich), d. 3/25/1802, New Germany, age 42 years, 9 months, 25 days (died in childbirth); buried in the same place (RDH:245)

WYCKOFF (also see WIKOFF)

Death Record

Wyckoff, Miss. Orpha, (dau. of John Wyckoff, resident of Cherry Valley), d. 8/13/1846, age 20 years, 6 months; buried on farm & removed to Cherry Valley Cemetry ca. 1864 (CVC:1)

WYLD

1790 Census

Wyld, Yost Henry   [Appendix B]

WYMER

1790 Census

Wymer, Andrew   [Appendix B]

WYNINGS

1790 Census

Wynings, Clark   [Appendix B]

WYNSI

Birth/Baptism

Wynsi, John (of Canajoh. Castle) & Rachel [?]: Georg, b. 2/28/1790, bapt. 4/2/1790 (SJC:24); Margretha, bapt. 6/24/1792 (SJC:60). Sponsors: Georg Haus & Maria Haus (re:1); Arend Alberti & Margretha Alberti (re:2).

WYSENBERK

Birth/Baptism

Wysenberk, Catharine & [?]: Mary, bapt. 10/14/1744 (FH:25). Sponsors: James Rogers, Helena Walleslous, Issabella Allen.

WYTH

1790 Census

Wyth, Ebenezer   [Appendix B]

———————

YALE

Birth/Baptism

Yale, Nate & Sarah (Hover): Mary, b. 9/18/1790; bapt. 10/24/1790 (DRC:90). Sponsors: Anthony Van Vechten & Maria Van Vechten.

YALES

1790 Census

Yales, Weight   [Appendix B]

YANNEY

Probate Abstract

Yanney, Henry, (of Johnstown), will dated 1/6/1827; probated 7/12/1830. Legatees: wife, Elizabeth; sons, James and Philip; brother, Christian; daus., Dolly Bedford, Susannah Younglove, Catharine Boshart, Margaret; grandchildren, Amasa, Christian, Henry, Anna

926

COMPENDIUM

Margaret, Clarissa and Elizabeth Stevens, John, George, Henry and Hiram Yanney, Susannah, Joseph and Catharine Quilhot; John Y. Edwards. Executors: sons, James and Philip. Witnesses: Louis Bedford, Aaron Haring, John Frats (1830, resident in British Province, Upper Canada). (WMC 57:278)

Tryon County Militia

Yanney, Christian   [Appendix A]
Yanney, Henry

1790 Census

Yannee, Christian   [Appendix B]

YANSER

1790 Census

Yanser, Hendrickus   [Appendix B]

YANTUS

1790 Census

Yantus, Bartholomew   [Appendix B]

YATCHT

Marriage

Yatcht, John m. Peggy Funda, 11/11/1785 (DRC:164)

YATES

Marriage

Yates, Abram m. Anna Maragrita Herring, 4/27/1778 (DRC:162)

Yates, John J. (of Canajoharie) m. Sally Crane (of Canajoharie), 12/27/1825 (PCBC:51)

Yates, Robert, Jr. m. Turckje Gardinier, 9/9/1770 (RDSA:190)

Birth/Baptism

Yates, Christopher [Major] & Maria [?]: Margretha, b. 11/28/1781; bapt. 12/2/1781 (DRGF:51). Sponsors: Margretha Cox (widow; maiden name Frey).

Yates, Peter & [?]: Sara, b. 3/20/1781; bapt. 5/19/1781 (DRGF:45). Sponsors: Abraham Yates & Maria Yates.

Yates, Peter A. & Catrina (Doxteder): Elizabeth, b. 3/3/1783, bapt. 4/14/1783 (DRC:65); Margrita, b. 7/6/1785, bapt. 7/29/1785 (DRC:74); John, b. 11/16/1790, bapt. 12/15/1790 (DRC:91). Sponsors: Mark Doxteder & Elizabeth Doxteder (re:1); Hendrik J. Doksteder & Maria Doksteder (re:2); [none named] (re:3).

Death Record

Yates, John Xt.[?], d. 3/?/1812, age 58 years; buried 3/13/1812 (DFP:94)

Probate Abstract

Yates, Abraham A., (of Root), will dated 7/7/1830; probated 9/16/1830. Legatees: sons, Robert A., John L. and Abraham, Jr.

927

Executors: John Lenardson, Jr., Robert Lenardson, Abraham Yates, Jr. Witnesses: Simeon Snow, James G. Van Voast, Frederick Lenardson. (WMC 57:277)

Yates, Catharine, (of Root), will dated 9/16/1826; probated 6/27/1831. Legatees: sons, Abraham and John; daus., Sarah (wife of Nicholas Dockstader, Jr.), Elizabeth (wife of John R. Van Everin), Margaret (wife of Aaron T.[?] Dockstader). Executors: [unknown]. Witnesses: [unknown]. (WMC 57:279)

Yates, Christopher, (of Johnstown), will dated 6/15/1798; probated 1/28/1815. Legatees: wife, Catharine; sons, Christopher, Gerrit, Peter, Obadiah, Evert, Sander and John; dau., Catalina (wife of Henry V. Fonda). Executors: son, Evert; Cornelius Veeder, James Lansing, Abraham Van Horne. Witnesses: Volkert Veeder, Robert Lotteridge, James Lansing. (WMC 56:393)

Yates, Christopher P., (of Canajoharie), will dated 12/27/1814; probated 12/20/1816. Legatees: wife, Maria; son, Henry F.; daus., Sarah, Margaret, Ann, Elisabeth, Maria, Susan and Catharine. Bequest: Land in Johnstown to son, Henry F. Executor: son, Henry F. Witnesses: Henry F. Cox, Jeremiah Brumfield, Henry I. Frey. (WMC 57:163)

Yates, Dirikie, (widow of Robert Yates, of Glen), will dated 9/4/1826; probated 10/22/1828. Legatees: Isaiah Depuy and wife, Nelly; brother, John A. Gardinier; Dirikie (dau. of Nicholas Gardinier); Eliza Albright (dau. of Jacob). Executor: friend, Isaiah Depuy. Witnesses: Rynier Gardinier, Isaiah Hardenburgh, Howland Fish. (WMC 57:272)

Yates, Peter A., (of Charleston), will dated 3/26/1814; probated 5/25/1824. Legatees: wife,

Catharine; sons, John P. and Abraham P.; daus., Catharine, Elizabeth Van Ever, Laney Dockstader, Margaret Veeder and Mary Smith; brothers, Abraham and Robert. Executors: brother, Robert; John Leanderson, Jr. Witnesses: William L. Holliday, Cristen Leathers, John Mears[?]. (WMC 57:178-179)

Yates, Robert, (of Charleston), will dated 11/18/1819; probated 7/26/1821. Legatees: wife, Dirkie; Joseph N. Yates. Executrix: wife. Witnesses: John Morrell, Giles and Henry I. Fonda. (WMC 57:172)

Tryon County Militia

Yates, Christopher P.   [Appendix A]
Yates, Peter
Yates, Robert

Pension Abstract

Yates, Christopher P., b. 3/29/1750; m. Maria Frey, 2/14/1774; d. 2/20/1815, Canajoharie, Montgomery Co., N.Y. (Maria Yates, b. 9/6/1752, dau. of Hendrick Frey.) Children: Sarah, b. 1/18/1775; Henry Frey, b. 12/28/1776; Peter, b. 7/19/1779, d. 1/30/1797; Margaret, b. 11/28/1781; Anne, b. 2/15/1784; Elizabeth, b. 2/26/1786; Catharine, b. 4/27/1788, d. 5/3/1835; Maria, b. 8/26/1790; Susanna, b. 9/17/1792, d. 10/14/1829. Christopher entered the Continentals in July 1775 and was said to have "distinguished himself as one of the most prominent Characters in [the] then County of Tryon, in supporting and prosecuting the Commencement of the Revolution, against the Government of Great Britain"; he marched on Gen. Montgomery's expedition to Quebec and was appointed major in Col. Goose Van Schaick's 1st. Regt. of the N.Y. Line until leaving the regiment near the end of 1777; he then served

COMPENDIUM

in the commissary department until the end of the war. Following the war, Christopher was "frequently elected by the people of Montgomery county to represent them in the Legislature of New York". (RWPA: #W16486)

Deed Abstract

Yates, Christopher, of Schenectady Township, Albany Co. to Marten Johannes Van Alstyn, of Canajoharie, Tryon Co. Deed dated 3/12/1773; recorded 3/17/1773. Description: Fourth part of Lot #4 (devised to Marten Joh's. Van Alstyn in the Will of his grandfather, Marten Van Alstyn, decd.) which is to adjoin the fourth part of the same Lot #4 (devised in said Will to Marten Abraham Van Alstyn); also the fourth part of Lot #6 (named in said Will). This land in Canajoharie contains in all (220 acres). Remarks: Christopher Yates conveyed this land, sold to him on 7/23/1772 by Gysbert Fonda, of Albany, merchant. Consideration: L14.11.0. Witnesses: Honterscott [Hunter Scott] Quackenbos, Peter P. B. Quackenbos. (MVL:40)

1790 Census

Yates, Abraham   [Appendix B]
Yates, Abraham, Jr.
Yates, Christopher P.
Yates, John
Yates, Peter
Yates, Robert, Jr.
Yates, Samuel

YATTAN

1790 Census

Yattan, Adam   [Appendix B]
Yattan, Nicholas
Yattan, Peter

YEOMANS

Tryon County Militia

Yeomans, Joseph   [Appendix A]

YERTER

Birth/Baptism

Yerter, Henrich & Maria [?]: Jacob, b. 8/15/1782; bapt. 8/25/1782 (DRGF:60). Sponsors: Jacob Wallrath & Magdalena.

YORAM

Tryon County Militia

Yoram, Jacob   [Appendix A]

YORAN

Tryon County Militia

Yoran, Jacob   [Appendix A]

YORDAN (also see JORDAN)

Pension Abstract

Yordan, John P., b. 1/1/1766, Canajoharie, N.Y.; applied on 2/1/1844 for pension which was rejected because "proof of six months of service, required by the pension law, was not furnished". John stated that he volunteered for duty in 1778 and 1779 under Cols. Willett and Gansevoort; he served six months each year as a private in Capt. Adam Lipe's Co., Col. Samuel Clyde's 1st. Regt., Tryon Co. Militia and assisted in the construction of Fort Clyde; John also said that he served from 1780 through 1782 as a guard at Fort Clyde under Sgt. John Peter Dunkle. (RWPA: #R11943)

1790 Census

Yordon, Casper   [Appendix B]
Yordon, George
Yordon, John

YOST (also see JOST)

Birth/Baptism

Yost, Peter & Mari Madalena (Sheets): Mari Madalena, b. 3/20/1782; bapt. 7/19/1782 (DRC:63). Sponsors: [none named].

Probate Abstract

Yost, Peter, (of Johnstown), will dated 6/13/1810; codicil dated 2/2/1811; probated 2/20/1811. Legatees: wife, Mary Magdalen; sons, John, William, Nicholas, Jacob (& his dau., Margaret); daus., Mary (wife of Joseph Ely) and Elizabeth (wife of John Foote); [number of children varies from six to seven in document; also states four sons & two daus.); grandson, Andrew Settle [may be child of dau., not named]; Peter Witmore. Executors: John McCarthy, Abrm. B. Vosburgh, Eli Parsons; son, William. Witnesses: Corn. Van Beuren, James Lansing, Charles Loughery. Witnesses to codicil: James Lansing, Charles Loughery, Abijah Lobdell. (WMC 56:381)

Tryon County Militia

Yost, Peter   [Appendix A]

1790 Census

Yost, Peter   [Appendix B]

YOUHE

1790 Census

Youhe, James   [Appendix B]

YOUKER (also see YUCKER)

1790 Census

Youker, George   [Appendix B]
Youker, Jacob
Youker, John
Youker, Solomon

YOUNCK

1790 Census

Younck, Peter   [Appendix B]

COMPENDIUM

Younck, William

YOUNG

Marriage

Young, David (son of Andreas Jung) m. Elisabeth Leib (dau. of Jost Leib, decd.), 11/3/1788 (DFP:38)

Young, Dewald m. Margretha Hauss, 6/14/1763 (RDSA:172)

Young, Georg m. Catharina M. Petri, 1/8/1786 (DRGF:202)

Young, George m. Elizabeth Coss, both of Warrensbush, 6/7/1787 (JDR:#66)

Young, Jacob (son of Andreas Jung) m. Anna Norden (dau. of Seblon Norden), 1/23/1791 (DFP:43)

Young, Jean (son of Jemmy Jung, decd.) m. Betsey Spalsberger (dau. of Jean Spalsberger), 6/30/1789 (DFP:39)

Young, Joh. Thom. (son of Christian Jung) m. Nancy Heckeni (dau. of Johann Heckeni), 8/5/1789 (DFP:41)

Young, Johan Fridrich m. Catharina Schumacher (widow of Melchior Bell, Little Falls), 3/18/1762 (RDSA:171)

Young, Johann (son of Joh. Christ. Jung) m. Maria Elisabeth Oehl (dau. of Peter Oehl), 7/21/1789 (DFP:39)

Young, Johann Thomas m. Maria Elisabeth Helmer, 9/18/1770 (RDSA:190)

Young, Johannes m. Maria Riebsamen, 1/12/1783 (DRGF:197)

Young, Michael m. Anna Eker, 2/16/1794 (RDSA:199)

Young, Michael (of Rome) m. Miss. Flint (of Cherry Valley), 7/25/1826 (PCBC:51)

Birth/Baptism

Young, Adam & [?]: [?], b. 6/?/1776; bapt. 6/17/1776 (DRGF:18). Sponsors: [data obliterated].

Young, Adam & Catterina Lis. (Schremling): Johanes, bapt. 1742 (RDSA:4); Henrich, b. 8/17/1762, bapt. 8/18/1762 (RDSA:35); Abraham, b. 8/17/1762, bapt. 8/18/1762 (RDSA:35). Sponsors: Fridrich Jung, Thoredea Hess (re:1); Captn. Henrich Frei & his wife, Elisabeth (re:2); George Schromling & his wife, Catharina (re:3).

Young, Adam, Jr. & Anna Margreth [?]: Georg, b. 2/8/1771; bapt. 3/8/1771 (RDSA:109). Sponsors: Georg Snell & Anna Eva.

Young, Andreas & Catharina [?]: Catharina, b. 7/18/1784; bapt. 7/22/1784 (DRGF:85). Sponsors: Johannes Laux & Catharina.

Young, Andreas & Elisabetha [?]: Theobald, b. 12/30/1761; bapt. 1/7/1762 (RDSA:30). Sponsors: Theobald Jung & Magdalena.

Young, Barnt & Elisabet [?]: Margaret, b. 8/3/1792 (LTSA:75). Sponsors: John Koch, Bezi Seber.

Young, Dewald & Margaretha [?]: Dewald, b. 8/27/1770 (LTSA:33). Sponsors: Dewald Hess,

Elisabetha Schremling.

Young, Dieterich/Dederick & Christina (Scharmann): Margaretha, b. 1/29/1780, bapt. 2/2/1780 (LTSA:59); Pieter, b. 2/25/1782, bapt. 3/2/1782 (DRGF:55); Margaretha, b. 1/25/1789, bapt. 2/25/1789 [parents of Schneidersbusch] (SJC:10); Philip, b. 9/15/1797 (LTSA:100). Sponsors: Johann Koch & Magdalena (re:1); Pieter Jung & Engel Merckel, widow (re:2); Mr. Paul Hochstrasser & Mrs. Margaretha Paris (re:3); Philip Dehas & Anna Eva (re:4).

Young, Emmanuel & [?], N. Amsterdam: Barnt, bapt. 7/22/1798 (JDR:11).

Young, Henrich & Magdalena [?]: Elisabetha, b. 1/15/1770 (LTSA:30). Sponsors: Nicolaus Haffner & Elisabetha, his wife.

Young, Jacob & [?]: Daniel, bapt. 2/22/1784 (DRGF:80). Sponsors: Andreas Keller & Elisabeth.

Young, Jacob & [?]: Maria, b. 11/7/1781; bapt. 11/9/1781 (DRGF:50). Sponsors: Nicolas Windekker & Maria.

Young, Jacob & Eva [?]: Jacob, b. 12/23/1783; bapt. 1/12/1784 (DRGF:79). Sponsors: Johann Jost Snell & Margretha Jung.

Young, Jacob (of Canandaya Lake) & Eva (Knieskern): George, b. 12/15/1789, bapt. 1/24/1790 (SJC:22); Johannes, bapt. 2/5/1792 (SJC:53). Sponsors: Georg Young & Eva Knieskern (re:1); Johannes Knieskern & Eva Young (re:2).

Young, James & Hannah (Snyder), Saratoga: Elizabeth, bapt. 7/27/1783 (JDR:12).

Young, Joh. Friederich & Catharina [?]: Dorothea, b. 1/26/1764; bapt. 1/29/1764 (RDSA:44). Sponsors: Felix Keller & Dorothea Elisabeth.

Young, Johannes & Catharina [?]: Daniel, b. 11/18/1770 (LTSA:34). Sponsors: Daniel Jung, Elisabeta Mattes.

Young, Johannes & Dorothea [?]: Elisabetha, b. 12/6/1782, bapt. 1/6/1783 (DRGF:65); Wilhelm, b. 2/5/1785, bapt. 2/13/1785 (DRGF:93). Sponsors: Jost Kraemer & Elisabeth Diel (re:1); Wilhelm Walrath & Margreth Mac Caffry (re:2).

Young, Johannes & Margretha [?]: Barendt, b. 8/27/1766; bapt. 8/31/1766 (RDSA:67). Sponsors: Johannes Kajser & Catharina Wallrad.

Young, John & Elisabet [?]: James, b. 8/11/1790 (LTSA:72). Sponsors: [none named].

Young, John (of Canajoharie) & Margaretha [?]: Anna, bapt. 2/22/1789 (SJC:10); Johann Georg, bapt. 6/23/1793 (SJC:77). Sponsors: Jacob Cordimann & Anna Cordimann (re:1); Georg Dumm with wife (re:2).

Young, Joseph/Jost & Jannetje/Jennitje (Flint): Maria, b. 9/28/1783, bapt. 11/10/1783 (DRGF:77); Peter, b. 5/4/1785, bapt. 5/22/1785 (DRC:73). Sponsors: Hermanes van Aalstein & Elisabeth (re:1); David Cox & Caty Hikky (re:2).

Young, Michel & Anna [?]: Maria, b. 6/12/1794 (LTSA:84). Sponsors: Peter Suz & Magdalena.

Young, Peter & Ann Eve [?]: Maria Catharina, bapt. 6/1/1740 (FH:11); Eve, bapt. 10/24/1742

COMPENDIUM

(FH:18); Helena, bapt. 2/3/1743/4 (FH:22). Sponsors: Joseph Walleslous, Margaret Snock, Barbara Toetendorf (re:1); Johns Cleyn, [?] Salts (re:2); Helena Wallslous, Helena [?] (re:3).

Young, Peter & Elisabeth [?]: Elisabeth, b. 3/7/1782; bapt. 3/10/1782 (DRGF:56). Sponsors: Jacob Jung & Dorothea.

Young, Peter & Magdalena [?]: Henrich, b. 8/11/1762; bapt. 8/18/1762 (RDSA:35). Sponsors: Henrich Schremling & Catharina Frei.

Young, Peter (of Fort Plain) & Elisabeth (Sever): Jacob, b. 3/9/1790; bapt. 3/14/1790 (SJC:24). Sponsors: Jacob Young & Maria Young.

Young, Philipp & Anna Maria [?]: Elisabetha, b. 12/12/1763, bapt. 1/11/1764 (RDSA:44); Philippus, b. 9/2/1765, bapt. 9/10/1765 (RDSA:57). Sponsors: Elisabeth Franck & Georg Henrich Bell (re:1); Johann Jost Hergheimer & Catharina (re:2).

Young, Pieter & Marlena [?]: Mari Lena, b. 8/27/1767; bapt. 9/24/1767 (RDSA:77). Sponsors: Lena & Pieter Serves.

Young, Seth & Martha (Farley), Schenectady: Charles, bapt. 9/26/1785 (JDR:10).

Young, Theobald & Margretha [?]: Friedericus, b. 6/23/1764; bapt. 7/1/1764 (RDSA:48). Sponsors: Friderich Blanck & his wife, Ottilia.

Young, Thomas & Elisabetha [?]: Elisabetha, b. 9/13/1782; bapt. 9/22/1782 (DRGF:62). Sponsors: Conrad Pieter Miller & Catharina.

Death Record

Young, [?], (widow), d. 11/10/1812, age 58 years, 4 months (DFP:95)

Young, Anna, (wife of Godfried Young), d. 8/25/1807, age 53 years, 8 months, 10 days (DFP:91)

Young, Elisabeth, (dau. of Johann Christ Jung), b. 7/15/1789; d. 8/16/1793, age 4 years, 2 months, 1 day; buried 8/18/1793 (DFP:84)

Young, Elizabeth Cuming, (wife of Jacob Young), b. 6/2/1788; d. 4/27/1862; buried Fort Plain Cemetery, Minden (FPC 44:127)

Young, George Y., (son of John S. & Jane M. Young), d. 8/1/1836, age 11 years; buried sect. 6, Colonial Cemetery (JC:190)

Young, Jacob, b. 2/19/1780; d. 4/7/1863; buried Fort Plain Cemetery, Minden (FPC 44:127)

Young, Jacob, d. 12/29/1795, age 42 years, less 6 days ["well respected Elder in this congregation, died suddenly from apoplexy"]; left behind, besides his wife, five children: 3 sons & 2 daus.; buried 1/1/1796 (DFP:87)

Young, James C., (resident of Cherry Valley), d. 3/29/1826, age 24 years; removed ca. 1864 to Cherry Valley Cemetery (CVC:2)

Young, Jane, d. 1/?/1813, age about 45 years; buried 2/1/1813 (DFP:95)

Young, John Christ., d. 3/?/1813, age 86 years [had eight children, sixty-six grandchildren & forty-five great-grandchildren]; buried 3/2/1813 (DFP:95)

Young, John Henry, b. 1/31/1739; d. 4/5/1808, age 69 years, 2 months, 5 days; buried 4/7/1808 (DFP:92)

Young, Margaretha, (widow of Joh. Jung), b. 1727; d. 8/1/1789; buried 8/2/1789 (DFP:78 & 79)

Young, Maria Elisabeth, d. 4/?/1811, age 73 years; buried 4/29/1811 (DFP:94)

Probate Abstract

Young, Han Christ, (of Minden), will dated 5/28/1807; probated 6/12/1813. Legatees: sons, Thomas, Godfry, John, Han Christ (& his son, Christian); daus., Christina, Anna and Elizabeth. Executors: Nicholas Lesker, Abraham Shoemaker. Witnesses: John Dygert, Jacob H. Walrath, Jr., Robert McFarlan. (WMC 56:388)

Young, Jacob, (of Canajoharie), will dated 3/22/1790; probated 3/17/1795. Legatees: wife, Dorothy; sons, Jacob, Peter and Hendrick; daus., Catharine, Margaret and Elisabeth. Executors: sons, Jacob and Peter. Witnesses: John Seeber[?], Elizabeth Vanderlip, Christopher P. Yates. (WMC 56:148)

Young, William, (of the town of Florida), will dated 11/12/1811; probated [date not stated]. Legatees: wife, Rachel; brothers, Peter (& his son, Peter), George (& his son, William); sister's son, William Frederick. Executors: David Cady, Peter Young, Jr. Witnesses: David and John W. Cady, George Serviss. (WMC 56:383)

Youngs, George, (of the town of Florida), will dated 2/24/1820; probated 6/5/1820. Legatees: wife, Elizabeth; sons, George, Peter, William, Jacob and Smith; daus., Eve, Elizabeth and

Lenean. Executors: Samuel Jackson; friend, Peter Youngs, Jr. Witnesses: John G. Sweet, John Taylor, James Smith. (WMC 57:170)

Tryon County Militia

Young, Adam	[Appendix A]
Young, Andrew	
Young, Christian	
Young, Christian A.	
Young, Frederick	
Young, George	
Young, Godfrey	
Young, Henry	
Young, Henry P.	
Young, Jacob	
Young, Jacob, Jr.	
Young, Jeremiah	
Young, John	
Young, Joseph	
Young, Ludwig	
Young, Nicholas	
Young, Peter	
Young, Richard	
Young, Robert	
Young, Thomas	
Young, William	

Pension Abstract

Young, George, b. [date not given], Philadelphia, Pa.; m. Catharine Petrie, 1/8/1787, at the house of Casper Cook in Palatine, N.Y. by Rev. Abraham Rosencrantz; the couple moved to Manheim, Montgomery Co., N.Y. shortly after their marriage and George Boachus "helped to build them a log house"; d. 12/14/1824, Manheim, N.Y. Children: John, b. 1787/8 (eldest son and resident of Charleston Twp., Tioga Co., Pa. in 1846). [There were also four sons and four daughters not named in the file.] Grandchild: Harvey Young, b. 1828/9 (resident of

COMPENDIUM

Charleston Twp., Tioga Co., Pa. on 2/8/1855). George served under Capt. McBrion and fought in the battles of Bunker Hill, Schuylkill and Fort Montgomery; George stated that he "suffered most at the battle of Fort Montgomery where they were so scarce of provisions that they roasted and scraped all the horse bones & eat what could be obtained"; he was at Fort Plain when peace was first declared and they "roasted an ox whole & dipped up liquor and drank with their shoes". (RWPA: #R11951)

Young, Godfrey, b. 1752; m. [wife not named; living on 3/31/1831]; d. 7/31/1830, Herkimer Co., N.Y. Godfrey was a corporal in Capt. Copeman's Co., Col. Samuel Clyde's 1st. Regt., Tryon Co. Militia; he fought in the battle of Oriskany where "he became disabled in the service of the United States in consequence of a Wound in the lower part of his Belly on the sixth Day of August 1777". Godfrey was granted a pension for his disability on 4/22/1786. (RWPA: #S26974)

Young, Joseph, m. Jane Flint, 1777 at Fort Plain, Tryon Co., N.Y.; d. 3/?/1830, Columbia, Herkimer Co., N.Y. (Jane Young, d. 5/21/1842, Lee, Oneida Co., N.Y.) Children: Isaac, b. 1799/1800 (resident of Rome, Oneida Co. in 1836); Peter (resident of Litchfield, Oneida Co. in 1836); Hannah (m. [?] Beckwith); John, William, Archibald and Peter [all living in Elmira, Chemung Co., N.Y. in 1836]. Peter served in the 1st. Regt., Tryon Co. Militia and in 1780 he enlisted as a batteauman under Capt. Lefler in the N.Y. Line; he fought in the battles of Oriskany and Johnstown and was engaged in the skirmish at West Canada Creek. After their marriage Joseph and Jane Young lived with his parents in their home near Cherry Valley. An Indian attack on the Youngs' resulted in the burning of their home, the murder of Joseph's parents; several of his [Joseph's] children, and the capture of his wife, Jane, who was taken to Canada where she was held for sixteen months before being allowed to return home to the Mohawk Valley. (RWPA: #W20146)

Young, Peter, b. 7/?/1759, Minden, N.Y.; resident of Minden, Montgomery Co. on 9/19/1832. Peter was drafted in May 1778 to serve in Capt. Adam Lipe's Co., Col. Samuel Clyde's 1st. Regt., Tryon Co. Militia and was promoted to the rank of sergeant; he was called upon to help bury the dead after the Cherry Valley massacre in November 1778; Peter served under Col. Van Schaick in April 1779 and assisted in transporting the baggage and property of the government from the Mohawk River across to Wood Creek; he fought in the battles of Durlock and Johnstown. (RWPA: #S11922)

Young, Richard, b. 10/24/1753, Minden, N.Y.; resident of Ephratah, Montgomery Co., N.Y. on 9/20/1832. Richard enlisted from Minden in the spring of 1776 as a private under Capt. Krouse in Col. William Seeber's 1st. Regt., Tryon Co. Militia and was promoted to the rank of sergeant in July of the same year; he also served in Col. Jacob Klock's 2nd. Regt. and continued on various tours of duty into 1783; Richard fought in the battles of Oriskany and Lampman's Field. (RWPA: #S11923)

Youngs, Jeremiah, b. 1754/5, Rhinebeck (now Carlisle, Schoharie Co., N.Y.), son of Peter Youngs; m. [wife not named]; d. 3/3/1845, Seward, Schoharie Co., N.Y. Children: John, Christian, Abraham, Jacob, Martines, b. 1794/5; Cornelius, Adam (living in Seward, N.Y. in 1844); Hannah, Elisabeth, Laura/Lana[?] and Mary. Grandchild: Jeremiah P. Youngs (living in Seward, N.Y. in 1852).

Jeremiah enlisted on 4/1/1778 as a private in Capt. James Dickenson's Co. of the N.Y. Troops for nine months; he volunteered in June 1779 and was a private and corporal under Major Adrian Wynkoop for five months; Jeremiah was appointed ensign in Capt. Matthew Brown's Co., Col. Clyde's 1st. Regt., Tryon Co. Militia and served for four months; he served for five months, beginning in the summer of 1780, as a private in Capt. Isaac Bogart's Co., Col. John Harper's 5th. Regt., Tryon Co. Militia. (RWPA: #S9533)

Deed Abstract

Young, Adam, of Youngsfield, Tryon Co. to Isaac Paris, of Stone Arabia, Tryon Co. Deed dated 5/16/1774; recorded 3/14/1775. Description: Land situated on the south side of the Mohawk River in a patent granted to Philip Livingston and nineteen others. Three lots known and distinguished as: Lot #8 (400 acres), Lot #16 (400 acres), and Lot #25 (543 acres) next to the Otsquage Creek. Consideration: L270. Witnesses: William Seeber, Chris. P. Yates. (MVL:41)

1790 Census

Young, Adam   [Appendix B]
Young, Andrew (2)
Young, Christian, Jr.
Young, Christian, Sr.
Young, George (3)
Young, Godfry
Young, Jacob
Young, Jacob, Jr.
Young, Jeremiah
Young, John (7)
Young, Joseph (2)
Young, Lodowick
Young, Nancy
Young, Peter (3)
Young, Seth (2)
Young, Thomas (2)
Young, William

YOUNGLOVE

Birth/Baptism

Younglove, David & Anna [?]: Jesajas, b. 8/24/1783; bapt. 9/8/1783 (DRGF:75). Sponsors: Joh: Jost Helmer & Magdalena Fheling.

Tryon County Militia

Younglove, David   [Appendix A]

Pension Abstract

Younglove, Moses, b. ca. 1755, Cambridge, Washington Co., N.Y.; m. Polly Patterson, 7/11/1781; d. 1/31/1829, Columbia Co., N.Y. (Polly Younglove, b. ca. 1762; d. 10/13/1847, Hudson, Columbia Co., N.Y.) Children: [sine prole]. Moses was appointed surgeon's mate in Col. Samuel Elmore's Continental New York Regt. in Albany on 9/29/1776; he was appointed surgeon of General Nicholas Herkimer's Brigade, Tryon Co. Militia in July 1777; he was captured at the battle of Oriskany on 8/6/1777 and taken to Canada where he was paroled in December of the same year; Moses returned to serve as surgeon of the Tryon Co. Militia through 1779. (RWPA: #W4410)

Deed Abstract

Younglove, Moses, Doctor, of Palatine District, Tryon Co. to Michael Bader, yeoman, of the same place. Deed dated 7/3/1774; recorded 9/24/1787. Description: Land situated in Palatine District within the bounds of a patent bearing date of 10/19/1723. Land begins west from the house where Adam Loux [Loucks] dwells, thence along the road west, then east, then north to the place of beginning (18 acres). Consideration: L350. Witnesses: Johann Daniel Gros, Peter S. Deygert, Saml. Clyde. (MVL:41)

YOUNGS see **YOUNG**

YOURAN (also see **YORAN**)

Tryon County Militia

Yuran, Jacob   [Appendix A]

1790 Census

Youran, Jacob   [Appendix B]

YUCKER (also see **YOUKER**)

Marriage

Yucker, Jacob m. Magdalena Dussler, 9/16/1781 (DRGF:195)

Yucker, Johannes m. Anna Catharina Rinckel, 1/13/1784 (DRGF:199)

Birth/Baptism

Yucker, Jacob & Magdalena (Dusler): Elisabetha, b. 10/11/1781, bapt. 10/14/1781 (DRGF:49); Johannes, b. 2/6/1785, bapt. 2/8/1785 (DRGF:93); Maria, bapt. 4/5/1789

(SJC:15); Anna, bapt. 5/3/1791 (SJC:42) [parents of Palatine for bapts. 3 & 4]. Sponsors: Wilhelm Dussler & Elisabeth Jucker (re:1); Johannes Snell & Elisabeth (re:2); Andreas Scheffer & Maria Wallrath (re:3); Jacob Dusler & Anna Dusler (re:4).

Yucker, Johannes & Anna Catharina [?]: Anna, b. 3/27/1785; bapt. 3/29/1785 (DRGF:94). Sponsors: Salomon Jukker & Margreth Schall.

Yucker, Johannes (of Yukersbusch) & Anna (Ringel): Georg, bapt. 6/20/1790 (SJC:29). Sponsors: Georg Yuker & Elisabeth Yuker.

Yucker, Johannes George (of Palatine) & Elisabeth (Schall): Johannes, bapt. 2/8/1789 (SJC:9); Elisabeth, bapt. 8/7/1791 (SJC:45).

Yucker, Rudolph & Anna (Windlor): Rudolph, bapt. 4/11/1752 (RDSA:12); Zusanna, b. 6/6/1756 (LTSA:18). Sponsors: Rudolph Keller, Elisabeth Diebendorff (re:1); Jacob Keller & his wife, Zusanna (re:2).

Yucker, Solomon (Palatine) & Elisabeth [?]: Rudolf, bapt. 5/3/1791 (SJC:42); Margretha, bapt. 12/9/1792 (SJC:67). Sponsors: Adolph Haus & Anna Eva Scheffer (re:1); Jacob Palsli & Margretha Haus (re:2).

Pension Abstract

Yucker, George, b. 2/16/1757, Canajoharie, N.Y.; resident of Oppenheim, Montgomery Co., N.Y. on 9/20/1832. George enlisted in the spring of 1775 and served at various times as a corporal in Capt. Christian House's Co., Col. Jacob Klock's 2nd. Regt., Tryon Co. Militia until 4/1/1782; he also served for nine months as a private in Capt. Abner French's Co., Col. Frederick Fisher's 3rd. Regt. and was discharged from the military on 1/1/1783.

(RWPA: #S29566)

Yucker, Jacob, b. 10/26/1757, Palatine, N.Y.; resident of Oppenheim, Montgomery Co., N.Y. on 9/22/1832. Jacob served as a minute man for six months in 1777 under the command of Capt. Samuel Gray in Col. Jacob Klock's 2nd. Regt., Tryon Co. Militia; he was also a private in Capt. Christian House's Co. of the same regiment; Jacob was on garrison duty at Riememsnyder's Fort [between Little Falls and Fairfield] and was out on a scouting mission with George Adle on 3/2/1782 when the two soldiers were captured by a company of about fifty Tories and Indians, taken to Buck's Island and on to Montreal where Jacob Yucker was kept until late October [about eight months] when he and another prisoner [not named] escaped and returned home; Jacob was called out again and joined in pursuit of Walter Butler who was then on his retreat from Johnstown. (RWPA: #S11925)

Yucker, John, m. Anna Catharina Rinckel, 1/13/1784, by Rev. Abraham Rosencrantz; d. 9/14/1831. (Anna Catharina Yucker, b. 4/?/1762; resident of Oppenheim, Fulton Co., N.Y. on 2/20/1839 and still living there in 1854.) Children: Jacob J. (resident of Oppenheim, N.Y. in 1839.) John enlisted and was a private for more than nine months in 1781 and 1782 under Capts. Christian House and Lawrence Gross in the regiments of Cols. Wagoner, Willett and Klock; John fought in the battle of Durlock. (RWPA: #W22709)

YUEL

Birth/Baptism

Yuel, James & Margretha [?]: James, b. 9/12/1780, bapt. 9/27/1780 (DRGF:40); Margretha, b. 9/4/1782, bapt. 9/8/1782 (DRGF:61); Nicolaus, b. 11/4/1784, bapt. 11/9/1784 (DRGF:88). Sponsors: Jacob Boshaar & Catharina (re:1); Jacob Christmann & Margreth Gettmann (re:2); Friedrich Fox & Elisabeth (re:3).

ZANG

Birth/Baptism

Zang, Peter & Elisabeth (Braun): Maria Sybilla, b. 12/10/1779; bapt. 12/17/1779 (DRGF:37). Sponsors: Jacob Dunches & Maria Sybilla.

ZEE

1790 Census

Zee, David   [Appendix B]

ZERENER

1790 Census

Zerener, Lewis   [Appendix B]

938

ZESSINGER

Tryon County Militia

Zessinger, Nicholas   [Appendix A]

ZIELE (also see SIELE)

Marriage

Ziele, Adam (of Schoharie) m. Alita Conne, 12/3/1763 (RDSA:173)

Ziele, Thomas m. Anna Merckel, 1/29/1788 (RDSA:192)

Probate Abstract

Zieley, John, [residence not stated], will dated 1/20/1825; probated 12/7/1825. Legatees: sons, David, Thomas (& his Henry and Jacob); daus., Elizabeth (widow of Adam S. Vrooman), Margaret (wife of Henry Suits), Cornelia (wife of Robert Scadden/Schedder[?]), Jane (wife of Adam Guardinear); granddau., Elizabeth (wife of Herman Dewandelaer and dau. of John Brown). Executors: David I. Zeilley, Martinus Warmouth. Witnesses: Adam H. Van Slyck, John I. Neahr, John D. Zielley. (WMC 57:185)

Tryon County Militia

Zieley, John   [Appendix A]

Pension Abstract

Zielie, Martinus, b. Middleburgh, Schoharie, N.Y.; m. [wife not named; d. 1813, Aurelius, N.Y.]; moved in 1818 to Friendship, Allegany Co., N.Y. where he lived with his son, Peter, for nine years; d. 11/2/1833, Oil Creek,

Crawford Co., Pa. Children: Peter, b. ca. 1786 (resident of Mentz, Cayuga Co., N.Y. on 8/16/1844); David (resident of Oil City, Pa.); Cornelia (m. John Rose and resident of Elmira, Chemung Co., N.Y.); Ann (lived with her brother, Peter, in Mentz, N.Y.); Agnes (m. Isaac Ward and resident of Painted Post, Steuben Co., N.Y.). [All children alive in 1844.] Martinus enlisted from Middleburgh in 1776 and served as a lieutenant in Col. Peter Vrooman's Regt. of N.Y. Troops until February 1781. (RWPA: #S28960)

Zielley, Thomas, b. 4/?/1760, son of John Zielley; m. [wife not named]; d. 7/3/1844, Howard, Steuben Co., N.Y. Children: Henry (eldest heir of Thomas Zielley on 12/20/1852). Thomas entered the military from Palatine in April 1780 and served under Capt. John Bigbread in Col. Jacob Klock's 2nd. Regt., Tryon Co. Militia; he was in the battle of Stone Arabia at which time his father, Lt. John Zielley, commanded the company in the absence of Capt. Bigbread; Thomas, stationed at Fort Keyser, was ordered out to Johnstown where he joined Col. Willett's forces in the battle of Johnstown; he was appointed a corporal in the same company in 1782 and remained at Fort Keyser as a guard. (RWPA: #R11988)

ZILLEBACH (also see SILLEBACH)

Marriage

Zillebach, Christian m. Elisabeth Weaver (dau. of Joh: N. Weaver), 1/8/1792 (DRGF:208)

Death Record

Zillebach, Christian, (widower), d. 10/28/1807,

Herkimer, age 45 years [a blacksmith and formerly Deacon of our church]; buried in cemetery near the new church in Herkimer (RDH:259)

ZIMMERMAN (also see TIMMERMAN)

Marriage

Zimmerman, Adam (son of Deobald Zimmermann, decd.) m. Margaretha Mathaeus (dau. of Jacob Mathaeus), 2/15/1789 (DFP:39)

Zimmerman, Christian (son of Friederich Zimmermann of Hohen Solms County) m. Anna Eva Saltzmann (dau. of George Saltzmann of Stone Arabia), 5/20/1778 (LTSA:285)

Zimmerman, Conrad m. Margretha Riebsaamen, 7/11/1769 (RDSA:186)

Zimmerman, Henrich m. [?] Feling, 12/4/1770 (RDSA:190)

Zimmerman, Henrich Lorentz m. Elisabeth Keller (dau. of Henrich Keller), 10/26/1784 (DRGF:200)

Zimmerman, Johann Jacob m. Magdalena Fheling (dau. of Nic. Fheling), 2/22/1784 (DRGF:199)

Zimmerman, Johannes G. m. Sara Glock (dau. of Jac. Glock), 5/23/1786 (DRGF:203)

Zimmerman, John m. Anna Diefendorff, 2/10/1795 (DFP:53)

Birth/Baptism

Zimmerman, Adam & Caterina (Nellis): Anna

Eva, bapt. 1743 (RDSA:5). Sponsors: Robert Nelles, Eva Zimmerman.

Zimmerman, Adam D. (of Canajoharie) & Margretha (Matheus): Elisabeth, bapt. 4/18/1790 (SJC:25); Anna, bapt. 11/13/1791 (SJC:50); Maria, bapt. 2/2/1794 (SJC:90). Sponsors: Conrad Matheus & Elisabeth Zimmerman (re:1); Jacob Matheus & Anna Matheus (re:2); Jacob Matheus & Maria Zimmerman (re:3).

Zimmerman, Christian & Anna Eva [?]: Maria, b. 3/31/1779, bapt. 4/5/1779 (LTSA:57); Catharina, b. 8/31/1781, bapt. 9/3/1781 (DRGF:47). Sponsors: Johann Loescher & Maria (re:1); Henrich Salsmann & Froena (re:2).

Zimmerman, Conrad & Magdalena/Marlena (Schnell): Johannes, b. 4/27/1785, bapt. 5/15/1785 (DRGF:96); Maria, bapt. 11/15/1789 [parents of Schnellenbusch] (SJC:19). Sponsors: Johannes Snell & Anna (re:1); John Jost Schnell & Maria Schnell (re:2).

Zimmerman, Conrad & Margretha [?]: Delia, b. 12/5/1783; bapt. 12/14/1783 (DRGF:78). Sponsors: Johannes Majer & Lena Zimmermann.

Zimmerman, Conrad C. (Schnellenbusch) & Margretha [?]: Catharina, bapt. 6/24/1792 (SJC:60). Sponsors: Friderich Raspach & Catharina Raspach.

Zimmerman, Conrad L. (Palatine Town) & Margretha [?]: Gertrud, bapt. 4/12/1792 (SJC:57). Sponsors: Adam Zimmerman & Gertrud Zimmerman.

Zimmerman, Deobald & Elisabetha [?]:

Elisabetha, b. 9/23/1765, bapt. 9/28/1765 (RDSA:58); Thomas, b. 5/22/1769, bapt. 5/28/1769 (RDSA:94). Sponsors: Elisabetha Hess & Conrad Zimmerman (re:1); Lena Klock & Conrad Zimmermann (re:2).

Zimmerman, Georg & Anna Elisabeth [?]: Margretha, b. 5/16/1764, bapt. 5/22/1764 (RDSA:47); Lena, b. 5/14/1766, bapt. 5/19/1766 (RDSA:64). Sponsors: Margretha Glock & Conrad Zimmermann (re:1); Lena Klock & Conrad Zimmermann (re:2).

Zimmerman, Henrich & Catharina [?]: Margretha, b. 8/29/1764, bapt. 9/7/1764 (RDSA:49); Margretha, b. 3/1/1766, bapt. 3/5/1766 (RDSA:62). Sponsors: Delia Fox & Conrad Zimmermann (re:1); Delia Fox & Conrad Zimmermann, jun. (re:2).

Zimmerman, Henrich (of Canajoharie Castle) & Elisabeth [?]: Alida, bapt. 8/2/1789 (SJC:16); Susanna, bapt. 3/14/1792 (SJC:57). Sponsors: Adam Zimmermann & Dorothea [?]hoff (re:1); Jacob C. Zimmerman & Susanna Zimmerman (re:2).

Zimmerman, Henrich & Margretha [?]: Henrich, b. 11/9/1769, bapt. 11/19/1769 (RDSA:98); Adam, b. 2/1/1771, bapt. 2/24/1771 (RDSA:109); Johannes, b. 3/13/1782, bapt. 3/16/1782 (DRGF:56); Anna Eva, b. 7/10/1784, bapt. 7/16/1784 (DRGF:85). Sponsors: Henrich Bellinger & Anna Eva Zimmermann (re:1); Henrich Zimmermann & Margreth Zimmermann (re:2); Johannes Zimmermann & Elisabeth Zimmermann (re:3); Adam Zimmermann & Anna Fheling (re:4).

Zimmerman, Henrich (of Schnellenbusch) & Margaretha (Bellinger) (of Palatine): Magdalena, bapt. 9/16/1788 (SJC:4); Gertrud,

bapt. 3/17/1790 (SJC:24); Peter, bapt. 3/3/1793 (SJC:74). Sponsors: Peter Bellinger & Magdalena Fehling (re:1); Jacob Zimmerman & Anna Zimmerman (re:2); Peter A. Bellinger & Elisabeth Bellinger (re:3).

Zimmerman, Henrich H.[?] (Palatine Town) & Appollonia [?]: Johann Adam, b. 10/25/1793; bapt. 11/4/1793 (SJC:84). Sponsors: Joh: Adam Zimmerman & Catharina Zimmerman.

Zimmerman, Henrich L. (Palatine) & Elisabeth [?]: Anna, bapt. 12/29/1793 (SJC:86). Sponsors: Isaac Christman & Anna C. Zimmerman.

Zimmerman, Jacob & Anna Elisabeth [?]: Jacob, b. 9/13/1781; bapt. 9/16/1781 [posthumously] (DRGF:48). Sponsors: Jacob Fheling & Elisabeth D. Fheling.

Zimmerman, Jacob (of Palatine) & Magdalena (Fehling): Anna, bapt. 7/5/1789 (SJC:16); Catharina, bapt. 10/30/1791 (SJC:50). Sponsors: Johannes Fehling & Elisabeth Fehling (re:1); Johannes Zimmerman & Elisabeth Zimmerman (re:2).

Zimmerman, Joh: Jacob & Magdalena [?]: Elisabeth, b. 11/22/1784; bapt. 11/23/1784 (DRGF:89). Sponsors: Debald Zimmerman & Elisabeth.

Zimmerman, Johannes & [?]: Elisabeth, bapt. 9/14/1788 (SJC:4). Sponsors: [none named].

Zimmerman, Johannes & Elisabeth [?]: Anna, b. 12/4/1781; bapt. 12/23/1781 (DRGF:51). Sponsors: Adam Zimmermann & Lena Fheling.

Zimmerman, Johannes G. (Royal Grant) & Sara [?] (Palatine): Gertrud, bapt. 1/10/1791 (SJC:38); Johann Jost, bapt. 2/17/1793

COMPENDIUM

(SJC:73). Sponsors: John Herchimer & Gertrud Zimmerman (re:1); Johann Jost Snel & Margretha Zimmerman (re:2).

Zimmerman, Wilhelm/William & Catharina (Fehling): Jacob, b. 8/7/1782, bapt. 8/11/1782 (DRGF:60); Conrath, b. 1/29/1785, bapt. 2/6/1785 (DRGF:92); Johann Dieterich, bapt. 3/22/1789 (SJC:12); Peter, bapt. 11/20/1791 (SJC:51); Catharina, bapt. 12/30/1793 (SJC:87) [note: parents were of Palatine for bapts. # 3,4 & 5]. Sponsors: Jacob Fheling & Margretha (re:1); Conrath Zimmermann & Magdalena (re:2); Dieterich Fehling & Elisabeth Zimmerman (re:3); Peter Warmuth & his wife (re:4); Heinrich J. Fehling & Catharina Zimmerman (re:5).

Death Record

Zimmerman, [?], (child of John Zimerman), d. 12/?/1807, age 7 months, 15 days; buried 12/27/1807 (DFP:91)

Zimmerman, [?], (widow Timmerman), d. 8/?/1812, age 78 years, 6 months, 2 days; buried 8/24/1812 (DFP:95)

Zimmerman, Adam, d. 7/?/1808, age 45 years, 1 month, 20 days; buried 7/8/1808 (DFP:92)

Probate Abstract

Zimmerman, George, (of Manheim), will dated 2/7/1800; probated 2/7/1801. Legatees: son, John and his son (Daniel, called Timmerman); daus., Caty, Margrate, Lana, Elizabeth, Anna, Mary, Annis, Gartrute (wife of William Smith), Annaleas Syver. Executors: son, John; Abnor Reed, Cornelius C. Beekman. Witnesses: John Ja Failing, Jacob Zimmerman, Cornelius C. Beekman. (WMC 56:150)

Zimmerman, Henrich, (of Manheim), will dated 8/25/1805; probated 4/13/1808. Legatees: wife, Margrate; sons, Henry, Adam, Jacob, John and Frederich; brothers, George and Lowrance; five or more daughters, one named Delean. Executors: son-in-law, Jacob Snell; sons, Henry, Jacob, Adam. Witnesses: Lorence Zimerman, Conrad Zimerman, Cornelius C. Beekman. (WMC 56:158)

Tryon County Militia

Zimmerman, Christian   [Appendix A]
Zimmerman, Conrad
Zimmerman, Frederick

Pension Abstract

Zimmerman, Christian, b. 7/16/1748, Frankfort in the Main, Germany [stated in 1811 to be Hoenzollern in the Empire of Germany]; naturalized at Johnstown, Montgomery Co., N.Y. on 1/19/1811; resident of Sullivan, Madison Co., N.Y. on 10/9/1832. Christian was drafted in 1778 to serve for nine months in Capt. John Bickbread's Co., Col. Jacob Klock's 2nd. Regt., Tryon Co. Militia; he was in the "engagement at Cherry Valley [with] Joseph Brandt"; Christian volunteered in the spring of 1781 for a nine month tour of duty in Capt. Garret Putman's Co., Col. Marinus Willett's Regt.; he fought in the battles of Stone Arabia and Johnstown. (RWPA: #S11928)

Zimmerman, Jacob, b. 9/1/1758, Canajoharie, N.Y.; m. Magdalena Failing, 2/22/1784 at Canajoharie; d. 1/18/1835, Oppenheim, N.Y. (Magdalena Zimmerman, b. 7/18/1763, dau. of Nicholas Failing; resident of St. Johnsville, N.Y. on 5/15/1838.) Children: Elizabeth, b. 11/22/1784; Mary, b. 9/9/1786; Nancy, b. 7/2/1789; Catherine, b. 10/28/1791; Jacob, b.

2/28/1795 (m. Elizabeth Gray, 3/7/1822); Nicholas, b. 7/14/1797; Eva, b. 5/15/1800; Christiana, b. 3/17/180?; Daniel, b. 3/15/1806 (m. Lavinia Fox, 4/24/1828); David, b. 10/16/1808. Jacob enlisted in 1775/76 and was a private under Capts. Winn, House, Zilley and Fox in Col. Jacob Klock's 2nd. Regt., Tryon Co. Militia; he served at various times until 8/9/1781 or 8/10/1781, when he was wounded in the neck and throat by Indians while on a scouting party near Fort Zimmerman and taken prisoner to Canada where he remained until late in 1782. (RWPA: #W20002)

Zimmerman, John, m. Elizabeth [?] 11/4/1770, by Rev. Abraham Rosencrantz; d. about 8/9/1781. (Elizabeth Zimmerman, b. 1752/3; resident of Oppenheim, Montgomery Co., N.Y. on 5/10/1837.) Children: "a number of children" [not named in the file]. Grandchild: Jacob H. Zimmerman. John was a lieutenant in Capt. Christian House's Co., Col. Jacob Klock's 2nd. Regt., Tryon Co. Militia; John was reporting for military duty about 8/9/1781 and upon leaving his home "was shot & scalped by the Indians—— that the report of the enemies guns was heard & some of her [Elizabeth Zimmerman] neighbors went in the direction & found her husband [John Zimmerman] mortally wounded & carried him to his house where after a short time he expired". (RWPA: #W16489)

Zimmerman, William, m. Catharine Failing, 9/8/1777; d. 4/4/1830 or 4/24/1830. (Catharine Zimmerman, b. 4/7/1759, dau. of Jacob Failing [he died prior to 1838]. She lived in Manheim, Herkimer Co., N.Y. on 12/26/1838 when she was denied a pension because of failure to provide the necessary proof of William's military service.) William enlisted in the spring of 1775 and served for short periods of duty each year into 1782 as a private under the command of Capts. Christian House, Jacob W. Seeber, and Nicholas Richter in the regiments of Cols. Klock, Dayton, Cox and Waggoner; he was stationed at Ticonderoga, Stillwater, Cherry Valley and at Forts Zimmerman and Herkimer. (RWPA: #R11990)

1790 Census

Zimerman, Elizabeth   [Appendix B]

ZIRAN

Birth/Baptism

Ziran, Christoph & Gertraut [?]: Apollonia, b. 11/11/1774, bapt. 11/13/1774 (LTSA:46); Dorothea, b. 3/17/1778, bapt. 3/22/1778 (LTSA:52). Sponsors: Peter Lowenstein & his wife, Apollonia (re:1); Dieterich Laucks & Dorothea (re:2).

ZIRENIUS

Birth/Baptism

Zirenius, Maria & [?]: Johannes, b. 11/29/1792 (LTSA:76). Sponsors: Johannes Potman & Barbara.

ZOLLER

Marriage

Zoller, Caspar m. Sussanna Keller (dau. of Hen: Keller), 3/29/1795 (DRGF:212)

COMPENDIUM

Zoller, Henry m. Catharine Wallrath, 5/31/1795 (DFP:53)

Zoller, Henry m. Margaretha Dockstader, 10/16/1796 (DFP:55)

Death Record

Zoller, [?], (child of [?] Zoller), d. 12/11/1810, age 2 weeks, 2 days (DFP:94)

1790 Census

Zuller, Henry   [Appendix B]

ZOLLINGER

Birth/Baptism

Zollinger, Henry & Anna [?]: Anna, b. 11/22/1788 (LTSA:61). Sponsors: John Jung, Elisabeth Brukmann.

Death Record

Zollinger, Catharine, (dau. of Heinrich Zollinger), b. 12/3/1792; d. 8/1/1796, age 3 years, 8 months, less 2 days; buried 8/3/1796 (DFP:89)

ZUPHIN

1790 Census

Zuphin, John   [Appendix B]

ZUTPHIN (also see SUTPHEN)

1790 Census

Zutphin, John   [Appendix B]
Zutphin, Richard

Abbott
  Grace 442
Ackerman
  Margaret 23
Adair
  Elizabeth 847
  Jean 465
  Margaret 655
Adami
  Catharina 744
Adams
  Caty 72
  Polly 72
Adamy
  Maria 738
Adle
  George 938
Aekelson
  Catharina 270
Aesius
  Anna 253
Aitken
  Ellon 109
  William 109
Akre
  Catharine 126
Albrant
  Annatje 897
  Barbara 460
Albright
  Eliza 928
  Jacob 928
Alexander
  James 827
Algire
  Anna 413
  Elizabeth 425
  Maragrita 388
  Sophia 201
Allen
  Henry 571
  Nelly 413
  Rachel 825
  Sarah 244
Almsbury
  Almond 45
  Peggy 45
Alt
  Anna Catharina 859
Anderson
  Ann 540
  James 540
  Margaret 540

Andrews
  Sarah 504
Aney
  Godfrey 564
Angenberg
  Magdalena 908
Angst
  Catharina 575
  Elizabeth 724
Anters
  Sally 31
Antis
  Rachel 383
Appleton
  Susannah 695
Arent
  Jacob 491
Armagh
  Sophia 15
Armentage
  John 82
Armstrong
  Dorothea 33
Arndorff
  Catharine 408
Arndt
  Abraham 803
Arnold
  Benedick 71
Astor
  John Jacob 199
Auck
  Catrina 832
Aultenburgh
  George H. 432
  Mary 432
Austin
  Freeborn, Jr. 410
  Rhoda 410
  Wm. 330
Avery
  Eve 878
  Henry 878
Baardt
  Anna 907
Backer
  Adam, Jr. 560
  Maria 560
Bader
  Michael 936
Baird
  Obedient 78
  Sally 340

Bajer
  Anna Barbara 316
  Barbara 19
  Catharina Val. 35
  Gertraud 300
  Leonhard 19
  Maria 238
Baker
  Cornelia 690
  Elizabeth 597
  Eve 2
  Obediah 2
  Thankful 764
Baloon
  Margaretha 419
Bangbourn
  Lidia 907
Bannister
  Edward 220
Bant
  Caty 608
  Samuel 608
Barber
  Elias 553
  Mary 55
  Nancy 553
  Sanford 55
Bargy
  Garret 55
  Jacob 55
Barks
  Nancy 255
  Philantron 255
Barlass
  Ann 680
Barlat
  John 847
Barlet
  Catrina 724
  Elizabeth 480
  Eva 480
  John 920
  Marey 920
Barmoor
  Christiana 686
Barnhard
  Anne 95
Barnhart
  Elizabeth 382, 683
  Mary 334
Barret
  Nancy 208
Barrett

945

Maria Elisabeth 788
Peter 285, 614, 917
Peter P. 614
Pieter 275
[?] A. 611
Bellong
Margaretha 419
Bemer
Catharina 638
Bender
Maria 713
Benedict
Charity 533
Bennet
Amos 403
Anna 615
Ide 476
Nanse 615
Bennett
Charlotte 146
Bently
Anna 513
Juliana 513
William 513
Beove
Calva 779
Berlet
Eva 164
Pryna 718
Berleth
Veronica 715
Berleths
Eva 163
Hans Wolff 163
Bernard
Sarah 102
Bernhart
Elizabeth 674
Sarah 718
Bernhert
Christina 393
Berns
Elisabeth Margreth 891
Berry
Daniel 646
Mary 646, 648
Sibyll 569
Syrus 569
Bertolph
Nancy 299
Betsinger
Anna 696
Catharina 114

Betten
Gertraut 546
Margretha 547
Bettinger
Jacob 623
Magdalena 744
Martin 744
Bettli
Maria 693
Bevan
Ebenezer 59
Beviel
Alita 85
Beyer
Maragrita 640
Biddle
Bethseba 145
Mary 172
Nancy 173
Bidwill
Hester 564
Bierman
Elizabeth 707
Biggam
Jean 744
Biggs
Phineas 829
Rachel 829
Bikkert
Anna 845
Lea 22
Margreth 845
Biller
Henrich 922
Sophia 922
Billington
Anna 866
John 31
Nancy 31
Binder
Catharina 442
Bingam
Permilia 205
Bitley
Eva 667
Blaans
Cornelia 340
Blake
Florah 608
Blanck
Catharine 665
George Adam 665
Blank

Cornelius 489
Elizabeth 489
Blevins
Rachel 177
Boachus
George 934
Bodine
Isaac 842
Mary 842
Bogen
Dirkje 134
Bohm
[?] 744
Bolton
Nancy 507
Bombach
Mary Magdalen 323
Philip 323
Boom
Elisabeth 210
Margaret 885
Margretha 883
William 885
Boon
Rachel 3
Boormand
Abraham 214
Anna 214
Borckert
Margreta 794
Borden
Barbara 410
Joseph 410
Borst
Peggy 468
Boschardt
Catharina 419
Boschkirk
Dorothea 862
Boshart
Catharine 926
Jacob 795
Nancy 795
Bottman
Elisabeth 339
Bottmann
Cornelia 328
Elisabeth 275, 889
Bowen
Daniel 610
Lynda 610
Maragrita 335, 336
Bowman

Anna 258
Anna Catharina 881
John 3
Maragrita 134
Obed[iah] 27
Susanna 258
[?] 119, 401, 769
Bowton
Betsey 307
Boyer
Elizabeth 587
Brader
Polly 618
Bradford
Jane 811
Bradpick
John 472
Bradt
Aaron 800
Engel 717
Lena 893
Maryche 643
Susanna 645, 648
Braik
[?] 133
Brainard
Polly 882
Bratt
Cataleyuntje 91
Kinyet 622
Braun
Elisabeth 938
Margaretha 434
Maria 414
Sara 296
Breadalbane
Isobel 97
Janet 230
Jean 230
Breitenbacher
Margretha 662
Breitenbucher
[?] 456
Brentop
Anna Margreth 780
Brettli
Elisabetha 183
Brewer
Elizabeth 249
Rebecca 836
Bries
Neeltje 263
Brietenbucher

[?] 570
Briggam
Elizabeth 522
Briggs
Eliza 326
Else 805
Squire 805
Brightman
David 854
Sarah 854
Brigs
Amanda 83
Aurela 83
Benjamin 83
Caleb 83
Eliza 83
Lavina 83
Lyman 83
Matilda 83
Britten
Sarah 95
Britton
Fanny 715
Broadbake
John 736
Brod
Catherine 424
Henry 424
Brodder
Balli 621
Bronnel
Catrina 873
Bronner
Elizabeth 696
Brookman
John 623
Brouwer
Agnittje 893
Anganieta 893
Catarina 253
Brower
Anne 829
Hendrick 827
Mary 318
Marytie 299
Polly 896
Brown
Catrina 703
Christina 425
Cornelius 186
Cynthia 920
Dorothy 186
Elisabeth 238

Elizabeth 939
John 300, 939
Joseph 474
Millicent 300
Polly 361
Brownell
George 880
Mary 880
Bruckmann
Elisabeth 190
Gottfried 190
Brugen
Sarah 803
Brugman
Gatfrit 292
Brundige
Susannah 128
Brunner
Catharina 696
Elisabeth 696
Buchanan
John 119
Mary 119
Buck
Catrina 338
Bundy
Stephen 82
Burgie
Ali 566
Burk
Henry Pawling 607
John 607
Burr
Amarillus 558
James 558
Bushart
Elizabeth 88
Buskark
Barnhardt 724
John 724
Martin 724
Bussert
Christina 125
Butler
Deborah 871
Maria 336, 393
Mary 335
Polly 336
Walter 697, 725
Butten
Polley 632
Buttler
Mary 203

948

Elisabeth 62
Margreth 71
Chrouch
Polly 661
Cirle
Annatje 821
Claese
Lawrence 827
Clarck
Sara 637
Clark
Christy 671
Darius 781
Esther 898
Nancy 131, 869, 922, 923
Parris G. 898
Rachel 348
Stephen 161
Clarke
Anna 511
Clas
Maria 271
Susanna 650
Clause
Helena 223
Jacob 223
Sarah 885
Clayton
Sally 602
Clement
Adam 567
Elizabeth 3
John 360
John F. 913
Lewis 360
Maria 146
Mary Ann 913
Clepsattle
Andreas 213, 625, 776
Catharina 213, 218
Margaretha 733
[?] 551
Clide
Jane 119
Mathias 119
Clock
Catharina 550
Clute
Alida 913
Jemima 641
John G. 641
Monah 331
Peter I. 913

Tanecka 908
Clyde
Joseph 187
Julia 187
Margreth 187
Samuel 4
Clyne
Anna 658
Cnouts
John 583
Mary 583
Codington
Angelica 31
Thomas J. 31
Coeymans
Andries 827
Cognath
Catharin 1
Cognet
Marrigrita 226
Coieman
Gerritie 24
Coit
Elizabeth B. 468
Colbert
Becca 69
Colby
Nancy 28
Cole
Hanah 920
Colier
Neeltje 585
Nelytje 644
Colley
[?] 615
Collier
Catharina 897
Catrina 293
Machtel 648
Madalena 643
Magdalen 648
Magdalena 554
Collins
Anne 325
John 827
Colvin
Elizabeth 379
Margaret 379
Comerson
Elizabeth 726
Commins
Benjamin 569
Deborah 36

Lois 569
Conant
Ebenezer 59
Concklin
Sarah 600
Cone
Arriana 744
Coneyn
Alida 861
Congar
Mary Ann 532
McKinney 532
Conine
Helena 477
John 477
Conklin
Eliza M. 96
Rhoda 269
Sally 143
Conne
Alita 939
Connelly
Alice 527
Catharine 723
Elizabeth 519
Mary 532
Connely
Nancy 527
Conner
Cristiner 143
Jude 678
Connor
Mary 502
Conradt
Mary 20
Philip 20
Conterman
Elizabeth 385
John 385
Contermann
Gertraud 293
Conturman
Catherine 391
John 391
Conyne
Debora 631
Cook
Anna 379
Anna Eve 665
Caspar C. 665
Casper 934
Magdalane 314
Phineas 608

CROSS-INDEX

Rudolph 885
Samuel 314
William 679
[?] 647

Cool
Catharine 432
Henry 432
Maria 761
Philip, Jr. 761

Cooley
Marjory 615

Cooly
Peter 220

Coonrad
Anna 560

Coonraet
Gertruy 667

Coons
Catharina 286

Cooper
Jane 474

Copeman
Abraham 661

Copley
Seeber 716

Coppernoll
Catharina 794
Eva 367
Georg 794

Coren
Bethay 576

Corey
Mareitje 821

Cornute
Elisabeth 588

Cosaadt
Nancy 584
Susanna 281

Coss
Elizabeth 931

Cothrill
Isabell 137

Cottes
Dina 907
Martha 466

Cotton
Bibye L. 518
Mary 763

Couch
George 143

Coughnut
Catharine 826
Jacob 409

Nancy 409

Counderman
George, Jr. 765
Rachel 765

Counterman
Anna Eva 47

Countreman
[?] 555

Countriman
Margaret 923

Countryman
Abalona 515
Andrew 191
Anna Rosina 623
Catharine 515
Caty 390
Conrad 357
Elizabeth 191, 206, 390
Frederic 515
George 661
John I. 390
Marcus 515
Maria 918
Mark 390
Nancy 257

Covenhoven
Cathrain 331
Rachel 711
Sally 711

Cover
Fransyntje 187

Cowen
James A. 197
Phoebe 197
William H. 197

Cowenhoven
Albert 146
Jacob 146
Jannetje 330
Lea 524
Maria 146
Patience 146

Cox
Anna 240, 242
Margreth 127
Nancy 242
Ruth 615

Cradle
Elizabeth 373
Thomas 681

Craemer
Eva 450
Heinrich 450

Sophia 496

Crafts
Griffin 207

Cramer
Caty 256
Dolly 214
Gadfrey 214
Jacob J. 580
Lana 580

Crampton
Eli 838
Lucy 838

Crane
Sally 927

Crantz
Catharina 776
Maria 595

Crasin
Maragriet 157

Crembs
Christina 896

Cremer
Anna 903
Catharina 762
Joh. 903
Johannes 762

Crems
Dorothea 270
Peter 270

Crief
Clara 720

Criehoof
Elizabeth 573

Crims
Christina 896
Heinrich 896

Crommel
Annatje 617
Aron 441
Echje 598
Ege 11
Flora 40
Jannetje 10

Crommell
Annatje 617
Echje 130

Cromwell
Magdalin 484
Philip 484

Cronnern
Salome 868

Croset
[?] 201

951

Peter 860
Rachel 860
De Lyn
Elizabeth 509
De Pue
Sarah 336
De Wandelaer
Rachel 451
Deal
Margaret 883
[?] 819
Dean
Peggy 619
Debus
Barbara 547
Deek
Mary 338
Deforest
Annaetje 856
Defy
Maria 831
Degoljah
Mary 106
Degraff
Mary 851
Dehart
Jane 199
Dehors
Maria 349
Deifendorff
Elisabeth 763
Deinman
Maria 302
Deixin
Cath. 859
Delaney
Barbara 366
Peter 366
Deline
Elizabeth 405
Hannah 592
Yaniche 620
Delong
Elianora 207
Delyne
Jannetje 618
Susanna 688
DeMelt
Jane 373
Deming
Anna W. 220
Demuth
Catharina M. 363

Delia 480
G: 611
Gertraud 611, 673, 887
Johan Jost 480
M: 673
Denison
Hannah 300
Samuel 300
Dens
Anna 638
Depuy
Isaiah 928
Nelly 928
Derry
Cathy 132
Devan
Catharine 333
Devendorf
Anna 829
Augustus 867
David 829
Mary 867
Devis
Denglas 660
Devoe
Catharine 317
Dewandelaer
Elizabeth 939
Herman 939
Dey
Stephen B. 133
Susan 133
Deygert
Anna 547
Dorothea 361
Elisabeth 316
Dibble
Cloe 147
Dickenson
Phebe 117
Dickeson
Elizabeth 104, 519
Dickson
James 609
Diefendorf
Adam 449
Barbara 910
Catherine 449
Caty 449
Daniel 449
Henry 841
John 449
Rosina 841

Diefendorff
Anna 940
Anna Rosina 866
Catharina 240
Elisabeth 143, 270
Henry 829
John Jacob 270
Rosina 829
Diefendorfff
Elisabeth 653
Dieffendorf
Barbara 829
Diel
John 715
Margaretha 715
Dienstmann
Christine 432
Derius 432
Dieterich
Catharina 407
Dievendorf
Catrina 568
Diffindorf
George Jacob 911
Henry 911
John 911
Dikenson
Sarah 674
Dillebach
Catharina 268
Maria 296, 425
Dillenbach
Anna Margareth 659
Anna Maria 493
Barbara Elis. 582
Christina 287
Delia 704
Elisabeth 582
Henrich 582
Lena 860
Peter 704
Dillenback
Abraham 456
Betsey 456
Elizabeth 240
Martinus I. 240
Dillenbag
Magdalena 421
Dinges
Elisabeth 53
Johannes 53
Dingman
[?] 747

Dinke
    Mary 497
Diore
    John 501
Disbrow
    Henry 659
    Magdalen 659
Divendorf
    Maragrita 45
Dixon
    Dorothy 186
Dockstader
    Aaron T. 928
    Adam 217
    Caty 227
    Frederick L. 227
    George 415
    George Adam 844
    Henry 415
    Henry F. 227
    John 749
    Laney 928
    Margaret 928
    Margaretha 944
    Maria 775
    Mary 749
    Nicholas, Jr. 928
    Peggy 227
    Sarah 928
Dodge
    Almina 131
    John 133
    Margaret 133
    Phineas Leach 474
Doehlern
    Eva 358
Dogsteder
    Cattrien 720
    Elisabeth 227
Doksteder
    Doretha 239
    Elizabeth 62
Dole
    Elizabeth 208
    Grisel 289
Dollar
    Catharine 875
    Henry I. 875
Donelson
    Hannah 878
    Robert 878
Doreschad
    Anna 396

Dorn
    John M. 150
    Nancy 150
Dornberberg
    Margreth 374
Dornberger
    Anna 43
    Catharina 423
    Elisabeth 865
Dorr
    Dinah 569
    Mathew 569
Dotch
    Abigail 524
Dotty
    Cloe 743
Downer
    Peggy 86
Downing
    Peggy 86
Doxstedder
    Sarah 80
    [?] 80
Doxteder
    Anna 659
    Annatje 681
    Catrina 813, 927
    Elizabeth 208
    Sarah 900
Drake
    Aaron 785
    Lois 785
Drammer
    Catharina 81
Drum
    Catherine 258
Dubois
    Peter 204, 707
Ducelion
    Polly 108
Ducken
    Anna 383
Duer
    Catrina 523, 528
Duff
    Agnes 219
Duguid
    Isabel 572
Duireback
    Cattelyntje 152
Dum
    Eve 740
Dunbar

John 827
Dunce
    Janet 767
Dunckell
    Anna 391
    Francis 391
Dunham
    Ebenezer 186
    Esther 119
    John 119
Dunigan
    Fanny 823
Dunkel
    Johann Peter 144
Dunkle
    Betsey 213
    Peter G. 213
Dunlap
    William 18
    [?] 101
Durell
    Dorothea 685
Durham
    Comfort 83
    Cyntha 465
Durot
    Anne 907
Durst
    Anne 907, 908
Dusler
    Anna 354
    Elisabeth 580
    Magdalena 937
    Margaret 32
Dussler
    Cath. 576
    Elisabeth 753
    Magdalena 937
    Maria 576
Dust
    Mathias 403
Duytzer
    Gabriel 650
    John 650
Dwight
    Abbley 899
    Daniel 300
    Margaret 300
Dye
    Abigail 118
    Dolly 149
    Silva 111
    William 149

Dyeslin
Anna 449
Henry 449

Dygert
Anna Peggy 857
Annet 421
Barbara 452
Catharina 872
Elisabeth 453, 737
Elisabetha 776, 807
Gertraut 470
Gertrude 192
Henry 857
Mary 1
Nicholas 1
Peter 452

Dyghart
Margreth 444

Eagleston
Benjamin 86
Elizabeth 86

Eaker
George, Jr. 736
Jacob 251
Margret 251
Maria 163

Earl
Sarah 244

Easton
Eva 876
Thomas 876

Eaten
Lydy 663

Eaton
John, Jr. 162

Ecker
Anna 553
Elisabeth 163
Georg 544
Margaretha 573
Margarita 80
Margretha 544
Maria Magdalena 484
Maria Philippina 353

Eckert
Abraham 573
Margaretha 573

Edle
Mary 36

Edwards
Albert 608
Levi 608

Eenie

Maragrita 6

Eglen
Catharine 199

Ehanisin
Anna Maria 719

Ehl
Anna 451, 898
Annatie 858
Elisabeth 210
Hermanus 451
Maria 192
Petrus 192

Ehle
Delia 579
Elizabeth 140, 167
Harmonus 167
Hermanus 140
John C. 346
Magdalena 354
Margareth 737
Peter M. 737
Peter P. 579

Ehmiche
Elisabeth 407

Eigenbrod
Anna 41

Eigenbrodt
George 306

Eisemann
Elisabetha 719

Eisenlord
Elisabeth 13
John 162, 459

Eker
Anna 931
Maria 303, 922

Ekher
Maria Elisabetha 212
Maria Esther 544

Ekker
Catharina H. 163
Elisabeth 890
John 923
Maria 164, 922, 923

Ellen
Mary 525

Ellice
James 4

Elliot
George 902
Percy 902
Relecty 902

Ellsworth

Elizabeth 118

Elwell
Lursine 96

Elwood
Elizabeth 829

Ely
Joseph 930
Mary 930

Eman
Dorothea 881

Emer
Elizabeth 549
Maragrita 739

Emeri
Catharina 6

Emgie
Adam 893
Johannes 73
Margaretha 708
Margretha 73
Polly 893

Empie
Anna Barbara 707
Anna Elisabetha 922
Anna Margaretha 107
Christina 458
Elisabetha 459
Jacob 707
Mary 924

Enders
Jacob, Sr. 780
John 294

England
Catrina 441

Enkish
Maria 223

Enos
Flavel 807
Hannah Polly 807

Enslin
Elis. 232

Ensly
Elisabeth 658

Enter
Elisabeth 374

Eppli
Anna 658
Johannes 658

Epply
Elizabeth 793
Jacob 793

Erbitsinger
Anna Maragrita 330

Foll
Philip 751
Ann 490
Jesse 490
Mary 490

Folmer
Catharin 405
Gertraut 666
Th: 666

Folts
Anna Margaretha 355
Margaret 904

Foltz
Anna 33, 749
Catharina 446, 749
Elisabeth 184, 749
Elisabeth P. 374
Elisabetha 613, 625
Jacob 160, 184, 213
Maria 160

Fonda
Annatje 853
Catalina 928
Elizabeth 854
Giles 72
Giles H. 72
Gysbert 929
Henry I. 854
Henry J. 854
Henry V. 928
Jelles 30, 166, 295
Jellis 148
John 913
Margarita 893
Maria 638, 639, 848
Mary 166, 848
Rachel 335

Fonteyn
Sophia 508

Foot
Celestia 558

Foote
Elizabeth 930
Horace 690
John 930
Mary 690

Forbes
Anna 726
John 726
Penelope 315
Peter 315

Forer
Catharina 266

Forgason
Ruey 111

Forks
Maria 638

Forncrook
Patty 474

Fort
Catharina 287
Deunge 820
Johanis 823
Magdalena 623

Forth
Marlena 60

Fosburgh
Catherin 143

Fosburry
Margaret 835

Fox
Anna 241, 367, 589
Anna Elisabeth 731
Anna Elizabeth 733
Anna Margaretha 448
Anna W. 576
Catharine 257, 580
Christopher 257, 796, 841
Christopher C. 459
Christopher W. 579, 793
Daniel 580
Delia 638, 794
Dority 459
Dorothea 251
Dorothy 252
Elisabeth 402, 425, 625
Elisabetha 275
Elizabeth 228, 626
Fr. 731
Fr: 625
Frederick 626
Gitty 833
Jacob W. 228
John 167, 551
Joseph H. 385, 390
Lavinia 943
Magdalena 255
Margareth 459, 579
Margreth 41
Margretha 190, 256
Maria 190, 191, 368, 592
Mary 385, 390, 551
Mathias W. 20
Nancy 579, 796
Peter 663
Peter C. 579

Phil. 190
Philip 459
Philipp 402
William 833

Fraest
Catharina 270

Fraley
Jacob 793
John 793
Mary Magdalene 793

Fralich
Abraham 191
Margaret 191

Frame
Eva 599

France
Elizabeth 771

Francisco
Ann 860
Daniel 860
Garet 620
Nancy 620

Franck
Anna Elisabeth 303
Annatye 635
Catharina 439
Catharine 57
Conrad 794
Elisabeth 270, 377, 794
Eva 408
Eva Barbara 275
Fr: 303, 502
Joh: 301, 408
Johannes 886
Lena 523
Margreth 301, 367, 886
Maria 303, 547
Maria Catharin 502
Maria Catharina 303
Michael 251
Steph. 377
Tim. 367

Francoss
Hannah 564

Frank
Albert 723
Andrew 723
Anna Elisabeth 306
Catharina 439
Catrina 459
Elisabeth 795
Elizabeth 388, 389
Eva 117

Evelina 723
Frederick 306
Lorence 45
Margareth 379
Margaretha 35
Margret 757
Maria 306, 733
Maria Catharina 883
Nancy 45
Timothy 733
Frans
Elizabeth 779
Fraser
Catharina 764
Geertruy 520
Frasher
Jinne 520
Frasod
James 765
Maris 765
Frass
Balli 648
Frederick
Annatje 267
Maria 841
Philip 841
Sophia 95
William 934
Frederik
Sophia 95
Fredrick
Anna 158
Eva 840
Maria 840
Freeman
Hanna 330
Meritje 857
Nanse 604
Freemann
Nelly 109
French
Phebe 150
Frey
Catharina 468
Elisabetha 192
Hendrick 928
Henrich 192
John 148
Major 181
Maria 928
Freymaurer
Catharina 711

Gertrud 499
Freymeyer
Margretha 210
Fridrichsin
Maria Engel 710
Frieber
Margreth 69
Fries
Rachel 764
Friligh
Elizabeth 407
Frisbee
Priscilla 683
Fritcher
Catrina 453
Frits
Catrina 746
Fritscher
Barba 405
Gertraut 565
Joh. 425
Sara 425
Fritsher
Elisabeth 890
Froelich
Margareta 838
Fry
Catrina 728
Elizabeth 842
John 646
Mary 646
Frye
Elizabeth 313
Fuchs
Catharina 773
Christina 576
Dorothea 468
Fuller
Alva 876
David W. 876
Henry 876
Hester 429
Margaret 876
Mary 429
Mary Ann 876
Nancy 876
Peter 876
Fulmer
Barbara 595
Catharine 904
Jacob C. 379
Fults
Catharina 213

Jacobi 213
Funda
Alida 837
Peggy 927
Fungie
Lena 584
Furrey
Catherine 266
Rudolph 267
Fye
Elizabeth 842
Sarah 485, 486
Fykes
Catrina 125
Fyne
Maria 914
Merytje 914
Fyx
Rosina 349
F[?]eman
Dorothea 880
Gahe
Luisa 789
Gallier
Cornelia 831
Jeannetje 763
Pieter 831
Gamel
James 394
Maria 394
Gano
Mary 619
Gansevoort
Harme 841
Johannes 204
Gardanear
Abraham 484
Eave 484
Gardenier
Annatie 821
Catrina 821
Hester 405
Jacob 647
Rachel 585
Gardennier
Jacob N. 854
Mary 854
Gardiner
Catharine 342
Gardinier
Caty 222
Dirikie 928
Maria 25

Nelyltje 626
Nicholas 928
Rachel 154, 293, 586
Turckje 927

Garloch
Elisabeth 296

Garlock
Adam 224
Anna Maria 372
Delia 213
John 213
Lany M. 224
Magdalena 793

Garrison
Maria 81
Rebecca 639, 641
William Brower 81

Garrot
Catherine 894

Garter
Ann Eva 50
Robert 50

Gataker
Abigael 204

Gauncy
Margaret 724

Gemell
Christina 49

Gerlach
Anna Margretha 480
Carl 739
Catharina 341
Elisabeta 664
Elisabeth 739
Magdalena 236, 793
Margretha 275
Maria 448
Maria Margr. 60

Gerlogh
Catharina 221
Elisabeth 709

German
Christopher 107
Katherine 107

Gerngross
Maria 21

Gerrison
Marigrietje 335

Gerritson
Annatje 640

Gerryty
Mary 269

Gerster

Elisabet 795

Getman
Conrad 733
Elizabeth 665
Elsie 730
George S. 135
Jacob 704
Joseph 665
Margaret 135
Nancy 704
Peter 730

Gettmann
Anna Maria 550
Catharina 502
Margretha 741
Maria 460

Gibbs
Daniel 485
Magdalena 485

Gibson
Catharine 869

Giels
Catharina 763
J. Nic. 763

Gifford
Annanies 636

Gilbert
Benjamin 85

Gilchrist
Elizabeth 563

Giles
Abigail 882

Gill
Elisabeth 805
Eliza 123

Gillet
Lemuel 513
Mary 513

Gimel
Barbara Elisabeth 744

Glen
Catharine 858
Jacob S. 254, 858
John 855

Glock
Anna 669
Catharina 238
Conr: 238
Elisabeth 147
Jac. 940
Joh. 19
Joh: Adam 669
Lena 19, 238

Sara 940

Godmann
Anna Eva 704
Christian 704

Goedbrood
Elisabeth 54

Goedmann
Catharina 682

Gollinger
Elizabeth 805

Goodbroad
Elizabeth 57

Goodell
Eche 623
Elijah 623

Goodemoot
Jacob 282

Goodrich
Betsey 558
Charles 558
Susannah 593

Gordon
Sarah 151

Gotz
Anna 844

Gould
Rachel 813

Gouverneur
Abraham 827

Gowdie
Jane 5

Graham
Elizabeth 157

Grahe
Anna Maria 329

Grames
Sibble 151

Grant
Isabel 539
Maria 766
Nancy 303
Polly 766, 776

Grason
Sarah 511

Gray
David 923
Elias 599
Elizabeth 749, 943
Jacob 240
Nancy 240
Peter 749
William 689

Grayes

Hulday 205
Greah
Maria Magdalen 176
Green
Ann 118
James 201
Margaret 132
Greenfield
John 726
Sophia 726
Greenman
Elisa 62
Nancy 62
Phebe 62
Grems
Margaretha 270
Gress
Anna 866
Griffin
Joseph, Jr. 142
Lodowic 403
Phebe 403
Samuel 66
Sarah 66, 189
Smith 403
Grigs
Elizabeth 172
Lena 801
Grimm
Catharina 423
Gertraud 388
Jac: 388
Griswold
Chloe 511
Groat
Nancy 797
Simon 797
Groesbeeck
Geertruy 14
Groff
Catherine 135
John 135
Gronhard
Elisabeth 269
Groninger
Catharin L. 412
Groosbeck
Rebeca 263
Groot
Abraham 133
Elizabeth 851
Jeremiah 851
Sarah 133

Gros
Johann Daniel 567
Gross
Anna Maria 790
Catharina 45
Guardinear
Adam 939
Jane 939
Guile
Freelove 152
Gundel
Maria 697
Gunn
Caty 795
Matthias 795
Guntermann
Maria 918
Haack
Maria Eva 43
Haal
Johanna 73
Lidia 922
Simonis 922
Haas
Maria 870
Hadcock
Daniel 389
Hadkok
Margretha 621
Haener
Maria Elisabeth 445
Haeuser
Catharina 698
Hagaman
Joseph 484
Matilda 484
Hagedorn
Margretha 771
Hagel
Catrina 487
Lena 107
Hager
Gitty 82
Hagerman
L. 900
Hahlenbek
Elis. 339
Haine
Anna Dorothea 694
Hakins
Maria 262
Halbeck
Johann 61

Halenbeck
Eva 40
Maragrita 640
Hall
Elizabeth 50
Hannah 750
Nensi 868
Phineas Leach 474
Shower 750
[?] 50
Hallenbeck
Maria 288
Hallenbek
Sarah 599
[?] 792
Hamell
Nancy 523
Hamil
Elizabeth 207
Margret 631
Hammond
Obadiah 899
Polly 898
Ruba 899
Hann
George 911
Hanse
Debora 264
Hansen
Angelica 265
Barent 360
Caty 444
Deborah 894
Douw 444
Ephraim 894
Hans 360
Hendrick 360
Henry 265
Maria 444
Nicholas 360
Peter 264, 827
Rachel 264
Richard 827
Hanson
Angelica 481
Cornelius 847
Daniel H. 481
Deborah 585
Dow 481
Engeltje 264
Jacob 481
Magdalen 847
Margareth 81

Catharina 33
Elisabeth 32, 363
Elisabetha 184
Elizabeth 104, 306
Frederich 184
Fried: 771
Gertraud 432, 458
H: 744
Jenny 94
Magdaleen 485
Margretha 353, 666, 744
Maria Elisabeth 931
Ph. 32
Sabina 771

Helmers
Adam 17, 666
Catharine 666
Elisabeth Margretha 17

Helsburg
Sally 107

Hendrickson
Catharine 197, 655

Heppel
Catharina 106

Heppelin
Jacob 457
Peggy 457

Herass
Dorothea Maria Carolina 344

Herbig
Catharin 33

Herchimer
Elisabeth 711

Herder
Anna 49, 50
Anna L: 46
Appollonia 547
Catharina 550, 883, 885
Elisabeth 731
Ernstine 51
Fr: 883
Frederick 885
Gertraud 403
Hen. 547
[?] 908

Hergheimer
Anna H. 89
Elisabeth H. 710
Lena 210

Herick
Lilla 325

Hering
Philippina 394

Herkemer
Gertrydt 670

Herkimer
John 396
John Jost 343, 803
Magdalena 214
Nicholas 51, 647, 677, 708

Herp
Catharina 207

Herrick
Avery 172
Elias 553
Hannah 553
John 30

Herring
Anna Maragrita 927

Herris
Elizabeth 355

Hersy
Hester 743

Herter
Christina 772
Ernestina 771
Frederic 515

Herwich
Elisabeth 33

Herwig
Anna Margretha 514

Hess
Anna 446
Augustinus 192
Catharina 271, 883
Catharine 190, 192
Daniel 796
Elisabeth 270, 654, 771
Elizabeth 796
John 273, 486
Lany 256
Margaret 706

Hesse
Gertraud 510
Hohn: 510

Hetkok
Catharina 418

Heveling
Maragrita 804

Heychet
Elizabeth 816

Hicks
Jonathan P. 513
Nancy 513

Hicky
Catrina 906

Hiels
Catharina 114, 744
Dorothea 43
Elisabeth 260
J: Nic: 114
Margretha 114

Hieltz
Maria Catharina 261

Hielz
Catharina 698
G: 698

Hikey
Catharina 257
George 257

Hill
Catherine 356
John 356
Nanse 478
Nansy 691

Hillegas
Catharina 658

Hillekas
[?] 431

Hiller
Anna Elisabeth 463
Joh: 173, 763
John 391
Margret 763
Maria 173, 391

Hilton
Abraham 884
Hiram 884
Peter 884

Hilts
Elisabeth 202
Nancy 736
Nicholas G. 736
Stophel 202

Hiltz
George 695
Sophia 695

Hitcock
Catrina 418

Hitshmann
Eva 857

Hoag
Mary 693

Hobbs
Olive 691

Hochstatter
Elisabeth 16

Hock
Elisabeth 143

CROSS-INDEX

John 143
Hodge
Elen 617
Sarah 743
Hoff
Anna 840
Catherine 643
Catrina 130, 643, 647
Maria 598
Hoffman
Anna Barbara 37
Hofstatter
Catharina 662
Christian 662
Hogeboom
Deborah 881
Hogoboom
Leona 763
Holder
Elizabeth 766
Holland
Rachel 371, 401
Hollenbeck
Chester 182
Lana 265
Mary 182
Peter 265
Holliday
Judith 851
Matthew 851
Holms
Elizabeth 124
Mary 495
Hook
Maria 480
Hop
Elizabeth 84
Hope
Mary Ann 563
Hopkins
Christina 553
Mary 244
Horn
Lany 894
Horning
Catharina 143
Catharine 489
John Dirk 377
Magdalena 297
Mary 377
Horsford
Joseph 310
Maria 310

Sarah G. 310
Horsmander
Daniel 3
Hosack
Simon 375, 376, 531
Hose
Elizabeth 432
Henry 432
Hough
Hannah 444
John 444
Houghtailing
Rebecca 72
Richard 72
Houghtaling
Mary 336
Mathias 336
Rebecca 336
Richard 336
House
Appolonia 145
Elisabeth 311
Elizabeth 911
Hannah 724
Jacob 231
John 750
Mary 724
Nicholas 911
Peter C. 724
Houseman
Hannah 619
Houss
John Jost 160
Mary 160
Hovel
Sophia 417
Hover
Anna 617
Catrina 553, 554
Elizabeth 832
Maria 504
Rachel 482, 483
Sarah 926
Susanna 710
Hovey
Lovina 543
Polly P. 543
Sally M. 543
Howk
Caty 149
Christina 149
Jacob 149
Peter 149

Hoxsie
Martha 144
Samuel 144
Thankful 144
Hubble
Rebecca 602
Hubbs
Anne 497
Cornelius 497
Eve 497
Grison John 497
Jeremiah 497
John Daniel 497
Molly 902
Peggy 497
Polly 497
Huber
Maria 610
Hudson
Abigail 847
Richard 847
Robert 811
Huff
Jane 415
Ruloff 415
Huffnagel
Anna 418
Christian 477
Margaretha 477
Huganin
Sarah 894
Hugeman
Jane 838
Richard 838
Hugenor
Catharine 646
Effie 646
James 646
Lambert 646
Hughes
Catharine 634
Huik
Baat 401
Huise
Hannah 619
Huisman
Hannah 619
Hultz
Catharina 439
Maria Magdalena 904
Sara 744
Stophel 439
Hunt

Mansfield 796
Mary 796
Sally 796
Sarah 590
Huntley
Benjamin 485
Margaret 485
Huppert
Anna 649
Hurler
Maria 747
Hurley
Timothy 307
Hurtick
Elisabeth 878
Hurtig
Catharina Elisabeth 85
Elisabeth 878
Rachel 704
Hutcherson
Eunus 5
Hutchinson
Ann 490
Huthmacher
Elizabeth 207
Huvel
Jacob 223
Margaret 223
Huyck
Catrina 59
Huyser
Catharina 666
Hyuck
Harvey 869
Iddig
Anna 285
Chr: 285
Christ: 731
Margretha 731
Ingals
James 190
Irving
Ann Sarah 199
Washington 199
William 199
Ittig
Christian 733
Conrad 733
Elisabeth 197, 367, 369, 733
Eva 369
Marc. 197
Michael 369
Jackson

Mary 728
Sarah 728
Jacobson
Jenny 843
Jacocks
Elizabeth 12
Janson
Charlotta 351
Efje 720
Willhelm 351
Jauncey
James 216
Jecocks
Elizabeth 12
Maragrita 6
Jillet
Silva 546
Johnson
Appollonia 720
Elizabeth 484
Francis 107
Katherine 107
Lydia 118
Nancy 141
Rachel 586
Ruliff 484
Ruth 244
Ruth Ann 690
Timothy 690
William 82, 721
Johnston
Agnes 463
Elizabeth 88, 736
Jones
Agnis 792
Jong
Maria 95
Jordan
Anna 106, 593
Anna Maria 457
Elisabeth 744
Georg 593
Joh. 106
Magdalena 890
Margaretha 744, 863
Maria Elisabeth 367
Maritje 151
Joyce
Jane 12
Judd
Margaret Ann 101
Jung
Anna 446

Anna Elisabeth 55
Anna Margretha 367
Dorothea Elisabeth 421
Elisabeth 326, 437
Joh: Christ: 55
Johann 701
Margaretha 701
Maria 778
Willm. 437
Jurdan
Peggy 312
Kahn
Anna 327
Kajser
Joh: 425
Margreth 425
Kamer
Maria 722
Kane
Almira 258
Hannah 924
Karsineress
Lena 237
Kast
Catharina 202
Friedr. 553
Gertraut 887
Margretha 553
Kayser
Catharina 468
Elisabeth 469
Joh. 468
Margaretha 533
Margretha 1
Keelen
Prudence 67
Keeler
Prudence 67
Keis
Laura 465
Kelder
Annatje 766
Keller
Apollonia 448
Appolonia 446
Catharin 911
Catharina 293
Christina 649
Elisabeth 191, 871, 911,
Hen: 943
Henrich 940
Jacob 579
Joh: 911

964

Klust
Baetta 199
Klyn
Catrina 626
Klyne
Anna 659
Barber 98
Dorothea 792
Elisabeth 412
Elizabeth 615
Maragrita 523, 528
Knap
Melee 95
Knauth
Catharina 116
Knauts
Anna 489
John 489
Knautz
Barbara 670
Knieskern
Eva 932
Margaret 712
Knights
David 109
Elison 109
Knouts
John 583
Knuh
Daniel 221
Elisabeth 221
Knute
Rachel 585
Koch
Anna 468, 544
Caspar 303
Catharina 488, 748
Elisabeth 303, 468, 470, 544
Margaretha 303
Margriet 70
Maria Catharina 744
Kochenath
Elisabeth 684
Koel
Elizabeth 617
Koelach
Elisabeth 914
Kok
Anna 216
Koppernol
Mary 251
Nicholas 251
Kraaft

Maria Magdalena 488
Kramer
Christina 2
Gertraud 372
Krankheit
Altje 183
Krankheyt
Elinora 239
Maria 197
Krantz
Catharina 776
Kraus
Maria Elisabetha 469
Maria Margaretha 391
Krauss
Catharina 446, 448
Krazzenberg
Sybilla 459
Krazzenberger
Sibylla 458
Krembs
Elisabetha 439
Krems
Barbara 232
Catharina 79
Elisabetha 225
Heinr. 79
Margaretha 455
Kress
Anna 391, 394
Johannes 391, 394
Krims
Catharina 476
Kring
John Lewis 305
Maria 305
Krouss
Gertroud 356
Jacob 356
Kuhl
Catharina 232
Kuhlmann
Christina 6
Kunz
Catharina 286
Kurn
Maria Christina 588
Kyne
Mary 317
Kyser
Catharine 167
Henry 167
Labagh

Isaac 388
Lake
Charlotte 146
[?] 146
Lambert
Caty 390
Peter 390
Sussanna 547
Lampert
Elisabeth 488
Peter 488
Lance
Mary 729
Landman
Catharina 476
Heinrich 476
Lane
Annatie 646
Hankinson 646
Margaret 301
Nancy 600
Langbergh
Magdalena 908
Lansing
Catrina 902
Christopher 856
Gertrude 893
Lidia 856
William 856
Lasher
George 31
Margaret 31
Lauchs
Anna Eva 90
Anna Magdalena 81
Catarina 452
Catharina 452
Elisabeth 236, 715
H: 452
Laucks
Adam A. 236, 793
Ana 454
Catharina 452
Elizabeth 236, 454, 793
Jacob 454
Magdalena 236, 793
Maria Barbara 74
Maria Cunigunda 212
Richard 454
William 236, 793
Lauder

Veronica 28
[?] 692
Makafery
Catharina 352
Makkis
Benjamin 701
Maria 701
Mannan
Liddy 101
March
Henry 449
John 449
Peter 449
Marines
Baada 477
Esther 643
Gertraud W. 315
Gertruyd 845
Margaretha 391
Wilhelm 391
Marinnis
Maria 391
Wilhelm 391
Marinus
Geertruy 151
Hester 476
Rebecca 705
Markel
Anna Eva 303
Markell
Anna 10
Elizabeth 10
Henry 250
Jacob W. 10
Margaret 10
Maria 250
Maria D. 753
Peggy 10
Peter 10
Richard 10
Teobald 753
William 10
Marlat
Eleanor 146
Elizabeth 281
Nelly 146
Marlatt
Garret 572
John 35
Peggy 383
Polly 444
Marselis
Gilbert 121

Mary 121
Marselus
Gysbert G. 65
Marsh
Elisha 679
Marshell
Hannah 16
Martin
Eleanor 38
Jannetje 510
Magdalena 38
Molly 679
Peter 86, 679
Robert 400
Mason
Anna 158, 727
Mary 386, 744
Tamzen 146
Mastin
Maria 826
Mathaeus
Christina 12
Conrad 488
Elisabeth 488
Jacob 940
Margaretha 940
Mattenje
Polly 507
Matthees
Catharina 17
Matthews
Anna 49
Gertrude 753
Nicel 753
Mattoon
Barbara 876
Jesse 876
Mauser
Mary 442
Mavi
Alita 547
Dorothea 509
Max
Anna Maria 60
Maxfield
Ann 829
Elias 829
Maxwell
Elizabeth 774
Isaac 774
Levi 903
Sally 903
May

H.M. 252
Mayer
Christina 750
Henrich 750
Maria 773
Veronica 28
Mc Colon
Mary 573
Mc Cown
Mary 98
Mc Graw
Hanna 815
McAllister
Elizabeth 264
John 264
McArthur
Aunt 534
Charles 121
John 536
Margaret 534, 536
Mary 655
McBean
Isabel 525
Jannet 525
John 525
Mary 525
McBeth
Christiana 672
John 672
McCall
Ira 593
Janette 767
Mary 593
Sarah 593
McCallum
Duncan 672
Hugh 672
John 672
McCarley
Betsy 767
McCarn
Elijah 242
Nancy 242
Sally 242
McCarthy
Anne 72
Elizabeth 54, 532, 638, 639
McCaughen
Nancy 37
McCay
Catrina 539
McClassin
Christina 361

McClean
Barbara 519
McClyman
Sarah 428
McColl
Margaret 540
McCollam
Alexander 142
McCollom
John 142
McCollon
Mary 98
McCrea
Martha 883
McDaniels
Alida 858
McDearmid
Agnes 534
Betsey 533
John 533
McDermot
James 521
McDermott
James 521
McDiarmid
Christiana 113
McDole
Jane 81
McDonald
Anna 314
Catrin 96
Caty 97
Elizabeth 315
James 99, 315
Mary 375, 526, 618
Nancy 314
McDonnel
Mary 565
McDowel
Andrew 162
McDugle
Daniel 389
McDurch
Molley 533
McGinnis
Elizabeth 342
McGlachlen
Betty 538
McGlasion
Jane 575
McGraw
Agnes 757
Mary 509

Polly 176
McGregor
Mary 97
McIntire
Duncan 201
Elizabeth 490
James 541
Margret 535
McIntyre
Anna 500
Barbara 154
Catharine 870
Daniel 154
Elizabeth 526
John 500, 526
Margaret 533
McKay
Jane 541
Margaret 515
McKee
Alexander 691
McKenney
Elizabeth 575
McKercher
Catharine 535
McKertie
Alexander 220
McKies
Catharina 38
McKillip
Mary 200
McKinlay
Peter 99
Sally 97
McKinley
Mary 540
McKoom
Sara 363
McKooms
Helena 363
McKown
Margaret 521
Mary 98
McLaren
Ann 540
Archibald 540
Catharine 520, 540
Christian 516
Christiana 517
Isabel 540
Isabella 429
Margaret 429, 540
Mary 540

McLarin
John 540
Peter 540
McLean
Batshaba 500
Hanna 152
McLyman
Ann 86
Bruce 86
McMannis
Susanna 542
McMarten
Jane 516
McMartin
Catharine 516, 538
Duncan, Jr. 500
Jane 672
Jean 500, 516
Malcolm 500
Margaret 500
Mary 520
Molly 534
McMichir
Rosenna 24
McMillen
Jennet 73
McMullen
[?] 690
McMuttle
Jane 529
McNaughton
Christian 672
Duncan 541
[?] 528
McNorton
Christina 536
Jannetje 517
Jennet 541
McPherson
Christian 801
Christie 376
McSillix
Sarah 178
McVean
Jean 522
Margaret 641
McWorth
Jane 529
Mebie
Anna 846
Catarina 853
Dorothea 509
Maria 395

CROSS-INDEX

Meebe
Catrina 608
Meeker
Eliza 543
Meigs
Benedict A. 14
Polly 14
Mejer
Anna Barbara 106
Anna Eva 225
Bally H. 200
Catharin 353, 363
Catharine 658
Elisabeth 363, 553
Fr: 353
Gertraud 98
Henr: 363
Jac: 402, 553, 658
John 883
Joseph 97, 225
Juliana 402
Maria 97, 883
Maria Magdalena 689
Mekie
Batje 764
Johann 764
Melona
Sarah 171
Melroy
Elisabeth 428
Merckel
Anna 939
Anna Maria 303
Engel 705
Johann Henrich 303
Johannes 303
Maria Elisabetha 251
Merckl
Anna 76
Merines
Baada 476
Geertruid 846
Magdelena 847
Merinus
Elsje 174
Merrill
Isaac 339
John 339
Merrit
Meritje 155
Merton
Hannah 509
Messenger

Thankful 563
Metcalf
Mrs. E. 9
Metzger
Maria 193
Meyer
Anna 425, 739
Anna Maria 363
Henry 739
Johannes 214
Margaretha 423
Marillis 214
Theobald 214
Meyers
Annatje 499
Barber 425
Miligan
Margaret 159
Miller
Alida 281
Anna 223, 231
Anna Eva 649
Anna Margreth 303
Catharina 546
Catharine 143
Catrina 871
Charity 366
Elizabeth 223, 785
Fr: 649
Gerhard 143
Hen. 686
Hendrick 154
Jacob 154
Jacobina 178
James W. 375, 376
Jellis 223
Joh. 303
John 389
John D. 231
Lena 686, 720
Magarete 154
Margaret 154, 357
Paul 223
Pieter 357
Sarah 375
Susanna 379
Sussanna 374
Valentin 178
Milligan
Anne 604
Elizabeth 626
Mills
Amarillis 475

Frederick 475
Martha 7
Milmine
George R. 848
Milton
Hanna 40
Minthorn
Lucy 198
Nancy 10
Minthorne
Mary 837
Polly 838
Minton
Ruth 145
Misseles
Catharina 404
Sara 35
Sueries 35
[?] 260
Misselis
Elisabeth 582
Gerret 582
Mitter
Naghty 331
Mitts
Christina 275
Elizabeth 727
Mock
Grates 654
Moer
Mary 128
Mohr
Anna Maria 284
Moke
Catharine 473
Mokin
Anna 653
MomBrute
Elsje 634
Mon Roe
Isabella 521
Monk
Anna 556
Johanes 556
Monro
George 154
Monrow
Mary 542
Sarah 183
Montanje
Elizabeth 495
Monteith
Jennett 109

David 231, 740
Elizabeth 373, 681, 868
Fanny 740
George H. 157
James 740
John J. 273
Magdalena 426, 868
Margaret 486
Margaretha 873
Margretha 876
Maria 740, 868
Mary 305
Nancy 795, 796
Peggy 231
Peter 765
Robert 740
William 358
William I. 868
William J. 868
William W. 868
William, Jr. 305
Nelson
Helena 519
Sara 909
Neps
Eva 821
Nestel
Margaretha 753
Nestle
Gotlieb 849
Mary 250
Newkerk
Anna 638
Douw 336
Newkirk
Albert 572
Anne 376
David 572
Geritje 798
John Peter 336
Maria 81, 850
Rachel 646, 648
William I. 646, 648
Newman
Elizabeth 36
Newton
Joseph 543
Sussanna 543
William 536
Nicholas
Elizabeth 690
William 690
Nichols

Anson 588
Else 269
Seth 588
Warren 588
Nickles
Drusilla 919
Nielson
William 4
Niewkerk
Annatje 376
Nigason
Rebecca 632
Niles
Gertrude 214
William 214
Nistel
Isiah 8
John 8
William 8
Nollin
Hannah 81
Noordtman
Uyltje 27
Norden
Anna 931
Seblon 931
Nortman
Elizabeth 376
Evah 276
Margaret 276
Maria 334
Mary 359
[?] 682
Nortmenn
Anna 675
Norton
Joseph 608
Truman 608
Nowell
Nanse 828
Nukerck
Abraham 298
Charles 526
Maria 298
Nukirk
Elizabeth 599
Maria 759
Nye
Ebenezer 363
Henry 363
Nykman
Catryna 851
O'Linda

Elisa 74
Oathoudt
Henry 844
Oathout
Mary 568
Och
Catharine 279
James 279
Peter 279
Ochsen
Elisabeth 58
Odell
Collins 781
Oehl
Maria Elisabeth 931
Peter 931
Ofenhauser
Margaretha 447
Oharon
Maria 872
Ohrendorf
Margaretha 262
Ohrendorff
Friedrich 408
Ohrndorff
Conr: 610
Eva 610
Ojons
Maria Margaretha 832
Olin
Annaatje 741
Olman
Elizabeth 497
Frederick 801
Maria 497
Omensetter
Elisabeth 912
Oosterhout
Cornelia 713
Sarah 638
Oosterman
Sophia 757
Orandt
Elizabeth 500
Orendorf
Anna Eva 731
Orlough
Elizabeth 497
Sophia 497
Orndorff
Con: 592
Gertraut 592
Orndt

Dorothea 293
Elizabeth 524
Engenietje 845
Maria 163, 482, 483
Neeltje 674
Rebecca 208

Philipson

Gertrud 805

Phillips

Elizabeth 111
Hannah 496
James 758
Mary 811
Philip 496

Philpse

Neylche 674

Phlepps

Agnitje 182

Phlipse

Angenietje 182
Annatje 510

Phlipson

Christina 340

Phrasier

Nancy 280

Phykes

Rosina 349

Pickard

Isaac 919

Pickert

Catharine 911
Frederic 911

Picket

Catrina 154

Picking

Anna 747

Pierce

Anna 318
Elizabeth 14
Joseph 318
Sophrona 882

Piere

Anna Sophia 347

Pikard

Lea 603
Margretha 846

Pine

Phebe 410

Pinkeny

Charity 723

Piper

Andrew 734
Elizabeth 51

[?] 51

Plank

Adam 760

Plants

Charlotte 186
Maria 348
Peter 186

Poff

Jane Ann 901

Polmuteer

Merytje 540

Porter

Mary 371

Portious

[?] 5

Post

Barbara 767
Garret P. 640
James 767
Margaret 640
Rebecca 640

Poter

Lea 108

Potman

Mary 71, 72
Victor 122

Pots

Catrina 328

Potter

Eseck 83
Harriet 83
Job 83
John 83
Nancy 333
Rachel 83

Pottman

Margaret 757

Pottmann

Catharina 45
Christina 69
Elisabeth 872
Jacomyntje 819
Saara 286

Powel

Charles 3, 119
Mary 416

Powell

Corally C. 809
Elizabeth 122
William 122

Powelson

Elizabeth 383

Powlson

Elizabeth 383

Prescot

Isabel 157

Price

Christene 367
Maragrita 276, 822
Sarah 830

Prime

Catrina 414
Harriet 135
Marcus H. 135
Margaret 383
Mary 113, 481
Marytje 506

Printup

Alida 618
Maragriet 780

Prior

Ebenezer 438
Mary 438

Priscot

Isabel 157

Pruyn

Elizabeth 638
John S. 466
Margaret 466

Pruyne

Hannah 561

Puffer

Ire 851
Mary 851

Pulver

Barbel 31
Jacob S. 860
Keziah 860
William 31

Putman

Aaron 248
Catherine 102, 859
Catrina 48, 442, 828
Christina 674
Cornelius 216, 646
Elisabeth 339
Elizabeth 47
Francis 264
Frederick 102
John 336
John A. 248
Katharine 336
Maragriet 781
Maragrita 852, 853
Margaret 383, 646
Maria 849

Rogers
  Catrina 172
  Charity 823
  Francis 444
  Martha 444
  Mary 628
Rohrig
  Dorothea 255
Romien
  Thomas 691
Rooff
  John 680, 706
Rooleson
  Elizabeth 563
Roop
  Abraham 456
  Christina 456
Rosa
  Catalina 646
  John 646
Rose
  Cornelia 939
  John 939
Roseboom
  Elisabeth 292
  John 292
Rosem
  Jane 647
Rosencrantz
  Margretha 731
Rosner
  Elisabetha 547
Ross
  Ephenes 560
  Mary 97
  Susanna 223
Row
  Cathlye 37
Rowe
  Amy 863
Rowland
  Sarah 417
Rredefort
  Mary 56
Ruby
  Phibee Fox 66
Rudd
  Ralph 77
  Ralph, Sr. 805
Rudo
  Elias 561
Rudulp
  Catrina 158

Ruff
  Barbara 820
  Johannis 343, 803
Ruggles
  Nathaniel 608
Rungen
  Elisabeth 462
Runions
  Hannah 69
Runjen
  Lena 226
Runkel
  John 497, 567
  Margareth 497
Runkle
  John 788
  Mary 788
Runniens
  Catrina 92
Runyons
  Sarah 290
Rupert
  Anna 290
  Maria 517
Ruppert
  Anna 856
  Elisabeth 125
Russel
  Hannah 618
  Mary 558
  Samuel 558
Russell
  Hannah 620
Rust
  A. 375
  Ann 375
  Catharine 375, 376
  Nancy 901
Ryon
  Lena 907
Sadleir
  Clement 685
  Frances 685
  Rebecca 685
Sadlier
  Clement 203
  Maria H. 203
Sadow
  Jacob 331
  Rebecca 331
Saeger
  Anna 687
Saert

Anna 211
Elisabeth 440
Sager
  Sarah 87
Sailsbury
  Susan 816
Sale[?]
  Catharine 31
  John 31
Salman
  Madelena 624
  Maragrita 634
Salsburg
  Susan 816
Salts
  Sophia 282
Saltsman
  Catharine 868
  Elisabeth 139
  Georg 139
  George 107
  Margreta 107
  Maria 174
  Maria Dorothea 578
  Sophonia 107
  William 868
Saltz
  Anna Eva 324
Saltzmann
  Anna Eva 940
  George 60, 940
  Magdalena 60
  Maria Elisabeth 19,
Salzmann
  Anna Maria 232
  Maria Dorothea 578
Sammons
  Elizabeth 862
  John 833
Sampell
  Mary 136
Sarje
  Sarah 13
Sarth
  Anna 307
Sater
  George Adam 322
  Gertrude 322
Saterlee
  Amey 118
  Daniel 118
Satman
  Margaret 875

Solomon 875

Saunderson
John J. 167
Magdalain 167

Sayle
Theoda H. 131

Scadden
Cornelia 939
Robert 939

Schade
Anna 394

Schafer
Anna 861

Schaffer
Henry 569

Schall
Anna 694
Catharina 351
Elisabeth 437, 937

Scharmann
Christina 932

Schaumann
Anna 205

Schedder
Cornelia 939
Robert 939

Scheffer
Catharina 173
Rosina Cath. 287

Schefin
Margarita 719

Schell
John 904

Schenck
Catharina 720
Dorothea 281

Schenk
Mary 738

Scherer
Anna 270
Catharina 546
Margreth 407

Schermann
Anna Eva 180
Jacob 180

Schermerhorne
Hannah 265
John 265

Scherp
Geertruy 205

Schever
Maria 667

Schiddi

Maria Marlena 419

Schiff
Maria G. 561
Marigreth 857

Schill
Maria 57

Schily
Maria 286

Schimmel
Elisabeth 553

Schmid
Anna Dorothea 679
Elisabeth 241

Schmidt
Catharina 79
Catharine 224
Maria 461
Rachel 790
Salvey 909

Schmitt
Margaretha 743

Schneck
Antis 218
Juliana 76

Schneider
Dorothea Sybilla 187
Elisabeth 879
Jacob 512
Magdalena 230, 512
Magdalene 231

Schnel
Anna Elisabeth 545

Schnell
Anna 679, 694
Appollonia 210
Catharina 838
Elisabeth 544
Eva 469
Jacob 679
Magdalena 940
Maria 210

Schnerr
Elisabeth 715

Scholl
Catharina 638
Elisabeth 753
Joh. 753
Maria 349

Schomaker
Anna Margarete 446
Thomas 446

Schonmaker
Yannitie 912

Schons
Anna 239

School
Elisabeth 347

Schremling
Catharina 293
Catrina 294
Catterina 821
Catterina Lis. 931
Elizabeth 912
Marigrietje 822

Schrimling
Hendrick 824

Schruyver
Stephen 491

Schuerman
Gertrude 365

Schuiler
John 711

Schuivets
Elizabeth 598

Schults
Annatje 640

Schultz
Anna 469, 470
Barbara 163, 164
Catharina 744
Elisabetha 163
Elisabetha Barbara 233
Jacob 163

Schulz
Maria 789

Schumacher
Catharina 594, 931
Dorothea 767

Schumniel
George L. 851
Nancy 851

Schunk
Anna Maria Magdalena 28
Margaret 323
Margaretha 872
Nicholas 323

Schut
Betsy 248

Schuyler
Cathrine 848
Elje 67
Gertruyd 584
Harmanus 67
Huldah 396
John 396, 403
Margaret 844

Margreth 652
Mary 721
Philip 844
William 721

Schyler

Alita 361, 891
Anna 710
Phil. 710

Scott

Esther 661
Henrica 414
John 35

Scouten

Annenia 258

Scribee

Mary 875
Stephen 875

Scubee

Mary 875
Stephen 875

Sealy

Catharine 251
John 251

Seamans

Charlotte 307
Lemira 307

Seber

Alida 494
Conrad 844
Eliza 710
Maria 421

Seddoman

Aganietje 402

See

Elizabeth 258

Seeber

Conrad 243
Elisabeth 432
Elizabeth 875
Jacob 432
Margaretha 845
Maria 4
Maria Elisabeth 547

Seedam

Elizabeth 141

Seelbach

Arnold 300
Maria 300

Seever

Jac: 720
Maria Catharina 720

Seghner

Anna 610

Paul 610

Segner

Catharina 432
Elisabeth P. 697
Maria P. 425
Paul 432

Seilin

Barbara 315

Semser

Maria 5

Senft

Frederick 489

Service

Anna 443
Catrina 674
Elisabeth 504
Eva 443
Maria 253, 673
Meritje 165
[?]na 93

Serviss

Elizabeth 808
Eva 630
George 735
John C. 640

Settle

Andrew 930

Seuffer

Catharin 664
Elisabeth 669
Maria 664

Sever

Elisabeth 933
Madelena 43

Seymour

Huldah 59
Levi 59
Martin 59

Seymoure

Mary 321

Shadock

Elizabeth 26

Shall

Catharine 580
Leonard 580

Shallop

Elizabeth 182

Shanly

Polly 856

Sharp

Catherine 51
Elizabeth 334, 359
[?] 51

Shaut

Anna 397

Shaver

Catrina 720
Dorothy 627
Frederick 735
Henry 422
Margareth 735
Peter 627

Shea

George 655

Sheets

Mari Madalena 930

Sheffler

Annatje 862

Shelden

Hanna 508

Sheley

Abraham 827

Shell

Maria 640

Sherman

Mable 891

Sheuerman

Gertrude 365

Shew

Jacob 490

Shimmel

Hannah 367

Shipperman

Christian 896

Shite

Peter 236

Shiverly

Betsey 488
Christian 488
Josiah 488

Shnyder

Johannes 385

Shober

Margariet 450

Shoefelt

Catherine 322
Peter 322

Shoemaker

Anna Dorothea 210
Barbara 366
Bolly 550
Elisabeth 884
Elizabeth 917
Ludolph 210
Utilia 311

Sholl

Anna Eve 305
Jost 305

Shool
Elisabeth 347

Shoots
Abelone 615
Catharine 100
Magdalene 216
Mary 137

Shottenkirk
Phineas Leach 474

Shout
Christina 580
George 580

Shuffler
[?] 862

Shult
Casparus 322
Lena 322

Shultes
Barbara 167
Jacob 167
Maria 638

Shultis
Catharine 579
Catherine 580
Christopher H. 314
Edward 314
George 579
John A. 314
Michael 580

Shults
Christopher 167
Johannis J. 472
Maria 665
Mary 167
Nancy 751
William H. 665

Shultz
George 173
Johannis 472
John S., Jr. 135
Maria 135

Shutinkirk
Ruth 690

Shutinkurk
Andrew 179

Sickers
Margaret 179

Sielie
Engelgen 80

Sikkels
Mary 199

Simmons
Elizabeth 861
Eve 854
Rachel 728
Sally 333

Simpser
Martin 348
Susannah 348

Simson
Elizabeth 490

Sinclair
Christiana 534

Singer
Catharina 771

Sisum
Jacob 787
Livey 787

Sits
Elisabeth 455
Lea 703

Sitts
Catharine 878
Henry 878

Sitz
Anna 432
Anna Maria 194
Dorothea 731
Elisabeth 862
Maria 432, 435
Mathalain 209

Siver
Elizabeth 619

Six
Anna Maria 194

Sixbury
Elizabeth 389
Robert 389

Skeanck
John J. 843
Sarah 843

Skinner
Anne 569
Levi 569
Stephen 691

Smaal
Anna Elisabeth 916

Small
Catharina 438

Smead
Jennie 806
[?] R. 806

Smeal
Jacob 114

Maria 114

Smidt
Anna 423
Anna Maria 918
Cornelies 852
Elisabeth 240, 702, 852
Elizabeth 243
Hilletje 710
Maria Sabina 704

Smith
Aaron 760
Abraham 704
Adam 760
Agnes 760
Amos 829
Ann 767
Anna 94
Anne 321
Catharine 704
Cornelius H. 167
Dorothea 618
Elizabeth 346, 599, 853
Eva 893
Gartrute 942
George 94
Gertruy 568
Harriet 899
Henry H., Jr. 646
Jannetje 839
Lany 206, 704
Margaret 276, 330
Margrate 646
Maria 167
Mary 511, 829
Mathew 346
Meritje 133
Nicholas F. 736
Obed 899
Olive 736
Peter 704
Sarah 671, 672, 798, 893
Smith 928
Susan 655
Ursula 761
William 761, 942

Sneck
Maria 248

Sneeden
Elizabeth 410

Sneider
Elisabeth 576
Ludw. 576

Snell

CROSS-INDEX

Abalona 515
Adam 515
Adam A. 251
Anna 693
Anna Elizabeth 515
Anna Eva 515
Catharina 227, 316, 768, 916
Catharine 317, 918
Catharine Elisabeth 469
Christopher 646
Elisabeth 242
Elisabetha 233
Elizabeth 251
Friedr. 768
Georg 361
George 317, 515
Henry N. 460
Jac. 916
Jacob 317, 918, 942
Jacob N. 460
Joh: 316
Lena 675
Loicy Margaret 251
Margaret 51
Margaretha 251, 480
Margretha 361
Maria 51, 316, 478
Maria Elisabeth 226, 227
Mary 317
Nancy 646
William 317
[?] 51
Snock
Elizabeth 326
Lena 634
Maria 72
Snoll
Laura 437
Truman 437
Snoock
Christina 615
Snook
Mary 615
Snyder
Catrina 880
Hannah 932
Jacob 231
Peggy 574
Sary 713
Soott
Jane 86
Sorm
Anna 378

Souse
Catrina 674
South
Marky 497
Southwick
Blondana 585
Spaanenburgh
George 72
Jane 72
Spaarbeck
Catharina 345
Spalsberger
Betsey 931
Jean 931
Spananbergh
Hannah 70
Spanneknebel
Anna Ursula 745
Spannenburg
Anna 91
Spawnenburgh
Polly 72
Speis
Justina 112
Spencer
Elisabeth 425
Spendeler
Magdalena 699
Spenser
Elizabeth 816
Spiess
Maria 238
Spitser
Anna 543
Spon
Catharina 395
Spoon
Anna 223
Catharina 327
Catharine 397
Lainy 51
[?] 51
Spoore
Elizabeth 851
Spraker
Angeline 690
John 690
Sprecher
Eva 193
Maragretha 864
St. John
Nancy 824
Staats

Elsje 645
Samuel 827
Stack
Deborah 586
Stahlee
Ad: 576
Maria Catharin 576
Stahring
Anna 137
Ernestina 908
Staley
Almy 415
Anna 724
Elizabeth 796
Joseph 415
Lydia 724
Mary 724
Rachel 842, 851
Sally 73
Seatty 199
Valentine 73
Staller
Christian 186
Lena 327
Michael 186
Phillip 186
Stamm
Barba 664
Barbara 455
Dorothea 60, 693
Elisabeth 401
Magdalena 440
Sussanna 469
[?] 307
Stanbury
Eva 234
Jacob 234
Stanhouse
Anna 477
Stansel
William 834
Stanton
Mary 670
Starckwetter
Sophia 905
Staring
Adam 51
Anna 45, 163
Anna Eva 776
Anna Margreth 374
Betsy 214
Catharina 165, 698
Catharina H. 352

982

Catharine 10
Elisabeth 13
Ernstine 51
H: 163
Henry 214
Jac: 394, 771
Joh: Nicol. Nic: 45
Joseph 776
Lena 394
Magdalena 395
Maria Eva 261
Sussanna 771
Starks
Daniel 856
David 856
James 856
Starkweather
Edward 220
John 220
Thomas 220
Starn
Annatje 644
Stauring
Elizabeth 134
Stears
Angelica 222
Steeresh
Engelie 220
Stehle
Dorothea 49
Stein
Juliana 607
Steinberg
Anna 61
Gerhardt 61
Maria 61
Steller
Peter 842
Stensel
Margaretha 90
Stenzel
Catharina 871
Stephany
Catty 837
Sterling
James 73
Jannet 73
John 73
Margaret 73
Peter 73
Stern
Catrina 467
Elizabeth 645

Maria 845, 846
Sarah 644
Sternberg
Catrina 234
Elizabeth 474
Eva 474
Jacob 474
Jacob Frederick 474
Sternberger
Adam 762
Anna 594
Catharina 445, 762
Elisabeth 240
Jac: 594
Maria 287
Sternbergh
Elizabeth 646
Jacob F. 646
Stevens
Amasa 927
Anna Margaret 927
Betsey 904
Christian 927
Clarissa 927
Elizabeth 927
Henry 927
Olive 120
Stevenson
James 828
John 828
Stewart
Ann 541
Donald 533
Janet 515
John 533
Mary 533
Molly 502
Peter 161
Sally 533
Stien
Catharine 387
Stiles
Clarissa 882
Still
Betty 189
Stillwell
Catherine 370
Isaiah D. 370
Lydia 831
Stimish
Jannetje 141
Stinsel
Margaret R. 91

Stoller
Dorothy 186
Michael 186
Stone
Edy 149
Ethan 149
Stoner
Nicholas 833
Stooner
Barbara 656
Caty 86
Storm
Christina 478
Storms
Caty 876
Gilbert 876
Story
Mary Jane 31
Robert 31
Stout
Hannah 752
Stowits
George 191, 192
Jacob 191
Margaret 191
Strahon
James 416
Strail
Evi 59
Straub
Dorothea 46
Strayer
Catharina 225
Streeter
Lydia 588
Margaret 263
Strong
George 197
Julia 197
Stroobeck
Catharin 576
Stuart
Christiana 328
Thomas 672
Stultz
Catharine 439
Stumerse
Janneche 141
Suits
Henry 939
Margaret 939
Peter 237
Sukee

Catharina 228
George 228
Sutfin
Anne 507
Suts
Barbara 226
Katherine 305
Richard 305
Sutton
Polly 811
Sutz
Amalia 874
Anna 210
Anna Margreth 760
Catharina 100, 316
Elisabeth 251, 640, 707
Margaretha 113
Peter 236
Suz
Amalia 215
Amelia 411
Dorothea 656
Swart
Catharine 849
Elizabeth 38, 179
Hillica 309
Josias 849
Nancy 179
Rachel 849
Rebecca 179
Sally 179
Susan 768
Swarthout
Cornelius 530
Jennie 530
Sweet
Charles N. 585
Sweetland
Jane 829
Joseph 829
Swits
Folkie 265
Gezina 179
Syber
Sophia 622
Sybergen
Madalena 816
Synes
Caty 593
Syver
Annaleas 942
Taft
Elizabeth 82

[?] 82
Talbot
Eliza 546
Talcot
Hezekia 751, 886
Taller
Alle 572
Sarah 422
Tanner
Jacob 484
Mary 484
Tayler
Mary 53
Taylor
Effy 711
Elizabeth 329
James Stuart 672
Jane 672
Mary 135
Teigert
Anna Catharina 189
Petrus 189
Tell
Catairen 383
Ten Broeck
Gerrit 843
Ten Eick
Sarah 843
Ten Eyck
Abraham 343
Barent 661
Henry 661
Jacob 661
John D.P. 661
Myndert S. 661
Rachel 661
Tobias 441, 661
Ten Eycks
Elizabeth 894
Ten Eyke
Maria 843
Tenbrook
Anne 803
Terrel
Catrina 383
Terwillegar
Mariah 23
Terwilleger
Catrina 644
TerWilliger
Catrina 642
Janetje 6
Maragrita 852

Margrita 853
Teughard
Maria 45
Tevendorf
Catrina 45
Thayre
Hannah 118
Jacob 118
Thimes
Rosina 884
Thomas
Caty 721
Elizabeth 721
Lydia 414
Osseltje 548
Thompson
Ann 500
Anna 506
Edward 524
Jinne 524
Jonathan S. 380
Mary 381
[?] 279
Thomsen
Mary 280
Thomson
Alexander A. 525
Anna 525
Mersi 88
Willemina 23
Thorn
Catharina 544
Throop
Abia 344
Thum
Agnes 212
Elisabeth 352
Margreth 698
Melch: 352
Melchior 653, 698
Thumb
Adam 740
Barbara 190
Margaret 740
Melc: 190
Thurston
Barent 185
John 185
Tice
Rebecca 30
Tick
Hannah 378
Tie

Peggy 479
Tillabagh
Maria Elizabeth 301
Tillenbach
Catharina 493
Henrich 493
Timmerman
Deobald 244
Lena G. 50
Margaret 243, 396
Tingmann
Cornelia 158
Tirwilger
Rebecca 566
Tivendorf
Barber 46
Tommon
Agnes 213
Tonner
Catharina 629
Torkey
John 214
Marillis 214
Tourteloot
Amasa 881
Elizabeth 881
Trichrat
Heinrich 218
Maria 218
Truman
Jenny 723
Tuble
Catharine 488
Tucker
Joseph 343, 803
Tulbak
Margaret 421
Tuller
Rosannah 596
Tuneclef
Bolly 595
Tuttle
Mary 799
Stephen 758
Tygart
Anna Elisabeth 916
Tyger
Elizabeth 716
Tygert
Cunigunda 771
Maria 864
Tyghart
Anna 445

Catharina 576
Catharina W. 315
Dorothea 576
Elisabetha 316
Johannes 316
Lena 753, 816
Maria Catharina 872
Sev: 576
W: 445, 872
Werner 816
Tymenson
Annatje 254
Tymese
Annatje 451
Catharina 892
Tymids
Margrita 313
Tysen
Catrina 643
Uhle
Magdalena 104
Ulshoefer
Dorothea 864
V. Dike
Hannah 486
v.d. Werken
Elisabeth 4
V.D. Willige
Yannatje 384
V: Antwerpe
Catarina 72
Vader
William 52
Valkenbourgh
Elisabeth 643
Valkenburg
Baata A. 293
Christina 678
Vallac
Catye 820
Van Aalen
Leentje 832
Rachel 509
Sarah 832
Van Aalsteen
Janitje 643
Van Aalstein
Cornelia 839
Cosen 839
Elisabeth 643
Maraytie 292
Van Aalsteyn
Catarina 645

Van Aalstyn
Derkje 832
Elizabeth 644
Marytje 102
Van Alen
Ann 18
Derick 18
Van Allen
Benjamin 809
Mary 809
Van Alstine
Cornelia 820
Cornelius 477
Derkje 644
Elizabeth 397
Lanai 129
Margaret 477
Maria 103
Van Alstyn
Dirckje 643
Jannetje 645
Maria 129
Marten 929
Marten Abraham 929
Marten Johannes 929
Van Alstyne
Agnitje 820
Cornelia 832
Eva 644
Janetge 293
Maria 140
Nelly 173
Nyltje 851
Van Antwerp
Angelica 109
Annatie 854
Annatje 237
Catharine 760
Daniel 133
Henry 760
John 760, 833
Margaret 760
Susan 648
Volkert 760
Van Antwerpen
Annatye 638
Neeltje 836
Van Beuren
Elizabeth 765
Martin 765
Van Braekel
Aelje 638
Van Braeklen

CROSS-INDEX

Anna Eva 377
Anna Rosina 46
Catharine 34
Elizabeth 488
Garret W. 391
Hendrick 196
Hendrick H. 196
Jacob 196
John 196, 488
Magdalena 868
Maria Catharina 447
Maria Margaretha 395
Wm. I. 868

Walter
Robert 827
Walther
Dorothea 508
Walts
Jacob 231
Maria 231
Waltz
Mary 878
Wample
Hannah 33
Wanner
Anna Margretha 740
Elizabeth 618
Wanple
Anna 634
Ward
Agnes 939
Isaac 939
Warmoeth
Anna P. 108
Warmuth
Anna Margaretha 193
Betsey 551
Margretha 272, 864
William C. 551
Warner
Ebenezer 300
Elizabeth 695
James 758
Maria 823
Molly 300
Warren
Catrina 255
Peter 403
Waters
Peggy 199
Watson
Mathew 30
Wauffel

Catharine 795
Weaver
Abraham 701
Anna 184
Catharina P: 45
Elisabeth 939
Eve 701
Georg 210
Gertraud 210
Hannickel 168
J: Nic. 184
Joh: N. 939
Margaret 924
Weber
Andreas 408, 500, 546
Barbara 408
Catharina 164, 365, 578, 771
Elisabeth 500, 637, 792
Elisabetha 445
Elizabeth 45
Lena 816
Margretha 177
Weeke
Maragrita 407
Weeks
Anna 14
Weemer
Catrina 6
Weever
Barbara 165
Maria 6
Weil
Catharina 710
Franz 710
Weiss
Sussanna 877
Wekeserin
Anna Barbara 6
Welch
Sarah 142
Welden
James D. 456
Peggy 456
Welds
Helen 500
Phebe 500
Susanna 500
Weller
William 834
Wells
James 475
Josiah 475
Prudence 475

Richard 609
Susannah 729
Wells
Job 729
Wemell
Elizabeth 549
Wemp
John 854
Susanna 543
Wempble
Annatje 327
Wemph
Jannetje 779
Wemple
Adriaentje 390
Alida 837
Anenetche 81
Ariaantje 182
Arriaantje 853
Arriana 852
Barent 264
Catharine 647
Catlyna 824
Catrina 643
Caty 854
Deborah 335
Jane 74, 322, 775, 779
Magdalen 855
Margaret 264
Maria 746
Mindert 854
Rebecca 81, 135
Sarah 81, 820
Susanna 499
Wendeker
Catharina 395
Lea 451
Wendel
Eleanor 858
John H. 858
Wendell
Aultie 265
Harmanus 122
Hermanus H. 834
John Babtist 204
Weniger
Maria 492
Wenne
Agnete 859
Wentworth
Dolly 420
Wentz
Anna Maria 776

Barbara 445

Wenz

Margaretha 776

Werdt

Efje 777

Wermuth

Eliza Margaret 129

Werner

Anna Barbara 19
Dorothea 595
Maria 351

Wert

Antje 384
Evah 784
Joseph 690
Mary Magdalen 126
Rachel 690

Wescot

Sally 217

Wessels

Eveline 838
Luke 838

Westermann

Catharina 311
Peter 311

Westervelt

Helen 23

Wetherwax

Catherine 50, 51
Christina 50
[?] 50

Wever

Barbara Elisabeth 98

Weyli

Sally 394

Whart

Evah 784

Wheeler

Annatje 564
Della 346
George W. 346
Isaac 614
Olive 466

While

Henry 134
Peggy 134

Whitaker

James A. 685
Nancy 815

Whitbeck

[?] 805

White

Lana 655

Laura 900
Maragrita 672
Margaret 672
Mary 96
Phebe 290

Whiting

Elizabeth 402
Martha 319
Mary 26

Whitney

Sarah 185

Wick

Catharina 443
Lana 551
Suffrenius 551

Wicks

Maragrita 290
Peggy 407

Wiederstein

Anna Maria 372
Henry 372

Wieler

Neyltje 628

Wies

Catharina 923

Wilcocks

B. 417

Wild

Rosina 805

Wilder

Nancy 342

Wildie

John Radliff 650
Mary 650

Wiles

Elizabeth 744

Wiley

Dorado 711
John 711

Wilkens

Martha 881

Wilkie

Anna 199

Willes

Minerva 36

Williams

Elizabeth 566
Jane 520
Margaret 319
Mary 674

Williamson

Delia 665
George 665

James 833
Mary 858

Willse

Mary 133
Thomas 133

Willsen

Rebecca 786

Willson

Thankful 546

Wilse

Merya 229

Wilson

Anatje 326
Anne 111
Catrina 173
Charles 678
Elisabeth 190
Elizabeth 490
Jane 782
Jannet 520
Jean 782
Johann 190
Maragrietje 154
Mary 572
Polly 826, 827
Rhoda 678
S.M. 91
Willard 678

Wilts

Fanny 524

Wimp

Sussanna 619

Wimpel

Ariaantje 596
Myndert 827
Volke 861

Wimple

Mary 91

Windecker

Anna 60, 427
Anna Elisabeth 270
Catharine 192
Frederic 427
Hartman 357

Windekker

Anna Barbara 611
Cathrina 394
Conrad 394

Windlor

Anna 937

Winigar

Lucy 202

Winkle

APPENDIX A

TRYON COUNTY MILITIA

On October 5, 1776 a "Resolution of Congress" was laid before the Tryon County Committee of Safety appointing Nicholas Herkimer, Esq., Brigadier General of the Brigade of Militia of the County of Tryon.

During the American Revolution there were five regiments, formed according to their geographical locations, which comprised the Tryon County Militia.

FIRST REGIMENT (Canajoharie District): Colonel Samuel Campbell, Lt. Colonel Samuel Clyde, Major Peter S. Dygert, Adjutant Jacob Seeber, Quarter Master John Pickard.

SECOND REGIMENT (Palatine District): Colonel Jacob Klock, Lt. Colonel Peter Wagner, Major Harmanus Van Slyck, Adjutant Samuel Gray, Quarter Master Jacob Ecker.

THIRD REGIMENT (Mohawk District): Colonel Frederick Fisher, Lt. Colonel Volkert Veeder, Major John Newkirk, Adjutant Peter Conyne, Quarter Master Simon Veeder.

FOURTH REGIMENT (German Flatts & Kingsland Districts): Colonel Peter Bellinger, Lt. Colonel Frederick Bellinger, Major John Eisenlord, Adjutant George Demuth, Quarter Master Rudolph Steele.

FIFTH REGIMENT (Frontier settlements of Tryon County to be protected by Ranger Companies. No roster of men in this regiment has been found): Colonel John Harper, Lt. Colonel William Wills, Major Joseph Harper, Adjutant St. Leger Cowley.

(See "key code" [NYR] in *References* for source of data on the Tryon County Militia.)

NAME	RANK	REGIMENT
Adamy, John	Lieutenant	Second
Adamy, Peter	Lieutenant	First
Adamy, Peter	Private	Second
Albrant, Henry	Private	Third
Algire, John	Private	Third
Allen, William	Private	Third
Anderson, William	Private	Third
Anguish, John	Private	Second
Antis, Conrad	Private	Third
Antis, John	Private	Third
Archer, Ananias	Private	Third
Armstrong, Archibald	Private	Fourth
Armstrong, John	Private	Fourth
Arndt, Abraham	Lieutenant	First
Baani, Ichabod	Private	Fourth
Badcock, John	Private	Fourth

APPENDIX A

TRYON COUNTY MILITIA

NAME	RANK	REGIMENT
Bader, Francis	Private	Third
Bader, Melchior	Private	Second
Bader, Michael	Private	Second
Baker, Adam	Private	Third
Balthaser, Breih	Private	Fourth
Barbat, John	Private	Third
Barclay, Isaas	Private	Third
Barhydt, Teunis	Private	Third
Barkill, Lewis	Private	Third
Barnes, Aaron	Private	Third
Barnes, Jacob	Private	Third
Barnes, John	Private	Third
Barnhart, Charles	Private	Third
Barnhart, John	Private	Third
Barth, Nicholas	Lieutenant	First
Baum, Frederick	Private	Second
Baum, Philip	Private	Second
Baumann, Adam	Private	Fourth
Baumann, Christopher	Private	Fourth
Baumann, Frederick	Private	Fourth
Baumann, George A.	Private	Fourth
Baumann, Jacob	Private	Fourth
Baumann, Johannes	Private	Fourth
Baumann, Nicholas	Private	Fourth
Baumann, Peter	Captain	First
Bayer, John	Private	Second
Bayer, John, Jr.	Private	Third
Becker, Henrich	Private	Fourth
Becker, Henry	Private	Second
Becker, Peter	Private	Second
Becker, Philip	Private	Second
Beekman, Ishmael	Private	Third
Beeler, Jacob	Private	Second
Beffer, Jacob	Private	Fourth
Bell, G. Henry	Private	Fourth
Bell, Jacob	Private	Fourth
Bell, John	Private	Third
Bell, Matthew	Private	Third
Bell, Nicholas	Private	Fourth
Bell, Thomas	Private	Fourth
Bellinger, Adam	Lieutenant	Second
Bellinger, Adam	Private	Second
Bellinger, Adam	Private	First
Bellinger, Adam P.	Private	Second
Bellinger, Christian	Private	Third
Bellinger, Christopher	Private	Fourth

TRYON COUNTY MILITIA

NAME	RANK	REGIMENT
Bellinger, Frederick	Private	Fourth
Bellinger, Frederick	Private	Second
Bellinger, Frederick	Private	First
Bellinger, Henrich	Private	Second
Bellinger, Johannes	Ensign	Fourth
Bellinger, Johannes	Private	Fourth
Bellinger, John L.	Ensign	First
Bellinger, Jost	Private	Second
Bellinger, Peter	Colonel	Fourth
Bellinger, Peter	Private	Fourth
Bellinger, Peter	Private	Second
Bellinger, Peter B.	Private	Fourth
Bellinger, Peter P.	Private	Fourth
Bellinger, Peter, Jr.	Quarter Master	Fourth
Bellinger, Philip	Private	Third
Bellinger, Philip	Private	First
Bellinger, William	Private	First
Bendel, Catren	Private	Fourth
Bender, Jacob	Private	Fourth
Bennet, Amos	Lieutenant	Third
Benrich, Frans	Private	Fourth
Berckie, Jacob	Private	Fourth
Berckie, Peter	Private	Fourth
Berdrick, Frantz	Private	Fourth
Berlet, John	Private	Third
Berry, Nicholas	Private	Third
Berry, William	Private	Third
Bersh, Ludwig	Private	Fourth
Bersh, Rudolph	Private	Fourth
Beshar, Jacob	Private	Fourth
Betrer, Jacob	Private	Fourth
Bettinger, Martin	Private	First
Beverly, David	Lieutenant	Third
Beverly, Thomas	Private	Third
Biddle, Benjamin	Private	Third
Billings, James	Private	Third
Bishop, Charles	Private	Second
Bliven, John	Major	Third
Bodin, John	Private	Third
Bogart, Henry	Private	Third
Boshart, John	Private	Third
Bost, Andreas	Private	Second
Bove, Nicholas	Private	Third
Bowman, John	Captain	First
Bowman, John	Private	Third
Bratt, Henry	Lieutenant	First

APPENDIX A

TRYON COUNTY MILITIA

NAME	RANK	REGIMENT
Bratt, Henry	Private	Second
Bratt, Jacob	Private	Second
Breadbake, John	Captain	Second
Breem, John	Private	Third
Breidenbucher, Baltus	Private	Fourth
Breitenbacher, Baltes	Private	First
Brewer, Harman	Lieutenant	Second
Brewster, John	Private	Third
Brothack, Bartholomew	Private	Fourth
Brothack, Jacob	Private	Fourth
Brothack, John	Private	Fourth
Brothers, John	Private	Third
Brower, William	Private	Second
Brown, Christian	Private	Second
Brown, Conrad	Lieutenant	First
Brown, Matthew	Captain	First
Brukman, Godfrey	Private	First
Brunner, Christian	Private	First
Brunner, Jacob	Private	Second
Bunn, Jacob	Private	Third
Bunn, John	Private	Third
Burch, Jeremiah	Private	Third
Bush, George	Private	First
Bush, Julius	Private	Second
Butler, Thomas	Private	Third
Cady, Nathaniel	Private	Third
Cagal, John	Private	Third
Caimon, Andrew	Private	Third
Caine, John	Private	Third
Caine, Peter	Private	Third
Caine, Thomas	Private	Third
Campbell, John	Private	Fourth
Campbell, John	Private	Third
Campbell, Ludwig	Private	Fourth
Campbell, Nathaniel	Private	Third
Campbell, Patrick	Lieutenant	Fourth
Campbell, Patrick	Private	Fourth
Campbell, Samuel	Colonel	First
Campbell, Samuel	Private	Third
Cane, Samuel	Private	Third
Cannan, Andrew	Private	Third
Canner, John	Private	Third
Cannon, Matthew	Private	First
Carey, William	Private	Third
Carrall, John	Private	Third

APPENDIX A

TRYON COUNTY MILITIA

NAME	RANK	REGIMENT
Carrol, George	Private	Fourth
Cartright, Henry	Private	Third
Casselman, John	Private	Second
Casselman, John	Private	Second
Casselman, John, Jr.	Private	Second
Casselman, Peter	Private	Second
Chitter, John	Private	Second
Chokin, Thomas	Private	Fourth
Christman, Frederick	Private	Fourth
Christman, Jacob	Private	Fourth
Christman, Jacob	Private	Second
Christman, John	Private	Fourth
Christman, John	Private	Second
Christman, John	Private	First
Christman, Nicholas	Private	Fourth
Clapper, Christian	Private	Second
Clapsattle, Andrew	Private	Fourth
Clapsattle, Andrew	Private	Second
Clapsattle, William	Private	Fourth
Clapsattle, William	Private	Second
Clark, William	Private	Third
Claus, George	Private	Second
Clement, John	Private	Third
Clement, Lambert	Private	Third
Clements, Jacob	Private	Fourth
Clements, Jacob	Private	Second
Clements, Philip	Private	Fourth
Clenicum, John	Private	Fourth
Cline, William	Private	Fourth
Clyde, Samuel	Lt. Colonel	First
Cochen, Thomas	Private	Fourth
Cochran, Andrew	Private	Third
Cock, Peter	Private	Third
Coleman, Henry	Private	Second
Collier, Isaac	Private	Third
Collier, Jacob	Private	Third
Collier, John	Private	Third
Collier, William	Private	Third
Colsh, John, Jr.	Private	Fourth
Colsh, John, Sr.	Private	Fourth
Comrie, James	Private	Third
Connelly, Hugh	Private	Third
Conner, James	Private	Third
Conrad, Joseph	Private	Third
Conrad, Nicholas	Private	Third
Conyne, John	Private	Third

APPENDIX A

TRYON COUNTY MILITIA

NAME	RANK	REGIMENT
Conyne, Peter	Adjutant	Third
Cook, Severines	Captain	Second
Copeman, Abraham	Major	First
Coppernoll, John	Private	Second
Coppernoll, Nicholas	Lieutenant	Second
Coppernoll, Richard	Lieutenant	Second
Coppernoll, William	Private	Second
Coughnut, Jacob	Private	Third
Countryman, Adam	Private	First
Countryman, Conrad	Private	First
Countryman, Frederick	Private	First
Countryman, George	Lieutenant	First
Countryman, John	Ensign	First
Countryman, John	Private	Second
Countryman, John J.	Private	First
Covenhoven, Abraham	Private	Third
Covenhoven, Isaac	Private	Third
Covenhoven, John	Private	Third
Covenhoven, Peter	Private	Third
Cox, Ebenezer	Colonel	First
Cox, Fasier	Private	Fourth
Cram, Jacob	Private	Fourth
Cranse, Jacob	Private	Second
Crantz, Henry	Private	Fourth
Crantz, Henry	Private	Third
Crim, Hendrick	Private	Second
Cronkhite, Abraham	Private	Third
Crook, Christopher F.	Private	Third
Crossett, Benjamin	Private	Third
Crossett, John	Private	Third
Crowley, Jeremiah	Private	Third
Crownhart, George	Private	Second
Crummel, Herman	Private	Third
Crysler, George	Private	Second
Cunningham, John	Private	Fourth
Cunningham, John	Private	Second
Cunningham, William	Private	Fourth
Cunningham, William	Private	Second
Dachstaeder, Adam	Private	Third
Dachstaeder, Frederick F.	Private	Third
Dachstaeder, Frederick H.	Private	Third
Dachstaeder, George	Private	Fourth
Dachstaeder, George	Private	Third
Dachstaeder, George A.	Private	Third
Dachstaeder, Henrich	Private	Third

APPENDIX A

TRYON COUNTY MILITIA

NAME	RANK	REGIMENT
Dachstaeder, Henry H.	Private	Third
Dachstaeder, Jacob	Private	Third
Dachstaeder, Joh. Nicholas	Private	Third
Dachstaeder, John	Private	Fourth
Dachstaeder, John	Private	Third
Dachstaeder, John	Private	First
Dachstaeder, John F.	Private	Third
Dachstaeder, John H.	Private	Third
Dachstaeder, Leonard	Private	Third
Dachstaeder, Marcus	Private	Third
Dachstaeder, Nicholas	Lieutenant	Third
Dachstaeder, Nicholas	Private	Third
Dachstaeder, Nicholas	Private	Second
Dachstaeder, Nicholas H.	Private	Third
Dachstaeder, Peter	Private	Fourth
Darrow, John	Private	Third
David, Adam	Private	Second
Davies, Jacob	Private	Second
Davis, Abraham	Private	Third
Davis, George	Private	Fourth
Davis, Isaac	Private	Third
Davis, Jacob	Private	Fourth
Davis, James, Jr.	Private	Third
Davis, John	Private	Fourth
Davis, John	Private	Third
Davis, Joseph	Private	Second
Davis, Peter	Private	Fourth
Davis, Thomas	Private	Third
Deacke, John	Private	Second
Deacker, Hendrick B.	Private	Second
Degraff, Emanuel	Captain	Third
Deharsh, Philip	Private	Second
Deisellman, Christian	Private	Fourth
Deline, Benjamin	Lieutenant	Third
Deline, Isaac	Private	Third
Deline, Ryer	Private	Fourth
Deline, William	Private	Third
Demuth, Deterich	Private	Fourth
Demuth, Dieterich	Private	First
Demuth, George	Adjutant	Fourth
Demuth, Hans Mark	Captain	Fourth
Demuth, Johannes	Lieutenant	Fourth
Demuth, John	Private	Fourth
Demuth, Marx	Private	Fourth
Dieffendorf, Jacob	Captain	First
Dieffendorf, Jacob	Private	Third

APPENDIX A

TRYON COUNTY MILITIA

NAME	RANK	REGIMENT
Dieffendorf, John	Private	First
Dieffendorf, John J.	Private	First
Dieffendorf, John, Jr.	Private	First
Dienstman, Antony	Private	First
Dienstman, Dennis	Private	First
Dillenbach, Baltus	Private	First
Dillenbach, Henrich	Private	Second
Dillenbach, John	Private	Second
Dillenbach, Martin	Private	Second
Dillenbach, Martin	Private	First
Dinges, Johannes	Private	Fourth
Dinghardt, Jacob	Lieutenant	Third
Dingman, Gerrit	Private	Third
Dingman, Peter	Private	Third
Dingman, Samuel	Private	Third
Dinus, Jacob	Private	Fourth
Dorn, Alexander	Private	Third
Dorn, David	Private	Third
Dorn, John	Private	Third
Dornenbergh, John	Private	Third
Dorp, Matthew	Private	Third
Doyle, Stephen	Private	Third
Dum, Adam	Private	Second
Dum, Conrad	Private	Second
Dum, Melchior	Private	Fourth
Dum, Melchior	Private	Second
Dum, Nicholas	Private	Second
Dum, Richard	Private	Third
Dunckel, Francis	Private	First
Dunckel, Garrett	Private	First
Dunckel, George	Private	First
Dunckel, Nicholas	Private	First
Dunckel, Peter	Private	First
Dunham, Ebenezer	Private	Third
Dunham, John	Private	First
Dunlap, John	Private	First
Dunlap, William	Private	First
Dunn, James	Private	Third
Dunn, John	Private	Third
Dussler, Jacob	Private	Second
Dussler, William	Private	Second
Dygert, George	Private	Second
Dygert, Henry	Private	Second
Dygert, Henry	Private	First
Dygert, Jost	Captain	First
Dygert, Nicholas	Lieutenant	First

APPENDIX A

TRYON COUNTY MILITIA

NAME	RANK	REGIMENT
Dygert, Nicholas	Private	First
Dygert, Peter J.	Private	Second
Dygert, Peter S.	Captain	Second
Dygert, Peter S.	Major	First
Dygert, Peter S.	Private	Second
Dygert, Peter W.	Private	Second
Dygert, Rudolph	Private	Second
Dygert, Severines	Private	Second
Dygert, Severines H.	Private	Second
Dygert, Severines P.	Private	Second
Dygert, Severines, Jr.	Private	Second
Dygert, Severinus	Private	First
Dygert, Theobald	Private	First
Dygert, William	Private	Second
Dygert, William A.	Private	Fourth
Dygert, William H.	Private	Second
Dygert, William, Jr.	Private	Second
Earnest, Jacob	Private	Third
Eaton, Eleazor	Private	Third
Eaton, Ephraim	Private	Third
Eaton, James	Private	Third
Eaton, Thomas	Private	Third
Eckler, Christopher	Private	First
Eckler, Henrich	Private	Second
Ehle, Anthony	Private	First
Ehle, Christian	Private	First
Ehle, Harmanus	Private	First
Ehle, John	Private	First
Ehle, Michael	Private	Second
Ehle, Nicholas	Private	Third
Ehle, Peter	Private	First
Ehle, William	Private	Second
Eigenbrodt, George	Private	Second
Eigenbrodt, John	Lieutenant	Second
Eigenbrodt, John	Private	Second
Eigenbrodt, Peter	Private	Second
Eisenlord, John	Captain	Fourth
Eisenman, Johannes	Private	Fourth
Eisenman, Stephen	Private	Fourth
Ekher, Abraham	Private	Second
Ekher, George	Ensign	Second
Ekher, George	Private	Third
Ekher, George	Private	Second
Ekher, George, Jr.	Private	Second
Ekher, Jacob	Quarter Master	Second

TRYON COUNTY MILITIA

NAME	RANK	REGIMENT
Ekher, Johannes	Private	Second
Ekher, John	Private	Third
Ekher, Nicholas	Private	Second
Elliot, Andrew	Private	Third
Elliot, Jacob	Private	Third
Elliot, Joseph	Private	Third
Ellis, John	Private	Third
Ellwood, Benjamin	Private	First
Ellwood, Isaac	Private	Second
Ellwood, Isaac	Private	First
Ellwood, Peter	Private	First
Ellwood, Richard	Ensign	First
Empie, Adam	Private	Second
Empie, Andrew	Private	Second
Empie, Frederick	Private	Second
Empie, John	Private	Second
Empie, John, Jr.	Private	Second
Empie, Philip	Private	Second
England, Benjamin	Private	Third
Eny, George	Private	Third
Eny, Godfrey	Private	Third
Eny, Jacob	Private	Third
Eny, John	Private	Third
Epply, Jacob	Private	Second
Epply, Philip	Private	Second
Ergersinger, John	Private	Third
Erichman, Godfrey	Private	Second
Erksen, John	Private	Second
Ernest, Christ	Lieutenant	Third
Everson, Adam	Private	Third
Everson, John, Jr.	Private	Third
Failing, Andreas	Private	First
Failing, Henry	Private	First
Failing, Jacob	Private	Second
Failing, Jacob	Private	First
Failing, John	Private	Second
Failing, Nicholas	Private	First
Failing, Peter	Private	First
Farrell, Charles	Private	First
Feelis, Jacob	Private	Fourth
Ferguson, Daniel	Private	Third
Ferguson, William	Private	Third
Fey, George	Ensign	Second
Fey, George, Jr.	Private	Third
Fey, George, Jr.	Private	Second

APPENDIX A

TRYON COUNTY MILITIA

NAME	RANK	REGIMENT
Files, John	Private	Third
Fine, Andrew	Private	Third
Fine, Francis	Private	Third
Fink, Andrew	Private	Second
Fink, Christian	Private	Second
Fink, Johannes Jost	Private	Second
Fink, John	Lieutenant	Second
Fink, John	Private	Second
Fink, William, Jr.	Private	Second
Finster, John	Private	Fourth
Fisher, Frederick	Colonel	Third
Fisher, Harmanus	Private	Third
Fisher, John	Captain	Third
Fitzpatrick, Peter	Private	Third
Flack, Peter	Private	Fourth
Flander, Dennis	Private	Second
Flander, Henry	Private	Second
Flander, Jacob	Private	Second
Flander, John	Private	Second
Flint, Adam	Ensign	First
Flint, Alexander	Private	First
Flint, Cornelius	Private	First
Flint, John	Private	First
Flint, Robert	Private	First
Folke, John George	Surgeon	Third
Follick, Thomas	Private	Fourth
Folmer, Christian	Private	Fourth
Folmer, Conrad	Private	Fourth
Folmer, Thomas	Private	Fourth
Folmer, William	Private	Fourth
Folts, Conrad	Private	Fourth
Folts, Conrad C.	Private	Fourth
Folts, George	Private	Fourth
Folts, Jacob	Private	Fourth
Folts, John Jost	Private	Fourth
Folts, Jost	Private	Fourth
Folts, Melchior	Private	Fourth
Folts, Peter	Private	Fourth
Fonda, Adam	Private	Third
Fonda, Jellis	Captain	Third
Fonda, John	Private	Third
Forbush, Bartholomew	Private	Second
Forbush, Johannes	Private	First
Forrest, Matthew	Private	Third
Fort, Andreas	Private	Second
Fowler, James	Private	Third

APPENDIX A

TRYON COUNTY MILITIA

NAME	RANK	REGIMENT
Fox, Christian William	Major	Second
Fox, Christopher	Major	Second
Fox, Daniel	Private	Second
Fox, Frederick	Private	Fourth
Fox, John	Private	Fourth
Fox, Joseph	Private	Second
Fox, Peter	Private	Second
Fox, Peter	Private	First
Fox, William	Lieutenant	Second
Fox, William	Private	Second
Fox, William	Private	First
Frank, Adam	Private	Third
Frank, Adam	Surgeon	First
Frank, Albert	Private	Third
Frank, Andrew	Private	Third
Frank, Frederick	Captain	Fourth
Frank, Henry	Private	Fourth
Frank, Henry	Private	Third
Frank, John	Private	Fourth
Frank, Timothy	Lieutenant	Fourth
Frederick, Francis	Private	Third
Frederick, Jacob	Private	Third
Frederick, Peter	Private	Third
Frederick, Philip	Private	Third
French, Ebenezer	Private	Third
French, Henrich	Private	Fourth
French, Joseph	Private	Third
Frey, Jacob	Private	Second
Frey, John	Lieutenant	Second
Fritcher, Henry	Private	Second
Froelich, Francis	Private	Second
Froelich, Jacob	Private	Second
Froelich, Valentine	Private	Second
Fuller, Abraham	Private	Third
Fuller, Isaac	Private	Third
Fuller, Michael	Private	Third
Furneay, John	Private	Second
Fykes, George	Private	Second
Fykes, Philip	Private	Second
Gallenger, Henry	Private	Third
Gardenier, Abraham	Private	Third
Gardenier, Jacob	Captain	Third
Gardenier, Martin	Private	Third
Gardenier, Martin J.	Private	Third
Gardenier, Matthew	Private	Third

TRYON COUNTY MILITIA

NAME	RANK	REGIMENT
Gardenier, Nicholas	Private	Third
Gardenier, Nicholas T.	Private	Third
Gardenier, William	Private	Third
Garlock, Adam	Private	Second
Garlock, Adam	Private	First
Garlock, Christian	Private	Second
Garlock, George	Private	Second
Garlock, George	Private	First
Garlock, George P.	Private	First
Garlock, George W.	Private	First
Garlock, Henry	Private	First
Garlock, Jacob	Private	First
Garlock, Joh. Christian	Private	First
Garlock, Philip	Private	Second
Garlock, Philip	Private	Second
Garlock, William G.	Private	Second
Garrison, John	Private	Second
Gerter, Henrich	Private	Second
Getman, Christian	Private	Second
Getman, Conrad	Private	Fourth
Getman, Frederick	Captain	Fourth
Getman, Frederick	Private	Fourth
Getman, Frederick	Private	Second
Getman, Frederick, Jr.	Private	Fourth
Getman, George	Private	Second
Getman, Johannes	Private	Second
Getman, Peter	Private	Fourth
Getman, Peter	Private	Second
Getman, Thomas	Private	Second
Gibson, William	Private	Third
Giles, John	Private	Third
Gortner, Peter	Private	Fourth
Grace, Owen M.	Private	Third
Graff, Christian	Private	Second
Graft, Jacob	Private	Third
Grant, John	Private	Second
Grass, Philip	Private	Third
Gray, Adam	Private	Second
Gray, Andrew	Private	Second
Gray, John	Private	Second
Gray, Robert	Private	Second
Gray, Samuel	Adjutant	Second
Gray, Samuel	Private	Second
Gros, Lawrence	Private	Second
Guywitz, Frederick	Private	Second

APPENDIX A

TRYON COUNTY MILITIA

NAME	RANK	REGIMENT
Hagal, John	Private	Third
Hagal, Magal	Private	Third
Haines, John	Private	Third
Hall, Jacob	Private	Third
Hall, John	Private	Third
Hall, Peter	Private	Third
Hall, William	Lieutenant	Third
Hall, William	Private	Third
Hanes, Jacob	Ensign	First
Hanna, James	Private	Third
Hanna, William	Private	Third
Hanson, John	Private	Third
Hanson, Nicholas	Private	Third
Hanson, Richard	Private	Third
Hanson, Victor	Private	Third
Hare, James	Private	Third
Harlam, Adam	Private	fourth
Harper, Archibald	Private	Third
Harper, John	Colonel	Fifth
Harper, Joseph	Major	Fifth
Harrison, Harmanus	Private	Third
Harrison, Peter	Private	Third
Harrison, Thomas	Ensign	Third
Harrison, Thomas	Private	Third
Hart, Conrad	Private	Second
Hart, Daniel	Private	Second
Hart, John	Private	Second
Hartch, Adam	Private	Fourth
Hartman, Adam	Private	Fourth
Haselman, John	Captain	Second
Hatz, Peter	Private	Fourth
Hayney, Frederick	Private	Second
Hayney, George	Private	Second
Hayney, Henry	Private	Second
Hebrissen, Martin	Private	Fourth
Heer, Casper	Private	Second
Heering, Henry	Private	Second
Hees, Johanes	Private	Second
Heintz, Andreas	Private	Second
Hellegas, Conrad	Private	Second
Hellegas, Peter	Private	Second
Hellenbold, Andrew	Private	Second
Hellenbold, Dennis	Private	Second
Hellenbold, Tunis	Private	Second
Heller, John	Private	Fourth
Helmer, Adam	Private	Second

TRYON COUNTY MILITIA

NAME	RANK	REGIMENT
Helmer, Frederick	Private	Fourth
Helmer, Frederick A.	Private	Fourth
Helmer, George	Lieutenant	Fourth
Helmer, Henrich	Private	Second
Helmer, John	Private	Second
Helmer, John	Private	Third
Helmer, John	Private	First
Helmer, John G.	Private	First
Helmer, Jost	Private	First
Helmer, Leonard	Private	Second
Helmer, Leonard L.	Private	Second
Helmer, Philip	Captain	Second
Helmer, Philip	Private	Fourth
Helwig, John	Private	Second
Hendert, John	Private	Fourth
Herkimer, Abraham	Private	Fourth
Herkimer, Abraham	Private	Second
Herkimer, George	Private	Fourth
Herkimer, George	Private	Second
Herkimer, John	Private	Fourth
Herkimer, Jost	Private	Fourth
Herkimer, Nicholas	Private	Fourth
Herkimer, Nicholas	Private	Second
Herring, John, Sr.	Private	Fourth
Herter, Frederick, Jr.	Private	Fourth
Herter, Henrick	Captain	Fourth
Herter, John	Private	Fourth
Herter, Lorentz	Private	Fourth
Herter, Lorentz F.	Private	Fourth
Herter, Lorentz N.	Private	Fourth
Herter, Lorentz P.	Private	Fourth
Herter, Nicholas	Private	Fourth
Herter, Nicholas F.	Private	Fourth
Herter, Philip	Private	Fourth
Herter, Philip F.	Private	Fourth
Hess, Augustinus	Private	Fourth
Hess, Christian	Private	Fourth
Hess, Christian	Private	Second
Hess, Conrad	Private	Fourth
Hess, Daniel	Private	Second
Hess, Frederick	Private	Fourth
Hess, George	Private	Fourth
Hess, George	Private	First
Hess, Henry	Private	Second
Hess, Henry	Private	First
Hess, John	Captain	Second

APPENDIX A

TRYON COUNTY MILITIA

NAME	RANK	REGIMENT
Hess, John	Private	Fourth
Hess, John	Private	Second
Hessler, Martin	Private	Fourth
Heyer, George	Private	Fourth
Heyer, George Frederick	Private	Fourth
Heyer, Peter	Private	Fourth
Hickey, George	Private	Fourth
Hickey, Michael	Private	First
Hilts, John	Private	Second
Hiltz, George	Private	Fourth
Hiltz, George G.	Private	Fourth
Hiltz, George N.	Private	Fourth
Hiltz, George, Jr.	Private	Fourth
Hiltz, Godfrey	Private	Fourth
Hiltz, Johannes	Private	Fourth
Hiltz, Lawrence	Private	Fourth
Hiltz, Nicholas	Private	Fourth
Hird, Leonard	Private	Third
Hoch, George	Private	Third
Hochstrasser, Christian	Private	Fourth
Hodges, Abraham	Private	Third
Hoff, Richard	Private	Third
Hoff, Richard, Jr.	Private	Third
Hoffstader, Christian	Private	Fourth
Hogeboom, Dirik	Captain	Third
Hogoboom, Christian	Private	Third
Hogoboom, John	Private	Third
Hogoboom, Peter	Private	Third
Hohenschield, George	Private	Second
Holdenbergh, Abraham	Private	Third
Hoover, Jacob	Private	First
Horn, James	Private	Third
Horn, Matthew	Private	Third
Horning, Adam	Private	First
Horning, Dieterich	Lieutenant	First
Horning, Dieterich	Private	First
Horning, George	Private	First
Horning, John	Private	First
Horning, Leonard	Private	First
House, Adam	Private	Second
House, Adam	Private	First
House, Christian	Captain	Second
House, Elias	Private	Second
House, Frederick	Private	Second
House, George	Private	Second
House, George	Private	First

TRYON COUNTY MILITIA

NAME	RANK	REGIMENT
House, Harmanus	Private	Second
House, Henrick	Private	First
House, Jacob	Private	Third
House, Jacob	Private	First
House, John	Private	First
House, Joseph	Captain	First
House, Joseph	Private	First
House, Jost C.	Private	First
House, Nicholas	Private	First
House, Peter	Private	First
Hubbs, Alexander	Private	Third
Hubbs, Charles	Lieutenant	Third
Hubbs, Charles	Private	Third
Huber, Henry	Captain	Fourth
Huber, John	Private	Fourth
Huffnagel, Christian	Private	Second
Hulsperger, Adam	Private	Third
Hunt, Timothy	Private	Third
Hutcheson, Edward	Private	Third
Hutmacher, Adam	Private	Second
Hyser, Martin	Private	Fourth
Irvin, Andrew	Adjutant	Second
Ittig, Christian	Private	Fourth
Ittig, Conrad	Private	Fourth
Ittig, Frederick	Private	Fourth
Ittig, George	Private	Fourth
Ittig, Jacob	Private	Fourth
Ittig, Jacob J.	Private	Fourth
Ittig, Marcus	Private	Fourth
Ittig, Michael	Captain	Fourth
Johnson, Andrew	Private	Third
Johnson, John	Private	Third
Johnson, Robert	Private	Third
Johnson, Rudolph	Private	Third
Johnston, William	Private	Second
Johnston, Witter	Private	Third
Jones, Harmanus	Private	Third
Jones, James	Private	Third
Jones, Richard	Private	Third
Jordan, Casper	Private	Second
Jordan, Casper	Private	First
Jordan, Casper L.	Private	First
Jordan, George	Private	Second
Jordan, George	Private	First

APPENDIX A

TRYON COUNTY MILITIA

NAME	RANK	REGIMENT
Jordan, John	Private	First
Jordan, John Peter	Private	First
Jordan, Nicholas	Private	First
Jordan, Peter	Private	First
Juman, David	Private	Third
Jurry, John	Private	Third
Kaiser, Barent	Private	Second
Kaiser, Henry	Private	Second
Kaiser, Johannes Jost	Private	Second
Kaiser, Johannes	Captain	Second
Kaiser, Michael	Private	Second
Karle, George	Private	Fourth
Kast, Frederick	Private	Fourth
Keech, George	Private	Third
Keech, James	Private	Third
Keelman, Jacob	Private	Third
Keith, Jacob	Private	Third
Keith, Jacob	Private	Third
Keller, Andreas	Private	First
Keller, Andrew	Private	Second
Keller, Casper	Private	First
Keller, Felix	Private	Second
Keller, Felix	Private	First
Keller, Jacob	Private	Third
Keller, Jacob R.	Private	First
Keller, Nicholas	Private	Fourth
Keller, Peter	Private	Second
Kelly, George	Private	Second
Kelly, Peter	Private	Third
Kelly, Thomas	Private	Second
Kelsch, John, Jr.	Private	Fourth
Kelsch, John, Sr.	Private	Fourth
Kennedy, James	Private	Third
Kennedy, Robert	Private	Third
Kern, Betus	Private	Second
Kern, Carl	Private	Second
Kern, John	Private	Second
Kern, Michael	Private	Second
Kessler, Conrad	Private	Fourth
Kessler, Conrad	Private	Second
Kessler, Jacob	Private	Fourth
Kessler, Jacob H.	Private	Fourth
Kessler, Jacob John	Private	Fourth
Kessler, John	Private	Fourth
Kessler, John P.	Private	Fourth

APPENDIX A

TRYON COUNTY MILITIA

NAME	RANK	REGIMENT
Kessler, John T.	Private	Fourth
Kessler, Joseph	Private	Fourth
Kessler, Joseph	Private	Second
Kessler, Melchior	Private	Fourth
Kessler, Melchior	Private	Second
Kessler, Nicholas	Private	Fourth
Ketchum, Ephraim	Private	Third
Kiley, Henry	Private	Third
Kilts, Adam	Private	Second
Kilts, Conrad	Private	Second
Kilts, Nicholas	Private	Second
Kilts, Peter	Private	Second
Kilts, Peter N.	Private	Second
Kilts, Philip	Private	Second
Kiltz, George	Private	Fourth
Kiltz, Lawrence	Private	Fourth
King, John	Private	Second
Kitts, John	Private	Second
Kitts, John, Jr.	Private	Third
Kleppsattel, George	Private	First
Kleppsattel, William	Private	First
Kline, Adam	Private	Third
Kline, John	Private	Third
Kline, Martin	Private	Third
Klock, Adam	Private	Second
Klock, George G.	Private	Second
Klock, Hendrick	Private	Second
Klock, Hendrick J.	Private	Second
Klock, Jacob	Colonel	Second
Klock, Jacob H.	Private	Second
Klock, John	Private	Second
Klock, Joseph	Private	Second
Klock, Joseph	Private	First
Klock, Severines	Captain	Second
Knapp, William	Private	Second
Knautz, John	Private	First
Koch, Beadus	Private	Second
Koch, Casper, Jr.	Private	Second
Koch, John	Lieutenant	Second
Koch, John	Private	Second
Koch, Jost	Private	Fourth
Koch, Rudolph	Captain	Second
Koch, Rudolph, Jr.	Private	Second
Krackenberg, Adam	Private	Third
Krackenberg, George	Private	Third
Kramer, Andreas	Private	Second

APPENDIX A

TRYON COUNTY MILITIA

NAME	RANK	REGIMENT
Kramer, Godfrey	Private	First
Kramer, John	Private	Second
Kramer, John	Private	First
Kramer, Jost	Private	First
Krantz, Henrich	Private	Fourth
Krantz, Michael	Private	Fourth
Krauss, Frederick	Private	First
Krauss, Jacob	Private	Second
Krauss, Jost	Private	Second
Krauss, Leonard	Private	Second
Kreim, Jacob	Private	Fourth
Kremps, Hendrick	Private	Second
Kremps, John	Private	Second
Kremps, Peter	Ensign	Second
Kremps, Peter, Jr.	Private	Second
Kring, Johannes	Private	Second
Kring, John Louck	Private	Second
Kuhl, Philip	Private	Second
Kuhlman, Henry	Private	Second
Kuran, Michael	Private	Fourth
Kyler, Nicholas	Private	Fourth
Lambert, Peter	Private	Second
Lambert, Peter	Private	First
Lampman, Henrich	Private	Second
Lampman, Peter	Private	Second
Lane, Daniel	Private	Third
Lane, Jacob	Private	Third
Lannen, Richard	Private	Third
Lansing, John G.	Adjutant	Third
Lapdon, Daniel	Private	Second
Lard, William	Lieutenant	Third
Lasher, Garret	Private	Second
Lasher, John	Private	Second
Laucks, Adam	Private	Second
Laucks, Adam A.	Private	Second
Laucks, Conrad	Private	Second
Laucks, Dieterich	Private	Second
Laucks, George	Private	Second
Laucks, Hendrick	Private	Second
Laucks, Henry W.	Private	Second
Laucks, Jacob	Private	Second
Laucks, John	Private	Second
Laucks, Peter	Private	Second
Laucks, William	Private	Second
Ledder, Christian	Private	Second

APPENDIX A

TRYON COUNTY MILITIA

NAME	RANK	REGIMENT
Ledder, John	Private	Second
Lenardson, James	Private	Third
Lenardson, John	Private	Third
Lenardson, Timothy	Private	Third
Lentner, George	Private	First
Lentz, Jacob	Private	Fourth
Lentz, Jacob	Private	Second
Lentz, John	Private	Fourth
Lentz, John, Jr.	Private	Fourth
Lentz, Peter	Private	Fourth
Lepper, Frederick	Private	Second
Lepper, John	Private	Third
Lepper, Wiand	Private	Second
Lewis, Adam	Private	Third
Lewis, David	Private	Third
Lewis, David, Jr.	Private	Third
Lewis, Frederick	Private	Third
Lewis, Henry	Ensign	Third
Lewis, John	Private	Third
Lewis, William	Private	Third
Lighthall, Abraham	Private	Fourth
Lighthall, George	Private	Fourth
Lighthall, Nicholas	Private	Fourth
Link, John	Private	Third
Lipe, Adam	Captain	First
Little, John	Captain	Third
Lloyd, Daniel	Private	Third
Long, Hendrick	Private	Second
Low, Lawrence Gras	Private	First
Lutz, George	Private	Second
Lyke, John, Sr.	Private	Second
Mabee, David	Private	First
Mabee, Joseph	Private	First
Mabee, Joseph	Private	First
Mabie, Harmanus	Captain	Third
Macknod, James	Private	Second
Malone, John	Private	Third
Manderback, John	Private	Fourth
Manness, Hugh M.	Private	Third
March, Stephen	Private	Second
Marines, Abraham	Private	Second
Marlatt, Abraham	Private	Third
Marlatt, Gideon	Adjutant	Third
Marlatt, Gideon	Ensign	Third
Marlatt, Gideon	Private	Third

APPENDIX A

TRYON COUNTY MILITIA

NAME	RANK	REGIMENT
Marlatt, John	Private	Third
Marlatt, Michael	Private	Third
Marlatt, Thomas	Private	Third
Marselus, Isaac	Captain	Third
Martin, Alexander	Private	Second
Martin, John W.	Private	Third
Martin, Peter M.	Private	Third
Martin, Philip	Private	Third
Martin, Philip	Private	Second
Mashel, John	Private	Third
Mason, Jacob	Private	Third
Mason, John	Private	Third
Matthews, Jacob	Lieutenant	First
Mayer, Frederick	Private	Fourth
Mayer, H. Henry	Private	First
Mayer, Henry	Private	Fourth
Mayer, Jacob	Private	Third
Mayer, Jacob	Private	First
Mayer, Jacob S.	Private	First
Mayer, Jacob, Jr.	Private	Third
Mayer, John	Ensign	Fourth
Mayer, John	Private	Fourth
Mayer, Joseph	Private	Fourth
Mayer, Matthew	Private	Fourth
Mayer, Michael	Private	Fourth
Mayer, Nicholas	Private	Fourth
Mayer, Peter	Private	Fourth
McArthur, Daniel	Private	Third
McArthur, Donald	Private	Third
McArthur, Duncan	Private	Third
McArthur, Duncan	Private	Second
McArthur, John	Private	Second
McClumpha, Thomas	Private	Third
McCollom, Findlay	Private	Third
McCollom, John	Private	Third
McCredy, William	Private	Third
McDonald, James	Private	Third
McDonald, Nicholas	Private	Third
McDougall, Daniel	Private	Second
McGraw, Christopher	Private	Third
McGraw, Daniel	Private	Third
McGraw, Dennis	Private	Third
McGraw, John	Private	Third
McGraw, William	Private	Third
McKenny, Daniel	Private	Third

APPENDIX A

TRYON COUNTY MILITIA

NAME	RANK	REGIMENT
McKillip, John	Private	First
McMaster, David	Captain	Third
McMaster, Hugh	Private	Third
McMaster, James	Lieutenant	Third
McMaster, James	Private	Third
McMaster, Robert	Private	Third
McMaster, Thomas	Private	Third
McNaughton, Peter	Private	Third
McNutt, James	Private	Fourth
McTaggert, James	Private	Third
Merckel, Dewalt	Private	Second
Merckel, Jacob	Private	Second
Merckel, Peter	Private	Second
Merckel, Richard	Private	Second
Meyer, Dewalt	Private	Second
Meyer, Henrick	Private	First
Meyer, Henrick S.	Private	First
Meyer, Jacob	Private	Second
Meyer, Jacob R.	Private	First
Meyer, John	Private	Second
Meyer, Matthew	Private	First
Meyer, Solomon	Private	First
Miller, Adam	Private	Third
Miller, Conrad	Private	Second
Miller, Conrad	Private	First
Miller, Dionysius	Private	First
Miller, Frederick	Private	Third
Miller, Garret	Private	Second
Miller, Garret	Private	First
Miller, George	Private	Third
Miller, Henrich	Private	Fourth
Miller, Henry	Captain	Second
Miller, James	Private	Third
Miller, Jellis	Private	Third
Miller, John	Private	Fourth
Miller, John	Private	Third
Miller, John	Private	Second
Miller, John	Private	First
Miller, John C.	Private	First
Miller, John, Jr.	Private	Fourth
Miller, Nicholas	Private	Fourth
Miller, Philip	Private	Second
Miller, Samuel	Private	Second
Miller, Valentine	Private	Fourth
Milloy, Alexander	Private	Third

APPENDIX A

TRYON COUNTY MILITIA

NAME	RANK	REGIMENT
Montgomery, Peter	Private	Third
Moon, Jacob	Private	Third
Moore, Conrad	Private	Third
Moore, John	Private	Third
Mount, Joseph	Private	Third
Mount, Samuel	Private	Third
Mour, George	Private	Third
Mower, Barent	Private	Third
Mower, Henry	Private	Third
Multer, Jacob	Private	Fourth
Multer, Peter	Private	Fourth
Murphy, Henry	Private	First
Murphy, Thomas	Private	First
Murray, David	Private	Third
Murray, Thomas	Private	Third
Myer, Henry	Ensign	First
Myer, Jacob	Lieutenant	Fourth
Myers, George	Private	Third
Myers, Peter	Private	Third
Nash, James	Private	Fourth
Nellis, Andreas	Private	Second
Nellis, Christian	Private	First
Nellis, George	Private	Second
Nellis, George	Private	First
Nellis, Henry	Private	Second
Nellis, Henry	Private	First
Nellis, Henry N.	Private	First
Nellis, Jacob	Private	First
Nellis, John	Private	Second
Nellis, John	Private	First
Nellis, Joseph	Private	Second
Nellis, Ludwig	Lieutenant	Second
Nellis, Ludwig	Private	Second
Nellis, Peter	Private	Second
Nellis, Philip	Private	Second
Nellis, William	Private	Second
Nestel, Andrew	Private	Second
Nestel, George	Private	Second
Nestel, Gotlieb	Private	Second
Nestel, Henry	Private	Second
Nestel, Martin	Private	Second
Newkirk, Abraham	Private	Third
Newkirk, Benjamin	Private	Fourth
Newkirk, Garret	Private	Third
Newkirk, Gerrit C.	Private	Third

TRYON COUNTY MILITIA

NAME	RANK	REGIMENT
Newkirk, Gerritt	Lieutenant	Third
Newkirk, Jacob	Private	Third
Newkirk, John	Major	Third
Newman, Joseph	Private	Second
Och, George	Private	Fourth
Ogden, Daniel, Sr.	Private	Third
Ogden, David	Private	Third
Ohrendorph, Frederick, Jr.	Private	Fourth
Ohrendorph, Frederick, Sr.	Private	Fourth
Ohrendorph, George	Private	Fourth
Ohrendorph, Peter	Private	Fourth
Oline, Benjamin	Lieutenant	Third
Osterhout, John	Private	Fourth
Osteroth, Frederick	Private	Second
Palmateer, John	Private	Third
Palmateer, Thomas	Private	Third
Palmateer, William	Private	Third
Patteson, Adam	Private	Third
Percy, Ephraim	Private	Third
Pesausie, John	Private	Fourth
Peters, Joseph	Private	Third
Peters, Joseph	Private	Second
Peters, Joseph, Jr.	Private	Third
Petry, Daniel	Private	Fourth
Petry, Dieterich	Private	Fourth
Petry, Jacob	Ensign	Fourth
Petry, Jacob	Private	Fourth
Petry, Johannes	Private	Fourth
Petry, Johannes Jost	Private	Second
Petry, John Marx	Private	Fourth
Petry, Joseph	Private	Fourth
Petry, Marx	Private	Fourth
Petry, William	Surgeon	Third
Pettingell, Henry	Private	Third
Pettingell, Jacob	Private	Third
Pettingell, John	Private	Third
Pettingell, Joseph	Private	Third
Pettingell, Samuel	Private	Third
Pettingell, William	Private	Third
Philips, Abraham	Private	Third
Philips, Harmanus	Private	Third
Philips, Henry	Private	Third
Philips, Jacob	Private	Third
Philips, James	Private	Third

TRYON COUNTY MILITIA

NAME	RANK	REGIMENT
Philips, James	Private	Second
Philips, John	Private	Third
Philips, Lewis	Private	Third
Philips, Phillip	Private	Third
Philips, Volkert	Private	Third
Philips, William	Private	Third
Phoenix, Michael	Private	Second
Pickert, Adolph	Private	Second
Pickert, Adolph	Private	First
Pickert, Conrad	Private	Second
Pickert, Conrad	Private	First
Pickert, George	Private	First
Pickert, Jacob	Private	Second
Pickert, John	Ensign	First
Pickert, John	Private	Second
Pickert, John	Quarter Master	First
Pickert, Nicholas	Private	First
Pierce, Ephraim	Ensign	Third
Piper, Andrew	Aprivate	Fourth
Piper, Jacob	Private	Fourth
Piper, Jost	Private	Fourth
Plank, Adam	Private	Third
Plank, John	Private	Third
Plantz, Johannes	Private	Second
Plapper, Christian	Private	Second
Powell, Charles	Lieutenant	First
Prentiss, Daniel	Private	Third
Prentiss, Joseph	Lieutenant	Third
Price, John	Private	Second
Prime, David	Private	Third
Prime, Henry	Private	Third
Prime, John	Private	Third
Prime, Peter	Private	Third
Printup, Joseph	Lieutenant	Third
Printup, William	Private	Third
Pruyn, Daniel	Private	Third
Pruyn, Francis F.	Lieutenant	Third
Pruyn, Henry	Private	Third
Pruyn, John	Private	Third
Pruyn, Lewis	Private	Third
Putman, Aaron	Private	Third
Putman, Adam	Private	Third
Putman, Arent	Private	Second
Putman, Cornelius, Jr.	Private	Third
Putman, David	Private	Third
Putman, David	Private	Second

APPENDIX A

TRYON COUNTY MILITIA

NAME	RANK	REGIMENT
Putman, Francis	Ensign	Third
Putman, Frederick	Private	Third
Putman, George	Private	Third
Putman, Gerrit	Captain	Third
Putman, Hendrik	Private	Third
Putman, Henry	Private	Third
Putman, Jacob	Private	Third
Putman, John	Private	Third
Putman, Lewis	Private	Third
Putman, Ludwig	Private	Third
Putman, Richard	Ensign	Third
Putman, Victor	Lieutenant	Third
Putman, Victor	Private	Third
Putman, William	Private	Third
Quackenbush, Abraham	Lieutenant	Third
Quackenbush, Abraham, Jr.	Private	Third
Quackenbush, David	Private	First
Quackenbush, David	Private	Third
Quackenbush, Hunter Scot	Private	First
Quackenbush, Isaac	Private	Third
Quackenbush, Isaac	Private	First
Quackenbush, Jeremiah	Private	First
Quackenbush, John	Private	First
Quackenbush, John G.	Private	Third
Quackenbush, Myndert W.	Lieutenant	Third
Quackenbush, Nicholas	Private	Third
Quackenbush, Peter	Private	First
Quackenbush, Peter	Private	Third
Quackenbush, Vincent	Lieutenant	Third
Quackenbush, William	Private	Third
Rabold, George	Private	Fourth
Raisner, Jacob	Private	Second
Rapspel, Frederick	Private	Second
Rasbach, John	Private	Fourth
Rattenauer, George	Private	First
Rattenauer, Jacob	Private	Second
Rattenauer, Jacob	Private	First
Ready, Charles	Private	Third
Reed, Conrad	Private	Third
Reed, John	Private	Second
Reeder, Hendrick	Private	Second
Rees, Samuel	Captain	Third
Reyner, Francis	Lieutenant	Third
Richardson, Jonathan	Private	Third

APPENDIX A

TRYON COUNTY MILITIA

NAME	RANK	REGIMENT
Richter, Nicholas	Captain	Second
Rickel, Christian	Private	Fourth
Rickert, Bartholomew	Private	Second
Rickert, Jacob	Private	Second
Rickert, John	Private	Second
Rickert, Ludwig	Private	Second
Rickert, Nicholas	Private	Second
Riebsamen, Matthew	Private	First
Riebsamen, William	Private	First
Riemensnyder, John	Private	Second
Rigel, Frederick	Private	Fourth
Rigel, Godfrey	Private	Fourth
Rimah, George	Private	Fourth
Rimah, John	Private	Fourth
Rimah, John, Jr.	Private	Fourth
Ritter, Johannes	Sergeant	Second
Ritzman, Johanes	Private	Second
Rob, George	Private	Second
Rob, John	Private	Second
Roberson, Robert	Private	Third
Robison, George	Private	Third
Robison, Joseph	Private	Third
Roelofson, Abraham	Private	Third
Rogers, John	Private	Third
Rogers, Samuel	Private	Third
Rogers, Samuel	Private	First
Roller, Andrew	Private	Second
Rombough, Ausmus	Private	Third
Romine, Abraham	Private	Third
Romine, Theodorus F.	Quarter Master	Third
Roof, John	Captain	First
Roof, Michael	Private	Second
Root, Christian	Private	Second
Rosecrantz, George	Private	Second
Rosecrantz, Nicholas	Private	Fourth
Rosecrantz, Nicholas	Private	Second
Roth, John	Private	First
Runyons, Henry	Private	Third
Runyons, John	Private	Third
Rury, Henry	Private	Third
Ruse, Jacob	Private	Third
Russ, Johannes	Captain	Second
Russ, John	Captain	First
Rust, George	Private	Second
Ryan, John	Private	Fourth

APPENDIX A

TRYON COUNTY MILITIA

NAME	RANK	REGIMENT
Salisbury, John	Private	Third
Saltsman, George	Private	Second
Saltsman, Henry	Private	Second
Saltsman, John	Private	Second
Sammons, Frederick	Private	Third
Sammons, Thomas	Private	Third
Scarbury, William	Private	Third
Schaffer, James	Private	Third
Schaffer, John	Private	Third
Schall, George	Private	Second
Schall, Johannes Jost	Private	Second
Schall, John	Lieutenant	Second
Schefer, Adam	Private	First
Schefer, Bartholomew	Private	Second
Schefer, Henrich	Private	Second
Schefer, Henry	Private	First
Schefer, John	Private	Second
Schefer, Nicholas	Private	Second
Schell, Christian	Private	Fourth
Schell, Johannes	Private	Fourth
Schenck, George	Private	Fourth
Schiff, George	Private	Fourth
Schimmel, Dieterich	Private	First
Schneck, George	Private	First
Schneider, Jacob	Lieutenant	First
Schneider, Michael	Private	First
Scholl, Han Yost	Lieutenant	Second
Schoonmaker, Thomas	Private	Third
Schot, Joseph	Private	Third
Schremling, Dewald	Private	Third
Schremling, Henry	Lieutenant	First
Schremling, Henry	Private	Third
Schuler, Lorentz	Lieutenant	Third
Schuler, Lorentz	Private	Third
Schultz, Hendrick	Private	Second
Schultz, Jacob	Private	Second
Schultz, John	Private	Second
Schupp, Nicholas	Private	Second
Schuts, Joseph	Private	Third
Schuyler, David	Private	First
Schuyler, Jacob	Private	First
Schuyler, John Jost	Private	First
Schuyler, Nicholas	Private	First
Schuyler, Peter P.	Private	First
Scott, James	Private	Third
Scott, Joseph	Private	Third

APPENDIX A

TRYON COUNTY MILITIA

NAME	RANK	REGIMENT
Seeber, Conrad	Private	Second
Seeber, Jacob	Adjutant	First
Seeber, Jacob	Private	First
Seeber, John	Lieutenant	First
Seeber, John	Private	Second
Seeber, John	Private	First
Seeber, John W.	Private	First
Seeber, William	Lieutenant	First
Seelbach, Johannes	Private	Second
Seimer, Isaac	Private	Fourth
Semple, Hugh	Private	Third
Semple, Samuel	Private	Third
Service, Christian	Private	Third
Service, Frederick	Private	Third
Service, George	Private	Third
Service, John	Private	Third
Service, Philip	Private	Third
Service, Richard	Private	Third
Shaddock, James	Private	Third
Shaddock, Thomas	Private	Third
Shall, Frederick	Private	Fourth
Sharpenstine, Jacob	Private	Third
Shasha, Abraham	Private	Third
Shasha, William	Private	Third
Sheham, Butler	Private	Third
Shew, Godfrey	Private	Third
Shew, Henry	Private	Third
Shew, Jacob	Private	Third
Shew, John	Private	Third
Shew, Stephen	Private	Third
Shiele, Mantus	Private	Second
Shilip, Christian	Private	Third
Shilip, Frederick	Private	Third
Shoemaker, Christopher	Private	Fourth
Shoemaker, Frederick	Private	Fourth
Shoemaker, Hanjost	Private	Fourth
Shoemaker, John	Private	Fourth
Shoemaker, Jost	Private	Fourth
Shoemaker, Rudolph	Private	Third
Shoemaker, Thomas	Private	Fourth
Shoemaker, Thomas	Private	Third
Shultheis, George	Private	Second
Shultheis, Johannes	Private	Second
Shute, Frederick	Private	Fourth
Shute, William	Private	Fourth
Sillebach, Christian	Private	Third

APPENDIX A

TRYON COUNTY MILITIA

NAME	RANK	REGIMENT
Sillebach, John	Private	Third
Simpson, Henry	Private	Third
Simpson, Nicholas	Private	Third
Sits, Baltes	Private	First
Sits, George	Private	Second
Sits, Hendrick	Private	Second
Sits, Hendrick	Private	First
Sits, John	Private	First
Sits, Nicholas	Private	First
Sits, Peter	Private	First
Sitz, Peter	Ensign	Second
Sixberry, Adam	Private	Third
Sixberry, Bangnen	Private	Third
Sixberry, Cornelius	Private	Third
Sixberry, Cornelius, Jr.	Private	Third
Skinner, John	Private	Third
Skinner, Thomas	Private	Third
Slack, Martin	Private	Third
Small, Jacob	Captain	Fourth
Smith, Adam	Private	Fourth
Smith, Baltus	Private	Second
Smith, Baltus S.	Private	Second
Smith, Frederick	Private	Fourth
Smith, George	Private	Fourth
Smith, George	Private	Second
Smith, Harmanus	Private	Third
Smith, Henry	Private	Second
Smith, James	Private	Second
Smith, John	Lieutenant	Fourth
Smith, John	Private	Fourth
Smith, John	Private	First
Smith, Jost	Private	Fourth
Smith, Matthew	Private	Second
Smith, Nicholas	Private	Fourth
Smith, Nicholas	Private	Second
Smith, Nicholas, Jr.	Private	Second
Smith, Peter	Private	Fourth
Smith, Philip	Private	First
Smith, William	Private	Fourth
Smith, William	Private	Second
Snell, Adam	Private	Second
Snell, George	Private	Second
Snell, Jacob	Private	Second
Snell, John	Private	Second
Snell, John F.	Private	Second
Snell, John J.	Private	Second

TRYON COUNTY MILITIA

NAME	RANK	REGIMENT
Snell, John P.	Private	Second
Snell, John, Jr.	Private	Second
Snell, Nicholas	Private	Second
Snell, Peter	Private	Second
Snell, Severines	Private	Second
Snell, Thomas Jacob	Private	Second
Snook, Henry	Private	Third
Snook, William	Captain	Third
Snook, William	Lieutenant	Third
Snyder, Adam	Private	Third
Southworth, William	Private	Third
Spalsberger, John	Private	Second
Spanknable, John	Private	Second
Spencer, Aaron	Private	Third
Spencer, Jonathan	Private	Third
Spencer, Nathan	Private	Third
Spohn, Nicholas	Private	Fourth
Spohn, Werner	Private	Fourth
Spoor, John	Private	Third
Spoor, Nicholas	Private	Third
Spracher, Conrad	Private	Second
Spracher, George	Private	Second
Spracher, George, Jr.	Private	Second
Spracher, John	Private	Second
Stabitz, Michael	Private	Third
Staley, George	Private	Third
Staley, Henry	Private	Third
Staley, Joseph	Private	Third
Staley, Rudolph	Private	Third
Stall, Rudolph	Private	Second
Stamm, George	Private	Second
Stamm, Jacob	Private	Second
Stamm, Lawrence	Private	Second
Stansil, George	Private	Second
Stansil, Nicholas	Private	Second
Stansil, William	Private	Second
Staring, Adam	Private	Third
Staring, Adam	Private	Second
Staring, Adam A.	Ensign	Fourth
Staring, Adam J.	Private	Fourth
Staring, Adam, Sr.	Private	Fourth
Staring, Conrad	Private	Fourth
Staring, Frederick	Private	Third
Staring, George	Private	Fourth
Staring, Henrich	Captain	Fourth
Staring, Henrich	Private	Fourth

TRYON COUNTY MILITIA

NAME	RANK	REGIMENT
Staring, Jacob	Private	Second
Staring, John	Private	Third
Staring, Joseph	Private	Third
Staring, Margred	Private	Fourth
Staring, Nicholas	Private	Fourth
Staring, Nicholas N.	Private	Fourth
Staring, Peter	Private	Fourth
Staring, Philip	Private	Third
State, George	Private	Fourth
Steele, Adam	Private	Fourth
Steele, Deterich	Private	Fourth
Stephens, Amasa	Private	Third
Sterman, Christian	Private	Third
Stern, Nicholas	Private	Third
Sternbergh, Christian	Private	Third
Sternbergh, Jacob	Private	Third
Stine, William	Private	Third
Stone, Conrad	Ensign	Third
Stone, George	Ensign	Third
Strader, Nicholas	Private	Second
Straher, John	Private	Second
Straub, William	Private	Second
Straubel, Christopher	Private	Fourth
Strubel, Christian	Private	Second
Struble, Christopher	Private	Second
Stuart, William	Private	Third
Sutz, Derick	Private	Second
Sutz, John	Lieutenant	Second
Sutz, John	Private	Second
Sutz, John P.	Lieutenant	Second
Sutz, Peter	Private	Second
Sutz, Peter P.	Private	Second
Swart, Benjamin	Private	Third
Swart, Isias J.	Lieutenant	Third
Swart, Jeremiah	Lieutenant	Third
Swart, John	Private	Third
Swart, Tunis	Private	Third
Swart, Walter	Private	Third
Swart, William	Lieutenant	Third
Syphert, Godfrey	Private	Second
Tanner, Jacob	Private	Third
Terwilliger, Hermanus	Private	Third
Terwilliger, James	Private	Third
Thompson, Aaron	Private	First
Thompson, James	Private	Third

TRYON COUNTY MILITIA

NAME	RANK	REGIMENT
Thompson, John	Private	First
Thompson, Thomas	Private	First
Thompson, William	Private	First
Timmerman, Christian	Private	Third
Timmerman, Conrad	Ensign	Second
Timmerman, Hendrick	Lieutenant	Second
Timmerman, John	Lieutenant	Second
Tims, Michael	Private	Third
Tinis, Jacob	Private	Fourth
Tinis, John	Private	Fourth
Tucker, George	Private	Second
Tucker, Jacob	Private	Second
Tucker, Johannes	Private	Second
Ulman, Barent	Private	Third
Ulman, Johannes	Private	Third
Ulman, Leonard	Private	Third
Ulshever, Bastian	Private	First
Ulshever, Stephen	Private	First
Usner, Peter George	Private	Fourth
Utt, Francis	Private	Second
Vach, Johann George	Surgeon	Second
Van Allen, Jacob	Private	Third
Van Alstyne, Abraham	Private	Third
Van Alstyne, Abraham	Private	First
Van Alstyne, Abraham C.	Private	First
Van Alstyne, Cornelius	Private	Third
Van Alstyne, Cornelius	Private	First
Van Alstyne, Cornelius C.	Private	First
Van Alstyne, Cornelius J.	Private	First
Van Alstyne, Gilbert	Private	Third
Van Alstyne, Harmanus	Private	First
Van Alstyne, Isaac	Private	Third
Van Alstyne, Jacob	Private	Third
Van Alstyne, John	Private	Third
Van Alstyne, John	Private	First
Van Alstyne, John G.	Private	First
Van Alstyne, John M.	Private	First
Van Alstyne, Martin	Private	First
Van Alstyne, Martin A.	Private	First
Van Alstyne, Martin C.	Private	Second
Van Alstyne, Martin G.	Private	First
Van Alstyne, Nicholas	Private	Second
Van Alstyne, Peter	Private	First
Van Alstyne, Philip	Private	First

APPENDIX A

TRYON COUNTY MILITIA

NAME	RANK	REGIMENT
Van Antwerp, John, Jr.	Private	Third
Van Antwerp, John, Sr.	Private	Third
Van Brakelen, Alexander	Private	Third
Van Brakelen, Garett S.	Lieutenant	Third
Van Brakelen, Garret G.	Private	Third
Van Brakelen, Garrett G.	Ensign	Third
Van Brakelen, Gysbert	Private	Third
Van Brakelen, Melchior	Private	Third
Van Camp, Cornelius	Private	First
Van Camp, Isaac	Private	First
Van Dusen, Abraham	Private	Third
Van Dusen, Gilbert	Private	Third
Van Dusen, Harpert	Private	Third
Van Dusen, Matthew	Private	Third
Van Eps, John	Private	Third
Van Etten, Jacob	Private	Second
Van Etten, Samuel	Lieutenant	Second
Van Every, Cornelius	Ensign	First
Van Every, John	Lieutenant	First
Van Every, Ryner	Captain	First
Van Geisling, Peter	Private	Third
Van Heusen, Albert	Private	Third
Van Horn, Abraham	Quarter Master	Third
Van Horn, Henry	Private	Third
Van Horn, John	Private	Third
Van Horn, Thomas	Lieutenant	Third
Van Loon, John	Private	Second
Van Olinda, Benjamin	Private	Third
Van Olinda, Jacob	Private	Third
Van Olinda, Peter	Lieutenant	Third
Van Sice, Cornelius	Private	Third
Van Sickle, Ryner	Private	Third
Van Slyck, Adam	Private	Second
Van Slyck, Garret	Private	First
Van Slyck, George	* Private	First
Van Slyck, Jacob	Private	Fourth
Van Slyck, Jacob	Private	Second
Van Slyck, John	Lieutenant	Second
Van Slyck, John	Private	Second
Van Slyck, John	Private	First
Van Slyck, Nicholas	Ensign	Second
Van Slyck, Nicholas	Private	Third
Van Slyck, Nicholas	Private	Second
Van Slyck, Nicholas G.	Private	Second
Van Slyck, Samuel	Private	Second
Van Slyck, William	Private	Second

APPENDIX A

TRYON COUNTY MILITIA

NAME	RANK	REGIMENT
Van Vaughn, Teunis	Ensign	Third
Van Vechten, Derick	Lieutenant	Third
Van Vechten, John	Private	Third
Van Vorst, John	Private	Third
Vanderwerken, Casper	Private	Third
Vanderwerken, Harmanus	Private	First
Vanderwerken, John	Private	Third
Vanderwerken, John	Private	Second
Vanderwerken, Joshua	Private	First
Vanderwerken, Thomas	Private	Third
Vanderwerken, Thomas	Private	Second
Vanderwerken, William	Private	Third
Vanderwerken, William	Private	Second
Veeder, Abraham	Captain	Third
Veeder, Abraham	Private	Third
Veeder, Albert	Private	Third
Veeder, Arnout	Private	Second
Veeder, Cornelius	Private	Third
Veeder, Isaac	Private	Third
Veeder, John	Private	Third
Veeder, John J.	Private	Third
Veeder, Simon	Quarter Master	Third
Veeder, Volkert	Lt. Colonel	Third
Vrooman, Henry B.	Private	Third
Vrooman, Henry H.	Lieutenant	Third
Vrooman, Henry H.	Private	Third
Vrooman, Isaac	Private	Third
Vrooman, John J.	Private	Third
Vrooman, Peter	Ensign	Third
Vrooman, Peter	Private	Third
Vrooman, Simon	Private	Third
Wafle, Adam	Private	Second
Wafle, George	Private	Second
Wafle, Hendrick	Private	Second
Wafle, Henry	Private	Second
Wafle, John	Private	Second
Wafle, William	Private	Second
Wagner, Engelhard	Private	Second
Wagner, Engelhard	Private	First
Wagner, Englehardt	Lieutenant	First
Wagner, George	Ensign	Second
Wagner, George	Private	Second
Wagner, George	Private	First
Wagner, Isaac	Private	First
Wagner, Jacob	Private	First

APPENDIX A

TRYON COUNTY MILITIA

NAME	RANK	REGIMENT
Wagner, Joseph	Private	Second
Wagner, Peter	Lt. Colonel	Second
Wallrath, Adam	Private	Second
Wallrath, Adolph	Private	Third
Wallrath, Adolph	Private	Second
Wallrath, Adolph	Private	First
Wallrath, Frederick	Private	Second
Wallrath, Frederick	Private	First
Wallrath, George	Private	First
Wallrath, Gerhart	Private	Second
Wallrath, Henrich	Private	Second
Wallrath, Henry	Ensign	First
Wallrath, Henry	Private	First
Wallrath, Isaac	Private	Second
Wallrath, Jacob	Private	Second
Wallrath, Jacob	Private	First
Wallrath, Jacob H.	Private	Second
Wallrath, Johannes	Private	First
Wallrath, John	Private	Second
Wallrath, Nicholas	Ensign	Second
Wallrath, Nicholas	Private	Second
Wallrath, Peter	Private	Second
Wallrath, William	Private	First
Walls, Conrad	Private	First
Walls, Conrad, Jr.	Private	First
Walter, Adam	Private	Second
Walter, Christian	Private	Second
Walter, George	Private	Second
Waltz, Conrad	Private	Second
Waltz, George	Private	Second
Waltz, Jacob	Private	First
Warmouth, Christian	Private	Second
Warmouth, John	Private	First
Warmouth, John	Private	Second
Warmouth, Matthew	Private	Second
Warmouth, Nathaniel	Private	Second
Warmouth, Peter	Private	Second
Warmouth, Peter	Private	First
Warmouth, Peter J.	Private	Second
Warmouth, William	Private	Second
Wart, Andrew	Private	Third
Wart, Matthew	Private	Third
Water, George	Private	Second
Weaver, Frederick	Private	Fourth
Weaver, Frederick G.	Private	Fourth
Weaver, Frederick, Jr.	Private	Fourth

TRYON COUNTY MILITIA

NAME	RANK	REGIMENT
Weaver, George	Private	Fourth
Weaver, George F.	Private	Fourth
Weaver, George M.	Private	Fourth
Weaver, George, Jr.	Private	Fourth
Weaver, Jacob	Private	Fourth
Weaver, Jacob	Private	Second
Weaver, Jacob G.	Private	Fourth
Weaver, Jacob J.	Private	Fourth
Weaver, Jacob N.	Private	Fourth
Weaver, Johannes	Private	Fourth
Weaver, Michael	Private	Fourth
Weaver, Nicholas	Private	Third
Weaver, Nicholas	Private	Third
Weaver, Nicholas	Private	Second
Weaver, Nicholas G.	Private	Fourth
Weaver, Nicholas H.	Private	Fourth
Weaver, Peter	Private	Fourth
Weber, George A.	Lieutenant	Fourth
Weber, Peter	Lieutenant	Fourth
Weimer, Andrew	Private	Second
Weiser, John	Private	Third
Weiser, Nicholas	Captain	First
Weiser, Nicholas	Private	Third
Wemple, Abraham	Captain	Third
Wemple, Barent	Private	Third
Wemple, Cornelius	Private	Third
Wemple, Hendrick	Private	Third
Wemple, John	Captain	Third
Wemple, John	Private	Third
Wemple, John T.	Private	Third
Wemple, Myndert	Private	Third
Wemple, William	Private	Third
Wents, George	Private	Fourth
Werner, Alexander	Private	Second
Werner, Andrew	Private	Second
Werner, Charles Alexander	Private	Second
Werner, Christian	Private	Second
Wessel, Adam	Private	Second
Wessel, George	Private	Second
Wessel, Henry	Private	Second
Wessel, John	Private	Second
Wessel, William	Private	Second
Wheeler, Isaac	Private	Third
White, Edward	Private	Third
Wick, John	Private	Second
Wick, Michael	Private	Second

APPENDIX A

TRYON COUNTY MILITIA

NAME	RANK	REGIMENT
Wicks, Samuel	Private	Third
Widerstein, Henry	Private	Fourth
Widrig, Conrad	Private	Fourth
Widrig, George	Private	Fourth
Widrig, Michael	Private	Fourth
Wile, Christian	Private	Third
Wiles, George	Private	Second
Wiley, Nicholas	Private	Third
Williams, Daniel	Private	Third
Williams, Eliser	Private	Second
Wills, William	Colonel	Fifth
Wilson, Abner	Private	Third
Wilson, Andrew	Private	Third
Wilson, James	Private	First
Wilson, Japes	Captain	First
Wilson, John	Private	Third
Wilson, Samuel	Private	Third
Windecker, Frederick	Private	Second
Windecker, Frederick	Private	First
Windecker, Jacob	Private	Second
Windecker, Johannes	Lieutenant	First
Windecker, Nicholas	Private	Second
Windecker, Nicholas	Private	First
Winkle, John	Private	Second
Winn, John	Private	Second
Winn, John	Private	First
Witbeck, Leonard	Private	Third
Wohleben, Abraham	Private	Fourth
Wohleben, Jacob	Private	Fourth
Wohleben, Nicholas	Private	Second
Wohleben, Peter	Private	Fourth
Wohlever, Peter	Private	Second
Wohlgemuth, John	Private	First
Wohlgemuth, William	Private	First
Woldorf, Johannes	Private	First
Wolf, Jacob	Private	First
Wolff, Johannes	Private	Fourth
Wollever, John	Private	First
Wollever, Nicholas	Private	First
Won, Nicholas	Private	Fourth
Wood, William	Private	Third
Woodcock, Abraham	Private	Third
Woodcock, John	Private	Third
Woodcock, Peter	Private	Third
Woodworth, Selah	Private	Third
Woodworth, Solomon	Lieutenant	Third

APPENDIX A

TRYON COUNTY MILITIA

NAME	RANK	REGIMENT
Wright, David	Private	Third
Yanney, Christian	Private	Third
Yanney, Christian	Private	Second
Yanney, Henry	Private	Third
Yates, Christopher P.	Private	First
Yates, Peter	Lieutenant	Third
Yates, Robert	Captain	Third
Yeomans, Joseph	Captain	Third
Yoram, Jacob	Private	Second
Yoran, Jacob	Private	Third
Yost, Peter	Private	Third
Young, Adam	Private	Second
Young, Adam	Private	First
Young, Andrew	Private	Second
Young, Andrew	Private	First
Young, Christian	Private	Second
Young, Christian	Private	First
Young, Christian A.	Private	First
Young, Frederick	Private	First
Young, George	Private	Third
Young, Godfrey	Private	First
Young, Godfrey	Private	Second
Young, Henry	Private	First
Young, Henry P.	Private	First
Young, Jacob	Private	Second
Young, Jacob	Private	First
Young, Jacob, Jr.	Private	Second
Young, Jeremiah	Ensign	First
Young, John	Private	First
Young, Joseph	Private	First
Young, Ludwig	Private	Second
Young, Ludwig	Private	Third
Young, Ludwig	Private	First
Young, Nicholas	Private	Second
Young, Peter	Lieutenant	Third
Young, Peter	Private	First
Young, Richard	Private	Second
Young, Robert	Private	First
Young, Thomas	Private	First
Young, William	Private	Third
Younglove, David	Surgeon	First
Yucker, George	Private	Second
Yucker, Jacob	Private	Second
Yucker, John	Private	Second
Yuran, Jacob	Private	Second

APPENDIX A

TRYON COUNTY MILITIA

NAME	RANK	REGIMENT
Zessinger, Nicholas	Private	Second
Zieley, John	Captain	Second
Zimmerman, Christian	Private	Second
Zimmerman, Conrad	Private	Second
Zimmerman, Frederick	Ensign	Second

APPENDIX B

1790 FEDERAL CENSUS, MONTGOMERY COUNTY, NY

In 1790 Montgomery County (formerly Tryon and changed on April 2, 1784 to honor Revolutionary War General Richard Montgomery) had eleven towns within its boundaries. They were: Canajoharie, Caughnawaga, Chemung, Chenango, German Flatts, Harpersfield, Herkimer, Mohawk, Otsego, Palatine, and Whites. There were nearly five thousand "Heads of Families" enumerated in this record and the entire population of the county totaled nearly twenty-nine thousand persons.

The 1790 Federal Census entry column identifiers have been abbreviated from the complete headings as written in the original record. These identifiers, followed by the original headings are: HOF (Head of Family); TOWN (Town); M 16+ (Free white males of 16 years and upwards, including heads of families); M -16 (Free white males under 16 years); F (Free white females, including heads of families); OFP (All other free persons); S (Slaves).

(See "key code" [C1790] in *References* for source of data on the 1790 Census.)

HOF	TOWN	M 16+	M -16	F	OFP	S
Abbott, William	Otsego	3	5	2	0	?
Acker, Abraham	Canajoharie	2	4	2	0	0
Adams, Darius	Canajoharie	2	2	4	0	0
Adams, Isaac	Chemung	1	1	1	0	0
Adams, John	Canajoharie	1	1	4	0	0
Adams, John	Mohawk	1	2	3	?	?
Adams, John	Otsego	1	1	4	0	0
Adams, Robert	Caughnawaga	4	1	3	0	3
Adamy, Peter	Canajoharie	1	0	3	0	0
Adear, John	Mohawk	2	0	2	0	0
Adear, John, Jr.	Mohawk	1	0	2	0	0
Adimy, Henry	Canajoharie	1	0	2	0	0
Ailworth, Philip	Whites	1	0	4	0	0
Aingier, John	Whites	2	0	2	0	?
Ajutant, Nathan	Harpersfield	1	2	2	0	0
Ajutant, Peter	Harpersfield	1	1	1	0	0
Albrunt, Hannah	Caughnawaga	2	0	2	0	0
Alderman, Elijah	Mohawk	1	2	4	0	0
Alger, Stoughton	Otsego	2	2	3	?	?
Alin, James	Otsego	1	6	2	0	0
Allback, John	Palatine	1	3	4	0	0
Alleburt, White	Palatine	1	2	3	?	?
Allen, [?]	Caughnawaga	1	0	2	0	0
Allen, Barnabas	Canajoharie	2	4	3	0	0
Allen, Eastwood	Otsego	3	0	2	0	0
Allen, Elias	Canajoharie	1	1	1	0	0
Allen, Gideon	Whites	3	3	2	0	0
Allen, Isaac	Whites	3	0	1	0	0

APPENDIX B

1790 FEDERAL CENSUS, MONTGOMERY COUNTY, NY

HOF	TOWN	M 16+	M -16	F	OFP	S
Allen, Jeremiah	Whites	1	0	2	0	0
Allen, John	Canajoharie	1	2	2	0	?
Allen, John	Caughnawaga	2	0	0	0	0
Allen, John	Whites	8	2	4	0	0
Allen, Jonathan, Jr.	Mohawk	1	1	?	?	?
Allen, Moses	German Flatts	4	0	3	0	0
Allen, Nathan	Canajoharie	2	0	2	0	0
Allen, Pheneas	Whites	1	1	3	0	0
Allen, Philip	Mohawk	1	2	2	0	0
Allen, Robert	Mohawk	1	1	2	0	0
Allen, Seth	German Flatts	1	3	2	0	0
Allen, Thomas	Caughnawaga	2	0	1	0	0
Allen, William	Mohawk	1	0	3	0	0
Allen, William	Mohawk	1	2	5	0	?
Alpatty, Charles	Canajoharie	1	0	5	0	0
Alridge, Nicholas	German Flatts	3	0	5	0	0
Alter, Jacob	Otsego	1	0	?	?	?
Alverson, Uriah	Whites	8	0	2	0	0
Ames, Robert	Whites	1	0	0	0	0
Anders, Jonathan	Chemung	1	1	1	0	0
Anderson, David	Canajoharie	1	2	1	0	0
Anderson, Duncan	Caughnawaga	1	3	4	0	0
Anderson, Elijah	Canajoharie	2	1	2	0	0
Anderson, Ezekel	Caughnawaga	1	1	2	0	0
Anderson, James	Canajoharie	1	0	0	0	?
Anderson, John	Canajoharie	1	1	3	0	0
Anderson, John	Caughnawaga	3	1	2	0	0
Anderson, John, Jr.	Canajoharie	1	0	1	0	?
Anderson, Samuel	Canajoharie	1	1	2	0	?
Andrees, David	Whites	1	1	1	0	0
Andrees, John	Herkimer	1	1	2	0	?
Andrew, David	Herkimer	1	6	4	0	?
Andrews, Isaac	Canajoharie	1	0	1	0	0
Andrews, John	German Flatts	1	1	1	0	0
Andrews, Samuel	Harpersfield	1	2	3	0	0
Andrews, Seth	Harpersfield	3	0	0	0	0
Antes, Conradt	Mohawk	1	1	1	0	0
Antes, John	Mohawk	1	4	3	0	0
Anthony, Peter	Canajoharie	2	0	2	0	0
Anthony, Seth	Harpersfield	1	2	6	0	?
Apple, Hendrick	Harpersfield	1	2	2	0	0
Applegate, Moses	Mohawk	1	1	2	0	?
Arackesinger, Baltus	Caughnawaga	2	4	2	0	0
Arackesinger, Baltus, Jr.	Caughnawaga	2	1	3	0	0
Aracksinger, Philip	Caughnawaga	1	1	2	0	0

1035

1790 FEDERAL CENSUS, MONTGOMERY COUNTY, NY

HOF	TOWN	M 16+	M -16	F	OFP	S
Archy, John	Canajoharie	1	1	1	0	0
Armstrong, Archibald	Whites	2	2	2	0	0
Armstrong, John	German Flatts	1	2	1	0	0
Arndt, Abraham	Canajoharie	1	0	1	0	?
Arnold, David	Whites	3	0	1	0	0
Arnold, Edward	Herkimer	1	2	3	0	?
Arnold, Gidion	Otsego	1	1	2	0	?
Arnold, Hopkins	Whites	1	1	2	0	?
Askins, James	Chemung	1	2	3	0	0
Askins, Lemuel	Chemung	1	3	7	0	0
Askins, Squire	Chemung	1	0	1	0	0
Asson, Isaac	Canajoharie	1	0	4	0	0
Aston, Thomas	Chemung	1	2	2	0	0
Atkins, Samuel	Chemung	1	2	4	0	?
Atkins, William	Canajoharie	1	0	0	0	0
Atwater, Aseph	Whites	1	1	0	0	?
Aumick, Thomas	Mohawk	1	2	2	0	0
Ausman, Philip	German Flatts	1	1	2	0	0
Ausmuck, Abraham	Mohawk	1	3	3	0	0
Austen, Abel	Herkimer	1	3	3	?	?
Austen, David	Otsego	1	1	3	0	0
Austen, Stephen	Canajoharie	1	5	4	?	?
Austin, Nathaniel	Whites	1	3	1	0	0
Averell, James	Otsego	1	2	1	0	0
Averell, Josiah	Canajoharie	3	2	1	0	0
Averell, Thomas	Harpersfield	1	2	2	0	?
Averell, William	Canajoharie	2	3	4	0	0
Averson, John	Canajoharie	1	1	2	?	?
Avery, Noel	Mohawk	1	0	1	0	?
Avery, Richard	Mohawk	1	1	1	0	?
Avery, Samuel	Canajoharie	1	3	3	0	0
Avery, Sarah B.	Herkimer	1	0	3	0	0
Avery, Thomas	Mohawk	2	0	1	0	?
Awmuck, William	Mohawk	1	1	2	0	?
Axtol, Aaron	Harpersfield	1	2	1	0	0
Axtol, Daniel	Harpersfield	1	2	1	0	0
Ayle, Harmanus	Canajoharie	2	0	1	0	0
Ayle, Honchrist	Canajoharie	1	2	5	0	0
Ayle, John	Canajoharie	1	0	0	0	?
Ayle, John	Canajoharie	1	1	3	0	?
Ayle, Michael	Palatine	4	2	3	0	?
Ayle, Peter	Canajoharie	2	2	4	0	?
Ayle, Peter	Canajoharie	1	1	4	0	0
Ayle, Petres	Palatine	3	2	5	0	4
Ayle, William	Palatine	1	4	4	0	0

1790 FEDERAL CENSUS, MONTGOMERY COUNTY, NY

HOF	TOWN	M 16+	M -16	F	OFP	S
Ayres, John	Caughnawaga	2	1	3	0	0
Ayres, Nathaniel	Mohawk	1	1	4	0	0
Ayson, Robert	Canajoharie	1	2	3	0	?
Babcock, Jonathan	Otsego	2	1	1	0	?
Babet, Alcanor	Caughnawaga	2	1	2	0	0
Backer, David	Caughnawaga	2	1	1	0	0
Backer, Henry	Herkimer	1	2	5	0	0
Backer, Lodowick	Canajoharie	1	1	2	0	0
Backer, Philip	Canajoharie	1	1	3	0	0
Backwell, James	Chemung	2	5	3	0	?
Bacon, Gould	Harpersfield	1	0	0	0	0
Bacon, Joel	Chemung	2	1	2	0	?
Badcock, David	Whites	2	2	1	0	0
Badcock, Jonathan	Otsego	1	2	1	0	0
Badcock, Jonathan	Whites	3	1	8	0	0
Bader, Melchor	Palatine	2	2	?	?	?
Bader, Ulrick	Palatine	2	4	5	0	0
Badger, Edmund	Harpersfield	2	0	2	0	?
Badger, Lemuel	Harpersfield	2	2	5	0	?
Badger, Nathaniel	Chemung	2	3	4	0	0
Bailey, Jessee	Chemung	1	0	3	0	0
Baker, Asa	Chemung	2	5	3	0	?
Baker, Daniel	Otsego	2	2	3	0	0
Baker, David	Herkimer	2	1	3	0	0
Baker, Ebenezer	Otsego	1	1	4	0	0
Baker, Elnathan	Otsego	1	2	2	0	0
Baker, Joel	German Flatts	2	0	0	0	0
Baker, John	Chemung	2	0	2	0	?
Baker, Joseph	Canajoharie	1	0	4	0	0
Baker, Nathan	Herkimer	1	1	3	0	?
Balcom, Azte	Otsego	1	0	1	0	?
Balcom, Francis	Otsego	3	1	1	0	?
Balcom, Uriah	Otsego	1	0	0	0	?
Balding, Isaac	Chemung	1	0	1	0	0
Balding, Isaac, Jr.	Chemung	2	2	2	0	0
Balding, Thomas	Chemung	4	3	5	0	0
Balding, William	Chemung	1	2	2	0	0
Ball, Nathaniel	German Flatts	1	0	0	0	0
Ballard, Luke	Whites	2	1	2	0	?
Ballow, Benjamin	German Flatts	5	0	1	0	?
Baltsly, Andrew	Palatine	2	1	3	0	0
Baltsly, Peter	Palatine	2	1	2	0	0
Balyea, Henry	German Flatts	2	1	1	0	?
Baneseler, Thomas	Mohawk	1	?	?	?	?

APPENDIX B

1790 FEDERAL CENSUS, MONTGOMERY COUNTY, NY

HOF	TOWN	M 16+	M -16	F	OFP	S
Barber, Amaziah	Harpersfield	2	2	2	0	0
Barberow, John	Mohawk	1	0	0	0	?
Bardet, Catherine	Canajoharie	2	1	1	0	?
Bardsley, John	Whites	2	0	2	0	0
Bardy, Luther	Chemung	1	4	2	0	?
Barker, John	Chemung	3	2	2	0	0
Barker, Jonathan	Chemung	1	2	2	0	0
Barker, Simeon	Whites	2	3	2	0	0
Barlett, John	Mohawk	1	3	5	0	0
Barnard, Moses	Whites	4	4	4	0	0
Barnard, Samuel	Whites	3	6	4	0	0
Barne, Thomas	Mohawk	1	3	?	?	?
Barnes, Asa	Whites	1	1	1	0	0
Barnes, Benjamin	Whites	3	2	2	0	0
Barnes, Henry	Palatine	1	0	2	0	0
Barnes, Jacob	Caughnawaga	3	1	2	0	0
Barnes, Thomas O.	Palatine	1	1	2	0	0
Barnet, Cimon	Otsego	0	1	3	0	?
Barnhart, Frederick	Canajoharie	2	2	5	0	?
Barree, Seth	Harpersfield	1	1	1	0	0
Barret, Israel	Whites	1	1	2	0	0
Barrett, Benjamin	Whites	1	0	0	0	0
Barrett, Stephen	Whites	2	0	3	0	0
Barrs, Hezekiah	Harpersfield	1	0	1	0	0
Bars, Ludwick	German Flatts	1	1	2	0	0
Barsh, Adam	Palatine	2	2	2	0	0
Barsh, Rudolph	Palatine	1	1	2	0	0
Bartholemew, Benjamin	Canajoharie	1	3	3	0	0
Bartholemew, Charles	Canajoharie	1	2	3	0	0
Bartholemew, Joseph	Canajoharie	2	3	4	0	0
Bartholemew, Theobald	Canjoahrie	2	2	5	0	0
Bartlet, Levy	Harpersfield	1	0	2	0	0
Bartlet, Nathaniel	Mohawk	3	0	2	0	0
Bartlet, William	Canajoharie	4	2	4	0	0
Bartlet, William	Canajoharie	3	2	3	0	0
Barton, Izra	Canajoharie	1	1	2	0	0
Basel, Ephraim	Chemung	2	1	6	0	0
Bashasha, Hannah	Canajoharie	0	0	4	0	?
Basshor, Jacob	German Flatts	2	1	2	0	2
Batchelor, Zepheniah	Caughnawaga	2	3	2	0	0
Bates, Augustus	Harpersfield	3	0	0	0	1
Bates, Benjamin	Chemung	2	0	3	0	0
Bates, David	Otsego	4	1	2	0	?
Bates, Elisha	Chemung	1	1	1	0	0
Bates, John	Chemung	1	1	1	0	0

1790 FEDERAL CENSUS, MONTGOMERY COUNTY, NY

HOF	TOWN	M 16+	M -16	F	OFP	S
Bates, Jonathan	Chemung	1	3	4	0	0
Bates, Joshua	Mohawk	1	2	2	0	0
Bates, Luke	Chemung	1	1	2	0	0
Bates, William	Chemung	2	1	6	0	0
Batterson, Abijah	Chemung	2	1	2	0	?
Battles, John	Harpersfield	1	1	2	0	0
Bauder, Michael	Palatine	1	2	1	0	0
Baum, Hendrick	Canajoharie	1	0	1	0	?
Baum, Philip	Canajoharie	1	0	2	0	0
Bauman, John	Canajoharie	2	3	5	0	0
Baut, Nicholas	Canajoharie	2	4	4	0	0
Baxter, Andrew	Caughnawaga	2	1	2	0	?
Baxter, Thomas	Canajoharie	3	2	4	0	0
Bayard, Martin	Canajoharie	2	2	2	0	?
Bayley, Oliver	German Flatts	1	2	2	0	0
Beacon, Abner	Canajoharie	2	3	3	0	0
Beard, Abijah	Harpersfield	1	3	1	0	0
Bearsley, Dyer	Otsego	2	2	3	0	0
Bearsley, Levy	Otsego	1	1	3	0	0
Bearsley, Obediah	Otsego	1	1	2	0	0
Bearsley, Patridge Thatcher	Otsego	1	0	3	0	0
Beauman, Adam A.	Herkimer	1	2	1	0	0
Beauman, Jacob	Canajoharie	1	1	1	0	?
Beauman, Jacob	Herkimer	1	2	3	0	?
Beauman, John A.	Herkimer	4	0	2	0	0
Beauman, John, Jr.	Canajoharie	1	1	1	0	?
Beauverie, Solomon	Chemung	2	3	5	0	0
Bebee, Joseph	Chemung	1	0	1	?	?
Bebee, Samuel	Harpersfield	3	0	1	0	0
Beck, John	Palatine	1	2	2	0	?
Becker, Christian	Canajoharie	1	0	2	0	0
Becker, Henry	Palatine	1	3	4	0	?
Becker, John	Otsego	2	1	2	0	0
Becker, Matthew	Mohawk	2	0	1	0	0
Becker, Philip	Caughnawaga	1	1	2	0	0
Beckwith, Asa	Whites	1	1	2	0	0
Beckwith, Reuben	Whites	2	2	1	0	0
Beckwith, Silas	Caughnawaga	1	0	3	0	0
Beech, Abigail	Harpersfield	1	2	4	0	0
Beech, Amos	Mohawk	1	1	8	0	0
Beech, Ashbel	Whites	2	1	1	0	?
Beech, Gershom	Herkimer	3	0	2	0	0
Beech, Ira	Canajoharie	1	2	3	0	?
Beech, Moses	Herkimer	1	0	2	0	0
Beedle, Barnard	Caughnawaga	2	1	6	0	0

1790 FEDERAL CENSUS, MONTGOMERY COUNTY, NY

HOF	TOWN	M 16+	M -16	F	OFP	S
Beekman, Alice	Mohawk	1	2	2	0	0
Beekman, Henry	Mohawk	0	0	0	3	?
Beekman, Henry	Palatine	1	0	1	0	?
Beekman, William	Canajoharie	1	3	4	0	?
Beels, Abraham	Otsego	1	5	3	0	0
Beels, Nabby	Otsego	0	2	4	0	0
Beeman, Bulah	Harpersfield	1	1	1	0	0
Beers, Ephraim	Harpersfield	1	4	5	0	0
Bees, William	Palatine	2	0	3	0	4
Begford, Samuel	Caughnawaga	2	3	4	0	0
Belden, Charles	Caughnawaga	3	1	1	0	0
Belding, Pearl	Chemung	2	0	3	0	0
Belknap, Abel	Canajoharie	2	2	6	0	0
Belknap, Jessee	Canajoharie	1	5	2	0	?
Bell, Andrew	German Flatts	1	2	3	0	0
Bell, Hendrick	Canajoharie	2	2	2	0	2
Bell, Hezekiah	Canajoharie	1	1	0	0	0
Bell, Jacob	Herkimer	1	1	4	0	0
Bell, John	Caughnawaga	1	1	4	0	0
Bell, John	Otsego	1	0	4	0	?
Bell, Philip	Herkimer	1	0	1	0	?
Bell, Thomas	Herkimer	1	1	1	0	?
Bell, William	Harpersfield	1	1	1	0	0
Bellinger, Adam	Palatine	3	1	5	0	?
Bellinger, Adam A.	Palatine	2	2	2	0	0
Bellinger, Adam B.	Canajoharie	1	2	3	0	?
Bellinger, Christian	Herkimer	1	1	4	0	0
Bellinger, Christopher	Herkimer	1	1	2	0	?
Bellinger, Frederick	Canajoharie	1	2	2	0	0
Bellinger, Frederick	German Flatts	1	2	5	0	?
Bellinger, Frederick	Palatine	2	2	3	0	0
Bellinger, Henry	Palatine	1	2	4	0	0
Bellinger, Henry	Palatine	2	1	7	0	3
Bellinger, John	German Flatts	2	2	3	0	?
Bellinger, John	Whites	1	1	4	0	0
Bellinger, John L.	Palatine	1	1	1	0	?
Bellinger, Joseph	Mohawk	1	3	3	0	?
Bellinger, Peter	Palatine	1	0	3	0	?
Bellinger, Peter F.	Herkimer	2	1	5	0	?
Bellinger, Peter, Sr.	German Flatts	4	0	2	0	1
Bellinger, Philip	German Flatts	2	0	2	0	0
Bellinger, Philip	Herkimer	1	4	1	0	0
Bellinger, William	Canajoharie	2	4	5	0	0
Bellows, Jonas	Chemung	2	1	2	0	0
Belnap, John	Whites	3	4	4	0	?

1790 FEDERAL CENSUS, MONTGOMERY COUNTY, NY

HOF	TOWN	M 16+	M -16	F	OFP	S
Belor, Jacob	Palatine	1	1	2	0	0
Bender, [?]mumus	Herkimer	1	0	1	0	0
Benedick, Enock	Otsego	1	3	5	?	?
Benedict, Avey	German Flatts	1	1	1	0	?
Benedict, Elias	German Flatts	1	2	2	0	?
Benedict, Silas	Harpersfield	1	1	1	0	0
Benjamin, Abel	Otsego	4	4	4	0	0
Benjamin, Jessee	Canajoharie	1	1	3	0	?
Bennedick, Stephen	Otsego	1	1	1	0	0
Bennerd, Caleb	Harpersfield	2	2	4	0	?
Bennet, Abraham	Chemung	1	2	2	0	0
Bennet, Amos	Mohawk	3	4	4	0	?
Bennet, Andrew	Herkimer	2	0	0	0	?
Bennet, Ephraim	Chemung	2	1	1	0	0
Bennet, Ephraim, Jr.	Chemung	1	2	4	0	0
Bennet, Gersham	Chemung	1	3	2	0	0
Bennet, Hendrick	Mohawk	2	3	4	0	0
Bennet, John	Canajoharie	2	2	3	0	0
Bennet, Jonathan	Canajoharie	1	0	1	0	0
Bennet, Justiss	Chemung	1	5	2	0	?
Bennet, Nathan	Canajoharie	1	0	3	0	0
Bennet, Phineas	Harpersfield	4	1	4	0	0
Bennet, Reuben	Harpersfield	2	1	2	0	0
Bennet, Robinson	Canjoharie	1	0	2	0	0
Bennet, Silas	Harpersfield	2	0	3	0	0
Bennet, Thadeus	Chemung	1	2	4	?	?
Bennett, Francis	Canajoharie	2	5	6	0	0
Bent, Elijah	Mohawk	3	2	3	0	0
Bentley, Azte	Otsego	2	0	2	?	?
Bentley, Benedict	Caughnawaga	1	2	5	?	?
Bentley, Joseph	Caughnawaga	1	1	3	0	0
Bentley, William	Canajoharie	2	2	2	0	0
Bently, Green	Chemung	2	1	3	0	0
Benton, Nathaniel	Chemung	1	1	1	0	0
Bentsley, David	Herkimer	1	2	2	0	?
Bentsley, Joseph	Herkimer	1	3	1	0	?
Bergin, William	Mohawk	1	2	4	0	0
Berkey, Jacob	Herkimer	1	2	3	0	0
Berkey, Peter	Herkimer	1	0	1	0	0
Bethoom, William	Herkimer	1	2	3	0	?
Betinger, Martin	Canajoharie	2	2	2	0	0
Betts, Millard	Caughnawaga	1	3	2	0	0
Beuel, Soloman	Chemung	1	2	3	0	0
Bevee, Abraham	Mohawk	3	2	3	0	?
Bevee, Anthony	Palatine	1	0	3	0	?

1790 FEDERAL CENSUS, MONTGOMERY COUNTY, NY

HOF	TOWN	M 16+	M -16	F	OFP	S
Bevee, Nicholas	Mohawk	1	1	2	0	?
Beverly, David	Mohawk	1	2	3	0	0
Beverly, Thomas	Mohawk	2	2	3	0	?
Bewell, Samuel	Otsego	4	2	9	0	?
Bezer, John	Canajoharie	1	1	3	0	0
Bick, Dirick C.A.	Canajoharie	1	0	2	0	0
Bidleman, Peter Simon	Canajoharie	1	4	4	0	0
Bidwell, Samuel	Otsego	1	4	2	0	0
Biers, Abel	Caughnawaga	1	2	3	0	0
Bighams, William	Mohawk	1	0	4	0	?
Billings, James	Mohawk	1	3	4	0	?
Bingham, Royal	Caughnawaga	1	3	3	0	0
Bird, Benjamin	Chemung	2	2	4	0	0
Bishop, Charles	Palatine	1	2	6	0	0
Bishop, Jeremiah	Chemung	1	1	3	0	?
Bishop, Jeremiah, Jr.	Chemung	1	0	5	0	?
Bishop, Joel	Mohawk	1	0	4	0	?
Bishop, John	Harpersfield	2	3	4	0	?
Bishop, Luther	Caughnawaga	1	3	3	0	?
Bixley, Samuel	Harpersfield	5	0	0	0	0
Black, Allred	Caughnawaga	1	2	2	0	0
Black, John	Caughnawaga	1	2	1	0	?
Black, John	German Flatts	1	2	5	0	0
Blackmer, Ephraim	Whites	3	0	2	0	?
Blackmer, Joseph	Whites	1	1	2	0	?
Blackmer, Joseph, Sr.	Whites	1	0	1	0	?
Blair, Joel	Whites	1	1	2	0	0
Blair, John	Caughnawaga	4	1	4	0	0
Blair, John	Whites	2	2	4	0	0
Blakeley, John	Canajoharie	1	0	4	0	0
Blanchard, Andrew	Whites	1	0	5	0	?
Blanden, John	Chemung	1	1	1	0	0
Blandge, Luther	Mohawk	1	0	2	0	?
Blank, Case	Canajoharie	1	1	3	0	0
Bliss, Elijah	Canajoharie	1	1	1	0	0
Bliss, Reuben	Palatine	1	0	3	?	?
Bliss, Timothy	Chemung	1	1	2	0	?
Blodget, Elijah	Whites	6	3	2	0	0
Blodget, Joseph	Whites	1	3	3	0	?
Blodget, Ludam	Whites	1	0	2	0	?
Blodget, Rufus	Whites	3	0	2	0	?
Blodget, Solomon	Whites	2	3	2	0	?
Bloom, George	Chemung	1	1	5	0	?
Bloomfield, John	Mohawk	1	0	3	0	0
Blunt, Samuel	Whites	2	2	4	0	?

APPENDIX B

1790 FEDERAL CENSUS, MONTGOMERY COUNTY, NY

HOF	TOWN	M 16+	M -16	F	OFP	S
Boardman, Thadeus	Harpersfield	2	2	4	0	?
Bodwell, John	Canajoharie	3	0	1	0	?
Bohall, Adam	Canajoharie	2	2	4	0	?
Bohall, Casper	Canajoharie	2	1	2	0	0
Bohall, Hooper	Canajoharie	2	2	3	0	?
Boldman, John, Jr.	Caughnawaga	3	0	3	0	0
Bome, Frederick	Palatine	1	2	1	0	0
Bone, Peter	Caughnawaga	3	1	4	0	?
Bone, William	Caughnawaga	1	2	1	0	0
Bonesteel, Philip	Mohawk	1	4	3	0	?
Bonta, Hendrick	Caughnawaga	1	1	1	0	0
Boon, Abraham	German Flatts	2	1	4	0	?
Bordman, Benajah	Chemung	3	2	5	0	0
Boshart, Margaret	Caughnawaga	2	0	2	0	?
Bostick, Zedock	Chemung	3	1	3	0	0
Bostwick, Henry	Mohawk	1	1	1	0	0
Bostwick, Jessee	Mohawk	3	0	3	0	?
Bostwick, Milo	Mohawk	1	0	2	0	?
Bosworth, Benajah	Chemung	2	2	2	0	?
Bosworth, David	Chemung	1	3	2	0	?
Bosworth, Samuel	Otsego	2	0	1	0	0
Bouch, Henry	Canajoharie	3	1	5	0	0
Boundy, Stephen	Canajoharie	1	0	0	0	0
Bovee, Matthias	Mohawk	3	1	2	0	?
Bovee, Nicholas	Mohawk	3	0	1	0	0
Bowen, Benjamin	Herkimer	1	3	4	0	2
Bowers, Daniel	Canajoharie	2	0	3	0	0
Bowker, Ester	Chemung	2	2	4	0	?
Bowker, Silas	Chemung	1	1	2	0	?
Bowman, Frederick	German Flatts	1	1	4	0	?
Boyer, Falatine	Palatine	1	1	2	0	?
Boyer, John	Palatine	4	2	7	0	?
Bradford, James	Mohawk	2	3	6	0	0
Bradley, John	German Flatts	1	0	0	0	?
Bradner, Josiah	Canajoharie	2	1	2	0	?
Bradt, Henry	Canajoharie	2	3	4	0	0
Brame, John	Palatine	1	0	3	0	?
Bramer, Jesse	Caughnawaga	1	2	1	0	0
Bramer, Ludwick	Canajoharie	1	3	3	0	?
Bramhall, Joseph	Harpersfield	1	3	6	0	?
Branard, Jeptha	Whites	3	4	3	0	0
Branch, Walter	Harpersfield	1	0	3	0	?
Brand, John	Caughnawaga	1	0	1	0	0
Brannan, Seabury	Whites	3	1	1	0	?
Brant, Simeon	Canajoharie	1	2	1	0	0

1790 FEDERAL CENSUS, MONTGOMERY COUNTY, NY

HOF	TOWN	M 16+	M -16	F	OFP	S
Braot, Henry	Palatine	1	0	2	0	0
Bratt, Samuel	Mohawk	1	0	2	0	?
Breadback, John	Palatine	2	0	3	0	7
Brett, Joshua H.	Harpersfield	3	2	0	0	0
Brewer, Aaron	Palatine	2	0	2	?	?
Brewer, Abraham	Chemung	1	1	4	0	0
Brewer, Herman	Palatine	4	1	4	0	?
Brewster, Nathan	Caughnawaga	1	2	1	0	?
Brickman, Lodowick	Canajoharie	4	3	5	0	0
Bricks, Eliakim	Herkimer	1	2	1	0	?
Bridgman, Orlanden	Chemung	2	2	2	0	0
Bridgman, Reuben	Chemung	1	2	1	0	0
Briggs, Ellis	Mohawk	2	2	4	0	0
Briggs, Joseph	Caughnawaga	1	1	2	0	0
Briggs, Joshua	Caughnawaga	1	1	3	0	0
Briggs, Perez	Otsego	1	1	3	0	0
Briggs, William	Whites	7	0	1	0	0
Brigham, Lyman	Whites	1	0	0	0	0
Brigham, Stephen	Whites	2	4	5	0	0
Brink, James	Chemung	1	1	3	0	?
Bristol, Eli	Whites	2	0	4	0	0
Bristol, Joel	Whites	5	0	2	0	?
Bristol, Richard	Harpersfield	2	0	2	0	0
Brittain, Abraham	Mohawk	1	2	5	0	0
Broadhack, Jacob	Herkimer	1	3	4	0	0
Broadhack, John	Herkimer	1	1	1	?	?
Brockway, Ephraim	Mohawk	1	2	3	0	0
Brodhock, Bartholomew	German Flatts	1	2	3	0	0
Brombly, Eden	Mohawk	1	0	2	0	?
Bronk, Matthew	Caughnawaga	1	2	4	0	0
Brookins, Thadeus	Canajoharie	1	0	3	0	?
Brookman, Godfry	Canajoharie	2	1	3	0	3
Brooks, Benjamin	Canajoharie	1	0	4	0	0
Brooks, Cornelius	Chemung	1	1	7	0	0
Brooks, John	Chemung	1	1	1	0	0
Brothers, John	Caughnawaga	1	2	4	0	0
Brower, Francis	Caughnawaga	1	0	1	0	0
Brower, John	Caughnawaga	2	1	2	0	0
Brower, Wilhelmus	Caughnawaga	1	1	0	0	1
Brower, William	Caughnawaga	2	0	4	0	0
Brown, Adam	Canajoharie	1	1	1	0	?
Brown, Benajah	Chemung	2	2	2	0	?
Brown, Christian	Canajoharie	1	1	7	0	0
Brown, Conradt	Canajoharie	3	0	4	0	0
Brown, Daniel	Chemung	1	0	1	0	0

1790 FEDERAL CENSUS, MONTGOMERY COUNTY, NY

HOF	TOWN	M 16+	M -16	F	OFP	S
Brown, Daniel	Whites	1	0	0	0	0
Brown, David	German Flatts	1	2	2	0	?
Brown, David	Herkimer	1	0	1	0	?
Brown, Ebenezer	Otsego	1	3	2	0	0
Brown, Elisha	Chemung	1	0	1	0	0
Brown, Ezekiel	Chemung	2	1	3	0	0
Brown, Ezra	Caughnawaga	1	1	1	0	0
Brown, Godlip	Palatine	1	2	1	0	0
Brown, James	Harpersfield	1	1	0	0	0
Brown, John	Harpersfield	1	2	2	0	0
Brown, John M.	Canajoharie	2	7	2	0	?
Brown, Jonathan	Chemung	3	0	0	0	?
Brown, Jonathan	Otsego	3	0	0	0	?
Brown, Levy	Whites	1	4	7	0	0
Brown, Moses	Chemung	1	2	2	0	?
Brown, Nathaniel	Herkimer	1	0	0	0	?
Brown, Philip	Palatine	2	0	3	0	?
Brown, Simon	Canajoharie	1	0	3	0	?
Brown, Stephen	Canajoharie	1	0	3	0	?
Brown, Stephen	Canajoharie	1	0	1	0	0
Brown, Thomas	Caughnawaga	1	2	6	0	0
Brown, William	Caughnawaga	3	0	5	0	1
Brownrice, Samuel	Chemung	2	1	2	0	?
Brownson, Solomon	Whites	1	1	0	0	0
Brunson, Asiel	Whites	1	0	0	0	0
Brutherton, Abel	Canajoharie	1	2	2	0	?
Buck, Elijah	Chemung	3	4	2	0	?
Buckland, John	Herkimer	1	2	3	0	?
Buckland, William	Herkimer	1	1	1	0	?
Bull, John	Canajoharie	1	4	3	?	?
Bullen, David	Whites	2	1	4	0	?
Bullen, John	Whites	3	3	9	0	0
Buman, Uriah	Mohawk	2	2	4	0	?
Bumer, John	Mohawk	1	0	0	0	0
Bun, Jacob	Mohawk	1	3	3	0	?
Bun, Jacob, Jr.	Mohawk	1	0	2	0	0
Bun, John Peter	Mohawk	2	1	1	0	0
Bun, John, Jr.	Mohawk	1	1	2	0	0
Bundy, Elisha	Harpersfield	1	1	2	0	0
Bundy, Peter	Harpersfield	1	3	3	0	0
Bundy, Simeon	Chemung	1	2	4	0	?
Bunn, Jobe	Canajoharie	1	1	1	0	0
Bunt, James	Mohawk	1	2	2	0	0
Bunts, Abraham	Mohawk	1	2	5	0	0
Burch, Jeremiah	Mohawk	3	5	3	0	0

1790 FEDERAL CENSUS, MONTGOMERY COUNTY, NY

HOF	TOWN	M 16+	M -16	F	OFP	S
Burch, Nathan	Harpersfield	1	2	5	0	?
Burch, Thomas	Canajoharie	1	2	4	0	0
Burchet, Elias	Harpersfield	1	0	0	0	?
Burdock, Jessee	Canajoharie	1	2	1	0	0
Burger, John	Canajoharie	1	2	1	0	0
Burgess, John	Otsego	6	0	2	0	0
Burget, Henry	Harpersfield	1	2	4	0	?
Burget, Joharikam	Harpersfield	1	4	2	0	?
Burk, James	Caughnawaga	1	0	2	0	0
Burkdorff, John	German Flatts	1	2	2	0	0
Burnap, Joseph	Mohawk	1	3	2	0	?
Burnard, Samuel	Mohawk	3	0	5	0	?
Burnham, Asel	Chemung	1	1	3	0	?
Burnham, Isaac	Canajoharie	1	1	2	0	?
Burnham, Keeny	Chemung	1	0	2	0	?
Burns, William	Mohawk	1	2	6	0	0
Burr, Horras	Caughnawaga	1	1	1	0	0
Burr, Nathaniel	Caughnawaga	3	2	1	0	0
Burr, Salem	Caughnawaga	1	1	2	0	0
Burt, Benjamin	Chemung	1	2	3	0	?
Burt, David	Chemung	1	1	2	0	?
Burt, Luther	Harpersfield	2	1	3	0	0
Burt, Thomas	Chemung	1	1	5	0	?
Burtil, Nathan	Mohawk	1	2	2	0	?
Burton, Isaac	Mohawk	1	2	1	0	0
Burton, Oliver	Mohawk	4	2	4	0	0
Burton, Stephen	Mohawk	1	0	1	0	?
Bush, Charles	Chemung	1	0	1	0	0
Bush, George	Palatine	1	7	3	0	0
Bush, Henry	Chemung	1	4	1	0	?
Bush, Japhet	Chemung	1	2	2	0	0
Bush, Joseph	Chemung	2	0	2	0	0
Bush, Samuel	Caughnawaga	2	0	2	0	0
Bushnel, Stephen	Whites	2	1	4	0	?
Buss, Christian	Canajoharie	2	1	1	0	0
Butler, [?]	Caughnawaga	1	0	3	0	0
Butler, Ebenezer	Whites	1	0	2	0	0
Butler, Ebenezer, Jr.	Whites	4	0	3	0	?
Butler, John	Canajoharie	3	6	1	0	?
Butler, John	Chemung	1	0	2	0	0
Butler, Salmon	Whites	1	0	1	0	0
Butler, Thomas	Chemung	1	2	1	0	0
Butler, Zachariah	Canajoharie	1	2	5	0	?
Butterfield, James	Otsego	1	5	2	0	0
Butterfield, Levy	Herkimer	1	1	2	0	0

1790 FEDERAL CENSUS, MONTGOMERY COUNTY, NY

HOF	TOWN	M 16+	M -16	F	OFP	S
Button, Benjamin	Canajoharie	1	2	2	0	0
Button, Peter	Mohawk	1	3	2	0	0
Buye, John	Palatine	2	1	5	0	?
Byington, John	Herkimer	1	0	3	0	0
Cacrelle, Francis	Otsego	1	1	3	0	0
Cadle, George	Palatine	2	1	3	0	?
Cady, Charles	Caughnawaga	1	3	2	0	0
Cady, David	Mohawk	1	2	3	0	?
Cady, David, Jr.	Mohawk	2	2	1	?	?
Cady, John	Mohawk	1	2	4	0	0
Cady, Manassah	Chemung	3	1	3	0	0
Cady, Zebulan	Chemung	2	2	4	0	0
Caldwell, William	Caughnawaga	1	2	3	0	0
Caler, Peter	Caughnawaga	1	2	2	0	0
Calhoon, Benjamin	Palatine	3	0	1	?	?
Calhoon, Joseph	Palatine	3	1	1	0	0
Calhoon, Rennolds	Palatine	1	0	1	0	0
Cameron, Angus	Caughnawaga	1	3	3	0	0
Cameron, Charles	Caughnawaga	1	0	7	?	?
Cameron, John	Caughnawaga	1	1	3	?	?
Cammeron, Even	German Flatts	1	0	1	0	?
Camp, Benjamin	Canajoharie	1	1	2	0	0
Campbell, Alexander	Canajoharie	1	1	4	0	0
Campbell, Barbelez	German Flatts	2	3	3	0	0
Campbell, Ephraim	Otsego	2	2	5	0	?
Campbell, Hugh	Mohawk	1	4	4	0	0
Campbell, James	Canajoharie	4	0	7	0	0
Campbell, James	Caughnawaga	1	1	2	0	0
Campbell, John	Canajoharie	1	2	5	0	0
Campbell, John	Harpersfield	1	1	4	0	0
Campbell, John	Mohawk	3	4	5	0	?
Campbell, John, Sr.	Canajoharie	3	0	4	0	0
Campbell, Ludwick	German Flatts	1	4	2	0	0
Campbell, Nathaniel	Caughnawaga	1	1	2	?	?
Campbell, Nathaniel	Mohawk	3	4	3	0	0
Campbell, Patrick	German Flatts	2	2	6	1	?
Campbell, Richard	Mohawk	1	0	0	0	0
Campbell, Samuel	Canajoharie	2	1	4	0	0
Campbell, Samuel, Sr.	Canajoharie	6	0	4	0	1
Canady, Henry	Caughnawaga	2	1	2	0	0
Canady, James	Caughnawaga	2	1	4	?	?
Canady, James	Otsego	1	4	3	0	0
Canady, James	Otsego	2	1	3	0	?
Canady, James, Jr.	Caughnawaga	1	3	4	?	?

1790 FEDERAL CENSUS, MONTGOMERY COUNTY, NY

HOF	TOWN	M 16+	M -16	F	OFP	S
Canady, Robert	Caughnawaga	1	0	2	0	0
Canady, Robert	Caughnawaga	1	4	3	?	?
Canady, Samuel	Caughnawaga	1	0	3	0	0
Canady, William	Otsego	1	2	2	0	?
Canfield, Jonathan	Caughnawaga	3	3	3	0	0
Canine, Abraham	Caughnawaga	1	1	3	0	1
Canine, John	Mohawk	1	2	1	0	1
Canine, Peter	Caughnawaga	2	3	5	0	3
Cannan, Andrew	Canajoharie	2	2	5	0	?
Cannan, James	Canajoharie	3	3	4	0	0
Canute, Isaac	Mohawk	1	0	3	0	?
Card, Benjamin	Otsego	3	0	0	0	0
Care, Thomas	Palatine	2	1	1	0	?
Carman, Charles	Palatine	1	3	3	0	0
Carman, John	Chemung	2	3	4	0	0
Carmichael, James	Caughnawaga	1	2	?	?	?
Carne, Michael	Canajoharie	1	3	3	0	0
Carni, Peter	Mohawk	1	0	3	0	?
Carpenter, Augustus	Mohawk	1	2	2	0	?
Carpenter, Barnard	Mohawk	1	0	3	0	?
Carpenter, Joshua	Chemung	4	3	4	0	0
Carpenter, Michael	Mohawk	1	2	4	0	0
Carpenter, Stephen	Herkimer	1	0	1	0	?
Carpenter, Thomas	Mohawk	1	0	3	0	?
Carpenter, William	Whites	2	0	0	0	0
Carr, David	Canajoharie	1	3	4	?	?
Carr, Percerfur	Otsego	4	2	5	0	?
Carr, Robert	Otsego	6	3	4	0	0
Carrell, Michael	Chemung	2	3	3	0	0
Carroll, John	Mohawk	1	6	2	0	?
Carroll, William	Mohawk	2	0	1	0	0
Carroll, William, Jr.	Mohawk	1	1	3	0	0
Cartener, Henry	Canajoharie	1	1	1	0	0
Carter, Henry	Palatine	3	0	6	0	?
Carter, Robert	Canajoharie	1	1	2	0	0
Carver, Henry	Palatine	1	3	3	0	?
Cary, Anson	Chemung	1	1	3	0	?
Cary, Jessee	Canajoharie	2	2	5	0	?
Case, [?]arius	Caughnawaga	2	3	3	0	0
Case, Aseph	German Flatts	1	0	0	0	0
Case, Benjamin	Whites	1	1	1	0	0
Case, Elihu	Caughnawaga	1	2	2	0	0
Case, Elijah, Jr.	German Flatts	1	2	2	0	0
Case, Gabriel	German Flatts	1	3	3	0	0
Case, Reuben	Caughnawaga	2	1	0	0	0

HOF	TOWN	M 16+	M -16	F	OFP	S
Cassady, Edward	Mohawk	1	1	3	0	?
Cassady, Robert	Chemung	1	3	4	0	0
Cassady, Thomas	Whites	2	0	0	0	0
Cassey, Robert	Mohawk	1	2	2	0	?
Casslear, Conradt	German Flatts	1	2	4	0	0
Casslear, Jacob J.N.	German Flatts	1	0	1	0	0
Casslear, Jacob Jacob [sic]	German Flatts	1	2	2	0	0
Casslear, Jacob John	German Flatts	2	1	8	0	0
Casslear, Jacob N.	German Flatts	2	1	2	0	0
Casslear, Jacob, Sr.	German Flatts	1	0	1	0	0
Casslear, John	Herkimer	2	5	5	0	0
Casslear, John Jacob	German Flatts	1	3	2	0	0
Casslear, John, Sr.	German Flatts	1	0	?	?	?
Casslear, Marks	German Flatts	1	0	4	0	0
Casslear, Richard	German Flatts	1	1	2	0	0
Castlear, Adam	Canajoharie	2	0	2	0	0
Castlear, John	Canajoharie	2	0	2	0	0
Castlear, John	Canajoharie	1	1	3	0	0
Castlear, Nicholas I.	Canajoharie	1	1	2	0	0
Castlear, Nicholas John	Canajoharie	1	0	2	0	0
Castlear, Thomas	Canajoharie	1	2	4	0	?
Caswell, David	Canajoharie	2	3	2	0	0
Catlin, James	Whites	3	1	2	0	0
Catlin, Jessee	Whites	1	0	1	0	?
Caugh, Bodus	Palatine	2	2	3	0	0
Caugh, George	Caughnawaga	3	1	2	0	?
Caugh, Gosper	Palatine	3	1	5	0	0
Caugh, Henrick	Palatine	4	2	6	0	1
Caugh, John	Palatine	2	1	?	?	?
Caugh, Nicholas	Palatine	1	0	4	0	0
Caugh, Peter	Palatine	1	3	3	0	0
Caugh, Rudolph	Palatine	2	2	5	0	?
Caugh, Severinius	Palatine	2	3	7	0	0
Caussant, Francis	Mohawk	1	3	3	0	?
Causselman, Bartly	Palatine	1	1	3	0	0
Causselman, John	Palatine	4	3	2	0	0
Causselman, John, Jr.	Palatine	1	0	3	0	?
Cesler, Nicholas	Palatine	1	1	3	0	1
Chalkgo, Nicholas	Palatine	3	2	2	0	?
Chamberlain, Aaron	Harpersfield	1	1	2	0	?
Chamberling, Luther	Chemung	2	0	1	0	0
Chambers, Moses	Chemung	1	1	1	0	?
Chapins, [?]	Otsego	1	1	2	0	0
Chapins, Samuel	Otsego	3	3	1	0	0
Chapman, Joseph	German Flatts	1	0	2	0	0

1790 FEDERAL CENSUS, MONTGOMERY COUNTY, NY

HOF	TOWN	M 16+	M -16	F	OFP	S
Chapple, Noah	Canajoharie	1	2	5	0	?
Chapple, William	Otsego	1	0	0	0	0
Chard, Baree	Caughnawaga	1	0	4	0	0
Charlesworth, John M.	Canajoharie	2	1	3	0	0
Chase, Ebin	Mohawk	2	0	4	0	0
Chase, Jeremiah	Mohawk	1	0	1	?	?
Chatfield, Cornelius	Herkimer	1	3	2	0	0
Cheney, Howard	Otsego	1	0	2	0	0
Cheney, William	Otsego	2	1	2	0	0
Chepley, David	Harpersfield	1	2	2	0	0
Chesholm, Keneth	Harpersfield	3	0	4	0	0
Chidwell, Benjamin	Canajoharie	2	0	0	0	0
Chilner, Christopher	Canajoharie	1	2	2	0	?
Chittington, Gerard	Whites	1	0	1	0	?
Chivers, Ebenezer	Palatine	1	1	2	0	0
Cholett, Samuel	Mohawk	3	0	2	0	0
Christian, John	Harpersfield	1	1	3	0	0
Christiancy, Solomon	Mohawk	0	1	2	2	?
Christie, James	Caughnawaga	1	0	0	0	0
Christie, John	Caughnawaga	1	4	3	0	?
Christman, Jacob	Whites	4	3	5	0	0
Church, Amasa	Otsego	2	2	2	0	?
Church, Cady	Otsego	1	0	2	0	?
Church, Isac	Chemung	1	1	2	0	?
Church, James	Canajoharie	2	1	2	0	0
Church, Richard	Harpersfield	1	2	2	0	?
Church, Willard	Otsego	2	0	2	0	?
Churchell, Isaac	Herkimer	1	2	3	0	0
Churchell, Stephen	Harpersfield	2	2	4	0	0
Cisseller, Joseph	Palatine	1	2	3	0	0
Clapsaddle, Andrew	German Flatts	2	2	4	0	0
Clapsaddle, George	German Flatts	2	2	5	0	3
Clapsaddle, William	German Flatts	1	3	3	0	0
Clark, Aaron	Whites	2	1	3	0	?
Clark, Abel	Otsego	1	0	1	?	?
Clark, Asa	Caughnawaga	1	1	2	0	?
Clark, Caleb	Mohawk	1	1	2	0	0
Clark, Christopher	Caughnawaga	2	2	5	0	0
Clark, Ezekel	Otsego	3	0	2	0	?
Clark, Gardner	Caughnawaga	1	0	2	0	?
Clark, Jeremiah	Caughnawaga	1	0	1	0	?
Clark, John	Caughnawaga	3	5	2	0	?
Clark, John	Harpersfield	3	1	3	0	0
Clark, Matthew	Caughnawaga	3	0	0	0	?
Clark, Oliver	Caughnawaga	2	2	3	0	0

APPENDIX B

1790 FEDERAL CENSUS, MONTGOMERY COUNTY, NY

HOF	TOWN	M 16+	M -16	F	OFP	S
Clark, Robert	Caughnawaga	1	1	1	0	?
Clark, Robert	Caughnawaga	1	0	2	0	?
Clark, Robert	Chemung	1	1	2	0	0
Clark, Samuel	Canajoharie	1	0	0	0	?
Clark, Willett	Caughnawaga	1	3	2	0	?
Clark, William	Mohawk	2	1	7	0	0
Clary, William	Whites	5	0	1	0	0
Claus, Peter	Palatine	3	1	4	0	0
Clayton, Nathan	Caughnawaga	1	1	2	0	1
Cleavland, Samuel	Caughnawaga	1	2	1	0	0
Clement, James	Mohawk	1	3	2	0	0
Clement, Lambertus	Caughnawaga	1	0	2	0	0
Clement, Rachel	Caughnawaga	2	0	3	0	0
Clements, [?]	Herkimer	1	2	3	0	0
Clerk, Moses	Harpersfield	1	1	2	0	?
Cleveland, Gardner	Whites	1	0	0	0	0
Cline, Jacob	Mohawk	2	0	1	0	0
Cline, John	Mohawk	3	0	1	0	0
Cline, Martinus	Mohawk	1	1	1	0	0
Cline, William	Caughnawaga	3	5	5	?	?
Clock, Conradt	Canajoharie	3	0	3	0	0
Close, Abel	Mohawk	1	0	0	0	0
Close, Reuben	Mohawk	2	1	4	0	0
Closs, John	Canajoharie	2	1	2	0	0
Clough, Benjamin	Otsego	3	0	4	0	0
Clump, Thomas	Otsego	4	1	5	0	?
Clute, Dirick	Mohawk	2	0	2	0	?
Clute, Garrit	Mohawk	1	2	2	0	?
Clute, Jacob	Mohawk	1	3	1	0	?
Clute, John	Mohawk	3	1	5	0	?
Clyde, Samuel	Canajoharie	4	0	3	0	?
Cock, Charles	Caughnawaga	1	0	2	0	0
Cock, Peter	Caughnawaga	2	3	6	0	0
Cockner, Jacob	Caughnawaga	2	1	7	0	0
Cockner, John E.	Caughnawaga	2	1	4	0	?
Cockner, Yost	Caughnawaga	1	0	2	0	0
Cocknut, Luke	Caughnawaga	1	1	2	0	?
Cockran, Andrew	Mohawk	1	2	4	0	?
Cockran, John	Canajoharie	2	1	2	0	0
Cody, Joseph	Mohawk	1	1	1	0	?
Coe, Amos	Herkimer	1	0	0	0	0
Coe, Andrew	Herkimer	1	0	0	0	0
Coe, Joel	Otsego	2	0	1	0	0
Coe, John	Herkimer	1	2	2	0	0
Coe, Robert	Otsego	2	1	1	0	0

1790 FEDERAL CENSUS, MONTGOMERY COUNTY, NY

HOF	TOWN	M 16+	M -16	F	OFP	S
Coe, Zachariah	Otsego	1	1	2	0	?
Coffin, Edward	Herkimer	1	4	2	0	0
Cogen, Thomas	German Flatts	2	1	4	0	0
Cogsdell, John	Chemung	1	0	0	0	0
Cogsdell, William	Chemung	3	0	1	0	?
Cogswell, Mason	Otsego	2	1	2	0	0
Cogswell, Robert	Otsego	1	2	1	0	0
Colbreath, William	Whites	2	2	3	0	0
Cole, Daniel	Chemung	3	4	2	0	0
Cole, Ebenezer	Herkimer	1	1	2	0	?
Cole, Ezra	Harpersfield	1	3	3	0	0
Cole, Matthew	Chemung	1	2	4	0	0
Cole, Silas	Chenango	1	0	3	0	?
Cole, Tobias	Caughnawaga	1	1	2	0	0
Coleby, William	Caughnawaga	1	2	4	0	?
Colgrove, [?]	Otsego	1	1	2	0	0
Colgrove, Andrew	Canajoharie	1	0	3	0	0
Coller, William	Harpersfield	1	2	2	0	0
Collier, [?]	Mohawk	1	1	1	0	0
Collier, Isaac	Otsego	2	?	?	?	?
Collier, Jacob	Mohawk	1	2	4	0	0
Collins, Cornelius	Canajoharie	1	3	4	0	0
Collins, Mary	Canajoharie	2	0	2	0	?
Collins, Oliver	Whites	4	1	2	0	?
Collins, Samuel	Whites	2	2	1	0	?
Collister, James	Whites	1	0	1	0	0
Colon, William	Mohawk	2	2	4	0	0
Commings, Francis	Herkimer	1	2	5	0	0
Compton, David	Chemung	1	1	2	0	?
Compton, Jacob	Harpersfield	3	0	3	0	?
Comree, Alexander	Caughnawaga	1	1	2	0	?
Comstock, Ebenezer	Mohawk	1	2	4	0	0
Comstock, William	Otsego	3	4	4	0	0
Conant, Amost	German Flatts	1	1	2	0	0
Conant, Ebenez	German Flatts	1	0	4	0	0
Conckle, John	Chemung	1	2	3	0	0
Concklin, Sillas	Canajoharie	1	4	2	0	0
Concklin, Thomas	Canajoharie	1	2	2	0	0
Cone, Osias	Whites	1	3	4	0	0
Cone, Walter	Whites	1	1	1	0	0
Conestican, Peter	Canajoharie	3	2	3	0	0
Conett, Roger	Chemung	1	5	4	0	0
Connolly, Hugh	Mohawk	1	1	4	0	0
Connolly, Patrick	Mohawk	2	0	3	0	0
Connor, Daniel	Caughnawaga	1	0	7	0	0

1790 FEDERAL CENSUS, MONTGOMERY COUNTY, NY

HOF	TOWN	M 16+	M -16	F	OFP	S
Connor, Owen	Caughnawaga	3	0	2	?	?
Conradt, John	Canajoharie	2	2	5	0	?
Conradt, Joseph	Canajoharie	3	3	2	0	0
Conradt, Michael	Canajoharie	1	2	5	0	0
Conradt, Nicholas	Canajoharie	1	0	3	0	0
Conradt, Peter	Mohawk	1	2	2	0	0
Consolly, James	Chemung	1	1	2	0	0
Conwell, William	Harpersfield	1	3	5	0	?
Conyngham, James	Harpersfield	1	1	3	0	0
Conyngham, John	Canajoharie	1	2	3	0	?
Conyngham, John	Chemung	1	0	1	0	0
Conyngham, John	German Flatts	2	0	5	0	?
Conyngham, William	German Flatts	2	0	5	0	?
Conyngham, William, Jr.	Palatine	2	0	1	0	0
Cook, Abner	Canajoharie	2	0	1	0	0
Cook, Comfort	Otsego	2	3	1	0	0
Cook, Elijah	Canajoharie	3	2	3	0	?
Cook, John	Otsego	1	3	2	0	?
Cook, Joseph	Caughnawaga	1	0	1	0	0
Cook, Joshua	Canajoharie	2	0	3	0	?
Cook, Pepperly	Canajoharie	4	0	1	0	0
Cook, Samuel	Whites	2	1	4	0	0
Cook, Samuel	Whites	1	1	2	0	?
Cook, Selah	Whites	1	2	1	0	?
Cook, Severenus	Canajoharie	1	2	3	0	0
Cook, Trueworthy	Whites	1	2	2	0	?
Cook, William	Whites	1	4	1	0	?
Cook, William E.	Canajoharie	1	1	2	0	?
Cook, William I.	Canajoharie	3	1	2	0	?
Coolage, Charles	Whites	1	0	0	0	0
Cooley, Peter	Mohawk	4	1	4	0	?
Coombs, Peter	Canajoharie	1	4	1	0	0
Coone, William	Caughnawaga	1	2	3	0	0
Cooper, William	Otsego	2	0	0	1	?
Cooperax, Joseph	Mohawk	1	2	2	0	0
Copeland, Samuel	Caughnawaga	2	0	2	0	0
Copeley, William	Mohawk	1	1	2	0	?
Coppernall, Adam	Palatine	1	2	3	0	?
Coppernall, John	Palatine	2	1	3	0	?
Coppernall, Nicholas	Palatine	1	3	4	1	?
Coppernall, Richard	Palatine	1	2	4	0	?
Coppernall, William	Palatine	2	0	6	0	?
Copps, David	Canajoharie	1	1	2	0	?
Coral, George	German Flatts	1	4	2	0	?
Corban, Samuel	Harpersfield	4	1	3	0	0

1790 FEDERAL CENSUS, MONTGOMERY COUNTY, NY

HOF	TOWN	M 16+	M -16	F	OFP	S
Cordin, Joseph	Chemung	1	0	4	0	0
Corkins, Daniel	Mohawk	1	0	0	0	0
Corkins, Nathaniel	Otsego	4	4	3	0	?
Corneau, Daniel	Canajoharie	2	2	3	0	?
Corneau, Wissel	Canajoharie	1	0	1	0	?
Cornell, David	Mohawk	1	1	3	0	?
Cornish, Stephen	Herkimer	1	1	2	0	?
Cornwell, [?]	Caughnawaga	1	2	2	0	?
Cornwell, Banjamin	Mohawk	1	1	?	?	?
Cornwell, Daniel	Chemung	2	2	4	0	0
Cornwell, John	Otsego	1	2	3	0	?
Corteauld, George	Caughnawaga	1	1	?	?	?
Cortright, John	Chemung	1	0	1	0	?
Coss, George	Mohawk	1	0	0	0	0
Costle, John	Canajoharie	2	0	2	0	0
Cotrin, Nathaniel	Mohawk	1	0	1	0	0
Cotton, Rowland	Canajoharie	3	1	2	0	?
Cotton, William	Chemung	1	1	1	0	0
Coughman, Anthony	Palatine	1	0	2	0	?
Councilman, Philip	Chemung	1	4	3	0	0
Countryman, Adam	Canajoharie	2	1	4	0	0
Countryman, Conradt	Canajoharie	1	2	3	0	0
Countryman, Conradt	Canajoharie	1	0	1	0	0
Countryman, George	Canajoharie	3	1	6	0	0
Countryman, John	Canajoharie	3	1	5	0	0
Countryman, John A.	Canajoharie	1	2	2	0	0
Countryman, John M.	Canajoharie	2	1	3	0	?
Countryman, Marelus	Canajoharie	1	0	3	0	0
Countryman, Markus	Canajoharie	2	0	3	0	0
Court, John	Canajoharie	1	2	2	0	0
Covell, Micajah	Mohawk	1	1	5	0	0
Covenhoven, Abraham	Mohawk	1	1	5	0	?
Covenhoven, Albert	Mohawk	2	3	5	0	0
Covenhoven, Isaac	Mohawk	1	4	3	0	0
Covenhoven, Jacob	Caughnawaga	1	4	2	0	0
Covenhoven, John	Mohawk	1	2	4	0	0
Covenhoven, Roluff	Mohawk	1	1	1	0	1
Cox, Fassert	Herkimer	1	3	6	0	0
Cox, William	Mohawk	3	1	5	0	0
Cradle, Thomas	Canajoharie	1	2	3	0	?
Craft, Benjamin	Caughnawaga	1	1	3	0	?
Craft, Griffin	Canajoharie	5	2	5	0	?
Craft, Joseph	Canajoharie	1	0	0	0	0
Craft, Joseph	Chemung	1	0	0	0	0
Crafts, Samuel	Canajoharie	2	3	3	0	?

1790 FEDERAL CENSUS, MONTGOMERY COUNTY, NY

HOF	TOWN	M 16+	M -16	F	OFP	S
Cramer, Christian	Palatine	1	1	2	0	0
Cramer, Jacob	Canajoharie	1	0	2	0	0
Cramer, John	Canajoharie	2	1	5	0	?
Cramer, John	Canajoharie	1	2	2	0	0
Cramer, Yost	Canajoharie	1	1	2	0	0
Crandle, John	Caughnawaga	1	4	3	0	0
Crandle, John	Whites	1	4	3	0	0
Crane, Enos	Otsego	2	0	2	0	0
Crane, Josiah	Palatine	2	1	2	0	5
Crane, Josiah, Jr.	Palatine	1	1	3	0	?
Crank, Cornelius	Canajoharie	1	2	2	0	0
Crank, Henry	Canajoharie	2	1	2	0	?
Crank, Henry, Jr.	Canajoharie	1	0	1	0	?
Crank, Teunis	Canajoharie	1	3	2	0	0
Cranker, Cutlip	Mohawk	1	5	3	0	0
Crants, Marks	Herkimer	1	1	2	0	0
Crantsinger, George	Canajoharie	2	2	3	0	?
Craturs, Balsur	German Flatts	1	3	3	0	0
Creighton, Daniel	Caughnawaga	2	0	0	0	0
Cress, Christian	Chemung	3	0	3	0	0
Cress, Jacob	Chemung	1	2	1	0	?
Cresser, Simeon	Caughnawaga	1	2	3	0	0
Cressy, Naughton	Palatine	1	0	2	0	?
Cring, John	Palatine	3	1	5	0	0
Cringe, John Ludwick	Palatine	2	1	4	0	0
Crisler, Adam	Caughnawaga	1	1	3	0	0
Crissler, John	Canajoharie	1	2	2	?	?
Cristman, Frederick	German Flatts	1	1	5	0	0
Cristman, Jacob	Canajoharie	1	1	5	0	?
Cristman, John	Canajoharie	1	2	3	0	0
Cristman, John	Herkimer	2	2	3	0	?
Cristman, John	Palatine	2	3	3	0	?
Cristman, Nicholas	Palatine	1	4	2	0	0
Croker, Eziekel	Chemung	1	0	0	0	0
Crommell, Philip	Caughnawaga	2	4	6	0	2
Cromwell, Philip	Mohawk	1	2	4	0	2
Cromwell, Stephanus	Mohawk	1	1	4	0	5
Cromwell, Thomas	Mohawk	1	2	0	0	0
Cronk, [?]	Caughnawaga	1	2	2	0	0
Cronkite, Abraham	Caughnawaga	1	3	2	0	0
Crosby, Lott	Otsego	3	1	3	0	0
Cross, Ebenezer	Canajoharie	3	2	4	0	0
Cross, Jacobus	Palatine	1	2	1	0	0
Cross, Jedediah	Canajoharie	1	2	3	0	?
Cross, Jirus	Canajoharie	1	0	1	0	0

1790 FEDERAL CENSUS, MONTGOMERY COUNTY, NY

HOF	TOWN	M 16+	M -16	F	OFP	S
Cross, Lemuel	Canajoharie	1	4	4	0	0
Crossett, Benjamin	Caughnawaga	1	3	5	0	0
Crossett, John	Caughnawaga	1	5	3	0	?
Crossitt, Benjamin	Caughnawaga	1	0	0	?	?
Crotsenbarack, Conradt	Caughnawaga	9	0	3	0	0
Crouse, John	Palatine	1	2	6	0	0
Crouse, Leonard	Palatine	1	2	4	0	0
Crowell, Isaiah	Canajoharie	1	1	1	0	0
Crowfoot, Nehemiah	Chemung	1	3	2	0	?
Crowley, Jeremiah	Caughnawaga	1	2	?	?	?
Crownheart, George	German Flatts	2	2	3	0	?
Cruger, Daniel	Chemung	1	0	0	0	0
Crush, Francis	Mohawk	2	1	5	0	0
Culley, David	Otsego	1	2	1	0	0
Culley, John	Otsego	3	2	5	0	0
Culley, Matthew	Otsego	3	2	4	0	0
Culley, Thomas	Otsego	2	2	1	0	0
Culman, Henry	Palatine	1	1	5	0	?
Culver, Aaron	Chemung	1	0	1	0	0
Culver, Jabez	Chemung	2	2	1	0	0
Culver, Jabez, Jr.	Chemung	1	1	2	0	0
Culver, Joseph	Otsego	1	1	2	0	?
Culver, Nathan	Chemung	1	1	1	0	0
Cummings, David	Harpersfield	1	1	2	0	0
Cummings, Ephraim	Mohawk	1	1	1	0	0
Cummings, Thomas	Canajoharie	1	2	3	0	?
Cummings, William	Mohawk	2	1	8	0	0
Cummings, William	Otsego	1	3	1	0	0
Cunning, Matthew	Canajoharie	1	0	2	0	0
Curby, Reuben	Harpersfield	1	0	3	0	?
Cure, William	Harpersfield	2	2	3	0	0
Curry, Jon	Caughnawaga	1	3	5	0	0
Curtis, Ebenezer	Palatine	1	1	4	0	0
Curtis, Edmond	Canajoharie	1	1	4	0	0
Curtis, Frederick	Canajoharie	2	0	0	0	0
Curtis, Jessee	Whites	1	2	1	0	?
Curtis, Nathaniel	Palatine	1	4	2	0	0
Curtis, Samuel	Otsego	1	0	2	0	0
Curtner, Peter	Canajoharie	2	0	1	0	?
Cushow, Jacob	Caughnawaga	1	2	3	0	0
Cussant, James	Mohawk	1	3	5	0	0
Cusselman, William	Caughnawaga	1	1	2	0	0
Custleman, John	Caughnawaga	1	1	1	0	0
Cutler, Joseph	Whites	6	0	4	0	?
Cuyler, Cornelius	Caughnawaga	2	1	1	?	?

1790 FEDERAL CENSUS, MONTGOMERY COUNTY, NY

HOF	TOWN	M 16+	M -16	F	OFP	S
Dabush, Henry	Canajoharie	1	2	4	0	0
Dagan, John	Caughnawaga	1	1	3	0	0
Dagen, Stephen	Canajoharie	1	2	1	0	0
Daily, Nathan	Otsego	1	1	3	?	?
Damewood, Richard	Whites	2	2	5	0	0
Damon, Elbe	Harpersfield	1	0	0	0	?
Damon, Jonathan	Harpersfield	1	1	3	0	?
Danna, James	Canajoharie	3	2	3	0	0
Dannalson, Altimont	Otsego	2	3	4	0	0
Danute, Anna	German Flatts	1	3	5	0	?
Darling, Moses	Canajoharie	1	0	2	0	0
Darnal, Ruth	Otsego	1	0	2	?	?
Darrah, George	Canajoharie	1	2	1	0	0
Darrah, John	Canajoharie	1	0	1	0	0
Davenport, Humphry	Canajoharie	1	2	2	0	1
Davidson, John	German Flatts	1	1	2	0	?
Davie, Adam	Otsego	1	7	3	0	?
Davis, [?]	Otsego	2	0	0	0	0
Davis, Elijah	Whites	2	0	0	0	0
Davis, Garrit	Caughnawaga	1	0	1	0	0
Davis, Isaac	Caughnawaga	2	3	3	0	0
Davis, Jacob	Palatine	1	5	1	0	?
Davis, John	Canajoharie	1	1	3	0	?
Davis, John	Mohawk	1	1	1	0	?
Davis, Joseph	Caughnawaga	1	0	3	0	0
Davis, Joshua	Whites	1	0	0	0	0
Davis, Nehemiah	Harpersfield	2	0	2	0	0
Davis, Thomas	Canajoharie	3	1	2	0	0
Davis, Thomas	Caughnawaga	1	2	4	0	0
Davison, John, Jr.	Otsego	1	0	1	0	0
Davison, John, Sr.	Otsego	1	1	1	0	?
Davison, Nathan	Otsego	4	0	3	0	0
Davison, Patrick	Canajoharie	3	2	4	0	?
Davy, Mary	Canajoharie	0	1	5	0	?
Daway, Peter	Herkimer	1	1	5	0	0
Day, Beventer	Chemung	3	1	3	0	0
Day, Ithamy	German Flatts	3	1	6	0	0
Day, Joseph	German Flatts	1	0	1	0	0
Dayton, Nathaniel	Mohawk	1	3	4	0	0
De Grove, Emanuel	Caughnawaga	2	3	5	0	0
De Grove, Frederick	Caughnawaga	3	4	4	0	0
De Grove, Jeremiah	Caughnawaga	2	3	5	0	1
De Gulliar, Joseph	Caughnawaga	3	1	1	0	0
De Riemer, Samuel	Mohawk	3	0	1	0	1
De Villers, Lewis	Otsego	4	0	2	0	0

1790 FEDERAL CENSUS, MONTGOMERY COUNTY, NY

HOF	TOWN	M 16+	M -16	F	OFP	S
De Vine, John	Mohawk	1	0	1	0	0
De Witt, Daniel	Chemung	1	1	3	0	?
De Witt, Joseph	Chemung	1	3	4	0	?
Deacon, Joseph	Herkimer	1	1	1	0	0
Dean, James	Whites	4	1	2	?	?
Dean, Jonathan	Whites	4	0	6	0	0
Dean, Nathan	Harpersfield	2	2	3	0	0
Dean, Parley	Chemung	2	0	1	?	?
Dean, William	Whites	2	1	4	0	0
Debell, Zachariah	Mohawk	1	4	6	0	0
Debow, Jacob	Canajoharie	1	1	2	0	?
Dederick, Diabald	German Flatts	2	3	5	0	0
Dederick, John	Mohawk	1	1	1	0	0
Deer, John	Chemung	1	0	3	0	0
Deline, Isaac	Mohawk	1	2	2	0	0
Deline, William	Mohawk	1	3	1	0	0
Delyne, Benjamin	Caughnawaga	3	1	4	0	?
Demmar, Solomon, Sr.	Mohawk	3	0	4	0	0
Demmins, Joseph	Mohawk	1	4	2	0	0
Demont, Joseph	Whites	1	2	3	0	0
Demster, James	Mohawk	1	0	1	0	?
Demude, Dederick	Herkimer	1	0	3	0	0
Demude, John	Herkimer	1	1	2	0	?
Demude, Marks	Herkimer	3	2	3	0	0
Denic, Joseph	Harpersfield	1	2	2	0	?
Denic, William	Harpersfield	1	0	1	0	?
Denman, Zebulan	Mohawk	1	2	8	0	0
Dennend, Humphry	Canajoharie	2	0	3	0	0
Denney, Barant	Caughnawaga	2	0	0	0	0
Denney, Nicholas	Caughnawaga	1	1	2	0	0
Dennison, John	Caughnawaga	3	0	3	0	0
Denny, Jacob	Caughnawaga	2	2	2	0	0
Densmore, John	Mohawk	1	0	0	0	0
Denston, John	Harpersfield	1	1	3	0	0
Desbrow, Henry	Mohawk	1	2	3	0	0
Desler, Jacob	Palatine	3	4	6	0	0
Devendorff, Isaac	Herkimer	1	0	2	0	0
Devendorff, Jacob	Canajoharie	2	1	3	0	0
Devendorff, Jacob, Jr.	Canajoharie	1	1	1	0	0
Devendorff, Jacob, Sr.	Canajoharie	3	3	6	?	?
Devendorff, John	Canajoharie	4	1	6	0	4
Devendorff, John	Herkimer	1	0	3	0	0
Devendorff, John Jacob	Canajoharie	5	2	7	0	0
Devendorff, Rosena	Canajoharie	4	1	6	0	0
Dewell, Samuel	Chemung	1	3	1	0	0

1790 FEDERAL CENSUS, MONTGOMERY COUNTY, NY

HOF	TOWN	M 16+	M -16	F	OFP	S
Dewey, Elias	Whites	1	1	1	0	?
Dick, Henry	Canajoharie	1	1	2	0	0
Dickens, John	Otsego	1	1	1	?	?
Dickinson, Jessee	Harpersfield	13	2	3	0	0
Diel, Hendrick	Canajoharie	3	0	3	1	?
Dienstman, Teunis	Canajoharie	1	0	1	0	?
Dill, Henry	Mohawk	1	2	3	0	0
Dillance, Benjamin	Mohawk	1	3	4	0	0
Dinghman, Harmanus	Caughnawaga	2	1	1	0	0
Dingman, Jacob	Mohawk	2	2	5	0	0
Dingman, Peter	Caughnawaga	3	3	3	0	0
Dingman, Samuel	Mohawk	1	2	2	0	0
Divendorph, Jacob	Mohawk	2	1	4	0	7
Dixon, Robert	Canajoharie	1	2	2	0	?
Dixon, Thomas	Harpersfield	1	2	2	0	0
Dixon, William	Canajoharie	2	0	1	0	0
Dixon, William, Sr.	Canajoharie	3	0	2	0	?
Dobbin, William	Chemung	1	3	6	0	0
Dochety, Charles	Herkimer	1	1	7	0	?
Dockstader, Christian	Canajoharie	3	1	3	0	?
Dockstader, Elizabeth	Caughnawaga	2	0	3	0	2
Dockstader, Frederick F.	Caughnawaga	3	0	2	0	0
Dockstader, Frederick H.	Caughnawaga	2	2	5	0	1
Dockstader, George	Caughnawaga	2	2	3	0	1
Dockstader, George	Herkimer	4	6	6	0	?
Dockstader, Jacob	Caughnawaga	1	2	1	0	0
Dockstader, John	Caughnawaga	1	2	3	0	?
Dockstader, John	Palatine	1	4	1	?	?
Dockstader, Leonard	Caughnawaga	2	2	7	0	0
Dockstader, Markus	Caughnawaga	2	0	2	0	4
Dockstader, Nicholas	Canajoharie	2	1	5	0	0
Dockstader, Nicholas	Caughnawaga	2	2	5	0	0
Dockstader, Nicholas H.	Mohawk	1	2	3	0	?
Dodds, Bartholemew	Mohawk	4	2	8	0	?
Dodge, Daniel	Caughnawaga	1	3	5	0	?
Dodge, Elisha	Canajoharie	1	1	5	0	1
Dodge, Elisha	Canajoharie	1	2	3	0	0
Dodge, Francis	Canajoharie	1	2	2	0	?
Dodge, John	Harpersfield	6	1	3	0	0
Dodge, Josiah	Canajoharie	1	0	1	0	0
Dodge, Nathaniel	Herkimer	1	1	4	0	0
Dodge, Noah	Canajoharie	1	0	0	0	?
Dodge, Richard	Caughnawaga	1	1	2	0	?
Dodge, Richard	Caughnawaga	1	0	1	0	?
Dodge, Richard	Mohawk	1	0	0	0	?

1790 FEDERAL CENSUS, MONTGOMERY COUNTY, NY

HOF	TOWN	M 16+	M -16	F	OFP	S
Dodge, Rufus	Canajoharie	1	1	4	0	0
Dodge, Rufus	Mohawk	3	1	3	0	?
Dolby, Jonathan	Otsego	1	2	1	0	0
Dolittle, Abraham	Chemung	2	3	2	0	0
Dolittle, George	Whites	4	1	4	0	0
Dolittle, Joel	Canajoharie	2	2	1	0	0
Dolittle, John	Chemung	2	4	2	0	0
Dolittle, Nathan	Mohawk	2	5	2	0	0
Dolittle, Samuel	Otsego	2	2	4	0	0
Dolson, John	Chemung	1	4	4	0	?
Dolson, Tuenis	Chemung	1	3	3	0	?
Donn, Cornelius	Caughnawaga	1	1	2	0	4
Donnaghe, Henry	Otsego	1	2	2	0	0
Doren, John	Caughnawaga	3	0	6	0	0
Dorne, Alexander	Mohawk	1	3	7	0	0
Doty, John	Mohawk	1	0	6	0	0
Doty, Reuben	Mohawk	2	4	4	0	0
Doty, Samuel	Mohawk	1	2	3	0	0
Douglass, James	Harpersfield	4	1	3	0	0
Douglass, John	Palatine	1	0	2	0	0
Downs, Timothy	Caughnawaga	2	2	2	0	0
Drake, Elijah	Chemung	1	0	1	0	?
Drake, Joseph	Chemung	1	2	2	0	?
Draper, Amos	Chemung	3	0	2	0	0
Drisselman, Christian	German Flatts	1	0	0	0	?
Drummond, Moses	Mohawk	1	1	1	0	0
Drury, Josiah	Whites	1	0	0	0	?
Ducky, John	Palatine	2	2	3	0	0
Duffin, Edward	Mohawk	1	0	2	0	0
Dum, Melchor	Herkimer	2	1	7	0	?
Dumont, Peter	Canajoharie	1	2	3	0	?
Dunburger, Frederick	Herkimer	1	0	3	0	0
Duncan, John, Jr.	Palatine	1	1	2	0	?
Dunham, Ebenezer	Caughnawaga	1	2	3	0	0
Dunham, Elijah	Caughnawaga	1	3	1	0	?
Dunham, Obediah	Canajoharie	2	0	1	0	0
Dunkel, Peter	Canajoharie	5	3	0	0	0
Dunlap, Andrew	Canajoharie	1	0	1	0	0
Dunlap, Andrew	Chemung	1	0	2	0	?
Dunlap, John	Canajoharie	2	4	3	0	0
Dunlap, John	Canajoharie	1	0	3	0	?
Dunlap, Samuel	Canajoharie	2	1	3	0	?
Dunlap, William	Canajoharie	2	2	4	0	?
Dunn, [?]	Caughnawaga	2	2	1	0	0
Dunn, James	Caughnawaga	2	2	3	0	0

1790 FEDERAL CENSUS, MONTGOMERY COUNTY, NY

HOF	TOWN	M 16+	M -16	F	OFP	S
Dunn, Joseph	Whites	1	3	4	0	0
Dunn, Richard	Caughnawaga	1	3	5	0	0
Durell, Dorothy	German Flatts	0	0	3	0	0
Durham, Jacob	Chemung	2	2	3	0	0
Dursey, James	Harpersfield	1	1	2	0	0
Dust, Matthias	Mohawk	1	1	4	0	?
Dutcher, John	Canajoharie	3	2	3	0	0
Dutcher, Low	Canajoharie	2	2	6	0	0
Dye, John	Caughnawaga	1	5	5	?	?
Dye, John	Mohawk	1	1	1	0	0
Dygert, Peter W.	Herkimer	1	2	2	0	0
Dygert, William, Jr.	Herkimer	1	3	3	0	0
Dylleback, Baltus	Palatine	4	1	6	0	0
Dylleback, Henry	Palatine	2	4	5	0	2
Dylleback, John	Palatine	4	2	5	0	0
Dylleback, Richard	Palatine	1	2	6	?	?
Dymuck, Timothy, Sr.	Otsego	5	2	4	0	0
Eadle, Honyost	Palatine	1	0	3	0	0
Eagan, Ann	Caughnawaga	0	0	3	0	?
Eagen, William	Caughnawaga	1	0	?	?	?
Eaget, Abel	Mohawk	1	0	0	0	?
Eaget, Stephen	Mohawk	1	2	3	0	?
Eaker, Adam	Caughnawaga	1	1	2	0	0
Eaker, George	Caughnawaga	1	1	4	0	0
Eaker, George	Palatine	1	1	5	1	3
Eaker, Henry	Caughnawaga	2	0	3	0	0
Eaker, Jacob	Palatine	1	4	5	0	0
Eaker, John	Caughnawaga	1	0	5	0	0
Eaker, Mary Elizabeth	Palatine	2	1	1	0	6
Earhart, John	Canajoharie	1	0	1	0	?
Earl, Joseph	Mohawk	1	2	2	0	0
Earl, Reuben	Caughnawaga	2	1	3	0	0
Earness, Charles	Chemung	2	3	4	0	?
Earnest, Peter	Mohawk	1	1	?	?	?
Earnst, John	Canajoharie	1	0	0	0	0
Eastman, Peter	Whites	3	0	1	0	0
Eastwood, Daniel	Otsego	2	2	4	0	0
Eastwood, John	Otsego	1	1	4	0	0
Eastwood, Nathaniel	Canajoharie	1	1	5	0	0
Eaton, Benjamin	Mohawk	2	0	3	0	0
Eaton, Calvin	Mohawk	1	1	1	0	0
Eaton, Ebenezer	German Flatts	1	0	0	0	0
Eaton, Elisha	Herkimer	1	0	1	0	?
Eaton, Ezra	Chemung	1	0	2	0	?

1790 FEDERAL CENSUS, MONTGOMERY COUNTY, NY

HOF	TOWN	M 16+	M -16	F	OFP	S
Eaton, Jacob	Mohawk	1	2	2	0	0
Eaton, John	Herkimer	4	2	2	0	?
Ebball, Lewis	Otsego	1	0	0	0	?
Ecgenbrodt, John	Palatine	2	0	1	0	0
Ecgenbrodt, Peter	Palatine	1	1	2	0	0
Ecker, Adam	Canajoharie	1	0	2	0	?
Ecker, Conradt	Canajoharie	1	1	3	0	0
Ecker, John	Canajoharie	3	2	4	0	?
Ecker, Nicholas	Palatine	2	1	4	1	0
Eckler, Hendrick	Canajoharie	1	0	2	?	?
Eckler, Henry	Canajoharie	1	0	2	?	?
Eckler, John	Canajoharie	1	6	2	0	?
Eckler, Leonard	Canajoharie	1	1	2	?	?
Eckler, Peter	Canajoharie	1	3	3	0	?
Ecler, Christopher	German Flatts	1	3	3	0	0
Eddy, William	Otsego	4	1	4	0	0
Edich, Jacob	Herkimer	1	4	2	0	?
Edick, George	Herkimer	1	1	3	0	?
Edminster, Joseph	Chemung	3	2	6	0	0
Edminster, William	Chemung	1	1	2	0	0
Edmunds, Patience	Harpersfield	0	3	3	0	0
Edwards, Talmage	Caughnawaga	1	2	1	0	?
Egbert, Abraham	Mohawk	1	0	3	0	0
Eggeston, Game	Canajoharie	1	3	3	0	0
Eggliston, Jessee	Mohawk	1	1	1	0	0
Eights, Christian	Canajoharie	4	0	3	0	?
Eisenman see Izeman						
Eldrickon, Artenus	Mohawk	1	1	1	0	0
Ellenwood, Hananiah	Whites	3	2	4	0	?
Ellis, Ebenezer	Chemung	1	3	2	0	0
Ellis, Ebenezer, Jr.	Chemung	1	1	3	0	0
Ellis, Eliazer	Mohawk	2	0	1	0	0
Ellis, Henry	Canajoharie	1	1	2	0	?
Ellis, John	Caughnawaga	1	0	3	0	?
Ellis, John	Mohawk	1	0	1	0	?
Ellis, Nancy	Canajoharie	0	1	2	0	0
Ellison, John	Chemung	2	1	3	0	0
Ellison, William	Otsego	3	0	?	?	?
Ellot, Andrew	Mohawk	2	1	3	0	0
Ellot, Andrew, Jr.	Mohawk	1	5	3	0	0
Ellot, George	Mohawk	1	2	3	0	0
Ellot, Gideon	Mohawk	1	0	3	0	0
Ellot, Jacob	Mohawk	1	3	3	0	0
Ellot, John	Mohawk	1	0	1	0	0
Ellot, Jonathan	Canajoharie	1	0	2	0	0

1790 FEDERAL CENSUS, MONTGOMERY COUNTY, NY

HOF	TOWN	M 16+	M -16	F	OFP	S
Ellwood, Benjamin	Canajoharie	2	3	4	0	0
Elmore, Isaac	Mohawk	3	5	3	0	0
Elnor, Ira	Mohawk	1	0	0	0	0
Elridge, David	Mohawk	1	1	?	?	?
Elwell, Ebenezer	German Flatts	1	0	0	0	?
Elwell, Samuel	German Flatts	1	0	3	0	?
Elwood, Isaac	Canajoharie	2	4	5	0	0
Elwood, Peter	Canajoharie	1	1	3	0	0
Elwood, Richard	Canajoharie	1	2	6	0	0
Empatty, Henry	Canajoharie	1	4	2	0	0
Empie, John	Herkimer	2	1	3	0	0
Empier, [?]	Palatine	3	1	6	0	0
Empier, John	Palatine	2	0	5	0	0
Empier, John, Jr.	Palatine	1	4	3	0	1
Enders, Jacob	Mohawk	2	3	4	0	5
England, Benjamin	Caughnawaga	1	1	3	0	0
Engle, Conradt	Canajoharie	4	1	4	0	?
Engush, John	Palatine	1	1	2	0	0
Eno, John	Whites	1	0	2	0	?
Enos, Abijah	Caughnawaga	2	5	3	0	0
Enos, Joab	Chemung	4	1	3	?	?
Ensign, Samuel	Whites	4	2	2	0	0
Erenbrodt, [?]	Palatine	2	1	3	0	0
Esnart, John	Mohawk	1	3	1	0	0
Etick, Christian	German Flatts	2	4	3	0	0
Etick, Frederick	German Flatts	2	0	3	0	0
Etick, George Jacob	German Flatts	1	3	2	0	0
Etick, Michael	German Flatts	3	0	4	0	0
Evans, Samuel	Caughnawaga	1	0	3	0	?
Evens, Joseph	Mohawk	1	1	3	0	?
Everett, John	Caughnawaga	1	1	2	0	0
Everitt, Ebenezer	Harpersfield	1	1	3	0	0
Everitt, John	GermanFlatts	2	0	0	0	0
Everson, Adam	Caughnawaga	1	0	3	0	0
Eversor, John	Caughnawaga	2	0	1	0	1
Eyre, Elizabeth	Herkimer	1	0	3	0	0
Eyre, Frederick	Herkimer	1	0	1	0	0
Fagan, William	Caughnawaga	1	0	1	0	?
Fairchild, David	Chenango	1	3	2	0	?
Fairchild, Ebenezer	Harpersfield	1	1	4	0	0
Fairchild, Matthew	Caughnawaga	1	3	4	0	?
Falckers, John	Canajoharie	2	0	4	0	?
Falkenburgh, Matthew	Mohawk	1	1	4	0	0
Fancher, Rufus	Harpersfield	1	1	1	0	?

1790 FEDERAL CENSUS, MONTGOMERY COUNTY, NY

HOF	TOWN	M 16+	M -16	F	OFP	S
Fancher, Thomas	Whites	3	3	4	0	?
Fancher, William	Chemung	2	0	1	0	0
Fangworth, Josiah	Harpersfield	1	1	1	0	?
Fanning, William	Whites	3	0	0	?	?
Fanshor, Eaton	German Flatts	2	2	1	0	0
Farewell, Joseph	Whites	1	1	5	0	0
Farmer, [?]	Herkimer	1	0	2	0	0
Farrington, Thomas	Harpersfield	4	0	4	0	?
Fash, Christian	Canajoharie	1	2	2	0	?
Faulkener, Caleb	Canajoharie	1	2	2	0	0
Faulkener, William	Canajoharie	1	4	4	0	0
Fealing, Andrew	Canajoharie	2	1	6	0	0
Fealing, Hendrick I.	Canajoharie	1	3	5	0	1
Fealing, Henry	Palatine	1	3	4	0	?
Fealing, Jacob	Palatine	4	0	3	0	?
Fealing, Jacob J.	Palatine	1	3	1	0	?
Fealing, John	Canajoharie	1	1	4	0	0
Fealing, Richard	Palatine	3	4	6	0	1
Feavel, John	Palatine	1	3	3	0	0
Fecter, Andrew	Canajoharie	3	0	6	0	0
Fecter, William	Herkimer	1	4	3	0	0
Fedderly, Eve	Herkimer	0	2	2	0	0
Fedderly, George	Canajoharie	3	0	4	?	?
Fedderly, John	Herkimer	1	0	5	0	0
Fedderly, Thomas	Herkimer	1	2	2	0	0
Fellows, Roswell	Whites	2	1	4	0	0
Felton, John	Canajoharie	3	2	4	0	?
Fenton, Nathaniel	Otsego	2	0	0	0	?
Fergo, Aaron	Canajoharie	1	1	4	0	0
Ferguson, Daniel	Mohawk	2	1	3	0	?
Ferguson, Enos	Mohawk	2	0	2	0	?
Ferguson, Gilbert	Mohawk	1	0	3	0	0
Ferguson, John	Canajoharie	1	3	2	0	?
Ferguson, Peter	Mohawk	1	0	3	0	0
Ferguson, Robert	Canajoharie	2	0	4	0	0
Ferguson, Samuel	Canajoharie	2	1	1	0	?
Ferguson, Samuel	Whites	1	1	1	0	?
Ferguson, Samuel, Sr.	Whites	2	0	0	0	?
Ferguson, William	Canajoharie	2	1	5	0	?
Ferguson, William	Mohawk	1	1	2	0	?
Ferguson, William	Otsego	3	0	0	0	0
Ferrel, [?]	Mohawk	2	4	4	0	0
Ferrers, Justice	Mohawk	1	2	1	0	0
Ferris, Caleb	Harpersfield	2	1	1	0	0
Ferris, Samuel	Harpersfield	1	0	4	0	0

1790 FEDERAL CENSUS, MONTGOMERY COUNTY, NY

HOF	TOWN	M 16+	M -16	F	OFP	S
Ferster, George	Canajoharie	4	2	5	0	0
Fiddle, Godfry	Canajoharie	1	2	4	0	0
Field, Nathan	Otsego	5	0	1	0	0
Finch, Benjamin	Mohawk	1	0	1	0	?
Finch, James	Caughnawaga	1	2	3	0	?
Finch, Jessee	Harpersfield	1	3	4	0	?
Finch, Simeon	Mohawk	1	3	1	0	0
Fine, Andrew	Mohawk	1	1	2	1	?
Fine, Francis	Mohawk	0	2	1	1	?
Finis, Michael	Canajoharie	1	3	4	0	0
Fink, Andrew	Palatine	1	3	2	0	4
Fink, Christian	Palatine	2	6	3	?	?
Fink, Honyost	Palatine	1	0	1	0	0
Fink, John	German Flatts	1	1	4	0	1
Fink, William	Palatine	2	3	4	0	3
Finsler, John	Herkimer	1	3	2	0	0
Fishback, Jacob	Caughnawaga	1	5	2	0	0
Fisher, Amos	Canajoharie	1	2	4	0	0
Fisher, Frederick	Caughnawaga	3	5	6	1	2
Fisher, Jacob	Canajoharie	1	2	4	0	0
Fisher, Jeremiah	Caughnawaga	1	0	1	0	0
Fisher, John	Otsego	3	2	3	0	0
Fisher, Peter	Caughnawga	1	0	2	0	0
Fisk, Abraham	Whites	3	0	0	0	0
Fisk, John	Canajoharie	2	2	5	0	?
Fisk, Jonathan	German Flatts	3	1	1	0	0
Fisk, Samuel	Otsego	1	3	2	0	0
Fitch, Jonathan	Chemung	2	2	5	0	?
Fitch, Lemore	Harpersfield	1	2	2	0	0
Fitch, Lendal	Harpersfield	1	1	1	0	0
Fitch, Stephen	Otsego	1	2	3	0	0
Fitcher, Henrick	Caughnawaga	1	1	2	0	0
Fitts, Moses	Caughnawaga	1	1	3	0	0
Flagg, Peter	German Flatts	1	2	3	0	0
Flanaghan, John	Caughnawaga	1	0	0	0	0
Flander, John	Palatine	1	0	4	0	0
Flander, Teunis	Palatine	1	4	3	0	0
Fletcher, Conradt	Canajoharie	1	3	2	0	0
Flin, James	Caughnawaga	2	1	3	0	0
Flint, Adam	Canajoharie	2	2	5	0	?
Flint, Alexander	Canajoharie	2	3	7	0	0
Flint, Cornelius	Canajoharie	3	4	2	0	0
Flint, John	Canajoharie	3	1	6	0	0
Flint, Robert	Canajoharie	1	4	2	0	1
Flint, Robert, Jr.	Canajoharie	1	2	2	0	0

1790 FEDERAL CENSUS, MONTGOMERY COUNTY, NY

HOF	TOWN	M 16+	M -16	F	OFP	S
Flint, Zacheus	Otsego	1	2	1	0	?
Flip, [?]lkert	Caughnawaga	4	3	5	0	0
Foarncrook, Christopher	Mohawk	1	1	6	0	?
Foekus, Yohan Hendrick	Palatine	1	0	4	?	?
Follet, James	Harpersfield	2	0	0	0	?
Folts, Conradt	Herkimer	1	3	3	0	0
Folts, Honyost	Hekimer	2	2	4	0	0
Folts, Peter	Herkimer	1	2	3	0	0
Foltz, George	Herkimer	2	2	3	0	?
Foltz, Melchor	Herkimer	1	3	2	0	?
Fonclair, John Vonde	Caughnawaga	4	1	2	0	0
Fonda, Adam	Caughnawaga	2	1	2	0	0
Fonda, Jacob G.	Canajoharie	1	1	3	0	0
Fonda, Jellis	Palatine	3	0	3	0	?
Fonda, John	Caughnawaga	1	4	2	0	?
Foot, Brunson	Whites	1	3	2	?	?
Foot, Ira	Whites	1	2	2	0	0
Foot, Isaac	Chemung	2	1	2	0	0
Foot, Luther	Whites	1	2	1	0	0
Foot, Moses	Whites	2	1	2	0	0
Foot, Timothy	Caughnawaga	2	2	4	0	0
Forbes, Peter	Caughnawaga	1	2	2	0	0
Forbus, Hannah	Canajoharie	1	1	3	0	0
Forbus, Jacob	Canajoharie	3	0	3	0	0
Forbus, Jacob, Jr.	Canajoharie	1	1	2	0	0
Forbus, James	Palatine	1	3	2	0	?
Forbus, Mabus	Palatine	3	2	5	0	0
Forbus, Nicholas	Canajoharie	1	2	4	0	0
Ford, Benoni	Herkimer	1	3	4	0	0
Ford, Freelove	Otsego	2	2	4	0	0
Ford, John	Canajoharie	1	0	5	0	0
Ford, Joseph	Otsego	1	0	1	0	0
Ford, Nathaniel	Canajoharie	2	3	2	0	0
Forsyth, William	Otsego	1	1	2	0	0
Fort, Abijah	Palatine	1	4	1	0	0
Fort, Andrew	Palatine	1	4	5	0	0
Fortner, Thomas	Harpersfield	1	0	2	0	0
Fortune, Enoch	Whites	0	0	0	3	0
Fosberry, Abraham	Caughnawaga	1	4	1	0	2
Fosberry, Abraham	Caughnawaga	2	0	3	0	1
Fosberry, Barent	Caughnawaga	3	0	2	0	1
Fosberry, Henry	Caughnawaga	1	1	1	0	0
Fosberry, Peter	Caughnawaga	1	0	2	0	0
Fosgate, Ezekel	Mohawk	3	1	2	?	?
Foster, John	Canajoharie	2	0	0	0	?

HOF	TOWN	M 16+	M -16	F	OFP	S
Foster, Nathan	Canajoharie	1	1	3	0	0
Foster, William	Canajoharie	2	3	2	0	?
Fouks, Peter	Palatine	2	0	1	0	?
Fowler, Reuben	Whites	3	0	1	0	0
Fox, Christopher	Palatine	4	4	?	?	?
Fox, Christopher W.	Palatine	2	3	1	0	?
Fox, Daniel	Palatine	2	2	?	?	?
Fox, Frederick	German Flatts	2	3	5	0	2
Fox, George	Palatine	3	0	3	0	2
Fox, Honyost	Palatine	1	1	3	0	0
Fox, John	German Flatts	2	2	5	0	?
Fox, Peter	Canajoharie	4	3	4	0	?
Fox, Peter	Herkimer	1	0	3	0	0
Fox, Philip	Canajoharie	3	2	3	0	?
Fox, Philip	Palatine	1	1	2	0	0
Fox, William	Canajoharie	1	1	2	0	1
Fox, William	Caughnawaga	1	1	3	0	?
Fox, William	Palatine	2	2	5	0	?
Fox, William W.	Palatine	2	2	3	0	?
Francisberry, William	Caughnwaga	2	2	3	0	0
Frank, Adam	Mohawk	2	2	6	0	0
Frank, Albert	Mohawk	1	2	4	0	0
Frank, Andrew	Mohawk	1	2	3	0	0
Frank, Frederick	German Flatts	1	2	3	0	1
Frank, Henry	German Flatts	3	0	7	0	0
Frank, John	German Flatts	3	1	8	0	0
Frank, Lawrence	German Flatts	2	4	3	0	0
Frank, Michael	Canajoharie	1	2	1	0	0
Frank, Sussanah	Palatine	0	0	2	0	0
Frank, Timothy	German Flatts	1	0	3	0	0
Franklin, Moses	Canajoharie	1	0	1	0	0
Franks, John S.	German Flatts	3	1	7	0	0
Frantz, Bastian	Canajoharie	3	1	2	0	0
Frantz, Christopher	Canajoharie	1	1	2	0	0
Frarey, Elisha	Chenango	1	0	0	0	?
Frasier, James	Caughnawaga	2	0	3	0	0
Fratz, Henry	Canajoharie	3	1	4	0	0
Frazier, John	Canajoharie	1	1	1	0	?
Frear, Casper	Otsego	2	6	1	0	?
Frear, Peter	Palatine	2	1	1	0	0
Frederick, Francis	Mohawk	1	3	3	0	0
Frederick, Jacob	Caughnawaga	2	3	4	0	0
Frederick, Peter	Mohawk	1	3	5	0	0
Frederick, Philip	Mohawk	1	0	1	0	2
Freeman, Edward	Canajoharie	2	0	3	0	0

1790 FEDERAL CENSUS, MONTGOMERY COUNTY, NY

HOF	TOWN	M 16+	M -16	F	OFP	S
Freeman, Isaac	Canajoharie	1	1	2	0	0
Freeman, Moses	Canajoharie	1	1	2	0	0
Freeman, Robert	Harpersfield	1	3	2	0	0
Freeman, Samuel	Caughnawaga	1	2	5	0	0
Freer, John S.	Caughnawaga	4	0	3	0	0
Frehugh, Francis	Palatine	1	1	1	?	?
Freleg, Clement	Canajoharie	2	0	3	0	0
Freleg, Jacob	Canajoharie	1	3	4	0	0
Frelich, Felter	Mohawk	1	3	2	0	0
French, Abner	Mohawk	1	0	3	0	0
French, Ashel	Mohawk	1	0	1	0	?
French, David, Jr.	Otsego	2	1	2	0	0
French, David, Sr.	Otsego	2	1	2	0	0
French, Ebenezer	Mohawk	2	0	2	0	?
French, Jasper	Whites	1	0	0	0	0
French, John	Harpersfield	1	1	1	0	0
French, John	Otsego	1	3	3	0	?
French, Joseph	Mohawk	1	1	1	0	?
French, Samuel	Mohawk	1	3	2	0	0
French, William	Harpersfield	1	2	3	0	0
Fretcher, Henry	Canajoharie	1	2	3	0	?
Freveau, Francis	German Flatts	1	1	0	0	?
Frey, Francis	Caughnawaga	4	1	4	0	0
Frey, Hendrick	Canajoharie	4	1	3	0	?
Frey, Jacob	Palatine	2	2	4	?	?
Frey, John	Palatine	2	1	2	0	4
Frey, John	Palatine	1	1	2	?	?
Frey, Rhodes	Otsego	1	4	2	0	0
Friday, Michael	Canajoharie	1	1	2	0	0
Frisby, Gideon	Harpersfield	1	2	3	0	?
Frisby, Grickson	Canajoharie	2	0	1	0	0
Frisby, Samuel	Canajoharie	1	1	2	0	0
Fritz, Conradt C.	German Flatts	1	3	1	0	0
Fritz, Ernest	Canajoharie	2	3	5	0	0
Frowgood, Rienholt	Canajoharie	1	1	1	0	0
Frymier, John	Canajoharie	2	1	2	0	0
Frymier, Michael	Canajoharie	1	2	2	0	0
Fulison, Abraham	Mohawk	1	3	4	0	0
Fullam, Elisha	Otsego	3	2	6	0	0
Fuller, Abraham	Chemung	1	1	4	0	0
Fuller, Benjamin	Harpersfield	1	3	4	0	?
Fuller, Isaac	Chemung	2	1	3	0	0
Fuller, Michael	Otsego	3	2	5	0	?
Fulmer, Conradt	Herkimer	1	3	1	0	0
Fulmer, Thomas	Herkimer	3	3	5	0	0

1790 FEDERAL CENSUS, MONTGOMERY COUNTY, NY

HOF	TOWN	M 16+	M -16	F	OFP	S
Fulmer, William	German Flatts	1	1	5	0	0
Fultz, Conrad I.	German Flatts	2	4	3	0	0
Fultz, Jacob, Sr.	German Flatts	1	0	2	0	0
Furgeson, John	Mohawk	1	1	1	0	0
Furguson, Jeremiah	Mohawk	1	4	4	0	0
Furman, Russel	German Flatts	1	6	1	0	0
Fyck, Adam	Caughnawaga	4	3	6	0	?
Fyckle, John	Palatine	1	0	2	0	0
Fys, George	Palatine	5	1	5	0	0
Gallop, Thomas	Chemung	1	2	3	0	0
Gallord, Levy	Harpersfield	1	0	3	0	0
Gallord, Levy, Jr.	Harpersfield	1	1	3	0	0
Galloway, James	Chemung	2	1	2	0	0
Gansey, Ebenezer	Chemung	2	1	2	0	?
Gardeneer, Abraham	Canajoharie	1	2	6	0	0
Gardeneer, Adam	Caughnawaga	1	1	1	?	?
Gardeneer, Jacob	Mohawk	3	1	1	0	1
Gardeneer, John	Mohawk	1	2	0	0	0
Gardeneer, John	Mohawk	1	0	2	0	0
Gardeneer, Martin	Mohawk	1	1	2	0	1
Gardeneer, Matthew	Canajoharie	4	3	4	0	?
Gardeneer, Matthew	Mohawk	1	1	2	0	?
Gardeneer, Nicholas	Mohawk	1	3	2	0	4
Gardeneer, Nicholas A.	Mohawk	2	1	2	0	0
Gardeneer, Samuel	Mohawk	3	0	3	0	0
Gardenhouse, Stephen	Chemung	1	0	0	0	0
Gardner, [?] (Schoolmaster)	Canajoharie	1	1	3	0	0
Gardner, Andrew	Chemung	1	1	2	0	0
Gardner, Bennah	Otsego	2	2	3	0	?
Gardner, Caleb	Otsego	2	0	0	0	0
Gardner, Calib	Chemung	4	0	3	0	?
Gardner, James	Otsego	1	3	3	?	?
Gardner, Nicholas	Caughnawaga	2	1	3	?	?
Gardner, Paul	Otsego	1	0	0	0	0
Gardner, Robert	Canajoharie	1	1	1	0	0
Gardner, Solomon	Chemung	1	0	1	?	?
Gardner, Stephen	Chemung	2	2	2	0	0
Gardner, Westcoat	Herkimer	2	4	3	0	?
Garlock, Adam	Palatine	3	1	5	0	?
Garlock, George P.	Canajoharie	2	7	4	0	0
Garlock, George W.	Canajoharie	1	3	5	?	?
Garlock, Jacob	Canajoharie	1	1	3	0	?
Garlock, William	Canajoharie	3	3	3	0	0
Garnsy, David	Chemung	1	1	6	0	0

1790 FEDERAL CENSUS, MONTGOMERY COUNTY, NY

HOF	TOWN	M 16+	M -16	F	OFP	S
Garris, Joseph	Chemung	1	1	4	0	0
Garrit, Robert	Otsego	2	3	1	0	?
Gasper, Peter	Canajoharie	2	1	2	0	0
Gaston, David	Caughnawaga	1	2	3	0	0
Gates, Nathaniel	Chemung	1	3	3	0	?
Gault, William	Canajoharie	6	0	4	0	?
Gaylard, Eleazor	Caughnawaga	1	2	2	0	?
Gaylord, Jedediah	Harpersfield	1	0	1	0	0
Gaylord, Joel	Harpersfield	1	0	2	0	?
Gaylord, Josiah	Canajoharie	1	1	3	0	?
Gaylord, Jotham	Whites	4	0	1	0	0
Geadeau, Lewis	Mohawk	1	3	3	0	?
Gellaspie, Thomas	German Flatts	1	0	3	0	0
Gennee, Francis	Caughnawaga	1	3	2	0	?
Gennee, Isaac	Caughnawaga	1	0	4	0	0
Gerry, Moses	Chemung	1	2	2	0	0
Getman, Conradt	German Flatts	1	1	2	0	0
Getman, Frederick	Herkimer	1	2	3	0	0
Getman, Frederick	Palatine	2	1	5	0	2
Getman, John	German Flatts	1	1	2	0	0
Getman, Peter	German Flatts	1	1	2	0	0
Getman, Peter	Palatine	1	0	3	0	0
Gibbs, Calep	Harpersfield	3	0	2	0	0
Gibbs, Simeon	Canajoharie	1	1	4	0	0
Gibbs, Zenas	Whites	1	0	2	0	1
Gibson, Abel	Harpersfield	2	4	3	0	0
Gibson, John	Mohawk	1	1	3	0	0
Gibson, William	Mohawk	1	1	6	0	?
Gilbert, Abijah	Otsego	4	1	1	0	1
Gilbert, Allen	Canajoharie	1	0	5	0	0
Gilbert, Benjamin	Canajoharie	2	3	2	0	?
Gilbert, Butler	Canajoharie	1	5	2	0	?
Gilbert, Elisha	Chemung	1	1	6	0	0
Gilbert, Giles	Canajoharie	1	4	2	0	?
Gilbert, Jessee	Harpersfield	1	1	3	0	0
Gilbert, Nathaniel	Whites	2	5	4	0	0
Gildeusleaf, (Widdow)	Chemung	0	0	1	0	0
Gillet, Sepheus	Palatine	2	1	1	0	0
Gillet, Stephen	Caughnawaga	1	2	5	0	0
Gillett, Charles	Mohawk	2	1	4	0	0
Gillett, Eli	German Flatts	1	1	1	0	0
Gillett, John	Mohawk	1	1	4	0	?
Gillett, Timothy	Whites	2	3	3	0	0
Gilson, John	Harpersfield	2	2	5	0	0
Gilson, Samuel	Harpersfield	1	2	3	0	0

1790 FEDERAL CENSUS, MONTGOMERY COUNTY, NY

HOF	TOWN	M 16+	M -16	F	OFP	S
Gipson, William	Chenango	1	0	0	0	?
Girtman, George	Palatine	1	3	3	0	0
Girtman, John	Palatine	4	3	3	0	0
Girtman, John	Palatine	1	6	4	0	0
Girtman, Thomas	Palatine	1	3	3	0	1
Glasgow, Hugh	Herkimer	2	0	4	0	?
Glazier, Christopher	Canajoharie	1	0	2	0	0
Gleason, Joseph	Whites	3	0	2	0	?
Gleason, Solomon	Whites	3	0	1	0	?
Godfrey, Annie	Caughnawaga	2	1	1	0	0
Goff, Calvert	Herkimer	1	2	3	0	0
Goff, David	Otsego	2	2	0	0	0
Goff, Nathan	Otsego	4	0	1	0	0
Goff, Rosel	Chemung	1	0	3	0	?
Goodale, Elijah	Mohawk	1	0	3	0	0
Goodale, Simeon	Canajoharie	1	0	3	0	?
Goodbroadt, William	Herkimer	1	1	2	0	0
Goodcourage, John	Mohawk	1	1	3	0	0
Goodrich, Elijah	Harpersfield	1	2	1	0	0
Goodrich, Jarid	Harpersfield	2	1	4	0	0
Goodrich, Michael	Harpersfield	1	3	4	0	0
Goodrich, Michael, Jr.	Harpersfield	1	3	3	0	0
Goodrich, Rosel	Whites	1	1	3	0	0
Goodrich, Wait	Harpersfield	2	2	2	0	0
Goodrich, Zenas	Caughnawaga	3	1	3	0	0
Goodrich, Zenas	Mohawk	1	1	1	0	0
Goodspeed, Nathaniel	Chemung	1	6	2	0	0
Goodwell, Frederick	Chemung	1	1	1	0	0
Gordon, Joseph	Mohawk	1	3	4	0	?
Gordon, Mary	German Flatts	0	1	?	?	?
Gordon, Timothy	Mohawk	1	3	4	0	0
Gordon, William	Harpersfield	1	3	3	0	?
Gould, Philip	Canajoharie	1	1	4	0	?
Gould, Simeon	Camajoharie	1	3	1	0	0
Gower, John	Mohawk	2	1	4	0	?
Graft, Jacob	Caughnawaga	2	2	3	0	0
Graft, Philip	Caughnawaga	1	0	0	0	0
Graham, George	Caughnawaga	1	4	2	0	0
Graham, James	Chemung	2	2	4	0	0
Graham, John	Harpersfield	2	0	1	0	0
Graham, John, Jr.	Harpersfield	1	1	3	0	0
Graham, William	Caughnawaga	1	0	0	0	?
Graneger, John	Canajoharie	1	1	5	0	0
Grant, John	Caughnawaga	2	0	1	0	?
Grant, Lewis	Harpersfield	1	4	1	0	0

1790 FEDERAL CENSUS, MONTGOMERY COUNTY, NY

HOF	TOWN	M 16+	M -16	F	OFP	S
Grant, William	Caughnawaga	2	1	1	?	?
Grass, George	Canajoharie	1	0	1	0	0
Grauss, George	Canajoharie	2	3	3	0	0
Graves, Belah	Harpersfield	1	3	2	0	0
Graves, Jacob	Whites	3	1	2	0	0
Graves, John	Canajoharie	1	2	3	0	0
Graves, Josiah	Canajoharie	1	1	2	0	0
Graves, Nathaniel	Whites	1	1	2	0	?
Graves, Recompence	Otsego	1	1	4	0	0
Gray, [?]	Palatine	1	2	3	0	0
Gray, Adam	Palatine	4	1	4	0	0
Gray, James	Harpersfield	1	2	2	0	0
Gray, John	Palatine	2	1	2	0	0
Gray, Nathaniel	Mohawk	4	0	4	0	?
Gray, Samuel	Palatine	1	6	2	0	0
Green, Aden	Chemung	1	1	1	0	0
Green, Eben	Chemung	3	1	2	0	0
Green, Ebenezer	Chemung	1	0	7	0	?
Green, Isaac	Canajoharie	3	0	0	0	0
Green, Jabez	Harpersfield	1	1	2	0	?
Green, James	Caughnawaga	1	2	2	0	0
Green, James	Caughnawaga	1	2	4	0	0
Green, Jedediah	German Flatts	1	4	3	0	?
Green, Jessee	Canajoharie	1	4	3	0	0
Green, Joseph	Chemung	1	1	2	0	?
Green, Joseph	Mohawk	1	2	3	0	?
Green, Josiah	Chemung	1	3	3	0	?
Green, Nathan	Canajoharie	1	1	2	0	0
Green, Solomon	Harpersfield	3	0	0	0	?
Green, Timothy	Caughnawaga	2	0	0	0	?
Green, William	Chemung	1	1	3	0	?
Greenman, Abner	Mohawk	1	4	4	0	0
Greenwalt, Jacob	Caughnawaga	1	0	2	0	0
Greenwood, Oliver	Canajoharie	2	0	0	0	0
Gregg, James	German Flatts	1	0	0	0	0
Greggery, Ezra	Harpersfield	1	3	3	0	0
Grenwell, George	Caughnawaga	1	2	1	?	?
Greswold, Jano	Canajoharie	2	1	2	0	0
Greves, Silvenus	Harpersfield	1	1	3	0	?
Gridley, Abraham	Whites	2	2	2	0	0
Gridley, Jobe	Whites	2	2	3	0	0
Gridley, Theodorus	Whites	1	2	2	0	0
Griffen, Kirkland	Whites	3	2	2	0	0
Griffin, Benjamin	Canajoharie	6	2	5	0	?
Griffin, Jonas	Canajoharie	1	3	4	0	0

1790 FEDERAL CENSUS, MONTGOMERY COUNTY, NY

HOF	TOWN	M 16+	M -16	F	OFP	S
Griffin, Joseph	Canajoharie	2	3	3	0	0
Griffin, Nathaniel	Whites	2	4	3	0	?
Griffin, Nijah	Mohawk	1	1	1	0	0
Griffin, Samuel	Canajoharie	1	3	4	0	?
Griffin, William	Mohawk	4	3	3	0	0
Griffith, Daniel	Canajoharie	2	2	4	0	?
Griggs, John	Chemung	1	4	3	0	0
Grim, Adam	German Flatts	1	0	1	0	0
Grim, Henry	German Flatts	1	3	1	0	0
Grim, Jacob	German Flatts	1	3	4	0	0
Grinman, Hallet	Mohawk	1	2	1	0	0
Grinman, Joseph	Caughnawaga	1	3	1	0	?
Grinman, Richard	Caughnawaga	1	0	1	0	?
Grippen, Silas	Canajoharie	1	6	1	0	0
Grisman, Jacob	Palatine	1	5	3	0	?
Griswell, Aaron	Caughnawaga	2	3	4	0	?
Griswell, Elijah	Chemung	1	0	1	0	0
Griswell, Francis	Caughnawaga	3	3	4	0	0
Griswell, Isaac Colton	Caughnawaga	1	0	1	0	?
Griswell, Johial	Caughnawaga	1	0	1	0	?
Griswold, David	Chemung	2	2	2	0	0
Griswold, Edward	Herkimer	1	1	3	0	0
Griswold, Elijah	Chemung	3	0	1	0	0
Griswold, Francis	Herkimer	1	0	0	0	0
Griswold, Gidion	Chemung	1	3	1	0	0
Groat, Lewis	Caughnawaga	2	0	2	0	1
Groat, Simon	Caughnawaga	1	3	4	0	0
Groesbeck, Garrit	Canajoharie	1	2	2	0	0
Groff, John	Mohawk	1	2	2	0	?
Grog, Godfrey	Canajoharie	1	3	3	0	0
Gross, Henry	Caughnawaga	1	2	2	0	1
Gross, Lawrence	Canajoharie	1	3	3	0	0
Grouts, Henry	German Flatts	1	2	3	0	0
Grove, Christian	Palatine	4	0	3	1	0
Grover, Eberiah	Otsego	3	3	3	0	0
Grover, Isaiah	Otsego	1	0	0	0	0
Grover, John, Sr.	Caughnawaga	4	1	2	0	?
Grover, Joseph	Canajoharie	2	2	3	0	?
Grover, Peter	Caughnawaga	4	2	5	0	?
Groves, [?]etire	Whites	2	2	4	0	0
Grow, Jacob	Mohawk	1	0	0	0	0
Grummon, Ezekiel	Otsego	2	1	2	0	0
Guide, William	Canajoharie	1	1	0	0	0
Guile, Abraham	Mohawk	1	0	0	0	?
Guile, Elijah	Whites	1	0	0	0	0

1790 FEDERAL CENSUS, MONTGOMERY COUNTY, NY

HOF	TOWN	M 16+	M -16	F	OFP	S
Guile, Israel	Otsego	2	1	1	0	?
Guile, John	Canajoharie	4	1	4	0	?
Guiles, Henry	Canajoharie	1	1	2	0	0
Gurney, Bezelial	Whites	2	0	3	0	?
Guthrie, James	Chemung	1	3	1	0	0
Guthrie, William	Chemung	2	0	4	0	0
Guthry, Joseph	Harpersfield	1	0	3	0	0
Haan, Johannes	Palatine	1	0	2	0	0
Hackney, William	Canajoharie	2	1	2	0	0
Hadcock, John	Herkimer	3	5	3	0	0
Hadley, Joseph	Harpersfield	1	2	3	0	?
Hadlock, James	Harpersfield	2	3	4	0	?
Hadly, Ebenezer	Canajoharie	1	5	1	0	0
Hagadorn, Bartholemew	Canajoharie	1	1	2	0	0
Hagadorn, Henderick	Canajoharie	4	0	3	0	0
Hagerty, John	Chemung	1	1	1	0	0
Hagle, John	Caughnawaga	1	2	1	0	0
Hagle, Michael	Caughnawaga	2	0	4	0	1
Haight, Silvenius	Caughnawaga	1	2	4	0	0
Hails, William	German Flatts	4	1	2	0	?
Hakey, George	Canajoharie	1	4	4	0	0
Hakey, John	Canajoharie	1	0	3	0	0
Hakey, John, Jr.	Canajoharie	1	0	2	0	0
Hakey, Michael	Canajoharie	2	2	6	0	0
Halbert, Azariah	Canajoharie	1	1	4	0	0
Hale, Eliphilet	Canajoharie	1	2	2	0	?
Hale, Minerva	Whites	1	0	1	0	0
Hale, Theodore	Mohawk	1	0	5	0	0
Hale, Thomas	Whites	1	0	4	0	?
Halenbeck, John	Caughnawaga	2	0	2	0	0
Hall, Barnabas	Whites	1	1	2	0	?
Hall, Benjamin	Caughnawaga	1	2	6	0	0
Hall, Elihu	Herkimer	2	1	8	0	0
Hall, Jacob	Mohawk	1	0	3	0	0
Hall, Jeremiah	Mohawk	1	0	2	0	0
Hall, John	Mohawk	2	4	2	0	0
Hall, Jonathan	Whites	3	4	3	0	?
Hall, Timothy	Caughnawaga	1	1	6	0	0
Hall, William	Mohawk	3	3	5	0	0
Hallete, Joseph	Caughnawaga	1	0	0	?	?
Halley, Abner	Harpersfield	5	1	7	0	0
Hallister, [?]	Mohawk	1	0	2	0	1
Halsey, Edward	Otsego	1	3	8	0	0
Halsted, Amos	Mohawk	1	0	3	0	?

HOF	TOWN	M 16+	M -16	F	OFP	S
Hamel, Robert	Canajoharie	2	1	7	0	?
Hamilton, Ezra	Caughnawaga	1	0	2	0	?
Hamilton, George	Caughnawaga	4	0	2	0	0
Haminway, Isaac	Whites	4	1	3	0	0
Hamlen, Giles	Palatine	1	1	3	0	?
Hamlin, Abraham	Mohawk	1	1	2	0	?
Hamlin, Barnabas	Otsego	1	0	1	0	0
Hamlin, David	Otsego	1	2	3	0	0
Hamlin, Ephraim	Mohawk	1	1	1	0	0
Hammel, William	Canajoharie	5	0	3	0	0
Hammelton, Eden	Harpersfield	1	4	1	0	0
Hammond, Benjamin	Whites	1	1	6	0	0
Hammond, David	Chemung	2	0	4	0	0
Hammond, Jonathan	Chemung	1	2	2	0	0
Hammond, Lebeus	Chemung	1	1	3	0	0
Hammond, Matthew	Chemung	1	0	1	0	0
Hand, Mark	Mohawk	1	2	2	0	0
Handford, Evershom	Harpersfield	1	0	0	0	0
Handmore, David	Canajoharie	1	2	2	0	0
Handy, John	Chemung	2	2	4	0	?
Handy, Thomas	Chemung	1	1	3	0	?
Hannah, Alexander	Mohawk	1	1	5	0	?
Hannah, Alexander, Sr.	Mohawk	1	0	0	0	?
Hannah, James	Mohawk	1	3	5	0	?
Hannah, William	Otsego	2	1	4	0	?
Hansor, John	Caughnawaga	1	1	4	0	0
Hansor, Nicholas	Caughnawaga	1	3	3	0	0
Hansor, Peter	Caughnawaga	3	1	3	0	?
Hansor, Richard	Caughnawaga	1	4	5	0	0
Hansor, Victor	Caughnawaga	1	2	4	1	0
Hardenburg, Cornelius	Mohawk	2	1	4	0	2
Hardenburgh, Jacob	Caughnawaga	1	2	3	0	?
Hardever, Abraham	Mohawk	1	0	1	0	0
Harding, Archibald	Chemung	1	0	1	0	0
Harding, Oliver	Chemung	1	4	1	0	0
Harding, Thomas	Chemung	2	2	5	0	0
Hardy, Charles	Canajoharie	1	2	2	0	0
Hardy, William	Canajoharie	1	3	2	0	0
Hare, John	Caughnawaga	1	0	1	0	0
Haring, Cornelius	Caughnawaga	3	4	2	0	1
Haring, Henry	Palatine	3	2	4	?	?
Harman, John	Caughnawaga	3	1	4	0	?
Harman, Sarah	Caughnawaga	1	4	3	0	0
Harp, George	Caughnawaga	1	0	2	0	0
Harper, Alexander	Harpersfield	3	3	5	0	0

1790 FEDERAL CENSUS, MONTGOMERY COUNTY, NY

HOF	TOWN	M 16+	M -16	F	OFP	S
Harper, Archibald	Harpersfield	1	1	1	0	0
Harper, George	Chemung	1	1	2	0	?
Harper, John	Harpersfield	4	0	6	0	0
Harper, Joseph	Harpersfield	1	1	3	0	0
Harper, William	Harpersfield	1	0	2	0	0
Harper, William	Mohawk	1	1	3	0	0
Harris, Daniel	Harpersfield	3	1	2	0	0
Harris, George	Mohawk	1	3	2	0	?
Harris, James	Whites	1	3	2	0	0
Harris, Joseph	Whites	1	2	2	0	0
Harris, Robert	Harpersfield	1	0	1	0	0
Harris, William	Palatine	1	0	2	0	0
Harrison, Elisha	Whites	1	1	1	0	0
Harrison, Harmanus	Caughnawaga	1	1	2	0	0
Harrison, Joseph	Canajoharie	2	0	1	0	?
Harrison, Joseph	Canajoharie	1	1	1	0	0
Harrison, Peter	Caughnawaga	2	2	1	0	0
Harrison, Thomas	Caughnawaga	1	2	3	0	0
Harrow, David	Harpersfield	2	0	2	0	0
Harrow, David, Jr.	Harpersfield	1	0	2	0	0
Hart, Conradt	Palatine	3	0	4	0	0
Hart, Daniel	Palatine	1	0	3	0	0
Hart, John	Palatine	1	3	5	0	0
Hartman, John	Canajoharie	1	1	3	0	0
Hartshorne, [?]	Caughnawaga	1	0	2	0	0
Hartshorne, Jacob	Caughnawaga	1	1	3	0	0
Hartshorne, Richard, Sr.	Caughnawaga	1	0	2	0	0
Hartwick, Aaron	Palatine	1	0	1	?	?
Harvey, John	Chemung	2	5	3	0	?
Haskins, William	Canajoharie	1	3	5	0	?
Hasleton, Solomon	Harpersfield	1	0	2	0	?
Hatch, John	Otsego	1	2	3	0	?
Hatch, Peter	German Flatts	2	2	3	0	?
Hatch, William	Caughnawaga	1	3	2	0	?
Hatfield, Abner	Chemung	1	2	3	0	0
Hatmaker, Adam	Canajoharie	1	0	2	0	0
Haun, Jacob	Canajoharie	1	1	2	0	0
Havens, Nathaniel	Otsego	1	1	5	0	?
Hawkins, (Widdow)	Whites	0	3	4	0	?
Hawkins, Christopher P.	Herkimer	1	0	3	0	0
Hawkins, David	Whites	2	1	1	0	?
Hawkins, Elijah	Otsego	2	2	4	0	0
Hawks, Daniel	German Flatts	4	2	5	0	0
Hawley, Rice	Whites	1	1	2	0	?
Hayden, Jonathan	Whites	1	0	2	0	0

1790 FEDERAL CENSUS, MONTGOMERY COUNTY, NY

HOF	TOWN	M 16+	M -16	F	OFP	S
Haynes, Henry	Canajoharie	1	2	4	0	1
Haynes, Jacob	Canajoharie	1	3	3	0	1
Haynes, Jacob, Jr.	Canajoharie	1	4	2	0	0
Haynes, Jessee	Mohawk	2	0	1	0	?
Haynes, John	Caughnawaga	2	0	1	0	?
Haynes, Solomon	Mohawk	2	1	8	0	0
Haynes, William	Canajoharie	2	2	5	0	0
Hays, Philip	Otsego	1	3	4	0	0
Hazard, James	Mohawk	1	0	5	0	0
Hazard, Joshua	Mohawk	1	1	3	0	0
Hazard, Raymond	Mohawk	1	1	3	0	?
Haze, Henry	Palatine	1	5	4	0	0
Haze, John	Palatine	2	4	6	0	0
Headcock, Daniel	Palatine	1	1	6	0	?
Headsell, Samuel	Chemung	1	0	2	0	0
Heart, James	Mohawk	1	0	0	0	?
Hearter, Lawrence P.	German Flatts	1	2	5	0	?
Heartman, Adam	Herkimer	1	5	2	0	0
Hebner, Andrew	Canajoharie	2	2	1	0	0
Hebner, Honess	Canajoharie	1	3	1	0	0
Hecock, Noah	Caughnawaga	1	2	2	0	0
Hedrington, Isaac	Herkimer	1	0	0	0	0
Hellebolt, Teunis	Palatine	1	2	3	0	0
Hellebrant, Jacob	Caughnawaga	2	1	3	0	0
Hellebrant, John	Caughnawaga	1	1	3	0	0
Hellegas, Conradt	Palatine	2	2	5	0	?
Hellegas, Peter	Palatine	1	2	2	0	?
Hellenburgh, Cornelius	Palatine	1	2	4	0	0
Hellmuch, John	Palatine	1	1	5	0	0
Helmer, Adam	German Flatts	2	1	5	0	?
Helmer, Frederick A.	Herkimer	3	1	2	0	0
Helmer, Frederick F.	Herkimer	2	1	3	0	0
Helmer, George	German Flatts	3	2	5	?	?
Helmer, Henry	Herkimer	1	4	4	0	0
Helmer, Honyost	Palatine	1	0	2	0	?
Helmer, John	Herkimer	1	1	3	0	0
Helmer, John F.	Herkimer	1	0	0	0	0
Helmer, John G.	Palatine	1	1	3	0	?
Helmer, John P.	Palatine	1	3	3	0	0
Helmer, Leonard	Palatine	1	3	4	0	0
Helmer, Philip	Caughnawaga	3	1	2	0	?
Helmer, Philip	Palatine	2	4	4	0	0
Helmer, Philip F.	Herkimer	3	3	6	0	0
Helmer, Philip L.	Palatine	1	2	4	0	0
Henderson, Cornelius	Herkimer	1	2	2	0	0

1790 FEDERAL CENSUS, MONTGOMERY COUNTY, NY

HOF	TOWN	M 16+	M -16	F	OFP	S
Henderson, Daniel	Herkimer	3	6	3	?	?
Hendrick, Cornelius	Canajoharie	1	0	1	0	0
Hendrickson, John	Mohawk	1	0	2	0	?
Henex, Barnhart	Herkimer	1	0	1	0	0
Henman, David	Herkimer	2	0	1	0	0
Henry, David	Harpersfield	2	1	2	0	?
Henry, David	Harpersfield	2	1	2	0	0
Henry, John	Chemung	1	2	3	0	0
Henry, Malcom	Caughnawaga	1	0	2	0	0
Henry, Wells	Canajoharie	1	4	2	0	0
Henry, William	Harpersfield	1	2	1	0	?
Henry, William	Harpersfield	1	2	1	0	0
Herbert, Thomas	Mohawk	1	0	0	0	0
Herkemer, Abraham	Canajoharie	1	2	1	0	0
Herkemer, Alida	Canajoharie	2	1	6	0	9
Herkemer, Catherine	Canajoharie	0	0	3	0	0
Herkemer, George	German Flatts	1	0	4	0	0
Herkemer, Hendrick	Canajoharie	1	0	2	0	0
Herkemer, Nicholas	Canajoharie	1	0	1	1	0
Herkemer, Yost	German Flatts	2	0	6	0	0
Herman, John	Palatine	1	0	2	0	?
Herrick, [?]	Mohawk	1	0	0	0	0
Herrick, Amos	Mohawk	1	3	1	0	0
Herrick, Daniel	Mohawk	2	4	3	0	0
Herrick, Francis	Canajoharie	3	3	2	0	0
Herrick, John	Canajoharie	1	2	1	0	0
Herrick, John	Mohawk	1	2	2	0	0
Herrick, John, Jr.	Mohawk	1	1	5	0	0
Herrick, Samuel	Canajoharie	4	0	3	0	0
Herring, John	Mohawk	1	0	1	0	0
Herrington, Jonas	Chemung	2	2	4	0	0
Hess, Augustenus	German Flatts	1	5	4	0	0
Hess, Christian	German Flatts	1	2	3	0	?
Hess, Conradt	German Flatts	2	1	3	0	1
Hess, Daniel	Palatine	1	2	4	0	0
Hess, David	Palatine	2	3	4	0	0
Hess, Frederick	German Flatts	2	2	4	0	0
Hess, Frederick	Palatine	2	3	4	?	?
Hess, Henry	Canajoharie	2	1	3	0	?
Hess, John	German Flatts	1	5	4	0	0
Hess, John	Palatine	2	0	1	0	1
Hess, Yost	German Flatts	1	2	3	0	0
Hessler, Henry	Canajoharie	1	4	1	0	0
Heth, Josiah	Canajoharie	1	3	5	0	0
Heth, Thomas	Canajoharie	3	0	2	0	?

HOF	TOWN	M 16+	M -16	F	OFP	S
Hewes, Thomas	Caughnawaga	1	0	1	0	0
Hewett, Elisha	Caughnawaga	1	2	3	0	0
Hicks, John	Canajoharie	1	2	5	0	?
Higby, Joseph	Whites	4	2	3	0	?
Higby, Peter	Harpersfield	1	0	2	0	?
Higby, Roswell	Harpersfield	1	1	3	0	?
Higgins, Edward	Whites	3	5	4	0	?
Hight, Elihu	Palatine	2	4	4	0	0
Hill, Elijah	Herkimer	2	0	1	0	?
Hill, Henry	Mohawk	1	0	2	0	0
Hill, Henry	Mohawk	1	0	2	0	0
Hill, Jabez	Caughnawaga	1	1	2	0	0
Hill, Jonathan	Mohawk	1	1	2	0	0
Hill, Nicholas	Mohawk	1	0	3	0	0
Hill, Norman	Harpersfield	1	1	1	0	0
Hill, William	German Flatts	2	4	2	0	0
Hiller, John	Herkimer	1	2	6	0	0
Hills, George	Herkimer	2	1	4	0	0
Hills, Godfrey	Herkimer	1	3	3	0	?
Hills, John	Herkimer	1	2	3	0	?
Hills, John, Jr.	Herkimer	1	2	3	0	0
Hills, Lawrence	Herkimer	1	5	2	0	0
Hills, Nicholas	Herkimer	3	1	3	?	?
Hills, Samuel	Canajoharie	3	0	2	?	?
Hills, Samuel, Jr.	Canajoahrie	1	1	1	0	0
Hillsinger, Michael	Canajoharie	2	0	2	0	1
Hilman, John	Chemung	2	2	4	0	?
Hilsinger, Jacob	Canajoharie	1	0	1	0	?
Hilsinger, Peter	Canajoharie	1	0	2	0	?
Hilt, John	German Flatts	1	1	3	0	0
Hilton, David	Chemung	1	2	2	0	0
Hilton, John	Caughnawaga	1	1	3	?	?
Hindman, Benjamin	Herkimer	1	2	1	0	0
Hindman, Noah	Mohawk	1	2	4	0	?
Hining, George	Palatine	1	3	2	0	0
Hitchcock, David	Chemung	1	3	6	0	0
Hitchcock, Ebenezer	German Flatts	1	0	0	0	0
Hitchins, John	German Flatts	3	2	0	0	0
Hobbs, Alexander	Mohawk	3	1	5	0	0
Hobbs, Charles	Mohawk	2	3	3	0	0
Hodge, Daniel	Mohawk	1	7	2	0	0
Hodge, Hesekiah	Mohawk	1	0	2	0	0
Hodge, Isaac	Mohawk	2	1	8	0	0
Hodge, Isaac, Jr.	Mohawk	1	3	3	0	0
Hodge, Reuben	Mohawk	1	0	3	0	0

1790 FEDERAL CENSUS, MONTGOMERY COUNTY, NY

HOF	TOWN	M 16+	M -16	F	OFP	S
Hodgecase, David	Chemung	4	2	3	0	?
Hodgecase, Enock	Chemung	2	2	1	0	?
Hodges, Benjamin	Harpersfield	3	0	0	0	0
Hodswell, Joseph	Harpersfield	1	0	2	0	?
Hoege, Nathan	Mohawk	3	5	4	0	0
Hoege, Russel	Mohawk	1	0	4	0	?
Hoege, Samuel	Mohawk	2	2	3	0	0
Hoff, Richard, Jr.	Mohawk	1	2	2	0	0
Hoffman, Jacob	Canajoharie	2	0	1	0	0
Hofslader, Christian	Herkimer	1	4	2	0	0
Hogeboom, John	Mohawk	2	0	1	0	0
Hogeboom, Christian	Mohawk	2	1	4	0	0
Hoke, John	Canajoharie	1	1	3	0	0
Holbrook, David	Chemung	1	0	1	0	0
Holden, James	Canajoharie	1	5	4	0	0
Holden, John	Chemung	2	1	5	0	0
Holleday, Robert	Herkimer	1	1	3	0	0
Hollenbeck, John	Caughnawaga	1	1	2	0	0
Hollenbeck, Nathaniel	Canajoharie	1	0	1	0	0
Holley, Daniel	Otsego	2	1	2	0	?
Holliday, Francis	Canajoharie	1	0	2	0	0
Holliday, James	Mohawk	3	1	5	0	?
Hollinbeck, Matthias	Caughnawaga	2	2	4	0	0
Hollis, Daniel	Otsego	1	1	2	0	?
Hollis, Thomas	Harpersfield	1	1	4	0	0
Holmes, Asel	Chemung	1	2	0	0	0
Holmes, Benjamin	Mohawk	2	2	6	0	0
Holmes, John	Caughnawaga	1	2	5	0	?
Holmes, John	Chemung	1	1	1	0	0
Holmes, John	Harpersfield	2	1	3	0	?
Holmes, John	Mohawk	1	1	1	0	0
Holt, Daniel	Canajoharie	3	1	5	0	?
Holt, John	Canajoharie	1	2	4	0	0
Holt, Justice	Whites	3	0	1	0	0
Honk, Nicholas	Palatine	4	2	2	0	?
Honk, Tobias	Otsego	1	1	2	0	1
Hopkins, Abner	Otsego	3	0	2	0	0
Hopkins, Elias	Whites	2	3	1	0	0
Horduck, Andress	Palatine	1	?	?	?	?
Horduck, John	Palatine	1	2	3	?	?
Horn, [?]	Caughnawaga	1	0	3	0	0
Horn, Matthew	Mohawk	1	0	3	0	0
Hornell, George	Chemung	2	0	2	0	0
Horney, Derick	Canajoharie	4	0	2	0	0
Horton, Gilbert	Mohawk	1	0	1	0	?

1790 FEDERAL CENSUS, MONTGOMERY COUNTY, NY

HOF	TOWN	M 16+	M -16	F	OFP	S
Hose, Henry	Palatine	1	0	2	0	0
Hosen, Barnt	Mohawk	2	0	3	0	0
Hoskins, Micah	German Flatts	2	0	2	0	?
Hoskins, Timothy	Caughnawaga	2	3	2	0	?
Hosmer, Daniel	Caughnawaga	2	2	4	0	0
Hosmer, Eldad	Caughnawaga	1	1	5	0	0
Hosmer, Simeon	Caughnawaga	3	2	1	0	0
Hotchkiss, Joseph	Harpersfield	3	0	3	0	0
Hotchkiss, Roswell	Harpersfield	1	2	1	0	1
Hoten, Lemuel	Canajoahrie	2	2	3	0	0
Hough, George	Caughnawaga	1	1	4	0	0
Hough, Jerry	Caughnawaga	1	1	5	0	0
Hough, Jonathan	Mohawk	2	0	2	0	?
Hough, Zepheniah	Mohawk	1	2	3	0	?
Houghtalen, Hermanus	Harpersfield	1	1	2	?	?
Houghtalen, Jacob	Harpersfield	3	0	5	0	0
Houghtalen, John	Harpersfield	4	0	3	0	?
Houghtalen, Martin	Caughnawaga	3	2	3	0	0
Houghtalen, Matthias	Caughnawaga	3	0	3	0	0
Hougtalen, Abraham	Canajoharie	1	3	2	0	0
House and Pease	Whites	2	5	3	0	0
House, [Ha]nyost	Canajoharie	1	3	2	0	0
House, Adam	Palatine	2	1	6	0	0
House, Christian	Palatine	2	2	6	0	0
House, Conradt	Canajoharie	1	1	3	0	0
House, Conradt	German Flatts	1	3	2	0	?
House, Cornelius	Caughnawaga	1	1	5	0	?
House, Elias	Palatine	2	1	4	0	0
House, George	Canajoharie	1	3	2	0	?
House, George	Canajoharie	3	1	2	0	0
House, Henry	Canajoharie	1	0	3	0	0
House, John	Canajoharie	2	5	2	0	0
House, John	Chemung	1	0	3	0	0
House, Joseph	Canajoharie	2	1	6	0	?
House, Nicholas	Canajoharie	1	2	2	0	0
House, Peter	Canajoharie	1	1	2	0	0
House, Peter, Jr.	Canajoharie	2	1	2	0	0
Houseman, George	German Flatts	1	1	2	0	0
Houver, Jacob	Canajoharie	2	2	2	0	?
Hover, Jacob	Herkimer	1	2	1	0	?
Hovey, Benjamin	Otsego	1	2	2	0	?
Hovey, Jacob	Mohawk	1	0	1	0	0
Hovey, Moses	Otsego	2	3	3	0	?
Hovey, Solomon	Whites	3	2	3	0	0
How, Charles	Mohawk	2	2	2	0	?

1790 FEDERAL CENSUS, MONTGOMERY COUNTY, NY

HOF	TOWN	M 16+	M -16	F	OFP	S
How, Elijah	Canajoharie	2	1	2	0	0
How, Timothy	Canajoharie	1	1	3	0	0
How, Timothy	Chemung	2	2	3	0	0
Howard, John	Harpersfield	1	0	2	0	0
Howard, John	Otsego	2	0	?	?	?
Howard, Nathan	Chemung	1	3	7	0	?
Howard, Stephen	Whites	2	1	2	0	0
Hoyer, George F.	German Flatts	2	2	4	0	0
Hoyer, William	Canajoharie	1	1	3	0	0
Hoyt, Benjamin	Caughnawaga	5	0	1	0	?
Hoyt, Ebenezer	Harpersfield	1	4	4	0	0
Hoyt, Eliphalet	Mohawk	1	1	2	0	0
Hoyt, Elnathan	Mohawk	1	0	1	0	?
Hoyt, Jarid	Harpersfield	1	2	4	0	0
Hoyt, Nathan	Mohawk	1	0	1	0	0
Hoyt, Samuel	Mohawk	1	3	4	0	0
Hoyt, Silvenius	Mohawk	1	0	0	0	0
Hoyt, Thadeus	Harpersfield	2	1	1	0	0
Hubbard, Balter	Whites	1	0	1	0	0
Hubbard, Samuel	Whites	1	0	1	0	0
Hubbart, John	Harpersfield	1	2	2	0	0
Hubbell, Abijah	Otsego	1	2	2	0	0
Hubbell, Jabez	Otsego	4	1	2	0	0
Hubbs, [?]	Mohawk	2	1	1	0	0
Hubbs, Charles	Mohawk	1	4	5	0	0
Huckeboom, Peter	Caughnawaga	1	1	3	0	0
Hudson, Barnet	Canajoharie	1	2	3	0	0
Hudson, Daniel	Chemung	3	1	2	0	0
Hudson, Ephraim	Canajoharie	3	3	7	0	?
Huff, Benjamin	Mohawk	1	2	2	0	0
Huff, Cornelius	Mohawk	1	0	1	0	0
Huganor, Daniel	Mohawk	1	3	3	0	0
Hugenor, Lambert	Mohawk	1	0	2	0	0
Huggens, William	Whites	1	0	0	0	0
Hughes, Catherine	Canajoharie	1	0	2	0	0
Hughes, Timothy	Mohawk	1	2	4	0	0
Huginer, Peter	Mohawk	1	5	3	0	?
Hull, Eliphilet	Otsego	3	2	4	0	?
Hull, William C.	German Flatts	1	0	1	0	?
Hults, John	Harpersfield	2	2	2	0	0
Hulvert, Joshua	Whites	5	0	0	0	0
Humfry, Cornelius	Caughnawaga	2	2	3	0	0
Humfry, William	Palatine	3	0	4	0	0
Humphry, Abner	Harpersfield	1	0	2	0	0
Humphry, Noah	Whites	1	0	1	0	?

1790 FEDERAL CENSUS, MONTGOMERY COUNTY, NY

HOF	TOWN	M 16+	M -16	F	OFP	S
Hungeford, Levy	Mohawk	1	0	2	0	0
Hungeford, Stephen	Caughnawaga	3	5	7	0	0
Hungerford, Oliver	Harpersfield	1	1	1	0	0
Hunt, Elijah	Chemung	1	1	2	0	0
Hunt, Isaac	Mohawk	1	0	1	0	0
Hunt, Timothy	Mohawk	1	4	4	?	?
Huntington, Samuel	Otsego	2	0	1	0	?
Hurd, [?]	Mohawk	1	1	2	0	0
Hurd, Elijah	Chemung	2	2	4	0	?
Hurd, Roswell	Mohawk	1	0	2	0	?
Hurder, Adam	Herkimer	1	1	2	0	0
Hurder, Frederick, Sr.	Herkimer	4	0	3	0	0
Hurder, Henry	Herkimer	3	0	2	0	?
Hurder, Lawrence	Herkimer	4	3	5	0	?
Hurder, Lawrence F.	Herkimer	1	2	3	0	0
Hurder, Nicholas	Herkimer	3	1	3	0	?
Hurder, Philip	Herkimer	1	1	2	0	0
Hurning, George	Canajoharie	2	0	4	0	0
Hurning, Leonard	Canajoharie	2	1	3	0	?
Hurter, Nicholas	Herkimer	3	0	2	0	?
Huston, Caleb	Mohawk	1	0	3	0	0
Hutchins, Edward	Mohawk	1	1	2	0	?
Hutchins, William	Canajoharie	4	0	2	0	0
Hutson, Oliver	Canajoharie	1	2	3	0	0
Huver, Henry	Herkimer	1	5	3	0	?
Huver, John	Herkimer	1	0	3	0	?
Hyde, Asel	Harpersfield	1	0	0	0	0
Hyder, Daniel Vander	Caughnawaga	1	1	3	0	0
Hynes, Andrew	Canajoharie	2	1	3	0	0
Hynes, Christopher	Palatine	1	0	3	0	0
Hynes, Joseph	German Flatts	3	2	4	0	0
Hyser, Jacob	German Flatts	1	0	2	0	0
Iceman, John	Herkimer	2	2	6	0	0
Ichabroadt, Mary	Canajoharie	0	1	1	0	?
Ichanbroadt, Adam	Canajoharie	1	0	1	0	?
Ichanhour, Conradt	Herkimer	2	2	2	0	0
Ide, Timothy	Caughnawaga	1	3	2	0	0
Ingerson, Peter	Chemung	1	1	1	0	0
Ingerson, Thomas	Chemung	1	5	4	0	0
Inglis, James	Canajoharie	1	1	2	0	0
Inglis, James	Mohawk	1	1	3	?	?
Ingram, Joseph	Whites	4	0	1	0	0
Inkerson, Jesse	Palatine	1	2	3	?	?
Irish, John	Canajoharie	1	0	0	0	0

APPENDIX B

1790 FEDERAL CENSUS, MONTGOMERY COUNTY, NY

HOF	TOWN	M 16+	M -16	F	OFP	S
Irwin, James	Mohawk	1	1	3	0	0
Isdale, John	German Flatts	3	1	4	0	0
Ives, Amos	Whites	1	4	2	0	?
Ives, Benajah	Chemung	2	0	2	0	0
Ives, Titus	Chemung	3	0	2	0	0
Izeman, Stephanus	German Flatts	1	1	3	0	?
Jackson, Jeremiah, Jr.	Caughnawaga	2	1	2	0	0
Jackson, Johial	Otsego	1	1	0	0	?
Jackson, John	Canajoharie	1	1	1	0	0
Jackson, Robert	Caughnawaga	1	2	4	0	0
Jackson, William	Caughnawaga	2	2	4	0	0
Jacquess, William	Chemung	1	2	2	0	0
James, Abel	Herkimer	1	1	1	0	?
James, Howard	Herkimer	1	0	2	0	?
Jameson, John	Mohawk	2	2	3	0	0
Jareais, Bill	Otsego	1	3	2	0	0
Jarvais, John	Harpersfield	2	0	0	0	?
Jeffers, Lodowick	Caughnawaga	1	4	2	0	0
Jenkins, John	Canajoharie	1	3	2	0	0
Jenkins, William	Chemung	1	1	1	0	0
Jenks, Larraway	Otsego	1	0	3	0	0
Jennings, Elnathan	Canajoharie	1	0	2	0	0
Jennings, John	Chemung	1	0	2	0	?
Jennings, Joseph	Whites	4	2	2	0	?
Jennings, Reuben	Otsego	1	1	4	0	0
Jennings, Samuel	Palatine	2	4	?	?	?
Jerroliman, John	Caughnawaga	1	4	1	0	?
Jewell, Nathaniel	Otsego	2	4	4	0	0
Jewell, William	Otsego	3	1	1	0	0
Jewett, Samuel	Whites	1	0	0	0	0
Jinkins, Wilks	Chemung	1	0	1	0	0
Johnson, James	Palatine	2	0	1	0	?
Johnston, Abraham	Palatine	1	5	4	0	?
Johnston, Amasa	Whites	3	0	0	0	0
Johnston, Andrew	Mohawk	1	0	3	0	?
Johnston, Andrew, Jr.	Mohawk	1	0	4	0	?
Johnston, Barrakiah	Otsego	2	3	2	0	0
Johnston, Benjamin	Canajoharie	2	2	5	0	0
Johnston, Daniel	Mohawk	3	2	3	0	?
Johnston, Daniel	Otsego	1	0	3	0	0
Johnston, George	Otsego	2	2	3	0	0
Johnston, Isaiah	Herkimer	4	0	2	0	0
Johnston, John	Canajoharie	3	3	4	0	?
Johnston, John	Caughnawaga	1	4	3	0	0

1790 FEDERAL CENSUS, MONTGOMERY COUNTY, NY

HOF	TOWN	M 16+	M -16	F	OFP	S
Johnston, John	Mohawk	1	1	3	0	?
Johnston, John	Otsego	3	0	1	0	0
Johnston, Roluff	Mohawk	1	4	6	0	0
Johnston, Samuel	Harpersfield	4	3	5	0	0
Johnston, Samuel	Mohawk	1	1	1	0	0
Johnston, Silas	Harpersfield	1	1	1	0	0
Johnston, Thomas	Chemung	1	3	2	0	0
Johnston, William	Canajoharie	1	2	2	0	?
Johnston, William	Herkimer	1	1	3	0	0
Johnston, William	Mohawk	3	2	5	0	?
Johnston, Witter	Harpersfield	3	1	2	0	0
Jones, Asa	Caughnawaga	1	0	3	0	0
Jones, Benjamin	Harpersfield	2	0	1	0	?
Jones, David	Canajoharie	1	1	3	0	0
Jones, Ebenezer	Mohawk	1	2	2	0	?
Jones, Harman	Mohawk	1	0	0	0	0
Jones, Isaiah	Chemung	1	2	3	0	?
Jones, James	Mohawk	3	0	2	0	?
Jones, Joseph	Whites	1	2	3	0	?
Jones, Josiah	Otsego	2	2	2	0	0
Jones, Nehemiah	Whites	1	1	2	?	?
Jones, Richard	Herkimer	2	2	2	0	0
Jones, Simon	Chemung	1	1	1	0	0
Jones, Thomas	Canajoharie	1	0	3	0	0
Jones, William	Chemung	1	1	2	0	?
Jones, William Clark	German Flatts	1	0	0	0	0
Joshling, Freeborn	Otsego	1	4	3	0	0
Joy, Gershom	Caughnawaga	1	0	1	0	0
Judd, Freeman	Harpersfield	1	2	1	0	0
Judd, Thomas	Harpersfield	1	3	4	0	?
Kacky, Andrew	Mohawk	1	4	5	0	?
Kaler, Frederick	Caughnawaga	1	2	1	0	0
Kane, Elias	Canajoharie	3	0	1	0	?
Kane, Elisha	Whites	1	1	0	0	?
Kane, Thomas	Mohawk	1	1	4	0	0
Kane, William	Mohawk	1	2	1	0	0
Kane, William	Mohawk	1	0	3	0	0
Kapeman, Abraham	Canajoharie	2	5	3	0	0
Karell, Daniel	Chemung	1	0	2	0	0
Kaskadon, Robert	Palatine	1	0	2	0	0
Kass, Frederick	Herkimer	3	1	2	0	?
Kasson, Robert	Caughnawaga	3	1	5	0	?
Keagle, John	Caughnawaga	2	0	3	0	?
Kean, Barny	Mohawk	1	0	1	0	0

HOF	TOWN	M 16+	M -16	F	OFP	S
Kean, George	Mohawk	1	0	1	0	0
Kean, John	Mohawk	1	2	1	0	0
Kean, Joseph	Mohawk	1	0	2	0	?
Kean, Stephen	Mohawk	3	0	2	0	?
Kean, Thomas, Jr.	Mohawk	1	0	1	0	0
Kearn, John	Palatine	1	2	2	0	?
Keetch, George	Mohawk	3	3	4	0	0
Keller, Andrew	Canajoharie	2	0	5	0	1
Keller, Casper	Canajoharie	2	1	6	0	?
Keller, Henry	Canajoharie	2	0	4	0	?
Keller, Henry	Herkimer	2	2	4	0	?
Keller, Honess	Canajoharie	1	2	4	0	0
Keller, Jacob	Canajoharie	2	1	3	0	?
Keller, Jacob	Canajoharie	1	2	2	0	1
Keller, John	Herkimer	1	2	2	0	0
Keller, John	Mohawk	1	1	1	0	0
Keller, John	Palatine	2	1	7	0	?
Keller, Rudolp	Mohawk	3	0	2	0	?
Kellogg, Aaron	Whites	2	0	2	0	0
Kellogg, Amos	Whites	1	1	3	0	0
Kellogg, Benjamin	Harpersfield	3	1	2	0	0
Kellogg, Ezikel	Otsego	2	3	3	?	?
Kellogg, Frederick W.	Whites	1	2	3	0	0
Kellogg, Freeman	Whites	1	1	2	0	0
Kellogg, Jacob	Whites	1	1	1	0	0
Kellogg, Jessee	Whites	3	2	3	0	0
Kellogg, Pheneus	Whites	1	2	4	0	0
Kellogg, Soloman	Whites	2	8	2	0	0
Kellogg, Stephen	Whites	1	0	1	0	0
Kellogg, Thomas	Caughnawaga	1	2	1	0	0
Kelly, George	Palatine	1	1	2	0	0
Kelly, Henry	Canajoharie	1	1	4	0	0
Kelly, James	Canajoharie	1	1	1	0	0
Kelly, John	Canajoharie	2	3	6	0	?
Kelly, Robert	Canajoharie	1	0	1	0	0
Kelly, Thomas	Canajoharie	2	0	2	0	?
Kelly, Zariah	Mohawk	1	4	4	0	0
Kelsey, Abner	Chemung	3	0	6	0	0
Kelsey, Heth	Harpersfield	1	2	3	?	?
Kelsey, John	Harpersfield	2	1	2	?	?
Kelsey, Nathan	Whites	1	0	2	0	?
Kelts, Conradt	Canajoharie	1	1	3	0	?
Kelts, Nicholas	Canajoharie	2	1	4	0	?
Keltz, Philip	Whites	1	0	2	0	0
Kemble, David	Canajoharie	1	1	1	0	0

HOF	TOWN	M 16+	M -16	F	OFP	S
Kemble, Jessee	Canajoharie	1	1	4	0	?
Kemble, John	Canajoharie	2	1	2	0	0
Kemble, Timothy	Otsego	2	1	3	0	?
Kenedy, Patrick	Palatine	2	4	1	0	?
Kenescan, William	Canajoharie	1	3	4	0	0
Keney, Thomas	Chemung	1	3	4	0	?
Kennedy, Robert	Canajoharie	2	2	6	0	?
Kenny, Robert	Mohawk	2	4	3	0	0
Kenny, Roger	Mohawk	2	4	4	0	0
Kent, Stephen	Chemung	2	3	5	0	0
Kenter, Henry	Palatine	1	5	5	?	?
Kenyan, Enock	Chemung	1	2	3	0	0
Kenyon, Barney	Caughnawaga	3	2	1	0	0
Kenyon, Ezekiel	Otsego	1	0	4	0	0
Kenyon, James	Chemung	1	0	3	0	0
Kerker, Philip	Canajoharie	5	2	5	0	0
Kerkland, Samuel	Whites	4	0	2	0	?
Kesterd, Hendrick	Mohawk	2	3	1	0	0
Kestliar, Minert	Herkimer	2	1	8	0	0
Ketchem, Daniel	Chemung	1	2	2	0	0
Kettle, Daniel	Palatine	2	2	5	0	?
Kettle, Jacob	Palatine	1	1	1	0	?
Keyser, Barant	Palatine	1	3	?	?	?
Keyser, Henry	Palatine	4	1	6	0	2
Keyser, John	Palatine	2	2	3	0	?
Keyser, Peter	Caughnawaga	1	2	5	0	1
Keyser, Yost	Palatine	1	0	3	0	1
Khull, Hendrick	Palatine	2	2	3	0	0
Kidder, Abel	Harpersfield	3	0	10	0	?
Kidder, John	Harpersfield	2	4	5	0	?
Kiff, Andrew	Harpersfield	1	2	3	0	?
Kill, Christopher	Palatine	1	3	3	0	0
Killpatrick, Samuel	Canajoharie	1	0	1	0	0
Kilts, Adam	Palatine	1	4	5	?	?
Kilts, Peter N.	Palatine	1	1	2	?	?
Kilts, Philip	Palatine	1	2	7	?	?
Kimble, Lebbeas	Mohawk	1	2	2	0	0
King, [?]	Whites	1	0	0	0	0
King, Thomas	Canajoharie	1	3	4	0	0
Kirk, George	Caughnawaga	1	5	3	0	0
Kisner, William	Palatine	1	0	3	0	0
Kitchum, Stephen	Chenango	1	0	0	0	?
Kitts, Conradt	Palatine	2	1	5	0	?
Kitts, Jacob	Caughnawaga	4	4	5	0	0
Kitts, John	Caughnawaga	2	2	4	0	0

1790 FEDERAL CENSUS, MONTGOMERY COUNTY, NY

HOF	TOWN	M 16+	M -16	F	OFP	S
Kitts, John, Jr.	Caughnawaga	1	2	1	0	0
Kitts, Peter	Palatine	1	1	4	1	0
Kling, Ludwick	Canajoharie	2	3	5	0	?
Klock, Adam	Palatine	1	4	4	0	0
Klock, George G.	Palatine	2	4	5	0	2
Klock, Henry	Herkimer	1	3	6	0	0
Klock, Henry	Palatine	2	1	4	0	2
Klock, Honyost	Palatine	3	2	7	0	0
Klock, Jacob	Palatine	3	0	4	1	6
Klock, Jacob C.	Palatine	1	4	5	0	?
Klock, Jacob G.	Palatine	2	3	2	0	?
Klock, Jacob I.	Palatine	2	5	7	0	0
Klock, John	Palatine	2	?	?	?	?
Klock, John J.	Palatine	2	4	5	0	1
Klock, Joseph	Herkimer	1	1	1	0	0
Knap, Elijah	Herkimer	1	1	1	0	?
Knap, Henry	Mohawk	2	5	3	0	0
Knap, Jonathan	Mohawk	1	0	2	0	?
Knap, Joseph	Mohawk	1	2	2	0	0
Knap, Joseph	Mohawk	1	2	2	0	?
Knap, Joseph	Mohawk	1	2	2	0	0
Knapp, Samuel	Harpersfield	2	1	2	0	0
Knight, Daniel W.	Whites	2	0	1	0	0
Knight, Richard	Caughnawaga	1	2	2	0	0
Knouts, George Frederick	Canajoharie	3	1	6	0	?
Knouts, John	Canajoharie	2	0	3	0	0
Knox, James	Canajoharie	1	0	1	0	0
Knox, James	Harpersfield	1	2	2	0	0
Koch, Joseph	Herkimer	1	1	3	0	0
Kone, William	Caughnawaga	1	2	3	0	0
Kontz, Adam	Palatine	1	0	3	0	?
Kortright, John	Chemung	2	2	3	0	?
Kortright, John, Jr.	Chemung	1	1	3	0	0
Krams, John	Palatine	1	2	1	0	0
Kramts, Peter, Jr.	Palatine	2	0	2	0	2
Kramtz, Henry	Palatine	2	0	4	0	1
Kramtz, John	Palatine	2	0	6	0	2
Krennel, John	Herkimer	1	1	2	0	?
Kretzer, Leonard	Palatine	1	4	1	0	0
Krotz, Domini	Palatine	1	0	2	0	0
Krous, Gertrude	Palatine	0	0	3	0	0
Krull, Frederick	Mohawk	1	0	2	0	0
Krull, John	Mohawk	1	2	2	0	0
Kyes, Elias	Canajoharie	1	0	7	0	?
Kyes, John	Canajoharie	2	1	3	0	?

1790 FEDERAL CENSUS, MONTGOMERY COUNTY, NY

HOF	TOWN	M 16+	M -16	F	OFP	S
Kyes, Marshal	Canajoharie	1	1	2	0	0
Kyes, Paul	Canajoharie	5	5	3	0	0
Labdon, Daniel	Palatine	3	3	6	0	0
Lacy, Seth	Otsego	1	?	3	?	?
Ladder, John	Caughnawaga	1	7	2	0	0
Laffler, Martin	Caughnawaga	1	1	1	0	1
Laffler, Martin, Jr.	Caughanwaga	1	3	2	0	0
Laird, John	Whites	2	0	1	0	?
Laird, Samuel	Whites	1	1	3	0	0
Laird, William	Caughnawaga	1	6	2	0	0
Lamb, Christian	Canajoharie	4	3	5	0	0
Lambert, Peter	Otsego	3	0	2	0	?
Lambert, Peter, Jr.	Canajoharie	1	0	4	0	0
Lambsen, Nathaniel	Caughnawaga	1	1	2	0	0
Lamperson, Cornelius	Palatine	1	4	2	0	0
Lanathea, Asa	Caughnawaga	2	1	6	0	0
Lane, Daniel	Mohawk	1	2	5	0	0
Lane, Jacob	Mohawk	2	2	2	0	0
Lane, John	Mohawk	2	0	3	0	0
Lane, Matthias	Canajoharie	2	3	5	0	?
Lane, Nathan	Harpersfield	1	0	2	0	0
Lane, Nathan	Harpersfield	2	5	3	0	0
Lane, Solomon	Chemung	1	1	6	0	0
Lane, Stephen	Chemung	1	1	3	0	0
Lane, William	Canajoharie	1	2	3	0	0
Lansing, James	Caughnawaga	1	0	3	0	?
Lanthea, John	Chemung	1	0	2	0	0
Lapper, Jacob	Caughnawaga	1	5	3	?	?
Lapper, John	Caughnawaga	1	2	1	0	0
Larest, Peter	Caughnawaga	1	1	4	0	0
Lasher, Garrit	Palatine	3	2	5	?	?
Lasly, William	Caughnawaga	1	3	4	0	0
Latham, Benjamin	Herkimer	1	0	0	0	0
Latham, David	Herkimer	1	0	1	0	0
Latham, Peter	Herkimer	1	2	1	0	0
Launders, Ebenezer	Harpersfield	1	2	2	0	?
Launders, Isaiah	Harpersfield	1	0	2	0	?
Launders, Joseph	Harpersfield	1	0	4	0	?
Launtman, Peter	Palatine	3	1	5	0	1
Lavont, Frederick	Canajoharie	1	1	2	0	0
Lawson, Isaac	Caughnawaga	2	3	5	0	0
Lawyer, David	Canajoharie	1	2	3	0	0
Lawyer, Peter	Canajoharie	1	0	3	0	1
Layman, John	Palatine	1	2	4	0	0

1790 FEDERAL CENSUS, MONTGOMERY COUNTY, NY

HOF	TOWN	M 16+	M -16	F	OFP	S
Leadle, George	Harpersfield	1	0	1	0	0
Leak, Nicholas	Canajoharie	3	5	5	0	0
Leam, Jobe	Otsego	1	1	1	0	0
Leaper, Frederick	German Flatts	2	2	4	0	0
Leaper, Wyont	Palatine	3	5	2	0	0
Lee, Nathaniel	Chemung	2	0	2	0	0
Lee, William	Chemung	1	2	1	0	?
Lee, William	Palatine	1	3	4	0	0
Lee, William, Jr.	Palatine	1	0	1	0	0
Leech, Pheneas	Mohawk	2	2	5	0	?
Lemmon, Archibald	Canajoharie	2	2	3	0	0
Lenox, John	Mohawk	1	0	1	0	0
Lenox, John	Mohawk	1	0	1	0	0
Lentz, Jacob	German Flatts	1	2	3	0	0
Lentz, Peter	German Flatts	1	2	3	0	0
Leonard, Ebenezer	Otsego	1	2	4	0	0
Leonard, Joseph	Chemung	1	2	2	0	0
Lepper, John	Caughnawaga	1	1	4	0	0
Lesher, Garrit, Jr.	Palatine	1	1	4	0	0
Lesher, John	Palatine	4	0	5	0	0
Leveler, Martin	Caughnawaga	1	0	1	0	1
Leveler, Martin, Jr.	Caughnawaga	1	2	4	0	0
Levensworth, Lemuel	Whites	4	2	2	0	?
Lewis, Adam	Mohawk	1	1	4	0	0
Lewis, Benedict	Caughnawaga	1	1	2	0	0
Lewis, Benjamin	Canajoharie	1	0	3	0	0
Lewis, David	Canajoharie	2	0	2	0	?
Lewis, David	Mohawk	1	3	3	0	0
Lewis, Frederick	Canajoharie	1	4	5	0	?
Lewis, George Michael	Canajoharie	2	4	4	0	0
Lewis, Henry	Mohawk	1	0	3	0	1
Lewis, Henry, Jr.	Mohawk	2	2	5	0	0
Lewis, John	Mohawk	1	4	5	0	0
Lewis, Justis	Canajoharie	1	2	2	0	0
Lewis, Nathan	Canajoharie	1	0	0	0	0
Lewis, Peter	Mohawk	1	0	1	0	1
Lewis, Samuel	Canajoharie	1	1	6	0	0
Lewis, Seth	Chemung	4	1	5	0	0
Lewis, Vinton	Otsego	1	2	1	0	0
Lewis, William	Canajoharie	1	0	1	0	?
Lieb, Adam	Canajoharie	3	2	6	0	0
Lieb, John	Canajoharie	4	1	3	0	0
Lieb, John	Canajoharie	2	1	5	0	0
Lieb, Margaret	Canajoharie	1	2	1	0	0
Lienertson, James	Mohawk	1	3	2	0	1

APPENDIX B

1790 FEDERAL CENSUS, MONTGOMERY COUNTY, NY

HOF	TOWN	M 16+	M -16	F	OFP	S
Lienertson, John	Mohawk	1	0	1	0	3
Lienertson, John, Jr.	Mohawk	1	1	1	0	0
Lienertson, Timothy	Mohawk	1	2	1	0	1
Lientner, George	Canajoharie	3	2	3	0	0
Limback, Henry	German Flatts	1	1	2	0	?
Lincoln, Otis	Canajoharie	1	1	2	0	0
Lincolnfelter, Michael	Caughnawaga	3	1	2	0	?
Lincolnfelter, Michael	Caughnawaga	2	3	6	0	?
Lindersey, Banthy	Caughnawaga	2	2	3	0	0
Link, Jacob	Caughnawaga	1	0	3	0	0
Linsley, John	Harpersfield	1	4	3	0	0
Linsley, Matthias	Harpersfield	1	0	3	0	0
Litehall, Abraham	German Flatts	1	0	3	0	0
Litehall, Francis	Caughnawaga	1	1	3	0	0
Litehall, George	German Flatts	1	1	3	0	?
Little, William	Otsego	2	2	4	0	0
Livingston, James	Caughnawaga	1	4	5	0	3
Lobden, Joseph	Herkimer	1	0	3	0	0
Lock, Nathaniel	Chemung	2	0	0	0	0
Long, Christopher	Canajoharie	3	1	1	0	0
Longshore, Solomon	Canajoharie	1	0	0	0	0
Lonks, Peter	Caughnawaga	1	1	2	0	0
Lord, Timothy	Canajoharie	1	6	1	0	?
Lory, Jeremiah	Chemung	1	0	3	0	0
Lory, William	Canajoharie	1	5	4	0	?
Losa, John	Chemung	2	1	4	0	0
Losey, Jessee	Chemung	1	1	1	0	0
Lott, Abraham	Mohawk	3	3	4	0	2
Loughead, Samuel	Canajoharie	3	1	3	0	?
Louks, Adam	Palatine	2	3	4	0	1
Louks, Andrew	Canajoharie	2	0	2	0	?
Louks, Cornelius	Canajoharie	2	0	3	0	?
Louks, George	Palatine	3	1	2	0	0
Louks, George	Palatine	1	2	3	0	5
Louks, Henry	Palatine	3	3	3	0	?
Louks, Henry A.	Palatine	1	0	1	0	?
Louks, Jacob	Palatine	1	0	1	?	?
Louks, John	Canajoharie	3	2	2	0	?
Louks, John	Canajoharie	2	1	5	1	2
Louks, John	Mohawk	1	0	2	0	0
Louks, Joseph	Palatine	1	3	2	0	0
Louks, Peter	Canajoharie	1	3	2	0	?
Louks, Peter	Palatine	3	3	3	0	0
Louks, Peter H.	Palatine	3	0	3	0	?
Louks, Wendell	Palatine	1	0	1	0	?

1790 FEDERAL CENSUS, MONTGOMERY COUNTY, NY

HOF	TOWN	M 16+	M -16	F	OFP	S
Love, John	Canajoharie	2	0	2	0	?
Lovejoy, Nathan	Mohawk	1	2	4	0	0
Low, Anthony	Chemung	1	0	1	0	0
Low, Peter	Canajoharie	2	2	4	0	?
Low, Samuel	Palatine	1	0	3	0	2
Lower, Conradt	Palatine	1	5	4	0	?
Lucas, David	Canajoharie	2	2	2	0	0
Luce, Abraham	Chemung	1	1	2	0	0
Luce, Benjamin	Chemung	1	0	2	0	0
Luce, Benjamin, Sr.	Chemung	1	2	1	0	0
Luce, Nathan	Otsego	3	2	3	?	?
Luce, Othniel	Otsego	1	0	2	?	?
Ludwell, Thomas	Caughnawaga	2	2	1	0	?
Lufbury, Thomas	Mohawk	1	0	0	0	0
Luke, Christian	Chemung	1	3	2	0	0
Lull, Benjamin	Otsego	?	?	?	?	?
Lull, Joseph	Otsego	1	3	5	0	0
Lull, Nathan	Otsego	2	1	2	0	0
Lum, Elnathan	Mohawk	1	1	1	0	0
Lum, Reuben	Mohawk	1	1	2	0	0
Lummas, Alpheus	Canajoharie	2	1	3	0	0
Lummas, David	Caughnawaga	1	1	3	0	0
Lummas, Israel	Whites	2	2	2	0	0
Lummas, Nathan	Whites	1	2	1	0	0
Lummas, Samuel	Caughnawaga	1	0	1	?	?
Lummos, Zadock	Whites	2	3	1	0	0
Lupe, Martin	Chemung	1	2	2	0	0
Lupton, Silvenus	Mohawk	1	2	1	0	?
Lute, John	Mohawk	1	0	2	0	0
Lutridge, George	Caughnawaga	2	0	4	0	0
Lyning, Jacob	Palatine	1	1	4	0	0
Lyon, Abel	Canajoharie	1	0	0	0	?
Lyon, Abial	Otsego	1	2	1	0	0
Lyon, Henry	German Flatts	1	0	1	0	0
Lyon, James	Chemung	3	1	3	0	0
Lyon, John	Mohawk	1	1	2	0	0
Lyon, Jonathan	Harpersfield	2	0	2	0	?
Lyons, Hosiah	Canajoharie	1	1	3	0	?
Lysle, Alexander	Harpersfield	2	4	1	0	?
Lysle, Alexander, Jr.	Harpersfield	1	1	1	?	?
Lytle, [?]	Caughnawaga	1	3	3	0	0
Lytle, Andrew	Canajoharie	1	0	3	0	?
Lytle, John	Caughnawaga	2	0	5	0	?
Mabee, Albert	Canajoharie	2	3	2	0	0

1790 FEDERAL CENSUS, MONTGOMERY COUNTY, NY

HOF	TOWN	M 16+	M -16	F	OFP	S
Mabee, David	German Flatts	1	1	2	0	?
Mabee, Dolly	Canajoharie	0	0	2	0	0
Mabee, Hermanus	Mohawk	1	1	5	0	?
Mabee, Joseph	Canajoharie	2	2	4	0	?
Mack, Abner	Harpersfield	1	1	4	0	0
Mack, Daniel	Chemung	1	3	5	0	0
Mack, Daniel	Harpersfield	2	2	3	0	0
Mack, Joel	Harpersfield	1	2	3	0	0
Mack, John	Herkimer	1	1	2	0	0
Make, [?]ratsom	Herkimer	1	0	3	0	0
Malbridge, Henry	Otsego	3	2	1	0	0
Maleck, John	Canajoharie	1	2	3	0	0
Mallat, John	Mohawk	1	1	4	0	0
Mallery, Gidion	Chemung	3	0	0	0	?
Mallery, Stephen	Chemung	1	1	2	0	?
Mallet, Abraham	Mohawk	1	2	4	0	?
Mallet, Gidion	Mohawk	3	4	4	0	?
Mallock, Moses	Caughnawaga	1	0	2	0	0
Man, Thomas	Caughnawaga	1	5	2	0	0
Manheart, John	Chemung	1	2	3	0	0
Manly, Thomas	Herkimer	1	1	1	0	0
Mann, Abel	Herkimer	1	0	0	0	0
Mann, Abijah	Herkimer	1	1	2	0	0
Mansfield, Thomas	Harpersfield	1	2	2	0	?
Mapes, Burgess	Mohawk	2	0	2	0	?
Maples, Josiah	Otsego	1	0	0	0	0
March, Thomas	Canajoharie	1	3	1	0	0
Marenus, Jeremiah	Harpersfield	1	0	0	0	0
Mares, Thomas	Mohawk	1	0	2	0	1
Marinus, John	Canajoharie	1	0	3	0	0
Markham, Stephen	Whites	3	0	0	0	?
Marks, Abisha	Chemung	1	0	2	0	?
Marks, John	Mohawk	1	1	5	0	?
Marlet, Mark	Mohawk	1	0	3	0	0
Marlet, Michael	Mohawk	1	1	4	0	0
Marlett, Enock	Mohawk	1	0	1	0	0
Marrinius, William	Mohawk	1	2	4	0	?
Marrs, James	Otsego	2	0	2	?	?
Marsh, Asa	Whites	1	3	4	0	0
Marsh, Benjamin	Chemung	1	0	1	0	0
Marsh, John	Whites	1	0	1	0	0
Marsh, Marcus	Harpersfield	3	1	2	0	0
Marsh, Peter	Canajoharie	1	2	2	0	0
Marsh, Samuel	Whites	1	3	2	0	0
Marsh, Stephen	Palatine	1	2	2	0	1

APPENDIX B

1790 FEDERAL CENSUS, MONTGOMERY COUNTY, NY

HOF	TOWN	M 16+	M -16	F	OFP	S
Marshal, John	Mohawk	2	0	6	0	?
Marsielus, [?]uarius	Caughnawaga	3	3	3	0	3
Marsielus, Saunder	Palatine	1	2	2	0	0
Martice, Jacob	Canajoharie	5	1	7	0	?
Martin, Ethel	Otsego	1	0	2	0	0
Martin, James	Caughnawaga	2	1	4	0	?
Martin, James	Chemung	2	2	2	0	?
Martin, John	Caughnawaga	1	0	3	0	0
Martin, John	German Flatts	2	0	3	0	0
Martin, Mary	Mohawk	2	3	2	0	1
Martin, Nathan	German Flatts	1	1	3	0	0
Martin, Philip	Caughnawaga	1	3	1	0	0
Martin, Robert	Caughnawaga	1	0	4	0	0
Martin, Robert	Caughnawaga	1	0	2	0	?
Martin, Robert	German Flatts	1	0	1	0	0
Martin, Samuel	German Flatts	1	1	1	0	0
Martin, Veeder	Palatine	1	1	4	0	0
Martz, Philip Peter	German Flatts	1	2	3	0	0
Marvin, Abraham	Otsego	4	1	2	0	0
Marvin, James	Mohawk	3	4	3	0	0
Mason, Jeremiah	Caughnawaga	4	0	4	0	?
Mason, John	Caughnawaga	1	0	1	?	?
Masoner, John	Mohawk	2	2	1	0	0
Mather, James	Chemung	1	0	6	0	0
Matin, Peter	Palatine	1	0	5	0	?
Matthews, Henry	Caughnawaga	4	2	2	?	?
Matthews, John	Caughnawaga	6	1	4	?	?
Maxfield, James	Canajoharie	1	4	5	0	0
May, Luke	Canajoharie	1	5	2	?	?
Mayall, Joseph	Otsego	1	3	3	0	0
Maynard, Needham	Whites	2	2	5	0	?
Mayo, Elijah	Harpersfield	1	2	1	0	?
McAllum, Alexander	Canajoharie	3	3	2	0	0
McAllum, Daniel	Canajoharie	3	2	3	0	0
McAllum, James	Mohawk	2	3	3	0	?
McAllum, John	Caughnawaga	2	0	5	0	0
McArthur, Daniel	Caughnawaga	1	2	5	0	?
McArthur, Duncan	Caughnawaga	2	1	1	0	1
McArthur, John	Caughnawaga	3	1	4	?	?
McArthur, Peter	Caughnawaga	1	0	?	?	?
McArthy, John	Caughnawaga	2	0	0	?	?
McBean, John	Caughnawaga	2	0	0	?	?
McBean, John	Caughnawaga	1	2	4	0	0
McBean, John	Caughnawaga	1	1	5	0	?
McBieth, John	Caughnawaga	1	?	?	?	?

1790 FEDERAL CENSUS, MONTGOMERY COUNTY, NY

HOF	TOWN	M 16+	M -16	F	OFP	S
McCall, Alexander	Caughnawaga	1	3	4	0	0
McCall, Anson	Harpersfield	1	0	0	0	0
McCall, Benajah	Harpersfield	3	2	4	0	0
McCall, Ephraim	Harpersfield	2	2	3	0	0
McCallah, James	Caughnawaga	1	?	?	?	?
McCarron, John	Canajoharie	1	2	3	0	?
McCarthy, George	German Flatts	1	0	0	0	0
McCarthy, John	German Flatts	1	0	0	0	0
McCarthy, Michael	Mohawk	1	2	2	0	0
McCarthy, Timothy	Caughnawaga	2	0	1	0	?
McCharket, John	Caughnawaga	2	2	5	0	0
McClannen, James	Caughnawaga	1	0	0	0	?
McClaury, Thomas	Harpersfield	2	6	3	0	?
McClean, Peter	Caughnawaga	3	1	2	0	0
McCloud, George	Harpersfield	1	0	2	0	0
McClumply, Thomas	Mohawk	2	2	3	0	?
McColough, John	Harpersfield	1	1	1	0	?
McCombs, George	Herkimer	1	0	1	0	0
McConnell, Samuel	Chemung	2	0	0	0	0
McConnoly, Barsley	Caughnawaga	1	0	4	0	0
McCoon, Samuel	Chemung	1	3	2	0	0
McCormit, David	Chemung	2	2	1	0	?
McDanald, Daniel	Mohawk	1	2	4	0	?
McDonald, Benjamin	Mohawk	1	1	2	0	0
McDonald, Edward	Otsego	1	5	2	0	?
McDonald, John	Harpersfield	1	1	2	0	?
McDonald, John	Mohawk	1	0	1	0	?
McDougal, Alexander	Caughnawaga	1	0	3	0	0
McDougall, Allen	Caughnawaga	2	0	2	0	0
McDougall, Benjaman	Caughnawaga	1	0	0	0	?
McDougall, Eve	Palatine	0	1	4	0	0
McDougall, Peter	Caughnawaga	1	2	3	?	?
McDowel, Daniel	Chemung	2	2	3	0	?
McDurmot, James	Canajoharie	1	1	2	0	0
McEfee, Dudly	Harpersfield	1	1	1	0	0
McFarlan, Donald	Caughnawaga	4	1	0	0	0
McFarlan, Duncan	Caughnawaga	1	0	0	0	?
McFarlan, Robert	Canajoharie	1	0	0	0	0
McFarland, William	Harpersfield	3	0	2	0	0
McFarlen, Daniel	Caughnawaga	5	2	2	0	?
McFee, Alexander, Jr.	Canajoharie	1	4	2	0	0
McFie, Alexander	Canajoharie	1	0	3	0	0
McGee, William	Mohawk	1	1	6	0	?
McGlashing, Robert	Caughnawaga	1	2	1	0	?
McGraw, [?]	Mohawk	1	2	7	0	0

1790 FEDERAL CENSUS, MONTGOMERY COUNTY, NY

HOF	TOWN	M 16+	M -16	F	OFP	S
McGraw, Christopher	Mohawk	2	0	1	0	0
McGraw, Christopher, Jr.	Mohawk	2	2	4	0	0
McGraw, Daniel	Mohawk	1	1	3	0	0
McGraw, Edward	Mohawk	1	1	3	0	0
McGraw, Margaret	Mohawk	0	0	2	0	0
McGreggor, Duncan	Caughnawaga	1	4	3	0	0
McIntire, Daniel	Caughnawaga	3	1	4	?	?
McIntire, Daniel, Jr.	Caughnawaga	2	0	0	0	0
McIntire, Dugall	Harpersfield	1	1	6	0	0
McIntire, Duncan	Caughnawaga	2	0	4	?	?
McIntire, James	Whites	1	1	3	0	0
McIntire, Peter	Caughnawaga	3	1	2	0	?
McIntire, Peter	Caughnawaga	1	2	5	?	?
McJoch, John	Mohawk	1	3	4	0	?
McKean, Samuel	Canajoharie	1	1	2	0	0
McKean, William	Chemung	1	6	2	0	?
McKee, William	Harpersfield	2	3	2	0	0
McKell, James	Caughnawaga	2	2	3	0	?
McKellup, Archibald	Canajoharie	2	1	5	0	?
McKellup, John	Canajoharie	2	2	2	0	?
McKenny, Cornelius	Canajoharie	1	2	3	0	?
McKinley, John	Caughnawaga	3	2	3	0	0
McKinny, Daniel	Mohawk	3	3	6	0	?
McKown, Robert	Canajoharie	2	3	2	0	0
McLaren, James	Caughnawaga	2	4	1	0	?
McLean, Jacob	Caughnawaga	1	3	3	0	0
McLenan, John	Harpersfield	1	3	2	0	0
McLoud, Alexander	Mohawk	1	3	2	0	0
McMartin, Duncan	Caughnawaga	1	0	2	0	?
McMartin, Duncan, Jr.	Caughnawaga	1	1	3	0	?
McMartin, John	Caughnawaga	1	1	2	0	?
McMartin, Peter	Caughnawaga	1	5	2	0	?
McMaster, David	Mohawk	2	2	7	0	1
McMaster, Hugh	Mohawk	1	3	5	0	0
McMasters, James	Chemung	3	2	5	0	0
McaMasters, Thomas	Chemung	4	2	5	0	0
McMichael, Daniel	Mohawk	1	2	3	0	0
McMullen, Adam	Otsego	4	3	6	0	?
McNaughton, [?]	Caughnawaga	2	3	4	0	0
McNaughton, Angus	Caughnawaga	1	3	1	0	0
McNaughton, John	Caughnawaga	1	1	1	0	?
McNaughton, Peter	Caughnawaga	1	1	5	0	0
McNaughton, Robert	Caughnawaga	1	1	5	0	0
McNiel, John	Caughnawaga	1	4	4	0	0
McNutt, [?]	Caughnawaga	1	3	2	0	0

1790 FEDERAL CENSUS, MONTGOMERY COUNTY, NY

HOF	TOWN	M 16+	M -16	F	OFP	S
McNutt, Andrew	Caughnawaga	1	0	2	0	?
McQueen, Alexander	Caughnawaga	2	0	1	0	?
McReady, Robert	Mohawk	2	1	4	0	?
McSwine, Daniel	Chemung	1	4	1	0	?
McVain, Daniel	Caughnawaga	2	2	5	0	?
McVain, Daniel	Caughnawaga	1	1	1	0	0
McVain, Duncan	Caughnawaga	1	0	1	?	?
McVain, Duncan, Jr.	Caughnawaga	2	1	1	?	?
McVain, James	Caughnawaga	1	0	1	?	?
McVain, John	Caughnawaga	1	3	4	0	?
McVain, Peter	Caughnawaga	2	1	2	?	?
McWilliams, John	Mohawk	1	1	3	0	0
McWright, John	Chemung	1	3	5	0	0
Mead, Samuel	Mohawk	1	0	0	0	0
Mechem, Jeremiah	Otsego	1	1	2	0	0
Medaw, Elias	Chemung	1	4	4	0	?
Medaw, Samuel	Chemung	2	3	7	0	0
Meggs, Thomas	Harpersfield	1	2	4	0	0
Meltz, John	Caughnawaga	1	2	2	0	0
Mercerian, Joshua, Jr.	Chemung	2	1	1	0	1
Merkle, David	Palatine	3	0	2	0	1
Merkle, Frederick	Canajoharie	3	0	1	0	0
Merkle, Henry	Palatine	3	1	6	1	4
Merkle, Jacob	Canajoharie	3	0	5	0	0
Merkle, Michael	Canajoharie	1	1	1	0	0
Merkle, Samuel	Palatine	1	0	2	0	?
Merrel, Caleb B.	Whites	1	2	2	0	0
Merriman, Christopher	Whites	1	0	1	0	?
Merriman, Enock	Chemung	2	2	4	0	?
Merriness, Abraham	Canajoharie	2	3	4	?	?
Merry, Benjamin	Mohawk	1	2	?	?	?
Merry, Matichi	Canajoharie	3	2	4	0	0
Merry, Samuel, Jr.	German Flatts	1	0	2	0	0
Merry, Samuel, Sr.	German Flatts	5	2	3	0	0
Mertle, Henry, Jr.	Palatine	1	4	2	0	0
Milerd, Robert	German Flatts	1	0	2	0	?
Miles, Nathan	Canajoharie	2	1	3	0	0
Miller, [?]	Canajoharie	1	1	2	0	0
Miller, Abraham	Chemung	5	1	5	0	0
Miller, Adam	Mohawk	1	1	1	0	0
Miller, Amock	Whites	3	0	2	0	?
Miller, Andrew	Herkimer	1	1	3	0	?
Miller, Dionesias	Canajoahrie	1	2	3	0	0
Miller, Elton	Herkimer	2	1	4	0	0
Miller, Francis	Chemung	1	0	1	0	0

APPENDIX B

1790 FEDERAL CENSUS, MONTGOMERY COUNTY, NY

HOF	TOWN	M 16+	M -16	F	OFP	S
Miller, Garret	Canajoharie	2	2	6	0	0
Miller, George	Caughnawaga	1	5	3	0	?
Miller, Hendrick	Mohawk	2	1	2	0	0
Miller, Henry	German Flatts	2	3	2	0	0
Miller, Henry	Palatine	2	2	2	0	0
Miller, Icabod	Mohawk	1	4	3	0	?
Miller, Jessee	Chemung	2	2	0	0	0
Miller, John	Canajoharie	2	1	4	0	?
Miller, John	Caughnawaga	1	3	2	0	?
Miller, John	Chemung	3	0	2	0	0
Miller, John	Chemung	2	3	1	0	?
Miller, John	Herkimer	1	3	4	0	0
Miller, John	Mohawk	1	0	1	0	0
Miller, John	Otsego	2	0	5	0	0
Miller, John L.	Otsego	1	0	0	?	?
Miller, Nathaniel	Canajoharie	1	2	4	0	?
Miller, Peter	Canajoharie	2	2	2	0	0
Miller, Philip	Caughnawaga	4	1	7	0	?
Miller, Samuel	German Flatts	1	0	0	0	0
Miller, Silas	Chemung	2	2	2	0	0
Millington, Peter	Canajoharie	1	3	5	0	0
Mills, Alexander	Harpersfield	1	3	2	0	0
Mills, Bildad	Caughnawaga	1	0	2	0	?
Mills, Jesse	Caughnawaga	1	1	3	0	0
Mills, Kanah	Whites	1	0	2	0	?
Mills, William C.	Caughnawaga	4	1	4	0	1
Milroy, Alexander	Mohawk	1	0	0	0	?
Mindeline, John	Canajoharie	2	0	1	0	?
Minthorne, William	Caughnawaga	3	3	1	0	0
Minton, Stephen	Caughnawaga	3	1	2	0	?
Miracle, William	Caughnawaga	1	4	4	0	1
Mire, Garret	Canajoharie	1	0	2	0	0
Mitchell, Hugh	Canajoharie	2	2	3	0	?
Mitchell, James	Caughnawaga	1	4	3	0	0
Mitchell, John	Chemung	3	2	2	0	0
Mitchell, John	Mohawk	1	0	2	0	0
Moffat, Alexander Conky	Canajoharie	1	1	2	0	?
Moffat, Jonathan	Canajoharie	3	0	4	0	?
Moffatt, Bezilial	Otsego	2	3	3	0	?
Moffatt, Isaac	Canajoharie	1	0	1	0	0
Moke, Jacob	Canajoharie	1	3	4	0	?
Monk, Johannes	Canajoharie	1	5	3	0	0
Mont, John	Palatine	1	4	3	0	0
Montanic, Edward	Mohawk	1	1	2	0	0
Montanie, Abraham	Mohawk	1	3	2	0	?

1790 FEDERAL CENSUS, MONTGOMERY COUNTY, NY

HOF	TOWN	M 16+	M -16	F	OFP	S
Montanie, Joseph	Mohawk	1	3	1	0	?
Monteney, Joseph	Mohawk	1	2	1	0	?
Montgomery, [?]	Caughnawaga	1	1	1	0	0
Montgomery, James	Mohawk	1	2	1	0	0
Montgomery, Robert	Harpersfield	2	4	7	0	0
Montieth, William	Caughnawaga	1	1	?	?	?
Moon, Darius	Canajoharie	1	1	2	0	0
Moor, Andrew	Canajoharie	1	2	2	0	0
Moor, James	Chemung	1	3	3	0	0
Moor, Jonathan	Otsego	3	?	?	?	?
Moor, Roderick	Otsego	1	?	?	?	?
Moor, Roger, Sr.	Otsego	3	2	3	?	?
Moore, Hannah	Harpersfield	2	1	1	0	?
Moore, Jacob	Palatine	1	0	1	0	0
Moore, John	Caughnawaga	3	2	6	0	0
Moore, William	Harpersfield	2	2	4	0	?
Morehouse, Jabez	Canajoharie	2	1	7	0	?
Morenius, George	Harpersfield	1	3	2	0	0
Morenus, Christian	Harpersfield	1	0	2	0	?
Morery, Silvenus	Whites	2	2	4	0	0
Morey, Silas	Chemung	3	3	3	0	0
Morey, Soloman	Whites	2	1	2	0	0
Morgan, James	Mohawk	1	0	2	0	0
Morgan, John	Caughnawaga	4	4	5	0	?
Morgan, Nathaniel	Caughnawaga	1	1	2	0	0
Morris, David	Canajoharie	1	4	5	0	0
Morris, Jacob	Otsego	4	1	3	0	5
Morris, John	Caughnawaga	1	0	2	0	0
Morris, Richard	Mohawk	2	3	2	0	0
Morris, Thomas	Canajoharie	3	2	3	0	?
Morrow, David	Mohawk	1	2	1	0	?
Morse, Benjamin	Harpersfield	2	0	1	0	?
Morse, Daniel	Canajoharie	2	5	2	0	0
Morse, Joshua	Whites	1	4	4	0	0
Morse, Stephen	Mohawk	1	4	4	0	0
Morse, Stephen	Otsego	1	4	3	0	0
Morse, Timothy	Otsego	3	4	5	0	0
Mort, Augustus	Canajoharie	1	0	0	0	?
Mottoner, John	Herkimer	3	0	3	0	0
Moulder, Jacob	Herkimer	1	0	1	0	0
Moulder, Margaret	Herkimer	1	1	2	0	0
Mower, Conradt	Mohawk	2	1	0	0	0
Mower, Conradt, Jr.	Mohawk	1	2	4	0	?
Mower, George	Mohawk	1	2	3	0	?
Mower, Hendrick	Mohawk	1	1	1	0	0

1790 FEDERAL CENSUS, MONTGOMERY COUNTY, NY

HOF	TOWN	M 16+	M -16	F	OFP	S
Mower, John	Mohawk	1	2	0	0	?
Mower, Peter	Mohawk	1	1	0	0	?
Moyer, [?]	German Flatts	3	4	4	0	0
Moyer, [?]	Palatine	1	5	2	0	0
Moyer, David	Palatine	2	1	4	0	0
Moyer, Henry	German Flatts	2	0	3	0	0
Moyer, Joseph	German Flatts	2	2	6	?	?
Mudge, Abraham	Mohawk	1	2	3	0	?
Mudge, Ebenezer	Mohawk	1	0	2	0	0
Mudge, Joshua	Mohawk	1	2	?	?	?
Mudge, Reuben	Mohawk	2	0	4	0	0
Mudge, Samuel	Mohawk	2	2	3	0	0
Muke, [?]	Caughnawaga	1	0	1	0	0
Munro, Ashel	Mohawk	1	1	2	0	0
Munro, John	Mohawk	1	5	4	0	0
Munroe, Theodore	Whites	1	0	1	0	0
Munroe, William	Otsego	2	1	2	0	0
Munterbach, John	German Flatts	2	2	4	0	0
Murdoch, John	Harpersfield	4	2	2	0	?
Murphy, Henry	Canajoharie	3	0	2	0	0
Murphy, Thomas	Canajoharie	1	2	3	0	0
Murphy, Thomas	Mohawk	1	0	2	0	0
Murray, Daniel	Mohawk	2	3	4	0	0
Murray, Ezra	Mohawk	2	2	2	0	0
Murray, Ichabod	Mohawk	1	3	3	0	0
Murray, John	Caughnawaga	1	4	2	0	?
Myer, Adam	Herkimer	1	2	3	0	0
Myer, Catharine	Canajoharie	1	0	4	0	?
Myer, David	Canajoharie	1	1	2	0	0
Myer, Frederick	Herkimer	2	3	6	0	?
Myer, Hendrick	Canajoharie	3	2	8	0	0
Myer, Henry S.	Canajoharie	1	4	5	0	0
Myer, Honkendrick	Canajoharie	3	2	7	0	0
Myer, Jacob	Canajoharie	1	4	5	0	0
Myer, Jacob	Mohawk	1	1	3	0	?
Myer, Jacob	Whites	1	0	2	0	0
Myer, John	Canajoharie	1	3	3	0	0
Myer, Peter	Herkimer	1	0	1	0	?
Myer, Solomon, Jr.	Canajoharie	1	1	1	0	?
Myers, Christian	Mohawk	1	1	?	?	?
Myers, John	Mohawk	1	1	3	0	?
Myers, John	Mohawk	1	1	3	0	0
Myers, Joseph	Herkimer	1	2	2	0	0
Myers, Michael	Herkimer	2	4	5	1	0
Myers, Oliver	Otsego	3	2	1	0	0

1790 FEDERAL CENSUS, MONTGOMERY COUNTY, NY

HOF	TOWN	M 16+	M -16	F	OFP	S
Myles, Daniel	Caughnawaga	3	3	4	0	0
Mynegar, Christian	Chemung	1	5	5	0	?
Mynhert, Christian	Canajoharie	1	4	4	0	?
Nafe, Adam	Caughnawaga	1	1	2	0	0
Nafe, Jacob, Jr.	Caughnawaga	1	1	0	0	0
Nafe, Johannes	Caughnawaga	3	2	2	0	2
Nafe, John	Caughnawaga	1	1	1	0	0
Nafees, John	Canajoahrie	2	1	7	0	?
Nairn, Peter	Caughnawaga	1	1	1	0	?
Nancy, Conradt	Canajoharie	1	0	2	0	0
Nash, James	German Flatts	1	1	4	0	0
Nash, Johnston	Harpersfield	1	2	5	0	0
Near, George	Canajoharie	1	0	4	0	0
Near, Jacob	Canajoharie	1	1	1	0	0
Neely, John	Chemung	1	1	6	0	0
Neilson, Allen	Caughnawaga	1	2	1	?	?
Nelles, George	Canajoharie	1	1	4	0	?
Nellis, Adam	Palatine	2	0	3	0	0
Nellis, Andrew	Herkimer	1	4	2	0	0
Nellis, Christian	Palatine	4	0	2	0	3
Nellis, David	Palatine	2	1	4	0	0
Nellis, George	Herkimer	3	1	4	0	0
Nellis, Henry	Canajoharie	3	1	3	0	0
Nellis, Henry W.	Palatine	1	1	4	0	0
Nellis, John	Palatine	4	1	3	0	?
Nellis, John	Palatine	1	2	2	0	?
Nellis, John D.	Canajoharie	3	2	2	0	2
Nellis, John H.	Palatine	3	5	8	0	0
Nellis, Ludwick	Palatine	3	0	3	0	?
Nellis, Peter W.	Palatine	1	4	2	0	0
Nellis, Philip	Palatine	3	3	6	0	0
Nellis, Robert	Canajoharie	1	1	2	0	0
Nellis, William	Palatine	3	0	6	0	2
Nellis, Yost	Palatine	1	1	1	0	0
Nesley, William	Chenango	1	0	5	0	?
Nestle, Andrew	Canajoharie	2	1	1	0	0
Nestle, Godlip	Palatine	1	2	6	0	0
Nestle, Martin	Palatine	3	0	5	0	?
Newcomb, Eleazer	Chemung	1	0	3	0	?
Newell, Elisha	Whites	4	0	1	0	0
Newkerk, Garrit C.	Mohawk	1	0	2	0	0
Newkerk, Garrit Corns.	Mohawk	4	0	2	0	0
Newkerk, Garrit I.	Mohawk	2	0	4	0	0
Newkerk, Jacob	Mohawk	1	3	1	0	0

HOF	TOWN	M 16+	M -16	F	OFP	S
Newkerk, John	Mohawk	2	0	2	0	0
Newkerk, William	Mohawk	1	1	1	0	0
Newkirk, Garrit	Mohawk	1	3	3	0	?
Newman, Abner	Harpersfield	2	5	3	0	?
Newman, John	Palatine	1	2	2	0	?
Newnan, Kirby	Caughnawaga	1	3	5	0	0
Newton, Joseph	Caughnawaga	4	1	5	0	0
Newton, William	Otsego	2	?	?	?	?
Nichley, Michael	Caughnawaga	4	4	2	0	?
Nichols, Hesekiah	Palatine	1	1	1	0	0
Nichols, John	Canajoharie	2	1	3	0	0
Nichols, Simeon	Palatine	4	1	2	0	0
Nichols, Thomas	Herkimer	2	1	3	0	?
Nichols, William	Herkimer	1	2	3	0	?
Nicholson, Peter	Canajoharie	1	1	1	0	0
Nielson, Ball	Herkimer	1	3	3	0	0
Nielson, Thomas	Caughnawaga	1	0	4	0	?
Nielson, William	Mohawk	1	4	2	0	0
Night, John	Herkimer	1	0	1	0	?
Noff, Richard	Mohawk	2	2	2	0	0
North, Gabriel	Harpersfield	2	1	3	0	0
North, Robert	Harpersfield	1	2	2	0	0
Northhoop, Nathaniel	Harpersfield	1	2	2	0	?
Nortman, George	Mohawk	1	2	1	0	0
Nortman, Jacob	Mohawk	1	0	1	0	0
Norton, Christopher	Canajoharie	1	2	1	0	0
Norton, Zebulan	Otsego	1	1	3	0	?
Noten, Gideon A.	Canajoharie	1	2	4	0	0
Noyes, Amos	Whites	1	1	4	0	0
Noyes, Nehemiah	Otsego	1	0	4	0	0
Noyes, Samuel	Otsego	1	1	2	0	0
Nurse, Jonathan	Whites	2	3	2	0	0
Nurse, Joshua	Harpersfield	2	0	2	0	0
Nutting, Simeon	Whites	1	5	3	0	0
Oakh, George	Canajoharie	3	1	2	0	0
Oakly, John	Mohawk	1	1	4	0	0
Oaks, Samuel	Canajoharie	3	0	2	0	?
Obell, John	Canajoharie	4	1	2	0	1
Obits, Michael	Caughnawaga	1	1	3	0	0
Odell, Luke	German Flatts	1	0	2	0	0
Ogden, Daniel	Otsego	4	1	2	0	?
Ogden, Daniel, Jr.	Otsego	1	0	3	0	0
Ogden, David	Otsego	1	2	1	0	0
Ogden, John	Harpersfield	2	3	4	0	0

1790 FEDERAL CENSUS, MONTGOMERY COUNTY, NY

HOF	TOWN	M 16+	M -16	F	OFP	S
Ogden, Richard	Otsego	1	4	3	0	0
Ohrendorff, Conradt	German Flatts	2	2	5	0	2
Ohrendorff, Frederick, Sr.	German Flatts	2	0	1	0	?
Ohrendorff, Peter	German Flatts	2	2	3	0	0
Olden, Prince	Chemung	1	3	1	0	0
Oldman, [?]arant	Caughnawaga	1	1	2	0	0
Oldman, Frederick	Caughnawaga	1	2	3	0	0
Olea, Gilbert	Caughnawaga	1	1	2	0	0
Olen, Hendrick	Mohawk	1	0	2	0	?
Olendorfph, Daniel	German Flatts	1	2	5	0	0
Oliver, Alexander	Caughnawaga	1	1	5	0	0
Oliver, Isac	Otsego	0	0	0	4	0
Oller, Peter	Canajoharie	1	0	2	0	0
Olmsted, Ashbel	Whites	2	1	2	0	?
Olmsted, Barton	Harpersfield	1	0	3	0	0
Olmsted, Gamaliel	Whites	2	0	2	0	0
Omstead, Henry	Palatine	1	2	1	?	?
Oneal, John	German Flatts	1	2	3	0	0
Ones, Essenetus	Chemung	3	5	3	0	?
Oooley, Henry	German Flatts	1	2	6	0	1
Orendorph, Frederick, Jr.	German Flatts	1	2	6	0	?
Orton, David	Caughnawaga	1	1	2	0	0
Osburn, Samuel	Chemung	1	4	3	0	?
Osman, Henry	Palatine	1	1	3	0	0
Osterhout, Cornelius	Mohawk	1	2	5	0	?
Osterhout, Frederick	Palatine	2	4	4	0	0
Ostrom, Thomas	Mohawk	1	1	2	0	0
Ostroman, Christian	Mohawk	1	1	5	0	0
Ostrum, John	Mohawk	2	1	2	0	0
Ostrum, Joshua	Mohawk	1	0	1	0	0
Otman, Christian	Canajoharie	3	4	2	0	?
Otman, William	Canajoharie	1	1	1	0	?
Oultsaver, Bastian	Canajoharie	2	2	6	0	?
Ousterhout, John	German Flatts	1	3	5	0	0
Overacker, George	Canajoharie	1	1	4	0	0
Overback, Benjamin	Mohawk	2	1	5	0	?
Owens, Isaac	Mohawk	1	2	2	0	0
Ower, John	Herkimer	1	2	2	0	0
Paddock, Jobe	Caughnawaga	1	2	4	0	0
Paddock, Peter	Caughnawaga	1	2	4	0	0
Page, Abraham	Canajoharie	2	0	3	0	0
Page, Isaac	Chemung	4	2	1	0	0
Page, John	Canajoharie	1	0	0	0	0
Page, Jonathan	Chemung	1	0	3	0	0

HOF	TOWN	M 16+	M -16	F	OFP	S
Paine, Ezra	Harpersfield	1	1	2	0	?
Paine, Joshua	Whites	2	0	0	0	?
Paine, Philip	Herkimer	2	1	3	0	1
Palmer, Benjamin	Otsego	3	0	2	0	0
Palmer, Ichabod B.	Otsego	1	2	2	?	?
Palmer, Nathan	Otsego	2	0	1	0	0
Palnaton, John	Mohawk	1	3	3	0	?
Parcel, Jacob	Caughnawaga	1	1	4	0	?
Parcel, Paul	Caughnawaga	1	3	4	0	?
Paris, Anthony	Caughnawaga	1	2	3	0	0
Paris, Catherine	Canajoharie	3	0	1	0	1
Parkel, Nathaniel	Canajoharie	3	3	3	0	0
Parker, Andress	Otsego	1	1	3	0	0
Parker, Asa	Harpersfield	1	1	2	0	0
Parker, Daniel	Harpersfield	1	2	2	0	?
Parker, Daniel	Herkimer	1	0	4	0	0
Parker, Edward	Mohawk	2	2	4	0	?
Parker, Elijah	Canajoharie	1	2	1	0	0
Parker, Elijah, Jr.	Canajoharie	1	2	1	0	0
Parker, Henry	Herkimer	1	1	1	0	?
Parker, Jason	Whites	3	0	1	0	0
Parker, Jonathan	Canajoharie	1	4	2	0	0
Parker, Jonathan	Canajoharie	1	4	1	0	0
Parkhouse, Frederick	Caughnawaga	1	2	2	?	?
Parkman, Alexander	Whites	3	2	5	0	0
Parks, David	Mohawk	1	2	1	0	0
Parks, Ezra	Mohawk	1	1	3	0	0
Parks, John	Mohawk	1	0	1	0	0
Parks, Joseph	Mohawk	1	1	2	0	0
Parks, Robert	Whites	2	2	4	0	?
Parks, Squire	Chemung	1	1	2	0	?
Parkson, Reuben	Canajoharie	1	2	4	0	?
Parkson, Silvanus	Canajoharie	1	0	1	0	?
Parmella, Amos	Whites	2	1	3	0	0
Parry, Archer	Caughnawaga	1	0	1	0	?
Parshall, Israel	Chemung	2	0	4	0	?
Parsons, Chatwell	Canajoharie	1	1	2	0	?
Parsons, Eli	Canajoharie	2	1	5	0	0
Parsons, Moses	Canajoharie	1	2	1	0	?
Patchin, Freegift	Harpersfield	2	1	3	0	0
Patchin, John, Jr.	Harpersfield	1	0	1	0	0
Pater, Francis	Caughnawaga	1	0	2	0	?
Paterson, James	Caughnawaga	1	2	2	0	0
Patrick, Robert	Palatine	3	3	8	?	?
Patridge, Thomas	Chemung	1	3	1	0	0

HOF	TOWN	M 16+	M -16	F	OFP	S
Patterson, Edward	Chemung	1	3	2	0	0
Patterson, James	Mohawk	1	1	1	0	?
Paulding, Henry	Caughnawaga	1	3	1	0	0
Pauter, John	Mohawk	1	0	2	0	?
Pauter, Lodowick	Mohawk	1	0	2	0	?
Peak, James	Mohawk	1	4	4	0	?
Peas, Samuel	Chemung	2	0	0	0	0
Pease see House	Whites	2	5	3	0	0
Peck, Hermanus	Caughnawaga	1	2	3	0	0
Peck, Jedediah	Otsego	3	0	0	0	0
Peck, Joseph	Chemung	4	5	4	0	0
Peck, Luman	Caughnawaga	2	0	1	0	?
Peek, Moses	Mohawk	3	3	3	0	0
Peekle, John	Caughnawaga	1	1	6	0	1
Peekle, John, Jr.	Caughnawaga	1	1	4	0	0
Pellendom, James	Palatine	1	0	2	0	?
Pellett, Silas	Mohawk	2	1	2	0	0
Perkens, Silas	Whites	1	1	1	0	0
Perkins, Nathaniel	Caughnawaga	2	1	4	0	?
Perry, George H.	Whites	1	1	2	0	?
Perry, Jonas	Otsego	1	1	2	0	0
Perry, Jonathan	Canajoharie	2	1	1	0	0
Perry, Nathan	German Flatts	1	0	0	0	0
Perry, Thomas	Harpersfield	3	0	0	0	0
Person, Pool	Palatine	1	0	3	0	0
Peters, Benjamin	Whites	4	0	2	0	?
Peters, Samuel	Otsego	3	2	1	0	?
Peterson, Zachariah	Caughnawaga	2	1	3	0	0
Petiss, John	Canajoharie	1	0	0	0	0
Petree, Catherine	German Flatts	2	0	1	0	?
Petrie, Barbara	Palatine	1	2	2	0	?
Petrie, Daniel	Herkimer	1	2	3	0	0
Petrie, Honyost	Herkimer	1	2	5	0	0
Petrie, Honyost, Jr.	Herkimer	2	0	3	0	?
Petrie, Jacob	Herkimer	3	3	6	0	0
Petrie, John	Herkimer	3	1	3	0	0
Petrie, John D.	German Flatts	1	1	2	0	?
Petrie, John M.	Herkimer	2	6	2	0	?
Petrie, Marks	Herkimer	1	4	2	0	0
Petrie, Richard	Herkimer	1	0	2	0	0
Petrie, William	Herkimer	2	3	4	0	?
Pettebone, Amasa	Mohawk	1	0	2	0	?
Pettegrove, Thomas	Canajoharie	2	4	2	0	?
Pettingell, Wiliam	Mohawk	1	1	4	0	?
Pettingill, Benjamin	Mohawk	1	0	3	0	?

1790 FEDERAL CENSUS, MONTGOMERY COUNTY, NY

HOF	TOWN	M 16+	M -16	F	OFP	S
Pettingill, Benjamin	Mohawk	1	0	3	0	?
Pettingill, Joseph	Mohawk	1	1	4	0	?
Pettingill, Joseph	Mohawk	2	2	1	0	?
Pettingill, Martin	Mohawk	1	0	2	0	?
Pettingill, Samuel	Mohawk	1	1	2	0	?
Pfyfer, Andrew	Palatine	1	0	1	0	0
Phanormun, Daniel	Chenango	1	1	2	0	?
Phelps, Abijah	Otsego	4	3	1	0	0
Phelps, James	Harpersfield	2	1	4	0	?
Phelps, Jedediah	Whites	1	3	2	0	0
Phelps, John	Harpersfield	1	0	2	0	?
Phelps, Joseph	Whites	1	4	2	0	0
Phelps, Rufus	Caughnawaga	1	0	1	0	0
Phelps, Silas	Whites	1	5	3	0	0
Philips, Abraham	Canajoharie	1	0	1	0	0
Philips, Abraham	Caughnawaga	1	3	2	0	0
Philips, Adam	Palatine	1	0	1	0	0
Philips, Amaziah	Otsego	1	3	4	0	?
Philips, Christian	Caughnawaga	1	3	3	0	0
Philips, Hermanus	Canajoharie	1	0	4	0	0
Philips, Hermanus	Caughnawaga	1	2	5	0	0
Philips, Jacob	Caughnawaga	1	4	3	0	0
Philips, James	Caughnawaga	1	3	7	0	0
Philips, John	Canajoharie	1	0	2	0	0
Philips, John	Canajoharie	4	1	3	0	0
Philips, John	Canajoharie	1	3	2	0	0
Philips, John	Caughnawaga	1	3	3	0	0
Philips, John	German Flatts	1	2	?	?	?
Philips, John	Mohawk	1	3	2	?	?
Philips, John, Jr.	Mohawk	1	2	1	0	0
Philips, Philip	Caughnawaga	1	1	3	0	0
Philips, Philip	Caughnawaga	1	1	4	0	0
Philips, Philip, Jr.	Caughnawaga	1	1	3	0	0
Philips, Philip, Sr.	Caughnawaga	1	1	1	0	4
Phillips, [?]	Mohawk	1	4	4	0	0
Phillips, Elijah	Mohawk	1	1	3	0	?
Phillips, John	Mohawk	1	1	2	0	?
Phillips, Lewis	Mohawk	3	3	6	0	?
Phillips, Richard	Mohawk	1	0	2	0	0
Phillips, Thomas	Mohawk	3	0	1	0	0
Phitis, Philip	Caughnawaga	1	1	1	0	0
Pickard, Isaac	Canajoharie	1	0	0	0	0
Pickard, Nicholas	Chenango	1	4	2	0	?
Pickart, Bartholimew	Palatine	4	3	4	0	?
Pickart, John	Palatine	1	0	4	0	0

1790 FEDERAL CENSUS, MONTGOMERY COUNTY, NY

HOF	TOWN	M 16+	M -16	F	OFP	S
Pickart, Joseph	Palatine	1	2	1	0	0
Pickerd, Adolph	Canajoharie	1	1	2	0	0
Pickerd, Conradt	Canajoharie	2	2	2	0	0
Pickerd, George	Canajoharie	2	1	2	0	0
Pickerd, John	Canajoharie	1	4	3	0	0
Pickerd, Nicholas I.	Canajoharie	1	2	5	0	0
Pier, David	Otsego	1	2	2	0	?
Pier, Ernest	Palatine	1	0	5	0	0
Pier, John	Otsego	1	5	3	0	?
Pier, Solomon	Otsego	2	1	2	0	?
Pier, Thomas	Otsego	2	1	1	0	0
Pierce, Abner	Otsego	1	2	2	0	0
Pierce, Ephraim	Mohawk	3	4	2	0	0
Pike, Jarvis	Caughnawaga	1	0	0	0	0
Pinckny, Jonathan	Mohawk	1	2	3	0	?
Pine, Joshua	Harpersfield	5	2	4	0	0
Pinew, Silveneus	Canajoharie	1	1	1	0	0
Piper, [?]	German Flatts	1	2	2	0	0
Piper, Jacob	Herkimer	4	1	6	0	?
Pippinger, Richard	Mohawk	4	0	3	0	0
Pire, Jonah	Chemung	1	1	4	0	0
Pixley, David	Chemung	8	0	0	0	0
Plank, Adam	Caughnawaga	3	5	3	0	?
Plank, Henry	Palatine	1	1	1	0	?
Plank, John	Caughnawaga	1	2	1	?	?
Plants, John	Caughnawaga	1	0	1	0	0
Plants, John, Jr.	Caughnawaga	1	1	1	0	0
Plants, Peter	Caughnawaga	1	1	1	0	0
Platner, Jacob	Harpersfield	2	0	0	0	1
Plato, James	Mohawk	1	2	2	0	0
Platts, George	Canajoharie	1	3	4	0	0
Plumb, Joseph	Whites	4	1	2	0	0
Plump, Gerard	Mohawk	1	0	3	0	?
Plumteau, John H.	Mohawk	1	0	3	0	0
Plupper, Christian	Palatine	1	3	3	?	?
Plymate, Bononi	Mohawk	1	2	3	0	?
Pollard, David	Harpersfield	2	2	3	0	?
Pollard, Jeremiah	Herkimer	2	1	2	0	0
Polly, Matthew	Chemung	1	0	1	0	0
Polly, Uriah	Chemung	1	0	3	0	0
Pond, Barnabas	Whites	2	3	1	0	?
Pond, Timothy	Whites	2	1	4	0	?
Pond, Timothy, Jr.	Whites	1	1	3	?	?
Pool, Simeon	Whites	4	0	4	0	0
Pooler, John	Harpersfield	1	4	2	0	0

APPENDIX B

1790 FEDERAL CENSUS, MONTGOMERY COUNTY, NY

HOF	TOWN	M 16+	M -16	F	OFP	S
Pope, Gersham	Otsego	4	2	4	0	0
Pope, Ichabod	Otsego	3	0	0	0	?
Pope, Izra	Otsego	1	0	1	0	0
Porteous, John	Herkimer	5	0	3	0	2
Porter, Alexander	German Flatts	1	1	2	0	0
Porter, Ashbel	Canajoharie	2	3	2	0	?
Porter, Benjlack	Harpersfield	1	0	3	0	0
Porter, Elijah	Otsego	2	0	0	0	?
Porter, Nathan	Otsego	1	2	4	0	?
Porter, Raphel	Whites	2	0	2	0	?
Porter, William	Mohawk	1	0	1	0	0
Poss, Nicholas	Palatine	1	2	5	0	0
Post, John	Whites	2	1	4	?	?
Postle, Francis	Herkimer	1	2	3	0	0
Potter, Aaron	Canajoharie	1	1	3	0	?
Potter, Aseph	Canajoharie	1	0	0	0	?
Potter, Ephraim	Caughnawaga	2	1	6	0	0
Potter, Jeremiah	Herkimer	4	2	3	0	0
Potter, John	Mohawk	1	2	1	0	?
Potter, Joseph	Chemung	3	2	3	0	?
Potter, Lemuel	Harpersfield	2	1	2	0	?
Potter, Michael	Palatine	4	4	2	0	1
Potter, Sheldon	Whites	1	1	1	0	0
Potter, Stephen	Whites	3	1	3	0	0
Potter, William	Otsego	3	2	4	0	?
Powell, Charles	Canajoharie	1	3	5	0	?
Powell, Isaac	Whites	1	1	1	0	?
Powell, Jeremiah	German Flatts	1	3	2	0	?
Power, Avery	Chenango	2	2	4	0	?
Powers, Jacob	Mohawk	1	0	1	0	0
Powers, James	Canajoharie	1	3	4	0	?
Powers, Joseph	Canajoharie	1	2	4	0	?
Powers, Oliver	Canajoharie	3	1	2	0	?
Powers, Oliver	Mohawk	1	1	4	0	0
Pratt, Chalker	Caughnawaga	1	0	4	0	0
Pratt, Izra	Chemung	1	2	6	0	0
Pratt, Jacob	Otsego	2	0	0	0	0
Pratt, Lemuel	Canajoharie	1	1	1	0	?
Pratt, Lemuel	Harpersfield	1	2	3	0	?
Pratt, William	Caughnawaga	1	1	3	0	0
Prentis, Samuel	Canajoharie	1	0	1	0	0
Prentup, Joseph	Mohawk	3	1	4	0	0
Prentup, William	Mohawk	1	0	1	0	4
Presser, Jonathan	Harpersfield	1	1	3	0	?
Preston, Jacob	Otsego	2	0	2	0	0

1790 FEDERAL CENSUS, MONTGOMERY COUNTY, NY

HOF	TOWN	M 16+	M -16	F	OFP	S
Preston, John	Canajoharie	1	1	1	0	0
Preston, Samuel	Canajoharie	1	1	4	0	0
Preston, Samuel	Otsego	2	?	?	?	?
Price, George	Canajoharie	1	4	2	0	0
Price, Jessu	Mohawk	1	1	1	0	0
Price, John	Palatine	1	2	1	0	?
Prime, David	Caughnawaga	4	0	4	0	?
Prime, Elizabeth	Palatine	1	0	2	0	?
Proper, Samuel	Canajoharie	1	4	3	0	0
Provoree, Henry	Chemung	2	2	3	0	?
Prunder, Frederick	Canajoharie	1	4	2	0	?
Prunder, Jacob	Canajoharie	2	2	4	0	?
Prunder, Jacob	Canajoharie	3	0	1	0	?
Pryme, Francis	Mohawk	4	0	2	0	?
Pryme, Hendrick	Mohawk	1	1	2	0	?
Pryme, Hendrick	Mohawk	1	3	2	0	0
Pryme, John	Mohawk	1	1	3	0	0
Pryme, Lewis	Mohawk	1	2	1	0	?
Pryor, Azariah	Whites	1	0	1	0	0
Puddy, John	Caughnawaga	1	2	4	?	?
Pudney, Thorne	Canajoharie	1	1	1	0	0
Puffer, Isaac	Canajoharie	2	2	2	0	0
Puffer, Jabez	Canajoharie	1	0	0	0	0
Pumpstade, Frederick	Canajoharie	1	3	2	0	0
Purdy, Daniel	Chemung	3	1	2	0	0
Putman, Aaron	Caughnawaga	1	1	1	0	0
Putman, Aaron	Mohawk	2	1	4	0	?
Putman, Adam	Mohawk	1	3	4	0	0
Putman, Cornelius	Mohawk	2	0	2	0	?
Putman, David	Caughnawaga	1	1	3	0	0
Putman, Derick	Caughnawaga	2	4	3	0	?
Putman, Frederick	Mohawk	2	3	3	0	?
Putman, Garrit	Mohawk	2	1	4	0	0
Putman, Hendrick	Mohawk	1	2	2	0	0
Putman, John	Caughnawaga	1	2	3	0	?
Putman, Lodowick	Mohawk	1	2	3	0	?
Putman, Victor	Mohawk	2	2	3	0	1
Putman, Victor D.	Mohawk	1	4	1	0	?
Putnam, Charles	Whites	2	3	7	0	1
Putnam, David	Canajoharie	1	1	5	0	0
Putnam, David	Caughnawaga	2	4	4	0	?
Putnam, Francis	Caughnawaga	1	1	4	0	?
Putnam, George	Otsego	1	1	5	0	0
Putnam, Jacob	Caughnawaga	3	3	2	0	?
Putnam, Jacob, Jr.	Caughnawaga	1	5	2	0	?

1790 FEDERAL CENSUS, MONTGOMERY COUNTY, NY

HOF	TOWN	M 16+	M -16	F	OFP	S
Putnam, Jacobus	Caughnawaga	2	2	4	0	?
Putnam, John	Caughnawaga	2	0	7	0	?
Putnam, Victor	Caughnawaga	1	2	4	0	?
Quackenbus, Abraham D.	Mohawk	2	3	4	0	0
Quackenbush, Isaac	Otsego	1	3	?	?	?
Quackenbuss, [?]	Mohawk	1	2	1	0	0
Quackenbuss, Abraham	Mohawk	1	0	1	0	?
Quackenbuss, Abraham I.	Mohawk	1	2	2	0	0
Quackenbuss, David H.	Canajoharie	1	2	1	0	0
Quackenbuss, David P.	Canajoharie	1	2	3	0	?
Quackenbuss, Hunter	Canajoharie	3	2	2	0	0
Quackenbuss, Jeremiah	Canajoharie	3	1	4	0	0
Quackenbuss, John	Mohawk	1	0	1	0	?
Quackenbuss, John	Mohawk	1	2	3	0	0
Quackenbuss, Nicholas	Mohawk	1	2	3	0	0
Quackenbuss, Peter	Mohawk	1	2	7	0	0
Quackenbuss, Peter, Sr.	Canajoharie	3	0	2	0	0
Quackenbuss, Vincent	Mohawk	2	0	4	0	?
Quackenbuss, William	Canajoharie	1	2	1	0	0
Quackenbuss, William	Mohawk	1	2	3	0	?
Quick, Elijah	Mohawk	1	1	2	0	0
Quilhot, [?]	Caughnawaga	1	3	1	0	1
Quilhot, John	Caughnawaga	2	0	2	?	?
Quilhot, Stephen	Caughnawaga	1	3	2	0	1
Radley, John	Mohawk	2	2	3	0	0
Radtly, Jacobus	Palatine	1	1	2	0	0
Ramsay, Ebenezer	German Flatts	1	0	0	0	0
Ramsey, Ebenezer	Canajoharie	1	0	0	0	0
Rancan, James	Herkimer	1	1	1	0	0
Randell, Nathaniel	Canajoharie	1	3	4	0	0
Ranney, James	Whites	1	3	1	0	0
Ranney, Seth	Whites	10	1	4	0	0
Ranney, Willett	Whites	2	1	2	0	0
Ransford, Haskil	Chenango	1	0	0	0	?
Ransome, John	Canajoharie	1	0	0	0	0
Ransome, Samuel	Chemung	2	2	2	0	0
Ransome, Thomas	Canajoharie	3	2	2	0	0
Rapelyee, Isaac	Canajoharie	1	0	2	0	0
Rapp, George	Canajoharie	1	0	1	0	?
Rarity, Timothy	Canajoharie	1	2	3	0	0
Rasbel, Marks	Herkimer	3	1	3	0	0
Rase, Daniel	Harpersfield	1	0	1	0	0
Rathbon, Edmund	Harpersfield	2	2	4	0	?

1790 FEDERAL CENSUS, MONTGOMERY COUNTY, NY

HOF	TOWN	M 16+	M -16	F	OFP	S
Rathbon, Perry	Harpersfield	1	2	3	0	?
Rawlens, Aaron	Canajoharie	1	1	1	0	0
Rawlens, Michael	Caughnawaga	2	1	2	0	?
Raymond, Daniel	Mohawk	2	3	5	0	0
Reaver, Andrew	Palatine	3	3	4	0	0
Redfield, Jared	Harpersfield	1	1	1	0	0
Redington, John	Canajoharie	2	1	2	0	0
Redway, Samuel	Chemung	2	1	6	0	0
Reed, Curtis	Herkimer	1	2	2	0	0
Reedenbaker, Baltus	Herkimer	1	5	4	0	0
Rees, Jonas	Palatine	2	1	3	?	?
Rees, Nicholas	Mohawk	4	4	5	0	0
Rees, Peter	Palatine	3	0	2	?	?
Rees, Samuel	Canajoharie	2	4	4	0	0
Reese, Adam	German Flatts	3	2	4	0	0
Reese, Jacob	Caughnawaga	2	4	3	0	0
Reeves, Abner	Caughnawaga	1	2	4	?	?
Remsen, Jonathan	Canajoharie	1	2	7	0	0
Remsen, Jonathan	Palatine	1	7	2	0	?
Rennalds, George	Caughnawaga	1	0	2	?	?
Renolds, Eli	Harpersfield	1	1	2	0	?
Renolds, Eli, Jr.	Harpersfield	1	2	4	0	?
Renquard, Andrew	Otsego	1	1	1	0	?
Reuby, Christopher	German Flatts	1	1	1	0	0
Rheel, Frederick	Herkimer	5	0	2	0	0
Rice, Amaziah	Whites	1	2	1	0	0
Rice, Hezekiah	Whites	3	0	0	0	0
Rice, Hezekiah	Whites	3	0	0	0	?
Rice, James	Caughnawaga	1	0	1	0	?
Rice, John	Canajoharie	3	1	2	0	?
Rice, John	Palatine	1	1	3	0	?
Rice, John, Jr.	Canajoharie	1	1	3	0	0
Rice, Pebetiah	Canajoharie	2	1	6	0	0
Rice, Seth	Canajoharie	1	1	3	0	0
Rice, William	Whites	1	0	3	0	0
Rich, Calvin	Canajoharie	1	1	1	0	?
Rich, Luther	Canajoharie	3	1	3	0	?
Rich, Moses	Canajoharie	1	3	3	?	?
Rich, Simon	Canajoharie	2	5	5	0	?
Richards, Moses	Otsego	2	4	4	0	0
Richardson, Daniel, Sr.	Caughnawaga	4	3	6	0	0
Richardson, Jonathan	Mohawk	1	2	4	0	0
Richardson, William	Caughnawaga	1	2	2	?	?
Richel, Christian	Herkimer	2	1	2	0	?
Richmond, Daniel	Herkimer	1	1	6	0	0

1790 FEDERAL CENSUS, MONTGOMERY COUNTY, NY

HOF	TOWN	M 16+	M -16	F	OFP	S
Richmond, Edward	Canajoharie	1	1	3	0	0
Richter, Nicholas	Palatine	2	2	5	?	?
Rickart, Conradt	Mohawk	2	0	3	0	?
Rickart, Conradt	Palatine	2	1	2	0	?
Rickart, Ludwick	Palatine	2	2	5	0	?
Ricker, Peter	Mohawk	1	2	5	?	?
Rickey, Andrew	Harpersfield	1	0	5	0	0
Rickhart, George	Canajoharie	3	2	5	0	?
Rickhart, John	Canajoharie	1	3	3	0	?
Riddle, Robert	Canajoharie	3	2	3	0	0
Rider, George	Palatine	1	1	2	0	0
Riechel, Godfrey	Herkimer	1	0	1	?	?
Ried, Abner	Herkimer	1	0	0	0	0
Ried, Conradt	Mohawk	1	2	3	0	0
Ried, Daniel	Chemung	2	2	5	0	?
Ried, Ebenezer	Caughnawaga	1	2	4	0	0
Ried, John	Palatine	1	2	1	0	?
Ried, Thomas	Caughnawaga	1	2	1	0	3
Riegel, Cornelius	Canajoharie	1	0	3	0	0
Riemau, Christian	Herkimer	1	0	1	0	0
Riemau, Jacob	Herkimer	1	1	3	0	0
Riemau, John	Herkimer	5	0	4	0	0
Riemensnider, John	Palatine	2	2	4	0	?
Rienhart, William	Canajoharie	1	0	0	0	0
Riensier, George	Canajoharie	1	1	4	0	0
Riepsome, Conradt	Canajoharie	2	1	3	0	?
Riker, Charles Sedam	Mohawk	1	1	3	0	0
Riker, Henry	Mohawk	4	1	2	0	0
Rims, Christopher	Canajoharie	2	5	2	0	0
Ripsome, Elizabeth	Canajoharie	3	0	3	0	?
Ripsome, Peter	Canajoharie	2	1	3	0	0
Ripsome, William	Canajoharie	1	0	3	0	0
Risley, Allen	Whites	2	0	2	?	?
Risley, Elijah	Whites	2	2	3	0	?
Ritmier, Henry	Mohawk	1	0	2	0	0
Ritmier, John	Mohawk	2	0	2	0	0
Ritter, Frederick	Palatine	1	1	2	0	0
Ritter, Henry	Palatine	1	1	2	0	?
Riverson, John Peter	Canajoharie	1	0	2	0	?
Rix, Michael	Caughnawaga	1	0	1	0	0
Robens, Ephraim	Whites	1	1	2	0	0
Roberts, James	Otsego	1	3	2	0	0
Roberts, John	Chemung	1	0	2	0	0
Roberts, Peter	Chemung	2	2	4	0	0
Robertson, Alexander	Caughnawaga	1	1	1	0	0

1790 FEDERAL CENSUS, MONTGOMERY COUNTY, NY

HOF	TOWN	M 16+	M -16	F	OFP	S
Robertson, Alexander	Mohawk	2	1	2	0	?
Robertson, John	Caughnawaga	1	0	1	0	0
Robinson, Hugh	Canajoharie	1	0	1	0	0
Robinson, John	Mohawk	1	4	3	0	0
Robinson, Matthew	Otsego	2	2	2	0	0
Robinson, Peter	Canajoharie	3	2	1	0	0
Robinson, Peter	Caughnawaga	2	2	2	0	?
Robinson, Robert	Caughnawaga	1	2	2	0	?
Robinson, Samuel	Canajoharie	1	0	0	0	0
Rock, Jonathan	Mohawk	1	2	2	0	0
Rockwell, Silas	Harpersfield	1	1	4	0	0
Rodenhour, Jacob	Canajoharie	1	1	5	0	0
Roe, William	Chemung	2	4	5	0	?
Rogers, Francis	Caughnawaga	3	1	2	?	?
Rogers, Simeon	Whites	1	0	1	0	0
Romyne, Abraham	Caughnawaga	3	1	4	?	?
Romyne, Thomas	Caughnawaga	3	2	1	0	?
Rooff, John	Canajoharie	3	3	4	0	2
Roorback, John	Canajoharie	4	0	2	2	2
Root, Daniel	Harpersfield	2	0	0	0	?
Root, Joseph, Sr.	Whites	3	1	3	0	?
Root, Josiah	Canajoharie	1	2	2	0	0
Root, Moses	Otsego	2	3	7	0	?
Root, Simeon	Whites	1	0	4	0	?
Rosback, Frederick	Palatine	2	2	4	0	0
Rose, Jacob	Chemung	1	2	3	0	?
Rose, William	Chemung	1	4	2	0	0
Roseboom, John	Canajoharie	4	2	2	0	?
Roseboom, Robert	Canajoharie	1	2	1	0	?
Rosegrants, Abraham	German Flatts	3	1	3	0	0
Rosen, Silas	Canajoharie	2	0	1	0	0
Rote, Charles	Palatine	2	1	3	0	?
Roth, John	Canajoharie	1	1	4	0	1
Rothbone, Benjamin	Canajoharie	3	2	3	0	0
Round, John	Mohawk	1	0	0	0	0
Round, Samuel	Mohawk	1	0	0	0	0
Rowland, Henry	Mohawk	2	1	3	0	?
Rowley, William	Chemung	2	1	6	?	?
Rowly, Daniel	Caughnawaga	1	0	5	0	0
Rowly, Joel	Mohawk	2	5	3	0	0
Rowly, Seth	Mohawk	1	0	3	0	0
Rown, Nicholas	Herkimer	2	0	2	?	?
Roxford, Ensign	Mohawk	1	1	1	0	0
Ruby, John	Canajoharie	1	0	1	0	?
Ruluffson, Lawrence	Mohawk	4	1	4	0	?

1790 FEDERAL CENSUS, MONTGOMERY COUNTY, NY

HOF	TOWN	M 16+	M -16	F	OFP	S
Rulufson, Samuel	Mohawk	1	0	0	0	0
Rumerfield, Anthony	Chemung	1	1	0	?	?
Rummer, John	Harpersfield	3	0	5	0	?
Runnelds, Jarid	Canajoharie	1	1	1	0	0
Runnells, Stephen	Mohawk	1	2	1	0	0
Runnels, Elijah	Chemung	2	1	2	0	?
Runnils, [?]	Palatine	3	1	4	0	0
Runyan, Benjamin	Palatine	1	1	2	0	0
Runyan, Henry	Mohawk	1	2	2	0	0
Runyan, John	Otsego	3	1	1	0	0
Runyan, Jonathan	Otsego	1	1	3	0	0
Runyan, Samuel	Caughnawaga	1	1	?	?	?
Rupulson, John	Mohawk	1	0	2	0	0
Rury, Henry	Mohawk	3	3	4	0	?
Rury, William	Mohawk	1	1	2	0	0
Russel, Samuel	Herkimer	2	0	0	0	?
Russell, Alexander	Caughnawaga	2	3	2	?	?
Russell, Daniel	Palatine	1	1	2	0	?
Russell, John	Otsego	1	3	1	0	0
Russell, Nathan	Canajoharie	1	0	3	0	0
Rust, Amaziah	Caughnawaga	1	1	3	?	?
Rust, Elijah	Whites	1	0	0	0	0
Rust, Samuel	Whites	1	1	3	0	0
Ryan, Magdalin	German Flatts	0	1	3	0	?
Ryne, Lawrence	Canajoharie	1	4	2	0	0
Rynes, John	Mohawk	1	3	1	0	0
Sabins, Walter	Chemung	1	?	4	0	?
Sable, William	Canajoharie	1	0	4	0	0
Safford, Darius	Mohawk	1	0	0	0	?
Sage, Silah	Chemung	1	4	4	0	?
Sagner, Conradt	German Flatts	1	1	2	0	?
Sagner, Paul	German Flatts	1	2	7	0	?
Sails, Darius	Whites	3	2	3	0	0
Sails, George	Whites	1	0	2	0	0
Sails, Jeremiah	Whites	1	0	0	0	0
Saler, Gasper	Canajoharie	2	2	4	0	0
Salisbury, Richard	Mohawk	1	0	2	0	?
Saltsman, George	Palatine	3	0	4	0	?
Saltsman, Henry	Palatine	4	2	4	0	0
Saltsman, John	Palatine	1	3	6	0	0
Saltsman, William	Palatine	1	2	1	0	1
Sample, Samuel	Mohawk	4	4	6	0	?
Sanders, Hendrick	Canajoharie	2	2	7	0	1
Sanford, Jonah	Whites	2	4	2	0	0

1790 FEDERAL CENSUS, MONTGOMERY COUNTY, NY

HOF	TOWN	M 16+	M -16	F	OFP	S
Sangor, Jedediah	Whites	6	1	3	0	?
Sarles, Lemuel	Chemung	1	1	4	0	0
Sarles, Reuben	Chemung	3	2	5	0	0
Sartel, John	Chemung	2	4	2	0	0
Sashy, Abraham	Mohawk	2	0	?	?	?
Satchel, William	Whites	2	2	3	0	?
Saterly, Selah	Chemung	1	3	4	0	0
Saunders, Henry	Caughnawaga	3	0	1	0	0
Savage, Gideon	Whites	2	3	4	?	?
Schermerhorn, Jacob H.	Mohawk	2	1	3	0	2
Schermerhorn, John	Mohawk	1	3	4	0	0
Scholl, George	Canajoharie	1	4	3	0	?
Schoten, Isaiah	Canajoharie	2	1	3	0	?
Schut, William	Canajoharie	1	0	3	0	0
Schuyler, Cimon	Mohawk	3	0	1	0	?
Schuyler, David A.	Canajoharie	1	3	2	0	?
Schuyler, David P.	Canajoharie	1	0	1	0	?
Schuyler, Jacob	Mohawk	2	2	2	0	0
Schuyler, John	Mohawk	2	3	3	0	0
Schuyler, Lear	Canajoharie	1	1	1	0	0
Schuyler, Nicholas	Canajoharie	1	3	1	0	?
Schuyler, Peter	Palatine	4	0	1	9	?
Schuyler, Peter D.	Canajoharie	1	0	3	0	?
Schuyler, Peter P.	Canajoharie	1	3	4	0	?
Scott, [?]	Caughnawaga	1	1	1	0	0
Scott, David	Palatine	1	0	2	0	0
Scott, Elijah	Harpersfield	1	1	1	0	0
Scott, Ezekel	Whites	1	1	3	0	?
Scott, Henry	Otsego	1	1	3	0	0
Scott, James	Canajoharie	2	0	2	0	?
Scott, John	Mohawk	5	3	1	0	0
Scott, John	Otsego	2	2	3	0	0
Scott, Joseph	Caughnawaga	2	4	7	0	0
Scott, Thomas	Palatine	1	3	4	0	0
Scramlin, David	Otsego	1	2	3	0	?
Scramlin, George	Otsego	2	2	3	?	?
Scramlin, Henry	Otsego	5	0	4	0	?
Scramling, Henry	Canajoharie	2	0	3	0	0
Scribner, Aaron	Herkimer	1	3	1	0	0
Seahouse, Yost	Canajoharie	1	3	2	0	0
Seamore, Ebenezer	Herkimer	1	1	4	0	?
Seamore, Enos	Caughnawaga	2	2	4	0	0
Seamore, Sarah	Caughnawaga	0	1	2	0	?
Seamore, Uriah	Whites	2	1	2	0	0
Sears, Allen	Caughnawaga	1	0	2	0	?

1790 FEDERAL CENSUS, MONTGOMERY COUNTY, NY

HOF	TOWN	M 16+	M -16	F	OFP	S
Sebor, Henry	Caughnawaga	2	1	2	0	0
Seeber, Conradt	Canajoharie	1	2	4	0	?
Seeber, James	Canajoharie	1	1	2	0	?
Seeber, John	Canajoharie	2	0	4	0	?
Seeber, William	Canajoharie	3	0	5	0	?
Seeley, James	Chemung	1	3	2	0	0
Seeley, Nathaniel	Chemung	1	1	2	0	0
Seeley, Nathaniel, Jr.	Chemung	3	0	2	0	1
Seeley, Samuel	Chemung	1	3	4	0	0
Seely, Bezeliel	Chemung	6	3	5	1	3
Segar, Thomas	Canajoharie	1	0	5	0	0
Seldon, Benjamin	Chemung	1	0	4	0	0
Seley, David	Mohawk	1	0	0	0	0
Seley, John	Palatine	3	3	5	0	1
Selleback, John	Palatine	1	2	3	0	?
Serenias, Christopher	Palatine	1	2	3	0	?
Service, Christian	Mohawk	3	2	4	0	0
Service, Christian	Mohawk	1	2	2	0	?
Service, Frederick	Mohawk	2	2	3	0	0
Service, George	Mohawk	2	6	2	0	0
Service, John	Mohawk	1	1	4	0	?
Service, Peter	Caughnawaga	3	2	3	0	0
Service, William	Mohawk	1	2	5	0	?
Severt, Jacob	Mohawk	1	2	2	0	0
Seward, Nathan	Whites	1	0	1	0	0
Sexton, James	Mohawk	1	3	3	0	0
Shaffee, Joseph	Canajoharie	1	0	4	0	?
Shaffer, Adam	Canajoharie	2	1	3	0	0
Shaffer, Henry	Palatine	3	4	4	0	0
Shaffer, Jacob	Canajoharie	1	2	3	0	?
Shaffer, John	Canajoharie	3	1	1	0	?
Shaffer, John	Palatine	4	1	4	0	0
Shallup, Hendrick	Mohawk	1	4	2	0	?
Shalop, Christian	Mohawk	1	0	4	0	0
Shankcling, Alexander	Canajoharie	2	2	3	0	0
Shares, Lenox	Caughnawaga	1	2	3	0	0
Sharpenstine, Jacob	Mohawk	4	1	6	0	0
Shaver, Adam	Canajoharie	4	1	3	0	0
Shaver, Henry	Canajoharie	1	1	1	0	0
Shaves, John	Caughnawaga	1	4	3	0	0
Shaw, Comfort	Caughnawaga	1	3	1	0	0
Shaw, Samuel	Whites	1	5	4	0	0
Sheaffer, Henry	Herkimer	3	0	4	0	?
Sheanhults, Frederick	Canajoharie	1	0	4	0	0
Shearman, James	Whites	1	4	0	0	?

1790 FEDERAL CENSUS, MONTGOMERY COUNTY, NY

HOF	TOWN	M 16+	M -16	F	OFP	S
Shearman, Levy	Whites	2	3	5	0	0
Shearman, Solomon	Harpersfield	1	2	1	?	?
Sheep, George F.	Caughnawaga	1	3	3	0	0
Sheer, Ludowick	Mohawk	1	1	5	0	0
Sheer, Manassa	Mohawk	1	2	3	0	0
Sheldon, Asa	Palatine	1	0	4	0	0
Sheldon, Elickim	Canajoharie	1	2	5	0	?
Sheldon, Elisha	Harpersfield	4	0	1	0	0
Sheldon, Stephen	Whites	3	0	0	0	0
Sheley, Martin	Canajoharie	2	0	3	0	?
Sheley, Martin, Jr.	Canajoharie	1	4	4	0	?
Shell, Frederick	Herkimer	2	0	2	0	0
Shell, John	Herkimer	4	0	6	0	0
Shell, Marks	Herkimer	1	0	0	0	0
Shell, Marks, Sr.	Herkimer	4	1	1	0	?
Shemell, Conradt	Canajoharie	1	1	1	0	0
Shemell, Francis	Canajoharie	4	2	4	0	0
Shepperd, Henry	Harpersfield	2	2	4	0	0
Shepperman, Christian	Palatine	1	1	3	0	0
Sherwood, Levy	Chemung	2	2	1	0	0
Shever, Partle	Palatine	1	5	3	0	0
Shill, Jacob	Palatine	1	2	1	0	0
Shilling, James	Mohawk	2	0	6	0	?
Shipman, David	Otsego	1	0	1	0	0
Shipman, Samuel	Otsego	2	2	5	0	0
Shippey, Ashkenius	Chemung	1	2	2	0	0
Shireman, Elizabeth	Canajoharie	0	2	1	0	0
Shoaf, Michael	Chemung	1	2	1	0	0
Shoe, Henry	Caughnawaga	1	1	3	0	?
Shoe, Jacob	Caughnawaga	1	1	1	0	?
Shoe, Stephen	Caughnawaga	1	1	2	0	0
Shoemaker, [?], Sr.	German Flatts	4	1	3	0	0
Shoemaker, Cartroudt	German Flatts	0	1	2	0	3
Shoemaker, Christopher	German Flatts	1	0	5	0	0
Shoemaker, Frederick	German Flatts	1	0	2	0	0
Shoemaker, Frederick, Sr.	German Flatts	2	2	2	0	0
Shoemaker, Rudolph	German Flatts	2	2	2	0	1
Shoemaker, Samuel	Chemung	1	4	1	0	?
Shoemaker, Thomas	German Flatts	4	3	8	0	?
Shoemaker, Yost	German Flatts	1	3	3	0	2
Shok, Zachariah	Palatine	1	?	?	?	?
Sholl, Bastian	Canajoharie	1	0	1	0	0
Sholl, Hendrick	Canajoharie	1	2	1	0	0
Sholl, Honyost	Palatine	1	1	8	?	?
Sholl, John	Canajoharie	1	3	1	0	?

APPENDIX B

1790 FEDERAL CENSUS, MONTGOMERY COUNTY, NY

HOF	TOWN	M 16+	M -16	F	OFP	S
Sholl, John	Palatine	1	3	3	0	0
Sholl, John, Sr.	Canajoharie	1	0	1	0	0
Sholl, Matice	Canajoharie	1	2	1	0	0
Short, Dorus	Canajoharie	4	0	1	0	0
Shotenkirk, Lydia	Caughnawaga	2	0	3	0	?
Shoults, Henry	Palatine	2	4	2	0	?
Shoults, John	Palatine	2	1	5	0	0
Shoults, John Jacob	Palatine	2	2	3	0	?
Shoultz, George	Palatine	4	1	6	0	0
Shoultz, Henry I.	Palatine	1	2	1	?	?
Shoultz, John I.	Palatine	2	1	6	0	0
Shoutz, Jacob	Palatine	2	1	3	0	1
Shuler, Jacob	Mohawk	1	1	1	0	0
Shuler, John	Mohawk	1	0	1	0	0
Shuler, Lawrence	Mohawk	1	1	2	0	5
Shuler, Solomon	Mohawk	1	1	1	0	0
Shurman, Jedediah	Whites	2	1	2	0	0
Shurman, Palmer	Whites	2	2	3	0	0
Shurman, Samuel	German Flatts	2	1	2	0	?
Shutes, William	Mohawk	1	0	2	0	0
Shutts, Christian	Caughnawaga	1	0	1	0	1
Sice, Gilbert	Caughnawaga	1	1	2	0	0
Siets, Henry	Canajoharie	3	2	7	0	0
Siets, Peter	Canajoharie	1	2	1	0	0
Silah, Josiah	Harpersfield	2	1	2	0	0
Siles, Jobe	Chemung	1	2	3	0	?
Sill, Andrew	Otsego	2	0	0	0	0
Silleback, Christian	Herkimer	1	0	0	0	0
Silsbury, Jonathan	Canajoharie	1	2	1	0	0
Silsbury, Jonathan, Jr.	Chemung	1	0	2	0	0
Simmons, Abraham	Palatine	1	2	1	?	?
Simmons, Benjamin	Caughnawaga	1	4	3	0	0
Simmons, Frederick	Caughnawaga	3	0	1	0	0
Simmons, Isaac	Canajoharie	1	2	2	0	0
Simmons, Jacob	Caughnawaga	1	2	4	0	0
Simmons, John	Chemung	2	0	2	0	?
Simmons, Martin	Canajoharie	3	0	1	0	0
Simpson, John	Canajoharie	1	1	3	0	?
Simpson, Joseph	Harpersfield	1	2	2	0	0
Simpson, Robert	Mohawk	1	0	3	0	?
Sims, William	Mohawk	1	1	1	0	0
Simser, Henry	Caughnawaga	1	2	3	0	0
Sines, Peter	Otsego	1	2	2	0	?
Siser, Samuel	Whites	6	3	4	0	0
Sitemore, John	Canajoharie	3	0	3	0	0

1790 FEDERAL CENSUS, MONTGOMERY COUNTY, NY

HOF	TOWN	M 16+	M -16	F	OFP	S
Sitemore, John, Jr.	Canajoharie	1	1	2	0	0
Sits, Baltus	Canajoharie	1	1	6	0	0
Sixbury, Adam	Caughnawaga	3	1	5	0	0
Sixbury, Cornelius	Caughnawaga	1	0	2	0	0
Sixbury, Hendrick	Caughnawaga	2	0	2	0	0
Skeal, Nathan	Mohawk	1	3	5	0	0
Skeal, Niram	Mohawk	1	1	1	0	0
Skeal, Thomas	Mohawk	1	0	0	0	0
Skiff, Benjamin	Mohawk	2	0	1	0	?
Skiff, Stephen	Mohawk	1	4	1	0	?
Skinner, David	Caughnawaga	1	0	1	0	?
Skinner, Gershom	Herkimer	1	1	4	0	0
Skinner, Jessee	Mohawk	1	3	6	0	?
Skinner, Jonathan	Harpersfield	1	0	3	0	0
Skinner, Josiah	Mohawk	1	2	4	?	?
Skinner, Levy	Mohawk	1	1	3	?	?
Skinner, Nathaniel	Harpersfield	2	1	2	0	0
Skipperd, Samuel	Whites	3	2	3	0	?
Skulgraft, Richard	Palatine	1	0	1	0	0
Sleeper, John, Sr.	Otsego	4	1	3	0	0
Sleeper, Joseph, Sr.	Otsego	1	0	1	0	0
Sleeper, Samuel	Otsego	1	1	1	0	0
Sliter, Cornelius	Otsego	1	0	1	0	?
Sliter, Jonas	Otsego	2	2	2	0	?
Sliter, Peter	Harpersfield	1	2	2	0	0
Sloan, Hugh	Harpersfield	1	2	2	0	?
Sloan, John	Canajoharie	3	1	5	0	0
Sloan, Peter	Caughnawaga	2	1	5	0	?
Smiley, William	Chenango	1	2	2	0	?
Smith, Aaron	Caughnawaga	3	1	3	0	?
Smith, Adam	Herkimer	2	1	7	0	?
Smith, Alexander	Harpersfield	4	1	1	0	?
Smith, Amos	Whites	1	3	2	0	?
Smith, Andrew	Canajoharie	1	0	1	0	0
Smith, Asa	Harpersfield	2	3	3	0	0
Smith, Baltus	Palatine	1	3	2	0	0
Smith, Benjamin	Whites	2	2	4	0	0
Smith, Bill	Whites	2	0	4	0	0
Smith, Christopher	Mohawk	1	1	4	0	0
Smith, Clark	Herkimer	1	1	2	0	0
Smith, Conradt	Canajoharie	1	1	2	0	0
Smith, Conradt	Chemung	1	0	3	0	?
Smith, Cornelius	Caughnawaga	1	2	4	0	2
Smith, David	Whites	2	0	0	0	0
Smith, Ebenezer	Whites	1	1	2	0	0

1790 FEDERAL CENSUS, MONTGOMERY COUNTY, NY

HOF	TOWN	M 16+	M -16	F	OFP	S
Smith, Edmund	Harpersfield	1	0	2	0	0
Smith, Edward	Harpersfield	2	0	2	0	0
Smith, Elijah	Whites	1	2	6	0	?
Smith, Ephraim	Mohawk	1	1	1	0	0
Smith, Frederick	Herkimer	1	1	2	0	?
Smith, George	Canajoharie	2	2	6	0	?
Smith, George	Herkimer	2	1	3	0	0
Smith, George	Palatine	2	4	4	0	0
Smith, Gerard	Mohawk	1	3	2	0	?
Smith, Gershom	Canajoharie	1	2	3	0	?
Smith, Gershom	Canajoharie	1	1	1	0	0
Smith, Gilbert	Harpersfield	1	1	2	0	0
Smith, Hendrick	Palatine	1	1	4	0	0
Smith, Hendrick, Jr.	Palatine	1	1	1	0	0
Smith, Henry	Canajoharie	1	0	1	0	?
Smith, Henry	Palatine	2	1	3	0	0
Smith, Hermanus	Caughnawaga	2	2	3	0	1
Smith, Isaac	Canajoharie	1	0	0	0	0
Smith, Israel	Harpersfield	5	1	3	0	0
Smith, Israel, Jr.	Harpersfield	1	0	1	0	0
Smith, Jacobala	Canajoharie	1	3	4	0	?
Smith, James	Canajoharie	4	0	1	0	0
Smith, James	Caughnawaga	2	0	1	0	?
Smith, James	Harpersfield	2	2	2	0	0
Smith, James	Whites	1	0	0	0	0
Smith, James	Whites	1	2	1	0	0
Smith, James	Whites	4	1	3	0	0
Smith, James, Jr.	Canajoharie	1	1	4	0	0
Smith, Jeremiah	Mohawk	1	3	2	0	0
Smith, Jeremiah	Palatine	1	1	2	0	0
Smith, Jessee	Chemung	1	4	1	0	0
Smith, John	Canajoharie	1	2	4	0	?
Smith, John	Canajoharie	2	1	2	0	0
Smith, John	Canajoharie	1	3	6	0	0
Smith, John	Caughnawaga	1	4	2	?	?
Smith, John	Chemung	1	1	2	0	0
Smith, John	German Flatts	4	3	6	0	0
Smith, John	Mohawk	2	1	2	0	0
Smith, John	Mohawk	2	1	1	0	0
Smith, John	Palatine	1	0	1	0	?
Smith, John	Whites	2	0	3	0	?
Smith, John M.	Herkimer	1	3	1	0	0
Smith, Joseph	Caughnawaga	1	0	3	0	?
Smith, Joshua	Canajoharie	1	0	1	0	0
Smith, Matthew	Canajoharie	3	0	1	0	0

1790 FEDERAL CENSUS, MONTGOMERY COUNTY, NY

HOF	TOWN	M 16+	M -16	F	OFP	S
Smith, Nathan	Whites	5	0	5	0	0
Smith, Nathaniel	Caughnawaga	1	2	4	0	0
Smith, Nicholas	Palatine	2	1	5	0	0
Smith, Noah	Herkimer	1	0	0	?	?
Smith, Peter	Canajoharie	1	1	1	0	0
Smith, Peter	Canajoharie	2	0	0	0	0
Smith, Peter	Whites	2	0	0	0	0
Smith, Philip	Canajoharie	3	1	2	0	0
Smith, Recompence	Canajoharie	1	0	2	0	?
Smith, Reuben	Canajoharie	2	4	2	0	0
Smith, Rosel	Chemung	2	3	4	0	?
Smith, Samuel	Mohawk	1	1	3	0	0
Smith, Shederick	Whites	1	2	5	0	0
Smith, Stephen, Jr.	Otsego	2	1	1	?	?
Smith, Stephen, Sr.	Otsego	2	3	2	?	?
Smith, Teunis	Canajoharie	1	0	1	0	0
Smith, Thomas	Mohawk	1	2	2	0	0
Smith, Yost	Herkimer	1	1	2	0	0
Snake, Frederick	Canajoharie	2	0	3	0	?
Sneaf, Lucas	Palatine	1	1	5	0	0
Snell, Adam	Canajoharie	1	1	1	0	?
Snell, Eve	Palatine	3	0	2	0	0
Snell, Jacob	Palatine	2	3	3	1	9
Snell, John	Palatine	4	3	3	0	0
Snell, John J.	Palatine	1	3	2	0	0
Snell, John S.	Palatine	1	3	2	0	0
Snell, Nicholas	Palatine	2	4	?	?	?
Snell, Peter	Palatine	1	8	4	0	0
Snell, Peter G.	Palatine	1	0	1	0	0
Snell, Severinius	Palatine	2	1	6	0	0
Snell, Zeely	Canajoharie	1	3	4	0	?
Snider, Cutlip	Canajoharie	1	3	2	0	0
Snider, Jacob	Canajoharie	1	0	7	0	?
Snider, John	Canajoharie	1	3	5	0	0
Snider, Michael	Canajoharie	2	1	3	0	0
Snider, William	Canajoharie	1	1	2	0	0
Snikerbacker, Francis	Chemung	1	0	2	0	0
Snook, Jacob	Caughnawaga	1	0	2	0	?
Snow, Elijah	German Flatts	1	2	4	0	0
Snow, Joseph	Caughnawaga	1	3	3	0	0
Snuke, Henry	Mohawk	1	2	1	0	0
Snuke, William	Mohawk	2	2	5	0	?
Soap, Michael	Harpersfield	1	0	1	0	0
Sodore, Isaac	Canajoharie	1	3	3	0	?
Souch, Peter	Palatine	2	3	5	0	?

HOF	TOWN	M 16+	M -16	F	OFP	S
Soul, Jonathan	Otsego	1	1	6	0	?
Soul, Joseph	Whites	4	1	4	0	0
Souls, Moses	Canajoharie	3	2	0	0	0
Soutch, George	Palatine	1	0	1	0	0
Soutch, John	Palatine	6	1	4	0	0
Soutch, John	Palatine	2	2	5	1	0
Soutch, John P.	Palatine	1	0	5	0	0
Soutch, Peter P.	Palatine	2	1	3	0	0
Soutel, Peter, Sr.	Caughnawaga	2	2	3	0	0
Southward, William	Canajoharie	2	3	1	0	?
Southward, William, Jr.	Canajoharie	1	1	2	0	?
Sparks, Pearl	Canajoharie	2	1	1	0	?
Spaulding, Amasa	Caughnawaga	1	3	3	0	?
Spaulding, Edward	Chemung	1	2	4	0	0
Spaulding, Nehemiah	Chemung	2	1	4	0	?
Spaulsberry, John	Canajoharie	2	1	4	0	0
Spencer, John	Herkimer	1	0	3	0	?
Spencer, Jonathan	Otsego	6	4	1	0	?
Spencer, Orange	Otsego	1	0	2	0	?
Spencer, Rufus	Herkimer	1	2	3	0	?
Spencer, William	Otsego	1	0	2	0	0
Spondable, John	Palatine	2	4	2	0	0
Sponenbarack, George	Caughnawaga	1	1	1	0	0
Spoon, Nicholas	Herkimer	3	2	3	0	0
Spoon, Warner	German Flatts	2	0	3	0	?
Spooner, Ruggles	Canajoharie	1	1	1	0	0
Spooner, Stephen	Canajoharie	2	0	1	0	0
Spoore, John	Harpersfield	1	1	4	0	?
Spore, Henry	Mohawk	1	0	2	0	?
Spore, John	Mohawk	1	0	1	0	0
Spore, Nicholas	Mohawk	2	1	4	0	1
Spraig, Jonathan	Chemung	1	1	4	0	0
Spraker, Conradt	Canajoharie	1	0	4	0	0
Spraker, George	Palatine	2	2	6	0	1
Spraker, John	Palatine	1	2	6	0	?
Spraker, Joseph	Palatine	1	0	2	?	?
Sprig, Alexander	Canajoharie	1	0	3	0	0
Springsteel, Jacob	Harpersfield	1	0	3	0	1
Springsteel, John	Harpersfield	2	0	2	0	0
Squire, John	Chemung	1	5	5	0	?
Squire, John, Jr.	Chemung	1	1	1	0	?
Squire, Zachariah	Chemung	3	4	3	0	?
Squires, Ichabod	Palatine	2	1	2	0	0
St. John, David	Harpersfield	1	1	3	0	0
Staals, Garret	Canajoharie	2	2	4	0	0

1790 FEDERAL CENSUS, MONTGOMERY COUNTY, NY

HOF	TOWN	M 16+	M -16	F	OFP	S
Staats, Francis	Mohawk	1	0	0	0	0
Stackweather, Elijah	Herkimer	1	1	4	0	0
Stacy, Isaac	Otsego	1	1	5	0	0
Stale, Adam	German Flatts	4	2	4	0	?
Stale, Dedrick	German Flatts	4	0	2	0	0
Stale, George	German Flatts	2	2	7	0	0
Stale, Rudolph	German Flatts	1	1	3	0	0
Stall, Anthony, Jr.	Caughnawaga	2	0	1	0	0
Stall, Joseph	Caughnawaga	4	1	8	0	?
Stally, Job	Caughnawaga	1	2	4	0	0
Staly, Hendrick	Mohawk	1	2	4	0	?
Staly, Jacob	Caughnawaga	2	1	1	0	?
Staly, John	Canajoharie	1	2	3	0	0
Staly, Ruloof	Mohawk	1	2	4	0	?
Staly, Silvanus	Mohawk	1	6	6	0	0
Stam, Elizabeth	Palatine	4	2	4	0	0
Standard, Oliver	Herkimer	1	0	3	0	0
Stanly, John	Whites	1	5	5	0	?
Stanson, George	Canajoharie	1	2	1	0	0
Stanson, John	Mohawk	1	1	1	0	0
Stanton, Daniel	Harpersfield	2	0	2	0	0
Stanton, Elijah	Mohawk	1	0	0	0	0
Stanton, John	Mohawk	2	3	2	0	?
Stanton, Rosel	Caughnawaga	1	0	0	?	?
Staples, George	Whites	7	0	4	0	0
Starenbarack, Adam	Mohawk	2	0	1	0	?
Starenburg, Joseph, Jr.	Mohawk	1	1	3	0	0
Staring, Adam	Herkimer	1	0	4	0	0
Staring, Adam	Herkimer	2	3	4	0	2
Staring, Adam	Mohawk	1	3	3	0	0
Staring, Adam A.	Herkimer	1	1	4	0	0
Staring, Adam N.	German Flatts	3	1	6	0	?
Staring, Adam, Sr.	German Flatts	3	2	2	0	0
Staring, Conradt	Palatine	1	2	4	0	?
Staring, Falatine	Herkimer	2	0	2	0	0
Staring, Frederick	Mohawk	2	2	2	0	0
Staring, George	Palatine	1	0	3	0	0
Staring, Henry	Herkimer	3	4	5	0	0
Staring, Henry N.	German Flatts	1	2	3	0	0
Staring, Jacob	Herkimer	1	0	2	0	0
Staring, Jacob	Palatine	2	0	3	0	0
Staring, John	Mohawk	1	3	2	?	?
Staring, Joseph	German Flatts	2	2	7	0	?
Staring, Nicholas	German Flatts	3	2	4	0	?
Staring, Philip	Mohawk	1	3	3	0	0

1790 FEDERAL CENSUS, MONTGOMERY COUNTY, NY

HOF	TOWN	M 16+	M -16	F	OFP	S
Staring, William	Mohawk	1	1	3	?	?
Starnbarack, Adam	Mohawk	1	1	4	0	0
Starr, Ebenezer	Harpersfield	1	2	2	0	0
State, Anthony, Jr.	Caughnawaga	1	0	1	0	0
Stebbins, Judah	Whites	3	0	2	0	0
Stebbins, Judah, Jr.	Whites	1	2	1	0	0
Steel, Hezekiah	Caughnawaga	1	0	2	0	0
Steel, James	Whites	3	5	2	?	?
Steel, Nathaniel	Harpersfield	1	4	3	0	0
Steel, Seth	Whites	1	3	3	0	?
Stempler, [?]	Palatine	1	3	6	0	0
Stephens, Adam	Chemung	1	5	2	0	0
Sternbarack, Nicholas	Canajoharie	1	2	2	0	?
Sterritt, Henry	Chemung	3	2	2	0	?
Steuart, Daniel	Caughnawaga	1	0	3	?	?
Steuart, Palatine [sic]	Palatine	2	2	4	0	0
Steuart, Thomas	Caughnawaga	1	0	1	0	?
Stevens, Daniel	Otsego	1	3	1	0	?
Stevens, James	Otsego	1	1	4	0	0
Stevens, Jeremiah	Otsego	1	1	3	0	?
Stevens, Josiah	Otsego	3	1	1	0	?
Stevens, William	Otsego	1	1	1	0	?
Stevenson, John	Caughnawaga	1	2	3	0	?
Steves, Jeremiah	Canajoharie	1	3	1	0	?
Stewart, Aaron	Harpersfield	3	1	3	0	0
Stewart, Allen	Caughnawaga	1	0	2	0	?
Stewart, Anna	Harpersfield	1	0	5	0	?
Stewart, Duncan	Caughnawaga	1	1	3	0	?
Stewart, Ebenezer	Canajoharie	2	1	3	0	0
Stewart, James	Canajoharie	2	1	4	0	0
Stewart, James	Chemung	3	1	2	0	0
Stewart, James	Harpersfield	2	2	5	0	0
Stewart, Jessee	Harpersfield	1	1	2	0	0
Stewart, John	Caughnawaga	1	0	3	0	?
Stewart, John	Otsego	1	2	2	0	?
Stewart, Robert	Caughnawaga	1	4	3	0	0
Stewart, William	Harpersfield	1	0	1	0	0
Stewart, William	Mohawk	2	3	3	0	?
Stickny, Joseph	German Flatts	1	0	0	0	0
Stien, Ludweek	Canajoharie	1	2	3	0	0
Stifford, David	Herkimer	1	0	4	0	0
Stifford, Jacob	Herkimer	1	1	2	0	0
Stifford, Richard	Herkimer	1	2	3	0	0
Stifford, Samuel	Herkimer	2	1	4	0	?
Stillman, Benjamin	Caughnawaga	2	0	2	0	0

1790 FEDERAL CENSUS, MONTGOMERY COUNTY, NY

HOF	TOWN	M 16+	M -16	F	OFP	S
Stilman, John	Whites	2	4	4	0	0
Stilman, Samuel	Whites	2	1	2	0	0
Stiltson, Amos	Mohawk	1	0	2	0	0
Stine, George	Mohawk	1	0	4	0	0
Stine, John	Mohawk	2	2	?	?	?
Stine, William	Mohawk	2	1	3	0	0
Stiver, Henry	Canajoharie	3	3	4	0	0
Stiversant, John	Caughnawaga	2	1	2	?	?
Stiversant, Samuel	Caughnawaga	1	1	1	?	?
Stocker, William	Canajoharie	1	2	2	0	0
Stoddard, Orange	Chemung	5	1	3	0	?
Stoel, Asa	Harpersfield	2	1	3	0	?
Stoel, Israel	Canajoharie	2	0	0	0	?
Stoel, Israel	Chemung	3	4	2	0	0
Stoell, Hezekiah	Chemung	4	1	8	0	0
Stoll, Jacob	Chemung	2	2	3	0	0
Stone, Charles	Chemung	2	0	0	0	0
Stone, Eaton	Caughnawaga	3	0	5	0	0
Stone, George	Palatine	3	1	5	0	0
Stone, Seth	Harpersfield	1	2	3	0	?
Stone, Squire	Mohawk	1	1	2	0	0
Stonemach, Philip	Mohawk	1	1	5	0	?
Stoner, John	Caughnawaga	1	1	2	?	?
Stoner, Nicholas	Caughnawaga	1	3	2	0	?
Stores, Nathaniel	Otsego	1	2	2	0	0
Stornbury, Jacob	Mohawk	1	1	1	0	1
Story, Benjamin	Otsego	1	1	3	0	0
Story, Oliver	Otsego	1	1	2	0	0
Stougton, Amaziah	Herkimer	2	0	0	0	0
Stout, James	Caughnawaga	1	1	3	?	?
Stoutinger, George	Harpersfield	1	0	4	0	?
Stow, Daniel	Chemung	1	0	3	0	0
Stow, David	Chemung	2	0	3	0	0
Stow, Josiah	Chemung	2	2	1	0	0
Stowids, George	Mohawk	1	1	2	0	0
Stowids, Samuel	Mohawk	1	0	2	0	0
Stoyle, Stephen	Harpersfield	2	1	1	0	0
Straback, Frederick	Palatine	3	2	3	?	?
Strader, Nicholas	Palatine	1	3	3	0	0
Strail, John	Mohawk	3	2	5	0	0
Strain, James	Canajoharie	1	0	1	0	0
Strain, James, Jr.	Canajoharie	1	1	1	0	0
Strayer, Jacob	Palatine	2	2	5	0	1
Street, Robert	Caughnawaga	2	0	3	?	?
Strickland, John	Canajoharie	1	1	2	0	?

1790 FEDERAL CENSUS, MONTGOMERY COUNTY, NY

HOF	TOWN	M 16+	M -16	F	OFP	S
Strickland, Noah	Canajoharie	1	0	6	0	?
Strong, Asher	Otsego	3	3	3	0	?
Stroud, Thomas	Canajoharie	1	2	4	0	0
Stroup, William	Palatine	1	0	1	0	?
Stroup, William, Jr.	Palatine	1	0	2	0	?
Strow, Baltus	Canajoharie	1	2	2	0	?
Strowback, Adam	Canajoharie	4	0	4	0	?
Strowback, Jacob	Canajoharie	1	0	1	0	0
Strowbridge, Philo	Canajoharie	1	3	3	0	?
Struble, Christopher	German Flatts	2	1	3	0	?
Strunck, Henry	Canajoharie	1	3	1	0	0
Stuley, Robert	Canajoharie	1	1	4	0	0
Stutson, Timothy	Otsego	3	4	4	0	0
Styles, Asel	Chemung	2	3	5	0	0
Sullivan, Edward	Canajoharie	1	4	2	0	0
Summers, John	Canajoharie	2	1	1	0	0
Summers, Nicholas	Canajoharie	1	2	3	0	0
Summers, Peter N.	Canajoharie	1	0	1	0	0
Summers, William	Canajoharie	1	2	4	0	0
Sutch, Derick	Caughnawaga	1	1	3	?	?
Swain, John	Canajoharie	1	3	2	0	0
Swart, (Widdow)	Mohawk	0	0	1	0	?
Swart, Benjamin	Mohawk	1	5	2	0	?
Swart, John	Caughnawaga	1	2	2	0	0
Swart, Josiah	Mohawk	1	2	2	0	?
Swart, Teunis	Mohawk	4	1	2	0	?
Swart, Walter	Mohawk	1	2	3	0	?
Swart, William	Mohawk	1	1	1	0	?
Swart, William, Sr.	Mohawk	2	0	2	0	?
Swartout, Moses	Canajoharie	1	2	3	0	0
Swat, Daniel	Chemung	1	0	7	0	0
Sweat, Isaac	Canajoharie	2	1	1	0	0
Sweep, Jacob	Harpersfield	2	0	1	0	0
Sweep, William	Harpersfield	1	0	1	0	?
Sweet, Caleb	Caughnawaga	1	4	1	0	?
Sweet, Jonathan	German Flatts	1	0	0	0	0
Sweet, William	Harpersfield	2	0	0	0	0
Swift, Ambross	Mohawk	1	1	3	0	0
Swoop, Michael	Caughnawaga	3	0	3	0	0
Sylleback, Garrit	Palatine	1	4	4	0	?
Symons, Anthony	Canajoharie	2	0	1	0	0
Syphert, John	Palatine	2	1	5	0	?
Sytez, George	Caughnawaga	1	1	1	?	?
Talbot, Silas	Caughnawaga	5	1	3	0	3

1790 FEDERAL CENSUS, MONTGOMERY COUNTY, NY

HOF	TOWN	M 16+	M -16	F	OFP	S
Talcot, Hesekiah	Herkimer	3	2	7	0	0
Talmage, Samuel	Caughnawaga	1	2	2	0	?
Tanner, Jacob	Mohawk	2	0	6	0	0
Taste, Stephen	Caughnawaga	1	2	3	0	?
Tayler, Ebenezer	Chemung	2	0	1	0	0
Taylor, Aaron	Palatine	3	4	3	0	?
Taylor, Israil	Mohawk	1	2	3	0	0
Taylor, John	Mohawk	4	0	1	0	0
Taylor, John, Jr.	Canajoharie	1	0	2	0	0
Taylor, John, Sr.	Canajoharie	2	0	1	0	0
Taylor, Joseph	Mohawk	1	0	0	0	0
Taylor, Niles	Caughnawaga	3	2	3	0	0
Taylor, Philip	Chemung	1	1	2	0	0
Taylor, Silas	Chemung	1	1	2	0	0
Taylor, Thomas	Mohawk	1	1	3	0	0
Taylor, William	Mohawk	1	0	0	0	0
Teal, Joseph	Herkimer	1	1	2	0	0
Teel, Timothy	Caughnawaga	1	1	?	?	?
Tehurst, Abraham	Palatine	1	0	4	?	?
Tehurst, Martin	Palatine	2	0	1	?	?
Tehurst, Philip	Palatine	1	2	3	0	0
Temple, Joseph	Canajoharie	2	1	3	0	0
Ten Eyck, Andrew	Canajoharie	1	2	1	0	?
Ten Eyck, Andrew	Caughnawaga	1	1	3	0	0
Tenant, John	Canajoharie	2	0	2	0	0
Tennant, Thomas	Canajoharie	1	3	4	0	0
Tenus, Jacob	German Flatts	2	1	3	0	0
Tenus, Jacob	German Flatts	2	1	3	0	0
Terrell, Hezekiah	Caughnawaga	1	0	1	0	0
Terry, [?]	Mohawk	1	4	4	0	0
Terry, Gamaliel	Otsego	2	0	?	?	?
Tewilleger, Isaac	Chemung	3	1	3	0	?
Thare, Ezra	Caughnawaga	1	0	3	0	0
Thare, John	Caughnawaga	1	2	2	0	0
Thare, Pheneas	German Flatts	1	1	2	0	?
Tharp, Daniel	Harpersfield	1	1	2	0	0
Tharp, Nathan	Harpersfield	2	4	3	0	0
Thomas, Henry	Caughnawaga	1	1	1	0	0
Thomas, Joel	Chemung	5	5	3	0	0
Thomas, Lewis	Caughnawaga	1	0	2	0	0
Thomas, Samuel	Otsego	1	0	1	0	0
Thompson, Aaron	Mohawk	1	3	5	0	?
Thompson, Alexander	Canajoharie	2	0	2	0	0
Thompson, Alpheus	Whites	1	1	3	0	?
Thompson, Hugh	Harpersfield	1	1	2	0	0

1790 FEDERAL CENSUS, MONTGOMERY COUNTY, NY

HOF	TOWN	M 16+	M -16	F	OFP	S
Thompson, James	Canajoharie	1	0	1	0	0
Thompson, James	Whites	2	2	2	0	?
Thompson, John	Canajoharie	1	1	2	0	0
Thompson, Jonathan	Harpersfield	2	0	3	0	0
Thompson, Nathan	Mohawk	1	2	3	0	?
Thompson, Phenius	Chemung	2	2	6	0	0
Thompson, Thomas	Canajoharie	1	0	1	0	?
Thompson, William	Canajoharie	3	1	4	0	?
Thompson, William	Canajoharie	1	0	2	0	0
Thompson, William	Otsego	1	1	1	0	?
Thompson, Zebulan	Whites	1	1	2	0	0
Thorne, Samuel	Palatine	1	5	4	0	2
Thorp, Joseph	Harpersfield	2	3	2	0	0
Thrasher, George	Herkimer	3	2	2	0	?
Thrasher, Stephen	Herkimer	1	0	1	0	?
Throup, George	Caughnawaga	1	0	1	0	0
Throup, George B.	Caughnawaga	2	1	3	0	?
Throup, Josiah	Caughnawaga	4	0	4	0	0
Thursten, Amos	Otsego	1	0	1	?	?
Thursten, Daniel	Chemung	1	3	3	0	0
Thursten, Edward	Otsego	1	1	1	0	?
Thursten, Increase	Otsego	1	2	2	?	?
Thursten, John	Caughnawaga	2	2	4	0	?
Thursten, Moses	Otsego	3	0	3	?	?
Tice, [?]	Canajoharie	2	0	2	0	1
Tickner, Benjamin	Mohawk	1	0	2	0	?
Tickner, Jonathan	Mohawk	1	0	2	0	?
Tickney, Jonathan	Otsego	1	1	2	0	0
Tidd, Samuel	Harpersfield	1	5	2	0	0
Tiffiny, Recompence	Mohawk	1	0	0	0	?
Tigmel, Asel	Harpersfield	1	2	3	0	?
Tilleback, Martinus	Canajoharie	1	3	2	0	0
Tilleback, William	Canajoharie	3	0	1	0	0
Tillotson, John	Whites	3	3	3	0	0
Timeson, Garret	Canajoharie	1	2	6	0	0
Timmerman, Adam	Canajoharie	3	0	5	0	1
Timmerman, Christian	Caughnawaga	1	?	?	?	?
Timmerman, George	Palatine	2	2	9	0	0
Timmerman, Henry	Palatine	1	1	3	0	?
Timmerman, Henry	Palatine	3	4	8	0	0
Timmerman, Jacob	Palatine	2	0	4	0	?
Timmerman, Lawrence	Palatine	3	2	12	0	0
Timmerman, William	Palatine	2	4	6	0	?
Tippet, Henry	Mohawk	2	3	7	0	0
Tirwilleger, Hermanus	Caughnawaga	2	0	1	0	0

1790 FEDERAL CENSUS, MONTGOMERY COUNTY, NY

HOF	TOWN	M 16+	M -16	F	OFP	S
Toby, Ephraim	Mohawk	1	4	4	0	0
Tower, Lidia	Otsego	1	0	1	0	0
Townsend, Absolem	Caughnawaga	1	0	0	0	0
Townshend, Gerdeus	Chemung	1	1	4	0	0
Townshend, Gerdeus	Chemung	2	1	4	0	0
Townshend, John	Whites	2	1	2	0	0
Townshend, Nathaniel	Whites	1	1	1	0	1
Townshend, Platt	Harpersfield	4	1	4	0	0
Tracy, Christopher	Chemung	1	0	2	0	0
Tracy, Jonathan	Chemung	3	2	3	0	0
Tracy, Nathan	Mohawk	1	0	0	0	?
Traver, Peter	Canajoharie	1	2	4	0	?
Travis, James	Chemung	2	1	5	0	0
Trempaw, Jacob	Canajoharie	1	1	4	0	0
Trip, Jaba	Caughnawaga	2	0	1	0	0
Trotts, John	Caughnawaga	1	1	2	0	0
Trowbridge, Samuel	Mohawk	1	1	1	0	0
Trull, John	Harpersfield	2	2	2	0	?
Trusdell, Justice	Mohawk	1	3	6	0	0
Tryon, Thomas	Whites	1	3	3	0	0
Tubbs, Enos	Chemung	1	3	2	?	?
Tubbs, Ezekiel	Otsego	2	0	3	0	0
Tubbs, Lebeus	Chemung	3	1	2	0	0
Tubbs, Samuel	Chemung	3	1	4	0	?
Tucker, Moses	Otsego	1	0	0	0	0
Tuller, James	Whites	1	0	2	0	?
Tum, Adam	Palatine	1	1	2	0	0
Tum, Conradt	Palatine	2	2	2	0	0
Tunn, Nicholas	Palatine	1	2	6	0	0
Tunnecliff, John	Otsego	7	1	4	0	0
Turner, Asa	Harpersfield	2	1	1	0	?
Turner, Nathan	Caughnawaga	1	2	3	0	0
Turner, William	Harpersfield	1	2	2	0	0
Tusler, Mark	German Flatts	1	0	3	0	0
Tussler, John	Canajoharie	1	1	2	0	0
Tutle, William Y.	Caughnawaga	1	1	1	0	?
Tuttle, Ezra	Mohawk	1	5	4	0	0
Tuttle, Samuel	Whites	3	2	2	0	0
Tuttle, Timothy	Whites	2	2	3	0	?
Tygart, Peter	German Flatts	5	0	6	0	?
Tygart, Severenius I.	Palatine	2	2	4	0	0
Tygart, Severinius	Palatine	3	1	4	0	0
Tygart, William, Sr.	German Flatts	3	0	4	0	0
Tyger, Andrew	Herkimer	1	1	2	0	0
Tygert, David	Canajoharie	1	0	1	0	0

1790 FEDERAL CENSUS, MONTGOMERY COUNTY, NY

HOF	TOWN	M 16+	M -16	F	OFP	S
Tygert, Henry	Canajoharie	2	2	3	0	0
Tygert, Nicholas	Canajoharie	1	3	2	0	0
Tygert, Peter H.	Canajoharie	1	2	4	0	0
Tygert, Peter S.	Canajoharie	3	0	1	0	0
Tyler, Ashbel	Whites	2	0	0	0	0
Tyler, Benjamin	Chemung	2	2	3	0	?
Tyler, Ephraim	Chemung	1	1	1	0	?
Tyler, Silas	Chemung	2	4	4	?	?
Underhill, David	Herkimer	1	0	0	0	0
Underwood, Elias	Caughnawaga	1	3	2	0	0
Underwood, Joseph	German Flatts	3	1	4	0	?
Underwood, Parker	German Flatts	1	0	3	0	0
Valentine, James	Mohawk	1	0	3	0	0
Van Alstine, Abraham	Canajoharie	2	1	3	0	0
Van Alstine, Abraham	Mohawk	1	3	3	0	?
Van Alstine, Abraham C.	Canajoharie	1	0	4	0	1
Van Alstine, Cornelius	Mohawk	1	0	2	0	0
Van Alstine, Cornelius C.	Canajoharie	4	1	4	0	0
Van Alstine, Cornelius I.	Palatine	1	1	8	0	5
Van Alstine, Elizabeth	Canajoharie	0	2	3	0	0
Van Alstine, Gilbert	Mohawk	1	3	3	0	?
Van Alstine, Jacob	Mohawk	1	3	4	0	0
Van Alstine, Jeremiah	Mohawk	1	0	2	0	?
Van Alstine, John	Canajoharie	1	1	2	0	0
Van Alstine, John	Canajoharie	1	3	2	0	?
Van Alstine, John	Canajoharie	3	0	3	0	0
Van Alstine, John	Mohawk	1	5	3	0	?
Van Alstine, Martin	Canajoharie	4	6	3	0	0
Van Alstine, Martin A.	Canajoharie	1	1	3	0	0
Van Alstine, Martin C.	Canajoharie	2	1	4	0	0
Van Alstine, Martin G.	Canajoharie	2	2	2	0	?
Van Alstine, Nicholas	Canajoharie	1	4	2	0	?
Van Alstine, Peter	Canajoharie	1	0	3	0	0
Van Alstine, Peter	Mohawk	1	2	4	0	?
Van Alstine, Philip	Canajoharie	1	0	4	0	?
Van Antwerp, [?]	Caughnawaga	2	1	4	0	0
Van Antwerp, Asmarius	Mohawk	1	2	3	0	0
Van Antwerp, John, Jr.	Caughnawaga	2	2	2	0	0
Van Ater, Samuel	Palatine	2	3	3	0	0
Van Awken, John	Mohawk	1	2	3	0	0
Van Brackle, Herbert	Herkimer	1	1	1	0	0
Van Brockle, Garrit	Caughnawaga	1	1	2	0	0
Van Brockle, Gisebert	Caughnawaga	1	5	5	0	0

APPENDIX B

1790 FEDERAL CENSUS, MONTGOMERY COUNTY, NY

HOF	TOWN	M 16+	M -16	F	OFP	S
Van Brute, William	Mohawk	4	0	3	0	?
Van Buren, Cornelius	Caughnawaga	2	1	2	0	?
Van Buren, Francis	Caughnawaga	3	1	2	0	7
Van Buren, Gosha	Mohawk	1	2	2	0	0
Van Buren, Peter	Caughnawaga	1	0	1	0	2
Van Camp, Cornelius	Canajoharie	2	0	2	0	0
Van Camp, Isaac	Canajoharie	1	1	3	0	0
Van Camp, Moses	Canajoharie	1	0	3	0	?
Van Daulson, Henry	Caughnawaga	1	2	2	0	0
Van Dorne, Christian	Mohawk	1	3	3	0	0
Van Dorne, William	Mohawk	1	0	3	0	0
Van Drusen, John	Palatine	2	1	3	0	0
Van Druser, John	Palatine	2	1	3	0	0
Van Duser, Abraham	Caughnawaga	3	1	2	?	?
Van Duser, Harpet	Caughnawaga	2	0	2	?	?
Van Duser, Hendrick	Chemung	1	2	2	0	0
Van Duser, Malachi	Chemung	2	1	1	0	0
Van Duser, Martin	Chemung	1	0	1	0	0
Van Duser, Matthew	Caughnawaga	1	0	5	?	?
Van Duser, Nelly	Caughnawaga	2	0	3	?	?
Van Elter, Peter	Palatine	1	1	4	0	0
Van Eps, Charles	Mohawk	2	1	2	0	1
Van Eps, Evert	Mohawk	1	1	1	0	0
Van Eps, John	Mohawk	1	2	2	0	0
Van Eps, John E.	Mohawk	1	0	0	0	0
Van Ever, Cornelius	Canajoharie	3	0	2	0	0
Van Ever, John	Canajoharie	1	3	3	0	0
Van Ever, John, Jr.	Canajoharie	1	0	2	0	?
Van Ever, Renier	Canajoharie	1	2	3	0	2
Van Gorder, Samuel	Chemung	1	2	2	0	0
Van Horn, [?]	Mohawk	2	3	6	0	0
Van Horn, Abraham	Canajoharie	3	1	2	1	?
Van Horn, Cornelius	Mohawk	2	2	5	0	0
Van Horn, Cornelius, Jr.	Mohawk	2	0	1	0	0
Van Horn, Hendrick	Mohawk	1	0	2	0	0
Van Horn, Thomas	Mohawk	1	1	5	0	?
Van Husen, Albert	Mohawk	3	1	5	0	?
Van Husen, Jacob	Mohawk	4	2	4	0	1
Van Inger, Joseph	Canajoharie	1	0	2	0	0
Van Neer, Peter	Canajoharie	1	0	2	0	0
Van Ness, George	Canajoharie	1	1	2	0	?
Van Ness, Henry	Caughnawaga	2	0	3	0	1
Van Ness, William	Palatine	1	0	3	0	?
Van Norman, Joseph	Chemung	2	3	3	0	0
Van Olenda, Benjamin	Mohawk	1	0	1	0	?

APPENDIX B

1790 FEDERAL CENSUS, MONTGOMERY COUNTY, NY

HOF	TOWN	M 16+	M -16	F	OFP	S
Van Olenda, Jacob	Mohawk	1	0	2	0	?
Van Olenda, Martin	Mohawk	3	3	4	0	1
Van Olenda, Peter	Mohawk	1	1	5	0	?
Van Ostrander, John	Caughnawaga	1	0	2	0	0
Van Schaack, William	Mohawk	3	1	4	0	1
Van Sickle, Renier	Canajoharie	1	0	2	0	0
Van Sickler, Rebecca	Caughnawaga	1	1	2	?	?
Van Slyk, Jacobus	Palatine	1	3	4	0	?
Van Slyk, Martin	Caughnawaga	3	2	5	0	0
Van Slyk, Nicholas	Mohawk	1	1	1	0	?
Van Slyk, Sylvanus	Palatine	1	1	5	0	2
Van Slyke, Adam	Canajoharie	1	0	1	0	0
Van Slyke, Elizabeth	Canajoharie	0	4	1	0	0
Van Slyke, Eve	Canajoharie	0	0	2	0	0
Van Slyke, George	Canajoharie	1	2	2	0	0
Van Slyke, Jacobus	Canajoharie	1	3	4	0	0
Van Slyke, John	Canajoharie	1	1	4	0	0
Van Slyke, Martenus	Canajoharie	1	2	3	0	0
Van Slyke, Nicholas	Palatine	2	1	3	0	4
Van Slyke, Peter	Palatine	1	1	1	0	0
Van Slyke, Samuel	Canajoharie	1	1	2	0	0
Van Slyke, William	Canajoharie	1	1	2	0	0
Van Vechten, Abraham	Caughnawaga	2	2	4	0	3
Van Vechten, Anthony	Caughnawaga	1	3	4	0	?
Van Vechten, Dirick	Mohawk	1	3	6	0	1
Van Lee, Andrew	Palatine	1	1	2	0	4
Van Vee, John	Palatine	1	3	4	0	2
Van Vleeck, Benjamin	Mohawk	1	1	4	0	?
Van Vleeck, John	Mohawk	1	0	1	0	0
Van Vleet, Dury	Palatine	1	0	2	0	?
Van Vleet, John	Mohawk	1	0	6	0	0
Van Vosen, Henry	Mohawk	1	4	2	0	2
Van Vost, Ellis	Caughnawaga	3	2	4	0	0
Van Vost, John	Canajoharie	1	0	0	0	0
Van Vronker, Dirick	Caughnawaga	1	3	4	0	0
Van Vronkin, Garrit	Caughnawaga	1	2	1	0	0
Van Vroonker, Richard	Caughnawaga	1	1	2	0	0
Van Vuver, Cornelius	Harpersfield	2	0	2	0	?
Van Waganer, Henry	Harpersfield	3	2	2	0	?
Van Wagener, Teunis	Canajoharie	1	2	3	0	?
Van Wormer, Peter	Caughnawaga	3	1	5	0	0
Van Zelan, Johannes	Caughnawaga	2	0	3	0	0
Vanbrackel, Garrit	Caughnawaga	3	2	3	0	0
Vander Belt, Henry	Caughnawaga	1	0	2	0	0
Vander Mater, John	Caughnawaga	1	1	2	0	?

1790 FEDERAL CENSUS, MONTGOMERY COUNTY, NY

HOF	TOWN	M 16+	M -16	F	OFP	S
Vander Veet, Garret	Mohawk	2	0	2	0	0
Vander Veet, Jacob	Mohawk	3	3	4	0	0
Vander Worker, Casper	Canajoharie	1	2	3	0	0
Vanderveer, Henry	Mohawk	2	0	1	0	1
Vanderwerker, Gersham	Otsego	1	1	3	?	?
Vanderwerker, John	Otsego	1	2	2	?	?
Vanderworker, Albert I.	Canajoharie	1	3	4	0	0
Vanderworker, Henry	Caughnawaga	1	3	4	0	0
Vanderworker, Jacobus	Canajoharie	1	4	4	0	0
Vanderworker, John	Mohawk	1	2	6	0	?
Vanderworker, Thomas	Palatine	1	1	3	0	?
Vanderwormer, John	Canajoharie	2	3	3	0	?
Vandeworker, William	Canajoharie	2	3	6	0	0
Vaughan, John	Whites	3	3	4	0	?
Vaughan, John, Jr.	Whites	1	2	2	0	?
Vaughan, Micajah	Mohawk	1	1	5	0	0
Vaughn, Joseph	Otsego	5	0	2	0	0
Veal, David	Mohawk	1	1	2	0	0
Veal, Stephen	Otsego	3	2	3	0	?
Vechta, John	Caughnawaga	4	1	4	0	0
Veder, John	Mohawk	1	2	3	0	?
Veeder, [?]	Caughnawaga	1	0	1	0	1
Veeder, [?]	Caughnawaga	3	2	6	0	0
Veeder, Abraham, Jr.	Caughnawaga	2	0	3	0	0
Veeder, Albert H.	Caughnawaga	3	3	4	0	0
Veeder, Arnold	Palatine	2	2	7	0	3
Veeder, Isaac	Caughnawaga	1	2	2	0	0
Veeder, Peter	Caughnawaga	1	1	1	0	0
Veeder, Peter V.	Caughnawaga	3	1	2	0	0
Veeder, Simon	Caughnawaga	2	4	4	0	0
Veeder, Simon	Caughnawaga	2	0	0	0	0
Veeder, Volkert	Caughnawaga	4	3	6	0	2
Venton, William	Mohawk	2	2	5	0	0
Vergil, James	Whites	1	6	3	0	0
Vernor, Andress	Palatine	1	0	2	0	0
Vicory, Thomas	Mohawk	1	3	3	0	0
Vinegar, Jacob	Mohawk	1	1	6	0	0
Vinegar, Samuel	Mohawk	2	3	2	0	0
Vinings, Jonas	Chemung	2	1	2	0	0
Vinton, Benoni	German Flatts	2	0	0	0	0
Vise, Samuel	Mohawk	1	1	4	0	0
Visger, John	Palatine	1	2	3	0	0
Visscher, John T.	Mohawk	2	3	3	0	3
Volkenburgh, [?]	Caughnawaga	3	1	3	0	0
Volkenburgh, Hendrick	Canajoharie	1	3	3	0	0

1790 FEDERAL CENSUS, MONTGOMERY COUNTY, NY

HOF	TOWN	M 16+	M -16	F	OFP	S
Voorhees, Andrew	Mohawk	1	0	1	0	0
Voorhees, Garrit	Mohawk	1	2	3	0	0
Voorhees, George	Caughnawaga	1	0	1	0	0
Voorhees, Hendrick	Mohawk	1	0	0	0	0
Voorhees, Henry	Mohawk	1	3	2	0	0
Voorhees, James	Mohawk	2	2	2	0	0
Voorhees, Peter	Mohawk	1	1	2	0	0
Vosburgh, Abraham	Canajoharie	1	4	5	0	0
Vosburgh, Evert	Canajoharie	1	1	1	0	0
Vosburgh, Isaac	Canajoharie	2	1	1	0	0
Vrooman, Abraham	Canajoharie	1	2	2	0	0
Vrooman, Abraham	Caughnawaga	1	1	1	0	0
Vrooman, Cimon	Mohawk	1	2	1	0	0
Vrooman, Henry B.	Caughnawaga	4	2	4	0	0
Vrooman, John	Mohawk	1	3	2	0	?
Vrooman, Martin	Canajoharie	2	1	5	0	0
Vrooman, Peter	Caughnawaga	1	1	3	0	?
Vrooman, Simon I.	Canajoharie	1	0	0	0	?
Waburn, Samuel	Chemung	2	2	4	0	0
Wade, Edward	Otsego	1	0	3	0	?
Wadham, Ichabod	Caughnawaga	2	0	1	0	0
Wadsworth, Israel	Caughnawaga	1	1	2	0	?
Waeres, John	Chemung	1	2	3	0	0
Waffle, George	Palatine	2	2	4	0	0
Waffle, Henry	Palatine	1	3	2	0	0
Waffle, John	Palatine	3	6	?	?	?
Wafle, George	Canajoharie	2	0	1	0	?
Wager, Henry	Whites	1	0	1	0	0
Waggoner, George	Canajoharie	4	2	2	0	0
Waggoner, George	Palatine	2	2	5	0	2
Waggoner, Honyost	Palatine	1	1	5	?	?
Waggoner, Inglehart	Canajoharie	4	1	6	0	?
Waggoner, Jacob	Canajoharie	2	0	4	0	?
Waggoner, John	Palatine	2	2	3	?	?
Waggoner, Peter	Palatine	3	4	5	0	9
Wait, John	Chenango	1	0	0	0	?
Waiton, John	Caughnawaga	1	2	?	?	?
Walden, Nathaniel	Canajoharie	1	1	1	0	0
Waldon, Simon	Harpersfield	1	1	2	0	0
Walker, David	Caughnawaga	1	2	4	0	0
Walker, Edward	German Flatts	2	2	3	0	?
Walker, George	Canajoharie	1	0	2	0	0
Walker, Jeremiah	Canajoharie	1	1	3	0	0
Walker, Phineas	Canajoharie	1	2	5	0	0

1790 FEDERAL CENSUS, MONTGOMERY COUNTY, NY

HOF	TOWN	M 16+	M -16	F	OFP	S
Wallace, William	Caughnawaga	1	1	1	0	?
Wallason, Christian	Palatine	1	0	3	0	0
Walradt, Adam	Palatine	3	4	4	0	?
Walradt, Adolph	Canajoharie	1	1	2	?	?
Walradt, Adolph	Palatine	1	1	4	0	0
Walradt, Adolph, Jr.	Canajoharie	1	2	4	0	1
Walradt, Frederick	Canajoharie	1	4	3	0	?
Walradt, Frederick A.	Canajoharie	1	4	3	0	0
Walradt, Garrit	Canajoharie	2	3	3	0	0
Walradt, George	Canajoharie	1	4	1	0	?
Walradt, Henry W.	Canajoharie	4	2	5	0	0
Walradt, Isaac	Palatine	1	1	5	0	0
Walradt, Jacob	Canajoharie	1	3	4	0	0
Walradt, Jacob A.	Canajoharie	1	1	2	0	0
Walradt, Jacob H.	Palatine	3	0	3	0	0
Walradt, John	Palatine	3	3	6	0	?
Walradt, John	Palatine	3	1	3	0	4
Walradt, John H.	Canajoharie	1	3	1	?	?
Walradt, John Peter	Canajoharie	1	2	4	0	1
Walradt, John S.	Canajoharie	1	0	2	0	1
Walradt, Nicholas	Palatine	2	3	9	0	0
Walradt, Peter	Canajoharie	1	0	3	0	0
Walradt, Peter H.	Palatine	1	1	3	0	0
Walradt, William	Canajoharie	1	3	2	0	?
Walsworth, Elisha	Canajoharie	1	1	2	0	?
Walsworth, Griswell	Canajoharie	1	0	0	0	0
Walsworth, James	Canajoharie	1	3	4	0	?
Walsworth, Jessee	Canajoharie	1	1	1	0	0
Walter, Christian	Canajoharie	1	2	2	0	0
Walter, George	Palatine	1	0	3	0	0
Walter, John	Canajoharie	1	1	1	0	0
Walter, Mary	Caughnawaga	1	0	2	0	0
Walts, Conradt	Canajoharie	1	0	2	0	0
Walts, Conradt	Canajoharie	3	1	3	0	0
Walts, Jacob	Canajoharie	1	0	3	0	0
Walts, Peter	Canajoharie	1	2	1	0	0
Wanger, Isaac	Palatine	1	0	1	0	0
Ward, John	Canajoharie	1	1	3	0	?
Ward, Joseph	Canajoharie	1	2	2	0	?
Ward, William	Canajoharie	1	3	3	0	?
Wardell, William	Harpersfield	1	0	3	0	0
Warne, Richard	Harpersfield	5	3	4	0	0
Warner, George	Canajoharie	3	2	5	0	0
Warner, Henry	German Flatts	1	0	2	0	0
Warner, Nicholas	Canajoharie	1	4	5	0	?

1790 FEDERAL CENSUS, MONTGOMERY COUNTY, NY

HOF	TOWN	M 16+	M -16	F	OFP	S
Warren, Darius	Otsego	3	1	4	0	?
Warren, James	Caughnawaga	1	2	6	0	0
Warren, John	Harpersfield	1	0	1	0	?
Wart, Matthias	Mohawk	3	1	2	0	0
Wasbrook, Samuel, Jr.	Chemung	3	3	4	0	?
Waterbury, [?]	Otsego	1	0	0	0	0
Waterhouse, Walter	Chemung	3	1	2	0	0
Waterman, John	Canajoharie	1	1	6	0	?
Waterman, Samuel	Canajoharie	1	0	2	0	?
Waters, John	Mohawk	1	0	3	0	0
Waters, Nathaniel	Caughnawaga	1	1	2	0	0
Waters, Samuel	Mohawk	1	1	2	0	0
Watson, Jud	Herkimer	1	0	2	0	0
Watson, Nathan	Herkimer	1	0	0	0	0
Watson, Samuel	Herkimer	1	1	2	0	0
Watterman, Adenijah	Caughnawaga	2	1	3	0	?
Wattles, John	Harpersfield	2	0	2	0	0
Wattles, Nathaniel	Harpersfield	5	4	3	0	0
Wattles, Sluman	Harpersfield	2	2	4	0	0
Way, Martin	Canajoharie	2	2	2	0	0
Weaver, Adam	German Flatts	1	2	1	0	0
Weaver, David	Palatine	1	4	2	0	?
Weaver, Frederick G.	Herkimer	2	0	2	0	0
Weaver, George	Herkimer	1	3	5	0	0
Weaver, George I.	Herkimer	1	0	1	0	0
Weaver, George I. N.	Herkimer	2	2	5	0	0
Weaver, George Michael	Herkimer	1	1	1	0	0
Weaver, Jacob	Herkimer	2	1	3	0	0
Weaver, Jacob H.	German Flatts	1	1	3	0	?
Weaver, John	German Flatts	2	1	2	0	0
Weaver, Nicholas G.	Herkimer	1	1	2	0	0
Weaver, Nicholas I.	Herkimer	1	1	4	0	0
Weaver, Peter	Caughnawaga	1	2	1	0	0
Weaver, Peter, Jr.	Herkimer	1	2	3	0	?
Webb, John	Mohawk	1	1	5	0	0
Webber, Christopher	Otsego	2	0	4	0	?
Weber, Frederick I.	Herkimer	1	2	2	0	?
Weber, Jacob G.	Herkimer	2	0	3	0	?
Weber, Jacob N.	Herkimer	2	2	2	0	?
Weber, Peter I.	Herkimer	2	3	2	0	0
Webster, Daniel	Whites	1	1	3	0	?
Webster, David	Whites	2	2	4	0	?
Wederick, Catherine	Herkimer	1	0	4	0	0
Wederick, George	Herkimer	2	2	4	0	1
Wederick, Jacob	Herkimer	2	1	3	0	0

1790 FEDERAL CENSUS, MONTGOMERY COUNTY, NY

HOF	TOWN	M 16+	M -16	F	OFP	S
Wederick, Michael	Herkimer	1	2	4	0	0
Wederstawn, Henry	Herkimer	2	1	4	0	0
Weeton, John	Canajoharie	1	0	2	0	0
Wells, Abner	Chemung	3	1	1	?	?
Wells, Benjamin	Caughnawaga	1	2	3	0	0
Wells, John	Caughnawaga	2	2	5	0	0
Wells, Josiah	Caughnawaga	1	2	3	0	0
Wells, Philip	Otsego	1	1	3	0	0
Wells, Samuel	Whites	2	0	1	0	?
Wells, Styles	Caughnawaga	1	2	2	0	0
Welsh, David	Caughnawaga	1	4	3	0	0
Welsh, Richard	Canajoharie	1	2	2	0	0
Wemple, Alida	Mohawk	0	0	2	0	0
Wemple, Barant	Caughnawaga	2	3	4	?	?
Wemple, Cornelius	Mohawk	1	1	3	0	0
Wemple, Cornelius E.	Mohawk	1	0	0	0	1
Wemple, Hagernet	Mohawk	0	1	5	0	1
Wemple, Hendrick	Mohawk	3	0	1	0	0
Wemple, John E.	Mohawk	1	0	0	0	0
Wemple, John J.	Mohawk	1	0	0	0	0
Wemple, Menert	Caughnawaga	2	0	2	0	?
Wemple, William E.	Mohawk	1	0	0	0	0
Wemple, Wyndert	Caughnawaga	1	0	1	1	1
Wentworth, Alpheus	Otsego	1	1	4	0	0
Wentworth, James	Otsego	2	0	3	0	0
Werner, Christian	Palatine	1	0	1	0	0
Werrington, Eber	Otsego	2	1	3	0	0
Werrington, Stephen	Otsego	2	0	0	0	0
Wert, Michael	Caughnawaga	1	0	1	0	0
Wert, Morris	Mohawk	1	2	5	0	0
Wert, Nicholas	Caughnawaga	3	0	4	0	0
West, Daniel	Caughnawaga	1	2	?	?	?
West, William	Caughnawaga	1	2	4	0	0
Westerman, Peter	Canajoharie	2	1	3	0	0
Westford, Cornelias	Chemung	1	2	1	0	1
Westles, Lucas	Mohawk	1	3	2	0	0
Weston, Jonathan	Whites	1	4	3	0	0
Whalen, John	Caughnawaga	2	1	2	0	0
Wharry, Evens	Herkimer	1	3	3	0	?
Wheeler, Timothy	Otsego	1	1	1	0	0
Whipple, Barnet	Otsego	2	0	0	0	0
Whipple, Calvin	Whites	4	2	2	0	0
Whipple, Israel	Whites	1	1	2	0	?
Whipple, Levy	Herkimer	1	2	1	0	0
Whipple, Nichols	Herkimer	1	1	2	0	0

1790 FEDERAL CENSUS, MONTGOMERY COUNTY, NY

HOF	TOWN	M 16+	M -16	F	OFP	S
Whipple, William	Herkimer	2	3	2	?	?
White, Abel	Chemung	1	3	5	0	0
White, Abijah	Canajoharie	1	1	2	0	?
White, Ansel	Whites	1	0	0	0	?
White, Daniel C.	Whites	7	2	4	0	0
White, David	Canajoharie	1	2	3	0	0
White, Edward	Caughnawaga	2	2	3	0	0
White, Henry	Canajoharie	2	3	4	0	0
White, Hugh, Jr.	Whites	4	1	1	0	0
White, Isaac	Canajoharie	2	2	6	0	?
White, Jeremiah	Chemung	2	1	5	0	0
White, John	Canajoharie	1	6	3	0	0
White, John	Canajoharie	2	0	3	0	?
White, Joseph	Canajoharie	2	1	1	0	0
White, Joseph	Whites	3	1	4	0	0
White, Lewis	Caughnawaga	1	1	2	0	0
White, Nathan	Canajoharie	2	0	0	0	0
White, Nathaniel	Canajoharie	1	1	2	0	?
White, Philo	Whites	1	1	1	0	?
White, Thomas	Caughnawaga	2	2	2	0	0
White, William	Canajoharie	1	2	3	0	?
Whitford, Joseph	Otsego	4	3	1	0	?
Whiting, John	Canajoharie	1	1	4	0	0
Whitman, Allen	Caughnawaga	3	4	6	0	0
Whitmore, Amos	Whites	8	2	3	0	0
Whitmore, Parsons	Whites	2	0	3	0	?
Whitmore, Peletiah	Harpersfield	1	0	1	0	0
Wick, John	Palatine	3	1	4	0	2
Wickham, William	Chemung	2	4	1	0	0
Widslow, Stephen	Mohawk	1	0	1	0	0
Wikoff, Christian	Mohawk	1	1	2	0	0
Wilaber, John	Canajoharie	2	1	3	0	0
Wilbur, Peter	Caughnawaga	2	3	1	0	0
Wilcocks, [?]	Mohawk	2	0	5	0	0
Wilcocks, Benjamin	Canajoharie	2	0	3	0	0
Wilcocks, Benjamin	Caughnawaga	1	1	2	0	0
Wilcocks, David	Canajoharie	2	4	4	0	0
Wilcocks, David	Whites	2	0	2	0	0
Wilcocks, Isaac	Mohawk	1	1	2	0	0
Wilcocks, Jessee	Harpersfield	1	1	1	0	?
Wilcocks, John	Harpersfield	1	0	2	0	0
Wilcocks, John	Mohawk	2	2	2	0	0
Wilcocks, Joseph	German Flatts	1	1	2	0	0
Wilcocks, Oseas	Whites	1	0	0	0	?
Wilcocks, Peter	Mohawk	1	0	4	0	?

1790 FEDERAL CENSUS, MONTGOMERY COUNTY, NY

HOF	TOWN	M 16+	M -16	F	OFP	S
Wilcooks, Samuel	Harpersfield	2	2	2	0	0
Wilks, John	Canajoharie	1	0	2	0	0
Willard, Lewis	Whites	2	2	2	0	0
Willard, Rufus	Whites	3	2	3	0	0
Williams, Andress	Mohawk	1	4	3	0	0
Williams, Cornelius	Mohawk	1	1	3	0	0
Williams, Daniel	Mohawk	2	1	4	0	0
Williams, David	Mohawk	1	1	1	0	?
Williams, David	Mohawk	1	5	3	0	?
Williams, Edward	Canajoharie	1	6	2	0	0
Williams, Elisha	Harpersfield	4	0	5	0	0
Williams, Ezekel	Whites	1	2	4	0	?
Williams, George	Chemung	2	3	2	0	0
Williams, George	Palatine	1	0	1	0	0
Williams, Gurden	Mohawk	2	0	1	1	0
Williams, Jabez	Canajoharie	1	1	4	0	0
Williams, Jacob	Mohawk	1	1	2	0	0
Williams, Josiah	Harpersfield	1	3	1	0	0
Williams, Thomas	Whites	1	2	3	0	?
Williams, William	Mohawk	1	1	2	0	?
Williamsen, John	Palatine	1	0	4	0	0
Williamson, James	Caughnawaga	1	0	4	0	0
Willis, Aseph	Herkimer	1	0	0	0	?
Willis, Caleb	Herkimer	1	0	0	0	?
Wills, Arnold	Whites	2	0	1	0	0
Willy, Benjamin	Mohawk	1	2	2	0	?
Willy, Bezllial	Whites	6	1	2	0	0
Wilsey, John	Canajoharie	2	2	2	0	0
Wilson, Alexander	Canajoharie	1	2	2	0	0
Wilson, Andrew	Canajoharie	1	1	4	0	?
Wilson, James	Canajoharie	3	0	2	0	?
Wilson, James	Canajoharie	2	2	2	0	0
Wilson, James	Caughnawaga	2	0	1	0	0
Wilson, John	Canajoharie	2	0	0	0	0
Wilson, John	Caughnawaga	1	1	3	?	?
Wilson, John	Caughnawaga	1	1	5	0	?
Wilson, John	Whites	3	2	5	0	0
Wilson, John, Jr.	Whites	1	0	0	0	0
Wilson, John, Sr.	Canajoharie	1	0	0	0	0
Wilson, Phenias	Canajoharie	1	0	1	0	?
Wilson, Robert	Mohawk	2	0	0	0	0
Wilson, Samuel	Canajoharie	1	0	2	0	?
Wilson, Samuel	Otsego	2	0	1	0	0
Wilson, William	Canajoharie	3	0	3	0	0
Wilson, William	Chemung	1	1	2	0	?

APPENDIX B

1790 FEDERAL CENSUS, MONTGOMERY COUNTY, NY

HOF	TOWN	M 16+	M -16	F	OFP	S
Winch, Samuel	Whites	1	0	4	0	0
Winchel, Benjamin	Chemung	2	0	1	0	?
Winchel, Ruggles	Chemung	2	3	2	0	?
Winchy, Jabez	Chemung	3	3	5	0	?
Windecker, Conradt	Palatine	3	3	4	0	?
Windecker, Frederick	Palatine	4	0	3	0	?
Windecker, John	Canajoharie	2	0	3	0	2
Wing, Wiliam	Mohawk	1	0	4	0	?
Winkler, John	Chemung	1	3	3	0	0
Winkoop, William	Chemung	2	1	3	0	?
Winn, John	Canajoharie	2	4	3	0	?
Winner, Conradt	Caughnawaga	1	2	2	0	0
Winner, Francis	Caughnawaga	3	2	3	0	0
Winner, Francis, Jr.	Caughnawaga	4	5	5	0	0
Winter, [?]venal	Canajoharie	2	2	1	0	0
Winter, Isaac	Canajoharie	1	2	2	0	0
Winters, William	Chemung	1	0	0	0	0
Wiser, Nicholas	Canajoharie	1	3	5	0	?
Wisselfel, Aaron	Mohawk	1	3	1	0	0
Wisselfel, Andrew	Mohawk	1	4	2	0	0
Wiswell, Samuel	Canajoharie	1	0	0	0	?
Witacer, Squire	Harpersfield	2	3	2	0	0
Witaker, Christopher	Canajoharie	1	2	4	0	?
Witaker, James	Canajoharie	2	2	2	0	0
Witaker, Thomas	Canajoharie	1	1	3	0	2
Witbeek, Gabriel	Mohawk	2	2	4	0	?
Witford, Storsly	Caughnawaga	1	2	3	0	0
Witney, Christopher	Chemung	1	2	3	0	0
Witney, Joshua	Chemung	2	3	5	0	0
Witney, Martha	Chemung	0	2	4	0	0
Witney, Thoms	Chemung	1	0	2	0	0
Witney, William	Chemung	2	1	4	0	0
Witt, Moses	Palatine	2	2	5	0	0
Wixen, Barnabas	Chemung	4	3	6	0	?
Wolff, Jacob	Harpersfield	1	2	3	0	0
Wood, Caleb	Canajoharie	1	2	2	0	0
Wood, David	Canajoharie	1	2	2	0	0
Wood, James	Caughnawaga	1	1	2	0	0
Wood, James	Chemung	1	4	3	0	0
Wood, John	Canajoharie	1	1	3	0	0
Wood, John	Herkimer	1	2	1	0	?
Wood, John	Otsego	1	1	4	0	?
Wood, Joseph	Whites	1	3	2	0	?
Wood, Palmer	Harpersfield	1	1	1	0	0
Wood, Thomas	Whites	2	0	3	0	0

1790 FEDERAL CENSUS, MONTGOMERY COUNTY, NY

HOF	TOWN	M 16+	M -16	F	OFP	S
Woodcock, Nicholas	Caughnawaga	1	5	5	0	0
Woodruff, Amasa	Otsego	1	0	0	0	?
Woodruff, Stephen	Caughnawaga	1	0	2	0	0
Woods, James	Caughnawaga	1	1	2	0	?
Woodward, David	Chemung	1	0	5	0	?
Woodward, James	German Flatts	1	0	?	?	?
Woodward, John	Chemung	1	2	4	0	0
Woodward, Oliver	Canajoharie	4	3	3	0	0
Woodworth, Ezekiel	Harpersfield	1	1	3	0	?
Woodworth, Samuel	Caughnawaga	1	0	1	0	0
Woodworth, Selah	Caughnawaga	2	?	?	?	?
Woodworth, Serenius	Caughnawaga	1	0	1	0	0
Woodworth, Solomon	Caughnawaga	1	0	2	0	0
Woolcot, William	Canajoharie	1	2	2	0	0
Woolever, Abraham	German Flatts	1	2	3	0	0
Woolever, Jacob	German Flatts	1	1	4	0	?
Woolever, Peter	Canajoharie	1	1	3	0	?
Woolever, Peter	German Flatts	2	2	4	0	0
Wooliber, Henry	Palatine	2	3	3	0	0
Woolkinwood, John	Palatine	2	2	4	0	0
Woolkinwood, John, Jr.	Palatine	2	2	8	0	0
Woolsey, David	Mohawk	1	1	2	0	0
Woolsey, John	Mohawk	1	1	0	0	0
Wormwood, Abraham	Caughnawaga	1	0	1	?	?
Wormwood, Christian	Canajoharie	1	2	2	0	?
Wormwood, John	Canajoharie	1	0	3	0	?
Wormwood, Matthias	Caughnawaga	1	3	2	?	?
Wormwood, Peter	Canajoharie	1	0	2	?	?
Wormwood, Peter	Palatine	3	2	5	0	7
Wormwood, Ryena	Palatine	0	4	1	0	?
Wright, Daniel	Canajoharie	1	2	2	0	0
Wright, Earl	Canajoharie	3	0	2	0	0
Wright, Ebenezer	Whites	4	2	2	0	0
Wright, Gabriel	Whites	3	0	0	0	0
Wright, Gideon	Canajoharie	2	2	2	0	0
Wright, Humphry	Canajoharie	1	1	4	0	0
Wright, Jacob	Canajoharie	1	3	4	0	0
Wright, Jacob	Caughnawaga	2	0	5	0	0
Wright, John	Canajoharie	1	3	1	0	0
Wright, Luther	Canajoharie	1	0	3	0	?
Wright, Samuel	Whites	2	4	3	0	0
Wright, Solomon	Whites	4	1	3	0	0
Wright, Thomas	Whites	5	2	5	0	0
Wyld, Yost Henry	Canajoharie	1	5	5	0	0
Wymer, Andrew	Palatine	1	1	2	0	0

1790 FEDERAL CENSUS, MONTGOMERY COUNTY, NY

HOF	TOWN	M 16+	M -16	F	OFP	S
Wynings, Clark	Chemung	1	2	6	0	?
Wyth, Ebenezer	Chemung	2	2	4	0	?
Yales, Weight	Caughnawaga	1	0	3	?	?
Yannee, Christian	Caughnawaga	2	2	2	0	0
Yanser, Hendrickus	Canajoharie	1	0	1	0	?
Yantus, Bartholomew	Harpersfield	3	1	4	0	0
Yates, Abraham	Mohawk	1	0	1	0	3
Yates, Abraham, Jr.	Mohawk	1	1	1	0	2
Yates, Christopher P.	Canajoharie	3	0	9	0	?
Yates, John	Caughnawaga	2	1	2	0	?
Yates, Peter	Mohawk	1	2	5	0	0
Yates, Robert, Jr.	Mohawk	2	0	?	?	?
Yates, Samuel	Canajoharie	1	2	4	0	0
Yattan, Adam	Canajoharie	1	1	2	0	0
Yattan, Nicholas	Canajoharie	1	1	1	0	0
Yattan, Peter	Canajoharie	1	1	3	0	0
Yordon, Casper	Canajoharie	3	0	7	0	0
Yordon, George	Canajoharie	1	2	2	0	0
Yordon, John	Canajoharie	1	4	4	0	?
Yost, Peter	Caughnawaga	2	4	3	0	0
Youhe, James	German Flatts	1	4	2	1	0
Youker, George	Palatine	1	4	6	0	0
Youker, Jacob	Palatine	1	2	3	0	0
Youker, John	Palatine	1	3	2	0	0
Youker, Solomon	Palatine	1	1	3	0	0
Younck, Peter	Canajoharie	4	0	3	0	?
Younck, William	Canajoharie	1	3	2	0	?
Young, Adam	Canajoharie	3	3	4	0	1
Young, Andrew	Caughnawaga	1	1	4	0	?
Young, Andrew	Otsego	4	1	6	?	?
Young, Christian, Jr.	Canajoharie	1	0	3	0	0
Young, Christian, Sr.	Canajoharie	1	0	2	0	0
Young, George	Canajoharie	2	2	1	0	0
Young, George	Mohawk	1	2	2	0	0
Young, George	Mohawk	2	1	1	0	0
Young, Godfry	Canajoharie	1	1	4	0	0
Young, Jacob	Canajoharie	3	1	4	0	0
Young, Jacob, Jr.	Canajoharie	2	3	4	0	0
Young, Jeremiah	Canajoharie	1	4	2	0	?
Young, John	Canajoharie	1	1	3	0	?
Young, John	Canajoharie	1	2	2	0	0
Young, John	Canajoharie	1	0	1	0	?
Young, John	Canajoharie	1	1	1	0	0
Young, John	Canajoharie	1	0	2	0	0

1790 FEDERAL CENSUS, MONTGOMERY COUNTY, NY

HOF	TOWN	M 16+	M -16	F	OFP	S
Young, John	Caughnawaga	1	4	3	0	0
Young, John	Whites	2	0	1	0	?
Young, Joseph	Canajoharie	1	2	2	0	0
Young, Joseph	Caughnawaga	1	2	3	0	0
Young, Lodowick	Caughnawaga	1	4	4	0	0
Young, Nancy	Canajoharie	2	0	1	0	?
Young, Peter	Caughnawaga	1	2	3	0	?
Young, Peter	Mohawk	2	1	2	0	0
Young, Richard	Canajoharie	2	2	4	0	0
Young, Seth	Palatine	1	3	3	0	?
Young, Seth	Palatine	1	5	2	0	0
Young, Thomas	Canajoharie	1	0	3	0	0
Young, Thomas	Canajoharie	2	0	2	0	0
Young, William	Mohawk	1	1	1	0	1
Youran, Jacob	Palatine	2	2	5	0	0
Zee, David	Canajoharie	1	3	3	0	0
Zerener, Lewis	Canajoharie	1	2	2	0	0
Zimerman, Elizabeth	Canajoharie	1	1	4	0	0
Zuller, Henry	Canajoharie	1	2	5	0	0
Zuphin, John	Canajoharie	2	1	5	0	?
Zutphin, John	Mohawk	1	0	8	0	0
Zutphin, Richard	Caughnawaga	1	0	3	0	0

REFERENCES

Each of the following references is preceded with a "key code" which will be found at the end of individual entries in the compendium. The one exception is in the case of birth/baptism where the key code is placed after the name of each child.

[AFC] "Private burying-ground on the Aarons farm, formerly owned by Mrs. Estella Finehout. Stones down and not well-kept." (Copied by Marian Finehout Scramlin (Mrs. Duane M.), Cherry Valley, N.Y. (1931) for Helen Lyons Wikoff (Mrs. Harry E.),member of Ft. Washington Chapter, N.S.D.A.R., New York City). *Collections of The New York State Daughters of the American Revolution*, Vol. 41.

[ARC] "Ames Rural Cemetery, Town of Canajoharie, Montgomery County, New York", compiled by John Kling. *Collections of Montgomery County, New York Department of History and Archives* (1977).

[BFC] "Private burying-ground on the Bowman farm, about two miles from the town of Hessville, Montgomery County, N.Y. About a half mile from the road, on a knoll. Many stones broken and lying on the ground and not well-kept." (Copied August 1931 by Helen Lyons Wikoff (Mrs. Harry E.), member of Ft. Washington Chapter, N.S.D.A.R., New York City). *Collections of The New York State Daughters of the American Revolution*, Vol. 41.

[C1790] *Heads of Families, At the First Census of the United States Taken In the Year 1790, New York*, pp. 99-116. Washington, D.C., 1908.

[CVC] "List of Cherry Valley Residents who were removed to Cherry Valley Cemetery around 1864, from private or the 'old' cemeteries". Collections of Montgomery County, New York Department of History and Archives (unpub. ms)

[DFP] "Records of the Dutch Reformed Church, Fort Plain", ed. by R. W. Vosburgh. *Collections of The New York Genealogical and Biographical Society*, Vol. I (1918).

[DRC] "Records of the Reformed Protestant Dutch Church of Caughnawaga", ed. by R. W. Vosburgh. *Collections of The*

REFERENCES

New York Genealogical and Biographical Society, Vol. I (1917).

[DRGF]   "Records of the Reformed Protestant Dutch Church of German Flatts", ed. by R. W. Vosburgh. *Collections of The New York Genealogical and Biographical Society*, Vol. I (1918).

[FH]   "Register of Baptisms, Marriages, Communicants & Funerals begun by Henry Barclay at Fort Hunter, January 26th 1734/5". Collections of The New-York Historical Society (unpub. ms #205).

[FPC]   "The Fort Plain Cemetery, about one-quarter of a mile from the village of Fort Plain, Montgomery County, New York. It is situated in the northwest corner of the Town of Minden." *Collections of The New York State Daughters of the American Revolution*, Vols. 44 and 56.

[JC]   "Gravestone Inscriptions from Johnstown Cemetery", by Rev. B. F. Livingston. Collections of Montgomery County, New York Department of History and Archives (unpub. ms)

[JDR]   "Reverend James Dempster's Records, Founder of Log Meeting House, 1778-1803", ed. by Robert M. Hartley. *Collections of Montgomery County, New York Department of History and Archives* (1934).

[JPC]   "Records of The Presbyterian Church of Johnstown in Fulton County, N.Y.", ed. by R. W. Vosburgh. *Collections of The New York Genealogical and Biographical Society* (1916).

[LTSA]   "Records of the Lutheran Trinity Church of Stone Arabia", ed. by R. W. Vosburgh. *Collections of The New York Genealogical and Biographical Society*, Vol. I (1916).

[MVL]   Penrose, Maryly B. *Mohawk Valley Land Records: Abstracts, 1738-1788.* Franklin Park, N.J.: Liberty Bell Associates, 1985.

[MVR]   Penrose, Maryly B. *Mohawk Valley In The Revolution: Committee of Safety Papers & Genealogical Compendium.* Franklin Park, N.J.: Liberty Bell Associates, 1978.

REFERENCES

[NYR]   Roberts, James A. *New York In The Revolution, As Colony and State*. Vol. I. Albany, N.Y., 1904.

[PCBC]   "Records of the Presbyterian Church of Bowman's Creek (Buel), Town of Canajoharie". Collections of Montgomery County, New York Department of History and Archives (unpub. ms)

[PCV]   "A Record of Deaths in the First Presbyterian Church & Congregation, Cherry Valley." Collections of Montgomery County, New York Department of History and Archives (unpub. ms)

[RDH]   "Records of the Reformed Protestant Dutch Church, Herkimer", ed. by R. W. Vosburgh. *Collections of The New York Genealogical and Biographical Society*, Vol. I (1918).

[RDSA]   "Records of the Reformed Dutch Church of Stone Arabia", ed. by R. W. Vosburgh. *Collections of The New York Genealogical and Biographical Society*, Vol. I (1916).

[RWPA]   Penrose, Maryly B. *Mohawk Valley Revolutionary War Pension Abstracts*. Bowie, MD.: Heritage Books, 1989.

[SC]   "Information copied from Seeber Cemetery, located on Clinton Road, on former Seeber Copley farm, near Sprout Brook, Town of Minden, County of Montgomery, State of New York." (Copied by Ileta Wiles Robinson, submitted by Carol H. Warner, Genealogical Chairman, Ft. Rensselaer Chapter, N.S.D.A.R., Canajoharie, N.Y.). *Collections of The New York State Daughters of the American Revolution*, Vol. 243.

[SJC]   "Records of the Dutch Reformed St. John's Church, St. Johnsville", ed. by R. W. Vosburgh. *Collections of The New York Genealogical and Biographical Society*, Vol. I (1914).

[UPSC]   "Records of the United Presbyterian Scotch Church, Town of Florida." Collections of Montgomery County, New York Department of History and Archives (unpub. ms)

[WMC]   "Abstracts of Wills, Montgomery County, N.Y.", compiled by Mrs. Edith Becker, *The New York Genealogical and Biographical Record*, Vols. 56 and 57 (1925-26).